SECOND EDITION

HTML5 Canvas

Steve Fulton and Jeff Fulton

Beijing · Cambridge · Farnham · Köln · Sebastopol · Tokyo

HTML5 Canvas, Second Edition

by Steve Fulton and Jeff Fulton

Printed in the United States of America.

Published by O'Reilly Media, Inc., 1005 Gravenstein Highway North, Sebastopol, CA 95472.

O'Reilly books may be purchased for educational, business, or sales promotional use. Online editions are also available for most titles (*http://my.safaribooksonline.com*). For more information, contact our corporate/institutional sales department: 800-998-9938 or *corporate@oreilly.com*.

Editors: Simon St. Laurent and Meghan Blanchette	**Indexer:** Lucie Haskins
Production Editor: Kara Ebrahim	**Cover Designer:** Randy Comer
Copyeditor: nSight, Inc.	**Interior Designer:** David Futato
Proofreader: nSight, Inc.	**Illustrator:** Rebecca Demarest

April 2013:   Second Edition

Revision History for the Second Edition:

2013-04-10:   First release

See *http://oreilly.com/catalog/errata.csp?isbn=9781449334987* for release details.

ISBN: 978-1-449-33498-7

[LSI]

For Pop

Table of Contents

Preface. xv

1. Introduction to HTML5 Canvas. 1
   What Is HTML5?   2
   The Basic HTML5 Page   3
      <!doctype html>   3
      <html lang="en">   4
      <meta charset="UTF-8">   4
      <title>...</title>   4
      A Simple HTML5 Page   4
   Basic HTML We Will Use in This Book   5
      <div>   5
      <canvas>   7
   The Document Object Model (DOM) and Canvas   7
   JavaScript and Canvas   7
      Where Does JavaScript Go and Why?   8
   HTML5 Canvas "Hello World!"   8
      Encapsulating Your JavaScript Code for Canvas   9
      Adding Canvas to the HTML Page   10
      Using the document Object to Reference the Canvas Element in JavaScript 11
      Testing to See Whether the Browser Supports Canvas   11
      Retrieving the 2D Context   12
      The drawScreen() Function   12
   Debugging with console.log   16
   The 2D Context and the Current State   17
   The HTML5 Canvas Object   18
   Another Example: Guess The Letter   19
      How the Game Works   20
      The "Guess The Letter" Game Variables   20

The initGame() Function   21
The eventKeyPressed() Function   21
The drawScreen() Function   23
Exporting Canvas to an Image   24
The Final Game Code   25
Hello World Animated Edition   25
Some Necessary Properties   26
Animation Loop   27
Alpha Transparency with the globalAlpha Property   28
Clearing and Displaying the Background   28
Updating the globalAlpha Property for Text Display   29
Drawing the Text   29
HTML5 Canvas and Accessibility: Sub Dom   31
Hit Testing Proposal   32
What's Next?   33

2. Drawing on the Canvas. 35
The Basic File Setup for This Chapter   35
The Basic Rectangle Shape   36
The Canvas State   37
What's Not Part of the State?   38
How Do We Save and Restore the Canvas State?   38
Using Paths to Create Lines   38
Starting and Ending a Path   39
The Actual Drawing   39
Examples of More Advanced Line Drawing   40
Advanced Path Methods   42
Arcs   42
Bezier Curves   44
The Canvas Clipping Region   45
Compositing on the Canvas   47
Simple Canvas Transformations   50
Rotation and Translation Transformations   50
Scale Transformations   56
Combining Scale and Rotation Transformations   57
Filling Objects with Colors and Gradients   60
Setting Basic Fill Colors   60
Filling Shapes with Gradients   61
Filling Shapes with Patterns   71
Creating Shadows on Canvas Shapes   75
Methods to Clear the Canvas   77
Simple Fill   77

      Resetting the Canvas Width and Height   77
      Resetting the Canvas clearRect Function   77
    Checking to See Whether a Point Is in the Current Path   79
    Drawing a Focus Ring   80
    What's Next?   80

3. The HTML5 Canvas Text API. **81**
    Canvas Text and CSS   81
    Displaying Basic Text   82
      Basic Text Display   82
      Handling Basic Text in Text Arranger   82
      Communicating Between HTML Forms and the Canvas   83
      Using measureText   84
      fillText and strokeText   85
    Setting the Text Font   89
      Font Size, Face, Weight, and Style Basics   89
      Handling Font Size and Face in Text Arranger   89
      Font Color   94
      Font Baseline and Alignment   96
      Text Arranger Version 2.0   101
    Text and the Canvas Context   101
      Global Alpha and Text   101
      Global Shadows and Text   103
    Text with Gradients and Patterns   106
      Linear Gradients and Text   107
      Radial Gradients and Text   109
      Image Patterns and Text   109
      Handling Gradients and Patterns in Text Arranger   110
    Width, Height, Scale, and toDataURL() Revisited   114
      Dynamically Resizing the Canvas   114
      Dynamically Scaling the Canvas   116
      The toDataURL() Method of the Canvas Object   117
    Final Version of Text Arranger   119
    Animated Gradients   128
    The Future of Text on the Canvas   132
      CSS Text   133
      Making Text Accessible   133
    What's Next?   133

4. Images on the Canvas. **135**
    The Basic File Setup for This Chapter   135
    Image Basics   136

Preloading Images   137
Displaying an Image on the Canvas with drawImage()   137
Resizing an Image Painted to the Canvas   139
Copying Part of an Image to the Canvas   140
Simple Cell-Based Sprite Animation   142
Creating an Animation Frame Counter   143
Creating a Timer Loop   143
Changing the Tile to Display   143
Advanced Cell-Based Animation   145
Examining the Tile Sheet   145
Creating an Animation Array   145
Choosing the Tile to Display   146
Looping Through the Tiles   146
Drawing the Tile   147
Moving the Image Across the Canvas   148
Applying Rotation Transformations to an Image   149
Canvas Transformation Basics   150
Animating a Transformed Image   153
Creating a Grid of Tiles   155
Defining a Tile Map   155
Creating a Tile Map with Tiled   156
Displaying the Map on the Canvas   158
Diving into Drawing Properties with a Large Image   161
Creating a Window for the Image   162
Drawing the Image Window   162
Changing the ViewPort Property of the Image   164
Changing the Image Source Scale   166
Panning to a Spot on the Source Image   167
Pan and Scale in the Same Operation   168
Pixel Manipulation   170
The Canvas Pixel Manipulation API   170
Application Tile Stamper   172
Copying from One Canvas to Another   179
Using Pixel Data to Detect Object Collisions   182
The Colliding Objects   183
How We Will Test Collisions   184
Checking for Intersection Between Two Objects   184
What's Next?   190

5. Math, Physics, and Animation. 191
Moving in a Straight Line   191
Moving Between Two Points: The Distance of a Line   194

Moving on a Vector 199
Bouncing Off Walls 204
    Bouncing a Single Ball 205
    Multiple Balls Bouncing Off Walls 208
    Multiple Balls Bouncing with a Dynamically Resized Canvas ... 214
    Multiple Balls Bouncing and Colliding 219
    Multiple Balls Bouncing with Friction 233
Curve and Circular Movement 239
    Uniform Circular Motion 239
    Moving in a Simple Spiral 243
    Cubic Bezier Curve Movement 245
    Moving an Image 251
    Creating a Cubic Bezier Curve Loop 255
Simple Gravity, Elasticity, and Friction 259
    Simple Gravity 260
    Simple Gravity with a Bounce 263
    Gravity with Bounce and Applied Simple Elasticity 266
    Simple Gravity, Simple Elasticity, and Simple Friction .. 270
Easing 273
    Easing Out (Landing the Ship) 273
    Easing In (Taking Off) 277
Box2D and the Canvas 281
    Downloading Box2dWeb 281
    How Does Box2dWeb Work? 281
    Box2D Hello World 282
    Including the Library 282
    Creating a Box2dWeb World 282
    Units in Box2dWeb 283
    Defining the Walls in Box2D 284
    Creating Balls 285
    Rendering b2debugDraw vs. Canvas Rendering 286
    drawScreen() 287
    Bouncing Balls Revisited 289
    Translating to the Canvas 290
Interactivity with Box2D 293
    Creating the Boxes 294
    Rendering the Boxes 295
    Adding Interactivity 296
    Creating Boxes 296
    Handling the Balls 297
Box2D Further Reading 303

What's Next?   303

6. Mixing HTML5 Video and Canvas. 305
    HTML5 Video Support   305
      Theora + Vorbis = .ogg   305
      H.264 + $$$ = .mp4   306
      VP8 + Vorbis = .webm   306
      Combining All Three   307
    Converting Video Formats   307
    Basic HTML5 Video Implementation   308
      Plain-Vanilla Video Embed   309
      Video with Controls, Loop, and Autoplay   311
      Altering the Width and Height of the Video   312
    Preloading Video in JavaScript   317
    Video and the Canvas   321
      Displaying a Video on HTML5 Canvas   321
      HTML5 Video Properties   327
    Video on the Canvas Examples   331
      Using the currentTime Property to Create Video Events   331
      Canvas Video Transformations: Rotation   335
      Canvas Video Puzzle   341
      Creating Video Controls on the Canvas   355
    Animation Revisited: Moving Videos   364
    Capturing Video with JavaScript   369
      Web RTC Media Capture and Streams API   370
      Example 1: Show Video   370
      Example 2: Put Video on the Canvas and Take a Screenshot   373
      Example 3: Create a Video Puzzle out of User-Captured Video   376
    Video and Mobile   378
    What's Next?   379

7. Working with Audio. 381
    The Basic <audio> Tag   381
    Audio Formats   382
      Supported Formats   382
      Audacity   382
      Example: Using All Three Formats   384
    Audio Tag Properties, Functions, and Events   385
      Audio Functions   385
      Important Audio Properties   385
      Important Audio Events   386
      Loading and Playing the Audio   387

Displaying Attributes on the Canvas	388
Playing a Sound with No Audio Tag	391
Dynamically Creating an Audio Element in JavaScript	392
Finding the Supported Audio Format	393
Playing the Sound	394
Look Ma, No Tag!	395
Creating a Canvas Audio Player	397
Creating Custom User Controls on the Canvas	398
Loading the Button Assets	399
Setting Up the Audio Player Values	400
Mouse Events	401
Sliding Play Indicator	402
Play/Pause Push Button: Hit Test Point Revisited	403
Loop/No Loop Toggle Button	406
Click-and-Drag Volume Slider	406
Case Study in Audio: Space Raiders Game	416
Why Sounds in Apps Are Different: Event Sounds	416
Iterations	416
Space Raiders Game Structure	417
Iteration #1: Playing Sounds Using a Single Object	426
Iteration #2: Creating Unlimited Dynamic Sound Objects	427
Iteration #3: Creating a Sound Pool	429
Iteration #4: Reusing Preloaded Sounds	431
Web Audio API	435
What Is the Web Audio API?	436
Space Raiders with the Web Audio API Applied	436
What's Next?	439
8. Canvas Games: Part I.	**441**
Why Games in HTML5?	441
Canvas Compared to Flash	442
What Does Canvas Offer?	442
Our Basic Game HTML5 File	442
Our Game's Design	444
Game Graphics: Drawing with Paths	444
Needed Assets	445
Using Paths to Draw the Game's Main Character	445
Animating on the Canvas	448
Game Timer Loop	448
The Player Ship State Changes	449
Applying Transformations to Game Graphics	451
The Canvas Stack	451

Game Graphic Transformations   453
  Rotating the Player Ship from the Center   453
  Alpha Fading the Player Ship   455
Game Object Physics and Animation   456
  How Our Player Ship Will Move   456
  Controlling the Player Ship with the Keyboard   458
  Giving the Player Ship a Maximum Velocity   462
A Basic Game Framework   463
  The Game State Machine   463
  The Update/Render (Repeat) Cycle   467
  The FrameRateCounter Object Prototype   469
Putting It All Together   471
  Geo Blaster Game Structure   471
  Geo Blaster Global Game Variables   475
The Player Object   476
Geo Blaster Game Algorithms   477
  Arrays of Logical Display Objects   477
  Level Knobs   479
  Level and Game End   480
  Awarding the Player Extra Ships   481
  Applying Collision Detection   481
The Geo Blaster Basic Full Source   483
Rock Object Prototype   484
Simple A* Path Finding on a Tile Grid   486
  What Is A*?   486
  A* Applied to a Larger Tile Map   493
  A* Taking Diagonal Moves into Account   498
  A* with Node Weights   502
  A* with Node Weights and Diagonals   506
  Moving a Game Character Along the A* Path   514
  Tanks That Pass Through Walls?   518
What's Next?   528

9. Canvas Games: Part II.   529
Geo Blaster Extended   529
  Geo Blaster Tile Sheet   530
  Rendering the Other Game Objects   535
  Adding Sound   541
  Pooling Object Instances   546
  Adding a Step Timer   548
Creating a Dynamic Tile Sheet at Runtime   550
A Simple Tile-Based Game   555

Micro Tank Maze Description   556
The Tile Sheet for Our Game   556
The Playfield   558
The Player   559
The Enemy   560
The Goal   561
The Explosions   561
Turn-Based Game Flow and the State Machine   562
Simple Tile Movement Logic Overview   566
Rendering Logic Overview   568
Simple Homegrown AI Overview   569
Micro Tank Maze Complete Game Code   570
Scrolling a Tile-Based World   570
First, a Tile Sheet That Contains the Tiles We Want to Paint to the Screen   570
Second, a Two-Dimensional Array to Describe Our Game World   571
Third, Paint the Tile-Based World to the Canvas   571
Coarse Scrolling vs. Fine Scrolling   572
The Camera Object   572
The World Object   573
Fine Scrolling the Row and Column Buffers   574
Coarse Scrolling Full Code Example   580
Fine Scrolling Full Code Example   585
What's Next?   589

10. Going Mobile!. 591
The First Application   591
The Code   592
Examining the Code for BSBingo.html   597
The Application Code   600
Scaling the Game for the Browser   601
Testing the Game on an Actual Device   606
Retro Blaster Touch   607
Mobilizing Retro Blaster Touch   610
Jumping to Full Screen   610
Touch Move Events   612
Retro Blaster Touch Complete Game Code   618
Beyond the Canvas   619
What's Next?   619

11. Further Explorations. 621
3D with WebGL   621
What Is WebGL?   621

How Does One Test WebGL?   622

How Do I Learn More About WebGL?   622

What Does a WebGL Application Look Like?   623

Further Explorations with WebGL   628

WebGL JavaScript Libraries   629

Multiplayer Applications with ElectroServer 5   630

Installing ElectroServer   631

The Basic Architecture of a Socket-Server Application   634

The Basic Architecture of an ElectroServer Application   634

Creating a Chat Application with ElectroServer   636

Testing the Application in Google Chrome   641

Further Explorations with ElectroServer   642

This Is Just the Tip of the Iceberg   645

Creating a Simple Object Framework for the Canvas   646

Creating the Drag-and-Drop Application   646

Application Design   647

Windows 8 Apps and the HTML5 Canvas   659

What's Next in HTML5.1 and Canvas Level 2?   663

HTML5.1 Canvas Context   663

Canvas Level-2   664

Conclusion   664

A. Full Code Listings.   667

Index.   711

Preface

Introduction to the Second Edition

In the past two years, since the release of this book, usage of the HTML5 Canvas has grown by leaps and bounds. The original edition of this book was one of the first publications dedicated to the Canvas. While we were proud to get out of the gate fast, it also meant that we had to do a lot of research and exploration of our own. Back in 2011, there were only a handful of examples of HTML5 Canvas applications, and still fewer tutorials. In 2013, the landscape has changed. There are many resources to choose from regarding the HTML5 Canvas, from frameworks and APIs to dedicated websites and books. To create this second edition, we took a hard look at what worked and what did not work the first time around. The following sections describe some of the exciting changes and updates that you can look forward to within these pages.

First Edition Updates

Most of the content from the first edition of this book remains intact. It remains because this book is geared towards a wide range of developers, from those who have never seen a Canvas to those who want to learn some intermediate-to-advanced ways to make use of the Canvas.

Every chapter has been revised with updated code and optimizations, as well as updates to address browser compatibility and other issues that have arisen over the past two years. A few parts have been removed. Some of the redundant code listings have been moved to the source distribution to make the book easier to read. We have also replaced parts of Chapter 4 with more, shorter demos, and we've completely rewritten Chapter 10 to remove the discussion of Phonegap because similar content is now widely available.

We have also added a ton of new content that we believe will help take your Canvas applications to the next level. This includes the following:

- A new animated Hello World application
- A discussion of accessibility and the sub-dom concept
- Multiple methods to clear the Canvas
- Finding points in the current path
- Drawing focus rings
- Animating gradients with text
- Using pixel data to detect collisions
- Five new examples that focus on using `Box2Dweb` for physics-based animations
- Using `getUserMedia()` to capture video on the Canvas
- Making use of the new Web Audio API
- A* path finding and animation
- Coarse and fine tile-based scrolling
- Development of mobile web (iOS) full-screen, scaled applications
- A new game named Retro Blaster Touch
- A new drag-and-drop example
- A discussion of building your own Canvas application framework
- A short tutorial for building an HTML5 application for Windows 8

What You Need to Run the Examples in the Book

The best part about the programming HTML5 Canvas is that the barrier to entry is very low. All you need is a modern web browser and a text editor.

As far as compatible browsers go, we suggest that you download and use the latest version of the following web browsers. The browsers are listed in the order that we suggest you test them:

- Chrome
- Safari
- Firefox
- Internet Explorer (version 10)
- Opera

Every example in this book was tested with Google Chrome, Safari, and Firefox. While we made every attempt to ensure that these examples worked across as many browsers as possible, we suggest that you use Google Chrome or Safari for the best results.

What You Need to Know

It would be good if you knew your way around programming in some kind of modern language like C, C++, C#, ActionScript 2, ActionScript 3, Java, or JavaScript. However, we will introduce the Canvas in the first chapter in a way that should ease you into web programming at the same time.

For Flash developers

> JavaScript and ActionScript 1 are essentially the same language. While Adobe took some liberties with ActionScript 2, you should be very comfortable with JavaScript. If you have experience with only ActionScript 3, JavaScript might feel like a step backwards.

For Silverlight/C# developers

> Take a deep breath, and think about a time before ASP.NET/C# when you might have had to develop web apps in VBScript. Keep your mind there, because that is just about the same space you are about to enter.

How This Book Is Organized

This book is organized into 11 chapters. All the chapters in the second edition have been updated, revised, and expanded. The first four chapters step you through the HTML Canvas API by example. The topics covered include text, images, and drawing. These chapters contain a few finished apps, but for the most part consist of demos designed to show you the facets of the Canvas API. The next six chapters build upon the Canvas API by expanding the scope of the examples to application length. In these chapters, we discuss math and physics applications, video, audio and games, and mobile. The final chapters introduce a few experimental areas: 3D, multiplayer, Windows 8, and a Canvas object model.

What you won't get in this book is a simple run-down and retelling of the published W3C Canvas API. While we cover portions of the API in detail, some of it is not applicable to games. However, if you want to explore the API further, you can find it at this site (*http://dev.w3.org/html5/2dcontext*).

Instead, we want to bring to light the ways the Canvas can be used to create animation, games, and entertainment applications for the Web and mobile web.

Conventions Used in This Book

The following typographical conventions are used in this book:

Italic

> Indicates new terms, URLs, email addresses, filenames, and file extensions.

Constant width

> Used for program listings, as well as within paragraphs to refer to program elements such as variable or function names, databases, data types, environment variables, statements, and keywords.

Constant width bold

> Shows commands or other text that should be typed literally by the user.

Constant width italic

> Shows text that should be replaced with user-supplied values or by values determined by context.

 This icon signifies a tip, suggestion, or general note.

 This icon indicates a warning or caution.

Using Code Examples

This book is here to help you get your job done. In general, if this book includes code examples, you may use the code in your programs and documentation. You do not need to contact us for permission unless you're reproducing a significant portion of the code. For example, writing a program that uses several chunks of code from this book does not require permission. Selling or distributing a CD-ROM of examples from O'Reilly books does require permission. Answering a question by citing this book and quoting example code does not require permission. Incorporating a significant amount of example code from this book into your product's documentation does require permission.

We appreciate, but do not require, attribution. An attribution usually includes the title, author, publisher, and ISBN. For example: "*HTML5 Canvas, Second Edition* by Steve Fulton and Jeff Fulton (O'Reilly). Copyright 2013 8bitrocket Studios, 978-1-449-33498-7."

If you feel your use of code examples falls outside fair use or the permission given above, feel free to contact us at *permissions@oreilly.com*.

Safari® Books Online

Safari Books Online (*www.safaribooksonline.com*) is an on-demand digital library that delivers expert content in both book and video form from the world's leading authors in technology and business.

Technology professionals, software developers, web designers, and business and creative professionals use Safari Books Online as their primary resource for research, problem solving, learning, and certification training.

Safari Books Online offers a range of product mixes and pricing programs for organizations, government agencies, and individuals. Subscribers have access to thousands of books, training videos, and prepublication manuscripts in one fully searchable database from publishers like O'Reilly Media, Prentice Hall Professional, Addison-Wesley Professional, Microsoft Press, Sams, Que, Peachpit Press, Focal Press, Cisco Press, John Wiley & Sons, Syngress, Morgan Kaufmann, IBM Redbooks, Packt, Adobe Press, FT Press, Apress, Manning, New Riders, McGraw-Hill, Jones & Bartlett, Course Technology, and dozens more. For more information about Safari Books Online, please visit us online.

How to Contact Us

Please address comments and questions concerning this book to the publisher:

O'Reilly Media, Inc.
1005 Gravenstein Highway North
Sebastopol, CA 95472
800-998-9938 (in the United States or Canada)
707-829-0515 (international or local)
707-829-0104 (fax)

We have a web page for this book, where we list errata, examples, and any additional information. You can access this page at *http://oreil.ly/html5-canvas-2edition*.

To comment or ask technical questions about this book, send email to *bookquestions@oreilly.com*.

For more information about our books, courses, conferences, and news, see our website at *http://www.oreilly.com*.

Find us on Facebook: *http://facebook.com/oreilly*

Follow us on Twitter: *http://twitter.com/oreillymedia*

Watch us on YouTube: *http://www.youtube.com/oreillymedia*

Acknowledgments

Steve Fulton

First off, I would like to thank my wife Dawn for the amazing patience and guidance she lovingly provided while this book was being written. I would also like to thank my girls—Rachel, Daphnie, and Kaitlyn—for not getting too frustrated every time I said "sure, yeah, in just a couple minutes" when they asked me to play with them while my head was in these pages and examples. I'd also like to thank my mom for taking her limited resources and creating a childhood where anything was possible. At the same time, I'd like to acknowledge my sisters, Mari and Carol, my mother-in-law Susan, and my uncle Richard, all of whom help guide me on a daily basis, whether they know it or not. Also thanks to the Martin, Fulton, Campi, Miller, Garnica, and Peters families for their love and support. Finally, I'd like to thank my dad, who sacrificed his dreams so that I could have my own.

Jeff Fulton

I would like thank my wonderful wife Jeanne, and sons Ryan and Justin for allowing me to devote the time necessary to complete the authoring process for a third time. They gave me the strength to keep going when times were rough and when examples were not working in even a single browser. I would also like to thank my mom, sisters Mari and Carol, as well as the entire Perry, Martin, Campi, and Backlar families for their love and support. Like Steve, I would like to thank my pop, who passed away right as we finished the first edition of this book. He taught me to chase my dreams while I still can because I have only a short time in which to realize them.

The authors would also like to acknowledge all the fine people at O'Reilly, especially Mike Loukides, who took the chance on us for this book, Simon St. Laurent, Meghan Blanchette, who led us out of the wilderness, and we'd also like to thank our technical reviewers Nick Pinkham, Kyle Nau, Tracey Oshiro, and Robert Brisita.

We'd also like to thank John and Sandy Santos of Producto Studios, everyone at Electrotank, Creative Bottle, Jet Morgan Games, Sprout, Nickelodeon, Mattel, and Adobe, plus James Becker, Ace The Super Villain, Richard Davey, Marty Goldman, Curt Vendel, Squize and nGFX from GamingYourWay.com (*http://gamingyourway.com*), Bonnie Kravis, Carl Ford and all at Crossfire Media, plus Jen and Mike Foti, Wesley Crews, Eric Barth, Brandon Crist, Ian Legler, Mike Peters, Jason Neifeld, John Campi, Arnie Katz, Bill Kunkel (R.I.P.), Chris Crawford, Rob Fulop, and Nolan Bushnell.

Introduction to HTML5 Canvas

HTML5 is the current iteration of HTML, the *HyperText Markup Language*. HTML was first standardized in 1993, and it was the fuel that ignited the World Wide Web. HTML is a way to define the contents of a web page using tags that appear within pointy brackets (< >).

HTML5 Canvas is an *immediate mode* bitmapped area of the screen that can be manipulated with JavaScript. Immediate mode refers to the way the canvas renders pixels on the screen. HTML5 Canvas completely redraws the bitmapped screen on every frame by using Canvas API calls from JavaScript. As a programmer, your job is to set up the screen display before each frame is rendered so that the correct pixels will be shown.

This makes HTML5 Canvas very different from Flash, Silverlight, or SVG, which operate in *retained mode*. In this mode, a display list of objects is kept by the graphics renderer, and objects are displayed on the screen according to attributes set in code (that is, the *x* position, *y* position, and alpha transparency of an object). This keeps the programmer away from low-level operations but gives her less control over the final rendering of the bitmapped screen.

The basic HTML5 Canvas API includes a 2D context that allows a programmer to draw various shapes, render text, and display images directly onto a defined area of the browser window. You can apply colors; rotations; gradient fills; alpha transparencies; pixel manipulations; and various types of lines, curves, boxes, and fills to augment the shapes, text, and images you place onto the canvas.

In itself, the HTML5 Canvas 2D context is a display API used to render graphics on a bitmapped area, but there is very little in that context to create applications using the technology. By adding cross-browser-compatible JavaScript functionality for keyboard and mouse inputs, timer intervals, events, objects, classes, sound, math functions, and so on, you can learn to take HTML5 Canvas and create stunning animations, applications, and games.

Here's where this book comes in. We are going to break down the Canvas API into digestible parts and then put it back together, demonstrating how to use it to create applications. Many of the techniques you will learn in this book have been tried and used successfully on other platforms, and now we are applying them to this exciting new technology.

Browser Support for HTML5 Canvas

With the exception of Internet Explorer 8, HTML5 Canvas is supported in some way by most modern web browsers, with specific feature support growing on an almost daily basis. The best support seems to be from Google Chrome, followed closely by Safari, Internet Explorer 10, Firefox, and Opera. We will utilize a JavaScript library named *modernizr.js* that will help us figure out which browsers support which Canvas features.

What Is HTML5?

Recently the definition of HTML5 has undergone a transition. When we wrote the first edition of this book in 2010, the W3C HTML5 specification was a distinct unit that covered a finite set of functionality. This included things like new HTML mark-up, <video>, <audio>, and <canvas> tags. However, in the past year, that definition has changed.

So, what *is* HTML5 now? The W3C HTML5 FAQ says this about HTML5:

> HTML5 is an open platform developed under royalty free licensing terms. People use the term HTML5 in two ways:
>
> - to refer to a set of technologies that together form the future Open Web Platform. These technologies include HTML5 specification (*http://www.w3.org/TR/html5*), CSS3 (*http://www.w3.org/Style/CSS/current-work#CSS3*), SVG (*http://www.w3.org/TR/SVG/*), MathML (*http://www.w3.org/TR/REC-MathML/*), Geolocation (*http://www.w3.org/TR/geolocation-API/*), XmlHttpRequest (*http://www.w3.org/TR/XMLHttpRequest/*), Context 2D (*http://www.w3.org/TR/2dcontext/*), Web Fonts (WOFF) (*http://www.w3.org/TR/WOFF*) and others. The boundary of this set of technologies is informal and changes over time.
> - to refer to the HTML5 specification (*http://www.w3.org/TR/html5*), which is, of course, also part of the Open Web Platform.

What we have learned through conversations and project work in the past few months is that, to the common person who does not follow this closely (or more likely, the common customer who needs something done right away), *it's all HTML5*, and therefore when someone says "HTML5," they are actually referring to the "Open Web Platform."

The one thing we are certain about regarding this "Open Web Platform" is that the one technology that was definitely left off the invite list was Adobe Flash.

So what is HTML5? In a nutshell, it is "not Flash" (and other like technologies), and HTML5 Canvas is the technology that has the best capability of replacing Flash functionality on the web and mobile web. This book will teach you how to get started.

The Basic HTML5 Page

Before we get to Canvas, we need to talk a bit about the HTML5 standards that we will be using to create our web pages.

HTML is the standard language used to construct pages on the World Wide Web. We will not spend much time on HTML, but it does form the basis of <canvas>, so we cannot skip it entirely.

A basic HTML page is divided into sections, commonly <head> and <body>. The new HTML5 specification adds a few new sections, such as <nav>, <article>, <header>, and <footer>.

The <head> tag usually contains information that will be used by the HTML <body> tags to create the HTML page. It is a standard convention to put JavaScript functions in the <head>, as you will see later when we discuss the <canvas> tag. There might be reasons to put some JavaScript in the <body>, but we will make every attempt to keep things simple by having all JavaScript in the <head>.

Basic HTML for a page might look like Example 1-1.

Example 1-1. A basic HTML page

```
<!doctype html>
<html lang="en">
<head>
<meta charset="UTF-8">
<title>CH1EX1: Basic Hello World HTML Page</title>
</head>
<body>
Hello World!
</body>
</html>
```

<!doctype html>

This tag informs the web browser to render the page in standards mode. According to the HTML5 spec from W3C, this is required for HTML5 documents. This tag simplified a long history of oddities when it came to rendering HTML in different browsers. This should always be the first line of HTML in a document.

<html lang="en">

This is the `<html>` tag with the language referenced: for example, "en" = English. Some of the more common language values are:

Chinese: `lang = "zh"`
French: `lang = "fr"`
German: `lang = "de"`
Italian: `lang = "it"`
Japanese: `lang = "ja"`
Korean: `lang = "ko"`
Polish: `lang = "pl"`
Russian: `lang = "ru"`
Spanish (Castilian): `lang = "es"`

<meta charset="UTF-8">

This tag tells the web browser which character-encoding method to use for the page. Unless you know what you're doing, there is no need to change it. This is a required element for HTML5 pages.

<title>...</title>

This is the title that will be displayed in the browser window for the HTML page. This is a very important tag, because it is one of the main pieces of information a search engine uses to catalog the content on the HTML page.

A Simple HTML5 Page

Now let's look at this page in a web browser. (This would be a great time to get your tools together to start developing code.) Open your chosen text editor, and get ready to use your preferred web browser: Safari, Firefox, Opera, Chrome, or IE.

1. In your text editor, type in the code from Example 1-1.
2. Save the code as *CH1EX1.html* in a directory of your choosing.
3. Under the File menu in Chrome, Safari, or Firefox, you should find the option Open File. Click that selection. You should then see a box to open a file. (On Windows using Chrome, you might need to press Ctrl+O to open a file.)
4. Locate the *CH1EX1.html* that you just created.

5. Click Open.

You should see something similar to Figure 1-1.

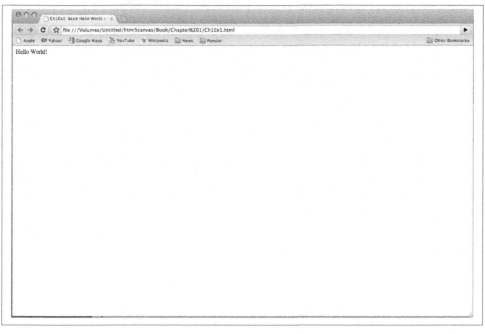

Figure 1-1. HTML Hello World!

Basic HTML We Will Use in This Book

Many HTML tags can be used to create an HTML page. In past versions of HTML, tags that specifically instructed the web browser on how to render the HTML page (for example, <font> and <center>) were very popular. However, as browser standards have become more restrictive in the past decade, those types of tags have been pushed aside, and the use of CSS (Cascading Style Sheets) has been adopted as the primary way to style HTML content. Because this book is not about creating HTML pages (that is, pages that don't have Canvas in them), we are not going to discuss the inner workings of CSS.

We will focus on only two of the most basic HTML tags: <div> and <canvas>.

<div>

This is the main HTML tag that we will use in this book. We will use it to position <canvas> on the HTML page.

Example 1-2 uses a `<div>` tag to position the words "Hello World!" on the screen, as shown in Figure 1-2.

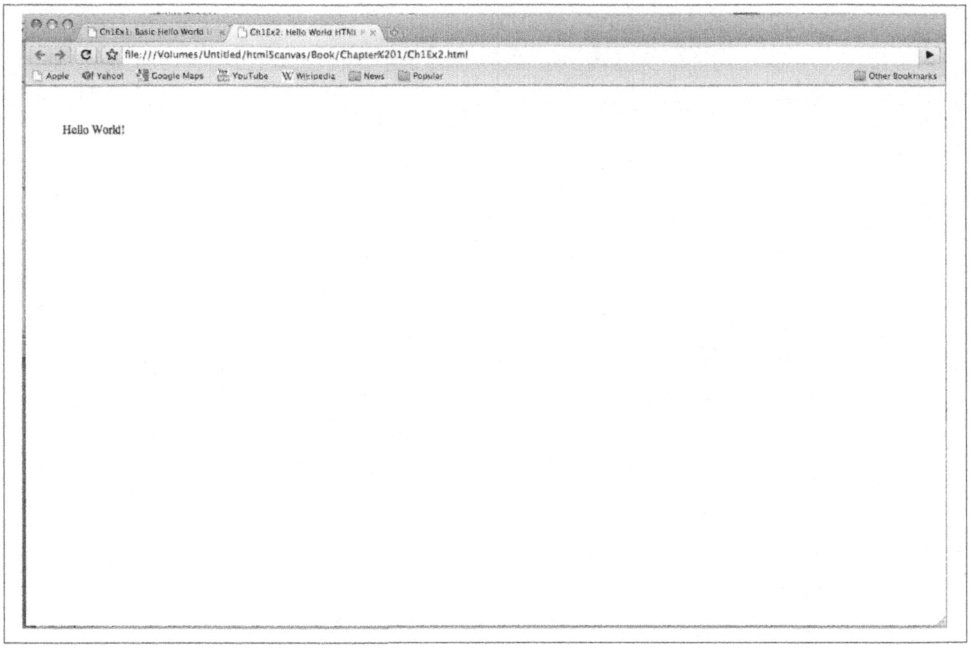

Figure 1-2. HTML5 Hello World! with a <div>

Example 1-2. HTML5 Hello World!

```
<!doctype html>
<html lang="en">
<head>
<meta charset="UTF-8">
<title>CH1EX2: Hello World HTML Page With A DIV </title>
</head>
<body>
<div style="position: absolute; top: 50px; left: 50px;">
Hello World!
</div>
</body>
</html>
```

The `style="position: absolute; top: 50px; left: 50px;"` code is an example of inline CSS in an HTML page. It tells the browser to render the content at the absolute position of 50 pixels from the top of the page and 50 pixels from the left of the page.

This `<div>` might position the Canvas in the web browser, but it will not help us when we try to capture mouse clicks on the Canvas. In Chapter 5, we will discuss a way to both position the Canvas and capture mouse clicks in the correct locations.

`<canvas>`

Our work with `<canvas>` will benefit from using the absolute positioning method with `<div>`. We will place our `<canvas>` inside the `<div>` tag, and it will help us retrieve information, such as the relative position of the mouse pointer when it appears over a canvas.

The Document Object Model (DOM) and Canvas

The *Document Object Model* represents all the objects on an HTML page. It is language-neutral and platform-neutral, allowing the content and style of the page to be updated after it is rendered in the web browser. The DOM is accessible through JavaScript and has been a staple of JavaScript, DHTML, and CSS development since the late 1990s.

The `canvas` element itself is accessible through the DOM in a web browser via the Canvas 2D context, but the individual graphical elements created on Canvas are not accessible to the DOM. As we stated earlier, this is because Canvas works in immediate mode and does not have its own objects, only instructions on what to draw on any single frame.

Our first example will use the DOM to locate the `<canvas>` tag on the HTML5 page so that we can manipulate it with JavaScript. There are two specific DOM objects we will need to understand when we start using `<canvas>`: `window` and `document`.

The `window` object is the top level of the DOM. We will need to test this object to make sure all the assets and code have loaded before we can start our Canvas applications.

The `document` object contains all the HTML tags that are on the HTML page. We will need to look at this object to find the instance of `<canvas>` that manipulates with JavaScript.

JavaScript and Canvas

JavaScript, the programming language we will use to create Canvas applications, can be run inside nearly any web browser in existence. If you need a refresher on the topic, read Douglas Crockford's *JavaScript: The Good Parts* (O'Reilly), which is a very popular and well-written reference on the subject.

Where Does JavaScript Go and Why?

Because we will create the programming logic for the Canvas in JavaScript, a question arises: where does that JavaScript go in the pages we have already created?

It's a good idea to place your JavaScript in the <head> of your HTML page because it makes it easy to find. However, placing JavaScript there means that the entire HTML page needs to load before your JavaScript can work with the HTML. This also means that the JavaScript code will start to execute before the entire page loads. As a result, you will need to test to see whether the HTML page has loaded before you run your JavaScript program.

There has been a recent move to put JavaScript right before the </body> at the end of an HTML document to make sure that the whole page loads before the JavaScript runs. However, because we are going to test to see whether the page has loaded in JavaScript before we run our <canvas> program, we will put our JavaScript in the traditional <head> location. If you are not comfortable with this, you can adapt the style of the code to your liking.

No matter where you put the code, you can place it inline in the HTML page or load an *external .js* file. The code for loading an external JavaScript file might look like this:

```
<script type="text/javascript" src="canvasapp.js"></script>
```

To make things simple, we will code our JavaScript inline in the HTML page. However, if you know what you are doing, saving an external file and loading it will work just as well.

 In HTML5, you no longer have to specify the script type.

HTML5 Canvas "Hello World!"

As we just mentioned, one of the first things we need to do when putting Canvas on an HTML5 page is test to see whether the entire page has loaded and all HTML elements are present before we start performing any operations. This will become essential when we start working with images and sounds in Canvas.

To do this, you need to work with *events* in JavaScript. Events are dispatched by objects when a defined event occurs. Other objects listen for events so that they can do something based on the event. Some common events that an object in JavaScript might listen for are keystrokes, mouse movements, and when something has finished loading.

The first event we need to listen for is a window object's load event, which occurs when the HTML page has finished loading.

To add a *listener* for an event, use the `addEventListener()` method that belongs to objects that are part of the DOM. Because `window` represents the HTML page, it is the top level of the DOM.

The `addEventListener()` function accepts three arguments:

Event: `load`
> This is the named event for which we are adding a listener. Events for existing objects like `window` are already defined.

Event handler function: `eventWindowLoaded()`
> Call this function when the event occurs. In our code, we will then call the `canva sApp()` function, which will start our main application execution.

`useCapture:` `true` *or* `false`
> This sets the function to capture this type of event before it propagates lower in the DOM tree of objects. We will always set this to `false`.

The final code we will use to test to see whether the `window` has loaded is as follows:

```
window.addEventListener("load", eventWindowLoaded, false);
function eventWindowLoaded () {
    canvasApp();
}
```

Alternatively, you can set up an event listener for the `load` event in a number of other ways:

```
window.onload = function()
    {
        canvasApp();
    }
```

or:

```
window.onload = canvasApp;
```

We will use the first method throughout this book.

Encapsulating Your JavaScript Code for Canvas

Now that we have created a way to test to see whether the HTML page has loaded, we can start creating our JavaScript application. Because JavaScript runs in an HTML page, it could be running with other JavaScript applications and code simultaneously. Usually, this does not cause any problems. However, there is a chance that your code might have variables or functions that conflict with other JavaScript code on the HTML page.

Canvas applications are a bit different from other apps that run in the web browser. Because Canvas executes its display in a defined region of the screen, its functionality is most likely self-contained, so it should not interfere with the rest of the page, and vice versa. You might also want to put multiple Canvas apps on the same page, so there must be some kind of separation of JavaScript when defining the code.

To avoid this issue, you can encapsulate your variables and functions by placing them inside another function. Functions in JavaScript are objects themselves, and objects in JavaScript can have both properties and methods. By placing a function inside another function, you are making the second function local in scope to the first function.

In our example, we are going to have the `canvasApp()` function that is called from the `window load` event contain our entire Canvas application. This "Hello World!" example will have one function named `drawScreen()`. As soon as `canvasApp()` is called, we will call `drawScreen()` immediately to draw our "Hello World!" text.

The `drawScreen()` function is now local to `canvasApp()`. Any variables or functions we create in `canvasApp()` will be local to `drawScreen()` but not to the rest of the HTML page or other JavaScript applications that might be running.

Here is the sample code for how we will encapsulate functions and code for our Canvas applications:

```
function canvasApp() {
    drawScreen();

    ...

    function drawScreen() {

        ...

    }

}
```

Adding Canvas to the HTML Page

In the `<body>` section of the HTML page, add a `<canvas>` tag using code such as the following:

```
<canvas id="canvasOne" width="500" height="300">
 Your browser does not support HTML5 Canvas.
</canvas>
```

Now, let's break this down to understand what we are doing. The `<canvas>` tag has three main *attributes*. In HTML, attributes are set within pointy brackets of an HTML tag. The three attributes we need to set are:

id

>   The `id` is the name we will use to reference this `<canvas>` tag in our JavaScript code. `canvasOne` is the name we will use.

`width`

The width, in pixels, of the canvas. The `width` will be 500 pixels.

`height`

The height, in pixels, of the canvas. The `height` will be 300 pixels.

 HTML5 elements, including canvas, have many more attributes: `ta bindex`, `title`, `class`, `accesskey`, `dir`, `draggable`, `hidden`, and so on.

Between the opening `<canvas>` and closing `</canvas>` tags, you can put text that will be displayed if the browser executing the HTML page does not support Canvas. For our Canvas applications, we will use the text "Your browser does not support HTML5 Canvas." However, you can adjust this text to say anything.

Using the document Object to Reference the Canvas Element in JavaScript

We will now make use of the DOM to reference the `<canvas>` we defined in HTML. Recall that the `document` object represents every element of an HTML page after it has loaded.

We need a reference to the `Canvas` object so that we will know where to display the Canvas API calls we will make from JavaScript.

First, we will define a new variable named `theCanvas` that will hold the reference to the `Canvas` object.

Next, we retrieve a reference to `canvasOne` by calling the `getElementById()` function of `document`, and passing the name `canvasOne`, which we defined as the `id` of the `<canvas>` tag we created in the HTML page:

```
var theCanvas = document.getElementById("canvasOne");
```

Testing to See Whether the Browser Supports Canvas

Now that we have a reference to the `canvas` element on the HTML page, we need to test to see whether it contains a *context*. The Canvas context refers to the drawing surface defined by a web browser to support Canvas. Simply put, if the context does not exist, neither does the Canvas. There are several ways to test this. This first test looks to see whether the `getContext` method exists before we call it using Canvas, as we have already defined it in the HTML page:

```
if (!theCanvas || !theCanvas.getContext) {
    return;
}
```

Actually, this tests two things. First, it tests to see whether `theCanvas` does not contain `false` (the value returned by `document.getElementById()` if the named `id` does not exist). Then, it tests whether the `getContext()` function exists.

The `return` statement breaks out and stops execution if the test fails.

Another method—popularized by Mark Pilgrim on his HTML5 website (*http://divein tohtml5.org*)—uses a function with a test of a dummy canvas created for the sole purpose of seeing whether browser support exists:

```
function canvasSupport () {
    return !!document.createElement('canvas').getContext;
}
function canvasApp() {
  if (!canvasSupport) {
     return;
  }

}
```

Our favorite method is to use the *modernizr.js* library (*http://www.modernizr.com/*). Modernizr—an easy-to-use, lightweight library for testing support for various web-based technologies—creates a set of static Booleans that you can test against to see whether Canvas is supported.

To include *modernizr.js* in your HTML page, download the code from *http://www.modernizr.com/* and then include the external *.js* file in your HTML page:

```
<script src="modernizr.js"></script>
```

To test for Canvas, change the `canvasSupport()` function to look like this:

```
function canvasSupport () {
    return Modernizr.canvas;
}
```

We are going to use the *modernizr.js* method because we think it offers the best approach for testing whether Canvas is supported in web browsers.

Retrieving the 2D Context

Finally, we need to get a reference to the 2D context so that we can manipulate it. HTML5 Canvas is designed to work with multiple contexts, including a proposed 3D context. However, for the purposes of this book, we need to get only the 2D context:

```
var context = theCanvas.getContext("2d");
```

The drawScreen() Function

It's time to create actual Canvas API code. Every operation we perform on Canvas will be through the `context` object, because it references the object on the HTML page.

We will delve into writing text, graphics, and images to HTML5 Canvas in later chapters, so for now, we will spend only a short time on the code of the `drawScreen()` function.

The "screen" here is really the defined drawing area of the canvas, not the whole browser window. We refer to it as such because within the context of the games and applications you will write, it is effectively the "window" or "screen" into the canvas display that you will be manipulating.

The first thing we want to do is clear the drawing area. The following two lines of code draw a yellow box on the screen that is the same size as the canvas. `fillStyle()` sets the color, and `fillRect()` creates a rectangle and puts it on the screen:

```
context.fillStyle = "#ffffaa";
context.fillRect(0, 0, 500, 300);
```

 Notice that we are calling functions of the `context`. There are no screen objects, color objects, or anything else. This is an example of the immediate mode we described earlier.

Again, we will discuss the text functions of Canvas in the next chapter, but here is a short preview of the code we will use to put the text "Hello World!" on the screen.

First, we set the color of the text in the same way that we set the color of the rectangle:

```
context.fillStyle  = "#000000";
```

Then we set the font size and weight:

```
context.font = "20px Sans-Serif";
```

Next, we set the vertical alignment of the font:

```
context.textBaseline = "top";
```

Finally, we print our text on the screen by calling the `fillText()` method of the con text object. The three parameters of this method are text string, x position, and y position:

```
context.fillText  ("Hello World!", 195, 80);
```

Let's add some graphics to our "Hello World!" text. First, let's load in an image and display it. We will dive into images and image manipulation in Chapter 4, but for now, let's just get an image on the screen. To display an image on the canvas, you need to create an instance of the `Image()` object, and set the `Image.src` property to the name of the image to load.

You can also use another canvas or a video as the image to display. We will discuss these topics in Chapter 4 and Chapter 6.

Before you display it, you need to wait for the image to load. Create an anonymous callback function for the Image load event by setting the onload function of the Image object. The anonymous callback function will be executed when the onload event occurs. When the image has loaded, you then call context.drawImage(), passing three parameters to put it on the canvas: Image object, x position, and y position:

```
var helloWorldImage = new Image();
helloWorldImage.onload = function () {
    context.drawImage(helloWorldImage, 160, 130);
}
helloWorldImage.src = "helloworld.gif";
```

Finally, let's draw a box around the text and the image. To draw a box with no fill, use the context.strokeStyle property to set a color for the stroke (the border of the box), and then call the context.strokeRect() method to draw the rectangle border. The four parameters for the strokeRect() method are the upper left x and y coordinates, the width, and the height:

```
context.strokeStyle = "#000000";
context.strokeRect(5,  5, 490, 290);
```

The full code for the HTML5 "Hello World!" application is shown in Example 1-3, and its results are illustrated in Figure 1-3.

Example 1-3. HTML5 Canvas Hello World!

```
<!doctype html>
<html lang="en">
<head>
<meta charset="UTF-8">
<title>CH1EX3: Your First Canvas Application </title>

<script src="modernizr.js"></script>
<script type="text/javascript">
window.addEventListener("load", eventWindowLoaded, false);

var Debugger = function () { };
Debugger.log = function (message) {
    try {
        console.log(message);
    } catch (exception) {
        return;
    }
}

function eventWindowLoaded () {
```

```
        canvasApp();
}

function canvasSupport () {
    return Modernizr.canvas;
}

function canvasApp () {

        if (!canvasSupport()) {
          return;
        }

    var theCanvas = document.getElementById("canvasOne");
    var context = theCanvas.getContext("2d");

    Debugger.log("Drawing Canvas");

      function drawScreen() {
       //background
       context.fillStyle = "#ffffaa";
       context.fillRect(0, 0, 500, 300);

       //text
       context.fillStyle  = "#000000";
       context.font = "20px Sans-Serif";
       context.textBaseline = "top";
       context.fillText  ("Hello World!", 195, 80 );

       //image
       var helloWorldImage = new Image();
       helloWorldImage.onload = function () {
          context.drawImage(helloWorldImage, 155, 110);
       }
       helloWorldImage.src = "helloworld.gif";

       //box
       context.strokeStyle = "#000000";
       context.strokeRect(5,  5, 490, 290);

    }

    drawScreen();

}

</script>

</head>
<body>
<div style="position: absolute; top: 50px; left: 50px;">
<canvas id="canvasOne" width="500" height="300">
 Your browser does not support HTML5 Canvas.
```

```
</canvas>
</div>
</body>
</html>
```

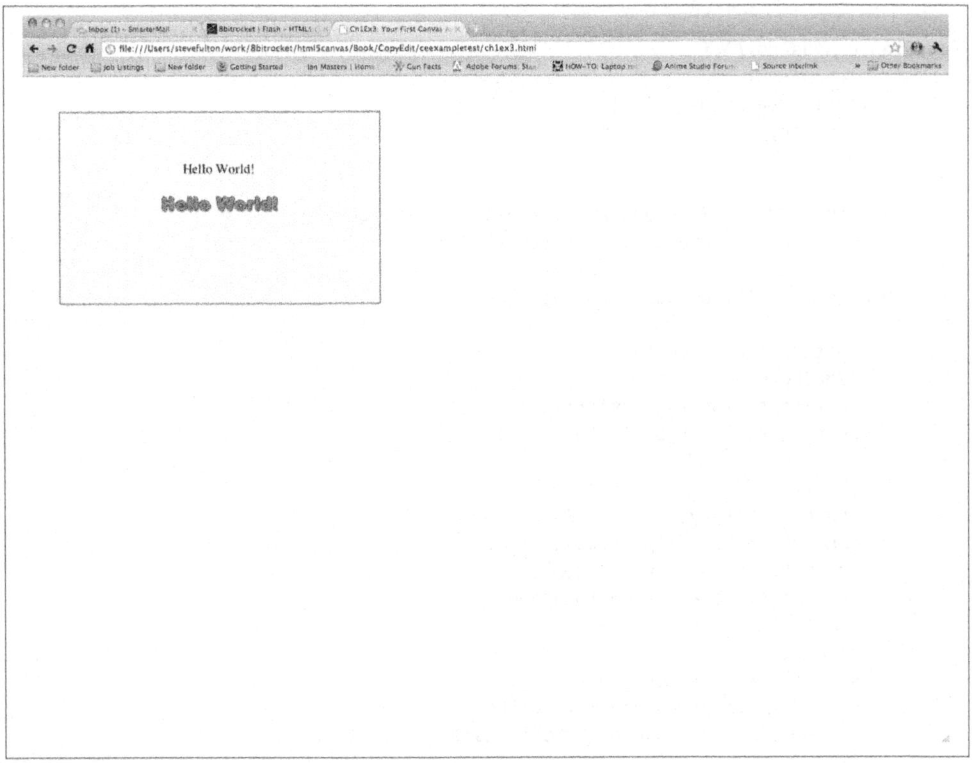

Figure 1-3. HTML5 Canvas Hello World!

Debugging with console.log

There is one more thing to discuss before we explore bigger and better things beyond "Hello World!" In this book, we have implemented a very simple debugging methodology using the `console.log` functionality of modern web browsers. This function lets you log text messages to the JavaScript console to help find problems (or opportunities!) with your code. Any browser that has a JavaScript console (Chrome, Opera, Safari, Firefox with Firebug installed) can make use of `console.log`. However, browsers without `console.log` support throw a nasty error.

To handle this error, we use a wrapper around `console.log` that makes the call only if the function is supported. The wrapper creates a class named `Debugger` and then creates a static function named `Debugger.log` that can be called from anywhere in your code, like this:

```
Debugger.log("Drawing Canvas");
```

Here is the code for the `console.log()` functionality:

```
var Debugger = function () { };
Debugger.log = function (message) {
    try {
        console.log(message);
    } catch (exception) {
        return;
    }
}
```

The 2D Context and the Current State

The HTML5 2D context (the `CanvasRenderingContext2D` object), retrieved by a call to the `getContext()` method of the `Canvas` object, is where all the action takes place. The `CanvasRenderingContext2D` contains all the methods and properties we need to draw onto the canvas. The `CanvasRenderingContext2D` (or context, as we will call it hereafter) uses a Cartesian coordinate system with 0,0 at the upper-left corner of the canvas, with coordinates increasing in value to the right and down.

However, all of these properties and methods are used in conjunction with *current state*, a concept that must be grasped before you can really understand how to work with HTML5 Canvas. The current state is actually a stack of drawing states that apply globally to the entire canvas. You will manipulate these states when drawing on the canvas. These states include:

Transformation matrix
    Methods for scale, rotate, transform, and translate.

Clipping region
    Created with the `clip()` method.

Properties of the context
    Properties include `strokeStyle`, `fillStyle`, `globalAlpha`, `lineWidth`, `lineCap`, `lineJoin`, `miterLimit`, `shadowOffsetX`, `shadowOffsetY`, `shadowBlur`, `shadowColor`, `globalCompositeOperation`, `font`, `textAlign`, and `textBaseline`.

Don't worry; these should not look familiar to you just yet. We will discuss these properties in depth in the next three chapters.

Remember earlier in this chapter when we discussed immediate mode versus retained mode? The canvas is an immediate mode drawing surface, which means everything needs to be redrawn every time something changes. There are some advantages to this; for example, global properties make it very easy to apply effects to the entire screen.

Once you get your head around it, the act of redrawing the screen every time there is an update makes the process of drawing to the canvas straightforward and simple.

On the other hand, retained mode is when a set of objects is stored by a drawing surface and manipulated with a display list. Flash and Silverlight work in this mode. Retained mode can be very useful for creating applications that rely on multiple objects with their own independent states. Many of the same applications that could make full use of the canvas (games, activities, animations) are often easier to code with a retained mode drawing surface, especially for beginners.

Our challenge is to take advantage of the immediate mode drawing surface, while adding functionality to our code to help it act more like it works in retained mode. Throughout this book, we will discuss strategies that will help take this immediate mode operation and make it easier to manipulate through code.

The HTML5 Canvas Object

Recall that the Canvas object is created by placing the <canvas> tag in the <body> portion of an HTML page. You can also create an instance of a canvas in code like this:

```
var theCanvas = document.createElement("canvas");
```

The Canvas object has two associated properties and methods that can be accessed through JavaScript: width and height. These tell you the current width and height of the canvas rendered on the HTML page. It is important to note that they are *not* read-only; that is, they can be updated in code and changed on an HTML page. What does this mean? It means that you can dynamically resize the canvas on the HTML page without reloading.

 You can also use CSS styles to change the scale of the canvas. Unlike resizing, scaling takes the current canvas bitmapped area and resamples it to fit into the size specified by the width and height attributes of the CSS style. For example, to scale the canvas to a 400×400 area, you might use this CSS style:

```
style="width: 400px; height:400px"
```

We include an example of scaling the Canvas with a transformation matrix in Chapter 3.

There are currently two public methods for the Canvas object. The first is getCon text(), which we used earlier in this chapter. We will continue to use it throughout this book to retrieve a reference to the Canvas 2D context so we can draw onto the canvas.

The second method is toDataURL(). This method will return a string of data that represents the bitmapped image of the Canvas object as it is currently rendered. It's like a snapshot of the screen. By supplying different MIME types as a parameter, you can retrieve the data in different formats. The basic format is an *image/png*, but *image/jpeg* and other formats can be retrieved. We will use the `toDataURL()` method in the next application to export an image of the canvas into another browser window.

 A third public method, `toBlob()`, has been defined and is being implemented across browsers. `toBlob([callback])` will return a file reference to an image instead of a base64 encoded string. It is currently not implemented in any browsers.

Another Example: Guess The Letter

Now we will take a quick look at a more involved example of a "Hello World!"–type application, the game "Guess The Letter." We've included this example to illustrate how much more Canvas programming is done in JavaScript than in the Canvas API.

In this game, shown in Figure 1-4, the player's job is to guess the letter of the alphabet that the computer has chosen randomly. The game keeps track of how many guesses the player has made, lists the letters he has already guessed, and tells the player whether he needs to guess higher (toward Z) or lower (toward A).

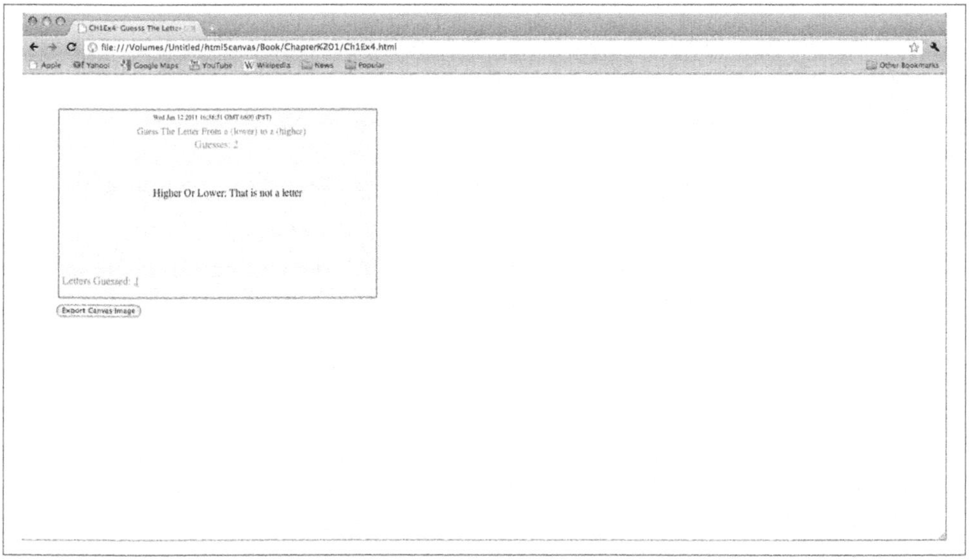

Figure 1-4. HTML5 Canvas "Guess The Letter" game

How the Game Works

This game is set up with the same basic structure as "Hello World!" `canvasApp()` is the main function, and all other functions are defined as local to `canvasApp()`. We use a `drawScreen()` function to render text on the canvas. However, there are some other functions included as well, which are described next.

The "Guess The Letter" Game Variables

Here is a rundown of the variables we will use in the game. They are all defined and initialized in `canvasApp()`, so they have scope to the encapsulated functions that we define locally:

guesses
> This variable holds the number of times the player has pressed a letter. The lower the number, the better he has done in the game.

message
> The content of this variable is displayed to give the user instructions on how to play.

letters
> This array holds one of each letter of the alphabet. We will use this array to both randomly choose a secret letter for the game and to figure out the relative position of the letter in the alphabet.

today
> This variable holds the current date. It is displayed on the screen but has no other purpose.

letterToGuess
> This variable holds the current game's secret letter that needs to be guessed.

higherOrLower
> This variable holds the text "Higher" or "Lower," depending on where the last guessed letter is in relation to the secret letter. If the secret letter is closer to "a," we give the "Lower" instruction. If the letter is closer to "z," we give the "Higher" instruction.

lettersGuessed
> This array holds the current set of letters that the player has guessed already. We will print this list on the screen to help the player remember what letters he has already chosen.

gameOver
> This variable is set to `false` until the player wins. We will use this to know when to put the "You Win" message on the screen and to keep the player from guessing after he has won.

Here is the code:

```
var guesses = 0;
var message = "Guess The Letter From a (lower) to z (higher)";
var letters = [
            "a","b","c","d","e","f","g","h","i","j","k","l","m","n","o",
            "p","q","r","s","t","u","v","w","x","y","z"
            ];
var today = new Date();
var letterToGuess = "";
var higherOrLower = "";
var lettersGuessed;
var gameOver = false;
```

The initGame() Function

The initGame() function sets up the game for the player. The two most important blocks of code are as follows. This code finds a random letter from the letters array and stores it in the letterToGuess variable:

```
var letterIndex = Math.floor(Math.random() * letters.length);
letterToGuess = letters[letterIndex];
```

This code adds an event listener to the window object of the DOM to listen for the keyboard keydown event. When a key is pressed, the eventKeyPressed event handler is called to test the letter pressed:

```
window.addEventListener("keydown",eventKeyPressed,true);
```

Here is the full code for the function:

```
function initGame() {
    var letterIndex = Math.floor(Math.random() * letters.length);
    letterToGuess = letters[letterIndex];
    guesses = 0;
    lettersGuessed = [];
    gameOver = false;
    window.addEventListener("keydown",eventKeyPressed,true);
    drawScreen();
}
```

The eventKeyPressed() Function

This function, called when the player presses a key, contains most of the action in this game. Every event handler function in JavaScript is passed an event object that has information about the event that has taken place. We use the e argument to hold that object.

The first test we make is to see whether the gameOver variable is false. If so, we continue to test the key that was pressed by the player; the next two lines of code are used for that purpose. The first line of code gets the key-press value from the event and converts it to an alphabetic letter that we can test with the letter stored in `letterToGuess`:

```
var letterPressed = String.fromCharCode(e.keyCode);
```

The next line of code converts the letter to lowercase so that we can test uppercase letters if the player unintentionally has Caps Lock on:

```
letterPressed = letterPressed.toLowerCase();
```

Next, we increase the `guesses` count to display and use the `Array.push()` method to add the letter to the `lettersGuessed` array:

```
guesses++;
lettersGuessed.push(letterPressed);
```

Now it is time to test the current game state to give feedback to the player. First, we test to see whether `letterPressed` is equal to `letterToGuess`. If so, the player has won the game:

```
if (letterPressed == letterToGuess) {
    gameOver = true;
```

If the player has not won, we need to get the index of `letterToGuess` and the index of `letterPressed` in the `letters` array. We are going to use these values to figure out whether we should display "Higher," "Lower," or "That is not a letter." To do this, we use the `indexOf()` array method to get the relative index of each letter. Because we alphabetized the letters in the array, it is very easy to test which message to display:

```
} else {
    letterIndex = letters.indexOf(letterToGuess);
    guessIndex = letters.indexOf(letterPressed);
```

Now we make the test. First, if `guessIndex` is less than zero, it means that the call to `indexOf()` returned –1, and the pressed key was not a letter. We then display an error message:

```
if (guessIndex < 0) {
    higherOrLower = "That is not a letter";
```

The rest of the tests are simple. If `guessIndex` is greater than `letterIndex`, we set the `higherOrLower` text to "Lower." Conversely, if `guessIndex` is less than `letterIndex`, we set the `higherOrLower` test to "Higher":

```
    } else if (guessIndex > letterIndex) {
        higherOrLower = "Lower";
    } else {
        higherOrLower = "Higher";
    }

}
```

Finally, we call `drawScreen()` to paint the screen:

```
        drawScreen();
```

Here is the full code for the function:

```
function eventKeyPressed(e) {
    if (!gameOver) {
        var letterPressed = String.fromCharCode(e.keyCode);
        letterPressed = letterPressed.toLowerCase();
        guesses++;
        lettersGuessed.push(letterPressed);

        if (letterPressed == letterToGuess) {
            gameOver = true;
        } else {

            letterIndex = letters.indexOf(letterToGuess);
            guessIndex = letters.indexOf(letterPressed);
            Debugger.log(guessIndex);
            if (guessIndex < 0) {
                higherOrLower = "That is not a letter";
            } else if (guessIndex > letterIndex) {
                higherOrLower = "Lower";
            } else {
                higherOrLower = "Higher";
            }

        }
        drawScreen();
    }
}
```

The drawScreen() Function

Now we get to `drawScreen()`. The good news is that we have seen almost all of this
before—there are only a few differences from "Hello World!" For example, we paint
multiple variables on the screen using the Canvas Text API. We set `context.textBase
line = 'top';` only once for all the text we are going to display. Also, we change the
color using `context.fillStyle`, and we change the font with `context.font`.

The most interesting thing we display here is the content of the `lettersGuessed` array.
On the canvas, the array is printed as a set of comma-separated values, like this:

```
Letters Guessed: p,h,a,d
```

To print this value, all we do is use the `toString()` method of the `lettersGuessed` array,
which prints out the values of an array as—you guessed it—comma-separated values:

```
context.fillText ("Letters Guessed: " + lettersGuessed.toString(), 10, 260);
```

We also test the `gameOver` variable. If it is `true`, we put "You Got It!" on the screen in
giant `40px` text so that the user knows he has won.

Here is the full code for the function:

```
function drawScreen() {
      //Background
      context.fillStyle = "#ffffaa";
      context.fillRect(0, 0, 500, 300);
      //Box
      context.strokeStyle = "#000000";
      context.strokeRect(5,  5, 490, 290);

      context.textBaseline = "top";
      //Date
      context.fillStyle = "#000000";
      context.font = "10px Sans-Serif";
      context.fillText  (today, 150 ,10);
      //Message
      context.fillStyle = "#FF0000";
      context.font = "14px Sans-Serif";
      context.fillText  (message, 125, 30);       //Guesses
      context.fillStyle = "#109910";
      context.font = "16px Sans-Serif";
      context.fillText  ('Guesses: ' + guesses, 215, 50);
      //Higher Or Lower
      context.fillStyle = "#000000";
      context.font = "16px Sans-Serif";
      context.fillText  ("Higher Or Lower: " + higherOrLower, 150,125);
      //Letters Guessed
      context.fillStyle = "#FF0000";
      context.font = "16px Sans-Serif";
      context.fillText  ("Letters Guessed: " + lettersGuessed.toString(),
                           10, 260);
      if (gameOver) {
         context.fillStyle = "#FF0000";
         context.font = "40px Sans-Serif";
         context.fillText  ("You Got It!", 150, 180);
      }
   }
```

Exporting Canvas to an Image

Earlier, we briefly discussed the `toDataUrL()` property of the `Canvas` object. We are going to use that property to let the user create an image of the game screen at any time. This acts almost like a screen-capture utility for games made on Canvas.

We need to create a button in the HTML page that the user can press to get the screen capture. We will add this button to `<form>` and give it the `id` `createImageData`:

```
<form>
<input type="button" id="createImageData" value="Export Canvas Image">
</form>
```

In the init() function, we retrieve a reference to that form element by using the getE
lementById() method of the document object. We then set an event handler for the
button "click" event as the function createImageDataPressed():

```
var formElement = document.getElementById("createImageData");
formElement.addEventListener('click', createImageDataPressed, false);
```

In canvasApp(), we define the createImageDataPressed() function as an event handler. This function calls window.open(), passing the return value of the Canvas.toDa
taURl() method as the source for the window. Since this data forms a valid *.png*, the
image is displayed in the new window:

```
function createImageDataPressed(e) {

    window.open(theCanvas.toDataURL(),"canvasImage","left=0,top=0,width=" +
    theCanvas.width + ",height=" + theCanvas.height +",toolbar=0,resizable=0");
    }
```

 We will discuss this process in depth in Chapter 3.

The Final Game Code

Check out the final game code for "Guess The Letter" in *CH1EX4.html* in the code
distribution.

Hello World Animated Edition

The "Hello World" and "Guess The Letter" examples were fine, but they lacked an an-
swer to the question "why?"—as in the question, "Why use the HTML5 Canvas at all?"
Static images and text have been the realm of HTML since its inception, so why is the
Canvas so different? To answer that question, we are going to create a second "Hello
World" example that introduces the main feature that sets the Canvas from other methods of display in HTML: animation. In this example, we will simply fade the words
"Hello World" in and out in the screen. While very simple, this is our first small step
into the bigger world of the HTML5 Canvas. You can see an example of the final application in Figure 1-5.

Figure 1-5. HTML5 Canvas Animated Hello World

Some Necessary Properties

For this application we need a few properties to set everything up.

The `alpha` property is the value that we will apply to `context.globalAlpha` to set the transparency value for text that we will fade in and out. It is set to 0 to start, which means the text will start completely invisible. We will explain more about this in the next section.

The `fadeIn` property will tell our application if the text is currently fading in or fading out.

The `text` property holds the string we will display.

The `helloWorldImage` property will hold the background image we will display behind the fading text:

```
var alpha = 0;
var fadeIn = true;
var text = "Hello World";
var helloWorldImage = new Image();
helloWorldImage.src = "html5bg.jpg";
```

Animation Loop

To make anything move on the Canvas, you need an *animation loop*. An animation loop is a function called over and over on an interval. The function is used to clear the Canvas and redraw it with updated images, text, video, and drawing objects.

The easiest way to create an interval for animation is to use a simple `setTimeout()` loop. To do this, we create a function named `gameLoop()` (it can be called anything you like) that uses `window.setTimeout()` to call itself after a specified time period. For our application, that time period will be 20 milliseconds. The function then resets itself to call again in 20 milliseconds and then calls `drawScreen()`.

Using this method, `drawScreen()` is called every 20 milliseconds. We will place all of our drawing code in `drawScreen()`. This method does the same thing as using `setInterval()` but, because it clears itself and does not run forever, is much better for performance:

```
function gameLoop() {
    window.setTimeout(gameLoop, 20);
    drawScreen()
}

gameLoop();
```

requestAnimationFrame()

The *best* way to create an animation loop is by using the brand-new `window.requestAnimationFrame()` method. This new method uses a delta timer to tell your JavaScript program exactly when the browser is ready to render a new frame of animation. The code looks like this:

```
window.requestAnimFrame = (function(){
    return  window.requestAnimationFrame       ||
            window.webkitRequestAnimationFrame ||
            window.mozRequestAnimationFrame    ||
            window.oRequestAnimationFrame      ||
            window.msRequestAnimationFrame     ||
            function( callback ){
               window.setTimeout(callback, 1000 / 60);
            };
})();

(function animloop(){
    requestAnimFrame(animloop);
    render();
})();
(code originally developed by Paul Irish)
```

However, because this method is changing and has not been implemented across all browsers, we are going to use `window.setTimeout()` for applications in this book.

Alpha Transparency with the globalAlpha Property

We have chosen `context.globalAlpha` for this animation because it is very easy to explain and makes for an effective demonstration of animating on the Canvas. The `globalAlpha` property is the setting for transparency on the Canvas. The property accepts numbers from 0 through 1, representing a percentage of opaqueness for what will be drawn *after* the property is set. For example:

```
context.globalAlpha = 0;
```

The preceding code would set everything drawn afterward to be rendered 0% opaque, or completely transparent.

```
context.globalAlpha = 1;
```

The preceding code would set everything drawn afterwards to be rendered 100% opaque, or 0% transparent.

```
context.globalAlpha = .5;
```

The preceding code would set everything drawn afterwards to be rendered 50% opaque, or 50% transparent.

By manipulating these values over time, we can make things drawn onto the Canvas appear to fade in or out.

 `context.globalAlpha` affects *everything* drawn afterward, so if you don't want something drawn with the `globalAlpha` property of the last thing drawn, you need to reset the value before drawing onto the Canvas.

Clearing and Displaying the Background

In the `drawScreen()` function that is called every 20 milliseconds, we need to redraw the Canvas to update the animation.

Because our little application uses `globalAlpha` to change the transparency of things we are drawing, we first need to make sure to reset the property before we start our drawing operation. We do this by setting `context.globalAlpha` to 1 and then drawing the background (a black box). Next we set the `globalAlpha` property to `.25` and draw the `helloWorldImage` that we loaded. This will display the image at 25% opacity, with the black background showing through:

```
function drawScreen() {
   //background
   context.globalAlpha = 1;
   context.fillStyle = "#000000";
   context.fillRect(0, 0, 640, 480);
   //image
   context.globalAlpha = .25;
   context.drawImage(helloWorldImage, 0, 0);
```

Updating the globalAlpha Property for Text Display

Because the animation in this example is composed of fading text in and out on the Canvas, the main operation of the drawScreen() function is to update the alpha and fadeIn properties accordingly. If the text is fading in (fadeIn is true) we increase the alpha property by .01. If alpha is increased above 1 (the maximum it can be), we reset it back to 1 and then set fadeIn to false. This means that we will start fading out. We do the opposite if fadeIn is false, setting it back to true when the value of alpha hits 0. After we set the alpha value, we apply it to the Canvas by setting context.globalAlpha to the value of the alpha property:

```
if (fadeIn) {
    alpha += .01;
    if (alpha >= 1)  {
        alpha = 1;
        fadeIn = false;
    }
} else {
    alpha -= .01;
    if (alpha < 0)  {
        alpha = 0;
        fadeIn = true;
    }
}

context.globalAlpha = alpha;
```

Drawing the Text

Finally, we draw the text to the Canvas, and the drawScreen() function is complete. In 20 milliseconds, drawScreen() will be called again, the alpha value will be updated, and the text will be redrawn:

```
   context.font        = "72px Sans-Serif";
   context.textBaseline = "top";
   context.fillStyle   = "#FFFFFF";
   context.fillText (text, 150,200);
}
```

The full code for this example is as follows:

```
<!doctype html>
<html lang="en">
<head>
<meta charset="UTF-8">
<title>CH1EX5 : Hello World Animated </title>

<script src="modernizr.js"></script>
<script type="text/javascript">
window.addEventListener("load", eventWindowLoaded, false);

function eventWindowLoaded () {
    canvasApp();
}

function canvasSupport () {
    return Modernizr.canvas;
}

function canvasApp () {

        if (!canvasSupport()) {
           return;
        }

      var theCanvas = document.getElementById("canvasOne");
      var context = theCanvas.getContext("2d");

      function drawScreen() {
        //background
        context.globalAlpha = 1;
        context.fillStyle = "#000000";
          context.fillRect(0, 0, 640, 480);
        //image
        context.globalAlpha = .25;
        context.drawImage(helloWorldImage, 0, 0);


        if (fadeIn) {
            alpha += .01;
            if (alpha >= 1)  {
                alpha = 1;
                fadeIn = false;
            }
        } else {
            alpha -= .01;
            if (alpha < 0)  {
                alpha = 0;
                fadeIn = true;
            }
        }

        //text
        context.font         = "72px Sans-Serif";
```

```
        context.textBaseline = "top";


        context.globalAlpha = alpha;
        context.fillStyle   = "#FFFFFF";
        context.fillText  (text, 150,200);

    }

    var text = "Hello World";
    var alpha = 0;
    var fadeIn = true;
    //image
    var helloWorldImage = new Image();
    helloWorldImage.src = "html5bg.jpg";

    function gameLoop() {
        window.setTimeout(gameLoop, 20);
        drawScreen()
    }

    gameLoop();

}


</script>

</head>
<body>
<div style="position: absolute; top: 50px; left: 50px;">
<canvas id="canvasOne" width="640" height="480">
 Your browser does not support HTML 5 Canvas.
</canvas>
</div>
</body>
</html>
```

HTML5 Canvas and Accessibility: Sub Dom

The current method for implementing accessibility for the Canvas is referred to as the "Fallback DOM Concept," or "sub dom" (which involves adding text directly into the <canvas></canvas>).

It has been known for quite some time that the HTML5 Canvas, because it is an immediate mode bit-mapped area of the screen, does not lend itself to accessibility. There is no DOM or display list inherent in the Canvas to make it easy for accessibility devices (such as screen readers) to search for text and images and their properties drawn onto the Canvas. To make the Canvas accessible, a method known as "Fallback DOM Concept," or *sub dom (http://www.w3.org/wiki/Reading_text_in_canvas)*, was devised.

Using this method, developers create a DOM element to match each element on the Canvas and put it in the sub dom.

In the first Canvas "Hello World!" example we created (*CH1EX3.html*), the text "Hello World!" appeared above an image of the earth (see Figure 1-3). To create a sub dom for that example, we might do something like this:

```
<canvas id="canvasOne" width="500" height="300">
 <div>A yellow background with an image and text on top:
    <ol>
        <li>The text says "Hello World"</li>
        <li>The image is of the planet earth.</li>
        </ol>
    </div>
</canvas>
```

We should also make an accessible title for the page. Instead of:

```
<title>Ch1Ex6: Canvas Sub Dom Example </title>
```

Let's change it to:

```
<title>Chapter 1 Example 6 Canvas Sub Dom Example </title>
```

To test this, you need to get a screen reader (or a screen reader emulator). Fangs (*https://addons.mozilla.org/en-us/firefox/addon/fangs-screen-reader-emulator/*) is a screen reader emulator add-on for Firefox that can help you debug the accessibility of your web pages by listing out in text what a screen reader might say when your page is read. After you install the add-on, you can right-click on the web page and choose the "View Fangs" option to see what a screen reader would see on your page.

For the Canvas page we just created, Fangs tells us that the page would read as follows:

"Chapter one Example six Canvas Sub Dom Example dash Internet Explorer A yellow background with an image and text on top *List of two items one* The text says quote Hello World quote *two* The image is of the planet earth.*List end*"

For Google Chrome, you can get the Google Chrome extension Chrome Vox, which will attempt to verbally read all the content on your pages.

(For the full example, see *CH1EX6.html* in the code distribution.)

Hit Testing Proposal

The "sub dom" concept can quickly become unwieldy for anyone who has tried to do anything more intricate than a simple Canvas animation. Why? Because associating fallback elements with Canvas interaction is not always an easy task, and it is complicated by screen readers that need to know the exact position of an element on the Canvas so that they can interpret it.

To help solve this issue, the Canvas needs some way to associate sub dom elements with an area on the bitmapped Canvas. The new W3C Canvas Hit Testing proposal (*http://www.w3.org/wiki/Canvas_hit_testing*) outlines why this type of functionality should be added to the Canvas specification:

> In the current HTML5 specification, authors are advised to create a fallback DOM under the canvas element to enable screen readers to interact with canvas user interfaces. The size and position of those elements are not defined, which causes problems for accessibility tools—for example, what size/position should they report for these elements?
>
> Because canvas elements usually respond to user input, it seems prudent to solve the hit testing and accessibility issues with the same mechanism.

So what kind of mechanism are they suggesting?

The idea appears to be to create two new methods, `setElementPath(element)` and `clearElementPath(element)`, that will allow programmers to define (and delete) an area of the Canvas to use as a hit area, provided that it is associated with the fallback DOM element of the Canvas. It appears that you must have an accessible fallback DOM element to provide to `setElementPath()` in order to associate it for the hit detection. When a hit is detected, an event is fired, and all is right in the world.

So what does this mean for developers?

For user interfaces with stationary interfaces, it will make things a lot easier. How many times have you wanted to create a simple way to click buttons on a game interface but had to use the same hit detection routines you wrote for your in-game sprite interactions? (For us? Every time.) However, for moving sprites in your game, it might be less useful. You will have to update the `setElementPath()` method and the fallback DOM element with new coordinate data every time something moves, which means triple overhead for a game that is probably not accessible in the first place.

Still, this is a good move by the W3C, because making the Canvas accessible for user interfaces is another huge step in making it more widely accepted for web applications. We hope these two new methods are added to the specification as soon as possible. The good news is, as of December 2012, the "Hit Testing Proposal" has been incorporated into the specification for the next version of Canvas, dubbed Canvas Level-2.

What's Next?

So now you should have a basic understanding of the HTML and JavaScript that we will use to render and control HTML5 Canvas on an HTML page. In the next chapter, we will take this information and expand on it to create an interactive application that uses the canvas to render information on the screen.

Drawing on the Canvas

Using HTML5 Canvas effectively requires a strong foundation in drawing, coloring, and transforming basic two-dimensional shapes. While the selection of built-in shapes is relatively limited, we can draw any shape we desire by using a series of line segments called *paths*, which we will discuss in the upcoming section "Using Paths to Create Lines" on page 38.

 The HTML5 Canvas API is well covered in many online forms. The W3C site (*http://bit.ly/17ftf5F*) has an exhaustive and constantly updated reference that details the features of the Canvas 2D Drawing API.

However, this online reference lacks concrete examples on using the API. Rather than simply reprinting this entire specification, we will spend our time creating examples to explain and explore as many features as we have space to cover.

The Basic File Setup for This Chapter

As we proceed through the Drawing API, all the examples in this chapter will use the same basic file setup, shown below. Use this code as the basis for all of the examples we create. You will have to change only the contents of the drawScreen() function:

```
<!doctype html>
<html lang="en">
<head>
<meta charset="UTF-8">
<title>Ch2BaseFile - Template For Chapter 2 Examples</title>

<script src="modernizr.js"></script>
<script type="text/javascript">
window.addEventListener('load', eventWindowLoaded, false);
function eventWindowLoaded() {
```

```
            canvasApp();

    }

    function canvasSupport () {
        return Modernizr.canvas;
    }

    function canvasApp(){

    if (!canvasSupport()) {
            return;
        }else{
          var theCanvas = document.getElementById("canvas");
          var context = theCanvas.getContext("2d");
        }

        drawScreen();

        function drawScreen() {
          //make changes here.
          context.fillStyle = '#aaaaaa';
          context.fillRect(0, 0, 200, 200);
          context.fillStyle  = '#000000';
          context.font = '20px _sans';
          context.textBaseline = 'top';
          context.fillText  ("Canvas!", 0, 0);

        }
    }

    </script>

    </head>
    <body>
    <div style="position: absolute; top: 50px; left: 50px;">
    <canvas id="canvas" width="500" height="500">
     Your browser does not support HTML5 Canvas.
    </canvas>
    </div>
    </body>
    </html>
```

The Basic Rectangle Shape

Let's get our feet wet by looking at the single primitive, built-in geometric shape on
Canvas—the rectangle. On Canvas, basic rectangle shapes can be drawn in three different ways: filling, stroking, or clearing. We can also build rectangles (or any other
shape) by using paths, which we will cover in the next section.

First, let's look at the API functions used for these three operations:

`fillRect(x,y,width,height)`
> Draws a filled rectangle at position x,y for width and height.

`strokeRect(x,y,width,height)`
> Draws a rectangular outline at position x,y for width and height. This makes use of the current `strokeStyle`, `lineWidth`, `lineJoin`, and `miterLimit` settings.

`clearRect(x,y,width,height)`
> Clears the specified area and makes it fully transparent (using transparent black as the color) starting at position x,y for width and height.

Before we can use any of these functions, we will need to set up the fill or stroke style that will be used when drawing to the canvas.

The most basic way to set these styles is to use a color value represented by a 24-bit hex string. Here is an example from our first demonstration:

```
context.fillStyle = '#000000';
context.strokeStyle = '#ff00ff';
```

In Example 2-1, the fill style is simply set to be the RGB color black, while the stroke style is a classic purple color. The results are shown in Figure 2-1.

Example 2-1. Basic rectangles

```
function drawScreen() {
    context.fillStyle  = '#000000';
    context.strokeStyle = '#ff00ff';
    context.lineWidth  = 2;
    context.fillRect(10,10,40,40);
    context.strokeRect(0, 0,60,60);
    context.clearRect(20,20,20,20);

}
```

Figure 2-1. Basic rectangles

The Canvas State

When we draw on the Canvas context, we can make use of a stack of so-called drawing *states*. Each of these states stores data about the Canvas context at any one time. Here is a list of the data stored in the stack for each state:

- Transformation matrix information such as rotations or translations using the `context.rotate()` and `context.setTransform()` methods
- The current clipping region
- The current values for canvas attributes, such as (but not limited to):
  — `globalAlpha`
  — `globalCompositeOperation`
  — `strokeStyle`
  — `textAlign`, `textBaseline`
  — `lineCap`, `lineJoin`, `lineWidth`, and `miterLimit`
  — `fillStyle`
  — `font`
  — `shadowBlur`, `shadowColor`, `shadowOffsetX`, and `shadowOffsetY`

We will cover these states later in this chapter.

What's Not Part of the State?

The current path (which we will explore later in this chapter) and current bitmap (see Chapter 4) being manipulated on the Canvas context are *not* part of the saved state. This very important feature will allow us to draw and animate individual objects on the canvas. The section "Simple Canvas Transformations" on page 50 utilizes the Canvas state to apply transformations to only the current shape being constructed and drawn, leaving the rest of the canvas not transformed.

How Do We Save and Restore the Canvas State?

To save (push) the current state to the stack, call:

```
context.save()
```

To restore the canvas by "popping" the last state saved to the stack, use:

```
context.restore()
```

Using Paths to Create Lines

Paths are a method we can use to draw any shape on the canvas. A path is simply a list of points, and lines to be drawn between those points. A Canvas context can have only a single "current" path, which is not stored as part of the current drawing state when the `context.save()` method is called.

Context for paths is a critical concept to understand, because it will enable you to transform only the current path on the canvas.

Starting and Ending a Path

The beginPath() function call starts a path, and the closePath() function call ends the path. When you connect two points inside a path, it is referred to as a *subpath*. A subpath is considered "closed" if the final point connects to the first point.

 The current transformation matrix will affect everything drawn in this path. As we will see when we explore the upcoming section on transformations, we will always want to set the transformation matrix to the identity (or reset) if we do not want any transformation applied to a path.

The Actual Drawing

The most basic path is controlled by a series of moveTo() and lineTo() commands, as shown in Example 2-2.

Example 2-2. A simple line path

```
function drawScreen() {
   context.strokeStyle  = "black";
   context.lineWidth  = 10;
   context.lineCap  = 'square';
   context.beginPath();
   context.moveTo(20, 0);
   context.lineTo(100, 0);
   context.stroke();
   context.closePath();

}
```

Figure 2-2 shows an example of this output.

Figure 2-2. A simple line path

Example 2-2 simply draws a 10-pixel-wide horizontal line (or stroke) from position 20,0 to position 100,0.

We have also added the lineCap and strokeStyle attributes. Let's take a brief look at the various attributes we can apply to a line before we move on to some more advanced drawing. The `context.stroke();` command will finalize and draw the line we have constructed.

lineCap attributes

context.lineCap. The `lineCap` is the end of a line drawn on the context. It can be one of three values:

butt
> The default; a flat edge that is perpendicular to the edge of the line.

round
> A semicircle that will have a diameter that is the length of the edge of the line.

square
> A rectangle with the length of the line width and the height of half the line width, placed flat and perpendicular to the edge of the line.

lineJoin attributes

context.lineJoin. The `lineJoin` is the "corner" that is created when two lines meet. This is called a *join*. A filled triangle is created at the join, and we can set its basic properties with the `lineJoin` Canvas attribute:

miter
> The default; an edge is drawn at the join. The `miterLimit` is the maximum allowed ratio of miter length to line width. (The default is 10.)

bevel
> A diagonal edge is drawn at the join.

round
> A round edge is drawn at the join.

lineWidth

The `lineWidth` (default = 1.0) depicts the thickness of the line.

strokeStyle

The `strokeStyle` defines the color or style that will be used for lines and around shapes (as we saw with the simple rectangles in Example 2-2).

Examples of More Advanced Line Drawing

Example 2-3 shows these attributes in action; the results are depicted in Figure 2-3. There are a few oddities when drawing lines on the canvas, which we will point out along the way.

Example 2-3. Line cap and join

```
function drawScreen() {

    // Sample 1: round end, bevel join, at top left of canvas
    context.strokeStyle  = "black";
    context.lineWidth  = 10;
    context.lineJoin  = 'bevel';
    context.lineCap  = 'round';
    context.beginPath();
    context.moveTo(0, 0);
    context.lineTo(25, 0);
    context.lineTo(25,25);
    context.stroke();
    context.closePath();

    // Sample 2: round end, bevel join, not at top or left of canvas
    context.beginPath();
    context.moveTo(10, 50);
    context.lineTo(35, 50);
    context.lineTo(35,75);
    context.stroke();
    context.closePath();

    // Sample 3: flat end, round join, not at top or left of canvas
    context.lineJoin  = 'round';
    context.lineCap = 'butt';
    context.beginPath();
    context.moveTo(10, 100);
    context.lineTo(35, 100);
    context.lineTo(35,125);
    context.stroke();
    context.closePath();

}
```

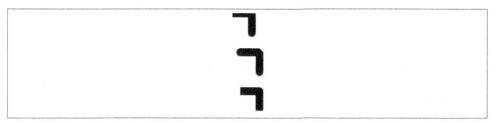

Figure 2-3. Line cap and join

These three line and join samples should help illustrate some of the combinations of attributes we can use to draw paths on the canvas.

The first sample attempts to draw starting at the top left of the canvas, resulting in a strange image. Canvas paths are drawn outward in both the *x* and *y* directions from the center of the pixel it begins on. For this reason, the top line in Sample 1 seems to be thinner than the 10 pixels we specified. In addition, the "round" end of the top-left horizontal line segment cannot be seen because both of these were drawn off the screen in the "negative" value areas of the screen coordinates. Furthermore, the diagonal "bevel" at the lineJoin is not drawn.

Sample 2 rectifies the problems in Sample 1 by offsetting the beginning of the drawing away from the top left. This allows the entire horizontal line to be drawn, as well as the "round" lineCap and the "bevel" lineJoin.

Sample 3 shows us eliminating the extra lineCap in favor of the default "butt," and changing the lineJoin to "round."

Advanced Path Methods

Let's take a deeper look at some of the other methods we can use to draw paths on the canvas, including arcs and curves that can be combined to create complex images.

Arcs

There are four functions we can use to draw arcs and curves onto the canvas. An arc can be a complete circle or any part of a circle.

context.arc()

Here is context.arc() (*http://www.w3schools.com/tags/canvas_arc.asp*) in action:

```
context.arc(x, y, radius, startAngle, endAngle, anticlockwise)
```

The x and y values define the center of our circle, and the radius will be the radius of the circle upon which our arc will be drawn. startAngle and endAngle are in radians, not degrees. anticlockwise is a true or false value that defines the direction of the arc.

For example, if we want to draw a circle with a center point at position 100,100 and with a radius of 20, as shown in Figure 2-4, we could use the following code for the contents of drawScreen():

```
context.arc(100, 100, 20, (Math.PI/180)*0, (Math.PI/180)*360, false);
```

Example 2-4 illustrates the code necessary to create a simple circle.

Example 2-4. A circle arc

```
function drawScreen() {
```

```
context.beginPath();
context.strokeStyle = "black";
context.lineWidth = 5;
context.arc(100, 100, 20, (Math.PI/180)*0, (Math.PI/180)*360, false);

//full circle
context.stroke();
context.closePath();
```

```
}
```

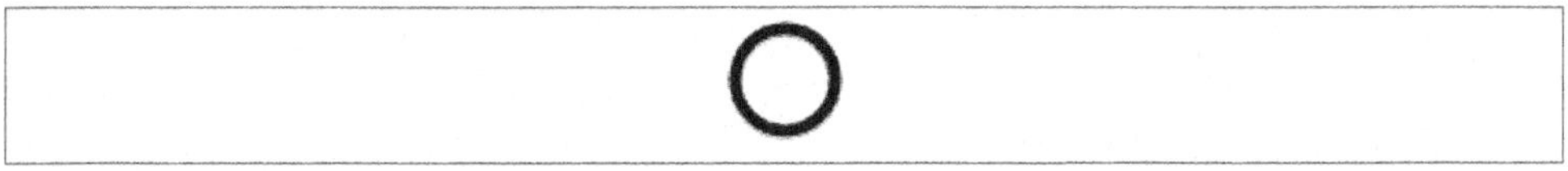

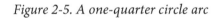

Figure 2-4. A basic circle arc

Notice that we have to convert our start angle (0) and our end angle (360) into radians
by multiplying them by (Math.PI/180). By using 0 as the start angle and 360 as the end,
we create a full circle.

We can also draw a segment of a circle by not specifying the entire 0 to 360 start and
stop angles. This code for drawScreen() will create one-quarter of a circle drawn clockwise, as shown in Figure 2-5:

```
context.arc(100, 200, 20, (Math.PI/180)*0, (Math.PI/180)*90, false);
```

Figure 2-5. A one-quarter circle arc

If we want to draw everything *but* the 0–90 angle, as shown in Figure 2-6, we can employ
the anticlockwise argument and set it to true:

```
context.arc(100, 200, 20, (Math.PI/180)*0, (Math.PI/180)*90, true);
```

Figure 2-6. A three-fourths circle arc

context.arcTo()

Here is context.arcTo() (*http://www.w3schools.com/tags/canvas_arcto.asp*) in
action:

```
context.arcTo(x1, y1, x2, y2, radius)
```

The arcTo method has been implemented only in the latest browsers—perhaps because its capabilities can be replicated by the arc() function. It takes in a point (x1,y1) and draws a straight line from the current path position to this new position. Then it draws an arc from that point to the y1,y2 point, using the given radius.

The context.arcTo method will work only if the current path has at least one subpath. So, let's start with a line from position 0,0 to position 100,200. Then we will build our small arc. It will look a little like a bent wire coat hanger (for lack of a better description), as shown in Figure 2-7:

```
context.moveTo(0,0);
context.lineTo(100, 200);
context.arcTo(350,350,100,100,20);
```

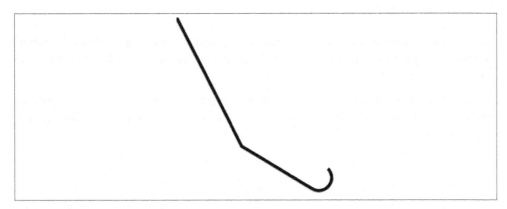

Figure 2-7. An arcTo() example

Bezier Curves

Bezier curves, which are far more flexible than arcs, come in both the cubic and quadratic types:

- context.bezierCurveTo(*cp1x, cp1y, cp2x, cp2y, x, y*) (*http://www.w3.org/ html/wg/drafts/2dcontext/html5_canvas/#dom-context-2d-beziercurveto*)
- context.quadraticCurveTo(*cpx, cpy, x, y*) (*http://www.w3.org/html/wg/ drafts/2dcontext/html5_canvas/#dom-context-2d-quadraticcurveto*)

The Bezier curve is defined in 2D space by a "start point," an "end point," and one or two "control" points, which determine how the curve will be constructed on the canvas. A normal cubic Bezier curve uses two points, while a quadratic version uses a single point.

The quadratic version, shown in Figure 2-8, is the simplest, needing only the end point (last) and a single point in space to use as a control point (first):

```
context.moveTo(0,0);
context.quadraticCurveTo(100,25,0,50);
```

Figure 2-8. A simple quadratic Bezier curve

This curve starts at 0,0 and ends at 0,50. The point in space we use to create our arc is 100,25. This point is roughly the center of the arc vertically. The 100 value for the single control point pulls the arc out to make an elongated curve.

The cubic Bezier curve offers more options because we have two control points to work with. The result is that curves—such as the classic "S" curve shown in Figure 2-9—are easier to make:

```
context.moveTo(150,0);
context.bezierCurveTo(0,125,300,175,150,300);
```

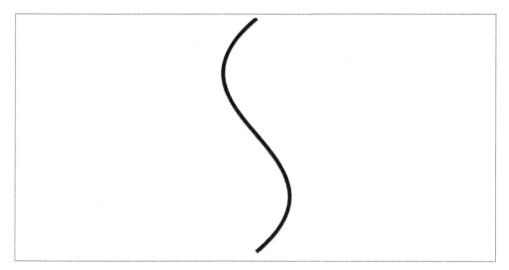

Figure 2-9. A Bezier curve with two control points

The Canvas Clipping Region

By using the Canvas clipping region, we can limit the drawing area for a path and its subpaths. We do this by first setting rect() attribute of the context to a rectangle that encompasses the region we would like to draw in and then calling the clip() function.

This will set the clip region to be the rectangle we defined with the rect() method call. Now, no matter what we draw onto the current context, it will display only the portion that is in this region. Think of this as a sort of mask that you can use for your drawing operations. Example 2-5 shows how this works, producing the clipped result shown in Figure 2-10.

In this example, we will implement the save() and restore() Canvas functions around the red circle. If we did not, the blue circle would not be drawn. You can test this for yourself by commenting out the save() and restore() lines in Example 2-5.

Example 2-5. The Canvas clipping region

```
function drawScreen() {

        //draw a big box on the screen
        context.fillStyle = "black";
        context.fillRect(10, 10, 200, 200);
        context.save();
        context.beginPath();        //clip the canvas to a 50×50 square starting at 0,0
        context.rect(0, 0, 50, 50);
        context.clip();

        //red circle
        context.beginPath();
        context.strokeStyle = "red";
        context.lineWidth = 5;
        context.arc(100, 100, 100, (Math.PI/180)*0, (Math.PI/180)*360, false);
        //full circle
        context.stroke();
        context.closePath();

        context.restore();

        //reclip to the entire canvas
        context.beginPath();
        context.rect(0, 0, 500, 500);
        context.clip();

        //draw a blue line that is not clipped
        context.beginPath();
        context.strokeStyle = "blue";
        context.lineWidth = 5;
        context.arc(100, 100, 50, (Math.PI/180)*0, (Math.PI/180)*360, false);
        //full circle
        context.stroke();
        context.closePath();


}
```

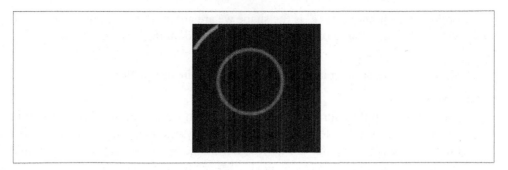

Figure 2-10. The Canvas clipping region

Example 2-5 first draws a large 200×200 black rectangle onto the canvas. Next, we set our Canvas clipping region to `rect(0,0,50,50)`. The `clip()` call then clips the canvas to those specifications. When we draw our full red circle arc, we see only the portion inside this rectangle. Finally, we set the clipping region back to `rect(0,0,500,500)` and draw a new blue circle. This time, we can see the entire circle on the canvas.

 Other Canvas methods can be used with the clipping region. The most obvious is the `arc()` function:

```
arc(float x, float y, float radius, float startAngle, float endAngle,
    boolean anticlockwise)
```

This can be used to create a circular clipping region instead of a rectangular one.

Compositing on the Canvas

Compositing refers to how finely we can control the transparency and layering effects of objects as we draw them to the canvas. There are two attributes we can use to control Canvas compositing operations: `globalAlpha` and `globalCompositeOperation`.

globalAlpha
> The `globalAlpha` Canvas property defaults to `1.0` (completely opaque) and can be set from `0.0` (completely transparent) through `1.0`. This Canvas property must be set before a shape is drawn to the canvas.

globalCompositeOperation
> The `globalCompositeOperation` value controls how shapes are drawn into the current Canvas bitmap after both `globalAlpha` and any transformations have been applied. (See the next section, "Simple Canvas Transformations" on page 50, for more information.)

In the following list, the "source" is the shape we are about to draw to the canvas, and the "destination" refers to the current bitmap displayed on the canvas:

copy
> Where they overlap, displays the source and not the destination.

destination-atop
> Destination atop the source. Where the source and destination overlap and both are opaque, displays the destination image. Displays the source image wherever the source image is opaque but the destination image is transparent. Displays transparency elsewhere.

destination-in
> Destination in the source. Displays the destination image wherever both the destination image and source image are opaque. Displays transparency elsewhere.

destination-out
> Destination out source. Displays the destination image wherever the destination image is opaque and the source image is transparent. Displays transparency elsewhere.

destination-over
> Destination over the source. Displays the destination image wherever the destination image is opaque. Displays the source image elsewhere.

lighter
> Source plus destination. Displays the sum of the source image and destination image, with color values approaching 1.0 as a limit.

source-atop
> Source atop the destination. Displays the source image wherever both images are opaque. Displays the destination image wherever the destination image is opaque but the source image is transparent. Displays transparency elsewhere.

source-in
> Source in the destination. Displays the source image wherever both the source image and destination image are opaque. Displays transparency elsewhere.

source-out
> Source out destination. Displays the source image wherever the source image is opaque and the destination image is transparent. Displays transparency elsewhere.

source-over
> (Default.) Source over destination. Displays the source image wherever the source image is opaque. Displays the destination image elsewhere.

xor

Source xor destination. Exclusive OR of the source image and destination image.

Example 2-6 shows how some of these values can affect how shapes are drawn to the canvas, producing Figure 2-11.

Example 2-6. Canvas compositing example

```
function drawScreen() {

    //draw a big box on the screen
    context.fillStyle = "black"; //
    context.fillRect(10, 10, 200, 200);

    //leave globalCompositeOperation as is
    //now draw a red square
    context.fillStyle = "red";
    context.fillRect(1, 1, 50, 50);

    //now set it to source-over
    context.globalCompositeOperation = "source-over";
    //draw a red square next to the other one
    context.fillRect(60, 1, 50, 50);        //now set to destination-atop
    context.globalCompositeOperation = "destination-atop";
    context.fillRect(1, 60, 50, 50);

    //now set globalAlpha
    context.globalAlpha = .5;

    //now set to source-atop
    context.globalCompositeOperation = "source-atop";
    context.fillRect(60, 60, 50, 50);

}
```

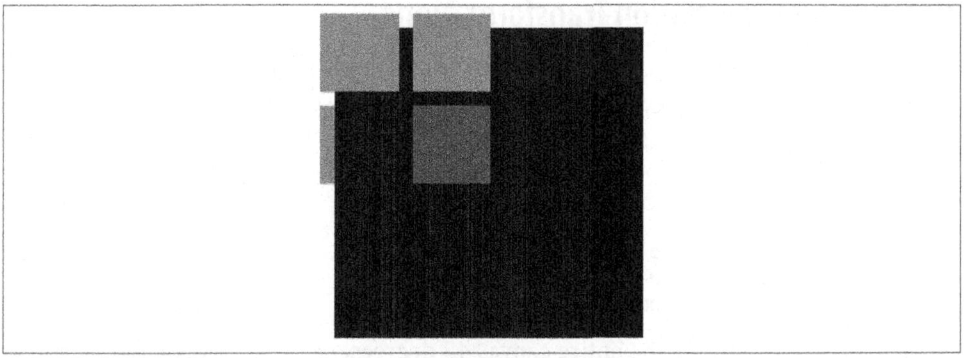

Figure 2-11. Canvas compositing example

Unfortunately `context.globalCompositeOperation = "destination-atop"` does not work properly in browsers any more.

As you can see in this example, we have toyed a little with both the `globalComposi teOperation` and the `globalAlpha` Canvas properties. When we assign the string `source-over`, we are essentially resetting the `globalCompositeOperation` back to the default. We then create some red squares to demonstrate a few of the various compositing options and combinations. Notice that `destination-atop` switches the newly drawn shapes under the current Canvas bitmap and that the `globalAlpha` property affects only shapes that are drawn after it is set. This means that we don't have to use the `save()` and `restore()` functions for the Canvas state to set the next drawn shape to a new transparency value.

In the next section, we will look at some transformations that affect the entire canvas. As a result, if we want to transform only the newly drawn shape, we will have to use the `save()` and `restore()` functions.

Simple Canvas Transformations

Transformations on the canvas refer to the mathematical adjustment of physical properties of drawn shapes. The two most commonly used shape transformations are scale and rotate, which we will focus on in this section.

Under the hood, a mathematical matrix operation applies to all transformations. Luckily, you do not need to understand this to use simple Canvas transformations. We will discuss how to apply rotation, translation, and scale transformations by changing simple Canvas properties.

Rotation and Translation Transformations

An object on the canvas is said to be at the 0 angle rotation when it is facing to the left. (This is important if an object has a facing side; otherwise, we will use this as a guide.) Consequently, if we draw an equilateral box (all four sides are the same length), it doesn't have an initial facing side other than one of the flat sides facing to the left. Let's draw that box for reference:

```
//now draw a red square
context.fillStyle = "red";
context.fillRect(100,100,50,50);
```

Now, if we want to rotate the entire canvas 45 degrees, we need to do a couple simple steps. First, we always set the current Canvas transformation to the "identity" (or "reset") matrix:

```
context.setTransform(1,0,0,1,0,0);
```

Because Canvas uses radians, not degrees, to specify its transformations, we need to convert our 45-degree angle into radians:

```
var angleInRadians = 45 * Math.PI / 180;
context.rotate(angleInRadians);
```

Lesson 1: Transformations are applied to shapes and paths drawn after the setTransform() or other transformation function is called

If you use this code verbatim, you will see a funny result...*nothing*! This is because the setTransform() function call affects only shapes drawn to the canvas *after* it is applied. We drew our square first and then set the transformation properties. This resulted in no change (or transform) to the drawn square. Example 2-7 gives the code in the correct order to produce the expected result, as illustrated in Figure 2-12.

Example 2-7. Simple rotation transformation

```
function drawScreen() {

    //now draw a red square
    context.setTransform(1,0,0,1,0,0);
    var angleInRadians = 45 * Math.PI / 180;
    context.rotate(angleInRadians);
    context.fillStyle = "red";
    context.fillRect(100,100,50,50);

}
```

Figure 2-12. Simple rotation transformation

We get a result this time, but it will probably differ from what you expect. The red box is rotated, but it looks like the canvas was rotated with it. The entire canvas did not rotate, only the portion drawn after the context.rotate() function was called. So, why did our square both rotate and move off to the left of the screen? The origin of the rotation was set at the "nontranslated" 0,0 position, resulting in the square rotating from the top left of the entire canvas.

Example 2-8 offers a slightly different scenario: draw a black box first, then set the rotation transform, and finally, draw the red box again. See the results in Figure 2-13.

Example 2-8. Rotation and the Canvas state

```
function drawScreen() {

    //draw black square
    context.fillStyle = "black";
    context.fillRect(20,20,25,25);

    //now draw a red square
    context.setTransform(1,0,0,1,0,0);
    var angleInRadians = 45 * Math.PI / 180;
    context.rotate(angleInRadians);
    context.fillStyle = "red";
    context.fillRect(100,100,50,50);

}
```

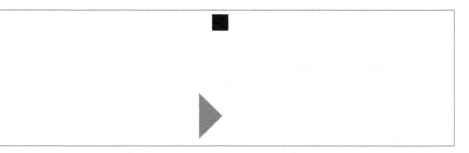

Figure 2-13. Rotation and the Canvas state

The small black square was unaffected by the rotation, so you can see that only the shapes drawn after the context.rotate() function was called were affected.

Again, the red box was moved far off to the left. To reiterate, this occurred because the canvas did not know what origin to use for the rotation. In the absence of an actual translated origin, the 0,0 position setting is applied, resulting in the context.ro tate() function rotating "around" the 0,0 point, which brings us to our next lesson.

Lesson 2: We must "translate" the point of origin to the center of our shape to rotate it around its own center

Let's change Example 2-8 to rotate the red square 45 degrees while keeping it in its current location.

First, we take the numbers we applied to the fillRect() function call to create a few variables to hold the red square's attributes. This is not necessary, but it will make the code much easier to read and change later:

```
var x = 100;
var y = 100;
```

```
var width = 50;
var height = 50;
```

Next, using the `context.translate()` function call, we must change the origin of the canvas to be the center of the red square we want to rotate and draw. This function moves the origin of the canvas to the accepted x and y locations. The center of our red square will now be the desired top-left corner x location for our object (`100`), plus half the width of our object. Using the variables we created to hold attributes of the red square, this would look like:

```
x+0.5*width
```

Next, we must find the y location for the origin translation. This time, we use the y value of the top-left corner of our shape and the height of the shape:

```
y+0.5*height
```

The `translate()` function call looks like this:

```
context.translate(x+0.5*width, y+0.5*height)
```

Now that we have translated the canvas to the correct point, we can do our rotation. The code has not changed:

```
context.rotate(angleInRadians);
```

Finally, we need to draw our shape. We cannot simply reuse the same values from Example 2-8 because the canvas origin point has moved to the center of the location where we want to draw our object. You can now consider 125,125 as the starting point for all draw operations. We get `125` for x by taking the upper-left corner of the square (`100`) and adding half its width (`25`). We do the same for the y origin position. The `translate()` method call accomplishes this.

We will need to draw the object starting with the correct upper-left coordinates for x and y. We do this by subtracting half the width of our object from the origin x, and half the height of our object from the origin y:

```
context.fillRect(-0.5*width,-0.5*height, width, height);
```

Why do we do this? Figure 2-14 illustrates the situation.

Consider that we want to draw our square starting at the top-left corner. If our origin point is at 125,125, the top left is actually 100,100. However, we have translated our origin so that the canvas now considers 125,125 to be 0,0. To start our box drawing at the nontranslated canvas, we have to start at −25,−25 on the "translated" canvas.

This forces us to draw our box as though the origin is at 0,0, not 125,125. Therefore, when we do the actual drawing of the box, we must use these coordinates, as shown in Figure 2-15.

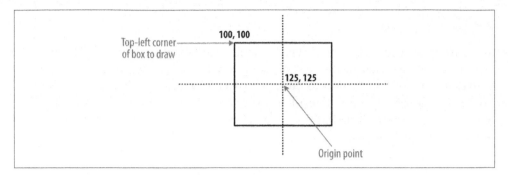

Figure 2-14. The newly translated point

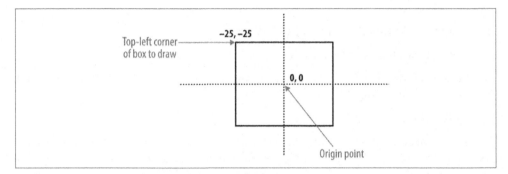

Figure 2-15. Drawing with a translated point

In summary, we needed to change the point of origin to the center of our square so that it would rotate around that point. But when we draw the square, we need our code to act as though the (125,125) point is actually (0,0). If we had not translated the origin, we could have used the (125,125) point as the center of our square (as in Figure 2-14). Example 2-9 demonstrates how this works, creating the result shown in Figure 2-16.

Example 2-9. Rotation around the center point

```
function drawScreen() {

    //draw black square
    context.fillStyle = "black";
    context.fillRect(20,20 ,25,25);

    //now draw a red square
    context.setTransform(1,0,0,1,0,0);
    var angleInRadians = 45 * Math.PI / 180;
    var x = 100;
    var y = 100;
    var width = 50;
    var height = 50;
```

```
context.translate(x+.5*width, y+.5*height);
context.rotate(angleInRadians);
context.fillStyle = "red";
context.fillRect(-.5*width,-.5*height , width, height);

}
```

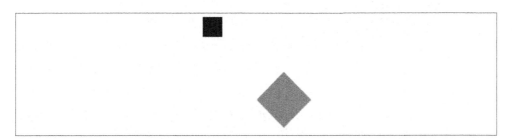

Figure 2-16. Rotation around the center point

Let's look at one final rotation example. Example 2-10 takes Example 2-9 and simply adds four separate 40×40 squares to the canvas, rotating each one slightly. The result is shown in Figure 2-17.

Example 2-10. Multiple rotated squares

```
function drawScreen() {

    //now draw a red square
    context.setTransform(1,0,0,1,0,0);
    var angleInRadians = 45 * Math.PI / 180;
    var x = 50;
    var y = 100;
    var width = 40;
    var height = 40;
    context.translate(x+.5*width, y+.5*height);
    context.rotate(angleInRadians);
    context.fillStyle = "red";
    context.fillRect(-.5*width,-.5*height , width, height);

    context.setTransform(1,0,0,1,0,0);
    var angleInRadians = 75 * Math.PI / 180;
    var x = 100;
    var y = 100;
    var width = 40;
    var height = 40;
    context.translate(x+.5*width, y+.5*height);
    context.rotate(angleInRadians);
    context.fillStyle = "red";
    context.fillRect(-.5*width,-.5*height , width, height);

    context.setTransform(1,0,0,1,0,0);
```

```
    var angleInRadians = 90 * Math.PI / 180;
    var x = 150;
    var y = 100;
    var width = 40;
    var height = 40;
    context.translate(x+.5*width, y+.5*height);
    context.rotate(angleInRadians);
    context.fillStyle = "red";
    context.fillRect(-.5*width,-.5*height , width, height);
    context.setTransform(1,0,0,1,0,0);
    var angleInRadians = 120 * Math.PI / 180;
    var x = 200;
    var y = 100;
    var width = 40;
    var height = 40;
    context.translate(x+.5*width, y+.5*height);
    context.rotate(angleInRadians);
    context.fillStyle = "red";
    context.fillRect(-.5*width,-.5*height , width, height);

}
```

Figure 2-17. Multiple rotated squares

Next, we will examine scale transformations.

Scale Transformations

The context.scale() function takes in two parameters: the first is the scale attribute
for the x-axis, and the second is the scale attribute for the y-axis. The value 1 is the
normal scale for an object. Therefore, if we want to double an object's size, we can set
both values to 2. Using the following code in drawScreen() produces the red square
shown in Figure 2-18:

```
context.setTransform(1,0,0,1,0,0);
context.scale(2,2);
context.fillStyle = "red";
context.fillRect(100,100 ,50,50);
```

Figure 2-18. A simple scaled square

If you test this code, you will find that scale works in a similar manner as rotation. We did not translate the origin of the scale point to double the size of the square; rather, we used the top-left corner of the canvas as the origin point. The result is that the red square appears to move farther down and to the left. What we would like is for the red square to remain in place and to scale from its center. We do this by translating to the center of the square before we scale, and by drawing the square around this center point (just as we did in Example 2-9). Example 2-11 produces the result shown in Figure 2-19.

Example 2-11. Scale from the center point

```
function drawScreen() {

        //now draw a red square
        context.setTransform(1,0,0,1,0,0);
        var x = 100;
        var y = 100;
        var width = 50;
        var height = 50;
        context.translate(x+.5*width, y+.5*height);
        context.scale(2,2);
        context.fillStyle = "red";
        context.fillRect(-.5*width,-.5*height , width, height);

}
```

Figure 2-19. Scale from the center point

Combining Scale and Rotation Transformations

If we want to both scale and rotate an object, Canvas transformations can easily be combined to achieve the desired results (as shown in Figure 2-20). Let's look in Example 2-12 at how we might combine them by using `scale(2,2)` and `rotate(an gleInRadians)` from our previous examples.

Example 2-12. Scale and rotation combined

```
function drawScreen() {
    context.setTransform(1,0,0,1,0,0);
    var angleInRadians = 45 * Math.PI / 180;
    var x = 100;
    var y = 100;
    var width = 50;
    var height = 50;
    context.translate(x+.5*width, y+.5*height);
    context.scale(2,2);
    context.rotate(angleInRadians);
    context.fillStyle = "red";
    context.fillRect(-.5*width,-.5*height , width, height);

}
```

Figure 2-20. Scale and rotation combined

Example 2-13 also combines rotation and scale, this time using a rectangle. Figure 2-21 reveals what it creates.

Example 2-13. Scale and rotate a nonsquare object

```
function drawScreen() {

    //now draw a red rectangle
    context.setTransform(1,0,0,1,0,0);
    var angleInRadians = 90 * Math.PI / 180;
    var x = 100;
    var y = 100;
    var width = 100;
    var height = 50;
    context.translate(x+.5*width, y+.5*height);
    context.rotate(angleInRadians);
    context.scale(2,2);

    context.fillStyle = "red";
    context.fillRect(-.5*width,-.5*height , width, height);

}
```

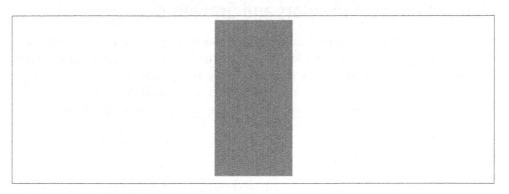

Figure 2-21. Scale and rotate a nonsquare object

Finding the Center of Any Shape

The rotation and scale of a rectangle or any other shape we draw on the canvas acts much like that of a square. As long as we are sure to translate to the center of our shape before we scale, rotate, or scale and rotate, we will see the results we expect from our simple transformations. Keep in mind that the "center" of any shape will be the x value that is half its width and the y value that is half its height. We need to use the *bounding box theory* when we attempt to find this center point.

Figure 2-22 demonstrates this theory. Even though the shape is not a simple square, we have been able to find a bounding box that encompasses each point of the object. Figure 2-22 is roughly square, but the same theory holds for rectangle-shaped bounding boxes.

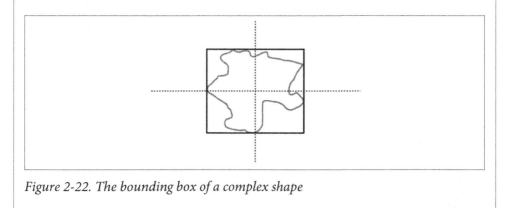

Figure 2-22. The bounding box of a complex shape

Filling Objects with Colors and Gradients

In this chapter, we have quickly looked at color and fill styles as we proceeded through the discussions of basic and complex shape construction. In this section, we will take a deeper look at coloring and filling shapes we draw on the canvas. In addition to these simple colors and fills, there are a number of different gradient styles that we can employ. Furthermore, Canvas also has a method to fill shapes with bitmap images. (See Chapter 4.)

Setting Basic Fill Colors

The Canvas `fillStyle` property is used to set a basic color for filling shapes on the canvas. We saw this earlier in the chapter when we used simple color names for our `fillStyle`. An example is:

```
context.fillStyle = "red";
```

Below is a list of the usable color string values from the HTML4 specification. As of this writing, the HTML5 color specification has not been set. In the absence of any additional HTML5-specific colors, the HTML4 colors will work properly in HTML5:

Black = #000000
Green = #008000
Silver = #C0C0C0
Lime = #00FF00
Gray = #808080
Olive = #808000
White = #FFFFFF
Yellow = #FFFF00
Maroon = #800000
Navy = #000080
Red = #FF0000
Blue = #0000FF
Purple = #800080
Teal = #008080
Fuchsia = #FF00FF
Aqua = #00FFFF

 All these color values will work with the `strokeStyle` property as well as the `fillStyle` property.

Of course, using a string for the color name is not the only available method of specifying a solid color fill. The following list includes a few other methods:

Setting the fill color with the rgb() *method*
> The rgb() method lets us use the 24-bit RGB value when specifying our fill colors:

```
context.fillStyle = "rgb(255,0,0)";
```

> This will result in the same red color as the string value above.

Setting the fill color with a hex number string
> We can also set the fillStyle color with a hex number in a string:

```
context.fillStyle = "#ff0000";
```

Setting the fill color with the rgba() *method*
> The rgba() method allows us to specify a 32-bit color value with the final 8 bits representing the alpha value of the fill color:

```
context.fillStyle = "rgba(255,0,0,1)";
```

> The alpha value can be from 1 (opaque) to 0 (transparent).

Filling Shapes with Gradients

There are two basic options for creating gradient fills on the canvas: linear and radial. A *linear* gradient creates a horizontal, vertical, or diagonal fill pattern; the *radial* variety creates a fill that "radiates" from a central point in a circular fashion. Let's look at some examples of each.

Linear gradients

Linear gradients come in three basic styles: horizontal, vertical, and diagonal. We control where colors change in our gradient by setting *color stops* at points along the length of the object we want to fill.

Linear horizontal gradients. Example 2-14 creates a simple horizontal gradient, as shown in Figure 2-23.

Example 2-14. A linear horizontal gradient

```
function drawScreen() {

    // horizontal gradient values must remain 0
    var gr = context.createLinearGradient(0, 0, 100, 0);

    // Add the color stops.
    gr.addColorStop(0,'rgb(255,0,0)');
    gr.addColorStop(.5,'rgb(0,255,0)');
    gr.addColorStop(1,'rgb(255,0,0)');
```

```
// Use the gradient for the fillStyle.
context.fillStyle = gr;
context.fillRect(0, 0,100,100);

}
```

Figure 2-23. A linear horizontal gradient

To create the horizontal gradient, we must first create a variable (gr) to reference the new gradient. Here's how we set it:

```
var gr = context.createLinearGradient(0,0,100,0);
```

The four parameter values in the createLinearGradient method call are the top-left *x* and *y* coordinates to start the gradient, as well as the two bottom-right points to end the gradient. Our example starts at 0,0 and goes to 100,0. Notice that the *y* values are both 0 when we create a horizontal gradient; the opposite will be true when we create a vertical gradient.

After we have defined the size of our gradient, we then add in color stops that take two parameter values. The first is a relative position origin point along the gradient to start with color, and the second is the color to use. The relative position must be a value from 0.0 to 1.0:

```
gr.addColorStop(0,'rgb(255,0,0)');
gr.addColorStop(.5,'rgb(0,255,0)');
gr.addColorStop(1,'rgb(255,0,0)');
```

Therefore, in Example 2-14, we have set a red color at 0, a green color at .5 (the center), and another red color at 1. This will fill our shape with a relatively even red to green to red gradient.

Next, we need to get the context.fillStyle to be the gradient we just created:

```
context.fillStyle = gr;
```

Finally, we create a rectangle on the canvas:

```
context.fillRect(0, 0, 100, 100);
```

Notice that we created a rectangle that was the exact size of our gradient. We can change the size of the output rectangle like this:

```
context.fillRect(0, 100, 50, 100);
context.fillRect(0, 200, 200, 100);
```

Example 2-15 adds these two new filled rectangles to Example 2-14 to create Figure 2-24. Notice that the gradient fills up the available space, with the final color filling out the area larger than the defined gradient size.

Example 2-15. Multiple gradient-filled objects

```
function drawScreen() {

    var gr = context.createLinearGradient(0, 0, 100, 0);

    // Add the color stops.
    gr.addColorStop(0,'rgb(255,0,0)');
    gr.addColorStop(.5,'rgb(0,255,0)');
    gr.addColorStop(1,'rgb(255,0,0)');

    // Use the gradient for the fillStyle.
    context.fillStyle = gr;
    context.fillRect(0, 0, 100, 100);
    context.fillRect(0, 100, 50, 100);
    context.fillRect(0, 200, 200, 100);

    }
```

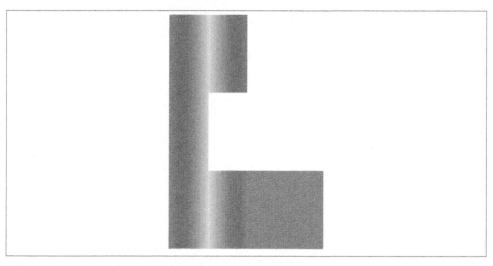

Figure 2-24. Linear horizontal gradient on multiple objects

Applying a horizontal gradient to a stroke. Gradients can be applied to any shape—even the stroke around a shape. Example 2-16 takes the filled rectangles from Example 2-15 and creates a `strokeRect` shape instead of a filled rectangle. Figure 2-25 shows the very different result.

Example 2-16. A horizontal stroke gradient

```
function drawScreen() {

    var gr = context.createLinearGradient(0, 0, 100, 0);

    // Add the color stops.
    gr.addColorStop(0,'rgb(255,0,0)');
    gr.addColorStop(.5,'rgb(0,255,0)');
    gr.addColorStop(1,'rgb(255,0,0)');

    // Use the gradient for the fillStyle.
    context.strokeStyle = gr;
    context.strokeRect(0, 0, 100, 100);
    context.strokeRect(0, 100, 50, 100);
    context.strokeRect(0, 200, 200, 100);

}
```

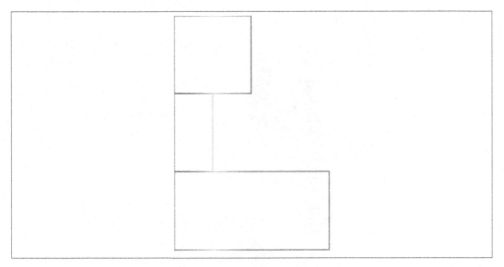

Figure 2-25. Horizontal stroke gradients

Applying a horizontal gradient to a complex shape. We can also apply a linear gradient to a "closed" shape made up of points, as shown in Example 2-17. A shape is considered closed when the final point is the same as the starting point.

Example 2-17. Horizontal gradient on a complex shape

```
function drawScreen() {

        var gr = context.createLinearGradient(0, 0, 100, 0);

        // Add the color stops.
        gr.addColorStop(0,'rgb(255,0,0)');
        gr.addColorStop(.5,'rgb(0,255,0)');
        gr.addColorStop(1,'rgb(255,0,0)');

        // Use the gradient for the fillStyle.
        context.fillStyle = gr;
        context.beginPath();
        context.moveTo(0,0);
        context.lineTo(50,0);
        context.lineTo(100,50);
        context.lineTo(50,100);
        context.lineTo(0,100);
        context.lineTo(0,0);
        context.stroke();
        context.fill();
        context.closePath();

    }
```

In this example, we use the `context.fill()` command to fill in our shape with the current `fillStyle`, creating the output shown in Figure 2-26.

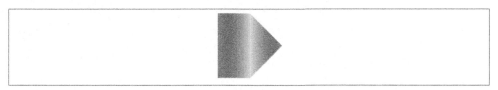

Figure 2-26. A horizontal gradient on a complex shape

Figure 2-26 shows the new shape we have created with points. As long as the points are closed, the fill will work as we expect.

Vertical gradients. Vertical gradients are created in a very similar manner as the horizontal variety. The difference is that we must specify a y value that is not 0, and the x values must both be 0. Example 2-18 shows the shape from Example 2-17 created with a vertical rather than a horizontal gradient to produce the output in Figure 2-27.

Example 2-18. Vertical gradients

```
function drawScreen() {

    var gr = context.createLinearGradient(0, 0, 0, 100);

    // Add the color stops.
    gr.addColorStop(0,'rgb(255,0,0)');
    gr.addColorStop(.5,'rgb(0,255,0)');
    gr.addColorStop(1,'rgb(255,0,0)');

    // Use the gradient for the fillStyle.
    context.fillStyle = gr;
    context.beginPath();
    context.moveTo(0,0);
    context.lineTo(50,0);
    context.lineTo(100,50);
    context.lineTo(50,100);
    context.lineTo(0,100);
    context.lineTo(0,0);
    context.stroke();
    context.fill();
    context.closePath();

}
```

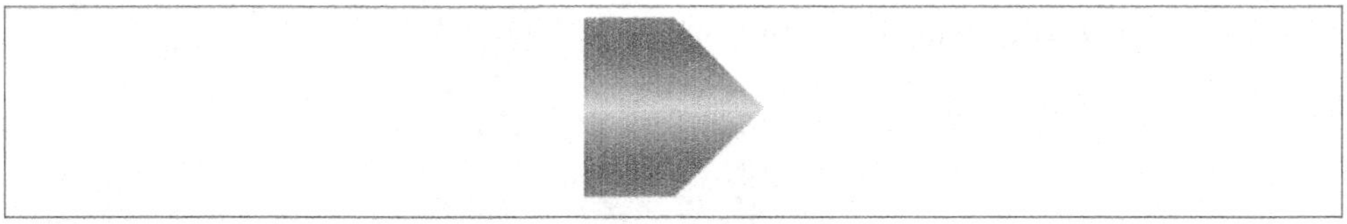

Figure 2-27. A vertical gradient example

The only difference between Example 2-18 and Example 2-17 is the line creating the linear gradient.

The horizontal version (Example 2-17):

```
    var gr = context.createLinearGradient(0, 0, 100, 0);
```

The new vertical version (Example 2-18):

```
    var gr = context.createLinearGradient(0, 0, 0, 100);
```

All of the same rules for strokes on horizontal gradients apply to vertical ones. Example 2-19 takes the shape from Example 2-18, stroking it with the gradient instead of filling it, producing the outline shown in Figure 2-28.

Example 2-19. A vertical gradient stroke

```
function drawScreen() {

    var gr = context.createLinearGradient(0, 0, 0, 100);

    // Add the color stops.
    gr.addColorStop(0,'rgb(255,0,0)');
    gr.addColorStop(.5,'rgb(0,255,0)');
    gr.addColorStop(1,'rgb(255,0,0)');

    // Use the gradient for the fillStyle.
    context.strokeStyle = gr;
    context.beginPath();
    context.moveTo(0,0);
    context.lineTo(50,0);
    context.lineTo(100,50);
    context.lineTo(50,100);
    context.lineTo(0,100);
    context.lineTo(0,0);
    context.stroke();
    context.closePath();

}
```

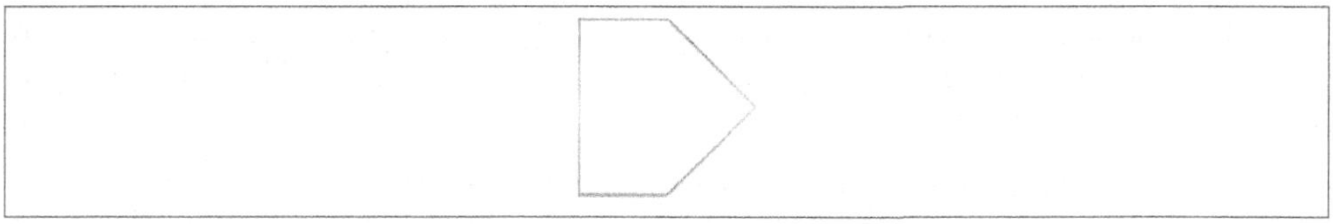

Figure 2-28. A vertical gradient stroke

Diagonal gradients. You can easily create a diagonal gradient by varying both the second x and second y parameters of the createLinearGradient() function:

```
    var gr= context.createLinearGradient(0, 0, 100, 100);
```

To create a perfect diagonal gradient, as shown in Figure 2-29, fill a square that is the same size as the diagonal gradient. The code is provided in Example 2-20.

Example 2-20. A diagonal gradient

```
function drawScreen() {

    var gr = context.createLinearGradient(0, 0, 100, 100);

    // Add the color stops.
    gr.addColorStop(0,'rgb(255,0,0)');
    gr.addColorStop(.5,'rgb(0,255,0)');
```

```
    gr.addColorStop(1,'rgb(255,0,0)');

    // Use the gradient for the fillStyle.
    context.fillStyle = gr;
    context.beginPath();
    context.moveTo(0,0);
    context.fillRect(0,0,100,100)
    context.closePath();

}
```

Figure 2-29. A diagonal gradient example

Radial gradients. The definition process for radial and linear gradients is very similar. Although a radial gradient takes six parameters to initialize rather than the four needed for a linear gradient, it uses the same color stop idea to create the color changes.

The six parameters are used to define the center point and the radii of two circles. The first circle is the "start" circle, and the second circle is the "end" circle. Let's look at an example:

```
    var gr = context.createRadialGradient(50,50,25,50,50,100);
```

The first circle has a center point of 50,50 and a radius of 25; the second has a center point of 50,50 and a radius of 100. This will effectively create two concentric circles.

We set color stops the same way we did with the linear gradients:

```
    gr.addColorStop(0,'rgb(255,0,0)');
    gr.addColorStop(.5,'rgb(0,255,0)');
    gr.addColorStop(1,'rgb(255,0,0)');
```

Example 2-21 puts this together to create the result shown in Figure 2-30.

Example 2-21. A simple radial gradient

```
function drawScreen() {

    var gr = context.createRadialGradient(50,50,25,50,50,100);

    // Add the color stops.
    gr.addColorStop(0,'rgb(255,0,0)');
    gr.addColorStop(.5,'rgb(0,255,0)');
    gr.addColorStop(1,'rgb(255,0,0)');
```

```
        // Use the gradient for the fillStyle.
        context.fillStyle = gr;
        context.fillRect(0, 0, 200, 200);

    }
```

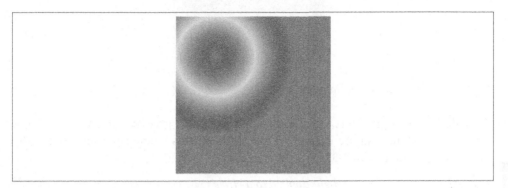

Figure 2-30. A simple radial gradient

Example 2-22 offsets the second circle from the first to create the effects shown in Figure 2-31.

Example 2-22. A complex radial gradient

```
function drawScreen() {

        var gr = context.createRadialGradient(50,50,25,100,100,100);

        // Add the color stops.
        gr.addColorStop(0,'rgb(255,0,0)');
        gr.addColorStop(.5,'rgb(0,255,0)');
        gr.addColorStop(1,'rgb(255,0,0)');

        // Use the gradient for the fillStyle.
        context.fillStyle = gr;
        context.fillRect(0, 0, 200, 200);

}
```

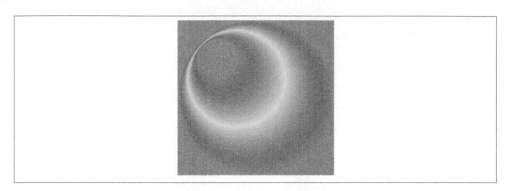

Figure 2-31. A complex radial gradient

As with the linear gradients, we can also apply the radial gradients to complex shapes. Example 2-23 takes an arc example from earlier in this chapter but applies a radial gradient to create Figure 2-32.

Example 2-23. A radial gradient applied to a circle

```
function drawScreen() {

    var gr = context.createRadialGradient(50,50,25,100,100,100);

    // Add the color stops.
    gr.addColorStop(0,'rgb(255,0,0)');
    gr.addColorStop(.5,'rgb(0,255,0)');
    gr.addColorStop(1,'rgb(255,0,0)');

    // Use the gradient for the fillStyle.
    context.fillStyle = gr;
    context.arc(100, 100, 100, (Math.PI/180)*0, (Math.PI/180)*360, false);
    context.fill();

}
```

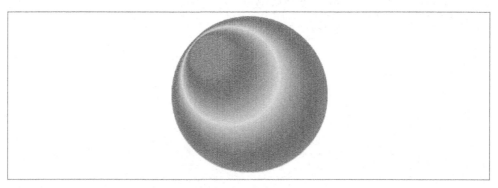

Figure 2-32. A radial gradient applied to a circle

Example 2-23 takes the radial gradient from Example 2-22 and applies it to a circle shape rather than a rectangle shape. This removes the red square from the background of the shape.

We can also apply our radial gradient to the stroke of our arc rather than the fill, as shown in Example 2-24 and Figure 2-33.

Example 2-24. An arc stroke gradient

```
function drawScreen() {

    var gr = context.createRadialGradient(50,50,25,100,100,100);

    // Add the color stops.
    gr.addColorStop(0,'rgb(255,0,0)');
    gr.addColorStop(.5,'rgb(0,255,0)');
    gr.addColorStop(1,'rgb(255,0,0)');

    // Use the gradient for the fillStyle.
    context.strokeStyle = gr;
    context.arc(100, 100, 50, (Math.PI/180)*0, (Math.PI/180)*360, false)
    context.stroke();

}
```

Figure 2-33. An arc stroke gradient

Example 2-24 created a circle that is smaller than the version in Example 2-23, so the radial gradient would show up on the stroke of the arc. If we left it the same size as Example 2-23, we would have a solid red fill because the radial gradient is solid red at the diameter edge of the circle.

Filling Shapes with Patterns

We will cover using bitmap images on the canvas in Chapter 4, but for now, let's take a quick look at how images can be used as fill patterns for shapes we draw.

Fill patterns are initialized with the createPattern() function, which takes two parameters. The first is an Image object instance, and the second is a String representing how to display the repeat pattern inside the shape. We can use a loaded image file or an entire other canvas as a fill pattern for a drawn shape.

There are currently four types of image fills:

1. repeat
2. repeat-x
3. repeat-y
4. no-repeat

Modern browsers have implemented these four types to various degrees, but standard repeat seems to be the most common. Let's look at it now, and then we will take a brief look at the other three.

Figure 2-34 shows a simple bitmap fill pattern that we can use to test this functionality. It is a 20×20 green circle on a transparent background, saved as a *.gif* file named *fill_20x20.gif*.

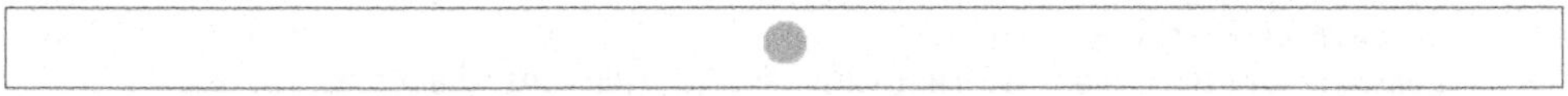

Figure 2-34. The fill_20x20.gif image for our fill

Example 2-25 tests this first with the repeat string to create a box full of little green circles, as shown in Figure 2-35.

Example 2-25. Filling with an image file using repeat

```
function drawScreen() {

    var fillImg = new Image();
    fillImg.src = 'fill_20x20.gif';
    fillImg.onload = function(){

        var fillPattern = context.createPattern(fillImg,'repeat');
        context.fillStyle = fillPattern;
        context.fillRect(0,0,200,200);

    }

}
```

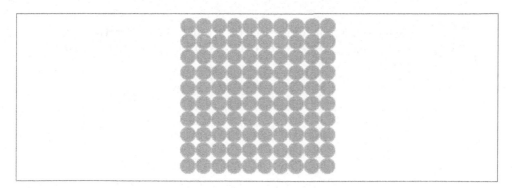

Figure 2-35. Repeat fill example

It is best not to use Image instances until they have loaded completely. We will cover this in detail in Chapter 4, but for now, we simply create an inline onload event handler function that will be called when Image is ready to be used. The repeat pattern string does a good job of completely filling the 200×200 square. Let's see the code for how the other repeat strings perform (in Example 2-26), and view the results in Figure 2-36 through Figure 2-38.

Example 2-26. Using the no-repeat, repeat-x, and repeat-y strings

```
function drawScreen() {

        var fillImg = new Image();
        fillImg.src = 'fill_20x20.gif';

        fillImg.onload = function(){

            var fillPattern1 = context.createPattern(fillImg,'no-repeat');
            var fillPattern2 = context.createPattern(fillImg,'repeat-x');
            var fillPattern3 = context.createPattern(fillImg,'repeat-y');

            context.fillStyle = fillPattern1;
            context.fillRect(0,0,100,100);

            context.fillStyle = fillPattern3;
            context.fillRect(0,220,100,100);


            context.translate(0,110);
            context.fillStyle = fillPattern2;
            context.fillRect(0,0,100,100);
        }

    }
```

Each browser will show these patterns in a different manner. These are always changing, so make sure to check with the new browsers you are developing.

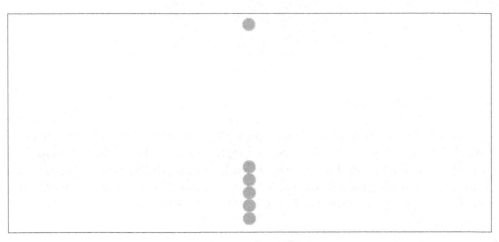

Figure 2-36. no-repeat, repeat-x, and repeat-y in Safari

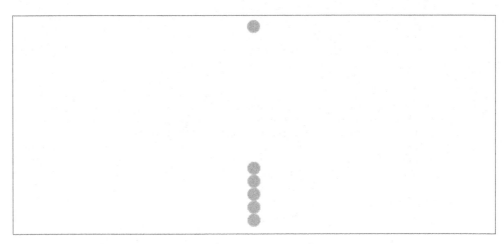

Figure 2-37. no-repeat, repeat-x, and repeat-y in Firefox

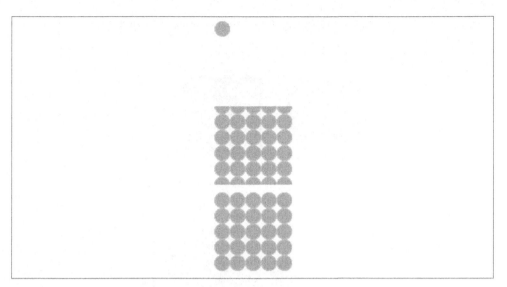

Figure 2-38. no-repeat, repeat-x, and repeat-y in Chrome

Note that to have a repeat-x fill work you have to translate to the x,y position that you want to draw into and then use 0,0 as the x,y coordinates in the fillRect function call.

Creating Shadows on Canvas Shapes

We can add shadows to shapes we draw on the canvas by using four parameters. As with the tiled fill patterns in the previous section, this feature has not been fully implemented on all HTML5-compliant browsers.

We add a shadow by setting four Canvas properties:

1. shadowOffsetX
2. shadowOffsetY
3. shadowBlur
4. shadowColor

The shadowOffsetX and shadowOffsetY values can be positive or negative. Negative values will create shadows to the left and top rather than to the bottom and right. The shadowBlur property sets the size of the blurring effect on the shadow. None of these three parameters is affected by the current Canvas transformation matrix. The shadow Color property can be any color set via HTML4 color constant string—rgb() or rgba() —or with a string containing a hex value.

Example 2-27 and Figure 2-39 show a few different boxes drawn with various shadow settings.

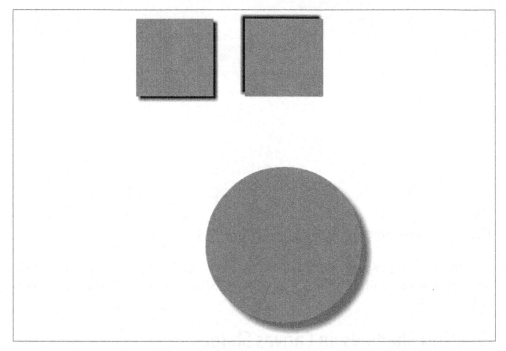

Figure 2-39. Adding shadows to drawn objects

Example 2-27. Adding shadows to drawn objects

```
function drawScreen() {

    context.fillStyle = 'red';

    context.shadowOffsetX = -4;
    context.shadowOffsetY = -4;
    context.shadowColor = 'black';
    context.shadowBlur = 4;
    context.fillRect(10,10,100,100);

    context.shadowOffsetX = -4;
    context.shadowOffsetY = -4;
    context.shadowColor = 'black';
    context.shadowBlur = 4;
    context.fillRect(150,10,100,100);

    context.shadowOffsetX = 10;
    context.shadowOffsetY = 10;
    context.shadowColor = 'rgb(100,100,100)';
```

```
        context.shadowBlur = 8;
        context.arc(200, 300, 100, (Math.PI/180)*0, (Math.PI/180)*360, false)
        context.fill();
}
```

As you can see, if we adjust the shadowOffset values along with the shadowBlur value, we create various shadows. We can also create shadows for complex shapes drawn with paths and arcs.

Methods to Clear the Canvas

We have explored refreshing the Canvas between animation operations in Chapter 1, and this will be covered more in depth in Chapter 4, but this chapter would not be complete without an examination of some methods used to completely clear the Canvas and refresh its contents.

Simple Fill

We can easily fill the entire Canvas with a new background color, thus erasing the current contents:

```
        context.fillStyle = '000000';
        context.fillRect(0,0,theCanvas.width, theCanvas.height)
```

Resetting the Canvas Width and Height

When the Canvas width or height (or both) are reset, the current contents of the Canvas are removed:

```
        var w=theCanvas.width;
        var h=theCanvas.height;
        theCanvas.width=w;
        theCanvas.height=h;
```

Resetting the Canvas clearRect Function

The clearRect() function takes in the start x,y location and the width and height to clear the Canvas:

```
        var w=theCanvas.width;
        var h=theCanvas.height;
        context.clearRect(0,0,w,h);
```

Let's test out using the clearRect() function by animating a path across the Canvas (Example 2-28). We will accomplish this by implementing the setTimeOut() function presented in Chapter 1. It will be used to repeatedly call our drawScreen() function and update the location of the path. The entire set of code for this example is presented because it is more involved than simply drawing a path or a shape on the Canvas at a single time.

Example 2-28. Using the clearRect() function

```
<!doctype html>
<html lang="en">
<head>
<meta charset="UTF-8">
<title>Chapter 2 Example 28: Animating a Path</title>

<script src="modernizr.js"></script>
<script type="text/javascript">
window.addEventListener('load', eventWindowLoaded, false);
function eventWindowLoaded() {

    canvasApp();

}

function canvasSupport () {
    return Modernizr.canvas;
}


function canvasApp(){


    if (!canvasSupport()) {
            return;
    }else{
        var theCanvas = document.getElementById('canvas');
        var context = theCanvas.getContext('2d');
    }

    var yOffset=0;

    function drawScreen(){

        context.clearRect(0,0,theCanvas.width,theCanvas.height);

        var currentPath=context.beginPath();
        context.strokeStyle = "red"; //need list of available colors
        context.lineWidth=5;
        context.moveTo(0, 0+yOffset);
        context.lineTo(50, 0+yOffset);
        context.lineTo(50,50+yOffset);
        context.stroke();
        context.closePath();
            yOffset+=1;

    }
```

```
    function gameLoop() {
        window.setTimeout(gameLoop, 20);
        drawScreen()

    }

    gameLoop();

}


</script>

</head>
<body>
<div style="position: absolute; top: 50px; left: 50px;">
<canvas id="canvas" width="500" height="500">
 Your browser does not support the HTML 5 Canvas.
</canvas>
</div>
</body>
</html>
```

In Example 2-28, we first create a variable called yOffset and set it to be 0. Next, we add a Canvas clearing function to our drawScreen() function. We then draw our path, adding the yOffset to each y-axis value.

As shown in Chapter 1, we create a gameLoop() function that we call a single time, and it, in turn, uses a setTimeout() function call to recursively call itself every 20 milliseconds. This results in the drawScreen() function repeatedly being called. At the bottom of the drawScreen() function, we simply add 1 to the current value of yOffset. This will create the illusion of the drawn path moving down the screen.

Checking to See Whether a Point Is in the Current Path

You can easily test whether a certain point is in the current path by using the isPoin tInPath() Canvas function:

```
context.strokeStyle = "red";
context.lineWidth=5;
context.moveTo(0, 0);
context.lineTo(50, 0);
context.lineTo(50,50);
context.stroke();

var isPoint1InPath1=context.isPointInPath(0, 0);
var isPoint1InPath2=context.isPointInPath(10, 10);
console.log("isPoint1InPath1=" + isPoint1InPath1);
console.log("isPoint1InPath2=" + isPoint1InPath2);
context.closePath();
```

The first point, (0,0), is in the current path and will output `true` to the console, while the second point, (10,10), is not and will output `false` to the console.

 This doesn't work the same in all browsers, *yet*. Compatibility is continuing to improve with each new browser build. You will need to test across a selection of browsers to see which have added full compatibility with this function.

Drawing a Focus Ring

Digging further into the Canvas Specification, we find some functions that have not yet been implemented. The `drawCustomFocusRing()` function applies to the Canvas current path and is used for accessibility. The `context.drawSystemFocusRing(element)` function should allow the given element to have a focus ring drawn around the current default path. Currently, almost no browsers support this function. Eventually, you should be able to apply this to the Canvas and also check to see whether the focus ring should be displayed by using the following function: `var shouldDraw = context.draw CustomFocusRing(theCanvas);`. If this returns `true`, a custom focus ring on the current path should be displayed.

What's Next?

We covered a lot of ground in this chapter, introducing the ways to construct primitive and complex shapes, and how we can draw and transform them on the canvas. We also discussed how to composite, rotate, scale, translate, fill, and create shadows on these shapes. But we've only just begun exploring HTML5 Canvas. In the next chapter, we will look at how to create and manipulate text objects on the canvas.

CHAPTER 3

The HTML5 Canvas Text API

The HTML5 Canvas Text API allows developers to render text on an HTML page in ways that were either tricky or next to impossible before its invention.

We are providing an in-depth analysis of the HTML5 Canvas Text API because it is one of the most basic ways to interact with the canvas. However, that does not mean it was the first Canvas API feature developed. In fact, for many browsers, it was one of the last parts implemented.

There was a time in the recent past when HTML5 Canvas Text API support in browsers was spotty at best. Back then, using *modernizr.js* to test for text support would have been a good idea. However, at this historic moment, all modern browser versions support the HTML5 Canvas Text API in some way.

This chapter will create an application named "Text Arranger" to demonstrate the features and interdependencies of the HTML5 Canvas Text API. This application will display a single line of text in an almost infinite number of ways. This is also a useful tool to see whether support for text is common among web browsers. Later in this chapter, you will see that some text features are incompatible when drawn on the canvas at the same time.

Canvas Text and CSS

The first thing you need to know about text on HTML5 Canvas is that it does not use CSS for style. While the properties of HTML5 Canvas look similar to CSS properties, they are not interchangeable. While your knowledge of CSS will help you understand text on the HTML5 Canvas, you can't rely solely on that knowledge to be successful with Canvas text. That being said, Canvas can take advantage of fonts defined in a CSS file using *@font-face*, and can fall back to multiple different fonts if the defined font is not available.

Displaying Basic Text

Displaying text on HTML5 Canvas is simple. We covered the basics in Chapter 1. Here, we will review these basics, and then we will show you how to make them work with the Text Arranger application.

Basic Text Display

The simplest way to define text to be displayed on the canvas is to set the `con text.font` style by using standard values for CSS font style attributes: `font-style`, `font-weight`, `font-size`, and `font-face`.

We will discuss each of these attributes in detail in the upcoming section "Setting the Text Font" on page 89. All you need to know now is that a font designation of some type is required. Here is a simple example of setting a 50-point serif font:

```
context.font = "50px serif";
```

You also need to set the color of the text. For filled text, you would use the `context.fill Style` attribute and set it using a standard CSS color, or with a `CanvasGradient` or `CanvasPattern` object. We will discuss the latter two options later in the chapter.

Finally, you call the `context.fillText()` method, passing the text to be displayed and the x and y positions of the text on the canvas.

The following is an example of all three basic lines of code required to display filled text on HTML5 Canvas:

```
context.font = "50px serif"
context.fillStyle = "#FF0000";
context.fillText ("Hello World", 100, 80);
```

If you do not specify a font, the default 10px sans-serif will be used automatically.

Handling Basic Text in Text Arranger

For Text Arranger, we are going to allow the user to set the text displayed by the call to `context.fillText()`. To do this, we will create a variable named `message` where we will store the user-supplied text. We will later use that variable in our call to `con text.fillText()`, inside the standard `drawScreen()` method that we introduced in Chapter 1 and will continue to use throughout this book:

```
var message = "your text";
...

function drawScreen() {
  ...
  context.fillStyle = "#FF0000";
```

```
    context.fillText (message, 100, 80);
    }
```

To change the text displayed on the canvas to the text entered by the user, we need to create an event handler for the text box keyup event. This means that whenever someone changes text in the box, the event handler function will be called.

To make this work, we are going to name our text box in our HTML `<form>` using an `<input>` form element. Notice that the `id` is set to the value `textBox`. Also notice that we have set the `placeholder=""` attribute. This attribute is new to HTML5, so it might not work in every browser. You can also substitute it with the `value=""` attribute, which will not affect the execution of this application:

```
<form>
    Text: <input id="textBox" placeholder="your text"/>
    <br>
</form>
```

Communicating Between HTML Forms and the Canvas

Back in our JavaScript code, we need to create an event handler for the keyup event of `textBox`. We do this by finding the form element by using the `document.getElement ById()` function of the DOM document object and storing it in the `formElement` variable. Then we call the `addEventListener()` method of `formElement`, setting the event to keyup and the event handler to the function `textBoxChanged`, which we have yet to define:

```
var formElement = document.getElementById("textBox");
formElement.addEventListener('keyup', textBoxChanged, false);
```

The final piece of the puzzle is to define the `textBoxChanged()` event handler. This function works like the event handlers we created in Chapter 1. It is passed one parameter when it is called, an `event` object that we universally name e because it's easy to remember.

The `event` object contains a property named `target` that holds a reference to the HTML form element that created the `change` event. In turn, the `target` contains a property named `value` that holds the newly changed value of the form element that caused the event to occur (that is, `textBox`). We retrieve this value and store it in the `message` variable we created in JavaScript. It is the very same `message` variable we use inside the `drawScreen()` method to paint the canvas. Now, all we have to do is call `drawScreen()`, and the new value of `message` will appear "automagically" on the canvas:

```
function textBoxChanged(e) {
    var target = e.target;
    message = target.value;
    drawScreen();
}
```

We just spent a lot of time describing how we will handle changes in HTML form controls with event handlers in JavaScript and then display the results on an HTML5 Canvas. We will repeat this type of code several more times while creating Text Arranger. However, we will refrain from explaining it in depth again, instead focusing on different ways to render and capture form data and use it with Canvas.

Using measureText

The HTML5 Canvas context object includes a useful method, measureText(). When supplied with a text string, it will return some properties about that text, based on the current context settings (font face, size, and so on) in the form of a TextMetrics object. Right now, the TextMetrics object has only a single property: width. The width property of a TextMetrics object gives you the exact width in pixels of the text when rendered on the canvas. This can be very useful when attempting to center text.

Centering text using width

For the Text Arranger application, we will use the TextMetrics object to center the text the user has entered in the textBox form control on the canvas. First, we retrieve an instance of TextMetrics by passing the message variable (which holds the text we are going to display) to the measureText() method of the 2D context and storing it in a variable named metrics:

```
var metrics = context.measureText(message);
```

Then, from the width property of metrics, we get the width value of the text in pixels and store it in a variable named textWidth:

```
var textWidth = metrics.width;
```

Next, we calculate the center of the screen by taking the width value of the canvas and dividing it in half (theCanvas.width/2). From that, we subtract half the width value of the text (textWidth/2). We do this because text on the canvas is vertically aligned to the left when it is displayed without any alignment designation (more on this a bit later). So, to center the text, we need to move it half its own width to the left and place the center of the text in the absolute center of the canvas. We will update this in the next section when we allow the user to select the text's vertical alignment:

```
var xPosition = (theCanvas.width/2) - (textWidth/2);
```

What about the height of the text?

So, what about finding the height of the text so that you can break text that is longer than the width of the canvas into multiple lines, or center it on the screen? Well, this poses a problem. The TextMetrics object does not contain a height property. The text font size does not give the full picture either, because it does not take into account font glyphs that drop below the baseline of the font. While the font size will help you estimate how to center a font vertically on the screen, it does not offer much if you need to break text into two or more lines. This is because the spacing would also need to be taken into account, which could be very tricky.

For our demonstration, instead of trying to use the font size to vertically center the text on the canvas, we will create the yPosition variable for the text by simply placing it at one-half the height of the canvas. The default baseline for a font is middle, so this works great for centering on the screen. We will talk more about baseline in the next section:

```
var yPosition = (theCanvas.height/2);
```

 In the chat example in Chapter 11, we will show you an example of breaking up text onto multiple lines.

fillText and strokeText

The context.fillText() function (as shown in Figure 3-1) will render solid-colored text to the canvas. The color used is set in the context.fillColor property. The font used is set in the context.font property. The function call looks like this:

```
fillText([text],[x],[y],[maxWidth]);
```

where:

text
    The text to render on the canvas.

x
    The x position of the text on the canvas.

y
    The y position of the text on the canvas.

maxWidth
    The maximum width of the text as rendered on the canvas. At the time of this writing, support for this property was just being added to browsers.

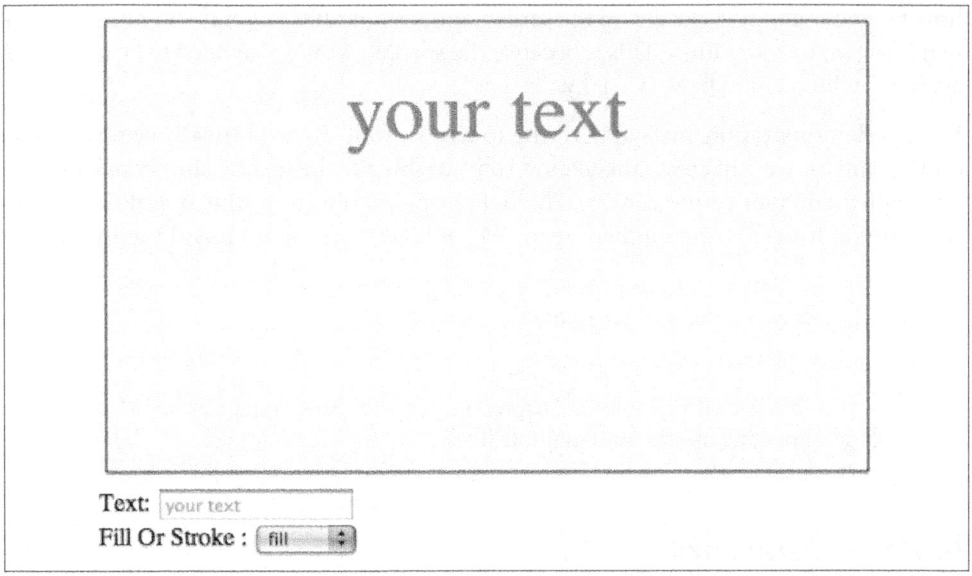

Figure 3-1. fillText in action

The `context.strokeText()` function (as shown in Figure 3-2) is similar, but it specifies the outline of text strokes to the canvas. The color used to render the stroke is set in the `context.strokeColor` property; the font used is set in the `context.font` property. The function call looks like:

```
strokeText([text],[x],[y],[maxWidth])
```

where:

text

> The text to render on the canvas.

x

> The x position of the text on the canvas.

y

> The y position of the text on the canvas.

maxWidth

> The maximum width of the text as rendered on the canvas. At the time of this writing, this property does not appear to be implemented in any browsers.

Figure 3-2. strokeText setting outline properties

The next iteration of Text Arranger adds the ability for the user to select `fillText`, `strokeText`, or `both`. Selecting `both` will give the `fillText` text a black border (the `strokeText`). In the HTML `<form>`, we will add a `<select>` box with the `id` `fillOr Stroke`, which will allow the user to make the selections:

```
<select id = "fillOrStroke">
  <option value = "fill">fill</option>
  <option value = "stroke">stroke</option>
   <option value = "both">both</option>
</select>
```

In the `canvasApp()` function, we will define a variable named `fillOrStroke` that we will use to hold the value selected by the user on the HTML `<form>`. The default value will be `fill`, which means Text Arranger will always show `fillText` first:

```
var fillOrStroke = "fill";
```

We will also create the event listener for a change in the `fillOrStroke` form element:

```
formElement = document.getElementById("fillOrStroke");
formElement.addEventListener('change', fillOrStrokeChanged, false);
```

And create the function `fillOrStrokeChanged()` to handle the event:

```
function fillOrStrokeChanged(e) {
    var target = e.target;
    fillOrStroke = target.value;
    drawScreen();
}
```

eval()

While we created a separate function for each event handler for the applications in this chapter, in reality, many of them work in an identical way. However, some developers might be inclined to use an eval() function, such as the following, as their event handler for changes made to the HTML element that controls Text Arranger:

```
var formElement = document.getElementById("textBox");
    formElement.addEventListener('keyup', function(e) {
        applyChange('message', e) }, false);
formElement = document.getElementById("fillOrStroke");
formElement.addEventListener('change', function(e) {
    applyChange('fillOrStroke', e) }, false);
function applyChange (variable, e) {
    eval(variable + ' = e.target.value');
    drawScreen();
}
```

The preceding code uses eval() to create and execute JavaScript code on the fly. It dynamically creates the name of the HTML element so that the multiple event handler functions do not need to be created individually. However, many developers are wary of using eval() because it opens up security holes, and makes debugging code more difficult. Use at your own risk.

In the drawScreen() function, we test the fillOrStroke variable to see whether it contains the value fill. Because we have three states (fill, stroke, or both), we use a switch statement to handle the choices. If the choice is both, we set the strokeStyle to black (#000000) as the highlight for the colored fillText.

If we use the xPosition and yPosition calculated using the width and height of the canvas, the message variable that contains the default or user-input text, and the fillOrStroke variable to determine how to render the text, we can display the text as configured by the user in drawScreen():

```
var metrics = context.measureText(message);
var textWidth = metrics.width;
var xPosition = (theCanvas.width/2) - (textWidth/2);
var yPosition = (theCanvas.height/2);

switch(fillOrStroke) {
   case "fill":
      context.fillStyle = "#FF0000";
      context.fillText  (message,  xPosition,yPosition);
      break;
   case "stroke":
      context.strokeStyle = "#FF0000";
      context.strokeText  (message, xPosition,yPosition);
      break;
```

```
    case "both":
        context.fillStyle = "#FF0000";
        context.fillText  (message, xPosition,yPosition);
        context.strokeStyle = "#000000";
            context.strokeText (message, xPosition,yPosition);
            break;
    }
```

Example 3-1 (*CH3EX1.html*) in the code distribution shows the full code for Text Arranger 1.0. Test it out to see how the user controls in HTML affect the canvas. There are
not many ways to change the text here, but you can see the difference between fill
Text and strokeText.

Setting the Text Font

In this section, we will update this application to configure and render the text in multiple ways. We will start with the text font.

Now that we have placed text on the canvas, it's time to explore some of the basics of
setting the context.font property. As you will see, specifying the font for displaying
basic text on Canvas is really no different from doing the same thing in HTML and CSS.

Font Size, Face, Weight, and Style Basics

It is very easy to style text that will be rendered on the canvas. It requires you to set the
size, weight, style, and font face in a CSS-compliant text string that is applied to the
context.font property. The basic format looks like this:

```
[font style] [font weight] [font size] [font face]
```

An example might be:

```
context.font = "italic bold 24px serif";
```

or:

```
context.font = "normal lighter 50px cursive";
```

After the context.font property is set, it will apply to *all* text that is rendered afterward
—until the context.font is set to another CSS-compliant string.

Handling Font Size and Face in Text Arranger

In Text Arranger, we have implemented only a subset of the available font options for
displaying text. We have chosen these to make the application work in as many browsers
as possible. Here is a short rundown of the options we will implement.

Available font styles

CSS defines the valid font styles as:

```
normal | italic | oblique | inherit
```

In Text Arranger, we have implemented all but `inherit`.

Here is the markup we used to create the font style `<select>` box in HTML. We made the `id` of the form control equal to `fontStyle`. We will use this `id` when we listen for a change event, which is dispatched when the user updates the value of this control. We will do this for all the controls in this version of Text Arranger:

```
<select id="fontStyle">
 <option value="normal">normal</option>
 <option value="italic">italic</option>
 <option value="oblique">oblique</option>
</select>
```

Available font weights

CSS defines the valid font weights as:

```
normal | bold | bolder | lighter | 100 | 200 | 300 | 400 | 500 | 600 | 700 | 800 | 900 | inherit
| auto
```

We have used only `normal`, `bold`, `bolder`, and `lighter` in Text Arranger. You can add the other values as you see fit.

Here is the markup we used to create the font weight `<select>` box in HTML:

```
<select id="fontWeight">
 <option value="normal">normal</option>
 <option value="bold">bold</option>
 <option value="bolder">bolder</option>
 <option value="lighter">lighter</option>
</select>
```

Generic font faces

Because we cannot be sure which font will be available in the browser at any time, we have limited the font face choices in Text Arranger to those that are defined as "generic" in the CSS specification: `serif`, `sans-serif`, `cursive`, `fantasy`, and `monospace`.

Here is the markup we used to create the font face `<select>` box in HTML:

```
<select id="textFont">
 <option value="serif">serif</option>
 <option value="sans-serif">sans-serif</option>
 <option value="cursive">cursive</option>
 <option value="fantasy">fantasy</option>
```

```
<option value="monospace">monospace</option>
</select>
```

Fallback and Custom Font Faces

While the preceding fonts are safe for every browser, you can specify any font that you are certain will be available for the user. For multiple fallback fonts, you can separate the font face designations with a comma, like this:

```
context.font = "normal lighter 50px arcade, monospace";
```

Also, as long as the fonts have been loaded, the Canvas can use custom fonts designated in CSS using @font-face like this:

```
@font-face {
    font-family: Arcade;
    src: url('arcade.otf');
}
```

Font size and HTML5 range control

To specify the size of the font, we have implemented the new HTML5 range form control. range is an <input> type that creates a slider on the HTML page to limit the numerical input to that specified in the range. A range is created by specifying range as the type of a form input control. range has four properties that can be set:

min
    The minimum value in the range

max
    The maximum value in the range

step
    The number of units to step when the range slider is moved

value
    The default value of the range

Here is the markup we used to specify the range in the Text Arranger HTML:

```
<input type="range" id="textSize"
 min="0"
 max="200"
 step="1"
 value="50"/>
```

If the browser does not support this range control, it will be rendered as a text box.

At the time of this writing, range did not render in Firefox or any version of Internet Explorer 10.

Creating the necessary variables in the canvasApp() function

In the `canvasApp()` container function, we need to create four variables—`fontSize`, `fontFace`, `fontWeight`, and `fontStyle`—that will hold the values set by the HTML form controls for Text Arranger. We create a default value for each so that the canvas can render text the first time the `drawScreen()` function is called. After that, `drawScreen()` will be called only when a change event is handled by one of the event handler functions that we will create for each form control:

```
var fontSize = "50";
var fontFace = "serif";
var fontWeight = "normal";
var fontStyle = "normal";
```

Setting event handlers in canvasApp()

Just like we did in version 1.0 of Text Arranger, we need to create event listeners and the associated event handler functions so that changes on the HTML page form controls can interact with HTML5 Canvas. All of the following event listeners listen for a change event on the form control:

```
formElement = document.getElementById("textSize");
formElement.addEventListener('change', textSizeChanged, false);

formElement = document.getElementById("textFont");
formElement.addEventListener('change', textFontChanged, false);

formElement = document.getElementById("fontWeight");
formElement.addEventListener('change', fontWeightChanged, false);

formElement = document.getElementById("fontStyle");
formElement.addEventListener('change', fontStyleChanged, false);
```

Defining event handler functions in canvasApp()

Following are the event handlers we need to create for each form control. Notice that each handler updates the variable associated with part of the valid CSS font string and then calls `drawScreen()` so that the new text can be painted onto the canvas:

```
function textSizeChanged(e) {
    var target = e.target;
    fontSize = target.value;
    drawScreen();
}
```

```
function textFontChanged(e) {
    var target = e.target;
    fontFace = target.value;
    drawScreen();
}

function fontWeightChanged(e) {
    var target = e.target;
    fontWeight = target.value;
    drawScreen();
}

function fontStyleChanged(e) {
    var target = e.target;
    fontStyle = target.value;
    drawScreen();
}
```

Setting the font in the drawScreen() function

Finally, in the `drawScreen()` function, we put all of this together to create a valid CSS font string that we apply to the `context.font` property:

```
context.font = fontWeight + " " + fontStyle + " " + fontSize + "px " + fontFace;
```

Figures 3-3 and 3-4 show the results.

Figure 3-3. Setting the font size and face

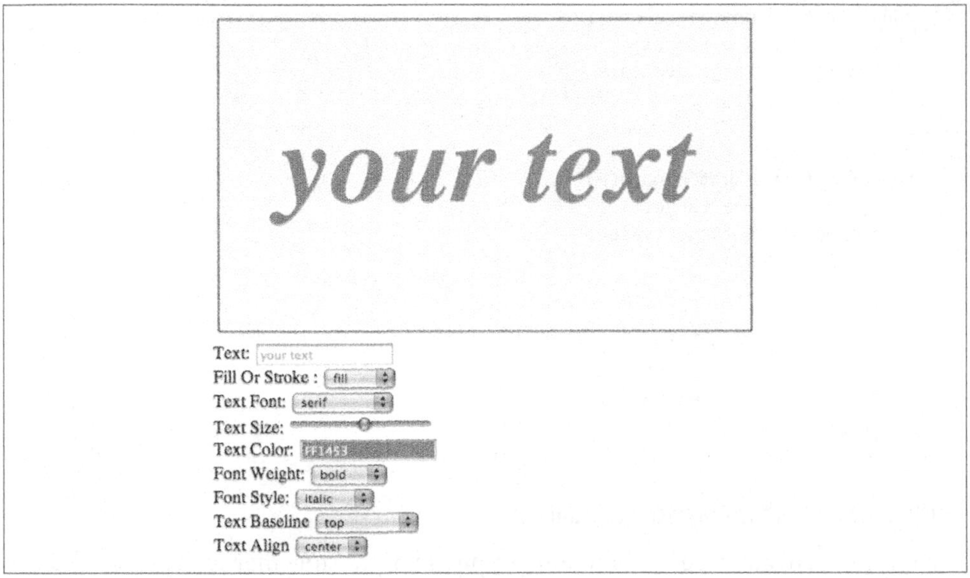

Figure 3-4. Setting the font as bold and italic

Font Color

Setting the font color for text rendered on HTML5 Canvas is as simple as setting the `context.fillStyle` or `context.strokeStyle` property to a valid CSS RGB color. Use the format #RRGGBB, where RR is the red component hexadecimal value, GG is the green component hexadecimal value, and BB is the blue component hexadecimal value. Here are some examples:

```
context.fillStyle = "#FF0000";
```
    Sets the text fill to red

```
context.strokeStyle = "#FF00FF";
```
    Sets the text stroke to purple

```
context.fillStyle = "#FFFF00";
```
    Sets the text fill to yellow

For Text Arranger, we will allow the user to select the text color. We could have made this a drop-down or a text box, but instead, we want to use the new HTML5 `<input>` type of `color`. This handy new form control works directly in the web browser, allowing users to visually choose a color from a beautifully designed color picker. At the time of this writing, only Chrome and Opera have implemented the `color` `<input>` object of the HTML5 specification.

However, because we could really use a nice color picker for Text Arranger, we will implement a third-party color picker, JSColor (*http://jscolor.com/*). The `jsColor` control creates a nice color picker in JavaScript (see Figure 3-5), similar to the one that will someday grace browsers supporting HTML5.

To implement `jsColor` and the color picker for Text Arranger, first download the *jscolor.js* library, and put it in the same folder as Text Arranger. Then add this line of code in the <head> to include `jsColor` in the HTML page:

```
<script type="text/javascript" src="jscolor/jscolor.js"></script>
```

Then add a new <input> element to the ever-growing HTML <form> on the Text Arranger HTML page, and give it the CSS class designation `color`:

```
<input class="color" id="textFillColor" value="FF0000"/>
```

When you pick a color with `jsColor`, it creates a text value that looks like "FF0000", representing the color value chosen. However, we already know that we need to append the pound (#) sign to the front of that value to work with HTML5 Canvas. The `text FillColorChanged` event handler does this by appending "#" to the value of the `text FillColor` form control:

```
function textFillColorChanged(e) {
        var target = e.target;
        textFillColor = "#" + target.value;
        drawScreen();
    }
```

And let's not forget the event listener that we must create so that we can direct and "change" events from the `textFillColor` <input> element to the `textFillColorCh anged()` event handler:

```
formElement = document.getElementById("textFillColor");
formElement.addEventListener('change', textFillColorChanged, false);
```

Finally, in the `canvasApp()` function, we need to create the `textFillColor` variable:

```
var textFillColor = "#ff0000";
```

We do this so that the variable can be updated by the aforementioned event handler and then implemented when that event handler calls the `drawScreen()` function:

```
switch(fillOrStroke) {
   case "fill":
      context.fillStyle = textFillColor;
      context.fillText (message, xPosition,yPosition);
      break;
   case "stroke":
      context.strokeStyle = textFillColor;
      context.strokeText (message, xPosition,yPosition);
      break;
   case "both":
      context.fillStyle = textFillColor;
      context.fillText (message, xPosition ,yPosition);
      context.strokeStyle = "#000000";
```

```
            context.strokeText (message, xPosition,yPosition);
            break;
    }
```

Notice that we needed to update the switch() statement created for Text Arranger version 1.0 so that it used textFillColor instead of hardcoded values. However, when both a stroke and a fill are chosen, we still render the stroke as black ("#000000"). We could have added an additional color picker for the strokeColor, but that is something you can do if you want to start expanding the application. Figure 3-5 illustrates what it looks like now.

Figure 3-5. Setting the font color

Font Baseline and Alignment

You have options to align text on HTML5 Canvas both vertically and horizontally. These alignments affect the text in relation to Canvas itself, but only to the invisible bounding box that would surround the text's topmost, bottommost, rightmost, and leftmost sides. This is an important distinction because it means that these alignments affect the text in ways that might be unfamiliar to you.

Vertical alignment

The font baseline is the vertical alignment of the font glyphs based on predefined horizontal locations in a font's `em square` (the grid used to design font outlines) in relation to font *descenders*. Basically, font glyphs like lowercase *p* and *y* that traditionally extend "below the line" have descenders. The baseline tells the canvas where to render the font based on how those descenders relate to other glyphs in the font face.

The HTML5 Canvas API online has a neat graphic that attempts to explain baseline. We could copy it here, but in reality, we think it's easier to understand by *doing*, which is one of the main reasons we wrote the Text Arranger application.

The options for the `context.textBaseline` property are as follows:

`top`
: The top of the text `em square` and the top of the highest glyph in the font face. Selecting this baseline will push the text the farthest down (highest y position) the canvas of all the baselines.

`hanging`
: This is a bit lower than the `top` baseline. It is the horizontal line from which many glyphs appear to "hang" from near the top of their face.

`middle`
: The dead vertical center baseline. We will use `middle` to help us vertically center the text in Text Arranger.

`alphabetic`
: The bottom of vertical writing script glyphs such as Arabic, Latin, and Hebrew.

`ideographic`
: The bottom of horizontal writing script glyphs such as Han ideographs, Katakana, Hiragana, and Hangul.

`bottom`
: The bottom of the `em square` of the font glyphs. Choosing this baseline will push the font the farthest up (lowest y position) the canvas.

So, for example, if you want to place your text with a `top` baseline, you would use the following code:

```
context.textBaseline = "top";
```

All text displayed on the canvas afterward would have this baseline. To change the baseline, you would change the property:

```
context.textBaseline = "middle";
```

In reality, you will probably choose a single baseline for your app and stick with it, unless you are creating a word-processing or design application that requires more precise text handling.

Horizontal alignment

The `context.textAlign` property represents the horizontal alignment of the text based on its x position. These are the available `textAlign` values:

center
: The dead horizontal center of the text. We can use this alignment to help center our text in Text Arranger.

start
: Text is displayed directly after the text y position.

end
: All text is displayed before the text y position.

left
: Text is displayed starting with the y position of the text in the leftmost position (just like `start`).

right
: Text is displayed with the y position in the rightmost position of the text (just like `end`).

For example, to set the text alignment to `center`, you would use the code:

```
context.textAlign = "center";
```

After this property is set, all text would be displayed with the y value of the text as the center point. However, this does not mean the text will be "centered" on the canvas. To do that, you need to find the center of the canvas and use that location as the y value for the text position. We will do this in Text Arranger.

These values can also be modified by the `dir` attribute of the `Canvas` object (inherited from the DOM `document` object). `dir` changes the direction of how text is displayed; the valid values for `dir` are `rtl` ("right to left") and `ltr` ("left to right").

Handling text baseline and alignment

We are going to handle the text baseline and alignment much like we handled the other text properties in Text Arranger. First, we will add some variables to the `canvasApp()` function in which Text Arranger operates that will hold the alignment values. Notice that we have set the `textAlign` variable to `center`, helping us simplify centering the text on the canvas:

```
var textBaseline = "middle";
var textAlign = "center";
```

Next, we add the `<select>` form elements for each new attribute to the HTML portion of the page:

```
Text Baseline <select id="textBaseline">
  <option value="middle">middle</option>
  <option value="top">top</option>
  <option value="hanging">hanging</option>
  <option value="alphabetic">alphabetic</option>
  <option value="ideographic">ideographic</option>
  <option value="bottom">bottom</option>
  </select>
  <br>
  Text Align <select id="textAlign">
  <option value="center">center</option>
  <option value="start">start</option>
  <option value="end">end</option>
  <option value="left">left</option>
  <option value="right">right</option>

  </select>
```

We then add event listeners and event handler functions so that we can connect the user interaction with the HTML form elements to the canvas display. We register the event listeners in the `canvasApp()` function:

```
formElement = document.getElementById("textBaseline");
formElement.addEventListener('change', textBaselineChanged, false);

formElement = document.getElementById("textAlign");
formElement.addEventListener('change', textAlignChanged, false);
```

Next, we need to create the event handler functions inside `canvasApp()`:

```
function textBaselineChanged(e) {
    var target = e.target;
    textBaseline = target.value;
    drawScreen();
}

function textAlignChanged(e) {
    var target = e.target;
    textAlign = target.value;
    drawScreen();
}
```

We then apply the new values in the `drawScreen()` function:

```
context.textBaseline = textBaseline;
context.textAlign = textAlign;
```

Finally, we change the code that centers the text horizontally on the screen. Because we used the center alignment for context.textAlign, we no longer need to subtract half the width of the text that we retrieved through context.measureText() like we did previously in Text Arranger 1.0:

```
var metrics = context.measureText(message);
var textWidth = metrics.width;
var xPosition = (theCanvas.width/2) - (textWidth/2);
```

Instead, we can simply use the center point of the canvas:

```
var xPosition = (theCanvas.width/2);
```

Remember, center is only the default alignment for the text. Because you can change this with Text Arranger, the text can still be aligned in different ways while you are using the application.

Figure 3-6 shows how a font set to start alignment with a middle baseline might appear on the canvas.

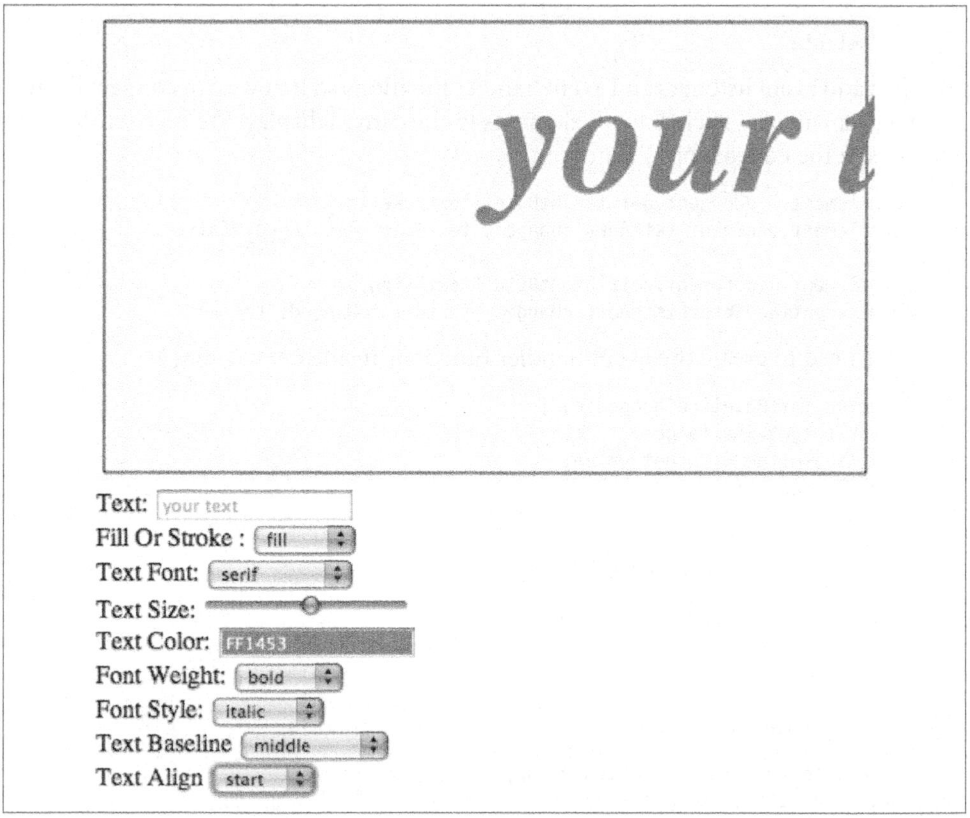

Figure 3-6. Font with start alignment and middle baseline

Text Arranger Version 2.0

Now try the new version of Text Arranger, shown in Example 3-2. It is *CH3EX2.html* in the code distribution. You can see that we have added a ton of new options that did not exist in version 1.0. One of the most striking things is how fluidly the text grows and shrinks as the font size is updated. Now, imagine scripting the font size to create animations. How would you do that? Could you create an application to record the manipulations the user makes with Text Arranger and then play them back in real time?

Also, notice how all the alignment options affect one another. Experiment with how changing the text direction affects the vertical alignment. Choose different font faces, and see how they affect the baseline. Do you see how an application like Text Arranger can help you understand the complex relationships of all the text properties on HTML5 Canvas in an interactive and—dare we say—fun way?

Text and the Canvas Context

We've already discussed a couple Canvas context properties that affect the canvas in a global fashion: `fillStyle` and `strokeStyle`. However, there are two areas that visually demonstrate how changes to the properties of the context can affect the entire HTML5 Canvas: alpha transparencies and shadows.

Global Alpha and Text

Using alpha is a cool way to make objects seem to be partially or fully transparent on HTML5 Canvas. The `globalAlpha` property of the Canvas context is used for this purpose. After `globalAlpha` is applied, it affects all drawing on the canvas, so you need to be careful when setting it.

The valid values for `context.globalAlpha` are numbers between 0.0 (transparent) and 1.0 (opaque), and they act as a percentage for the alpha value. For example, a 50% alpha value would be coded like this:

```
context.globalAlpha = 0.5;
```

A 100% alpha (no transparency) would be coded like this:

```
context.globalAlpha = 1.0;
```

Besides the now-familiar elements that we included for most of the other configurable options in Text Arranger, the `globalAlpha` property requires us to think a bit more about when we use it and how it will affect the rest of the canvas.

First, we create a variable named `textAlpha` in the `canvasApp()` function and initialize it with 1, which means the text will have no transparency when it is first displayed:

```
var textAlpha = 1;
```

Next, in the `drawImage()` function, we need to set the `globalAlpha` property twice—once before we draw the background and the bounding box frame:

```
function drawScreen() {
     //Background

     context.globalAlpha = 1;
```

And then again to the value stored in `textAlpha`, just before rendering the text to the canvas:

```
     context.globalAlpha = textAlpha;
```

This will reset `globalAlpha` so that we can draw the background, but it will still allow us to use a configurable alpha value for the displayed text.

We will use another HTML5 `range` control in our form, but this time we set the value range with a `min` value of 0.0 and a `max` value of 1.0, stepping 0.01 every time the range is moved:

```
Alpha: <input type="range" id="textAlpha"
       min="0.0"
       max="1.0"
       step="0.01"
       value="1.0"/>
```

The `textAlphaChanged()` function works just like the other event handler functions that we created in this chapter:

```
function textAlphaChanged(e) {
     var target = e.target;
     textAlpha = (target.value);
     drawScreen();
   }
```

Also, don't forget the event listener for the `textAlpha range` control:

```
formElement = document.getElementById("textAlpha");
formElement.addEventListener('change', textAlphaChanged, false);
```

The results will look like Figure 3-7.

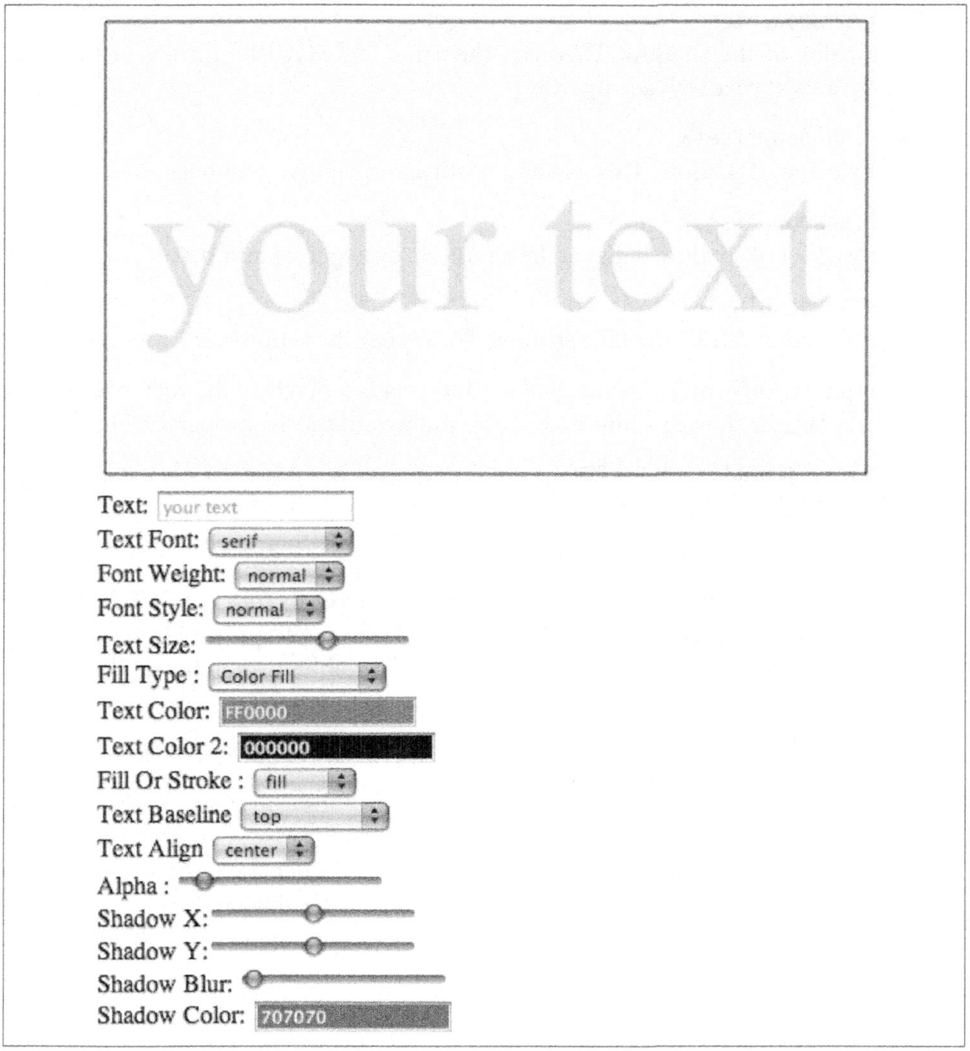

Figure 3-7. Text with globalAlpha applied

Global Shadows and Text

HTML5 Canvas includes a unique set of properties for creating a shadow for drawings. The `context.shadow` functions are not unique to text, but they can make some very good text effects with very little effort.

To create a `shadowEffect`, there are four properties of the Canvas context that need to be manipulated:

context.shadowColor

> The color of the shadow. This uses the same "#RRGGBB" format of the `fill Style` and `strokeStyle` properties.

context.shadowOffsetX

> The x offset of shadow. This can be a positive or negative number.

context.shadowOffsetY

> The y offset of shadow. This can be a positive or negative number.

context.shadowBlur

> The blur filter diffusion of the shadow. The higher the number, the more diffusion.

For example, if you want to create a red shadow that is 5 pixels to the right and 5 pixels down from your text, with a blur of 2 pixels, you would set the properties like this:

```
context.shadowColor = "#FF0000";
context.shadowOffsetX = 5;
context.shadowOffsetY = 5;
context.shadowBlur = 2;
```

Just as we saw with `globalAlpha`, we must reset the shadow properties before we draw the background for `textArranger`; otherwise, the shadow will apply to the entire image. First, in the `canvasApp()` function, we create a set of variables to hold the shadow values:

```
var textAlpha = 1;
var shadowX = 1;
var shadowY = 1;
var shadowBlur = 1;
var shadowColor = "#707070";
```

We then make sure to turn off the shadow before we render the background for `tex tArranger` in the `drawScreen()`. We don't have to reset the `shadowColor`, but we think it is good practice to update all the relative properties relating to any global change to the Canvas context:

```
context.shadowColor = "#707070";
context.shadowOffsetX = 0;
context.shadowOffsetY = 0;
context.shadowBlur = 0;
```

Later in `drawScreen()`, we render the shadow based on the settings in the four variables we created:

```
context.shadowColor = shadowColor;
context.shadowOffsetX = shadowX;
context.shadowOffsetY = shadowY;
context.shadowBlur = shadowBlur;
```

We also need to create the HTML to allow the user to update the shadow settings. We do this with three `range` controls, as well as another color picker using `jsColor`:

```
Shadow X:<input type="range" id="shadowX"
        min="-100"
        max="100"
        step="1"
        value="1"/>
<br>
Shadow Y:<input type="range" id="shadowY"
        min="-100"
        max="100"
        step="1"
        value="1"/>
<br>
Shadow Blur: <input type="range" id="shadowBlur"
        min="1"
        max="100"
        step="1"
        value="1" />
<br>
Shadow Color: <input class="color" id="shadowColor" value="707070"/>
```

Finally, we need to add the event listeners and event handler functions so that the HTML form elements can communicate with the canvas. See the results in Figure 3-8:

```
formElement = document.getElementById("shadowX");
formElement.addEventListener('change', shadowXChanged, false);

formElement = document.getElementById("shadowY");
formElement.addEventListener('change', shadowYChanged, false);

formElement = document.getElementById("shadowBlur");
formElement.addEventListener('change', shadowBlurChanged, false);

formElement = document.getElementById("shadowColor");
formElement.addEventListener('change', shadowColorChanged, false);
function shadowXChanged(e) {
    var target = e.target;
    shadowX = target.value;
    drawScreen();
}

function shadowYChanged(e) {
    var target = e.target;
    shadowY = target.value;
    drawScreen();
}

function shadowBlurChanged(e) {
    var target = e.target;
    shadowBlur = target.value;
    drawScreen();
}

function shadowColorChanged(e) {
```

```
        var target = e.target;
        shadowColor = target.value;
        drawScreen();
    }
```

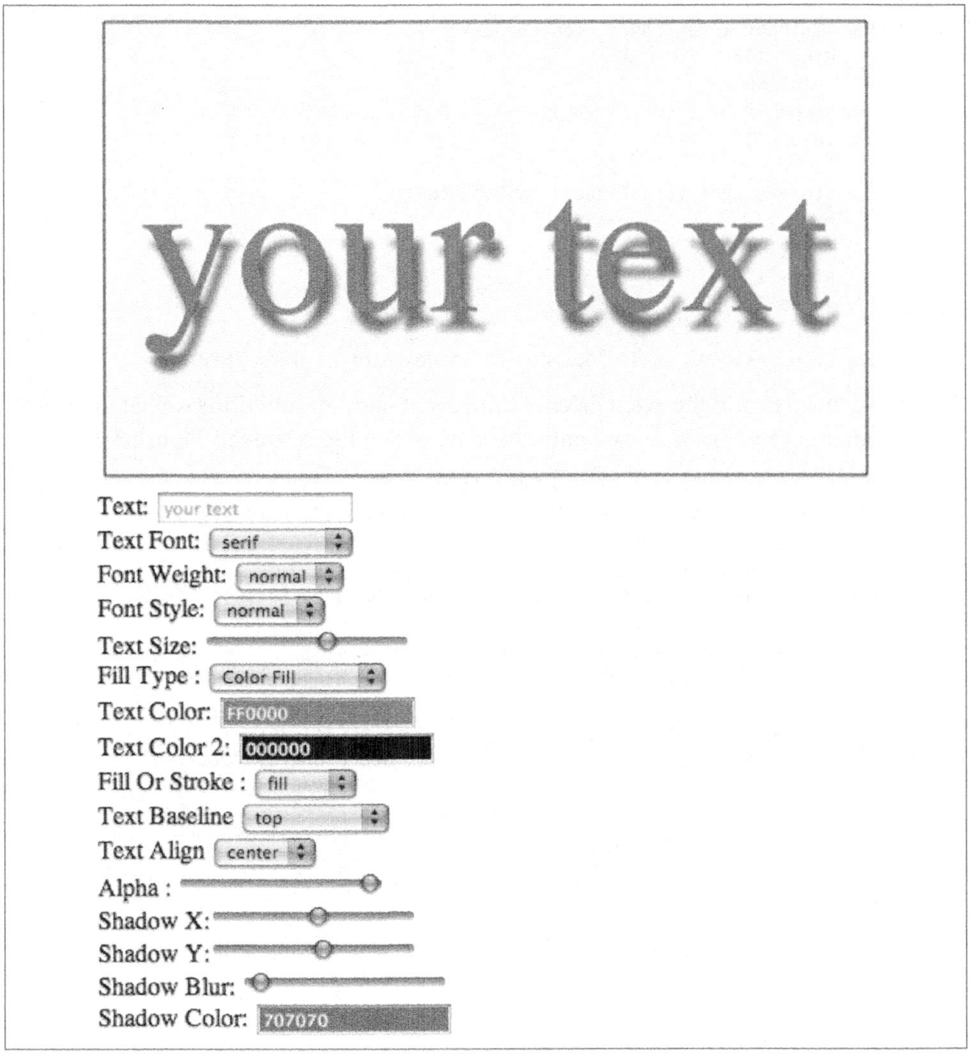

Figure 3-8. Text with global shadow applied

Text with Gradients and Patterns

We've already explored the fillColor and strokeColor properties of the Canvas context by setting those values to CSS-compliant colors. However, those very same properties can be set to refer to a few other objects defined in the Canvas API to create some stunning text effects. The objects are:

Linear gradient
> A linear color gradient with two or more colors

Radial gradient
> A circular color gradient with two or more colors

Image pattern
> An `Image` object used as a fill pattern

Linear Gradients and Text

To create a linear gradient, make a call to the context's `createLinearGradient()` method to create a `Gradient` object. The `createLinearGradient()` method accepts four parameters that all define the line of the linear gradient. The `x0` and `y0` parameters are the starting point of the line, and `x1` and `y1` represent the ending point of the line:

```
var gradient = context.createLinearGradient( [x0],[y0],[x1],[y1]);
```

For example, if you want to create a linear gradient that starts at the beginning of the text (located at 100,100) and has an endpoint that is the width of your text as displayed on the canvas, you might write the following code:

```
var metrics = context.measureText(message);
var textWidth = metrics.width;
var gradient = context.createLinearGradient(100, 100, textWidth, 100);
```

After you have created the line that represents the gradient, you need to add colors that will form the gradations of the gradient fill. This is done with the `addColorStop()` method, which requires two arguments, `offset` and `color`:

```
gradient.addColorStop([offset],[color]);
```

`offset`
> This is the offset on the gradient line to start the color gradation. The entire gradient is represented by the numbers between 0.0 and 1.0. The offset will be a decimal that represents a percentage.

`color`
> A valid CSS color in the format "#RRGGBB".

So, if you want black to be the first color in the gradient and red to be the second color that starts halfway down the gradient line, you would create two calls to `addColorStop()`:

```
gradient.addColorStop(0, "#000000");
gradient.addColorStop(.5, "#FF0000");
```

If you fail to add colors with addColorStop(), the text will be rendered invisible.

The results are shown in Figure 3-9.

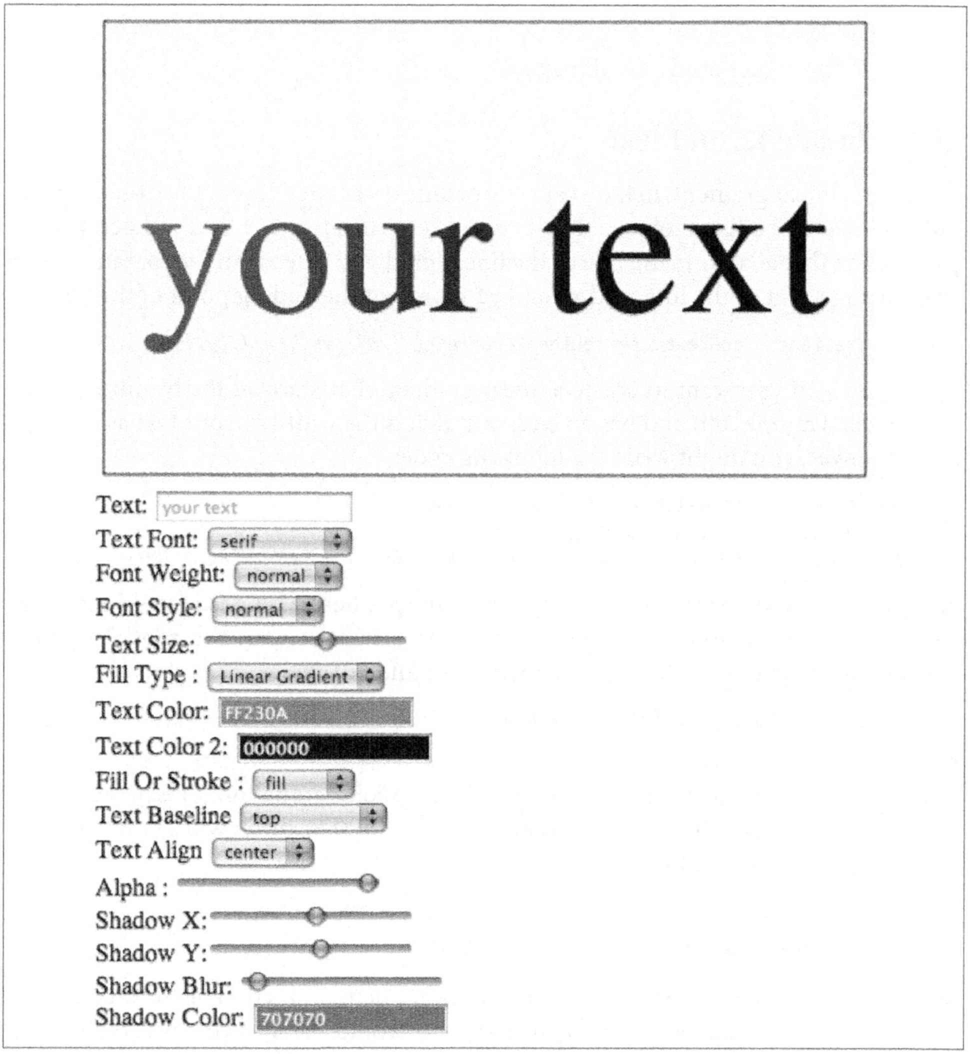

Figure 3-9. Text with linear gradient applied

Radial Gradients and Text

A radial gradient is created much like a linear gradient, except that it represents a cone —not a line. The cone is created by defining the center points and the radii of two different circles when calling the `createRadialGradient()` function of the Canvas context:

```
var gradient = context.createRadialGradient([x0],[y0],[radius0],[x1],[y1],
                                             [radius1]);
```

Let's say you want to create a radial gradient based on a cone. It starts with a circle that has its center point at 100,100 and a radius of 20, and it ends at a circle with its center point at 200,100 and a radius of 5. The code would look like this:

```
var gradient = context.createRadialGradient(100,100,20,200,100,5);
```

Adding color stops to a radial gradient works the same as with a linear gradient, except the color moves along the cone instead of the line:

```
gradient.addColorStop(0, "#000000");
gradient.addColorStop(.5, "#FF0000");
```

Image Patterns and Text

Another option for filling text on HTML5 Canvas is to use an `Image` object. We will devote all of Chapter 4 to using the Image API, so here we will discuss only the basics of how to use one as a pattern for a text fill.

To create an image pattern, call the `createPattern()` method of the Canvas context, passing a reference to an `Image` object, and an option for `repetition`:

```
var pattern = context.createPattern([image], [repetition]);
```

image

> A valid `Image` object that has been loaded with an image by setting the `pat tern.src` property and waiting for the image to load by setting an event listener for the `Image onload` event. The Canvas specification also allows for a `video` element or another `<canvas>` to be used here as well.

repetition

> The "tiling" of the image. This can have one of four values:

> repeat

> > The image is tiled on both the x- and y-axes.

> repeat-x

> > The image is tiled only on the x-axis (horizontally).

> repeat-y

> > The image is tiled only on the y-axis (vertically).

---

no-repeat
> The image is not tiled.

To use the image pattern, apply it to the `fillStyle` and `strokeStyle` properties of the context, just as you would apply a color:

```
context.fillStyle = pattern;
```

or:

```
context.strokeStyle = pattern;
```

For example, to load an image named *texture.jpg* and apply it to the `fillStyle` property so that it tiles on both the x- and y-axes, you would write code like this:

```
var patternImage = new Image();
patternImage.src = "texture.jpg"
patternImage.onload = function() {
var pattern = context.createPattern(patternImage, "repeat");
context.fillStyle = pattern;
...
}
```

Patterns with Video: The Bad News

The HTML5 Canvas API specifies that an HTML5 `video` element can be used as the source for `createPattern()` instead of an image. However, all of our attempts to do so emitted the following JavaScript error:

```
Uncaught Error: TYPE_MISMATCH_ERR: DOM Exception 17
```

According to the DOM reference (*http://www.gnu.org*), DOM Exception 17, TYPE_MISMATCH_ERR occurs "if the type of an object is incompatible with the expected type of the parameter associated to the object."

So it appears that most browsers have not included support for using video as the pattern for `createPattern()`. However, you can still load and play video on Canvas, which we will discuss in depth in Chapter 6.

Handling Gradients and Patterns in Text Arranger

Text Arranger 3.0 includes many changes that were implemented to support using gradients and image patterns with text on HTML5 Canvas. To see these changes in action, we first need to make sure that we have preloaded the *texture.jpg* image, which we will use for the `context.createPattern()` functionality. To do this, we will create a new function named `eventAssetsLoaded()` that we will set as the event handler for the `onload` event of the `Image` object that will hold the pattern. When that image has loaded, we will call `canvasApp()` in the same way we called it from `eventWindowLoaded()`:

```
function eventWindowLoaded() {
    var patternImage = new Image();
    patternImage.src = "texture.jpg";
    patternImage.onload = eventAssetsLoaded;
}

function eventAssetsLoaded() {

    canvasApp();
}
```

 We are not going to use the pattern variable we created in this function, because it does not have scope in the `canvasApp()` function. We are merely using it to make sure that the image is available before we use it.

In the `canvasApp()` function, we will create three variables to support this new functionality. `fillType` describes how the text will be filled (a regular color fill, a linear gradient, a radial gradient, or a pattern). The `textColorFill2` variable is the second color we will use for the gradient color stop. Finally, the `pattern` variable holds the `Image` object we preloaded, which we now need to create an instance of in `canvasApp()`:

```
var fillType = "colorFill";
var textFillColor2 = "#000000";
var pattern = new Image();
...
pattern.src = "texture.jpg";
```

Now, let's jump to the HTML of our `<form>`. Because we have created different ways to fill the text we are displaying, we need to build a selection that allows for this choice. We will create a `<select>` box with the `id` of `fillType` for this purpose:

```
Fill Type: <select id="fillType">
    <option value="colorFill">Color Fill</option>
    <option value="linearGradient">Linear Gradient</option>
    <option value="radialGradient">Radial Gradient</option>
    <option value="pattern">pattern</option>
    </select>
```

We need to add a second color selection that we can use for the gradient fills. We will use the `jsColor` picker and the `id` `textColorFill2`:

```
Text Color 2: <input class="color" id="textFillColor2" value ="000000"/>
    <br>
```

Back in `canvasApp()`, we need to create the event listeners for our two new form elements:

```
formElement = document.getElementById("textFillColor2");
formElement.addEventListener('change', textFillColor2Changed, false);
```

```
formElement = document.getElementById("fillType");
formElement.addEventListener('change', fillTypeChanged, false);
```

We also need to create the associated event handler functions for the new form elements:

```
function textFillColor2Changed(e) {
    var target = e.target;
    textFillColor2 = "#" + target.value;
    drawScreen();
}

function fillTypeChanged(e) {
    var target = e.target;
    fillType = target.value;
    drawScreen();
}
```

We need to add support to `drawScreen()` for this new functionality. First, we use the `measureText()` method of the context to get the width of the text, which we will use to create the gradients:

```
var metrics = context.measureText(message);
var textWidth = metrics.width;
```

Then, we need to decide how to format our "color" for the `fillStyle` or `strokeStyle` of the context. In this instance, it can be a CSS color, a gradient, or an image pattern; the following list provides more information:

Color fill
> If we are doing a simple color fill, we operate just like in previous versions of Text Arranger. All we need to do is make `tempColor` equal to the value of `textFillColor`.

Linear gradient
> For the linear gradient, we need to decide what line we are going to create for the gradient. Our line will start at the beginning of the text (xPosition-textWidth/2 because the text uses the `center` alignment), and runs horizontally to the end of the text (textWidth). We also add two color stops (at 0% and 60%)—the colors are textFillColor1 and textFillColor2.

Radial gradient
> For the radial gradient, we are going to create a cone that starts at the center of the text (xPosition,yPosition) with a radius the size of the font (fontSize). The cone will extend horizontally the width of the text (textWidth) with a radius of 1.

Pattern
> For this option, we create a pattern using the pattern `image` variable we previously created. We designate it to `repeat` so that it will tile horizontally and vertically.

Here's the code:

```
    var tempColor;
    if (fillType == "colorFill") {
       tempColor = textFillColor;
    } else if (fillType == "linearGradient") {
       var gradient = context.createLinearGradient(xPosition-
          textWidth/2, yPosition, textWidth, yPosition);
       gradient.addColorStop(0,textFillColor);
       gradient.addColorStop(.6,textFillColor2);
       tempColor = gradient;
    } else if (fillType == "radialGradient") {
       var gradient = context.createRadialGradient(xPosition, yPosition,
          fontSize, xPosition+textWidth, yPosition, 1);
       gradient.addColorStop(0,textFillColor);
       gradient.addColorStop(.6,textFillColor2);
       tempColor = gradient;
    } else if (fillType == "pattern") {
      var tempColor = context.createPattern(pattern,"repeat");
    } else {
       tempColor = textFillColor;
    }
```

Now, when we set our `fillStyle` or `strokeStyle`, we use `tempColor` instead of `text FillColor`. This will set the proper text fill choice that will be displayed on the canvas, as shown in Figure 3-10:

```
    context.fillStyle = tempColor;
```

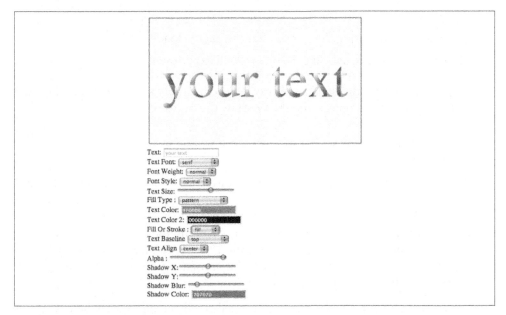

Figure 3-10. Text with image pattern applied

Width, Height, Scale, and toDataURL() Revisited

In Chapter 1, we briefly explained that you can set the width and height of the canvas, as well as the scale (style `width` and `height`) of the canvas display area, dynamically in code. We also showed you an example of using the `Canvas` object's `toDataURL()` method to export a "screenshot" of the Canvas application. In this section, we will revisit those functions as they relate to Text Arranger 3.0.

Dynamically Resizing the Canvas

In the code we developed in this chapter, we created a reference to the `Canvas` object on the HTML page—with the `id canvasOne`—and used it to retrieve the 2D context of the `Canvas` object:

```
var theCanvas = document.getElementById("canvasOne");
var context = theCanvas.getContext("2d");
```

While the 2D context is very important because we used it to draw directly onto the canvas, we did not spend any time discussing the `Canvas` object itself. In this chapter, we use the `width` property of the `Canvas` object to center text on the canvas. However, the `Canvas` object also includes another property named `height`, and both of these properties can be used to dynamically resize the `Canvas` object on demand. Why would you want to do this? There could be many uses, including the following:

- Updating the canvas to the exact size of a loaded `video` object
- Dynamically animating the canvas after the page is loaded
- Other, more creative uses like the one we will experiment with next

Resizing the canvas on the fly is quite easy. To do it, simply set the `width` and `height` properties of the `Canvas` object, and then redraw the canvas contents:

```
Canvas.width = 600;
Canvas.height = 500;
drawScreen();
```

The Canvas 2D API describes this function as a way to "scale" the canvas, but in practice, this does not appear to be true. Instead, the contents of the canvas are simply redrawn at the same size and same location on a larger canvas. Furthermore, if you don't redraw the canvas content, it appears to be invalidated, blanking the canvas back to white. To properly scale the canvas, you need to use the CSS `width` and `height` attributes, as described in the next section. We discuss using a matrix transformation to scale the canvas in both Chapter 2 and Chapter 4.

We will add the ability for the canvas to be resized at will, giving you a good example of how resizing works and what it does to your drawn content.

First, we will add a couple new range controls to the HTML <form>. As you might have already guessed, we really like this new HTML5 range control, so we've tried to find as many uses as possible for it—even though it's only tangentially related to HTML5 Canvas.

We will give the controls the ids canvasWidth and canvasHeight:

```
Canvas Width:  <input type="range" id="canvasWidth"
        min="0"
        max="1000"
        step="1"
        value="500"/>
    <br>

    Canvas Height:
    <input type="range" id="canvasHeight"
        min="0"
        max="1000"
        step="1"
        value="300"/>
    <br>
```

Next, we add event listeners for the new form elements in the canvasApp() function:

```
formElement = document.getElementById("canvasWidth");
formElement.addEventListener('change', canvasWidthChanged, false);

formElement = document.getElementById("canvasHeight");
formElement.addEventListener('change', canvasHeightChanged, false);
```

Finally, we add the event handlers. Notice that we set the width and height of theCan vas (the variable we created that represents the Canvas object on screen) right inside these functions. We also need to make sure that we call drawScreen() in each function so that the canvas is redrawn on the newly resized area. If we did not do this, the canvas on the page would blank back to white:

```
function canvasWidthChanged(e) {
    var target = e.target;
    theCanvas.width = target.value;
    drawScreen();
}

function canvasHeightChanged(e) {
    var target =  e.target;
    theCanvas.height =  target.value;
    drawScreen();
}
```

We also need to change the way we draw the background for the application in the drawScreen() function so that it supports a resized canvas. We do this by using the width and height attributes of theCanvas to create our background and bounding box:

```
context.fillStyle = '#ffffaa';
context.fillRect(0, 0, theCanvas.width, theCanvas.height);
//Box
context.strokeStyle = '#000000';
context.strokeRect(5,  5, theCanvas.width-10, theCanvas.height-10);
```

Dynamically Scaling the Canvas

Besides resizing the canvas using `theCanvas.width` and `theCanvas.height` attributes, you can also use CSS styles to change its scale. Unlike resizing, scaling takes the current canvas bitmapped area and resamples it to fit into the size specified by the `width` and `height` attributes of the CSS style. For example, to scale the canvas to a 400×400 area, you might use this CSS style:

```
style = "width: 400px; height:400px"
```

To update the `style.width` and `style.height` properties of the canvas in Text Arranger, we first create two more `range` controls in the HTML page:

```
Canvas Style Width:  <input type="range" id="canvasStyleWidth"
        min="0"
        max="1000"
        step="1"
        value="500"/>
  <br>

  Canvas Style Height:
  <input type="range" id="canvasStyleHeight"
        min="0"
        max="1000"
        step="1"
        value="300"/>
  <br>
```

Next, we set the event handler for each `range` control. However, this time we are using the same handler—`canvasStyleSizeChanged()`—for both:

```
formElement = document.getElementById("canvasStyleWidth");
formElement.addEventListener("change", canvasStyleSizeChanged, false);
formElement = document.getElementById("canvasStyleHeight");
formElement.addEventListener("change", canvasStyleSizeChanged, false);
```

In the event handler, we use the `document.getElementById()` method to get the values from both `range` controls. We then create a string that represents the style we want to set for the canvas:

```
"width:" + styleWidth.value + "px; height:" + styleHeight.value +"px;";
```

Finally, we use the `setAttribute()` method to set the "style":

```
function canvasStyleSizeChanged(e) {

    var styleWidth = document.getElementById("canvasStyleWidth");
```

```
var styleHeight = document.getElementById("canvasStyleHeight");
var styleValue = "width:" + styleWidth.value + "px; height:" +
    styleHeight.value +"px;";
theCanvas.setAttribute("style", styleValue );
drawScreen();
}
```

 While trying to change theCanvas.width and theCanvas.height attributes, you might notice some oddities if you try to change the scale
with CSS at the same time. It appears that after you change the scale
with CSS, the width and height attributes update the canvas in relation
to that scale, which might not be the effect you are expecting. Experiment with Text Arranger 3.0 to see how these different styles and attributes interact.

The toDataURL() Method of the Canvas Object

As we briefly explained in Chapter 1, the Canvas object also contains a method named
toDataURL(), which returns a string representing the canvas's image data. A call with
no arguments will return a string of image data of MIME type *image/png*. If you supply
the *image/jpg* as an argument, you can also supply a second argument between the
numbers 0.0 and 1.0 that represents the quality/compression level of the image.

We are going to use toDataURL() to output the image data of the canvas into a <tex
tarea> on our form and then open a window to display the actual image. This is just a
simple way to show that the function is working.

The first thing we do is create our last two form controls in HTML for Text Arranger.
We start by creating a button with the id of createImageData that, when pressed, will
create the image data with a call to an event handler named createImageData
Pressed().

We also create a <textarea> named imageDataDisplay that will hold the text data of
the image after the createImageData button is pressed:

```
<input type="button" id="createImageData" value="Create Image Data">
<br>

<br>
<textarea id="imageDataDisplay" rows=10 cols=30></textarea>
```

Next, we set up the event listener for the createImageData button:

```
formElement = document.getElementById("createImageData");
formElement.addEventListener('click', createImageDataPressed, false);
```

Then, in the `createImageDataPressed()` event handler, we call the `toDataURL()` method of the `Canvas` object (`theCanvas`) and set the value of the `imageDataDisplay` `<textarea>` to the data returned from `toDataURL()`. Finally, using the image data as the URL for the window, we call `window.open()`. When we do this, a window will pop open, displaying the actual image created from the canvas. (See Figure 3-11.) You can right-click and save this image, just like any other image displayed in an HTML page. Pretty cool, eh?

```
function createImageDataPressed(e) {

    var imageDataDisplay = document.getElementById('imageDataDisplay');
    imageDataDisplay.value = theCanvas.toDataURL();
    window.open(imageDataDisplay.value,"canvasImage","left=0,top=0,width=" +
        theCanvas.width + ",height=" + theCanvas.height +
        ",toolbar=0,resizable=0");
}
```

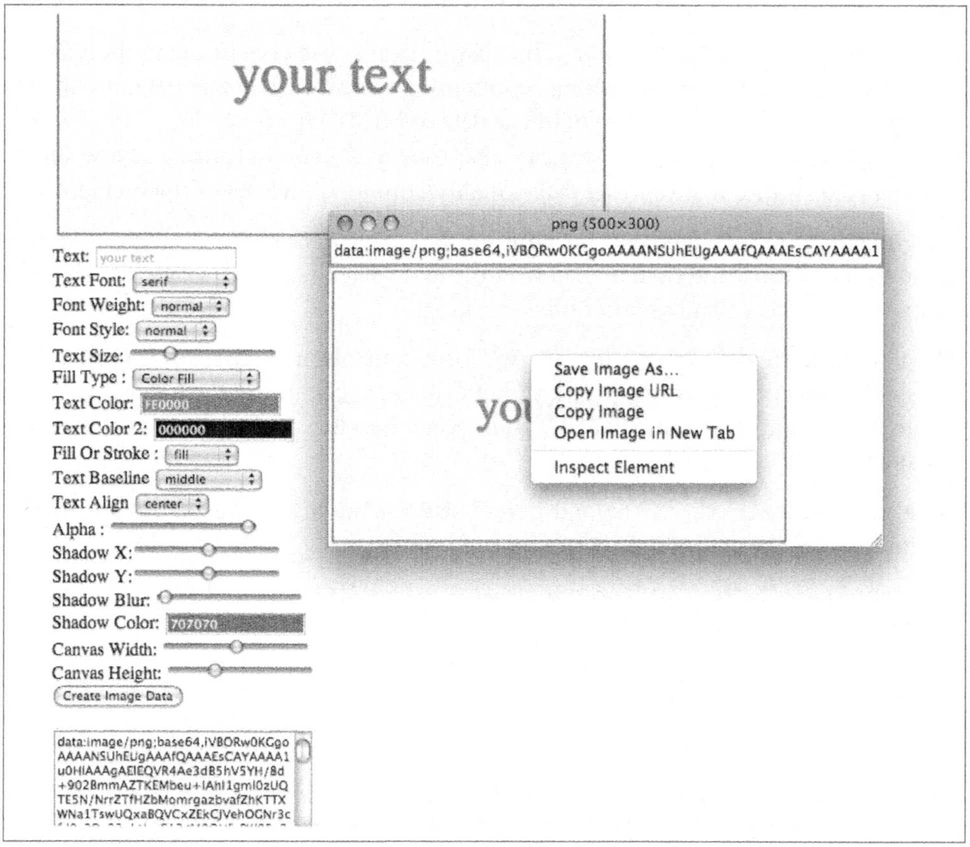

Figure 3-11. Canvas exported image with toDataURL()

Final Version of Text Arranger

The final version of Text Arranger (3.0) brings together all the HTML5 Text API features we have discussed in this chapter. (See Example 3-1.) Play with the final app, and see how the different options interact with one another. Here are a couple things you might find interesting:

- Increasing the text size with a pattern that is the size of the canvas changes the pattern on the text. (It acts like a mask or window into the pattern itself.)
- Canvas width and height are affected by the style width and height (scaling).

Example 3-1. Text Arranger 3.0

```
<!doctype html>
<html lang="en">
<head>
<meta charset="UTF-8">
<title>CH3EX3: Text Arranger 3.0</title>

<script src="modernizr.js"></script>
<script type="text/javascript" src="jscolor/jscolor.js"></script>
<script type="text/javascript">

window.addEventListener("load", eventWindowLoaded, false);
function eventWindowLoaded() {

    canvasApp();
}

function canvasSupport () {
    return Modernizr.canvas;
}

function eventWindowLoaded() {
    var patternPreload = new Image();
    patternPreload.onload = eventAssetsLoaded;
    patternPreload.src = "texture.jpg";
}
```

```
function eventAssetsLoaded() {

    canvasApp();
}

function canvasApp() {

    var message = "your text";
    var fontSize = "50";
    var fontFace = "serif";
    var textFillColor = "#ff0000";
    var textAlpha = 1;
    var shadowX = 1;
    var shadowY = 1;
    var shadowBlur = 1;
    var shadowColor = "#707070";
    var textBaseline = "middle";
    var textAlign = "center";
    var fillOrStroke ="fill";
    var fontWeight = "normal";
    var fontStyle = "normal";
    var fillType = "colorFill";
    var textFillColor2 = "#000000";
    var pattern = new Image();

    if (!canvasSupport()) {
            return;
        }

    var theCanvas = document.getElementById("canvasOne");
    var context = theCanvas.getContext("2d");

    var formElement = document.getElementById("textBox");
    formElement.addEventListener("keyup", textBoxChanged, false);

    formElement = document.getElementById("fillOrStroke");
    formElement.addEventListener("change", fillOrStrokeChanged, false);

    formElement = document.getElementById("textSize");
    formElement.addEventListener("change", textSizeChanged, false);

    formElement = document.getElementById("textFillColor");
    formElement.addEventListener("change", textFillColorChanged, false);

    formElement = document.getElementById("textFont");
    formElement.addEventListener("change", textFontChanged, false);

    formElement = document.getElementById("textBaseline");
    formElement.addEventListener("change", textBaselineChanged, false);

    formElement = document.getElementById("textAlign");
```

```
    formElement.addEventListener("change", textAlignChanged, false);

    formElement = document.getElementById("fontWeight");
    formElement.addEventListener("change", fontWeightChanged, false);

    formElement = document.getElementById("fontStyle");
    formElement.addEventListener("change", fontStyleChanged, false);

    formElement = document.getElementById("shadowX");
    formElement.addEventListener("change", shadowXChanged, false);

    formElement = document.getElementById("shadowY");
    formElement.addEventListener("change", shadowYChanged, false);

    formElement = document.getElementById("shadowBlur");
    formElement.addEventListener("change", shadowBlurChanged, false);

    formElement = document.getElementById("shadowColor");
    formElement.addEventListener("change", shadowColorChanged, false);

    formElement = document.getElementById("textAlpha");
    formElement.addEventListener("change", textAlphaChanged, false);

    formElement = document.getElementById("textFillColor2");
    formElement.addEventListener("change", textFillColor2Changed, false);

    formElement = document.getElementById("fillType");
    formElement.addEventListener("change", fillTypeChanged, false);

    formElement = document.getElementById("canvasWidth");
    formElement.addEventListener("change", canvasWidthChanged, false);

    formElement = document.getElementById("canvasHeight");
    formElement.addEventListener("change", canvasHeightChanged, false);

    formElement = document.getElementById("canvasStyleWidth");
    formElement.addEventListener("change", canvasStyleSizeChanged, false);

    formElement = document.getElementById("canvasStyleHeight");
    formElement.addEventListener("change", canvasStyleSizeChanged, false);

    formElement = document.getElementById("createImageData");
    formElement.addEventListener("click", createImageDataPressed, false);

    pattern.src = "texture.jpg";

    drawScreen();

    function drawScreen() {

      //Background
      context.globalAlpha = 1;
```

```
context.shadowColor = "#707070";
context.shadowOffsetX = 0;
context.shadowOffsetY = 0;
context.shadowBlur = 0;
context.fillStyle = "#ffffaa";
context.fillRect(0, 0, theCanvas.width, theCanvas.height);        //Box
context.strokeStyle = "#000000";
context.strokeRect(5,  5, theCanvas.width-10, theCanvas.height-10);

//Text
context.textBaseline = textBaseline;
context.textAlign = textAlign;
context.font = fontWeight + " " + fontStyle + " " + fontSize + "px " + fontFace;
context.shadowColor = shadowColor;
context.shadowOffsetX = shadowX;
context.shadowOffsetY = shadowY;
context.shadowBlur = shadowBlur;
context.globalAlpha = textAlpha;

var xPosition = (theCanvas.width/2);
var yPosition = (theCanvas.height/2);

var metrics = context.measureText(message);
var textWidth = metrics.width;

var tempColor;
if (fillType == "colorFill") {
   tempColor = textFillColor;
} else if (fillType == "linearGradient") {

   var gradient = context.createLinearGradient(xPosition-
      textWidth/2, yPosition, textWidth, yPosition);
   gradient.addColorStop(0,textFillColor);
   gradient.addColorStop(.6,textFillColor2);
   tempColor = gradient;
} else if (fillType == "radialGradient") {
   var gradient = context.createRadialGradient(xPosition, yPosition,
      fontSize, xPosition+textWidth, yPosition, 1);
   gradient.addColorStop(0,textFillColor);
   gradient.addColorStop(.6,textFillColor2);
   tempColor = gradient;
} else if (fillType == "pattern") {
   var tempColor = context.createPattern(pattern,"repeat")
} else {
   tempColor = textFillColor;
}

switch(fillOrStroke) {
   case "fill":
      context.fillStyle = tempColor;
         context.fillText  (message, xPosition,yPosition);
      break;
```

```
        case "stroke":
            context.strokeStyle = tempColor;
            context.strokeText  (message, xPosition,yPosition);
            break;
        case "both":
            context.fillStyle = tempColor;
                context.fillText  (message, xPosition,yPosition);
            context.strokeStyle = "#000000";
            context.strokeText  (message, xPosition,yPosition);
            break;
    }


}

function textBoxChanged(e) {
    var target = e.target;
    message = target.value;
    drawScreen();
}

function textBaselineChanged(e) {
    var target = e.target;
    textBaseline = target.value;
    drawScreen();
}

function textAlignChanged(e) {
    var target = e.target;
    textAlign = target.value;
    drawScreen();
}

function fillOrStrokeChanged(e) {
    var target = e.target;
    fillOrStroke = target.value;
    drawScreen();
}

function textSizeChanged(e) {
    var target = e.target;
    fontSize = target.value;
    drawScreen();
}

function textFillColorChanged(e) {
    var target = e.target;
    textFillColor = "#" + target.value;
    drawScreen();
}

function textFontChanged(e) {
```

```
    var target = e.target;
    fontFace = target.value;
    drawScreen();
}

function fontWeightChanged(e) {
    var target = e.target;
    fontWeight = target.value;
    drawScreen();
}

function fontStyleChanged(e) {
    var target = e.target;
    fontStyle = target.value;
    drawScreen();
}

function shadowXChanged(e) {
    var target = e.target;
    shadowX = target.value;
    drawScreen();
}

function shadowYChanged(e) {
    var target = e.target;
    shadowY = target.value;
    drawScreen();
}

function shadowBlurChanged(e) {
    var target = e.target;
    shadowBlur = target.value;
    drawScreen();
}

function shadowColorChanged(e) {
    var target = e.target;
    shadowColor = target.value;
    drawScreen();
}

function textAlphaChanged(e) {
    var target = e.target;
    textAlpha = (target.value);
    drawScreen();
}

function textFillColor2Changed(e) {
    var target = e.target;
    textFillColor2 = "#" + target.value;
    drawScreen();
}
```

```
        function fillTypeChanged(e) {
            var target = e.target;
            fillType = target.value;
            drawScreen();
        }

        function canvasWidthChanged(e) {
            var target = e.target;
            theCanvas.width = target.value;
            drawScreen();
        }
        function canvasHeightChanged(e) {
            var target = e.target;
            theCanvas.height = target.value;
            drawScreen();
        }

        function canvasStyleSizeChanged(e) {

            var styleWidth = document.getElementById("canvasStyleWidth");
            var styleHeight = document.getElementById("canvasStyleHeight");
            var styleValue = "width:" + styleWidth.value + "px; height:" +
                styleHeight.value +"px;";
            theCanvas.setAttribute("style", styleValue );
            drawScreen();
        }


        function createImageDataPressed(e) {

            var imageDataDisplay = document.getElementById("imageDataDisplay");
            imageDataDisplay.value = theCanvas.toDataURL();
            window.open(imageDataDisplay.value,"canvasImage","left=0,top=0,width=" +
                theCanvas.width + ",height=" + theCanvas.height +
                ",toolbar=0,resizable=0");

        }

}

</script>

</head>
<body>
<div style="position: absolute; top: 50px; left: 50px;">
<canvas id="canvasOne" width="500" height="300">
 Your browser does not support HTML5 Canvas.
</canvas>
<form>
  Text: <input id="textBox" placeholder="your text" />
  <br>
  Text Font: <select id="textFont">
```

```
<option value="serif">serif</option>
<option value="sans-serif">sans-serif</option>
<option value="cursive">cursive</option>
<option value="fantasy">fantasy</option>
<option value="monospace">monospace</option>
</select>
<br> Font Weight:
<select id="fontWeight">
<option value="normal">normal</option>
<option value="bold">bold</option>
<option value="bolder">bolder</option>
<option value="lighter">lighter</option>
</select>
<br>
Font Style:
<select id="fontStyle">
<option value="normal">normal</option>
<option value="italic">italic</option>
<option value="oblique">oblique</option>
</select>
<br>
Text Size: <input type="range" id="textSize"
      min="0"
      max="200"
      step="1"
      value="50"/>
<br>
Fill Type: <select id="fillType">
<option value="colorFill">Color Fill</option>
<option value="linearGradient">Linear Gradient</option>
<option value="radialGradient">Radial Gradient</option>
<option value="pattern">pattern</option>
</select>
<br>
Text Color: <input class="color" id="textFillColor" value="FF0000"/>
<br>
Text Color 2: <input class="color" id="textFillColor2" value ="000000"/>
<br>
Fill Or Stroke: <select id="fillOrStroke">
<option value="fill">fill</option>
<option value="stroke">stroke</option>
<option value="both">both</option>
</select>
<br>
Text Baseline <select id="textBaseline">
<option value="middle">middle</option>
<option value="top">top</option>
<option value="hanging">hanging</option>
<option value="alphabetic">alphabetic</option>
<option value="ideographic">ideographic</option>
<option value="bottom">bottom</option>
</select>
```

```html
<br>
Text Align <select id="textAlign">
<option value="center">center</option>
<option value="start">start</option>
<option value="end">end</option>
<option value="left">left</option>
<option value="right">right</option>
</select>
<br>
Alpha: <input type="range" id="textAlpha"
      min="0.0"
      max="1.0"
      step="0.01"
      value="1.0"/>
<br>
Shadow X:<input type="range" id="shadowX"
      min="-100"
      max="100"
      step="1"
      value="1"/>
<br>
Shadow Y:<input type="range" id="shadowY"
      min="-100"
      max="100"
      step="1"
      value="1"/>
<br>
Shadow Blur: <input type="range" id="shadowBlur"
      min="1"
      max="100"
      step="1"
      value="1" />
<br>
Shadow Color: <input class="color" id="shadowColor" value="707070"/>
<br>
Canvas Width:  <input type="range" id="canvasWidth"
      min="0"
      max="1000"
      step="1"
      value="500"/>
<br>
Canvas Height:
 <input type="range" id="canvasHeight"
      min="0"
      max="1000"
      step="1"
      value="300"/>
<br>
Canvas Style Width:  <input type="range" id="canvasStyleWidth"
      min="0"
      max="1000"
      step="1"
```

```
            value="500"/>
<br>
Canvas Style Height:
 <input type="range" id="canvasStyleHeight"
      min="0"
      max="1000"
      step="1"
      value="300"/>
<br>
<input type="button" id="createImageData" value="Create Image Data">
<br>

<br>
<textarea id="imageDataDisplay" rows=10 cols=30></textarea>
</form>

</div>
</body>
</html>
```

Animated Gradients

Before we leave the topic of text, we would like to introduce some animation into the mix. Everything you have seen so far in this chapter has been pretty much static. While text on HTML5 Canvas is really cool, it is not too far from what could be accomplished in standard HTML. Static text is static, and its utility when not being styled with CSS (again, the Canvas currently does not support CSS styling) might make you choose another solution for a pure text application.

However, animation is where the Canvas shows its utility beyond standard HTML. For this example, we will move away from Text Arranger and create some animated text by using only gradient fills. The gradient fills will "animate" by moving up in the text fill. The effect here is similar to what old video game and computer systems (especially those from Atari) used to create animated title screens.

Figure 3-12 shows what a single frame of the animation looks like on the Canvas.

Figure 3-12. Color cycle animation

The key to creating a gradient animation are the `createLinearGradient()` and `gradient.addColorStop` methods we discussed previously in this chapter, combined with the `setTimeout()` game loop functionality we developed in Chapter 1. First, we will set up a gradient "line" that represents the direction of the color gradient, and then we will create "color stops" that represent the colors in the gradient animation.

To get started, let's set up an animation loop:

```
function drawScreen() {
}
function gameLoop() {
    window.setTimeout(gameLoop, 20);
    drawScreen()
}
```

Next, we create a simple array of dynamic objects that represents the colors of the gradient (`color`) and the stop percentages for the gradient fill (`stopPercent`). This will act as a very simple "display list" of colors. Recall that since the Canvas runs in *immediate mode* and has no display list of objects, we need to simulate that functionality.

Color stops are a percentage of the gradient fill. We will start with red and then add yellow, blue, green, purple, and red again. We add red twice so that the color flows back to the beginning and looks fluid. Notice that the percentages for both reds are only 1/2 of the others (.125, instead of .25):

```
var colorStops = new Array(
 {color:"#FF0000", stopPercent:0},
 {color:"#FFFF00", stopPercent:.125},
 {color:"#00FF00", stopPercent:.375},
 {color:"#0000FF", stopPercent:.625},
 {color:"#FF00FF", stopPercent:.875},
 {color:"#FF0000", stopPercent:1});
```

Next, inside the `drawScreen()` function, we create the gradient. First we set up a gradient on the current path. The arguments to the `createLinerGradient()` function represent the "line" that the gradient will follow. Because we want the gradient to be in a straight vertical line, we center it in the middle of the canvas and draw it directly down to the bottom:

```
var gradient = context.createLinearGradient(
            theCanvas.width/2,
            0,
            theCanvas.width/2,
            theCanvas.height);
```

Next, we loop through the colorStops array calling gradient.addColorStop() for each color in the array. A gradient color stop method has two arguments: the *color* and the *percentage*. We already initialized these values in our array of dynamic objects, so now they are just applied in a loop.

After each gradient color stop is added, we increment the percentage of each color by .015. This effectively moves the color "down," because the greater the percentage, the larger the colors fills in the gradient. Because we are changing all of the colors each time, the effect is that they are all moving down in unison. If the gradient color stop percentage value goes above 1, we set it back to 0, which moves it back to the top of the gradient:

```
for (var i=0; i < colorStops.length; i++) {
    var tempColorStop = colorStops[i];
    var tempColor = tempColorStop.color;
    var tempStopPercent = tempColorStop.stopPercent;
    gradient.addColorStop(tempStopPercent,tempColor);
    tempStopPercent += .015;
    if (tempStopPercent > 1) {
        tempStopPercent = 0;
    }
    tempColorStop.stopPercent = tempStopPercent;;
    colorStops[i] = tempColorStop;
}
```

In reality, the gradient is not being "animated"; we are just changing the location of each color by changing the gradient colorStop percentage. However, the effect is the same. It looks like the colors are cycling.

Finally, we display the text using the gradient as the color for fillStyle:

```
context.fillStyle = gradient;
context.fillText ( message, xPosition ,yPosition);
```

To see the animation in action, type in the following code or load *CH3EX4.html* into your web browser.

Example 3-2 provides the full code for the color cycle example.

Example 3-2. Color cycle

```
<!doctype html>
<html lang="en">
<head>
<meta charset="UTF-8">
<title>CH.3 EX. 4: Color Cycle</title>

<script src="modernizr.js"></script>
<script type="text/javascript">

window.addEventListener("load", eventWindowLoaded, false);
function eventWindowLoaded() {

    canvasApp();
}

function canvasSupport () {
    return Modernizr.canvas;
}

function canvasApp() {
    if (!canvasSupport()) {
            return;
      }

    var message = "HTML5 Canvas";

    var theCanvas = document.getElementById("canvasOne");
    var context = theCanvas.getContext("2d");



    function drawScreen() {
        //Background

        context.fillStyle = "#000000";
        context.fillRect(0, 0, theCanvas.width, theCanvas.height);

        //Text

        context.font =  "90px impact"
        context.textAlign = "center";
        context.textBaseline = "middle";

        var metrics = context.measureText(message);
        var textWidth = metrics.width;
        var xPosition = (theCanvas.width/2);
        var yPosition = (theCanvas.height/2);

        var gradient = context.createLinearGradient( theCanvas.width/2,0,
            theCanvas.width/2,theCanvas.height);
        for (var i=0; i < colorStops.length; i++) {
```

```
            var tempColorStop = colorStops[i];
            var tempColor = tempColorStop.color;
            var tempStopPercent = tempColorStop.stopPercent;
            gradient.addColorStop(tempStopPercent,tempColor);
            tempStopPercent += .015;
            if (tempStopPercent > 1) {
                tempStopPercent = 0;
            }
            tempColorStop.stopPercent = tempStopPercent;;
            colorStops[i] = tempColorStop;
        }


        context.fillStyle    = gradient;
        context.fillText ( message,  xPosition ,yPosition);


    }

    function gameLoop() {
        window.setTimeout(gameLoop, 20);
        drawScreen()
    }
    var colorStops = new Array(
    {color:"#FF0000", stopPercent:0},
    {color:"#FFFF00", stopPercent:.125},
    {color:"#00FF00", stopPercent:.375},
    {color:"#0000FF", stopPercent:.625},
    {color:"#FF00FF", stopPercent:.875},
    {color:"#FF0000", stopPercent:1});
    gameLoop();


}

</script>

</head>
<body>
<canvas id="canvasOne" width="600" height="200">
 Your browser does not support HTML 5 Canvas.
</canvas>


</div>
</body>
</html>
```

The Future of Text on the Canvas

The W3C has been considering changes to the Canvas API to assist developers when rendering text.

CSS Text

As you might have noticed, while Canvas does a pretty good job of displaying a single line of text, displaying multiline text is another story. We have shown you one possible solution, but something else might be in order in the future. According to the W3C Canvas API specification, there might be a change in the future that opens the door for using CSS on the Canvas:

> A future version of the 2D context API may provide a way to render fragments of documents, rendered using CSS, straight to the canvas. This would be provided in preference to a dedicated way of doing multiline layout.

CSS would help developers render text on the Canvas and, at the same time, encourage developers to adopt the Canvas for text-based applications.

Making Text Accessible

The W3C Reading text in Canvas document (*http://www.w3.org/wiki/Read ing_text_in_canvas*) provides guidance on how future developers should handle text on the Canvas. To make text accessible, the W3C advises creating sub-dom elements for text. (See Chapter 1.) Here is what they say:

> When an author renders text on a canvas with fillText or strokeText, they must also add an html element (div or span) with the same text, styling and position to the canvas subdom. The bounding box of the text should be set with the setElementPath method. (See *http://www.w3.org/wiki/Canvas_hit_testing*.)

> This enables user agents to use the subdom text to deliver an accessible experience, as the subdom text acts as a proxy for the rendered text in the bitmap.

> User agents that support caret browsing can use the subdom text cursor position to indicate the current caret location on the screen. Authors that wish to enable text selection can keep the selection range (on the canvas) in sync with the text selection range in the canvas subdom element; user agents can use that information to render a selection indication on the screen.

What's Next?

In this chapter, we introduced you to the fundamentals of the HTML5 Canvas Text API, offered some general concepts relating to drawing on the canvas, and explained how to communicate with HTML form controls. As you can now see, the basic concept of writing text to HTML5 Canvas can be taken to very complex (and some might argue ludicrous) levels. The final application, Text Arranger 3.0, allows you to modify a single line of text in an almost infinite number of ways. In the next chapter, we move on to displaying and manipulating images on the canvas.

CHAPTER 4

Images on the Canvas

Like the Canvas Drawing API, the Canvas Image API is very robust. With it, we can load in image data and apply it directly to the canvas. This image data can also be cut and spliced to display any desired portion. Furthermore, Canvas gives us the ability to store arrays of pixel data that we can manipulate and then draw back to the canvas.

There are two primary Canvas functions that we can perform with images. We can display images, and we can modify them pixel by pixel and paint them back to the canvas. There are only a few Image API functions, but they open up a world of pixel-level manipulation that gives the developer the power to create optimized applications directly in the web browser without needing any plug-ins.

The Basic File Setup for This Chapter

All the examples in this chapter will use the same basic file setup for displaying our demonstrations as we proceed through the Drawing API. Use the following as the basis for all the examples we create—you will need to change only the contents of the drawScreen() function:

```
<!doctype html>
<html lang="en">
<head>
<meta charset="UTF-8">
<title>Ch4BaseFile - Template For Chapter 4 Examples</title>

<script src="modernizr-1.6.min.js"></script>
<script type="text/javascript">
window.addEventListener('load', eventWindowLoaded, false);
function eventWindowLoaded() {

    canvasApp();

}
```

```
function canvasSupport () {
    return Modernizr.canvas;
}

function canvasApp(){

    if (!canvasSupport()) {
            return;
      }else{
        var theCanvas = document.getElementById("canvas");
        var context = theCanvas.getContext("2d");
      }

drawScreen();

    function drawScreen() {
        //make changes here
        context.fillStyle = '#aaaaaa';
        context.fillRect(0, 0, 200, 200);
        context.fillStyle = '#000000';
        context.font = '20px sans-serif';
        context.textBaseline = 'top';
        context.fillText  ("Canvas!", 0, 0);
    }
}
</script>

</head>
<body>
<div style="position: absolute; top: 50px; left: 50px;">
<canvas id="canvas" width="500" height="500">
 Your browser does not support HTML5 Canvas.
</canvas>
</div>
</body>
</html>
```

Image Basics

The Canvas API allows access to the DOM-defined Image object type through the use of the drawImage() method. The image can be defined in HTML, such as:

```
<img src="ship1.png" id="spaceship">
```

Or it can be defined in JavaScript. We create a new JavaScript Image instance like this:

```
var spaceShip = new Image();
```

We can then set the file source of the image by assigning a URL to the src attribute of our newly created Image object:

```
spaceShip.src = "ship1.png";
```

Preloading Images

Before an image can be called in code, we must ensure that it has properly loaded and is ready to be used. We do this by creating an event listener to fire off when the `load` event on the image occurs:

```
spaceShip.addEventListener('load', eventSheetLoaded , false);
```

When the image is fully loaded, the `eventSheetLoaded()` function will fire off. Inside this function, we will then call `drawScreen()`, as we have in the previous chapters:

```
function eventSheetLoaded() {
    drawScreen();
}
```

 In practice, we would not create a separate event listener function for each loaded image. This code example works fine if your application contains only a single image. In Chapter 9, we will build a game with multiple image files (and sounds) and use a single listener function for all loaded resources.

Displaying an Image on the Canvas with drawImage()

After we have an image loaded in, we can display it on the screen in a number of ways. The `drawImage()` Canvas method is used for displaying image data directly onto the canvas. `drawImage()` is *overloaded* and takes three separate sets of parameters, each allowing varied manipulation of both the image's source pixels and the destination location for those pixels on the canvas. Let's first look at the most basic:

```
drawImage(Image, dx, dy)
```

This function takes in three parameters: an `Image` object, and x and y values representing the top-left corner location to start painting the image on the canvas.

Here is the code we would use to place our spaceship image at the 0,0 location (the top-left corner) of the canvas:

```
context.drawImage(spaceShip, 0, 0);
```

If we want to place another copy at 50,50, we would simply make the same call but change the location:

```
context.drawImage(spaceShip, 50, 50);
```

Example 4-1 shows the full code for what we have done so far.

Example 4-1. Load and display an image file

```
var spaceShip = new Image();
spaceShip.addEventListener('load', eventSheetLoaded , false);
```

```
spaceShip.src = "ship1.png";

function eventSheetLoaded() {
   drawScreen();
}

function drawScreen() {

   context.drawImage(spaceShip, 0, 0);
   context.drawImage(spaceShip, 50, 50);

}
```

Figure 4-1 shows the 32×32 *ship1.png* file.

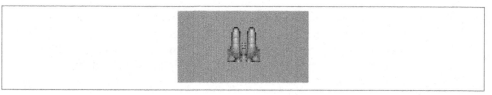

Figure 4-1. Load and display an image file

In practice, we would probably not put all of our drawing code directly into a function such as drawScreen(). It almost always makes more sense to create a separate function, such as placeShip(), shown here:

```
function drawScreen() {
   placeShip(spaceShip, 0, 0);
   placeShip(spaceShip, 50, 50);
}

function placeShip(obj, posX, posY, width, height) {
   if (width && height) {
     context.drawImage(obj, posX, posY, width, height);
   } else {
     context.drawImage(obj, posX, posY);
   }
}
```

The placeShip() function accepts the context, the image object, the x and y positions, and a height and width. If a height and width are passed in, the first version of the drawScreen() function is called. If not, the second version is called. We will look at resizing images as they are drawn in the next section.

The *ship1.png* file we are using is a 32×32 pixel *.png* bitmap, which we have modified from Ari Feldman's excellent SpriteLib. SpriteLib (*http://www.widgetworx.com/widget worx/portfolio/spritelib.html*) is a free library of pixel-based game sprites that Ari has made available for use in games and books.

The website for this book contains only the files necessary to complete the examples. We have modified Ari's files to fit the needs of this book.

Figure 4-2 shows two copies of the image painted to the canvas. One of the copies has the top-left starting location of 0,0, and the other starts at 50,50.

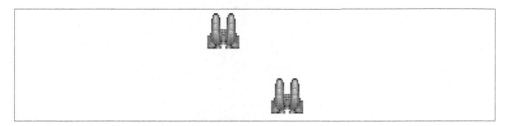

Figure 4-2. Draw multiple objects with a single source

Resizing an Image Painted to the Canvas

To paint and scale drawn images, we can also pass parameters into the `drawImage()` function. For example, this second version of `drawImage()` takes in an extra two parameters:

```
drawImage(Image, dx, dy, dw, dh)
```

dw and *dh* represent the width and height of the rectangle portion of the canvas where our source image will be painted. If we want to scale the image to only 64×64 or 16×16, we would use the following code:

```
context.drawImage(spaceShip, 0, 0,64,64);
context.drawImage(spaceShip, 0, 0,16,16);
```

Example 4-2 draws various sizes to the canvas.

Example 4-2. Resizing an image as it is drawn

```
function eventSheetLoaded() {
    drawScreen();
}

function drawScreen() {

    context.drawImage(spaceShip, 0, 0);
    context.drawImage(spaceShip, 0, 34,32,32);
    context.drawImage(spaceShip, 0, 68,64,64);
    context.drawImage(spaceShip, 0, 140,16,16);
}
```

See Figure 4-3 for the output to this example.

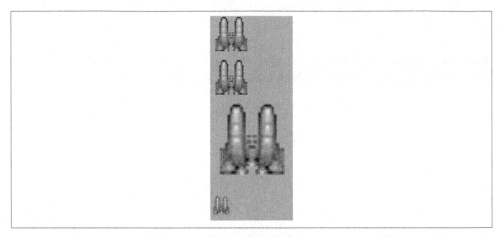

Figure 4-3. Resizing an image as it is drawn

In Example 4-2, we have added a gray box so that we can better see the placement of the images on the canvas. The image we placed on the screen can scale in size as it is painted, saving us the calculation and steps necessary to use a matrix transformation on the object. The only caveat is that the scale origin point of reference is the top-left corner of the object. If we used a matrix operation, we could translate the origin point to the center of the object before applying the scale.

We have placed two 32×32 objects on the canvas to show that these two function calls are identical:

```
context.drawImage(spaceShip, 0, 0);
context.drawImage(spaceShip, 0, 34,32,32);
```

Aside from the fact that the second is placed 34 pixels below the first, the extra 32,32 at the end of the second call is unnecessary because it is the original size of the object. This demonstrates that the scale operation does not translate (or move) the object on any axis. The top-left corner of each is 0,0.

Copying Part of an Image to the Canvas

The third set of parameters that can be passed into `drawImage()` allows us to copy an arbitrary rectangle of data from a source image and place it onto the canvas. This image data can be resized as it is placed.

We are going to use a second source image for this set of operations: spaceships that have been laid out on what is called a *tile sheet* (also known as a *sprite sheet*, a *texture sheet*, or by many other names). This type of file layout refers to an image file that is broken up physically into rectangles of data. Usually these rectangles have an equal width and height. The "tiles" or "sprites" we will be using are 32 pixels wide by 32 pixels high, commonly referred to as 32×32 tiles.

Figure 4-4 shows a tile sheet with the grid lines turned on in the drawing application. These grid lines separate each of the tiles on the sheet.

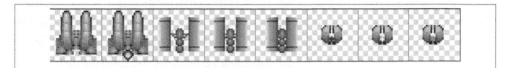

Figure 4-4. The tile sheet inside a drawing program

Figure 4-5 is the actual tile sheet—without grid lines—that we will use for our further examples.

Figure 4-5. The tile sheet exported for use in an application

The structure of the parameters for this third version of the drawImage() function looks like this:

```
drawImage(Image, sx, sy, sw, sh, dx, dy, dw, dh)
```

sx and *sy* represent the "source positions" to start copying the source image to the canvas. *sw* and *sh* represent the width and height of the rectangle starting at *sx* and *sy*. That rectangle will be copied to the canvas at "destination" positions *dx* and *dy*. As with the previous drawImage() function, *dw* and *dh* represent the newly scaled width and height for the image.

Example 4-3 copies the second version of our spaceship (tile number 2) to the canvas and positions it at 50,50. It also scales the image to 64×64, producing the result shown in Figure 4-6.

Example 4-3. Using all of the drawImage() parameters

```
var tileSheet = new Image();
tileSheet.addEventListener('load', eventSheetLoaded , false);

tileSheet.src = "ships.png";

function eventSheetLoaded() {
   drawScreen();
```

```
}

function drawScreen() {    //draw a background so we can see the Canvas edges
    context.fillStyle = "#aaaaaa";
    context.fillRect(0,0,500,500);
    context.drawImage(tileSheet, 32, 0,32,32,50,50,64,64);
}
```

As you can see, we have changed the name of our `Image` instance to `tileSheet` because it represents more than just the source for the single ship image.

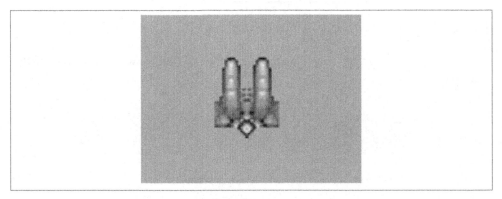

Figure 4-6. Using all of the drawImage() parameters

Now let's use this same concept to simulate animation using the tiles on our tile sheet.

Simple Cell-Based Sprite Animation

With a tile sheet of images, it is relatively simple to create what seems like cell-based or flip-book animation. This technique involves rapidly swapping images over time to simulate animation. The term *flip-book* comes from the age-old technique of drawing individual cells of animation in the top-left corner pages of a book. When the pages are rapidly flipped through, the changes are viewed over time, appearing to create a cartoon. *Cell-based animation* refers to a similar professional technique. Individual same-sized cells (or pages) of images are drawn to simulate animation. When played back rapidly with special devices in front of a camera, animated cartoons are recorded.

We can use the `drawImage()` function and the first two tiles on our tile sheet to do the same thing.

Creating an Animation Frame Counter

We can simulate the ship's exhaust firing by rapidly flipping between the first two tiles (or cells) on our tile sheet. To do this, we set up a counter variable, which is how we track the tile we want to paint to the canvas. We will use 0 for the first cell and 1 for the second cell.

We will create a simple integer to count which frame we are displaying on our tile sheet:

```
var counter = 0;
```

Inside drawScreen(), we will increment this value by 1 on each frame. Because we have only two frames, we will need to set it back to 0 when it is greater than 1:

```
counter++;
if (counter >1) {
    counter = 0;
}
```

Or use the following nice shortcut. This is a "bit-wise" operation that will simplify code, but we do not have the space to go into the full range of bit-wise operations in this text.

```
counter ^= 1;
```

Creating a Timer Loop

As it currently stands, our code will be called only a single time. Let's create a simple timer loop that will call the drawScreen() function 10 times a second, or once every 100 milliseconds. A timer loop that is set to run at a certain frame rate is sometimes referred to as a *frame tick* or *timer tick*. Each tick is simply a single iteration of the timer running all the code that we put into our drawScreen() function. We will also need a function that starts the timer loop and initiates the tick after the image has preloaded properly. We'll name this function startUp():

```
function eventShipLoaded() {
    startUp();
}
function startUp(){
    gameLoop();
}

function gameLoop() {
    window.setTimeout(gameLoop, 100);
    drawScreen();
}
```

Changing the Tile to Display

To change the tile to display, we can multiply the counter variable by 32 (the tile width). Because we have only a single row of tiles, we don't have to change the y value:

```
context.drawImage(tileSheet, 32*counter, 0,32,32,50,50,64,64);
```

 We will examine how to use a tile sheet consisting of multiple rows and columns in the next section, "Advanced Cell-Based Animation" on page 145.

Example 4-3 used this same line of code to draw our image. In Example 4-4, it will be placed on the canvas at 50,50 and scaled to 64×64 pixels. Let's look at the entire set of code.

Example 4-4. A simple sprite animation

```
var counter = 0;
var tileSheet = new Image();
tileSheet.addEventListener('load', eventSheetLoaded , false);
tileSheet.src = "ships.png";

function eventSheetLoaded() {
    startUp();
}

function drawScreen() {

    //draw a background so we can see the Canvas edges
    context.fillStyle = "#aaaaaa";
    context.fillRect(0,0,500,500);
    context.drawImage(tileSheet, 32*counter, 0,32,32,50,50,64,64);
      counter++;
      if (counter >1) {
         counter = 0;
      }
}

function startUp(){
   gameLoop();
}

function gameLoop() {
   window.setTimeout(gameLoop, 100);
   drawScreen();
}
```

When you run this code, you will see the exhaust on the ship turn off and on every 100 milliseconds, creating a simple cell-based animation.

Advanced Cell-Based Animation

In the previous example, we simply flipped back and forth between two tiles on our tile sheet. Next, we are going to create a method that uses a tile sheet to play through a series of images. First, let's look at the new tile sheet, created by using tiles from SpriteLib. Figure 4-7 shows the example sprite sheet, *tanks_sheet.png*; we will refer back to this figure throughout the chapter.

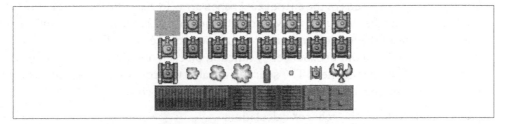

Figure 4-7. Example tile sheet

As you can see, it contains a number of 32×32 tiles that can be used in a game. We will not create an entire game in this chapter, but we will examine how to use these tiles to create a game screen. In Chapter 9, we will create a simple maze-chase game using some of these tiles.

Examining the Tile Sheet

The tile sheet is formatted into a series of tiles starting at the top left. As with a two-dimensional array, the numbering starts at 0—we call this *0 relative*. Moving from left to right and down, each tile will be referenced by a single number index (as opposed to a multidimensional index). The gray square in the top left is tile 0, while the tank at the end of the first row (the rightmost tank) is tile 7. Moving down to the next row, the first tank on the far left of the second row is tile 8, and so on until the final tile on row 3 (the fourth row down when we start numbering at 0) is tile 31. We have four rows with eight columns each, making 32 tiles with indexes numbered 0 to 31.

Creating an Animation Array

Next we are going to create an array to hold the tiles for the animation. There are two tanks on the tile sheet: one is green and one is blue. Tiles 1-8 are a series that—when played in succession—will make it appear as though the green tank's treads are moving.

 Remember, the tile sheet starts at tile 0, but we want to start with the first tank image at tile number 1.

We will store the tile IDs that we want to play for the tank in an array:

```
var animationFrames = [1,2,3,4,5,6,7,8];
```

We will use a counter to keep track of the current index of this array:

```
var frameIndex = 0;
```

Choosing the Tile to Display

We will use the frameIndex of the animationFrames array to calculate the 32×32 source rectangle from our tile sheet that we will copy to the canvas. First, we need to find the x and y locations of the top-left corner for the tile we want to copy. To do this, we will create local variables in our drawScreen() function on each iteration (frame) to calculate the position on the tile sheet. The sourceX variable will contain the top-left corner x position, and the sourceY variable will contain the top-left corner y position.

Here is pseudocode for the sourceX calculation:

```
sourceX = integer(current_frame_index modulo
the_number_columns_in_the_tilesheet) * tile_width
```

The modulo (%) operator gives us the remainder of the division calculation. The actual code we will use for this calculation looks like this:

```
var sourceX = Math.floor(animationFrames[frameIndex] % 8) *32;
```

The calculation for the sourceY value is similar, except we divide rather than use the modulo operation:

```
sourceY = integer(current_frame_index divided by
the_number_columns_in_the_tilesheet) *tile_height
```

Here is the actual code we will use for this calculation:

```
var sourceY = Math.floor(animationFrames[frameIndex] / 8) *32;
```

Looping Through the Tiles

We will update the frameIndex value on each frame tick. When frameIndex becomes greater than 7, we will set it back to 0:

```
frameIndex++;
    if (frameIndex == animationFrames.length) {
    frameIndex = 0;
    }
```

The animationFrames.length value is 8. When the frameIndex is equal to 8, we must set it back to 0 to start reading the array values over again, which creates an infinite animation loop.

Drawing the Tile

We will use drawImage() to place the new tile on the screen on each iteration:

```
context.drawImage(tileSheet, sourceX, sourceY,32,32,50,50,32,32);
```

Here, we are passing the calculated sourceX and sourceY values into the drawImage() function. We then pass in the width (32), the height (32), and the location (50,50) to draw the image on the canvas. Example 4-5 shows the full code.

Example 4-5. Advanced sprite animation

```
var tileSheet = new Image();
tileSheet.addEventListener('load', eventSheetLoaded , false);

tileSheet.src = "tanks_sheet.png";

var animationFrames = [1,2,3,4,5,6,7,8];
var frameIndex = 0;function eventSheetLoaded() {
   startUp();
}

function drawScreen() {

   //draw a background so we can see the Canvas edges
   context.fillStyle = "#aaaaaa";
   context.fillRect(0,0,500,500);

   var sourceX = Math.floor(animationFrames[frameIndex] % 8) *32;
   var sourceY = Math.floor(animationFrames[frameIndex] / 8) *32;

   context.drawImage(tileSheet, sourceX, sourceY,32,32,50,50,32,32);

   frameIndex++;
   if (frameIndex ==animationFrames.length) {
      frameIndex=0;
   }

}

function startUp(){
   gameLoop();
}

function gameLoop() {
   window.setTimeout(gameLoop, 100);
   drawScreen();
}
```

When we run the example, we will see the eight tile cell frames for the tank run in order and then repeat—the only problem is that the tank isn't going anywhere. Let's solve that little dilemma next and drive the tank up the screen.

Moving the Image Across the Canvas

Now that we have the tank treads animating, let's "move" the tank. By animating the tank treads and applying a simple movement vector to the tank's position, we can achieve the simulation of animated movement.

To do this, we first need to create variables to hold the current x and y positions of the tank. These represent the top-left corner where the tile from our sheet will be drawn to the canvas. In the previous examples, this number was set at 50 for each, so let's use that value here as well:

```
var x = 50;
var y = 50;
```

We also need a movement vector value for each axis. These are commonly known as deltaX (dx) and deltaY (dy). They represent the "delta" or "change" in the x or y axis position on each iteration. Our tank is currently facing in the "up" position, so we will use –1 for the dy and 0 for the dx:

```
var dx = 0;
var dy = -1;
```

The result is that on each frame tick, our tank will move *one* pixel up on the y-axis and *zero* pixels on the x-axis.

Inside drawScreen() (which is called on each frame tick), we will add the dx and dy values to the x and y values, and then apply them to the drawImage() function:

```
y = y+dy;
x = x+dx;
context.drawImage(tileSheet, sourceX, sourceY,32,32,x,y,32,32);
```

Rather than use the hardcoded 50,50 for the location of the drawImage() call on the canvas, we have replaced it with the current x,y position. Let's examine the entire code in Example 4-6.

Example 4-6. Sprite animation and movement

```
var tileSheet = new Image();
tileSheet.addEventListener('load', eventSheetLoaded , false);
tileSheet.src = "tanks_sheet.png";

var animationFrames = [1,2,3,4,5,6,7,8];
var frameIndex = 0;
var dx = 0;
var dy = -1;
var x = 50;
var y = 50;

function eventSheetLoaded() {
  startUp();
}
```

```
function drawScreen() {

   y = y+dy;
   x = x+dx;

   //draw a background so we can see the Canvas edges
   context.fillStyle = "#aaaaaa";
   context.fillRect(0,0,500,500);

   var sourceX = Math.floor(animationFrames[frameIndex] % 8) *32;
   var sourceY = Math.floor(animationFrames[frameIndex] / 8) *32;

   context.drawImage(tileSheet, sourceX, sourceY,32,32,x,y,32,32);

   frameIndex++;
   if (frameIndex==animationFrames.length) {
      frameIndex=0;
   }

}

function startUp(){
    gameLoop();
}

function gameLoop() {
    window.setTimeout(gameLoop, 100);
    drawScreen();
}
```

By running this example, we see the tank move slowly up the canvas while its treads play through the eight separate tiles of animation.

Our tile sheet has images of the tank facing only in the up position. If we want to have the tank move in other directions, we can do one of two things. The first option is to create more tiles on the tile sheet to represent the left, right, and down positions. However, this method requires much more work and creates a larger source image for the tile sheet. We are going to solve this problem in another way, which we will examine next.

Applying Rotation Transformations to an Image

In the previous section, we created an animation using tiles from a tile sheet. In this section, we will take it one step further and use the Canvas transformation matrix to rotate our image before drawing it to the canvas. This will allow us to use only a single set of animated tiles for all four (or more) rotated directions in which we would like to display our images. Before we write the code, let's examine what it will take to rotate our tank animation from the previous section.

In Chapter 2, we dove into applying basic transformations when drawing with paths. The same concepts apply to transforming images on the canvas. If you have not read the section "Simple Canvas Transformations" on page 50 in Chapter 2, you might want to review it before reading on.

Canvas Transformation Basics

Although we covered basic Canvas transformations in detail in Chapter 2, let's review what's necessary to transform an individual object on the canvas. Remember, the canvas is a single immediate-mode drawing surface, so any transformations we make are applied to the entire canvas. In our example, we are drawing two objects. First, we draw a gray background rectangle, and then we copy the current tile from our tile sheet to the desired location. These are two discrete objects, but once they are on the canvas, they are both simply collections of pixels painted on the surface. Unlike Flash or other platforms that allow many separate sprites or "movie clips" to occupy the physical space, there is only one such object on Canvas: the *context*.

To compensate for this, we create logical display objects. Both the background and the tank are considered separate logical display objects. If we want to draw the tank but rotate it with a transformation matrix, we must separate the logical drawing operations by using the save() and restore() Canvas context functions.

Let's look at an example where we rotate the tank 90 degrees, so that it is facing to the right rather than up.

Step 1: Save the current context to the stack

The save() context function will take the current contents of the canvas (in our case, the gray background rectangle) and store it away for "safekeeping":

```
context.save();
```

After we have transformed the tank, we will replace it with the restore() function call.

Step 2: Reset the transformation matrix to identity

The next step in transforming an object is to clear the transformation matrix by passing it values that reset it to the identity values:

```
context.setTransform(1,0,0,1,0,0)
```

Step 3: Code the transform algorithm

Each transformation will be slightly different, but usually if you are rotating an object, you will want to translate the matrix to the center point of that object. Our tank will be positioned at 50,50 on the canvas, so we will translate it to 66,66. Because our tank is a 32×32 square tile, we simply add half of 32, or 16, to both the x and y location points:

```
context.translate(x+16, y+16);
```

Next, we need to find the angle in radians for the direction that we want the tank to be rotated. For this example, we will choose 90 degrees:

```
var rotation = 90;
var angleInRadians = rotation * Math.PI / 180;
context.rotate(angleInRadians);
```

Step 4: Draw the image

When we draw the image, we must remember that the drawing's point of origin is no longer the 50,50 point from previous examples. After the transformation matrix has been applied to translate to a new point, that point is now considered the 0,0 origin point for drawing.

This can be confusing at first, but it becomes clear with practice. To draw our image with 50,50 as the top-left coordinate, we must subtract 16 from the current position in both the x and y directions:

```
context.drawImage(tileSheet, sourceX, sourceY,32,32,-16,-16,32,32);
```

Example 4-7 adds in this rotation code to Example 4-4. When you run the example now, you will see the tank facing to the right.

Example 4-7. Rotation transformation

```
var tileSheet = new Image();
tileSheet.addEventListener('load', eventSheetLoaded , false);

tileSheet.src = "tanks_sheet.png";

var animationFrames = [1,2,3,4,5,6,7,8];
var frameIndex = 0;
var rotation = 90;

var x = 50;
var y = 50;

function eventSheetLoaded() {
    drawScreen();
}

function drawScreen() {

    //draw a background so we can see the Canvas edges
    context.fillStyle = "#aaaaaa";
    context.fillRect(0,0,500,500);
```

```
    context.save();
    context.setTransform(1,0,0,1,0,0);

    context.translate(x+16, y+16);
    var angleInRadians = rotation * Math.PI / 180;
    context.rotate(angleInRadians);

    var sourceX = Math.floor(animationFrames[frameIndex] % 8) *32;
    var sourceY = Math.floor(animationFrames[frameIndex] / 8) *32;

    context.drawImage(tileSheet, sourceX, sourceY,32,32,-16,-16,32,32);

    context.restore();

}

function eventShipLoaded() {
    drawScreen();
}
```

Figure 4-8 shows the output for this example.

Figure 4-8. Applying a rotation transformation

Let's take this one step further by applying the animation technique from Example 4-5 and looping through the eight tiles while facing the tank at the 90-degree angle.

Animating a Transformed Image

To apply a series of image tiles to the rotated context, we simply have to add back in the frame tick loop code and increment the `frameIndex` variable on each frame tick. Example 4-8 has added this into the code for Example 4-7.

Example 4-8. Animation and rotation

```
var tileSheet = new Image();
tileSheet.addEventListener('load', eventSheetLoaded , false);

tileSheet.src = "tanks_sheet.png";

var animationFrames = [1,2,3,4,5,6,7,8];
var frameIndex = 0;
var rotation = 90;
var x = 50;
var y = 50;

function eventSheetLoaded() {
   startUp();
}

function drawScreen() {

   //draw a background so we can see the Canvas edges
   context.fillStyle = "#aaaaaa";
   context.fillRect(0,0,500,500);

   context.save();
   context.setTransform(1,0,0,1,0,0)
   var angleInRadians = rotation * Math.PI / 180;
   context.translate(x+16, y+16)
   context.rotate(angleInRadians);
   var sourceX = Math.floor(animationFrames[frameIndex] % 8) *32;
   var sourceY = Math.floor(animationFrames[frameIndex] / 8) *32;

   context.drawImage(tileSheet, sourceX, sourceY,32,32,-16,-16,32,32);
   context.restore();
   frameIndex++;
   if (frameIndex==animationFrames.length) {
       frameIndex=0;
   }

}

function startUp(){
    gameLoop();
}

function gameLoop() {
    window.setTimeout(gameLoop, 100);
```

```
    drawScreen();
}
```

When you test Example 4-8, you should see that the tank has rotated 90 degrees and that the tank treads loop through their animation frames.

As we did in Example 4-6, let's move the tank in the direction it is facing. This time, it will move to the right until it goes off the screen. Example 4-9 has added back in the dx and dy movement vectors; notice that dx is now 1, and dy is now 0.

Example 4-9. Rotation, animation, and movement

```
var tileSheet = new Image();
tileSheet.addEventListener('load', eventSheetLoaded , false);

tileSheet.src = "tanks_sheet.png";

var animationFrames = [1,2,3,4,5,6,7,8];
var frameIndex = 0;
var rotation = 90;
var x = 50;
var y = 50;
var dx = 1;
var dy = 0;

function eventSheetLoaded() {
   startUp();
}

function drawScreen() {
   x = x+dx;
   y = y+dy;

   //draw a background so we can see the Canvas edges
   context.fillStyle = "#aaaaaa";
   context.fillRect(0,0,500,500);

   context.save();
   context.setTransform(1,0,0,1,0,0)
   var angleInRadians = rotation * Math.PI / 180;
   context.translate(x+16, y+16)
   context.rotate(angleInRadians);
   var sourceX=Math.floor(animationFrames[frameIndex] % 8) *32;
   var sourceY=Math.floor(animationFrames[frameIndex] / 8) *32;

   context.drawImage(tileSheet, sourceX, sourceY,32,32,-16,-16,32,32);
   context.restore();

   frameIndex++;
   if (frameIndex ==animationFrames.length) {
      frameIndex=0;
   }
```

```
}

function startUp(){
    gameLoop();
}

function gameLoop() {
    window.setTimeout(gameLoop, 100);
    drawScreen();
}
```

When Example 4-9 is running, you will see the tank move slowly across the screen to the right. Its treads animate through the series of tiles from the tile sheet on a plain gray background.

So far, we have used tiles only to simulate sprite-based animated movement. In the next section, we will examine how to use an image tile sheet to create a much more elaborate background using a series of tiles.

Creating a Grid of Tiles

Many games use what is called a *tile-based environment* for backgrounds and level graphics. We are now going to apply the knowledge we have learned from animating an image on the canvas to create the background maze for our hypothetical game, *No Tanks!* We will use the same tile sheet from the previous tank examples, but instead of showing the tank sprite tiles, we will create a maze for the tank to move through. We will not actually cover the game-play portion of the code in this chapter because we want to focus on using images to render the screen. In Chapter 9, we will create a simple game using the type of examples shown here.

Defining a Tile Map

We will use the term *tile map* to refer to a game level or background built from a tile sheet. Take a look back at Figure 4-7, which shows the four-row by eight-column tile sheet from earlier in this chapter. If we were to create a maze-chase game similar to *Pac-Man*, we could define the maze using tiles from a tile sheet. The sequence of tiles for our game maze would be considered a tile map.

The first tile is a gray square, which we can use for the "road" tiles between the wall tiles. Any tile that a game sprite can move on is referred to as *walkable*. Even though our tanks are not literally walking but driving, the concept is the same. In Chapter 9, we will create a small game using these concepts, but for now, let's concentrate on defining a tile map and displaying it on the canvas.

Our tile map will be a two-dimensional array of tile ID numbers. If you recall, the tile ID numbers for our tile sheet are in a single dimension, numbering from 0 to 31. Let's say we are going to create a very small game screen consisting of 10 tiles in length and 10 tiles in height. This means we need to define a tile map of 100 individual tiles (10×10). If our tiles are 32 pixels by 32 pixels, we will define a 320×320 game screen.

There are many ways to define a tile map. One simple way is to use a tile map editor program to lay out a grid of tiles and then export the data to re-create the tile map in JavaScript. This is precisely how we are going to create our tile map.

Creating a Tile Map with Tiled

The program we are going to use, Tiled, is a great tile map editor that is available for Mac OS, Windows, and Linux. Of course, tile maps can be designed by hand, but map creation is much easier if we utilize a program such as Tiled to do some of the legwork for us. Tiled is available for free (*http://www.mapeditor.org/*) under the GNU free software license.

 As stated before, you do not need to use this software. Tile maps can be created with other good (and free) software such as Mappy (*http://tile map.co.uk/mappy.php*) and Tile Studio (*http://tilestudio.source forge.net/*), and even by hand using Microsoft Paint.

The goal of creating a tile map is to visually lay out a grid of tiles that represents the game screen and then export the tile IDs that represent those tiles. We will use the exported data as a two-dimensional array in our code to build the tile map on the canvas.

Here are the basic steps for creating a simple tile map in Tiled for use in the following section:

1. Create a new tile map from the File menu. When it asks for Orientation, select Orthogonal with a Map Size of 10×10 and a Tile Size of 32×32.

2. From the Map menu, import the *tanks_sheet.png* file to be used as the tile set. Select "New tileset" from this menu, and give it any name you want. Browse to find the *tanks_sheet.png* file that you downloaded from this book's website. Make sure that Tile Width and Tile Height are both 32; keep the Margin and Spacing both at 0.

3. Select a tile from the tile set on the bottom-right side of the screen. When selected, you can click and "paint" the tile by selecting a location on the tile map on the top-left side of the screen. Figure 4-9 shows the tile map created for this example.

4. Save the tile map. Tiled uses a plain text file format called *.tmx*. Normally, tile data in Tiled is saved out in a base-64-binary file format; however, we can change this by editing the preferences for Tiled. On a Mac, under the Tiled menu, there should

be a Preferences section. (If you are using the software on Windows or Linux, you will find this in the File menu.) When setting the preferences, select CSV in the "Store tile layer data as" drop-down menu. After you have done this, you can save the file from the File menu.

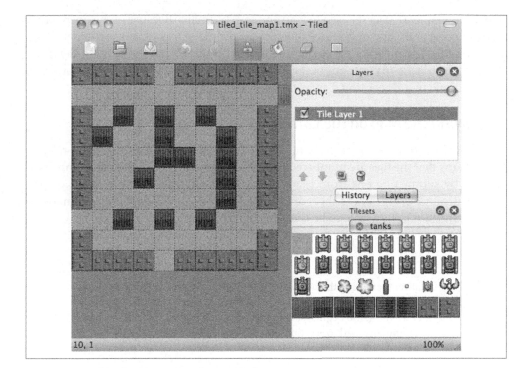

Figure 4-9. The tile map example in Tiled

Here is a look at what the saved *.tmx* file will look like in a text editor:

```
<?xml version="1.0" encoding="UTF-8"?>
<map version="1.0" orientation="orthogonal" width="10" height="10"
        tilewidth="32" tileheight="32">
  <tileset firstgid="1" name="tanks" tilewidth="32" tileheight="32">
  <image source="tanks_sheet.png"/>
  </tileset>
  <layer name="Tile Layer 1" width="10" height="10">
  <data encoding="csv">
32,31,31,31,1,31,31,31,31,32,
1,1,1,1,1,1,1,1,1,1,
32,1,26,1,26,1,26,1,1,32,
32,26,1,1,26,1,1,26,1,32,
32,1,1,1,26,26,1,26,1,32,
32,1,1,26,1,1,1,26,1,32,
32,1,1,1,1,1,1,26,1,32,
```

```
1,1,26,1,26,1,26,1,1,1,
32,1,1,1,1,1,1,1,1,32,
32,31,31,31,1,31,31,31,31,32
</data>
</layer>
</map>
```

The data is an XML data set used to load and save tile maps. Because of the open nature of this format and the simple sets of row data for the tile map, we can use this data easily in JavaScript. For now, we are concerned only with the 10 rows of comma-delimited numbers inside the <data> node of the XML—we can take those rows of data and create a very simple two-dimensional array to use in our code.

Displaying the Map on the Canvas

The first thing to note about the data from Tiled is that it is *1 relative*, not 0 relative. This means that the tiles are numbered from 1–32 instead of 0–31. We can compensate for this by subtracting one from each value as we transcribe it to our array, or programmatically during our tile sheet drawing operation. We will do it programmatically by creating an offset variable to be used during the draw operation:

```
var mapIndexOffset = -1;
```

 Rather than using the mapIndexOffset variable, we could loop through the array of data and subtract 1 from each value. This would be done before the game begins, saving the extra processor overload from performing this math operation on each tile when it is displayed.

Map height and width

We also are going to create two variables to give flexibility to our tile map display code. These might seem simple and unnecessary now, but if you get in the habit of using variables for the height and width of the tile map, it will be much easier to change its size in the future.

We will keep track of the width and height based on the number of rows in the map and the number of columns in each row:

```
var mapRows = 10;
var mapCols = 10;
```

Storing the map data

The data that was output from Tiled was a series of rows of numbers starting in the top left and moving left to right, and then down when the rightmost column in a row was completed. We can use this data almost exactly as output by placing it in a two-dimensional array:

```
var tileMap = [
        [32,31,31,31,1,31,31,31,31,32]
      ,   [1,1,1,1,1,1,1,1,1,1]
      ,   [32,1,26,1,26,1,26,1,1,32]
      ,   [32,26,1,1,26,1,1,26,1,32]
      ,   [32,1,1,1,26,26,1,26,1,32]
      ,   [32,1,1,26,1,1,1,26,1,32]
      ,   [32,1,1,1,1,1,1,26,1,32]
      ,   [1,1,26,1,26,1,26,1,1,1]
      ,   [32,1,1,1,1,1,1,1,1,32]
      ,   [32,31,31,31,1,31,31,31,31,32]

    ];
```

Displaying the map on the canvas

When we display the tile map, we simply loop through the rows in the `tileMap` array, and then loop through the columns in each row. The `tileID` number at [`row`][`col umn`] will be the tile to copy from the tile sheet to the canvas. `row *32` will be the y location to place the tile on the canvas; `col *32` will be the x location to place the tile:

```
for (var rowCtr=0;rowCtr<mapRows;rowCtr++) {
    for (var colCtr=0;colCtr<mapCols;colCtr++){

        var tileId = tileMap[rowCtr][colCtr]+mapIndexOffset;
        var sourceX = Math.floor(tileId % 8) *32;
        var sourceY = Math.floor(tileId / 8) *32;

        context.drawImage(tileSheet, sourceX,
          sourceY,32,32,colCtr*32,rowCtr*32,32,32);
    }

}
```

> The row, column referencing might seem slightly confusing because row is the *y* direction and column is the *x* direction. We do this because our tiles are organized into a two-dimensional array. The row is always the first subscript when accessing a 2D array.

We use the `mapRows` and the `mapCols` variables to loop through the data and to paint it to the canvas. This makes it relatively simple to modify the height and width of the tile map without having to find the hardcoded values in the code. We could have also done this with other values, such as the tile width and height, as well as the number of tiles per row in the tile sheet (8).

The `sourceX` and `sourceY` values for the tile to copy are found in the same way as in the previous examples. However, this time we find the `tileId` by using the [`rowCtr`] [`colCtr`] two-dimensional lookup and then adding the `mapIndexOffset`. The offset is a negative number (−1), so this effectively subtracts 1 from each tile map value, resulting in 0-relative map values that are easier to work with. Example 4-10 shows this concept in action, and Figure 4-10 illustrates the results.

Example 4-10. Painting the tile map to the Canvas

```
var tileSheet = new Image();
tileSheet.addEventListener('load', eventSheetLoaded , false);

tileSheet.src = "tanks_sheet.png";

var mapIndexOffset = -1;
var mapRows = 10;
var mapCols = 10;

var tileMap = [
        [32,31,31,31,1,31,31,31,31,32]
    ,   [1,1,1,1,1,1,1,1,1,1]
    ,   [32,1,26,1,26,1,26,1,1,32]
    ,   [32,26,1,1,26,1,1,26,1,32]
    ,   [32,1,1,1,26,26,1,26,1,32]
    ,   [32,1,1,26,1,1,1,26,1,32]
    ,   [32,1,1,1,1,1,1,26,1,32]
    ,   [1,1,26,1,26,1,26,1,1,1]
    ,   [32,1,1,1,1,1,1,1,1,32]
    ,   [32,31,31,31,1,31,31,31,31,32]

    ];

function eventSheetLoaded() {
    drawScreen()
}

function drawScreen() {
    for (var rowCtr=0;rowCtr<mapRows;rowCtr++) {
        for (var colCtr=0;colCtr<mapCols;colCtr++){

            var tileId = tileMap[rowCtr][colCtr]+mapIndexOffset;
            var sourceX = Math.floor(tileId % 8) *32;
            var sourceY = Math.floor(tileId / 8) *32;

            context.drawImage(tileSheet, sourceX,
            sourceY,32,32,colCtr*32,rowCtr*32,32,32);
        }

    }
}
```

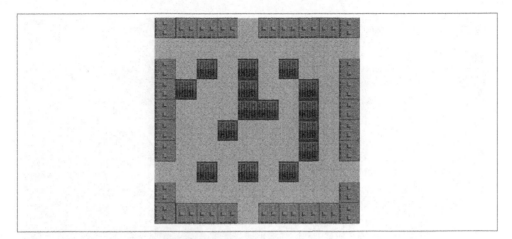

Figure 4-10. The tile map painted on the canvas

Next, we are going to leave the world of tile-based Canvas development. (See Chapter 9 for an example of a small game developed with these principles.) The final section of this chapter discusses building our own simple tile map editor. But before we get there, let's look at panning around and zooming in and out of an image.

Diving into Drawing Properties with a Large Image

In this section, we will examine some methods used to draw a large image on the canvas. The image we are going to use is from a recent vacation to Central California. It is a large *.jpg* file, measuring 3648×2736. Obviously, this is far too large to view in a single canvas, so we will build some examples that will allow us to use and manipulate the drawing properties for an image larger than the size of the canvas.

Figure 4-11 is a scaled-down version of this image.

Figure 4-11. A scaled-down version of the image we will zoom and pan

Creating a Window for the Image

The first thing we are going to do is create a logical window, the size of the canvas, where our image will reside. We will use the following two variables to control the dimensions of this window:

```
var windowWidth = 500;
var windowHeight = 500;
```

We will also create two variables to define the current top-left corner for the window. When we move on to the panning examples, we will modify these values to redraw the image based on this location:

```
var windowX = 0;
var windowY = 0;
```

Drawing the Image Window

To draw the image window, we will simply modify the standard `context.draw` `Image()` function call using the values in the four variables we just defined:

```
context.drawImage(photo, windowX, windowY, windowWidth, windowHeight, 0, 0,
                windowWidth,windowHeight);
```

Let's take a closer look at this for a refresher on how the `drawImage()` function operates. The values are passed in order:

photo
> The image instance we are going to use as our source for painting onto the canvas

windowX
> The top-left x location to start copying from the source image

windowY
> The top-left y location to start copying from the source image

windowWidth
> The width of the rectangle to start copying from the source image

windowHeight
> The height of the rectangle to start copying from the source image

0
> The top-left x destination location for the image on the canvas

0
> The top-left y destination location for the image on the canvas

viewPortWidth
> The width in pixels for the destination copy (can be modified to scale the image)

viewPortHeight
> The height in pixels for the destination copy (can be modified to scale the image)

When we draw from the image to the canvas, we will be modifying the `windowX` and `windowY` values to create a panning effect. Example 4-11 demonstrates how to get the image onto the canvas with the window location set to 0,0. Figure 4-12 shows an example of the output for Example 4-11.

Example 4-11. Placing an image on the canvas in a logical window

```
var photo = new Image();
photo.addEventListener('load', eventPhotoLoaded , false);

photo.src = "butterfly.jpg";

var windowWidth=500;
var windowHeight=500;
var viewPortWidth=500;
var viewPortHeight=500;

var windowX=0;
var windowY=0;
```

```
function eventPhotoLoaded() {
    drawScreen()
}

function drawScreen(){
        context.drawImage(photo, windowX, windowY,windowWidth,windowHeight,
                          0,0,viewPortWidth,viewPortHeight);
}
```

Figure 4-12. An image in a logical 500×500 window

Changing the ViewPort Property of the Image

We can change the ViewPort property of the drawn image by modifying the viewPort
Width and viewPortHeight values. Example 4-12 shows the image drawn into a 200×200
window, using the same pixels as the 400×400 copy from Example 4-11. Essentially, this
scales the image copy down to fit in a smaller space but uses the same source pixels:

```
var viewPortWidth=200;
var viewPortHeight=200;
```

Example 4-12 contains these simple changes.

Example 4-12. Changing scale with ViewPort properties

```
var photo=new Image();
photo.addEventListener('load', eventPhotoLoaded , false);
photo.src="butterfly.jpg";


var windowWidth=500;
var windowHeight=500;
var viewPortWidth=200;
var viewPortHeight=200;

var windowX=0;
var windowY=0;


function eventPhotoLoaded() {
    drawScreen()
}

function drawScreen(){
        context.drawImage(photo, windowX, windowY,windowWidth,windowHeight,
                        0,0,viewPortWidth,viewPortHeight);
}
```

When you test Example 4-12, you will see the exact same portion of the image copied into a smaller part of the canvas. Figure 4-13 shows an example of this scaled viewport window.

Figure 4-13. An image in a small logical window

Changing the Image Source Scale

Aside from using the viewport settings to scale an image when drawn to the canvas, we can also change the source height and width vales to display the image in a new scale. We will keep the view port height and width the same, but change the window height and window width values. When we make these greater than the size of the actual window, we will see more of the image in the 500×500 canvas, and the details will appear to be a little clearer. To scale an image, we need to change the final `width` and `height` values of the `drawImage()` function. Let's examine how we would scale to 2x of the original size of the image while panning at the same time. The `drawImage()` function will look like this:

```
context.drawImage(photo, windowX, windowY, windowWidth*2, windowHeight*2,
                  0, 0, viewPortWidth, viewPortHeight);
```

Example 4-13 modifies Example 4-12 and adds in the *2 to `windowHeight` and `window Width` for zooming out (2x zoom out) from the original image.

Example 4-13. Scale with source properties

```
var photo=new Image();
photo.addEventListener('load', eventPhotoLoaded , false);
photo.src="butterfly.jpg";


var windowWidth=500;
var windowHeight=500;
var viewPortWidth=500;
var viewPortHeight=500;

var windowX=0;
var windowY=0;



function eventPhotoLoaded() {
    drawScreen()
}

function drawScreen(){
        context.drawImage(photo, windowX, windowY,windowWidth*2,windowHeight*2,
                          0,0,viewPortWidth,viewPortHeight);
}
```

If you compare the output from Examples 4-12 and 4-13, you will notice that the image has been scaled down by 2x. This is best illustrated if we look at the butterfly in the image. To do that, we need to *pan* the image to the location of the butterfly and first look at it in the normal nonscaled source width and height.

Figure 4-14 shows an example of this scaled image.

Figure 4-14. The image scaled

Panning to a Spot on the Source Image

Example 4-14 changes the windowY and windowX locations to a sort that will display the butterfly. It removes any scaling from the draw operation:

```
var windowX=1580;
var windowY=1190;
```

When Example 4-14 is run, you should see the butterfly image take up most of the canvas.

Example 4-14. Pan an image using the widow draw destination properties

```
var photo=new Image();
    photo.addEventListener('load', eventPhotoLoaded , false);
    photo.src="butterfly.jpg";


    var windowWidth=500;
    var windowHeight=500;
    var viewPortWidth=500;
    var viewPortHeight=500;

    var windowX=1580;
    var windowY=1190;
```

```
function eventPhotoLoaded() {
    drawScreen()
}

function drawScreen(){
    context.drawImage
    (photo, windowX,windowY,windowWidth,windowHeight,0,0,viewPortWidth,
    viewPortHeight);
}
function gameLoop() {
    window.setTimeout(gameLoop, 100);
    drawScreen();
}
```

Figure 4-15 shows the pan to the butterfly in normal view scale mode.

Figure 4-15. Pan to the butterfly with no scale applied

Pan and Scale in the Same Operation

To pan and scale in the same operation, we simply need to pan using the same window and window properties as Example 4-14 and the same source scale factor as Example 4-15:

```
var windowX=1580;
var windowY=1190;
```

In the `drawScreen()` function, we will use this to draw the image:

```
context.drawImage(photo, windowX, windowY,windowWidth*2,windowHeight*2,
                  0,0,viewPortWidth,viewPortHeight);
```

Example 4-15 shows this powerful combination in action.

Example 4-15. Scale and pan to a spot on the image

```
var photo=new Image();
photo.addEventListener('load', eventPhotoLoaded , false);
photo.src="butterfly.jpg";


var windowWidth=500;
var windowHeight=500;
var viewPortWidth=500;
var viewPortHeight=500;

var windowX=1580;
var windowY=1190;


function eventPhotoLoaded() {
    drawScreen();
}

function drawScreen(){
      context.drawImage(photo, windowX,
      windowY,windowWidth*2,windowHeight*2,0,0,viewPortWidth,viewPortHeight);
}
```

When Example 4-15 is run, you will see that we have panned to a new spot on the large image and doubled the size of the image source rectangle. This acts as a zoom-out feature, and the butterfly becomes much clearer than in Example 4-14. Figure 4-16 shows this example in action.

Figure 4-16. Pan and scale applied to the butterfly image

Next we take a look at manipulating individual pixels on the canvas.

Pixel Manipulation

In this section, we will first examine the Canvas Pixel Manipulation API and then build a simple application demonstrating how to manipulate pixels on the canvas in real time.

The Canvas Pixel Manipulation API

The Canvas Pixel Manipulation API gives us the ability to "get," "put," and "change" individual pixels, utilizing what is known as the CanvasPixelArray interface. ImageData is the base object type for this manipulation, and an instance of this object is created with the createImageData() function call. Let's start there.

The createImageData() function sets aside a portion of memory to store an individual pixel's worth of data based on the following three constructors:

imagedata = context.createImageData(sw, sh)
> The *sw* and *sh* parameters represent the width and height values for the ImageData object. For example, imagedata=createImageData(100,100) would create a 100×100 area of memory in which to store pixel data.

imagedata = context.`createImageData(`*imagedata)*

The *imagedata* parameter represents a separate instance of `ImageData`. This constructor creates a new `ImageData` object with the same width and height as the parameter `ImageData`.

imagedata = context.`createImageData()`

This constructor returns a blank `ImageData` instance.

ImageData attributes

An `ImageData` object contains three attributes:

`ImageData.height`

This returns the height in pixels of the `ImageData` instance.

`ImageData.width`

This returns the width in pixels of the `ImageData` instance.

`ImageData.data`

This returns a single-dimensional array of pixels representing the image data. Image data is stored with 32-bit color information for each pixel, meaning that every fourth number in this data array starts a new pixel. The four elements in the array represent the red, green, blue, and alpha transparency values of a single pixel.

Getting image data

To retrieve a set of pixel data from the canvas and put it into an `ImageData` instance, we use the `getImageData()` function call:

imagedata = context.`getImageData(`*sx, sy, sw, sh)*

sx, sy, sw, and *sh* define the location and size of the source rectangle to copy from the canvas to the `ImageData` instance.

 A security error might be thrown if the origin domain of an image file is not the same as the origin domain of the web page. This affects local files (when running on your hard drive rather than on a web server running locally or on a remote server), because most browsers will treat local image files as though they are from a different domain than the web page. When running on a web server, this error will not be thrown with local files. The current versions of Safari (6.02), IE (10), and Firefox do not throw this error for local files.

Putting image data

To copy the pixels from an `ImageData` instance to the canvas, we use the `putImageData()` function call. There are two different constructors for this call:

```
context.putImageData (imagedata, dx, dy)
context.putImageData (imagedata, dx, dy [, dirtyX, dirtyY,
                      dirtyWidth, dirtyHeight ])
```

The first constructor simply paints the entire ImageData instance to the destina
tionX (dx) and destinationY (dy) locations. The second constructor does the same but
allows the passage of a "dirty rectangle," which represents the area of the ImageData to
paint to the canvas.

Application Tile Stamper

We are going to create a simple application that will allow the user to highlight a box
around some pixels on an image, copy them, and then use them as a stamp to paint back
to the canvas. It will not be a full-blown editing application by any means—it's just a
demonstration of one use of the ImageData object.

 This application will need to be run from a local or remote web server,
because most browsers will throw an exception if an application attempts to call getImageData() on a file—even in the same folder on a
local machine. The current version of Safari (6.02) does not throw this
error.

To create this simple application, we will use the tile sheet from earlier in this chapter.
The user will click on a spot on the tile sheet, highlighting a 32×32 square tile. That tile
can then be painted onto the bottom section of the canvas. To demonstrate pixel manipulation, we will set the color of the pixels to a new alpha value before they are painted
to the screen. This will be the humble beginning for making our own tile map editor.

Once again, we will use the *tanks_sheet.png* file from Figure 4-7.

How ImageData.data is organized

The ImageData.data attribute is a single-dimensional array containing four bytes for
every pixel in the ImageData object. We will be using 32×32 tiles in our example application. A 32×32 tile contains 1,024 pixels (or 1K of data). The ImageData.data attribute
for an ImageData instance that holds a 32×32 image would be 4,096 bytes (or 4K). This
is because a separate byte is used to store each of the red, green, blue, and alpha values
for each pixel. In our application, we will loop through each pixel and set its alpha value
to 128. Here is the code we will use:

```
for (j=3; j< imageData.data.length; j+=4){
    imageData.data[j] = 128;
}
```

We start our loop at 3, which is the fourth attribute in the array. The single-dimensional array contains a continuous set of values for each pixel, so index 3 represents the alpha value for the first pixel (because the array is 0 relative). Our loop then skips to every fourth value in the array and sets it to 128. When the loop is complete, all pixels will have an alpha value of 128.

 As opposed to other Canvas alpha manipulations where the alpha value is between 0 and 1, the alpha value is between 0 and 255 when manipulating it via the pixel color values.

A visual look at our basic application

Figure 4-17 is a screenshot of the simple Tile Stamper application we will create.

 Figure 4-17 is running in Safari 5.1 locally. As of this writing, this is the only browser that does not throw an exception when trying to manipulate the pixel data of a locally loaded file when not run on a web server.

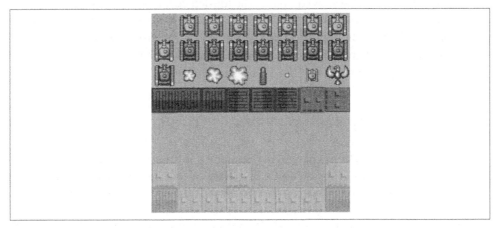

Figure 4-17. The Tile Stamper application

The screen is broken up into two sections vertically. The top section is the 256×128 tile sheet; the bottom is a tile map of the same size. The user will select a tile in the top section, and it will be highlighted by a red square. The user can then stamp the selected tile to the tile map drawing area in the lower portion. When a tile is drawn in this lower portion, we will set its alpha value to 128.

Adding mouse events to the canvas

We need to code our application to respond to mouse clicks and to keep track of the current x and y positions of the mouse pointer. We will set up two global application scope variables to store the mouse pointer's current position:

```
var mouseX;
var mouseY;
```

We will also set up two event listener functions and attach them to the theCanvas object:

```
theCanvas.addEventListener("mousemove", onMouseMove, false);
theCanvas.addEventListener("click", onMouseClick, false);
```

In the HTML, we will set up a single Canvas object:

```
<canvas id="canvas" width="256" height="256"  style="position: absolute;
    top: 50px; left: 50px;">
 Your browser does not support HTML5 Canvas.
</canvas>
```

In the JavaScript portion of our code, we will define the canvas:

```
theCanvas = document.getElementById("canvas");
```

Notice that we set the <canvas> position to top: 50px and left: 50px. This will keep the application from being shoved up into the top-left corner of the browser, but it also gives us a chance to demonstrate how to find correct mouse x and y values when the <canvas> tag is not in the top-left corner of the page. The onMouseMove function will make use of this information to offset the mouseX and mouseY values, based on the position of the <canvas> tag:

```
function onMouseMove(e) {
    mouseX = e.clientX-theCanvas.offsetLeft;
    mouseY = e.clientY-theCanvas.offsetTop;
}
```

The onMouseClick function will actually do quite a lot in our application. When the mouse button is clicked, this function will determine whether the user clicked on the tile sheet or on the tile map drawing area below it. If the user clicked on the tile sheet, the function will determine which exact tile was clicked. It will then call the highlight Tile() function and pass in the ID (0–31) of the tile clicked, along with the x and y locations for the top-left corner of the tile.

If the user clicked in the lower portion of the tile map drawing area, this function will again determine which tile the user clicked on and will stamp the current selected tile in that location on the tile map. Here is the function:

```
function onMouseClick(e) {

    if (mouseY < 128){
        //find tile to highlight
        var col = Math.floor(mouseX / 32);
```

```
        var row = Math.floor(mouseY / 32);
        var tileId = (row*7)+(col+row);
        highlightTile(tileId,col*32,row*32)
    }else{
        var col = Math.floor(mouseX / 32);
        var row = Math.floor(mouseY / 32);
        context.putImageData(imageData,col*32,row*32);
        }
    }
```

Let's take a closer look at the tile sheet click (`mouseY < 128`).

To determine the `tileId` of the tile clicked on the tile sheet, we first need to convert the x location of the mouse click to a number from 0–7, and the y location to a number from 0–3. We do this by calling the `Math.floor` function on the result of the current `mouseX` or `mouseY` location, divided by the tile width or height (they are both 32). This will find the `row` and `col` of the clicked tile:

```
var col = Math.floor(mouseX / 32);
var row = Math.floor(mouseY / 32)
```

To find the `tileId` (the 0–31 tile number of the tile sheet) of this row and column combination, we need to use the following calculation:

```
TileId = (row*totalRows-1) + (col+row);
```

The actual calculation, with values for our application, looks like this:

```
var tileId = (row*7)+(col+row);
```

For example, if the user clicks on the point where `mouseX = 50` and `mouseY = 15`, the calculation would work like this:

```
col = Math.floor(50/32);    // col = 1
row = Math.floor(15/32);    // row = 0
tileId = (0*7)+(1+0);       // tileId = 1
```

This position is the second tile on the tile sheet. The `onMouseClick()` function then passes the `tileId` and `col` value multiplied by 32, and the `row` value multiplied by 32, into the `highlightTile()` function. This tells the `highlightTile()` function the exact `tileId`, `row`, and `col` the user clicked.

If the user clicked the tile map drawing area in the lower portion of the screen, the code does the same row and column calculation. However, it then calls the `putImageData()` function and passes in the `ImageData` instance that holds the tile to stamp and the top-left location to place the tile:

```
var col = Math.floor(mouseX / 32);
var row = Math.floor(mouseY / 32);
context.putImageData(imageData,col*32,row*32);
```

The highlightTile() function

The `highlightTile()` function accepts three parameters:

- The 0–31 `tileId` of the tile on the tile sheet
- The top-left x coordinate of the tile represented by the `tileId`
- The top-left y coordinate of the tile represented by the `tileId`

 The x and y coordinates can be found by passing in the `tileId` value, but they are needed in the `onMouseDown` function, so we pass them in from there when calling `highlightTile()`. This way, we do not need to perform the calculation twice.

The first task `highlightTile()` tackles is redrawing the tile sheet at the top of the screen:

```
context.fillStyle = "#aaaaaa";
context.fillRect(0,0,256,128);
drawTileSheet();
```

It does this to delete the red box around the current tile, while preparing to draw a new red box around the tile represented by the `tileId` passed in.

The `drawTileSheet()` function then paints the *tanks_sheet.png* file to the canvas starting at 0,0:

```
function drawTileSheet(){
    context.drawImage(tileSheet, 0, 0);
}
```

Next, the `highlightTile()` function copies the new pixel data (with no red line around it yet) from the canvas and places it in the `ImageData` instance:

```
ImageData = context.getImageData(x,y,32,32);
```

The `ImageData` variable now contains a copy of the pixel data for the tile from the canvas. We then loop through the pixels in `ImageData.data` (as described previously in the section "How ImageData.data is organized" on page 172) and set the alpha value of each to 128.

Finally, now that the `ImageData` variable contains the correct pixels with the altered alpha values, we can draw the red line around the tile that's been selected to stamp on the tile map:

```
var startX = Math.floor(tileId % 8) *32;
var startY = Math.floor(tileId / 8) *32;
context.strokeStyle = "red";
context.strokeRect(startX,startY,32,32)
```

Example 4-16 is the entire set of code for this application.

Example 4-16. The Tile Stamper application

```
<!doctype html>
<html lang="en">
<head>
<meta charset="UTF-8">
<title>CH4EX16: Tile Stamper Application</title>

<script src="modernizr.js"></script>
<script type="text/javascript">
window.addEventListener('load', eventWindowLoaded, false);
function eventWindowLoaded() {

    canvasApp();

}

function canvasSupport () {
  return Modernizr.canvas;
}

function canvasApp(){

    if (!canvasSupport()) {
          return;
    }else{
       var theCanvas = document.getElementById("canvas");
       var context = theCanvas.getContext("2d");
    }

    var mouseX;
    var mouseY;

    var tileSheet = new Image();
    tileSheet.addEventListener('load', eventSheetLoaded , false);
    tileSheet.src = "tanks_sheet.png";

    var imageData = context.createImageData(32,32);

    function eventSheetLoaded() {
       startUp();
    }

    function startUp(){
       context.fillStyle = "#aaaaaa";
       context.fillRect(0,0,256,256);
       drawTileSheet();
    }

    function drawTileSheet(){
       context.drawImage(tileSheet, 0, 0);
```

```
        }

    function highlightTile(tileId,x,y){
        context.fillStyle = "#aaaaaa";
        context.fillRect(0,0,256,128);
        drawTileSheet();

        imageData = context.getImageData(x,y,32,32);
        //loop through imageData.data. Set every 4th value to a new value
        for (j=3; j< imageData.data.length; j+=4){
            imageData.data[j]=128;
        }

        var startX = Math.floor(tileId % 8) *32;
        var startY = Math.floor(tileId / 8) *32;
        context.strokeStyle = "red";
        context.strokeRect(startX,startY,32,32)
    }

    function onMouseMove(e) {
        mouseX = e.clientX-theCanvas.offsetLeft;
        mouseY = e.clientY-theCanvas.offsetTop;

    }

    function onMouseClick(e) {
        console.log("click: " + mouseX + "," + mouseY);
        if (mouseY < 128){
            //find tile to highlight
            var col = Math.floor(mouseX / 32);
            var row = Math.floor(mouseY / 32)
            var tileId = (row*7)+(col+row);
            highlightTile(tileId,col*32,row*32)
        }else{
            var col = Math.floor(mouseX / 32);
            var row = Math.floor(mouseY / 32);

            context.putImageData(imageData,col*32,row*32);


        }
    }

    theCanvas.addEventListener("mousemove", onMouseMove, false);
    theCanvas.addEventListener("click", onMouseClick, false);

}

</script>

</head>
<body>
```

```
<div>
<canvas id="canvas" width="256" height="256"  style="position: absolute;
    top: 50px; left: 50px;">
 Your browser does not support HTML5 Canvas.
</canvas>
</div>
</body>
</html>
```

 As of this writing, you must run this application from a web server in order to manipulate the local *tanks_sheet.png* file on the canvas. If you are using the Safari or Firefox browser (version 5.1 and 19.02, respectively, as of this writing), you can test the application on a local drive and it will function properly.

Copying from One Canvas to Another

The canvas allows us to use another canvas as the source of a bitmap drawing operation. Let's take a quick look at how we might utilize this functionality.

We will need to modify the base file for this chapter and create an extra <canvas> tag in our HTML. We will name this extra <canvas> element canvas2. (It can be given any ID as long as it is not the same ID as the first <canvas>.) Here is what our HTML <body> will look like now:

```
<body>
<div>
<canvas id="canvas" width="256" height="256"  style="position: absolute;
    top: 50px; left: 50px;">Your browser does not support HTML5 Canvas.</canvas>
<canvas id="canvas2" width="32" height="32"  style="position: absolute;
    top: 256px; left: 50px;">Your browser does not support HTML5 Canvas.</canvas>
</div>
</body>
```

We will place the second <canvas> below the original and give it a width and height of 32. We will also need to create a new context and internal reference variable for canvas2. Here is the code that will be used to provide a reference to both <canvas> elements:

```
if (!canvasSupport()) {
    return;

}else{

  var theCanvas = document.getElementById("canvas");
  var context = theCanvas.getContext("2d");
  var theCanvas2 = document.getElementById("canvas2");
  var context2 = theCanvas2.getContext("2d");
```

```
    }
```

Example 4-17 will use the tile sheet image from earlier examples and draw it to the first
canvas. It will then copy a 32×32 square from this canvas and place it on the second
canvas.

Example 4-17. Copying from one canvas to another

```
<!doctype html>
<html lang="en">
<head>
<meta charset="UTF-8">
<title>CH4EX17: Canvas Copy</title>

<script src="modernizr.js"></script>
<script type="text/javascript">
window.addEventListener('load', eventWindowLoaded, false);
function eventWindowLoaded() {

    canvasApp();

}

function canvasSupport () {

     return Modernizr.canvas;

}

function canvasApp(){
   if (!canvasSupport()) {
      return;
   }else{
      var theCanvas = document.getElementById("canvas");
      var context = theCanvas.getContext("2d");
      var theCanvas2 = document.getElementById("canvas2");
      var context2 = theCanvas2.getContext("2d");
   }

   var tileSheet = new Image();
   tileSheet.addEventListener('load', eventSheetLoaded , false);
   tileSheet.src="tanks_sheet.png";


   function eventSheetLoaded() {

      startUp();
   }

   function startUp(){
      context.drawImage(tileSheet, 0, 0);
      context2.drawImage(theCanvas, 32, 0,32,32,0,0,32,32);
```

```
        }
}
</script>

</head>
<body>
<div>
<canvas id="canvas" width="256" height="256"  style="position: absolute;
    top: 50px; left: 50px;"> Your browser does not support HTML5 Canvas.</canvas>

<canvas id="canvas2" width="32" height="32"  style="position: absolute;
    top: 256px; left: 50px;">Your browser does not support HTML5 Canvas.</canvas>

</div>
</body>
</html>
```

Figure 4-18 shows the canvas copy functions in operation.

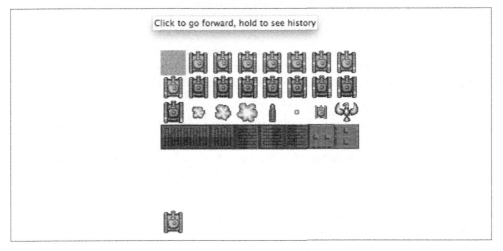

Figure 4-18. An example canvas copy operation

Canvas copy operations can be very useful when creating applications that need to share and copy image data across multiple <div> instances on (and the Canvas object within) a web page. For example, multiple Canvas elements can be spread across a web page, and as the user makes changes to one, the others can be updated. This can be used for fun applications, such as a "minimap" in a game, or even in serious applications, such as stock portfolio charting and personalization features.

Using Pixel Data to Detect Object Collisions

We can use the `context.getImageData()` function on two image objects to perform pixel-level collision detection between the images.

 As of this writing, you must run this application from a web server in order to manipulate the local file image data on the canvas. If you are using the Safari browser (version 5.1.7 as of this writing), you can test the application on a local drive and it will function properly.

This is not a simple task, but it is ultimately straightforward. We must remember that when we are using `getImageData()`, we are copying the color values from the actual canvas and not the images themselves. For this reason, we cannot simply use the `Image` object data as the source of our collision testing but must copy that data from the canvas to a variable and then use that data in the collision check.

 Visit the *http://www.playmycode.com* blog for further details about collision detection and other game related topics. This site was immensely helpful in finding a decent algorithm for `getImageData()`.

Testing the alpha value of each pixel against each pixel in two objects is an expensive operation. So, we are going to first test to see whether our objects' bounding boxes collide before we start to test each pixel in each object. Here is the `boundingBoxCollide()` function we will use. It is also used in Example 4-18, and in Chapter 8 and Chapter 9 when we create games for the Canvas:

```
function boundingBoxCollide(object1, object2) {
    var left1 = object1.x;
    var left2 = object2.x;
    var right1 = object1.x + object1.width;
    var right2 = object2.x + object2.width;
    var top1 = object1.y;
    var top2 = object2.y;
    var bottom1 = object1.y + object1.height;
    var bottom2 = object2.y + object2.height;

    if (bottom1 < top2) return(false);
    if (top1 > bottom2) return(false);

    if (right1 < left2) return(false);
    if (left1 > right2) return(false);

    return(true);
```

```
}
```

As you can see, this function takes in two parameters. These are the two logical objects that we want to test the collision on. As long as the object instances include x, y, width, and height attributes, the function will perform properly. First let's examine the objects that we are going to test collisions on.

The Colliding Objects

We are going to use two PNG image files as the design for our objects. They will both be 48-pixel by 48-pixel images. The first will be a blue plus sign, and the second will be a red circle with a round "bite" taken out of it. Figure 4-19 shows the drawing objects for our pixel-level collision detection.

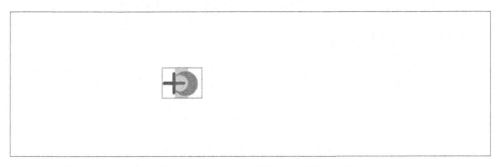

Figure 4-19. The drawing objects for our pixel-level collision detection

We will create two objects to hold the data for these images:

```
var blueObject={};
var redObject={};

blueObject.x=0;
blueObject.y=200;
blueObject.dx=2;
blueObject.width=48;
blueObject.height=48;
blueObject.image=new Image();
blueObject.image.src="blueplus.png";

redObject.x=348;
redObject.y=200;
redObject.dx=-2;
redObject.width=48;
redObject.height=48;
redObject.image=new Image();
redObject.image.src="redcircle.png";
```

We also need to draw each of the two images to the Canvas briefly and store the Image Data value for each:

```
context.drawImage(blueObject.image, 0, 0);
blueObject.blueImageData=context.getImageData(0, 0, blueObject.width,
                                              blueObject.height);
context.clearRect(0,0,theCanvas.width, theCanvas.height);redObject.x=348;

context.drawImage(redObject.image, 0, 0);
redObject.redImageData=context.getImageData(0, 0, redObject.width,
                                            redObject.height);
context.clearRect(0,0,theCanvas.width, theCanvas.height);
```

We draw at 0,0 for ease of use, but these could be drawn on a second hidden canvas or anywhere on the current canvas. We want to erase them right after we place them because we need to store only the pixel color data for each. Specifically, we will be using every fourth item in the array of pixel data. This is the transparency value of the pixel.

How We Will Test Collisions

We will employ a simple setTimeout loop to move these objects closer and closer together. As the bounding boxes of each collide, our code will then drop into an algorithm that will test the alpha value on each pixel at the overlap between the objects. If this alpha value is not 0, we know that the objects have collided.

Checking for Intersection Between Two Objects

After we have detected that we have a bounding box collision, we can simply loop through all of the pixels in each ImageData set, find the ones that match, and then check to see whether the alpha value for that pixel is 0. The problem with this approach is that it is *slow* and pretty much unusable for objects larger than a few pixels in width and height. Our 48×48 pixel images are each composed of 2,304 individual pixels. That is far too many to loop through on each frame tick, even for a single collision test. What we are going to do first is find where the two bounding boxes for our objects intersect and then check only those pixels.

Figure 4-20 shows an area of intersection where there would be a pixel-based collision.

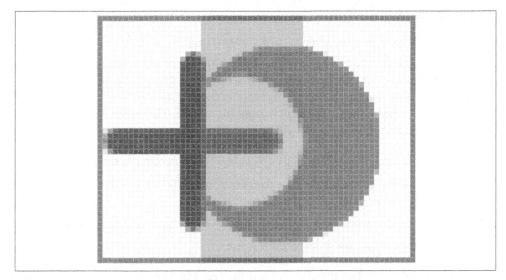

Figure 4-20. The area where a pixel based collision will take place

To check the pixels in only the area of intersection rather than the entire set of pixels in each object, we need to first find this area of intersection. We will accomplish this by using the `Math.min` and `Math.max` Javascript functions on the current object positions and their associated widths and heights:

```
var xMin = Math.max( blueObject.x, redObject.x );
var yMin = Math.max( blueObject.y, redObject.y );
var xMax = Math.min( blueObject.x+blueObject.width, redObject.x+redObject.width );
var yMax = Math.min( blueObject.y+blueObject.height, redObject.y+redObject.height
```

Based on the locations of the two objects and the width (or height, depending on the axis), these will give us four values needed to define the area in intersection.

`xMin` and `yMin` give us the location of the top-left corner of the intersection, and `xMax` and `yMax` give us the bottom-right corner of the intersection.

The next step is to create a nested loop where we iterate though all the horizontal (x) values in the intersection and through each vertical pixel (y). At each of these points, we find the transparency value for the pixel in each object at that point and compare it to 0.

The pixelX loop

```
for ( var pixelX = xMin; pixelX < xMax; pixelX++ )
```

Next we create a nested loop for the y positions in the intersection area.

The nested pixelY loop

```
for ( var pixelY = yMin; pixelY < yMax; pixelY++ )
```

When we have both a `pixelX` value and `pixelY` value, we need to find the transparency value for that pixel in each of our objects. Remember that `ImageData` objects are simply a single-dimensional array of four numbers for each pixel in the image. So, every fourth number in the array is the transparency value for a pixel. Therefore, the transparency value for a single pixel in our array will be found by using the following steps:

1. Subtract the current x value of our object from the current `pixelX` value.
2. Add the result of subtracting the current y of our object from the current `pixelY` value to the result in step 1.
3. Multiply the new value by 4 (because a pixel is every four values in our array).
4. Add 3 to this to find the transparency value.

It sounds complicated, but the code to find the red and blue object pixels comes out looking like this:

```
var bluepixel = ((pixelX-blueObject.x ) + (pixelY-blueObject.y )
                 *blueObject.width )*4 + 3 ;
var redpixel = ((pixelX-redObject.x) + (pixelY-redObject.y)
                 *redObject.width)*4 + 3 ;
```

The collision check

When we have the transparency value for both pixels, to see whether they collide is a simple matter of making sure that both `bluepixel` and `redpixel` in our `ImageData` arrays for the objects are both *not* 0:

```
if (( blueObject.blueImageData.data [ bluepixel ] !== 0 )
    &&( redObject.redImageData.data [ redpixel ] !== 0 )) {
    console.log("pixel collision")
    blueObject.dx=0;
    redObject.dx=0;
    break;
}
```

We have added a console log message and have set both of our objects' dx values to 0 so that they will stop on impact. Figure 4-21 shows the result of this collision.

Figure 4-21. The result on the Canvas of a pixel collision based impact

All of the code for this example

Example 4-18 contains the entire set of code needed to test out collisions, based on pixel color transparency values.

Example 4-18. Testing pixel collisions with color transparency values

```
<!doctype html>
<html lang="en">
<head>
<meta charset="UTF-8">
<title>Chapter 4 Example 18: Pixel Collisions</title>

<script src="modernizr.js"></script>
<script type="text/javascript">
window.addEventListener('load', eventWindowLoaded, false);
function eventWindowLoaded() {

    canvasApp();

}

function canvasSupport () {
    return Modernizr.canvas;
}


function canvasApp(){


    if (!canvasSupport()) {
            return;
    }else{
        var theCanvas = document.getElementById('canvas');
        var context = theCanvas.getContext('2d');


    }

    var blueObject={};
    var redObject={};
```

```
blueObject.x=0;
blueObject.y=200;
blueObject.dx=2;
blueObject.width=48;
blueObject.height=48;
blueObject.image=new Image();
blueObject.image.src="blueplus.png";

context.drawImage(blueObject.image, 0, 0);
blueObject.blueImageData=context.getImageData(0, 0, blueObject.width,
                                        blueObject.height);
context.clearRect(0,0,theCanvas.width, theCanvas.height);

redObject.x=348;
redObject.y=200;
redObject.dx=-2;
redObject.width=48;
redObject.height=48;
redObject.image=new Image();
redObject.image.src="redcircle.png";

context.drawImage(redObject.image, 0, 0);
redObject.redImageData=context.getImageData(0, 0, redObject.width,
                                        redObject.height);
context.clearRect(0,0,theCanvas.width, theCanvas.height);

function drawScreen() {
    blueObject.x+=blueObject.dx;
    redObject.x+=redObject.dx;

    context.clearRect(0,0,theCanvas.width, theCanvas.height);
    context.drawImage(blueObject.image, blueObject.x, blueObject.y);
    context.drawImage(redObject.image, redObject.x, redObject.y);

    console.log("redObject.redImageData.data[3]=" +
                redObject.redImageData.data[3]);


    if (boundingBoxCollide(blueObject, redObject)){
        console.log("bounding box collide");

        var xMin = Math.max( blueObject.x, redObject.x );
        var yMin = Math.max( blueObject.y, redObject.y );
        var xMax = Math.min( blueObject.x+blueObject.width,
                            redObject.x+redObject.width );
        var yMax = Math.min( blueObject.y+blueObject.height,
                            redObject.y+redObject.height );


        for ( var pixelX = xMin; pixelX < xMax; pixelX++ ) {
            for ( var pixelY = yMin; pixelY < yMax; pixelY++ ) {
```

```
                    var bluepixel = ((pixelX-blueObject.x ) + (pixelY-blueObject.y )
                    *blueObject.width )*4 + 3 ;
                    var redpixel = ((pixelX-redObject.x) +
                    (pixelY-redObject.y)*redObject.width)*4 + 3 ;

                    if (( blueObject.blueImageData.data [ bluepixel ] !== 0 ) &&
                        ( redObject.redImageData.data[ redpixel ] !== 0 )) {
                        console.log("pixel collision")
                        blueObject.dx=0;
                        redObject.dx=0;
                        break;
                    }
                }
            }


        }


    }

function boundingBoxCollide(object1, object2) {
    var left1 = object1.x;
    var left2 = object2.x;
    var right1 = object1.x + object1.width;
    var right2 = object2.x + object2.width;
    var top1 = object1.y;
    var top2 = object2.y;
    var bottom1 = object1.y + object1.height;
    var bottom2 = object2.y + object2.height;

    if (bottom1 < top2) return(false);
    if (top1 > bottom2) return(false);

    if (right1 < left2) return(false);
    if (left1 > right2) return(false);

    return(true);

};

function startUp(){
    gameLoop();
}

function gameLoop() {
    window.setTimeout(gameLoop, 100);
    drawScreen();
}

startUp();
```

```
    }

</script>

</head>
<body>
<div>
<canvas id="canvas" width="400" height="400"  style="position: absolute; top:
                                                  50px; left: 50px;">
 Your browser does not support the HTML 5 Canvas.
</canvas>
</div>

</body>
</html>
```

What's Next?

We covered quite a lot in this chapter, evolving from simply loading images to animating and rotating them. We looked at using tile sheets and tile maps, and then we built some useful applications with Canvas image functions and capabilities. In the first four chapters, we've covered most of what Canvas offers as a drawing surface. In the next six chapters, we will cover more advanced topics, such as applying 2D physics to `Canvas` objects, integrating the HTML5 `<video>` and `<audio>` tags with the `<canvas>` tag, creating games, and looking at some libraries and features that we can use to extend the functionality of HTML5 Canvas—even creating applications for mobile devices.

CHAPTER 5

Math, Physics, and Animation

Impressing users with animation involves more than knowing how to move objects—you also need to know how to move them in ways that users expect. That requires understanding some common algorithms for math-based movement and physics interactions. Simple movement based on points and vectors provides a foundation, and then it's time to create objects that bounce off walls and one another with a bit of friction added to the mix. After that, we will step back and talk about movement that goes beyond straight lines: circles, spirals, and complex Bezier curves. We will then cover how adding gravity can affect movement. Finally, we will finish this chapter by discussing easing and how it can have a positive effect on math-based animations.

Moving in a Straight Line

The simplest kinds of animations—moving objects in a straight line up and down the canvas—can take the form of adding a constant value to the x or y position of an object every time it is drawn.

So, to animate graphics, we will need to create an interval and then call a function that will display our updated graphics on every frame. Each example in this chapter will be built in a similar way. The first step is to set up the necessary variables in our `canvasApp()` function. For this first, basic example of movement, we will create a variable named `speed`. We will apply this value to the y position of our object on every call to `drawScreen()`. The x and y variables set up the initial position of the object (a filled circle) that we will move down the canvas:

```
var speed = 5;
var y = 10;
var x = 250;
```

After we create the variables, we set up an interval to call the drawScreen() function every 20 milliseconds. This is the loop we need to update our objects and move them around the canvas:

```
function gameLoop() {
    window.setTimeout(gameLoop, 20);
    drawScreen()
}
gameLoop();
```

In the drawScreen() function, we update the value of y by adding to it the value of the speed variable:

```
y += speed;
```

Finally, we draw our circle on the canvas. We position it using the current values of x and y. Because y is updated every time the function is called, the circle effectively moves down the canvas:

```
context.fillStyle = "#000000";
context.beginPath();
context.arc(x,y,15,0,Math.PI*2,true);
context.closePath();
context.fill();
```

To move the circle up the screen, we would make speed a negative number. To move it left or right, we would update the x instead of the y variable. To move the circle diagonally, we would update both x and y at the same time.

Example 5-1 shows the complete code needed to create basic movement in a straight line.

Example 5-1. Moving in a straight line

```
<!doctype html>
<html lang="en">
<head>
<meta charset="UTF-8">
<title>CH5EX1: Moving In A Straight Line</title>

<script src="modernizr.js"></script>
<script type="text/javascript">
window.addEventListener('load', eventWindowLoaded, false);
function eventWindowLoaded() {
    canvasApp();

}

function canvasSupport () {
    return Modernizr.canvas;
}

function canvasApp() {
```

```
    if (!canvasSupport()) {
         return;
       }

  function  drawScreen () {

    context.fillStyle = '#EEEEEE';
    context.fillRect(0, 0, theCanvas.width, theCanvas.height);
    //Box
    context.strokeStyle = '#000000';
    context.strokeRect(1,  1, theCanvas.width-2, theCanvas.height-2);


    // Create ball

    y += speed;

    context.fillStyle = "#000000";
    context.beginPath();
    context.arc(x,y,15,0,Math.PI*2,true);
    context.closePath();
    context.fill();

  }

  theCanvas = document.getElementById("canvasOne");
  context = theCanvas.getContext("2d");

  var speed = 5;
  var y = 10;
  var x = 250;

  function gameLoop() {
     window.setTimeout(gameLoop, 20);
     drawScreen()
  }
  gameLoop();

}

</script>

</head>
<body>
<div style="position: absolute; top: 50px; left: 50px;">

<canvas id="canvasOne" width="500" height="500">
 Your browser does not support HTML5 Canvas.
</canvas>
</div>
```

```
</body>
</html>
```

 The basic structure of the HTML for all the examples in this chapter will follow these rules. In the interest of saving space, we will refrain from discussing this code further, but it will appear in the examples provided.

Moving Between Two Points: The Distance of a Line

Movement based on constant changes to the x or y position of an object works well for some applications, but at other times you will need to be more precise. One such instance is when you need to move an object from point A to point B at a constant rate of speed.

In mathematics, a common way to find the length of an unknown oline is to use the Pythagorean theorem:

$$A^2 + B^2 = C^2$$

In this equation, C is the unknown side of a triangle when A and B are already known. However, we need to translate this equation into something that we can use with the points and pixels we have available on the canvas.

This is a good example of using a mathematical equation in your application. In this case, we want to find the distance of a line, given two points. In English, this equation reads like this:

> The distance equals the square root of the square of the difference between the x value of the second point minus the x value of the first point, plus the square of the difference between the y value of the second point minus the y value of the first point.

You can see this in Figure 5-1. It's much easier to understand in this format.

$$d = \sqrt{(x_2 - x_1)^2 + (y_2 - y_1)^2}$$

Figure 5-1. Distance equation

In the second example, we need to create some new variables in the `canvasApp()` function. We will still use a `speed` variable, just like in the first example, but this time we set it to 5, which means it will move 5 pixels on every call to `drawScreen()`:

```
var speed = 5;
```

We then create a couple of dynamic objects—each with an x and a y property—that will represent the two points we want to move between. For this example, we will move our circle from 20,250 to 480,250:

```
var p1 = {x:20,y:250};
var p2 = {x:480,y:250};
```

Now it is time to re-create the distance equation in Figure 5-1. The first step is to calculate the differences between the second and first x and y points:

```
var dx = p2.x - p1.x;
var dy = p2.y - p1.y;
```

To determine the `distance` value, we square both the values we just created, add them, and then use the `Math.sqrt()`function to get the square root of the number:

```
var distance = Math.sqrt(dx*dx + dy*dy);
```

Next, we need to use that calculated `distance` value in a way that will allow us to move an object a uniform number of pixels from p1 to p2. The first thing we do is calculate how many `moves` (calls to `drawScreen()`) it will take the object to move at the given value of `speed`. We get this by dividing the `distance` by the `speed`:

```
var moves = distance/speed;
```

Then we find the distance to move both x and y on each call to `drawScreen()`. We name these variables `xunits` and `yunits`:

```
var xunits = (p2.x - p1.x)/moves;
var yunits = (p2.y - p1.y)/moves;
```

Finally, we create a dynamic object named `ball` that holds the x and y value of p1:

```
var ball = {x:p1.x, y:p1.y};
```

And create the interval to call `drawScreen()` every 33 milliseconds:

```
function gameLoop() {
    window.setTimeout(gameLoop, 20);
    drawScreen()
}
gameLoop();
```

Drawing the ball

Let's draw the ball on the screen. In the `drawScreen()` function, we first check to see whether the `moves` variable is greater than zero. If so, we are still supposed to move the ball across the screen because we have not yet reached p2. We decrement moves (`moves--`) and then update the x and y properties of the ball object by adding the `xunits` to x and `yunits` to y:

```
if (moves > 0 ) {
    moves--;
```

```
        ball.x += xunits;
        ball.y += yunits;
    }
```

Now that our values have been updated, we simply draw the ball at the x and y coordinates specified by the x and y properties, and we are done—that is, until `drawScreen()` is called 33 milliseconds later:

```
context.fillStyle = "#000000";
context.beginPath();
context.arc(ball.x,ball.y,15,0,Math.PI*2,true);
context.closePath();
context.fill();
```

Let's try the example by executing it in a web browser. You can find it in the code distribution as *CH5EX2.html*, or you can type in Example 5-2. Watch the ball move from one point to another. If you update the *x* and *y* values of each point, or change the speed, watch the results. You can do a lot with this very simple example.

Tracing movement: A path of points

For many of the examples in this chapter, we will create a way to trace an object's movement on the canvas by drawing points to show its path. We have done this to help illustrate how objects move. However, in the real world, you would need to remove this functionality so that your application will perform to its potential. This is the only place we will discuss this code, so if you see it listed in any of the later examples in this chapter, refer back to this section to refresh your memory on its functionality.

First, we create an array in `canvasApp()` to hold the set of points we will draw on the canvas:

```
var points = new Array();
```

Next, we load a black 4×4 pixel image, *point.png*, which we will use to display the points on the canvas:

```
var pointImage = new Image();
pointImage.src = "point.png";
```

Whenever we calculate a point for an object we will move, we push that point into the `points` array:

```
points.push({x:ball.x,y:ball.y});
```

On each call to `drawScreen()`, we draw the set of points we have put into the `points` array. Remember, we have to redraw every point each time because the canvas is an immediate-mode display surface that does not retain any information about the images drawn onto it:

```
for (var i = 0; i< points.length; i++) {
    context.drawImage(pointImage, points[i].x, points[i].y,1,1);
}
```

In Figure 5-2, you can see what the ball looks like when moving on a line from one point to another and also what the `points` path looks like when it is drawn.

 This is the only time in this chapter where we will discuss the `points` path in depth. If you see the points being drawn, you will know how and why we have added that functionality. You should also have enough information to remove the code when necessary.

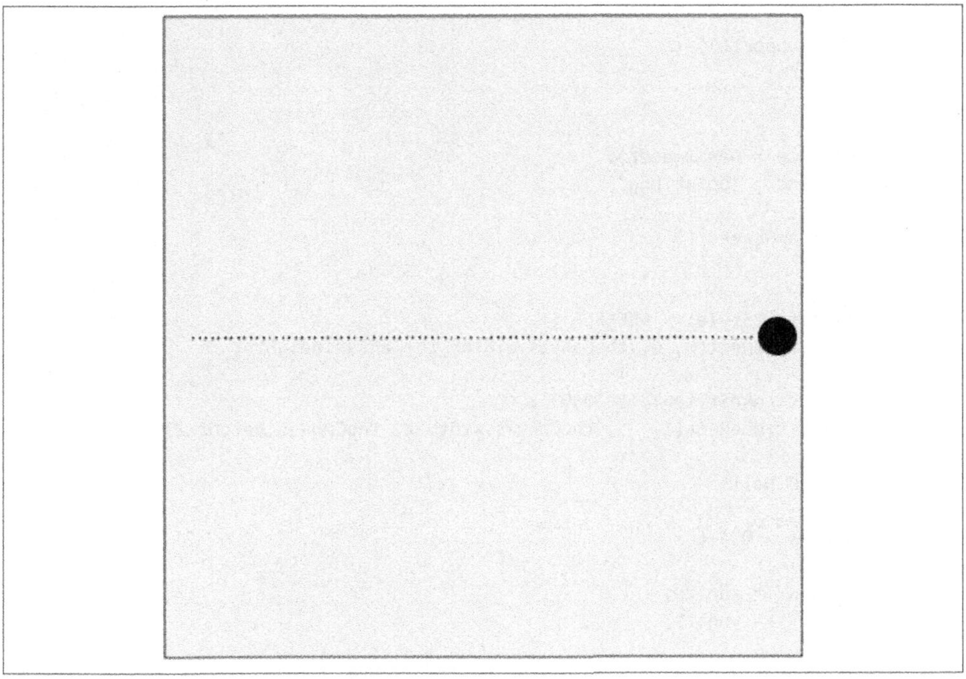

Figure 5-2. A ball moving from one point to another along the line, with the points drawn for illustration

Example 5-2 is the full code listing for *CH5EX2.html*.

Example 5-2. Moving on a simple line

```
<!doctype html>
<html lang="en">
<head>
```

```
<meta charset="UTF-8">
<title>CH5EX2: Moving On A Simple Line</title>

<script src="modernizr.js"></script>
<script type="text/javascript">
window.addEventListener('load', eventWindowLoaded, false);
function eventWindowLoaded() {
   canvasApp();

}

function canvasSupport () {
    return Modernizr.canvas;
}

function canvasApp() {

  if (!canvasSupport()) {
        return;
      }

  var pointImage = new Image();
  pointImage.src = "point.png";

  function  drawScreen () {


      context.fillStyle = '#EEEEEE';
      context.fillRect(0, 0, theCanvas.width, theCanvas.height);
      //Box
      context.strokeStyle = '#000000';
      context.strokeRect(1,  1, theCanvas.width-2, theCanvas.height-2);

      // Create ball

      if (moves > 0 ) {
         moves--;
         ball.x += xunits;
         ball.y += yunits;
      }

      //Draw points to illustrate path

      points.push({x:ball.x,y:ball.y});

      for (var i = 0; i< points.length; i++) {
         context.drawImage(pointImage, points[i].x, points[i].y,1,1);

      }

      context.fillStyle = "#000000";
      context.beginPath();
      context.arc(ball.x,ball.y,15,0,Math.PI*2,true);
```

```
        context.closePath();
        context.fill();

    }
    var speed = 5;
    var p1 = {x:20,y:250};
    var p2 = {x:480,y:250};
    var dx = p2.x - p1.x;
    var dy = p2.y - p1.y;
    var distance = Math.sqrt(dx*dx + dy*dy);
    var moves = distance/speed;
    var xunits = (p2.x - p1.x)/moves;
    var yunits = (p2.y - p1.y)/moves;
    var ball = {x:p1.x, y:p1.y};
    var points = new Array();

    theCanvas = document.getElementById("canvasOne");
    context = theCanvas.getContext("2d");

    function gameLoop() {
      window.setTimeout(gameLoop, 20);
      drawScreen()
    }
    gameLoop();


}

</script>

</head>
<body>
<div style="position: absolute; top: 50px; left: 50px;">

<canvas id="canvasOne" width="500" height="500">
 Your browser does not support HTML5 Canvas.
</canvas>
</div>
</body>
</html>
```

Moving on a Vector

Moving between two points is handy, but sometimes you don't have a point to move to, only a point to start from. In cases like this, it can be very useful to create a vector as a means to move your object.

A *vector* is a quantity in physics that has both magnitude and direction. For our purposes, the magnitude will be the speed value of the moving object, and the direction will be an angle value that the object will move upon.

The good news is that moving on a vector is very similar to moving between two points. In `canvasApp()`, we first set our `speed` value (magnitude). This is the number of pixels the object will move on every call to `drawScreen()`. We will set this to 5. We will also set the starting point (`p1`) for the object to 20,20:

```
var speed = 5;
var p1 = {x:20,y:20};
```

Now, we will set the `angle` value (direction) of movement for our object to 45 degrees. In mathematics, a flat, straight line usually represents the 0 angle, which means a vector with an angle of 45 degrees would be down and to the right on the canvas.

With our angle set, we now need to convert it to radians. Radians are a standard unit of angle measurement, and most mathematical calculations require you to convert an angle into radians before you can use it.

So why not just use radians and forget degrees altogether? Because it is much easier to understand movement in degrees when working with vectors and moving objects on a 2D surface. While a circle has 360 degrees, it has just about 6 radians, which are calculated counterclockwise. This might make perfect sense to mathematicians, but to move objects on a computer screen, angles are much easier. Therefore, we will work with angles, but we still need to convert our 45-degree angle into radians. We do that with a standard formula: `radians = angle * Math.PI/ 180`. And in the code:

```
var angle = 45;
var radians = angle * Math.PI/ 180;
```

Before we can discuss how we calculate the movement of our object along our vector, we need to review a couple trigonometric concepts. These are *cosine* and *sine*, and both relate to the arc created by our `angle` (now converted to `radians`), if it was drawn outward from the center of the circle.

cosine
> The angle measured counterclockwise from the x-axis (`x`)

sine
> The vertical coordinate of the arc endpoint (`y`)

You can see how these values relate to a 45-degree angle in Figure 5-3.

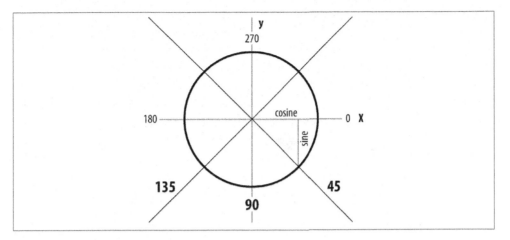

Figure 5-3. Angles on the canvas

This might seem complicated, but there is a very simple way to think about it: cosine usually deals with the x value, and sine usually deals with the y value. We can use sine and cosine to help us calculate movement along our vector.

To calculate the number of pixels to move our object on each call to drawScreen() (xunits and yunits), we use the radians (direction) we calculated and speed (magnitude), along with the Math.cos() (cosine) and Math.sin() (sine) functions of the JavaScript Math object:

```
var xunits = Math.cos(radians) * speed;
var yunits = Math.sin(radians) * speed;
```

In drawScreen(), we simply add xunits and yunits to ball.x and ball.y:

```
ball.x += xunits;
ball.y += yunits;
```

We don't check to see whether moves has been exhausted because we are not moving to a particular point—we are simply moving along the vector, seemingly forever. In the next section, we will explore what we can do if we want the moving object to change direction when it hits something, such as a wall.

Figure 5-4 shows what Example 5-3 looks like when it is executed in a web browser. Recall that the points are drawn for illustration only.

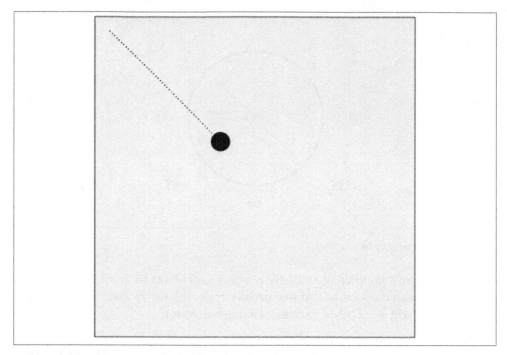

Figure 5-4. Moving an object on a vector

Example 5-3 gives the full code listing.

Example 5-3. Moving on a vector

```html
<!doctype html>
<html lang="en">
<head>
<meta charset="UTF-8">
<title>CH5EX3: Moving On A Vector</title>

<script src="modernizr.js"></script>
<script type="text/javascript">
window.addEventListener('load', eventWindowLoaded, false);
function eventWindowLoaded() {
   canvasApp();
}

function canvasSupport () {
    return Modernizr.canvas;
}

function canvasApp() {

  if (!canvasSupport()) {
        return;
      }
```

```javascript
var pointImage = new Image();
pointImage.src = "point.png";

function  drawScreen () {

    context.fillStyle = '#EEEEEE';
    context.fillRect(0, 0, theCanvas.width, theCanvas.height);
    //Box
    context.strokeStyle = '#000000';
    context.strokeRect(1,  1, theCanvas.width-2, theCanvas.height-2);

    ball.x += xunits;
    ball.y += yunits;

    //Draw points to illustrate path

    points.push({x:ball.x,y:ball.y});

    for (var i = 0; i< points.length; i++) {
       context.drawImage(pointImage, points[i].x, points[i].y,1,1);
    }

    context.fillStyle = "#000000";
    context.beginPath();
    context.arc(ball.x,ball.y,15,0,Math.PI*2,true);
    context.closePath();
    context.fill();

}   var speed = 5;
var p1 = {x:20,y:20};
var angle = 45;
var radians = angle * Math.PI/ 180;
var xunits = Math.cos(radians) * speed;
var yunits = Math.sin(radians) * speed;
var ball = {x:p1.x, y:p1.y};
var points = new Array();

theCanvas = document.getElementById("canvasOne");
context = theCanvas.getContext("2d");

function gameLoop() {
  window.setTimeout(gameLoop, 20);
  drawScreen()
}
gameLoop();


}

</script>
```

```
</head>
<body>
<div style="position: absolute; top: 50px; left: 50px;">

<canvas id="canvasOne" width="500" height="500">
 Your browser does not support HTML5 Canvas.
</canvas>
</div>
</body>
</html>
```

Bouncing Off Walls

While it's neat that we can create a vector with magnitude and direction and then move an object along it infinitely, it's probably not something you will need to do all that often. Most of the time, you will want to see that object react to the world around it by bouncing off horizontal and vertical walls, for example.

To help you understand how to do this, there is a simple rule in physics. Although this rule is usually applied to rays of light, it can be very useful when animating 2D objects —especially when they are bouncing off horizontal and vertical walls. This rule is known as *the angle of reflection*:

> The angle of incidence is equal to the angle of reflection.

The *angle of incidence* is the angle an object is traveling when it hits the walls, and the *angle of reflection* is the angle it travels after it bounces off the wall.

Figure 5-5 illustrates that when an object hits a wall on a line that forms a 45-degree angle with a perpendicular line drawn to the point of impact, it will bounce off (reflect) at a similar 45-degree angle.

In the next section, we will create a series of examples using this rule to animate objects. The first, Example 5-4, will simply allow a single ball to bounce off the edges of the canvas.

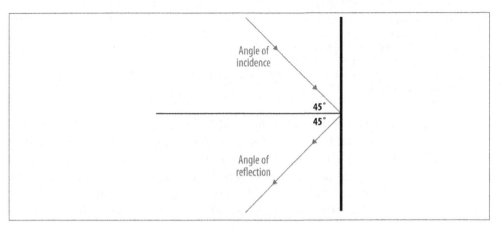

Figure 5-5. Angle of incidence is equal to the angle of reflection

Bouncing a Single Ball

In this first example, we will create a ball traveling on a vector. We will set the speed (magnitude) to 5 and the angle (direction) to 35 degrees. The rest of the variables are identical to those in Example 5-3. We are still moving on a vector, but now we will test to see whether the ball hits a "wall" (the edges of the canvas), in which case it will bounce off, using the rule of the angle of reflection. One big change from the previous vector example is the location in which we initialize the values for radians, xunits, and yunits. Instead of setting them up when we initialize the application in canvasApp(), we save that for a call to a new function named updateBall():

```
var speed = 5;
var p1 = {x:20,y:20};
var angle = 35;
var radians = 0;
var xunits = 0;
var yunits = 0;
var ball = {x:p1.x, y:p1.y};
updateBall();
```

The updateBall() function is called every time we set a new angle for the ball, because we need to recalculate the radians and find new values for xunits and yunits. A new angle value is generated when the app starts, as well as every time the ball bounces off a wall:

```
function updateBall() {
    radians = angle * Math.PI/ 180;
    xunits = Math.cos(radians) * speed;
    yunits = Math.sin(radians) * speed;
}
```

In drawScreen(), we update the position of the ball and then draw it on the canvas:

```
ball.x += xunits;
ball.y += yunits;
context.fillStyle = "#000000";
context.beginPath();
context.arc(ball.x,ball.y,15,0,Math.PI*2,true);
context.closePath();
context.fill();
```

Next, we test to see whether the ball has hit a wall before we draw it to the canvas. If the ball hits the right side (`ball.x > theCanvas.width`) or the left side (`ball.x < 0`) of the canvas, we set the angle to 180 degrees minus the angle of the vector on which the ball is traveling. This gives us the angle of reflection. Alternatively, if the ball hits the top (`ball.y < 0`) or bottom (`ball.y > theCanvas.height`) of the canvas, we calculate the angle of reflection as 360 degrees minus the angle of the vector on which the ball is traveling:

```
if (ball.x > theCanvas.width || ball.x < 0 ) {
      angle = 180 - angle;
      updateBall();
   } else if (ball.y > theCanvas.height || ball.y < 0) {
      angle = 360 - angle;
      updateBall();
   }
```

That's it. Example 5-4 demonstrates a ball that bounces off walls using the rules of physics. Figure 5-6 illustrates the code.

Example 5-4. Ball bounce

```
<!doctype html>
<html lang="en">
<head>
<meta charset="UTF-8">
<title>CH5EX4: Ball Bounce</title>

<script src="modernizr.js"></script>
<script type="text/javascript">
window.addEventListener('load', eventWindowLoaded, false);
function eventWindowLoaded() {
   canvasApp();
}

function canvasSupport () {
     return Modernizr.canvas;
}function canvasApp() {

  if (!canvasSupport()) {
        return;
      }

  function  drawScreen () {
      context.fillStyle = '#EEEEEE';
```

```
        context.fillRect(0, 0, theCanvas.width, theCanvas.height);
        //Box
        context.strokeStyle = '#000000';
        context.strokeRect(1,  1, theCanvas.width-2, theCanvas.height-2);
        ball.x += xunits;
        ball.y += yunits;
        context.fillStyle = "#000000";
        context.beginPath();
        context.arc(ball.x,ball.y,15,0,Math.PI*2,true);
        context.closePath();
        context.fill();

      if (ball.x > theCanvas.width || ball.x < 0 ) {
          angle = 180 - angle;
          updateBall();
      } else if (ball.y > theCanvas.height || ball.y < 0) {
          angle = 360 - angle;
          updateBall();
      }

    }

    function updateBall() {
        radians = angle * Math.PI/ 180;
        xunits = Math.cos(radians) * speed;
        yunits = Math.sin(radians) * speed;
    }

    var speed = 5;
    var p1 = {x:20,y:20};
    var angle = 35;
    var radians = 0;
    var xunits = 0;
    var yunits = 0;
    var ball = {x:p1.x, y:p1.y};
    updateBall();

    theCanvas = document.getElementById("canvasOne");
    context = theCanvas.getContext("2d");

    function gameLoop() {
      window.setTimeout(gameLoop, 20);
      drawScreen()
    }
    gameLoop();


}
</script>

</head>
<body>
<div style="position: absolute; top: 50px; left: 50px;">
```

```
<canvas id="canvasOne" width="500" height="500">
 Your browser does not support HTML5 Canvas.
</canvas>
</div>
</body>
</html>
```

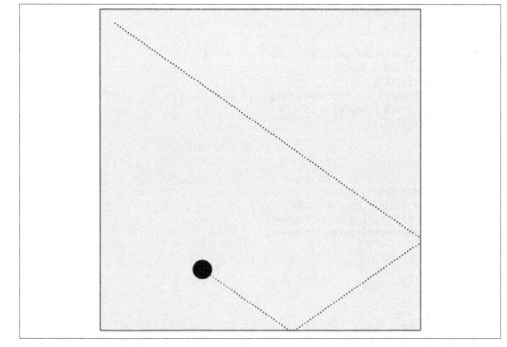

Figure 5-6. A single ball bouncing off a wall

 The points on the line are not drawn when executed in the web browser because they slow down the ball far too much. We left them in Figure 5-6 to illustrate the angles of incidence and reflection.

Multiple Balls Bouncing Off Walls

One ball is cool, but what about 100? Is the code 100 times more complicated? No, not at all. In fact, the code is only slightly more complicated, but it is also more refined. Most programming tasks that require only a single object of a type tend to allow you to be a bit lazy. However, when you need to build an application that must support *n* number of objects, you need to make sure the code will work in many different cases.

In the case of 100 balls bouncing on the canvas, we will need to create a ball object with a few more properties. Recall that the ball object we created previously had only x and y properties and looked like this:

```
var ball = {x:p1.x, y:p1.y};
```

All the other variables that represented the ball (speed, angle, xunits, yunits) were global in scope to the canvasApp(). We used global variables because we could get away with it. However, because we need to make sure everything works the same way in this app, we make all those values properties of each ball object.

For the multiple-ball-bounce application, we will create an object that holds all the pertinent information about each bouncing ball: x, y, speed, angle, xunits, and yunits. Because we are going to create 100 balls of various sizes, we also add a property named radius, which represents the size of the ball (well, half the size because it *is* a radius):

```
tempBall = {x:tempX,y:tempY,radius:tempRadius, speed:tempSpeed,
            angle:tempAngle, xunits:tempXunits, yunits:tempYunits}
```

Inside canvasApp(), we define some new variables to help manage the multiple balls that will bounce around the canvas:

numBalls
: The number of balls to randomly create

maxSize
: The maximum radius length for any given ball

minSize
: The minimum radius length for any given ball

maxSpeed
: The maximum speed any ball can travel

balls
: An array to hold all of the ball objects we will create

The following code shows the newly defined variables:

```
var numBalls = 100 ;
var maxSize = 8;
var minSize = 5;
var maxSpeed = maxSize+5;
var balls = new Array();
```

We also create a set of temporary variables to hold the values for each ball before we push it into the balls array:

```
var tempBall;
var tempX;
var tempY;
```

```
var tempSpeed;
var tempAngle;
var tempRadius;
var tempRadians;
var tempXunits;
var tempYunits;
```

Next, in `canvasApp()`, we iterate through a loop to create all the ball objects. Notice how `tempX` and `tempY` are created below. These values represent the ball's starting location on the canvas. We create a random value for each, but we offset it by the size of the ball (`tempRadius*2`). If we did not do that, some of the balls would get "stuck" in a wall when the app starts because their x or y location would be "through" the wall, but their `speed` would not be enough so that a "bounce" would get them back on the playfield. They would be stuck in bouncing limbo forever (which is kind of sad when you think about it).

When you try this app, you will see that occasionally a ball still gets stuck in a wall. There is a further optimization we need to make to prevent this, but it is a bigger subject than this little iteration. We will talk about it in the section "Multiple Balls Bouncing and Colliding" on page 219.

The `tempSpeed` variable is created by subtracting the value of `tempRadius` from the value of `maxSpeed`, which we created earlier. The `speed` is not random, but it is inversely proportional to the size (radius) of the ball. A larger ball has a larger radius, so the value you subtract from `tempSpeed` will be larger, thus making the ball move more slowly.

When you run *CH5EX5.html* in your web browser, you will notice that this little trick makes the ball appear more "real" because your brain expects larger objects to move more slowly.

```
for (var i = 0; i < numBalls; i++) {
    tempRadius = Math.floor(Math.random()*maxSize)+minSize;
    tempX = tempRadius*2 + (Math.floor(Math.random()*theCanvas.width)
            -tempRadius*2);
    tempY = tempRadius*2 + (Math.floor(Math.random()*theCanvas.height)
            -tempRadius*2);
    tempSpeed = maxSpeed-tempRadius;
    tempAngle = Math.floor(Math.random()*360);
    tempRadians = tempAngle * Math.PI/ 180;
    tempXunits = Math.cos(tempRadians) * tempSpeed;
    tempYunits = Math.sin(tempRadians) * tempSpeed;

    tempBall = {x:tempX,y:tempY,radius:tempRadius, speed:tempSpeed,
```

```
            angle:tempAngle,
        xunits:tempXunits, yunits:tempYunits}
      balls.push(tempBall);
  }
```

Now we need to draw the balls onto the canvas. Inside drawScreen(), the code to draw the balls should look very familiar because it is essentially the same code we used for one ball in Example 5-4. We just need to loop through the balls array to render each ball object:

```
for (var i = 0; i <balls.length; i++) {
        ball = balls[i];
        ball.x += ball.xunits;
        ball.y += ball.yunits;

        context.beginPath();
        context.arc(ball.x,ball.y,ball.radius,0,Math.PI*2,true);
        context.closePath();
        context.fill();

        if (ball.x > theCanvas.width || ball.x < 0 ) {
           ball.angle = 180 - ball.angle;
           updateBall(ball);
        } else if (ball.y > theCanvas.height || ball.y < 0) {
           ball.angle = 360 - ball.angle;
           updateBall(ball);
        }
    }
```

When you load Example 5-5 in your web browser, you will see a bunch of balls all moving around the screen independently, as shown in Figure 5-7. For the fun of it, why not change the numBalls variable to 500 or 1,000? What does the canvas look like then?

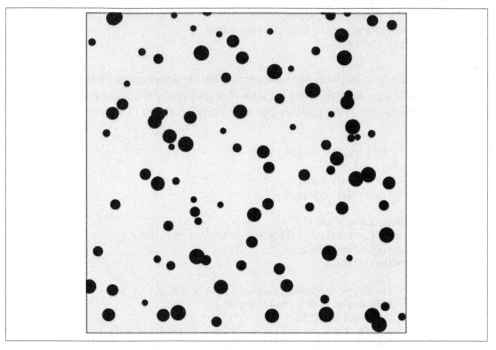

Figure 5-7. Multiple balls of different sizes bouncing off walls

Example 5-5. Multiple ball bounce

```
<!doctype html>
<html lang="en">
<head>
<meta charset="UTF-8">
<title>CH5EX5: Multiple Ball Bounce</title>

<script src="modernizr.js"></script>
<script type="text/javascript">
window.addEventListener('load', eventWindowLoaded, false);
function eventWindowLoaded() {
    canvasApp();
}

function canvasSupport () {
     return Modernizr.canvas;
}

function canvasApp() {   if (!canvasSupport()) {
          return;
        }

  function  drawScreen () {
```

```
        context.fillStyle = '#EEEEEE';
        context.fillRect(0, 0, theCanvas.width, theCanvas.height);

        //Box
        context.strokeStyle = '#000000';
        context.strokeRect(1,  1, theCanvas.width-2, theCanvas.height-2);

        //Place balls
        context.fillStyle = "#000000";
        var ball;

        for (var i = 0; i <balls.length; i++) {
            ball = balls[i];
            ball.x += ball.xunits;
            ball.y += ball.yunits;

            context.beginPath();
            context.arc(ball.x,ball.y,ball.radius,0,Math.PI*2,true);
            context.closePath();
            context.fill();

            if (ball.x > theCanvas.width || ball.x < 0 ) {
                ball.angle = 180 - ball.angle;
                updateBall(ball);
            } else if (ball.y > theCanvas.height || ball.y < 0) {
                ball.angle = 360 - ball.angle;
                updateBall(ball);
            }
        }

}

function updateBall(ball) {

    ball.radians = ball.angle * Math.PI/ 180;
    ball.xunits = Math.cos(ball.radians) * ball.speed;
    ball.yunits = Math.sin(ball.radians) * ball.speed;

}

var numBalls = 100 ;
var maxSize = 8;
var minSize = 5;
var maxSpeed = maxSize+5;
var balls = new Array();
var tempBall;
var tempX;
var tempY;
var tempSpeed;
var tempAngle;
var tempRadius;
var tempRadians;
```

```
    var tempXunits;
    var tempYunits;

    theCanvas = document.getElementById("canvasOne");
    context = theCanvas.getContext("2d");

    for (var i = 0; i < numBalls; i++) {
        tempRadius = Math.floor(Math.random()*maxSize)+minSize;
        tempX = tempRadius*2 + (Math.floor(Math.random()*theCanvas.width)-tempRadius*2);
        tempY = tempRadius*2 + (Math.floor(Math.random()*theCanvas.height)-tempRadius*2);
        tempSpeed = maxSpeed-tempRadius;
        tempAngle = Math.floor(Math.random()*360);
        tempRadians = tempAngle * Math.PI/ 180;
        tempXunits = Math.cos(tempRadians) * tempSpeed;
        tempYunits = Math.sin(tempRadians) * tempSpeed;

        tempBall = {x:tempX,y:tempY,radius:tempRadius, speed:tempSpeed, angle:tempAngle,
            xunits:tempXunits, yunits:tempYunits}
        balls.push(tempBall);
    }

    function gameLoop() {
        window.setTimeout(gameLoop, 20);
        drawScreen()
    }
    gameLoop();


    }


</script>

</head>
<body>
<div style="position: absolute; top: 50px; left: 50px;">

<canvas id="canvasOne" width="500" height="500">
 Your browser does not support HTML5 Canvas.
</canvas>
</div>
</body>
</html>
```

Multiple Balls Bouncing with a Dynamically Resized Canvas

Before we move on to more complex interaction among balls, let's try one more thing. Back in Chapter 3, we resized the canvas with some HTML5 form controls to display text in the center of the canvas. Well, let's do the same thing now with the ball example. This will give you a better idea of how we can make objects interact with a dynamically resizing canvas.

First, in the HTML, we create two HTML5 range controls, one for width and one for height, and set their maximum values to 1000. We will use these controls to set the width and height of the canvas at runtime:

```
<form>

  Canvas Width:  <input type="range" id="canvasWidth"
        min="0"
        max="1000"
        step="1"
        value="500"/>
  <br>
  Canvas Height:  <input type="range" id="canvasHeight"
        min="0"
        max="1000"
        step="1"
        value="500"/>
  <br>

</form>
```

In canvasApp(), we create the event listeners for the HTML5 form controls. We listen for the change event, which means that any time the range control is moved, the event handlers will be called:

```
formElement = document.getElementById("canvasWidth")
formElement.addEventListener('change', canvasWidthChanged, false);

formElement = document.getElementById("canvasHeight")
formElement.addEventListener('change', canvasHeightChanged, false);
```

The event handler functions capture the changes to the range, set theCanvas.width or theCanvas.height, and then call drawScreen() to render the new size. Without a call to drawScreen() here, the canvas will blink when the new size is applied in drawScreen() on the next interval:

```
function canvasWidthChanged(e) {
    var target = e.target;
    theCanvas.width = target.value;
    drawScreen();
}

function canvasHeightChanged(e) {
    var target = e.target;
    theCanvas.height = target.value;
    drawScreen();
}
```

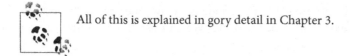

All of this is explained in gory detail in Chapter 3.

One last thing—let's increase the number of balls set in `canvasApp()` to 500:

```
var numBalls = 500 ;
```

Now, check out Example 5-6 (*CH5EX6.html* from the code distribution). When you run the code in a web browser, you should see 500 balls bounce around the canvas, as shown in Figure 5-8. When you increase the width or height using the `range` controls, they continue moving until they hit the new edge of the canvas. If you make the canvas smaller, the balls will be contained within the smaller space. If you adjust the size too rapidly, some balls will be lost off the canvas, but they will reappear when the canvas is resized. Neat, huh?

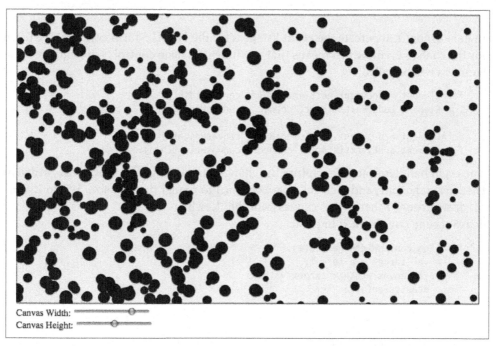

Figure 5-8. Multiple balls bouncing while the canvas is resized on the fly

Example 5-6. Multiple ball bounce with dynamically resized canvas

```
<!doctype html>
<html lang="en">
<head>
```

```
<meta charset="UTF-8">
<title>CH5EX6: Multiple Ball Bounce With Resize</title>

<script src="modernizr.js"></script>
<script type="text/javascript">
window.addEventListener('load', eventWindowLoaded, false);
function eventWindowLoaded() {
   canvasApp();
}function canvasSupport () {
     return Modernizr.canvas;
}

function canvasApp() {

  if (!canvasSupport()) {
        return;
      }

   formElement = document.getElementById("canvasWidth")
   formElement.addEventListener('change', canvasWidthChanged, false);

   formElement = document.getElementById("canvasHeight")
   formElement.addEventListener('change', canvasHeightChanged, false);

  function  drawScreen () {

      context.fillStyle = '#EEEEEE';
      context.fillRect(0, 0, theCanvas.width, theCanvas.height);
      //Box
      context.strokeStyle = '#000000';
      context.strokeRect(1,  1, theCanvas.width-2, theCanvas.height-2);

      //Place balls
      context.fillStyle = "#000000";
      var ball;

      for (var i = 0; i <balls.length; i++) {
         ball = balls[i];
         ball.x += ball.xunits;
         ball.y += ball.yunits;

         context.beginPath();
         context.arc(ball.x,ball.y,ball.radius,0,Math.PI*2,true);
         context.closePath();
         context.fill();

         if (ball.x > theCanvas.width || ball.x < 0 ) {
            ball.angle = 180 - ball.angle;
            updateBall(ball);
         } else if (ball.y > theCanvas.height || ball.y < 0) {
            ball.angle = 360 - ball.angle;
            updateBall(ball);
         }
```

```
        }

}

function updateBall(ball) {

    ball.radians = ball.angle * Math.PI/ 180;
    ball.xunits = Math.cos(ball.radians) * ball.speed;
    ball.yunits = Math.sin(ball.radians) * ball.speed;

}

var numBalls = 500 ;
var maxSize = 8;
var minSize = 5;
var maxSpeed = maxSize+5;
var balls = new Array();
var tempBall;
var tempX;
var tempY;
var tempSpeed;
var tempAngle;
var tempRadius;
var tempRadians;
var tempXunits;
var tempYunits;

theCanvas = document.getElementById("canvasOne");
context = theCanvas.getContext("2d");

for (var i = 0; i < numBalls; i++) {
    tempRadius = Math.floor(Math.random()*maxSize)+minSize;
    tempX = tempRadius*2 + (Math.floor(Math.random()*theCanvas.width)-tempRadius*2);
    tempY = tempRadius*2 + (Math.floor(Math.random()*theCanvas.height)-tempRadius*2);
    tempSpeed = maxSpeed-tempRadius;
    tempAngle = Math.floor(Math.random()*360);
    tempRadians = tempAngle * Math.PI/ 180;
    tempXunits = Math.cos(tempRadians) * tempSpeed;
    tempYunits = Math.sin(tempRadians) * tempSpeed;

    tempBall = {x:tempX,y:tempY,radius:tempRadius, speed:tempSpeed, angle:tempAngle,
        xunits:tempXunits, yunits:tempYunits}
    balls.push(tempBall);
}

function gameLoop() {
  window.setTimeout(gameLoop, 20);
  drawScreen()
}
gameLoop();
```

```
    function canvasWidthChanged(e) {
        var target = e.target;
        theCanvas.width = target.value;
        drawScreen();
    }

    function canvasHeightChanged(e) {
        var target = e.target;
        theCanvas.height = target.value;
        drawScreen();
    }

}

</script>

</head>
<body>
<div style="position: absolute; top: 50px; left: 50px;">

<canvas id="canvasOne" width="500" height="500">
 Your browser does not support HTML5 Canvas.
</canvas>
<form>

 Canvas Width:   <input type="range" id="canvasWidth"
        min="0"
        max="1000"
        step="1"
        value="500"/>
 <br>
 Canvas Height:  <input type="range" id="canvasHeight"
        min="0"
        max="1000"
        step="1"
        value="500"/>
 <br>

</form>
</div>
</body>
</html>
```

Multiple Balls Bouncing and Colliding

Now it's time to step it up again. Testing balls bouncing off walls is one thing, but what about balls bouncing off one another? We will need to add some pretty intricate code to handle this type of interaction.

Ball interactions in physics

For this example, we are going to create an *elastic collision*, which means that the total kinetic energy of the objects is the same before and after the collision. This is known as the *law of conservation of momentum* (Newton's third law). To do this, we will take the *x* and *y* velocities of two colliding balls, and draw a "line of action" between their centers. This is illustrated in Figure 5-9, which has been adapted from Jobe Makar and Ben Winiarczyk's *Macromedia's Flash MX 2004 Game Design Demystified* (Macromedia Press). Then we will create new *x* and *y* velocities for each ball based on this angle and the law of conservation of momentum.

To properly calculate conservation of momentum when balls collide on the canvas, we need to add a new property: mass. Mass is the measurement of how much a ball (or any object) resists any change in its velocity. Because collisions tend to change the velocity of objects, this is an important addition to the ball objects we will use on the canvas.

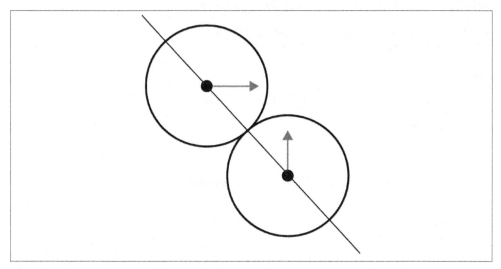

Figure 5-9. Two balls colliding at different angles with a line of action drawn between them

Making sure the balls don't start on top of each other

We will work from the code we created for Example 5-6 (*CH5EX6.html*). The first big change to that code is to make sure the balls don't randomly start on top of one another. If we let them start in the same location, they would be forever intertwined and would spin off into oblivion. To be honest, it looks pretty cool when that happens, but that's not the result we are looking to achieve.

In canvasApp(), we set a variable named tempRadius to 5. We will use this value as the radius for each ball we create. Next, we create another new variable named placeOK and

---

set it to `false`. When this is equal to `true`, we know we have found a place to put a ball that is not on top of another ball.

Next, we enter a `while()` loop that will continue to iterate as long as `placeOK` is `false`. Then, we set all the values for our new ball object:

```
tempRadius = 5;
var placeOK = false;
while (!placeOK) {
tempX = tempRadius*3 + (Math.floor(Math.random()*theCanvas.width)-tempRadius*3);
tempY = tempRadius*3 + (Math.floor(Math.random()*theCanvas.height)-tempRadius*3);
tempSpeed = 4;
tempAngle = Math.floor(Math.random()*360);
tempRadians = tempAngle * Math.PI/ 180;
tempvelocityx = Math.cos(tempRadians) * tempSpeed;
tempvelocityy = Math.sin(tempRadians) * tempSpeed;
```

Now, we need to make a dynamic object out of the values we just created and place that object into the `tempBall` variable. This is where we create a `mass` property for each ball. Again, we do this so that we can calculate the effect when the balls hit one another. For all the balls in this example, the `mass` will be the same—the value of `tempRadius`. We do this because, in our 2D environment, the relative size of each ball is a very simple way to create a value for `mass`. Because the `mass` and `speed` of each ball will be the same, they will affect each other in a similar way. Later we will show you what happens when we create ball objects with different `mass` values.

Finally, we create `nextX` and `nextY` properties that are equal to x and y. We will use these values as "look ahead" properties to help alleviate collisions that occur "between" our iterations, which lead to overlapping balls and other oddities:

```
tempBall = {x:tempX,y:tempY, nextX: tempX, nextY: tempY, radius:tempRadius,
    speed:tempSpeed, angle:tempAngle, velocityx:tempvelocityx,
    velocityy:tempvelocityy, mass:tempRadius};
```

Now that we have our new dynamic ball object represented by the `tempBall` variable, we will test to see whether it can be placed at the `tempX` and `tempY` we randomly created for it. We will do this with a call to a new function named `canStartHere()`. If `canStartHere()` returns `true`, we drop out of the `while()` loop; if not, we start all over again:

```
        placeOK = canStartHere(tempBall);
    }
```

The `canStartHere()` function is very simple. It looks through the `ball` array, testing the new `tempBall` against all existing balls to see whether they overlap. If they do, the function returns `false`; if not, it returns `true`. To test the overlap, we have created another new function: `hitTestCircle()`:

```
function canStartHere(ball) {
    var retval = true;
    for (var i = 0; i <balls.length; i++) {
        if (hitTestCircle(ball, balls[i])) {
```

```
            retval = false;
        }
      }
      return retval;
    }
```

Circle collision detection

The hitTestCircle() function performs a circle/circle collision-detection test to see whether the two circles (each representing a ball) passed as parameters to the function are touching. Because we have been tracking the balls by the center x and y of their location, this is quite easy to calculate. First, the function finds the distance of the line that connects the center of each circle. We do this using our old friend the Pythagorean theorem $(A^2+B^2 = C^2)$. We use the nextx and nexty properties of the ball because we want to test the collision before it occurs. (Again, if we test after by using the current x and y locations, there is a good chance the balls will get stuck together and spin out of control.) We then compare that distance value to the sum of the radius of each ball. If the distance is less than or equal to the sum of the radii, we have a collision. This is a very simple and efficient way to test collisions, and it works especially well with collisions among balls in 2D:

```
function hitTestCircle(ball1,ball2) {
    var retval = false;
    var dx = ball1.nextx - ball2.nextx;
    var dy = ball1.nexty - ball2.nexty;
    var distance = (dx * dx + dy * dy);
    if (distance <= (ball1.radius + ball2.radius) *
                    (ball1.radius + ball2.radius) ) {
        retval = true;
     }
    return retval;
  }
```

Figure 5-10 illustrates this code.

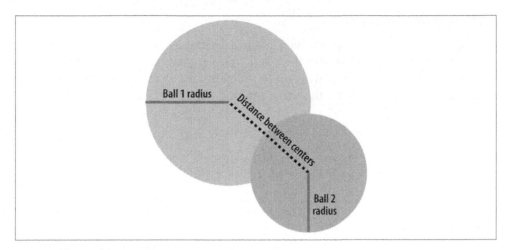

Figure 5-10. Balls colliding

Separating the code in drawScreen()

The next thing we want to do is simplify drawScreen() by separating the code into controllable functions. The idea here is that to test collisions correctly, we need to make sure some of our calculations are done in a particular order. We like to call this an *update-collide-render cycle.*

update()
> Sets the nextx and nexty properties of all the balls in the balls array.

testWalls()
> Tests to see whether the balls have hit one of the walls.

collide()
> Tests collisions among balls. If the balls collide, updates nextx and nexty.

render()
> Makes the x and y properties for each ball equal to nextx and nexty, respectively, and then draws them to the canvas.

And here is the code:

```
function  drawScreen () {

    update();
    testWalls();
    collide();
    render();

    }
```

Updating positions of objects

The `update()` function loops through all the balls in the `balls` array and updates the `nextx` and `nexty` properties with the x and y velocity for each ball. We don't directly update x and y here, because we want to test collisions against walls and other balls before they occur. We will use the `nextx` and `nexty` properties for this purpose:

```
function update() {
    for (var i = 0; i <balls.length; i++) {
        ball = balls[i];
        ball.nextx = (ball.x += ball.velocityx);
        ball.nexty = (ball.y += ball.velocityy);
    }
}
```

Better interaction with the walls

We discussed the interactions between balls and walls in the last example, but there is still one issue. Because we move the balls by the x and y location of their center, the balls would move halfway off the canvas before a bounce occurred. To fix this, we add or subtract the `radius` of the `ball` object, depending on which walls we are testing. For the right side and bottom of the canvas, we add the radius of the ball when we test the walls. In this way, the ball will appear to bounce exactly when its edge hits a wall. Similarly, we subtract the radius when we test the left side and the top of the canvas so that the ball does not move off the side before we make it bounce off a wall:

```
function testWalls() {
    var ball;
    var testBall;

    for (var i = 0; i <balls.length; i++) {
        ball = balls[i];

        if (ball.nextx+ball.radius > theCanvas.width) {
            ball.velocityx = ball.velocityx*-1;
            ball.nextx = theCanvas.width - ball.radius;          }
          else if (ball.nextx-ball.radius < 0 ) {
            ball.velocityx = ball.velocityx*-1;
            ball.nextx = ball.radius;

        } else if (ball.nexty+ball.radius > theCanvas.height ) {
            ball.velocityy = ball.velocityy*-1;
            ball.nexty = theCanvas.height - ball.radius;

        } else if(ball.nexty-ball.radius < 0) {
            ball.velocityy = ball.velocityy*-1;
            ball.nexty = ball.radius;
        }
    }
}
```

Collisions with balls

The `collide()` function tests to see whether any balls have hit another. This function uses two nested loops, both iterating through the `balls` array to ensure that we test each ball against every other ball. We take the ball from the first loop of the `balls` array and place it into the `ball` variable. Then we loop through `balls` again, placing each ball in the `testBall` variable, one at a time. When we have both `ball` and `testBall`, we make sure that they are not equal to one another. We do this because a ball will always have a false positive collision if we test it against itself. When we are sure that they are not the same ball, we call `hitTestCircle()` to test for a collision. If we find one, we call `colli deBalls()`, and then all heck breaks loose. (OK, not really, but the balls do collide, and some really interesting code gets executed.) See that code here:

```
function collide() {
    var ball;
    var testBall;
    for (var i = 0; i <balls.length; i++) {
        ball = balls[i];
        for (var j = i+1; j < balls.length; j++) {
            testBall = balls[j];
            if (hitTestCircle(ball,testBall)) {
                collideBalls(ball,testBall);
            }
        }
    }
}
```

Ball collisions in depth

So now we get to the most interesting code of this example. We are going to update the properties of each ball so that they appear to bounce off one another. Recall that we use the `nextx` and `nexty` properties because we want to make sure to test where the balls will be after they are drawn—not where they are right now. This helps keep the balls from overlapping in a way that will make them stick together.

 Sometimes the balls will still stick together. This is a common problem when creating collisions among balls. This happens when balls overlap one another before the collision test, and the reaction bounce is not enough to split them apart completely. We have made every attempt to optimize this function for the canvas, but we are sure further optimizations are possible.

The `collideBalls()` function takes two parameters: `ball1` and `ball2`. Both parameters are the `ball` objects that we want to make collide:

```
function collideBalls(ball1,ball2) {
```

First, we need to calculate the difference between the center points of each ball. We store this as dx and dy (difference *x* and difference *y*). This should look familiar because we did something similar when we tested for a collision between the balls. The difference is that now we know they have collided, and we want to know how that collision occurred:

```
var dx = ball1.nextx - ball2.nextx;
var dy = ball1.nexty - ball2.nexty;
```

To do this, we need to find the angle of the collision using the `Math.atan2()` function. This function gives us the angle in radians of the collisions between the two balls. This is the line of action or angle of collision. We need this value so that we can determine how the balls will react when they collide:

```
var collisionAngle = Math.atan2(dy, dx);
```

Next we calculate the velocity vector for each ball given the x and y velocities that existed before the collision occurred:

```
var speed1 = Math.sqrt(ball1.velocityx * ball1.velocityx +
    ball1.velocityy *   ball1.velocityy);
var speed2 = Math.sqrt(ball2.velocityx * ball2.velocityx +
    ball2.velocityy * ball2.velocityy);
```

Then, we calculate angles (in radians) for each ball given its current velocities:

```
var direction1 = Math.atan2(ball1.velocityy, ball1.velocityx);
var direction2 = Math.atan2(ball2.velocityy, ball2.velocityx);
```

Next we need to rotate the vectors counterclockwise so that we can plug those values into the equation for conservation of momentum. Basically, we are taking the angle of collision and making it flat so that we can bounce the balls, similar to how we bounced balls off the sides of the canvas:

```
var velocityx_1 = speed1 * Math.cos(direction1 - collisionAngle);
var velocityy_1 = speed1 * Math.sin(direction1 - collisionAngle);
var velocityx_2 = speed2 * Math.cos(direction2 - collisionAngle);
var velocityy_2 = speed2 * Math.sin(direction2 - collisionAngle);
```

We take the `mass` values of each ball and update their x and y velocities based on the law of conservation of momentum. To find the final velocity for both balls, we use the following formulas:

```
velocity1 = ((mass1 - mass2) * velocity1 + 2*mass2 * velocity2) / mass1 + mass2
velocity2 = ((mass2 - mass1) * velocity2 + 2*mass1 * velocity1)/ mass1+ mass2
```

Actually, only the x velocity needs to be updated; the y velocity remains constant:

```
var final_velocityx_1 = ((ball1.mass - ball2.mass) * velocityx_1 +
    (ball2.mass + ball2.mass) * velocityx_2)/(ball1.mass + ball2.mass);
var final_velocityx_2 = ((ball1.mass + ball1.mass) * velocityx_1 +
    (ball2.mass - ball1.mass) * velocityx_2)/(ball1.mass + ball2.mass);
```

```
var final_velocityy_1 = velocityy_1;
var final_velocityy_2 = velocityy_2
```

After we have our final velocities, we rotate our angles back again so that the collision angle is preserved:

```
ball1.velocityx = Math.cos(collisionAngle) * final_velocityx_1 +
    Math.cos(collisionAngle + Math.PI/2) * final_velocityy_1;
ball1.velocityy = Math.sin(collisionAngle) * final_velocityx_1 +
    Math.sin(collisionAngle + Math.PI/2) * final_velocityy_1;
ball2.velocityx = Math.cos(collisionAngle) * final_velocityx_2 +
    Math.cos(collisionAngle + Math.PI/2) * final_velocityy_2;
ball2.velocityy = Math.sin(collisionAngle) * final_velocityx_2 +
    Math.sin(collisionAngle + Math.PI/2) * final_velocityy_2;
```

Now we update `nextx` and `nexty` for both balls so that we can use those values in the `render()` function—or for another collision:

```
ball1.nextx = (ball1.nextx += ball1.velocityx);
ball1.nexty = (ball1.nexty += ball1.velocityy);
ball2.nextx = (ball2.nextx += ball2.velocityx);
ball2.nexty = (ball2.nexty += ball2.velocityy);
}
```

 If this is confusing to you, you are not alone. It took some serious effort for us to translate this code from other sources into a working example on HTML5 Canvas. The code here is based on *Flash Lite Effort: Embedded Systems and Pervasive Computing Lab* by Felipe Sampaio (*http:// wiki.forum.nokia.com/index.php/Collision_for_Balls*). It is also partly based on Jobe Makar and Ben Winiarczyk's work in *Macromedia Flash MX 2004 Game Design Demystified*, and Keith Peters' books on ActionScript animation.

Here is the full code listing for Example 5-7.

Example 5-7. Balls with simple interactions

```
<!doctype html>
<html lang="en">
<head>
<meta charset="UTF-8">
<title>CH5EX7: Balls With Simple Interactions</title>

<script src="modernizr.js"></script>
<script type="text/javascript">
window.addEventListener('load', eventWindowLoaded, false);
function eventWindowLoaded() {
    canvasApp();

}
```

```
function canvasSupport () {
    return Modernizr.canvas;
}

function canvasApp() {

  if (!canvasSupport()) {
        return;
      }

  function  drawScreen () {

      context.fillStyle = '#EEEEEE';
      context.fillRect(0, 0, theCanvas.width, theCanvas.height);
      //Box
      context.strokeStyle = '#000000';
      context.strokeRect(1,  1, theCanvas.width-2, theCanvas.height-2);

      update();
      testWalls();
      collide();
      render();

  }

  function update() {
      for (var i = 0; i <balls.length; i++) {
        ball = balls[i];
        ball.nextx = (ball.x += ball.velocityx);
        ball.nexty = (ball.y += ball.velocityy);
      }

  }

  function testWalls() {
      var ball;
      var testBall;

      for (var i = 0; i <balls.length; i++) {
        ball = balls[i];

        if (ball.nextx+ball.radius > theCanvas.width) {
           ball.velocityx = ball.velocityx*-1;
           ball.nextx = theCanvas.width - ball.radius;

        } else if (ball.nextx-ball.radius < 0 ) {
           ball.velocityx = ball.velocityx*-1;
           ball.nextx =ball.radius;

        } else if (ball.nexty+ball.radius > theCanvas.height ) {
           ball.velocityy = ball.velocityy*-1;
           ball.nexty = theCanvas.height - ball.radius;
```

```
      } else if(ball.nexty-ball.radius < 0) {
         ball.velocityy = ball.velocityy*-1;
         ball.nexty = ball.radius;
      }


   }

}

function render() {
   var ball;
   context.fillStyle = "#000000";
   for (var i = 0; i <balls.length; i++) {
      ball = balls[i];
      ball.x = ball.nextx;
      ball.y = ball.nexty;

      context.beginPath();
      context.arc(ball.x,ball.y,ball.radius,0,Math.PI*2,true);
      context.closePath();
      context.fill();
   }

}

function collide() {
   var ball;
   var testBall;
   for (var i = 0; i <balls.length; i++) {
      ball = balls[i];
      for (var j = i+1; j < balls.length; j++) {
         testBall = balls[j];
         if (hitTestCircle(ball,testBall)) {
            collideBalls(ball,testBall);
         }
      }
   }
}

function hitTestCircle(ball1,ball2) {
   var retval = false;
   var dx = ball1.nextx - ball2.nextx;
   var dy = ball1.nexty - ball2.nexty;
   var distance = (dx * dx + dy * dy);
   if (distance <= (ball1.radius + ball2.radius) *
                 (ball1.radius + ball2.radius) )
   {
         retval = true;
   }
   return retval;
```

```
    }

function collideBalls(ball1,ball2) {

    var dx = ball1.nextx - ball2.nextx;
    var dy = ball1.nexty - ball2.nexty;

    var collisionAngle = Math.atan2(dy, dx);

    var speed1 = Math.sqrt(ball1.velocityx * ball1.velocityx +
        ball1.velocityy * ball1.velocityy);
    var speed2 = Math.sqrt(ball2.velocityx * ball2.velocityx +
        ball2.velocityy * ball2.velocityy);

    var direction1 = Math.atan2(ball1.velocityy, ball1.velocityx);
    var direction2 = Math.atan2(ball2.velocityy, ball2.velocityx);

    var velocityx_1 = speed1 * Math.cos(direction1 - collisionAngle);
    var velocityy_1 = speed1 * Math.sin(direction1 - collisionAngle);
    var velocityx_2 = speed2 * Math.cos(direction2 - collisionAngle);
    var velocityy_2 = speed2 * Math.sin(direction2 - collisionAngle);

    var final_velocityx_1 = ((ball1.mass - ball2.mass) * velocityx_1 +
        (ball2.mass + ball2.mass) * velocityx_2)/(ball1.mass + ball2.mass);
    var final_velocityx_2 = ((ball1.mass + ball1.mass) * velocityx_1 +
        (ball2.mass - ball1.mass) * velocityx_2)/(ball1.mass + ball2.mass);

    var final_velocityy_1 = velocityy_1;
    var final_velocityy_2 = velocityy_2;

    ball1.velocityx = Math.cos(collisionAngle) * final_velocityx_1 +
        Math.cos(collisionAngle + Math.PI/2) * final_velocityy_1;
    ball1.velocityy = Math.sin(collisionAngle) * final_velocityx_1 +
        Math.sin(collisionAngle + Math.PI/2) * final_velocityy_1;
    ball2.velocityx = Math.cos(collisionAngle) * final_velocityx_2 +
        Math.cos(collisionAngle + Math.PI/2) * final_velocityy_2;
    ball2.velocityy = Math.sin(collisionAngle) * final_velocityx_2 +
        Math.sin(collisionAngle + Math.PI/2) * final_velocityy_2;

    ball1.nextx = (ball1.nextx += ball1.velocityx);
    ball1.nexty = (ball1.nexty += ball1.velocityy);
    ball2.nextx = (ball2.nextx += ball2.velocityx);
    ball2.nexty = (ball2.nexty += ball2.velocityy);
}

var numBalls = 200 ;
var maxSize = 15;
var minSize = 5;
var maxSpeed = maxSize+5;
var balls = new Array();
var tempBall;
var tempX;
```

```
    var tempY;
    var tempSpeed;
    var tempAngle;
    var tempRadius;
    var tempRadians;
    var tempvelocityx;
    var tempvelocityy;

    theCanvas = document.getElementById("canvasOne");
    context = theCanvas.getContext("2d");

    for (var i = 0; i < numBalls; i++) {
        tempRadius = 5;
        var placeOK = false;
        while (!placeOK) {
            tempX = tempRadius*3 + (Math.floor(Math.random()*theCanvas.width)
                -tempRadius*3);
            tempY = tempRadius*3 + (Math.floor(Math.random()*theCanvas.height)
                -tempRadius*3);
            tempSpeed = 4;
            tempAngle = Math.floor(Math.random()*360);
            tempRadians = tempAngle * Math.PI/ 180;
            tempvelocityx = Math.cos(tempRadians) * tempSpeed;
            tempvelocityy = Math.sin(tempRadians) * tempSpeed;

            tempBall = {x:tempX,y:tempY, nextX: tempX, nextY: tempY, radius:tempRadius,
                speed:tempSpeed, angle:tempAngle, velocityx:tempvelocityx,
                velocityy:tempvelocityy, mass:tempRadius};
            placeOK = canStartHere(tempBall);
        }
        balls.push(tempBall);
    }

    function canStartHere(ball) {
        var retval = true;
        for (var i = 0; i <balls.length; i++) {
            if (hitTestCircle(ball, balls[i])) {
                retval = false;
            }
        }
        return retval;
    }
    function gameLoop() {
      window.setTimeout(gameLoop, 20);
      drawScreen()
    }
    gameLoop();

}

</script>
```

```
</head>
<body>
<div style="position: absolute; top: 50px; left: 50px;"><canvas id="canvasOne"
    width="500" height="500">
 Your browser does not support HTML5 Canvas.
</canvas>
</div>
</body>
</html>
```

Now, when you execute Example 5-7 (*CH5EX7.html*), you will see a bunch of balls of the same size and mass bumping off of each other and the walls of the canvas, as shown in Figure 5-10. When you look at this demo, imagine all the ways you could modify it to do different things. You could create balls with different masses and different speeds, or even create balls that don't move but simply alter the direction of other balls that hit them. In Figure 5-11, we will take a slightly different look at this same code and add some new properties to make it more interesting.

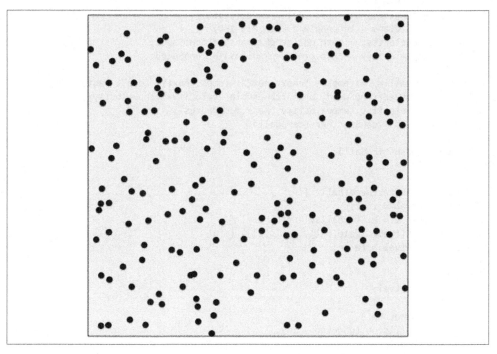

Figure 5-11. Balls of the same size bouncing off one another

Multiple Balls Bouncing with Friction

If we want the balls to slow down and eventually stop, we need to add friction to Example 5-7. For our purposes, simple friction is a value we use to modify the velocity of our objects every time they are drawn to the canvas.

In `canvasApp()`, we now want to create balls of various sizes. In the previous example, the balls were all the same size. It worked, but having balls of different sizes with different masses will create more interesting effects. To do this, we set `minSize` to 3 and `max Size` to 12, meaning that the radii for our balls will range from 3 to 12 pixels. We also add a new property named `friction`. This is a global property, so it will not be applied to each individual ball. We set it to `.01`, which means our balls will degrade their x and y velocities by `.01` pixels per frame (every time `drawScreen()` is called):

```
var numBalls = 50 ;
var maxSize = 12;
var minSize = 3;
var maxSpeed = maxSize+5;
var friction = .01;
```

We will now allow for various ball sizes. The mass of each ball will be different, and balls will have different effects on one another depending on their sizes. Recall that in Example 5-7 we needed a `mass` property so that we could calculate conservation of momentum when the balls collided. We are doing the same thing here, but now the masses are different depending on the size:

```
for (var i = 0; i < numBalls; i++) {
    tempRadius = Math.floor(Math.random()*maxSize)+minSize;
```

In `update()`, we apply the `friction` value by calculating the product of the current velocity multiplied by friction and then subtracting that value from the current velocity. We do this for both the x and y velocities. Why must we do this instead of simply subtracting the friction value from the x and y velocities? Because the x and y velocities are not always proportional to each other. If we simply subtract the friction, we might alter the velocity unintentionally. Instead, we need to subtract a value for the friction that is proportional to the velocity itself, and that value is the product of the velocity multiplied by the `friction` value. This method will give you a smooth degradation of the velocity when the `friction` value is applied:

```
function update() {
    for (var i = 0; i <balls.length; i++) {
        ball = balls[i];
        //Friction
        ball.velocityx = ball.velocityx - ( ball.velocityx*friction);
        ball.velocityy = ball.velocityy - ( ball.velocityy*friction);

        ball.nextx = (ball.x += ball.velocityx);
        ball.nexty = (ball.y += ball.velocityy);
    }
```

```
      }
```

You can see the full version of this code by executing *CH5EX8.html* from the code
distribution, or by typing in Example 5-8. You should notice that the smaller balls have
less of an effect on the larger balls when they collide, and vice versa. Also, the balls slow
down as they move, due to the applied friction.

Example 5-8. Balls with friction

```
<!doctype html>
<html lang="en">
<head>
<meta charset="UTF-8">
<title>CH5EX8: Balls With Friction</title>

<script src="modernizr.js"></script>
<script type="text/javascript">
window.addEventListener('load', eventWindowLoaded, false);
function eventWindowLoaded() {
    canvasApp();

}

function canvasSupport () {
      return Modernizr.canvas;
}

function canvasApp() {

    if (!canvasSupport()) {
        return;
        }

  function  drawScreen () {

      context.fillStyle = '#EEEEEE';
      context.fillRect(0, 0, theCanvas.width, theCanvas.height);
      //Box
      context.strokeStyle = '#000000';
      context.strokeRect(1,  1, theCanvas.width-2, theCanvas.height-2);

      update();
      testWalls();
      collide();
      render();

  }

  function update() {
     for (var i = 0; i <balls.length; i++) {
        ball = balls[i];
        //Friction
```

```
            ball.velocityx = ball.velocityx - ( ball.velocityx*friction);
            ball.velocityy = ball.velocityy - ( ball.velocityy*friction);

            ball.nextx = (ball.x += ball.velocityx);
            ball.nexty = (ball.y += ball.velocityy);
        }

    }

    function testWalls() {
        var ball;
        var testBall;

        for (var i = 0; i <balls.length; i++) {
            ball = balls[i];

            if (ball.nextx+ball.radius > theCanvas.width) {
                ball.velocityx = ball.velocityx*-1;
                ball.nextx = theCanvas.width - ball.radius;

            } else if (ball.nextx-ball.radius < 0 ) {
                ball.velocityx = ball.velocityx*-1;
                ball.nextx = ball.radius;

            } else if (ball.nexty+ball.radius > theCanvas.height ) {
                ball.velocityy = ball.velocityy*-1;
                ball.nexty = theCanvas.height - ball.radius;

            } else if(ball.nexty-ball.radius < 0) {
                ball.velocityy = ball.velocityy*-1;
                ball.nexty = ball.radius;
            }

        }

    }

    function render() {
        var ball;

        context.fillStyle = "#000000";
        for (var i = 0; i <balls.length; i++) {
            ball = balls[i];
            ball.x = ball.nextx;
            ball.y = ball.nexty;

            context.beginPath();
            context.arc(ball.x,ball.y,ball.radius,0,Math.PI*2,true);
            context.closePath();
            context.fill();
        }
```

```
}

function collide() {
    var ball;
    var testBall;
    for (var i = 0; i <balls.length; i++) {
        ball = balls[i];
        for (var j = i+1; j < balls.length; j++) {
            testBall = balls[j];
            if (hitTestCircle(ball,testBall)) {
                collideBalls(ball,testBall);
            }
        }
    }
}

function hitTestCircle(ball1,ball2) {
    var retval = false;
    var dx = ball1.nextx - ball2.nextx;
    var dy = ball1.nexty - ball2.nexty;
    var distance = (dx * dx + dy * dy);
    if (distance <= (ball1.radius + ball2.radius) * (ball1.radius + ball2.radius)
      ) {
            retval = true;
    }
    return retval;
}

function collideBalls(ball1,ball2) {

    var dx = ball1.nextx - ball2.nextx;
    var dy = ball1.nexty - ball2.nexty;

    var collisionAngle = Math.atan2(dy, dx);

    var speed1 = Math.sqrt(ball1.velocityx * ball1.velocityx +
        ball1.velocityy * ball1.velocityy);
    var speed2 = Math.sqrt(ball2.velocityx * ball2.velocityx +
        ball2.velocityy * ball2.velocityy);

    var direction1 = Math.atan2(ball1.velocityy, ball1.velocityx);
    var direction2 = Math.atan2(ball2.velocityy, ball2.velocityx);

    var velocityx_1 = speed1 * Math.cos(direction1 - collisionAngle);
    var velocityy_1 = speed1 * Math.sin(direction1 - collisionAngle);
    var velocityx_2 = speed2 * Math.cos(direction2 - collisionAngle);
    var velocityy_2 = speed2 * Math.sin(direction2 - collisionAngle);

    var final_velocityx_1 = ((ball1.mass - ball2.mass) * velocityx_1 +
        (ball2.mass + ball2.mass) * velocityx_2)/(ball1.mass + ball2.mass);
    var final_velocityx_2 = ((ball1.mass + ball1.mass) * velocityx_1 +
        (ball2.mass - ball1.mass) * velocityx_2)/(ball1.mass + ball2.mass);
```

```
        var final_velocityy_1 = velocityy_1;
        var final_velocityy_2 = velocityy_2;

        ball1.velocityx = Math.cos(collisionAngle) * final_velocityx_1 +
            Math.cos(collisionAngle + Math.PI/2) * final_velocityy_1;
        ball1.velocityy = Math.sin(collisionAngle) * final_velocityx_1 +
            Math.sin(collisionAngle + Math.PI/2) * final_velocityy_1;
        ball2.velocityx = Math.cos(collisionAngle) * final_velocityx_2 +
            Math.cos(collisionAngle + Math.PI/2) * final_velocityy_2;
        ball2.velocityy = Math.sin(collisionAngle) * final_velocityx_2 +
            Math.sin(collisionAngle + Math.PI/2) * final_velocityy_2;

        ball1.nextx = (ball1.nextx += ball1.velocityx);
        ball1.nexty = (ball1.nexty += ball1.velocityy);
        ball2.nextx = (ball2.nextx += ball2.velocityx);
        ball2.nexty = (ball2.nexty += ball2.velocityy);
}
var numBalls = 50 ;
var maxSize = 12;
var minSize = 3;
var maxSpeed = maxSize+5;
var balls = new Array();
var tempBall;
var tempX;
var tempY;
var tempSpeed;
var tempAngle;
var tempRadius;
var tempRadians;
var tempvelocityx;
var tempvelocityy;
var friction = .01;

theCanvas = document.getElementById("canvasOne");
context = theCanvas.getContext("2d");

for (var i = 0; i < numBalls; i++) {
    tempRadius = Math.floor(Math.random()*maxSize)+minSize;
    var placeOK = false;
    while (!placeOK) {
        tempX = tempRadius*3 + (Math.floor(Math.random()*theCanvas.width)
            -tempRadius*3);
        tempY = tempRadius*3 + (Math.floor(Math.random()*theCanvas.height)
            -tempRadius*3);
        tempSpeed = maxSpeed-tempRadius;
        tempAngle = Math.floor(Math.random()*360);
        tempRadians = tempAngle * Math.PI/ 180;
        tempvelocityx = Math.cos(tempRadians) * tempSpeed;
        tempvelocityy = Math.sin(tempRadians) * tempSpeed;

        tempBall = {x:tempX,y:tempY,radius:tempRadius, speed:tempSpeed,
```

```
                angle:tempAngle, velocityx:tempvelocityx, velocityy:tempvelocityy,
                mass:tempRadius*8, nextx: tempX, nexty:tempY};
            placeOK = canStartHere(tempBall);
        }
        balls.push(tempBall);
    }

    function canStartHere(ball) {
        var retval = true;
        for (var i = 0; i <balls.length; i++) {
            if (hitTestCircle(ball, balls[i])) {
                retval = false;
            }
        }
        return retval;
    }
    function gameLoop() {
        window.setTimeout(gameLoop, 20);
        drawScreen()
    }
    gameLoop();

}

</script>

</head>
<body>
<div style="position: absolute; top: 50px; left: 50px;">

<canvas id="canvasOne" width="500" height="500">
 Your browser does not support HTML5 Canvas.
</canvas>
</div>
</body>
</html>
```

Figure 5-12 illustrates how this code will look in the browser.

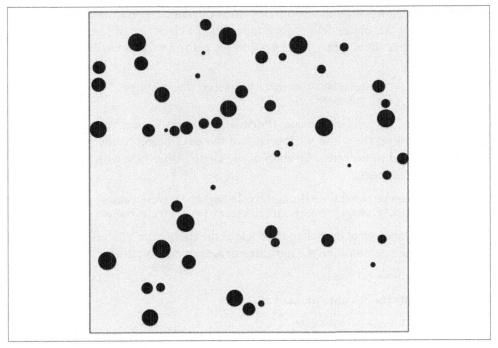

Figure 5-12. Multiple balls of different sizes bouncing off one another with friction applied

Curve and Circular Movement

Whew! Moving and colliding balls on vectors can create some cool effects. However, moving in straight lines is not the only way you might want to move objects. In this section, we will show you some ways to animate objects by using circles, spirals, and curves.

Uniform Circular Motion

Uniform circular motion occurs when we move an object along the distinct radius of a defined circle. When we know the radius, we can use our old friends cosine and sine to find the x and y locations of the moving object. The equations to find the locations of an object moving uniformly on a defined circle are as follows:

```
x = radius * cosine(angle)
y = radius * sine(angle)
```

We will create an example of uniform circular movement with a circle that has a radius of 125, with its center position at 250,250 on the canvas. We will move a ball along that circle, starting at an angle of 0.

In `canvasApp()`, we will define this circle path as a dynamic object stored in the `circle` variable. While this object defines the properties of a circle, we will not actually draw this circle on the canvas; rather, it defines only the path on which we will move our `ball` object:

```
var circle = {centerX:250, centerY:250, radius:125, angle:0}
var ball = {x:0, y:0,speed:.1};
```

In `drawScreen()`, we will incorporate the equations for uniform circular movement. To do this, we will set the x and y properties of the `ball` object to the products of the equations, added to the center location of the circle path on the canvas (`circle.cen terX`, `circle.centerY`):

```
ball.x = circle.centerX + Math.cos(circle.angle) * circle.radius;
ball.y = circle.centerY + Math.sin(circle.angle) * circle.radius;
```

We then add the speed of the ball to the angle of the circle path. This effectively sets the ball to move to a new location the next time `drawScreen()` is called:

```
circle.angle += ball.speed;
```

Finally, we draw the ball onto the canvas:

```
context.fillStyle = "#000000";
context.beginPath();
context.arc(ball.x,ball.y,15,0,Math.PI*2,true);
context.closePath();
context.fill();
```

You can see what the circle path looks like in Figure 5-13. We have drawn the points on the canvas to illustrate the circle path.

You can easily alter the location and size of the circle path by altering the `radius`, `centerX`, and `centerY` properties of the circle path object.

Example 5-9 shows the code for *CH5EX9.html.*

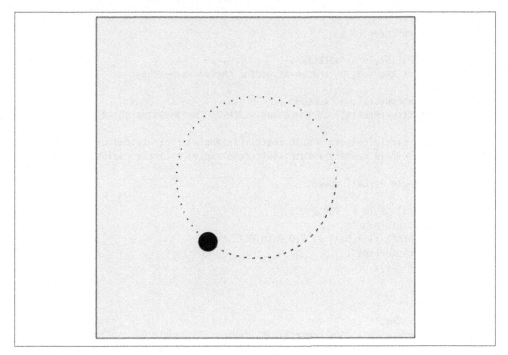

Figure 5-13. Moving an object in a circle

Example 5-9. Moving in a circle

```
<!doctype html>
<html lang="en">
<head>
<meta charset="UTF-8">
<title>CH5EX9: Moving In A Circle</title>

<script src="modernizr.js"></script>
<script type="text/javascript">
window.addEventListener('load', eventWindowLoaded, false);
function eventWindowLoaded() {
    canvasApp();

}

function canvasSupport () {
    return Modernizr.canvas;
}

function canvasApp() {

  if (!canvasSupport()) {
        return;
      }
```

```
    function  drawScreen () {

        context.fillStyle = '#EEEEEE';
        context.fillRect(0, 0, theCanvas.width, theCanvas.height);
        //Box
        context.strokeStyle = '#000000';
        context.strokeRect(1,  1, theCanvas.width-2, theCanvas.height-2);

        ball.x = circle.centerX + Math.cos(circle.angle) * circle.radius;
        ball.y = circle.centerY + Math.sin(circle.angle) * circle.radius;

        circle.angle += ball.speed;

        context.fillStyle = "#000000";
        context.beginPath();
        context.arc(ball.x,ball.y,15,0,Math.PI*2,true);
        context.closePath();
        context.fill();

    }

    var radius = 100;
    var circle = {centerX:250, centerY:250, radius:125, angle:0}
    var ball = {x:0, y:0,speed:.1};

    theCanvas = document.getElementById("canvasOne");
    context = theCanvas.getContext("2d");

function gameLoop() {
    window.setTimeout(gameLoop, 20);
    drawScreen()
    }
    gameLoop();

}

</script>

</head>
<body>
<div style="position: absolute; top: 50px; left: 50px;">

<canvas id="canvasOne" width="500" height="500">
 Your browser does not support HTML5 Canvas.
</canvas>
</div>
</body>
</html>
```

Moving in a Simple Spiral

There are many complicated ways to move an object on a spiral path. One such way would be to use the Fibonacci sequence, which describes a pattern seen in nature that appears to create perfect spirals. The Fibonacci sequence starts with the number 0, and continues with each subsequent number calculated as the sum of the two previous numbers in the sequence. Each subsequent rotation of the spiral is the sum of the two previous numbers (1, 2, 3, 5, 8, 13, 21, 34, 55, 89...). However, as you might imagine, the math used to create this sequence is quite involved, and it is also difficult to translate to object movement.

For our purposes, we can create a simple spiral by increasing the radius of the circle path on each call to drawScreen(). If we take the code from Example 5-9, we would add a radiusInc variable, which we will use as the value to add the radius movement path of the circle. We create this new variable in canvasApp():

```
var radiusInc = 2;
```

Then, in drawScreen(), we add the following code to increase the radius of the circle every time we move the object:

```
circle.radius += radiusInc;
```

In Figure 5-14, you can see what the resulting spiral looks like. (To illustrate the path, this example includes the points.)

If you want a tighter spiral, decrease the value of radiusInc. Conversely, if you want a wider spiral, increase the value of radiusInc.

Example 5-10 shows the code for *CH5EX10.html* from the code distribution.

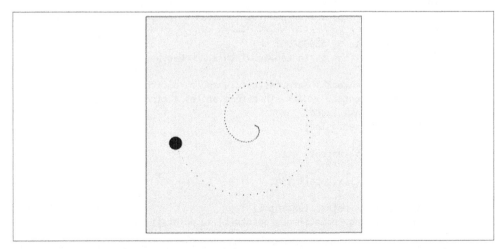

Figure 5-14. Moving an object in a simple spiral pattern

Example 5-10. Moving in a simple geometric spiral

```
<!doctype html>
<html lang="en">
<head>
<meta charset="UTF-8">
<title>CH5EX10: Moving In A Simple Geometric Spiral </title>

<script src="modernizr.js"></script>
<script type="text/javascript">
window.addEventListener('load', eventWindowLoaded, false);
function eventWindowLoaded() {
    canvasApp();

}

function canvasSupport () {
     return Modernizr.canvas;
}


function canvasApp() {

  if (!canvasSupport()) {
       return;
      }

  var pointImage = new Image();
  pointImage.src = "point.png";
  function  drawScreen () {


      context.fillStyle = '#EEEEEE';
      context.fillRect(0, 0, theCanvas.width, theCanvas.height);
      //Box
      context.strokeStyle = '#000000';
      context.strokeRect(1,  1, theCanvas.width-2, theCanvas.height-2);

      ball.x = circle.centerX + Math.cos(circle.angle) * circle.radius;
      ball.y = circle.centerY + Math.sin(circle.angle) * circle.radius;
      circle.angle += ball.speed;
      circle.radius += radiusInc;

      //Draw points to illustrate path

      points.push({x:ball.x,y:ball.y});

      for (var i = 0; i< points.length; i++) {
         context.drawImage(pointImage, points[i].x, points[i].y,1,1);
      }

      context.fillStyle = "#000000";
```

```
      context.beginPath();
      context.arc(ball.x,ball.y,15,0,Math.PI*2,true);
      context.closePath();
      context.fill();

  }

  var radiusInc = 2;
  var circle = {centerX:250, centerY:250, radius:2, angle:0, radiusInc:2}
  var ball = {x:0, y:0,speed:.1};
  var points = new Array();

  theCanvas = document.getElementById("canvasOne");
  context = theCanvas.getContext("2d");

  function gameLoop() {
    window.setTimeout(gameLoop, 20);
    drawScreen()
  }
  gameLoop();

}

</script>

</head>
<body>
<div style="position: absolute; top: 50px; left: 50px;">

<canvas id="canvasOne" width="500" height="500">
 Your browser does not support HTML5 Canvas.
</canvas>
</div>
</body>
</html>
```

Cubic Bezier Curve Movement

Cubic Bezier curves can be used to define a movement path for an object. Pierre Bezier first popularized these curves in the 1960s. They are widely used in 2D vector graphics to define smooth curves for drawing, but they can also be used in animation to define a path for motion.

A cubic Bezier curve is created using four distinct points—p0, p1, p2, and p3:

p0

    The starting point of the curve. We will refer to these x and y values as x0 and y0.

p3

    The ending point of the curve. We will refer to these x and y values as x3 and y3.

p1 *and* p2

> The control points for the curve. The curve *does not pass through* these points; instead, the equation uses these points to determine the arc of the curve. We will refer to these x and y values as x0, x1, x2, x3, y0, y1, y2, and y3.

 The usage of the p1 and p2 points is the biggest stumbling block for understanding Bezier curves. The easiest way to understand the relationship between these points and the curve is to draw them on a bitmapped canvas, which we will do several times in this chapter.

After you have the four points, you need to calculate six coefficient values that you will use to find the x and y locations as you move an object on the curve. These coefficients are known as ax, bx, cx, ay, by, and cy. They are calculated as follows:

```
cx = 3 * (x1 - x0)
bx = 3 *(x2 - x1) - cx
ax = x3 - x0 - cx - bx
cy = 3 * (y1 - y0)
by = 3 * (y2 - y1) - cy
ay = y3 - y0 - cy - by
```

After you've calculated the six coefficients, you can find the x and y locations based on the changing t value using the following equations. The t value represents movement over time:

```
x(t) = axt3 + bxt2 + cxt + x0
y(t) = ayt3 + byt2 + cyt + y0
```

For our purposes, the t value will be increased by the speed at which we want the object to move. However, you will notice that this value does not easily equate to the speed values we used elsewhere in this chapter. The reason is that the t value was not created with movement over time for animation in mind. The speed we specify must be smaller than 1 so that the movement on the curve will be incremental enough for us to see it as part of the animation. For our example, we will increase t by a speed of .01 so that we will see 100 points on the movement curve (1/100 = .01). This is advantageous because we will know our object has finished moving when the t value is equal to 1.

For Example 5-11 (*CH5EX11.html*), we will start by creating the four points of the Bezier curve in the canvasApp() function:

```
var p0 = {x:60, y:10};
var p1 = {x:70, y:200};
var p2 = {x:125, y:295};
var p3 = {x:350, y:350};
```

We then create a new ball object with a couple differing properties from those in the other examples in this chapter. The speed is .01, which means that the object will move

100 points along the curve before it is finished. We start the t value at 0, which means that the ball will begin at p0:

```
var ball = {x:0, y:0, speed:.01, t:0};
```

Next, in the drawScreen() function, we calculate the Bezier curve coefficient values (ax, bx, cx, ay, by, cy) based on the four points (p0, p1, p2, p3):

```
var cx = 3 * (p1.x - p0.x);
var bx = 3 * (p2.x - p1.x) - cx;
var ax = p3.x - p0.x - cx - bx;

var cy = 3 * (p1.y - p0.y);
var by = 3 * (p2.y - p1.y) - cy;
var ay = p3.y - p0.y - cy - by;
```

Then we take our t value and use it with the coefficients to calculate the x and y values for the moving object. First, we get the t value from the ball object, and we store it locally so that we can use it in our calculations:

```
var t = ball.t;
```

Next we add the speed to the t value so that we can calculate the next point on the Bezier path:

```
ball.t += ball.speed;
```

Then we use the t value to calculate the x and y values (xt, yt) using the Bezier curve equations:

```
var xt = ax*(t*t*t) + bx*(t*t) + cx*t + p0.x;
var yt = ay*(t*t*t) + by*(t*t) + cy*t + p0.y;
```

We add the speed to the t value of ball and then check to see whether t is greater than 1. If so, we don't increase it any further because we have finished moving on the curve:

```
ball.t += ball.speed;

if (ball.t > 1) {
    ball.t = 1;
}
```

Finally, when we draw the ball object on the canvas, we use the xt and yt values:

```
context.arc(xt,yt,5,0,Math.PI*2,true);
```

Figure 5-15 shows what Example 5-11 (*CH5EX11.html*) looks like when it is executed in a web browser. In addition to drawing the points of the path using the points array, we also draw the four points of the Bezier curve. These illustrate the relationship of the points to the curve itself. Notice that the curve does not pass through p1 or p2.

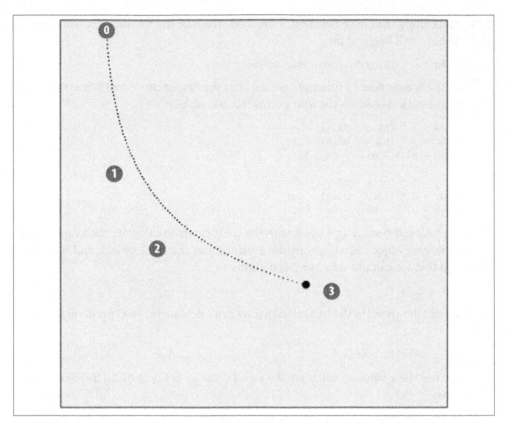

Figure 5-15. Moving a circle on a Bezier curve

Example 5-11 gives the full code listing for *CH5EX11.html*, including the code to draw the Bezier curve points on the canvas. You can find that code in the drawScreen() function following the //draw the points comment.

Example 5-11. Moving on a cubic Bezier curve

```
<!doctype html>
<html lang="en">
<head>
<meta charset="UTF-8">
<title>CH5EX11: Moving On A Cubic Bezier Curve </title>

<script src="modernizr.js"></script>
<script type="text/javascript">
window.addEventListener('load', eventWindowLoaded, false);
function eventWindowLoaded() {
    canvasApp();

}
function canvasSupport () {
```

```
        return Modernizr.canvas;
}

function canvasApp() {

  if (!canvasSupport()) {
        return;
      }

  var pointImage = new Image();
  pointImage.src = "point.png";

  function  drawScreen () {

      context.fillStyle = '#EEEEEE';
      context.fillRect(0, 0, theCanvas.width, theCanvas.height);
      //Box
      context.strokeStyle = '#000000';
      context.strokeRect(1,  1, theCanvas.width-2, theCanvas.height-2);

      var t = ball.t;

      var cx = 3 * (p1.x - p0.x)
      var bx = 3 * (p2.x - p1.x) - cx;
      var ax = p3.x - p0.x - cx - bx;

      var cy = 3 * (p1.y - p0.y);
      var by = 3 * (p2.y - p1.y) - cy;
      var ay = p3.y - p0.y - cy - by;

      var xt = ax*(t*t*t) + bx*(t*t) + cx*t + p0.x;
      var yt = ay*(t*t*t) + by*(t*t) + cy*t + p0.y;

      ball.t += ball.speed;

      if (ball.t > 1) {
         ball.t = 1;
      }        //draw the points

      context.font ="10px sans";
      context.fillStyle = "#FF0000";
      context.beginPath();
      context.arc(p0.x,p0.y,8,0,Math.PI*2,true);
      context.closePath();
      context.fill();
      context.fillStyle = "#FFFFFF";
      context.fillText("0",p0.x-2,p0.y+2);

      context.fillStyle = "#FF0000";
      context.beginPath();
      context.arc(p1.x,p1.y,8,0,Math.PI*2,true);
      context.closePath();
```

```
        context.fill();
        context.fillStyle = "#FFFFFF";
        context.fillText("1",p1.x-2,p1.y+2);

        context.fillStyle = "#FF0000";
        context.beginPath();
        context.arc(p2.x,p2.y,8,0,Math.PI*2,true);
        context.closePath();
        context.fill();
        context.fillStyle = "#FFFFFF";
        context.fillText("2",p2.x-2, p2.y+2);

        context.fillStyle = "#FF0000";
        context.beginPath();
        context.arc(p3.x,p3.y,8,0,Math.PI*2,true);
        context.closePath();
        context.fill();
        context.fillStyle = "#FFFFFF";
        context.fillText("3",p3.x-2, p3.y+2);

        //Draw points to illustrate path

        points.push({x:xt,y:yt});

        for (var i = 0; i< points.length; i++) {
            context.drawImage(pointImage, points[i].x, points[i].y,1,1);
        }

        context.closePath();

        //Draw circle moving

        context.fillStyle = "#000000";
        context.beginPath();
        context.arc(xt,yt,5,0,Math.PI*2,true);
        context.closePath();
        context.fill();

    }

var p0 = {x:60, y:10};
var p1 = {x:70, y:200};
var p2 = {x:125, y:295};
var p3 = {x:350, y:350};
var ball = {x:0, y:0, speed:.01, t:0};
var points = new Array();

theCanvas = document.getElementById("canvasOne");
context = theCanvas.getContext("2d");

function gameLoop() {
  window.setTimeout(gameLoop, 20);
```

```
        drawScreen()
    }
    gameLoop();

}

</script>

</head>
<body>
<div style="position: absolute; top: 50px; left: 50px;">

<canvas id="canvasOne" width="500" height="500">
 Your browser does not support HTML5 Canvas.
</canvas>
</div>
</body>
</html>
```

Moving an Image

Moving an image on a cubic Bezier curve path is just as easy as moving a circular drawing object, as we'll demonstrate in the next two examples. Suppose you are making a game where bull's-eyes move across the canvas and the player must shoot at them. You could use cubic Bezier curve paths to create new and interesting patterns for the bull's-eyes to move along.

For this example, we first create a global variable named bullseye, which we will use to hold the *bullseye.png* image that we will load to display on the canvas:

```
var bullseye;
function eventWindowLoaded() {
    bullseye = new Image();
    bullseye.src = "bullseye.png"
    bullseye.onload = eventAssetsLoaded;
}
```

In canvasApp(), we will create a different path for the curve from the one in the first example by setting new values for p0, p1, p2, and p3. Using these values, the bullseye will move on a parabola-like path. (Figure 5-16 shows the path of the curve.)

```
var p0 = {x:60, y:10};
var p1 = {x:150, y:350};
var p2 = {x:300, y:375};
var p3 = {x:400, y:20};
```

We also need to create a player object that represents the bull's-eye on the canvas:

```
var player = {x:0, y:0, speed:.01, t:0};
```

In drawImage(), after we calculate t, xt, and yt, we draw the image on the canvas:

```
        player.x = xt-bullseye.width/2;
        player.y = yt-bullseye.height/2;

        context.drawImage(bullseye,player.x,player.y);
```

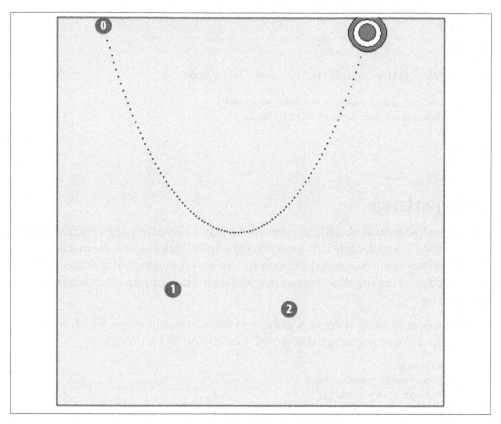

Figure 5-16. Moving an image on a cubic Bezier curve path

The rest of Example 5-12 works just like Example 5-11.

Example 5-12. Moving an image

```
<!doctype html>
<html lang="en">
<head>
<meta charset="UTF-8">
<title>CH5EX12: Moving An Image </title>

<script src="modernizr.js"></script>
<script type="text/javascript">
window.addEventListener('load', eventWindowLoaded, false);

var bullseye;
```

```
function eventWindowLoaded() {
    bullseye = new Image();
    bullseye.src = "bullseye.png"
    bullseye.onload = eventAssetsLoaded;
}

function eventAssetsLoaded() {

    canvasApp();
}

function canvasSupport () {
    return Modernizr.canvas;
}

function canvasApp() {

  if (!canvasSupport()) {
        return;
      }

  var pointImage = new Image();
  pointImage.src = "point.png";
  function  drawScreen () {

      context.fillStyle = '#EEEEEE';
      context.fillRect(0, 0, theCanvas.width, theCanvas.height);
      //Box
      context.strokeStyle = '#000000';
      context.strokeRect(1,  1, theCanvas.width-2, theCanvas.height-2);

      var t = player.t;

      var cx = 3 * (p1.x - p0.x)
      var bx = 3 * (p2.x - p1.x) - cx;
      var ax = p3.x - p0.x - cx - bx;

      var cy = 3 * (p1.y - p0.y);
      var by = 3 * (p2.y - p1.y) - cy;
      var ay = p3.y - p0.y - cy - by;

      var xt = ax*(t*t*t) + bx*(t*t) + cx*t + p0.x;

      var yt = ay*(t*t*t) + by*(t*t) + cy*t + p0.y;

      player.t += player.speed;

      if (player.t > 1) {
         player.t = 1;
      }       //draw the points

      context.font = "10px sans";
```

```
context.fillStyle = "#FF0000";
context.beginPath();
context.arc(p0.x,p0.y,8,0,Math.PI*2,true);
context.closePath();
context.fill();
context.fillStyle = "#FFFFFF";
context.fillText("0",p0.x-2,p0.y+2);

context.fillStyle = "#FF0000";
context.beginPath();
context.arc(p1.x,p1.y,8,0,Math.PI*2,true);
context.closePath();
context.fill();
context.fillStyle = "#FFFFFF";
context.fillText("1",p1.x-2,p1.y+2);

context.fillStyle = "#FF0000";
context.beginPath();
context.arc(p2.x,p2.y,8,0,Math.PI*2,true);
context.closePath();
context.fill();
context.fillStyle = "#FFFFFF";
context.fillText("2",p2.x-2, p2.y+2);

context.fillStyle = "#FF0000";
context.beginPath();
context.arc(p3.x,p3.y,8,0,Math.PI*2,true);
context.closePath();
context.fill();
context.fillStyle = "#FFFFFF";
context.fillText("3",p3.x-2, p3.y+2);

//Draw points to illustrate path

points.push({x:xt,y:yt});

for (var i = 0; i< points.length; i++) {
    context.drawImage(pointImage, points[i].x, points[i].y,1,1);
}

context.closePath();

player.x = xt-bullseye.width/2;
player.y = yt-bullseye.height/2;

context.drawImage(bullseye,player.x,player.y);

}

var p0 = {x:60, y:10};
var p1 = {x:150, y:350};
```

```
      var p2 = {x:300, y:375};
      var p3 = {x:400, y:20};
      var player = {x:0, y:0, speed:.01, t:0};
      var points = new Array();

      theCanvas = document.getElementById("canvasOne");
      context = theCanvas.getContext("2d");

      function gameLoop() {
        window.setTimeout(gameLoop, 20);
        drawScreen()
      }
      gameLoop();

   }

</script>

</head>
<body>
<div style="position: absolute; top: 50px; left: 50px;">

<canvas id="canvasOne" width="500" height="500">
 Your browser does not support HTML5 Canvas.
</canvas>
</div>
</body>
</html>
```

Creating a Cubic Bezier Curve Loop

You can create some very interesting paths using the four points in a cubic Bezier curve. One such effect is a loop. To create a loop, you need to make sure the points form an X, with p0 diagonal from p1, and p2 and p3 on an opposite diagonal from the other two points. p0 and p3 must be closer to the center of the canvas than p1 or p2. The points we will use to create this effect in Example 5-13 are as follows:

```
      var p0 = {x:150, y:440;
      var p1 = {x:450, y:10};
      var p2 = {x:50, y:10};
      var p3 = {x:325, y:450};
```

Because it is much easier to show than tell when it comes to cubic Bezier curves, look at Figure 5-17. It shows what the looping curve looks like when Example 5-13 is executed in a web browser.

This effect can be created only with the four points of a cubic Bezier curve. There is also a three-point Bezier curve known as a quadratic Bezier curve. You cannot create loops or S curves with quadratic Bezier curves because the three points are not as precise as the four points of a cubic Bezier curve.

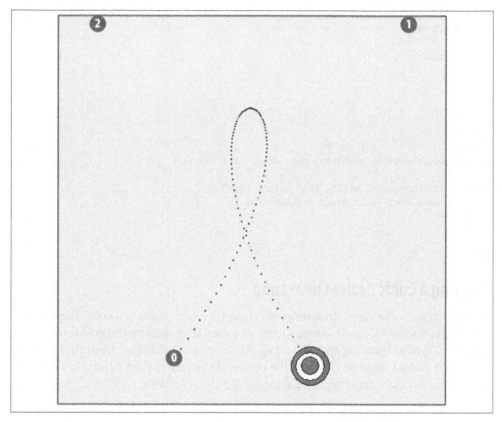

Figure 5-17. Moving an object in a loop using a cubic Bezier curve

Because the code for this example is essentially the same as in Example 5-12 (besides the four points), we have highlighted in bold the changed code in Example 5-13. We have done this to show you that—with relatively simple changes—you can create dramatic animation effects using cubic Bezier curves.

Example 5-13. Bezier curve loop

```
<!doctype html>
<html lang="en">
<head>
```

```
<meta charset="UTF-8">
<title>CH5EX13: Bezier Curve Loop </title>

<script src="modernizr.js"></script>
<script type="text/javascript">
window.addEventListener('load', eventWindowLoaded, false);

var bullseye;
function eventWindowLoaded() {
    bullseye = new Image();
    bullseye.src = "bullseye.png"
    bullseye.onload = eventAssetsLoaded;
}

function eventAssetsLoaded() {

    canvasApp();
}

function canvasSupport () {
    return Modernizr.canvas;
}

function canvasApp() {

    if (!canvasSupport()) {
            return;
        }

  var pointImage = new Image();
  pointImage.src = "point.png";
  function  drawScreen () {

      context.fillStyle = '#EEEEEE';
      context.fillRect(0, 0, theCanvas.width, theCanvas.height);
      //Box
      context.strokeStyle = '#000000';
      context.strokeRect(1,  1, theCanvas.width-2, theCanvas.height-2);

      var t = player.t;

      var cx = 3 * (p1.x - p0.x)
      var bx = 3 * (p2.x - p1.x) - cx;
      var ax = p3.x - p0.x - cx - bx;

      var cy = 3 * (p1.y - p0.y);
      var by = 3 * (p2.y - p1.y) - cy;
      var ay = p3.y - p0.y - cy - by;

      var xt = ax*(t*t*t) + bx*(t*t) + cx*t + p0.x;

      var yt = ay*(t*t*t) + by*(t*t) + cy*t + p0.y;
```

```
player.t += player.speed;

if (player.t > 1) {
    player.t = 1;
}
//draw the points

context.font = "10px sans";

context.fillStyle = "#FF0000";
context.beginPath();
context.arc(p0.x,p0.y,8,0,Math.PI*2,true);
context.closePath();
context.fill();
context.fillStyle = "#FFFFFF";
context.fillText("0",p0.x-2,p0.y+2);

context.fillStyle = "#FF0000";
context.beginPath();
context.arc(p1.x,p1.y,8,0,Math.PI*2,true);
context.closePath();
context.fill();
context.fillStyle = "#FFFFFF";
context.fillText("1",p1.x-2,p1.y+2);

context.fillStyle = "#FF0000";
context.beginPath();
context.arc(p2.x,p2.y,8,0,Math.PI*2,true);
context.closePath();
context.fill();
context.fillStyle = "#FFFFFF";
context.fillText("2",p2.x-2, p2.y+2);

context.fillStyle = "#FF0000";
context.beginPath();
context.arc(p3.x,p3.y,8,0,Math.PI*2,true);
context.closePath();
context.fill();
context.fillStyle = "#FFFFFF";
context.fillText("3",p3.x-2, p3.y+2);

points.push({x:xt,y:yt});

for (var i = 0; i< points.length; i++) {
    context.drawImage(pointImage, points[i].x, points[i].y,1,1);
}

context.closePath();

player.x = xt-bullseye.width/2;
player.y = yt-bullseye.height/2;
```

```
      context.drawImage(bullseye,player.x,player.y);

    }

    var p0 = {x:150, y:440};
    var p1 = {x:450, y:10};
    var p2 = {x:50, y:10};
    var p3 = {x:325, y:450};
    var player = {x:0, y:0, speed:.01, t:0};

    var points = new Array();

    theCanvas = document.getElementById("canvasOne");
    context = theCanvas.getContext("2d");

    function gameLoop() {
      window.setTimeout(gameLoop, 20);
      drawScreen()
    }
    gameLoop();
;

}

</script>

</head>
<body>
<div style="position: absolute; top: 50px; left: 50px;">

<canvas id="canvasOne" width="500" height="500">
 Your browser does not support HTML5 Canvas.
</canvas>
</div>
</body>
</html>
```

Simple Gravity, Elasticity, and Friction

Adding simulated gravity, elasticity, and friction to your objects adds a sense of realism that otherwise would not exist in 2D. These properties are major forces in nature that people feel and understand at nearly every moment of their lives. This means that people who play games expect objects to act in a particular way when these properties are applied. Our job is to simulate those effects as closely as possible, while minimizing the processing power necessary to create them. While there are some very complicated physics equations we could use to create these effects, we will use simplified versions that work well with the limited resources available to HTML5 Canvas in a web browser.

Simple Gravity

A very simple yet seemingly realistic gravitational effect can be achieved by applying a constant gravity value to the y velocity of an object moving on a vector. To do this, select a value for gravity, such as `.1`, and then add that value to the y velocity of your object on every call to `drawScreen()`.

For this example, let's simulate a ball with a `radius` of 15 pixels being shot from a cannon that rests near the bottom of the canvas. The ball will move at a `speed` of 4 pixels per frame, with an `angle` of 305 degrees. This means it will move up and to the right on the canvas. If we did not apply any gravity, the ball would simply keep moving on that vector until it left the canvas. (Actually, it would keep moving; we just would not see it any longer.)

You have seen the code to create an effect like this already. In the `canvasApp()` function, we would create the starting variables like this:

```
var speed = 4;
var angle = 305;
var radians = angle * Math.PI/ 180;
var radius = 15;
var vx = Math.cos(radians) * speed;
var vy = Math.sin(radians) * speed;
```

Next we create the starting point for the ball as `p1`, and then we create a dynamic object that holds all the values we created for the `ball` object:

```
var p1 = {x:20,y:theCanvas.height-radius};
var ball = {x:p1.x, y:p1.y, velocityx: vx, velocityy:vy, radius:radius};
```

If we want to add gravity to the application, we would first create a new variable named `gravity` and set it to a constant value of `.1`:

```
var gravity = .1;
```

Next, in the `drawScreen()` function, we apply this gravity value to the `ball` object when it is drawn to the canvas (`ball.velocityy += gravity`). We want the ball to stop moving when it hits the "ground" (the bottom of the canvas), so we test to see whether the y position of the `ball` plus the `radius` of the ball (the outer edge) has passed the bottom of the canvas (`ball.y + ball.radius <= theCanvas.height`). If so, we stop the ball's movement:

```
if (ball.y + ball.radius <= theCanvas.height) {
    ball.velocityy += gravity;
} else {
    ball.velocityx = 0;
    ball.velocityy = 0;
    ball.y = theCanvas.height - ball.radius;

}
```

Next we apply the constant x velocity and the new y velocity to `ball` and draw it to the canvas:

```
ball.y += ball.velocityy;
ball.x += ball.velocityx;

context.fillStyle = "#000000";
context.beginPath();
context.arc(ball.x,ball.y,ball.radius,0,Math.PI*2,true);
context.closePath();
context.fill();
```

Figure 5-18 shows what the path looks like when simple gravity is applied to a ball moving on a vector. We have added the points to illustrate the path.

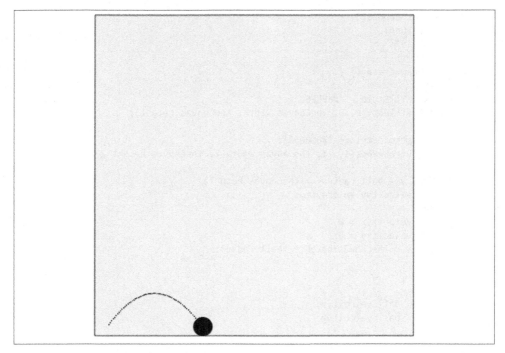

Figure 5-18. Simple gravity with an object moving on a vector

You can test out Example 5-14 with the file *CH5EX14.html* in the code distribution, or type in the full code listing below.

Example 5-14. Simple gravity

```
<!doctype html>
<html lang="en">
<head>
```

```
<meta charset="UTF-8">
<title>CH5EX14: Simple Gravity</title>

<script src="modernizr.js"></script>
<script type="text/javascript">
window.addEventListener('load', eventWindowLoaded, false);
function eventWindowLoaded() {
    canvasApp();
}

function canvasSupport () {
    return Modernizr.canvas;
}

function canvasApp() {

    if (!canvasSupport()) {
        return;
    }

  function  drawScreen () {

      context.fillStyle = '#EEEEEE';
      context.fillRect(0, 0, theCanvas.width, theCanvas.height);
      //Box
      context.strokeStyle = '#000000';
      context.strokeRect(1,  1, theCanvas.width-2, theCanvas.height-2);

      if (ball.y + ball.radius <= theCanvas.height) {
         ball.velocityy += gravity;
      } else {
         ball.velocityx = 0;
         ball.velocityy = 0;
         ball.y = theCanvas.height - ball.radius;

      }

      ball.y += ball.velocityy;
      ball.x += ball.velocityx;

      context.fillStyle = "#000000";
      context.beginPath();
      context.arc(ball.x,ball.y,ball.radius,0,Math.PI*2,true);
      context.closePath();
      context.fill();

  }
  var speed = 4;

  var gravity = .1;
  var angle = 305;
  var radians = angle * Math.PI/ 180;
  var radius = 15;
```

```
    var vx = Math.cos(radians) * speed;
    var vy = Math.sin(radians) * speed;

    theCanvas = document.getElementById("canvasOne");
    context = theCanvas.getContext("2d");

    var p1 = {x:20,y:theCanvas.height-radius};
    var ball = {x:p1.x, y:p1.y, velocityx: vx, velocityy:vy, radius:radius};

    function gameLoop() {
      window.setTimeout(gameLoop, 20);
      drawScreen()
    }
    gameLoop();


}

</script>

</head>
<body>
<div style="position: absolute; top: 50px; left: 50px;">

<canvas id="canvasOne" width="500" height="500">
 Your browser does not support HTML5 Canvas.
</canvas>
</div>
</body>
</html>
```

Simple Gravity with a Bounce

The last example showed what a cannonball might look like if it were shot out, landed on a surface, and stuck there with no reaction. However, even a heavy cannonball will bounce when it hits the ground.

To create a bouncing effect, we do not have to change the code very much at all. In drawScreen(), we first apply gravity on every frame; then, instead of stopping the ball if it hits the bottom of the canvas, we simply need to reverse the y velocity of ball when it hits the ground.

In *CH5EX14.html* you would replace this code:

```
    if (ball.y + ball.radius <= theCanvas.height) {
        ball.velocityy += gravity;
    } else {
        ball.velocityx = 0;
        ball.velocityy = 0;
        ball.y = theCanvas.height - ball.radius;
    }
```

With this:

```
ball.velocityy += gravity;
if ((ball.y + ball.radius) > theCanvas.height) {
   ball.velocityy = -(ball.velocityy)
}
```

This code will send the ball bouncing back "up" the canvas. Because it is still traveling on the vector and gravity is applied every time `drawScreen()` is called, the ball will eventually come down again as the applied `gravity` overtakes the reversed y velocity.

Figure 5-19 shows what the cannonball looks like when the bounce is applied.

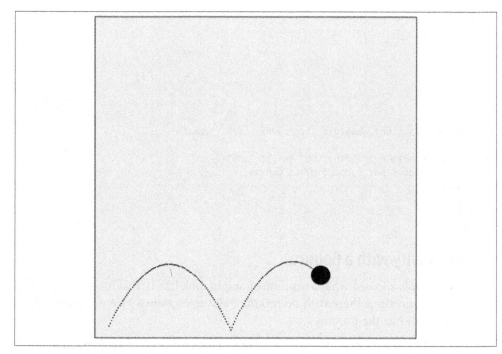

Figure 5-19. A ball moving on a vector with gravity and a bounce applied

> To achieve a nice-looking bounce for this example, we also changed the angle of the vector in `canvasApp()` to 295:
>
> ```
> var angle = 295;
> ```

Example 5-15 offers the full code.

Example 5-15. Simple gravity with a bounce

```
<!doctype html>
<html lang="en">
<head>
<meta charset="UTF-8">
<title>CH5EX15: Gravity With A Bounce</title>

<script src="modernizr.js"></script>
<script type="text/javascript">
window.addEventListener('load', eventWindowLoaded, false);
function eventWindowLoaded() {
   canvasApp();

}

function canvasSupport () {
     return Modernizr.canvas;
}

function canvasApp() {

   if (!canvasSupport()) {
          return;
        }

  function  drawScreen () {

      context.fillStyle = '#EEEEEE';
      context.fillRect(0, 0, theCanvas.width, theCanvas.height);
      //Box
      context.strokeStyle = '#000000';
      context.strokeRect(1,  1, theCanvas.width-2, theCanvas.height-2);

      ball.velocityy  += gravity;

      if ((ball.y + ball.radius) > theCanvas.height) {
         ball.velocityy = -(ball.velocityy)
      }
      ball.y += ball.velocityy;
      ball.x += ball.velocityx;

      context.fillStyle = "#000000";
      context.beginPath();
      context.arc(ball.x,ball.y,ball.radius,0,Math.PI*2,true);
      context.closePath();
      context.fill();

   }
   var speed = 5;

   var gravity = .1;
   var angle = 295;
```

```
    var radians = angle * Math.PI/ 180;
    var radius = 15;

    var vx = Math.cos(radians) * speed;
    var vy = Math.sin(radians) * speed;

    theCanvas = document.getElementById("canvasOne");
    context = theCanvas.getContext("2d");

    var p1 = {x:20,y:theCanvas.height-radius};
    var ball = {x:p1.x, y:p1.y, velocityx: vx, velocityy:vy, radius:radius};

    function gameLoop() {
      window.setTimeout(gameLoop, 20);
      drawScreen()
    }
    gameLoop();

}

</script>

</head>
<body>
<div style="position: absolute; top: 50px; left: 50px;">

<canvas id="canvasOne" width="500" height="500">
 Your browser does not support HTML5 Canvas.
</canvas>
</div>
</body>
</html>
```

Gravity with Bounce and Applied Simple Elasticity

In physics, the *elasticity* of a bouncing ball refers to how much energy is conserved when
a ball bounces off a surface. We already covered a bit about conservation of energy when
we discussed balls colliding, but when we are simulating objects falling, we need to take
a slightly different path with our code. In Example 5-15, we applied 100% elasticity and
the ball bounced forever. (Actually, this was only implied because we did not consider
elasticity at all.) However, in real life, balls usually lose some of their energy every time
they bounce off a surface. The amount of energy conserved depends on the material the
ball is made from, as well as the surface it is bouncing on. For example, a rubber Super
Ball is much more elastic than a cannonball and will bounce higher on the first bounce
off a surface. Both will bounce higher off a concrete surface than a surface made of thick
mud. Eventually, both will come to rest on the surface as all the energy is transferred
away from the ball.

We can simulate simple elasticity by applying a constant value to the ball when it bounces
off the ground. For this example, we will set the speed of the ball to 6 pixels per frame

and the `angle` to 285. We will keep our `gravity` at .1 but set a new variable named `elasticity` to .5. To make this more straightforward, we will also assume that the surface the ball is bouncing on does not add or subtract from the elasticity of the ball.

In `canvasApp()`, we would set the new properties like this:

```
var speed = 6;
var gravity = .1;
var elasticity = .5;
var angle = 285;
```

We then add the new `elasticity` property to the `ball` object because, unlike `gravity`, elasticity describes a property of an object, not the entire world it resides within. This means that having multiple balls with different values for elasticity would be very easy to implement:

```
var ball = {x:p1.x, y:p1.y, velocityx: vx, velocityy:vy, radius:radius,
    elasticity: elasticity};
```

In the `drawScreen()` function, we still add the `gravity` value to the y velocity (`velocityy`). However, instead of simply reversing the y velocity when the `ball` hits the bottom of the canvas, we also multiply the y velocity by the `elasticity` value stored in the `ball.elasticity` property. This applies the elasticity to the bounce, preserving the y velocity by the percentage value of `elasticity` for the object:

```
ball.velocityy += gravity;
if ((ball.y + ball.radius) > theCanvas.height) {
    ball.velocityy = -(ball.velocityy)*ball.elasticity;
}
ball.y += ball.velocityy;
ball.x += ball.velocityx;
```

In Figure 5-20, you can see what this application looks like when executed in a web browser.

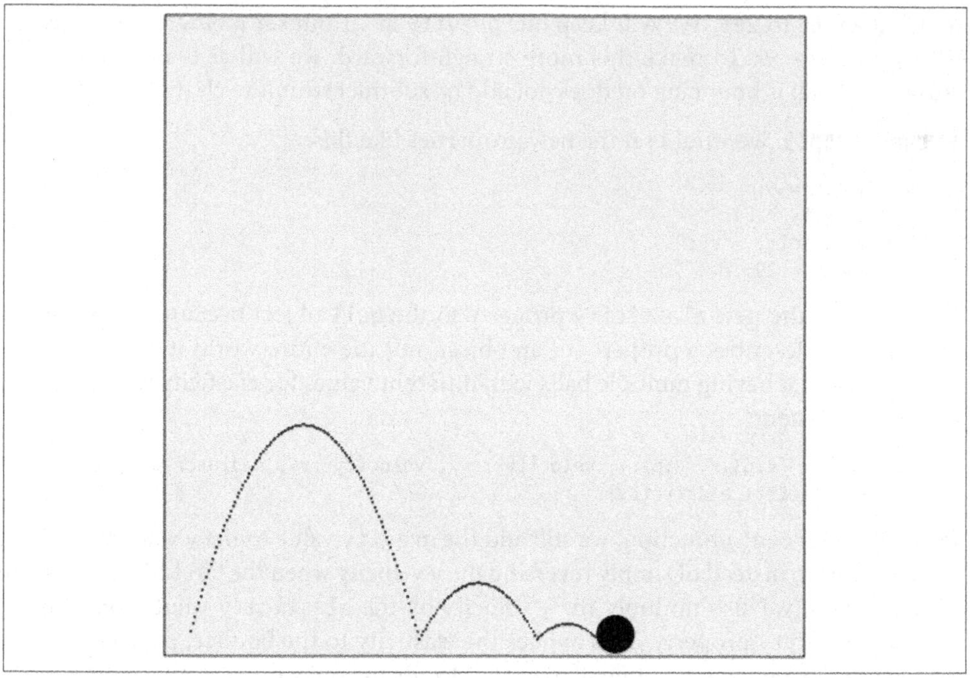

Figure 5-20. Ball bouncing with elasticity and gravity applied

> With gravity applied, the bounce is not exactly as you might expect. Gravity is always pulling down on our object, so the effect of a loss of y velocity due to an elastic bounce is pronounced.

The full code is shown in Example 5-16.

Example 5-16. Simple gravity with bounce and elasticity

```
<!doctype html>
<html lang="en">
<head>
<meta charset="UTF-8">
<title>CH5EX16: Gravity With A Vector With Bounce And Elasticity</title>

<script src="modernizr.js"></script>
<script type="text/javascript">
window.addEventListener('load', eventWindowLoaded, false);
function eventWindowLoaded() {
    canvasApp();

}

function canvasSupport () {
```

```
        return Modernizr.canvas;
}

function canvasApp() {

    if (!canvasSupport()) {
            return;
        }

  function  drawScreen () {

        context.fillStyle = '#EEEEEE';
        context.fillRect(0, 0, theCanvas.width, theCanvas.height);
        //Box
        context.strokeStyle = '#000000';
        context.strokeRect(1,  1, theCanvas.width-2, theCanvas.height-2);

        ball.velocityy += gravity;

        if ((ball.y + ball.radius) > theCanvas.height) {
            ball.velocityy = -(ball.velocityy)*ball.elasticity;
        }
        ball.y += ball.velocityy;
        ball.x += ball.velocityx;

        context.fillStyle = "#000000";
        context.beginPath();
        context.arc(ball.x,ball.y,ball.radius,0,Math.PI*2,true);
        context.closePath();
        context.fill();

    }
    var speed = 6;
    var gravity = .1;
    var elasticity = .5;
    var angle = 285;
    var radians = angle * Math.PI/ 180;
    var radius = 15;

    var vx = Math.cos(radians) * speed;
    var vy = Math.sin(radians) * speed;

    theCanvas = document.getElementById("canvasOne");
    context = theCanvas.getContext("2d");

    var p1 = {x:20,y:theCanvas.height-radius};
    var ball = {x:p1.x, y:p1.y, velocityx: vx, velocityy:vy, radius:radius,
        elasticity: elasticity};

    function gameLoop() {
      window.setTimeout(gameLoop, 20);
      drawScreen()
```

```
    }
    gameLoop();

}

</script>

</head>
<body>
<div style="position: absolute; top: 50px; left: 50px;">

<canvas id="canvasOne" width="500" height="500">
 Your browser does not support HTML5 Canvas.
</canvas>
</div>
</body>
</html>
```

Simple Gravity, Simple Elasticity, and Simple Friction

Now that we have a ball traveling on a vector that is affected by both gravity and elasticity, we have one more element to add to make the animation more realistic. In the previous example, the y velocity was affected by gravity and elasticity, but the ball still traveled on the x-axis without any degradation in velocity. We will fix this issue now by adding friction into the equation.

In physics, *friction* is a force that resists the motion of an object. We have already discussed friction as it applies to colliding balls, and this implementation is similar except that it affects only the x velocity. For our purposes, we will achieve simple friction by degrading the x velocity as gravity degrades the y velocity.

Taking the code from Example 5-16, in `canvasApp()` we create a new variable named `friction`. This is the amount of pixels to degrade the x velocity on every frame:

```
var friction = .008;
```

Notice that the amount is quite small. Friction does not have to be a large value to look realistic—it just needs to be applied uniformly each time `drawScreen()` is called. In `drawScreen()`, we apply `friction` to the x velocity like this:

```
ball.velocityx = ball.velocityx - ( ball.velocityx*friction);
```

This is the same type of proportional application of friction we used with the colliding balls, but again, this time we applied it only to the x velocity.

Figure 5-21 shows what this final version of our application looks like when executed in a web browser.

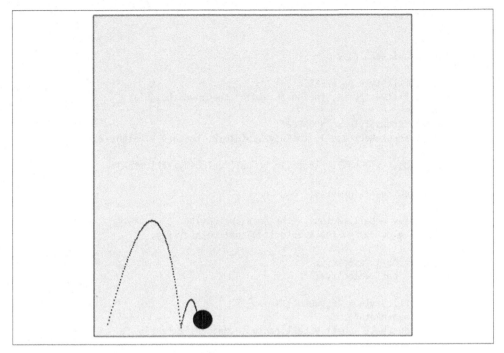

Figure 5-21. Ball bouncing with gravity, elasticity, and friction applied

Example 5-17 gives the full code for *CH5EX17.html*, the final code of our simple gravity, simple elasticity, and simple friction example.

Example 5-17. Gravity with a vector with bounce friction

```
<!doctype html>
<html lang="en">
<head>
<meta charset="UTF-8">
<title>CH5EX17: Gravity With A Vector With Bounce Friction</title>

<script src="modernizr.js"></script>
<script type="text/javascript">
window.addEventListener('load', eventWindowLoaded, false);
function eventWindowLoaded() {
    canvasApp();
}

function canvasSupport () {
     return Modernizr.canvas;
}

function canvasApp() {

    if (!canvasSupport()) {
```

```
            return;
        }

    function  drawScreen () {

        context.fillStyle = '#EEEEEE';
        context.fillRect(0, 0, theCanvas.width, theCanvas.height);
        //Box
        context.strokeStyle = '#000000';
        context.strokeRect(1,  1, theCanvas.width-2, theCanvas.height-2);

        ball.velocityx = ball.velocityx - ( ball.velocityx*friction);

        ball.velocityy += gravity;

        if ((ball.y + ball.radius) > theCanvas.height) {
            ball.velocityy = -(ball.velocityy)*ball.elasticity;
        }
        ball.y += ball.velocityy;
        ball.x += ball.velocityx;

        context.fillStyle = "#000000";
        context.beginPath();
        context.arc(ball.x,ball.y,ball.radius,0,Math.PI*2,true);
        context.closePath();
        context.fill();

    }
    var speed = 6;
    var gravity = .1;
    var friction = .008;
    var elasticity = .5;
    var angle = 285;
    var radians = angle * Math.PI/ 180;
    var radius = 15;

    var vx = Math.cos(radians) * speed;
    var vy = Math.sin(radians) * speed;

    theCanvas = document.getElementById("canvasOne");
    context = theCanvas.getContext("2d");

    var p1 = {x:20,y:theCanvas.height-radius};
    var ball = {x:p1.x, y:p1.y, velocityx: vx, velocityy:vy, radius:radius,
        elasticity: elasticity};

    function gameLoop() {
      window.setTimeout(gameLoop, 20);
      drawScreen()
    }
    gameLoop();
```

```
}

</script>

</head>
<body>
<div style="position: absolute; top: 50px; left: 50px;">

<canvas id="canvasOne" width="500" height="500">
  Your browser does not support HTML5 Canvas.
</canvas>
</div>
</body>
</html>
```

Easing

Easing is a technique used in animation to make an object smoothly enter or leave a location. The idea of easing is that instead of uniformly applying movement to every frame of animation, you instead increase (*easing in*) or decrease (*easing out*) the number of pixels you move on each frame. The result is that movement appears to be more realistic and smooth. There are many different ways to create easing animations. We will concentrate on two simple examples that will help pave the way for you to further explore the subject on your own.

Easing Out (Landing the Ship)

The process of easing out refers to easing at the end of an animation: an object moving from one point to another, starting out fast, and slowing down as it reaches the second point. To illustrate the concept, we will use the example of a spaceship landing. A spaceship starts out very fast, applies negative thrust to slow down, and by the time it reaches the ground, it's moving slowly enough to land without incident. If you've ever played the video game *Lunar Lander*, you will understand exactly the type of movement we are trying to accomplish.

To create this easing-out effect, we need to find two distinct points and then move an object between them, slowing down the object in linear fashion as it nears the second point. To achieve this effect, we first calculate the distance between the points. Next, we select a percentage value (easeValue) that we will use to move the object across that distance on each frame. As the distance gets shorter, the amount we move gets shorter as well. This gives the object the appearance of traveling slower and slower as it moves from the starting point to the ending point, as illustrated in Figure 5-22. We have drawn the points to show the easing values as the ship nears the bottom of the screen. Notice that the points get closer and closer until there is almost no distance between them.

Figure 5-22. Spaceship landing (easing out)

Figure 5-22 displays the results of *CH5EX18.html*. Now, let's look at how this example works in detail. First, we will load in the *ship.png* image the same way we have loaded images previously in this chapter:

```
var shipImage;
function eventWindowLoaded() {
   shipImage = new Image();
   shipImage.src = "ship.png"
   shipImage.onload = eventAssetsLoaded;
}

function eventAssetsLoaded() {

   canvasApp();
}
```

Then, in `canvasApp()`, we create a variable named `easeValue`, which represents the percentage to move the ship across the remaining distance between the two points. In our example, it is 5% (`.05`):

```
var easeValue = .05;
```

Next we create our two points. The first point, p1, is close to the middle of the canvas on the x-axis, and just above the top (–20) on the y-axis. The final point, p2, is in the same place on the x-axis, but near the bottom of the canvas (470) on the y-axis:

```
var p1 = {x:240,y:-20};
var p2 = {x:240,y:470};
```

Finally, we create a dynamic object for the ship that holds these values:

```
var ship = {x:p1.x, y:p1.y, endx: p2.x, endy:p2.y, velocityx:0, velocityy:0};
```

In drawScreen(), on every frame, we first find out the distance between the ship and the endpoint by subtracting the current x and y values for the ship from the endpoint x and y values. The distance will get shorter on each call to drawScreen() as the ship moves farther away from p1 and gets closer to p2. We do this for both x and y, even though, in our example, only the y value will change as the spaceship gets closer to p2:

```
var dx = ship.endx - ship.x;
var dy = ship.endy - ship.y;
```

When we have the distances, we multiply those values by easeValue to get the x and y velocities for the ship on this call to drawScreen():

```
ship.velocityx = dx * easeValue;
ship.velocityy = dy * easeValue;
```

Finally, we apply those values and draw the spaceship to the canvas:

```
ship.x += ship.velocityx;
ship.y += ship.velocityy;
context.drawImage(shipImage,ship.x,ship.y);
```

You can test this example by executing *CH5EX18.html* from the code distribution in your web browser, or by typing in the full code listing shown in Example 5-18.

Example 5-18. Easing out (landing the ship)

```
<!doctype html>
<html lang="en">
<head>
<meta charset="UTF-8">
<title>CH5EX18:  Easing Out (Landing The Ship)</title>

<script src="modernizr.js"></script>
<script type="text/javascript">
window.addEventListener('load', eventWindowLoaded, false);
var shipImage;
function eventWindowLoaded() {
    shipImage = new Image();
    shipImage.src = "ship.png"
    shipImage.onload = eventAssetsLoaded;
}

function eventAssetsLoaded() {
```

```
        canvasApp();
}

function canvasSupport () {
      return Modernizr.canvas;
}

function canvasApp() {

   if (!canvasSupport()) {
            return;
}

   var pointImage = new Image();
   pointImage.src = "pointwhite.png";
   function  drawScreen () {

        context.fillStyle = '#000000';
        context.fillRect(0, 0, theCanvas.width, theCanvas.height);
        //Box
        context.strokeStyle = '#ffffff';
        context.strokeRect(1,  1, theCanvas.width-2, theCanvas.height-2);
        var dx = ship.endx - ship.x;
        var dy = ship.endy - ship.y;

        ship.velocityx = dx * easeValue;
        ship.velocityy = dy * easeValue;

        ship.x += ship.velocityx;
        ship.y += ship.velocityy;

        //Draw points to illustrate path

        points.push({x:ship.x,y:ship.y});

        for (var i = 0; i< points.length; i++) {
           context.drawImage(pointImage, points[i].x+shipImage.width/2,
                           points[i].y,1,1);
        }

        context.drawImage(shipImage,ship.x,ship.y);

   }    var easeValue = .05;
   var p1 = {x:240,y:-20};
   var p2 = {x:240,y:470};

   var ship = {x:p1.x, y:p1.y, endx: p2.x, endy:p2.y, velocityx:0, velocityy:0};
   var points = new Array();

   theCanvas = document.getElementById("canvasOne");
   context = theCanvas.getContext("2d");
```

```
    function gameLoop() {
      window.setTimeout(gameLoop, 20);
      drawScreen()
    }
    gameLoop();

}

</script>

</head>
<body>
<div style="position: absolute; top: 50px; left: 50px;">

<canvas id="canvasOne" width="500" height="500">
 Your browser does not support HTML5 Canvas.
</canvas>
</div>
</body>
</html>
```

 We are showing the points in this example, but because the background is black, we load in a white bitmap point image named *pointwhite.png* instead of the all-black image, *point.png*.

Easing In (Taking Off)

Easing in is the opposite of easing out. When an animation *eases in*, it starts slowly and then gets faster and faster. If you have ever seen a video of a space shuttle taking off, you will understand this much better. The thrust builds up as the craft at first moves slowly and then gets faster and faster as it moves through the sky. We are going to use this "taking off" example as a way to develop code for an easing-in animation on HTML5 Canvas.

In canvasApp(), we start our code much the same way as in the last example—by creating a variable named easeValue:

```
    var easeValue = .05;
```

However, for easing in, instead of this being a percentage of the remaining distance between two points, it is simply a constant value added to the velocity of the ship on each frame. Figure 5-23 shows what this would look like. We have added the points again to illustrate how the animation speeds up as the ship takes off.

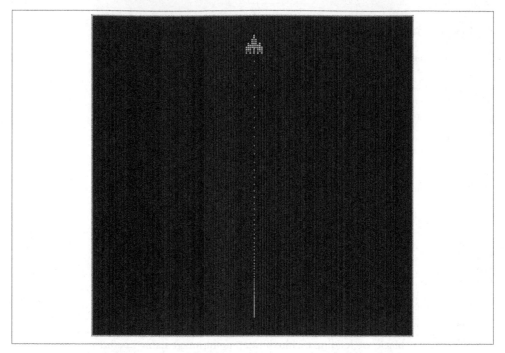

Figure 5-23. Ship taking off (easing in)

First, we set the beginning position of the ship (p1) to the bottom center of the canvas. Then we set the beginning speed of the ship very low (.5 pixels per frame) and set the angle to 270 (straight up the canvas). We then calculate the x and y velocity values for the ship:

```
var p1 = {x:240,y:470};
var tempSpeed = .5;
var tempAngle = 270 ;
var tempRadians = tempAngle * Math.PI/ 180;
var tempvelocityx = Math.cos(tempRadians) * tempSpeed;
var tempvelocityy  = Math.sin(tempRadians) * tempSpeed;

var ship = {x:p1.x, y:p1.y, velocityx:tempvelocityx, velocityy:tempvelocityy};
```

In drawScreen(), instead of finding the distance between two points, we add the ease Value to the x and y velocities on each frame and then apply it to the ship x and y values before drawing it to the canvas. This creates a linear increase in speed, resulting in the easing-in effect we want to see:

```
ship.velocityx = ship.velocityx + ( ship.velocityx*easeValue);
ship.velocityy = ship.velocityy + ( ship.velocityy*easeValue);

ship.x += ship.velocityx;
ship.y += ship.velocityy;
```

```
    context.drawImage(shipImage,ship.x,ship.y);
```

You can see this example by executing *CH5EX19.html* from the code distribution, or by typing in the code listing shown in Example 5-19.

Example 5-19. Easing in (taking off)

```
<!doctype html>
<html lang="en">
<head>
<meta charset="UTF-8">
<title>CH5EX19: Taking Off (Fake Ease In)</title>

<script src="modernizr.js"></script>
<script type="text/javascript">
window.addEventListener('load', eventWindowLoaded, false);
var shipImage;
function eventWindowLoaded() {
    shipImage = new Image();
    shipImage.src = "ship.png"
    shipImage.onload = eventAssetsLoaded;
}

function eventAssetsLoaded() {

    canvasApp();
}

function canvasSupport () {
    return Modernizr.canvas;
}

function canvasApp() {

    if (!canvasSupport()) {
        return;
        }

  var pointImage = new Image();
  pointImage.src = "pointwhite.png";
  function  drawScreen () {

    context.fillStyle = '#000000';
    context.fillRect(0, 0, theCanvas.width, theCanvas.height);
    //Box
    context.strokeStyle = '#ffffff';
    context.strokeRect(1,  1, theCanvas.width-2, theCanvas.height-2);

    ship.velocityx = ship.velocityx + ( ship.velocityx*easeValue);
    ship.velocityy = ship.velocityy + ( ship.velocityy*easeValue);

    ship.x += ship.velocityx;
```

```
        ship.y += ship.velocityy;

        //Draw points to illustrate path

        points.push({x:ship.x,y:ship.y});

        for (var i = 0; i< points.length; i++) {
           context.drawImage(pointImage, points[i].x+shipImage.width/2,
              points[i].y,1,1);
        }

        context.drawImage(shipImage,ship.x,ship.y);

    }

    var easeValue = .05;
    var p1 = {x:240,y:470};
    var tempX;
    var tempY;
    var tempSpeed = .5;
    var tempAngle = 270 ;
    var tempRadians = tempAngle * Math.PI/ 180;
    var tempvelocityx = Math.cos(tempRadians) * tempSpeed;
    var tempvelocityy  = Math.sin(tempRadians) * tempSpeed;

    var ship = {x:p1.x, y:p1.y, velocityx:tempvelocityx, velocityy:tempvelocityy};
    var points = new Array();

    theCanvas = document.getElementById("canvasOne");
    context = theCanvas.getContext("2d");

    function gameLoop() {
      window.setTimeout(gameLoop, 20);
      drawScreen()
    }
    gameLoop();

}

</script>

</head>
<body>
<div style="position: absolute; top: 50px; left: 50px;">

<canvas id="canvasOne" width="500" height="500">
 Your browser does not support HTML5 Canvas.
</canvas>
</div>
</body>
</html>
```

For more information about easing, check out Robert Penner's easing equations (*http://www.robertpenner.com/easing/*). These equations have been implemented in jQuery for JavaScript (*http://plugins.jquery.com/files/jquery.animation.easing.js.txt*).

Box2D and the Canvas

Now that we have discussed how to use math and physics to create animations on the Canvas, it's time to take this discussion to the next level and implement a popular JavaScript library named Box2D (*http://code.google.com/p/box2dweb/*). Box2D is a physics modeling library for 2D graphics. We will use it to replace some of the complex code we developed manually for some of the earlier examples in this chapter.

Box2D was originally developed for C++ by Erin Catto and gained popularity as a library named *Box2DFlashAS3* for making Flash games in ActionScript 3. There are two Box2D implementations for JavaScript. The first is *Box2Djs*, and the other is *Box2dWeb*. Box2dWeb is the latest and greatest and had has been updated to Box2D 2.1, so that is the version we will use in our examples. Box2dWeb was ported directly from Action-Script 3 for use on the HTML5 Canvas.

Downloading Box2dWeb

To start, we need to download the latest version of Box2dWeb (*http://code.google.com/p/box2dweb/*). At the time of this writing, the latest version was Box2dWeb-2.1a.3.

How Does Box2dWeb Work?

Box2dWeb is a physics modeling engine. It allows a developer to create a world with physics properties and add objects to that world that react to the properties of that world and to each other. However, the world is not displayed (not formally anyway, as you'll see in a bit). The job of the Canvas developer when using Box2dWeb is to define a physics model and then apply it to the Canvas.

Before we get started, here are some definitions in Box2dWeb related to the examples we are going to cover. (The World modeled with Box2D is more complicated than just this, but these are the things we will cover in the examples.)

Shape
    A geometrical object that exists 2D space. These are circles, squares, rectangles, and so on.

Fixture
    A logical object that binds a shape to body and give it properties like density, friction, and restitution.

Rigid Body
> A physical manifestation of an object in the 2D world, with a fixture and a shape applied.

World
> A 2D physics world that contains bodies that react to one another

In the examples that follow, we will show how these things relate to one another in Box2D.

Box2D Hello World

For our first example, we will create a box that contains balls that fall and bounce on the screen. See Figure 5-24 to see an example.

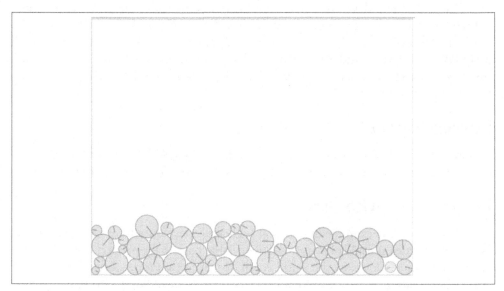

Figure 5-24. Box2D balls demo

Including the Library

The first thing we need to do is include the Box2dWeb library in JavaScript.

```
<script type="text/javascript" src="Box2dWeb-2.1.a.3.js"></script>
```

Creating a Box2dWeb World

Next we add the code to initialize the world. The variables created in the following code are shortcuts to the objects in Box2dWeb. They have shorter names make it much easier to define new objects in code. Not all the objects in Box2dWeb are represented here, so if you need a different one (such as a joint with b2JointDef), you will need to define a new shortcut (or just use the full object path name).

```
var     b2Vec2 = Box2D.Common.Math.b2Vec2
        , b2BodyDef = Box2D.Dynamics.b2BodyDef
        , b2Body = Box2D.Dynamics.b2Body
        , b2FixtureDef = Box2D.Dynamics.b2FixtureDef
        , b2World = Box2D.Dynamics.b2World
        , b2PolygonShape = Box2D.Collision.Shapes.b2PolygonShape
        , b2CircleShape = Box2D.Collision.Shapes.b2CircleShape
        , b2DebugDraw = Box2D.Dynamics.b2DebugDraw;
```

Now you create your world object. This will define your physics world. b2Vec() is a Box2D object that accepts two parameters: x-axis gravity and y-axis gravity. The second parameter is doSleep, which improves performance by not simulating inactive bodies if set to true.

```
var world = new b2World(new b2Vec2(0,10),  true);
```

Units in Box2dWeb

The first Box2D objects we will create are the four walls that define the area that holds our balls (a 500×400 Canvas). These walls are similar to the boundaries we defined in code for the earlier bouncing balls demos. We will define the walls as dynamic objects in an array, each with four properties:

```
{x:, x position, y: y position, w:width, h: height }
var wallDefs = new Array(
    {x:8.3,y:.03,w:8.3 ,h:.03},         //top wall
    {x:8.3,y:13.33,w:8.3 ,h:.03},       //bottom wall
    {x:0,y:6.67,w:.03 ,h:6.67},         //left wall
    {x:16.7,y:6.67,w:.03 ,h:6.67} );    //right wall
```

Notice that the values defined above do not look like anything we have used before. The values are in MTS units. As we stated earlier, MTS units refer to "meters-tonne-second" and are used represent large objects and spaces. However, because we draw everything in pixels on the Canvas, we need a way to think of MTS units in terms of the Canvas and vice versa.

To get these values, we need to choose a "scale" value to scale the Canvas pixels to MTS units. For this example (and all the examples in the rest of this chapter), we have chosen the value 30 as the scale value to translate pixels to MTS units.

At the same time, objects displayed in Box2D have their origin at the center (not the upper-left corner), so we need to compensate for that as well. Figure 5-25 shows how the units translate and the relative origins of the walls.

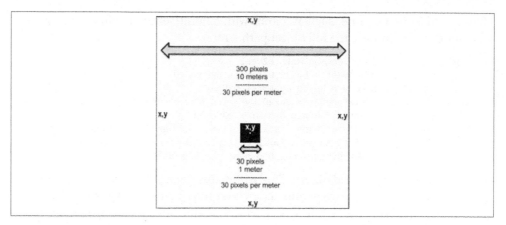

Figure 5-25. MTS conversion to pixels in Box2D

To get the sizes of the walls (width and height) we need to divide all the relative Canvas pixel values by 30. To get the location, we need to do the same but also make sure that we provide origins in the center, not the upper-left side of the object.

To top this off, the width and height passed to the Box2D `setAsBox()` method (width and height) are given in ½ width and ½ height. (We will discuss `setAsBox()` a little later in this chapter.)

So, for the top wall that we want to extend all the way across the Canvas with a height of 1 pixel, the code would be as follows:

```
{x:250/30, y:1/30, w:500/2/30, h:1/30}
```

Or, alternatively:

```
{x:8.3,y:.03,w:8.33 ,h:.03},        //top wall
```

The rest of the wall values use the same type of calculations to convert pixel values to MTS units for Box2D. Now let's use those units to make something.

What is interesting about this scale value is that when you use it uniformly (to convert to MTS units from pixels and from pixels to MTS units), the value can be *anything*. It just needs to be consistent. However, the value does have an effect on your physics world. The size of the value models the world in a different way. The smaller the scale value, the bigger the objects are in your world and vice versa. You will need to manipulate this scale value to tweak the physics for the world you are simulating.

Defining the Walls in Box2D

We now have our walls defined with locations and sizes based on MTS units. We can start defining the walls based on Box2D objects. We start by creating an array to hold our walls, and then we loop through the `wallDefs` array to create the four walls that bound the screen.

```
var walls = new Array();
for (var i = 0; i <wallDefs.length; i++) {
```

Next we start to define a wall by creating an instance b2BodyDef. A b2BodyDef object will hold the definitions we need to define a rigid body. Recall that a rigid body will have a *shape* and *fixture* applied to create a Box2D object that we can manipulate. We set the type to be `b2_staticBody`, which means that this object will never move and has infinite mass: perfect for the walls that bound our Canvas. We then set the position of `wall Def` to the position for this wall as set in the array of dynamic objects. Finally, we call `world.createBody(wallDef)` to create a rigid body in Box2D, based on the definitions set in the b2BodyDef object:

```
var wallDef = new b2BodyDef;
wallDef.type = b2Body.b2_staticBody;
wallDef.position.Set(wallDefs[i].x, wallDefs[i].y);
var newWall = world.CreateBody(wallDef)
```

Now it is time to create the fixture definition for the wall. Recall that a fixture binds a shape to the rigid body, and it contains properties for our Box2D object. First, we create a new `b2FixtureDef`, and then we set the `density` (mass per unit volume), `friction` (resistance, usually between 0 and 1), and the `restitution` (elasticity, usually between 0 and 1):

```
var wallFixture = new b2FixtureDef;
wallFixture.density = 10.0;
wallFixture.friction = 0.5;
wallFixture.restitution = 1;
```

Now that we have the fixture, we need to create the shape. We set the `shape` property of the fixture as `b2PolygonShape`, and then we call the shape's `setAsBox()` method (pass the `width` and `height` of the wall) to finish defining the shape. Next we close the loop by calling the `createFixture()` method of our rigid body, passing `wallFixture` as the parameter. This sets the fixture and shape to the rigid body. Finally, we add the rigid body to our walls array.

```
wallFixture.shape = new b2PolygonShape;
wallFixture.shape.SetAsBox(wallDefs[i].w, wallDefs[i].h);
newWall.CreateFixture(wallFixture);
walls.push(newWall);
}
```

Creating Balls

Creating the balls that will fall and bounce around in our demo is very similar to creating walls in Box2D. For this exercise, we will create 50 balls with random locations and sizes. The locations and sizes are (again) in MTS units. The only real difference from creating the walls is that we set the fixture shape property to b2CircleShape(size), where size is a random size in MTS units.

```
var numBalls = 50;
var balls = new Array();
for (var i=0; i < numBalls; i++) {
    var ballDef = new b2BodyDef;
    ballDef.type = b2Body.b2_dynamicBody;
    var ypos = (Math.random() * 8)+ 1;
    var xpos = (Math.random() * 14)+ 1;
    var size = (Math.random() * .4)+ 0.2;
    ballDef.position.Set(xpos, ypos);
    var ballFixture = new b2FixtureDef;
    ballFixture.density = 10.0;
    ballFixture.friction = 0.5;
    ballFixture.restitution = 1;
    ballFixture.shape =  new b2CircleShape(size);
    var newBall = world.CreateBody(ballDef)
    newBall.CreateFixture(ballFixture);
    balls.push(newBall);
}
```

Rendering b2debugDraw vs. Canvas Rendering

The b2debugDraw functionality of Box2D is just a way to test your physics world and see it working in a web browser. It is not an implementation of the physics for your application. We will use debugDraw to illustrate the objects we have created so that we can see them in action. In example *CH5EX22.html*, we will show you how to apply Box2D to the Canvas. For now, we just want to see the physics model we have created.

The following code is fairly boilerplate for getting b2debugDraw to work. The Set Sprite() method takes the Canvas context as a parameter. This means that the Canvas will be completely overwritten by the output from b2debugDraw. This is why it's just for testing. SetScaleFactor() takes the value we used to convert from pixels to MTS units (30*)*. SetFillAlpha() sets the transparency of the lines of the objects when displayed, and likewise, SetLineThickness() sets the thickness of those lines. The SetFlags() method accepts a single bit-wise parameter of options for display: e_shapeBit draws the shapes, and e_jointBit draws joints (but because we have not created any, you will not see them):

```
var debugDraw = new b2DebugDraw();
debugDraw.SetSprite (context2);
debugDraw.SetDrawScale(30);
debugDraw.SetFillAlpha(0.3);
debugDraw.SetLineThickness(1.0);
debugDraw.SetFlags(b2DebugDraw.e_shapeBit | b2DebugDraw.e_jointBit);
world.SetDebugDraw(debugDraw);
```

drawScreen()

Finally, we are ready to draw our Box2D physics models to the HTML5 Canvas. To make that work, we replace *all* of the code we have previously created in our `drawScreen()` function with following three lines:

```
world.Step(1 / 60, 10, 10);
world.DrawDebugData();
world.ClearForces();
```

`world.Step()` takes three parameters: time step, velocity iterations, and position iterations. The time step is how much time in the simulation to simulate on every call. For our application, we are simulating 1/60 of a second. The other two parameters set the precision of the iterations and should be left alone for now. `world.DrawDebugData()` draws the `b2DebugDraw` to the Canvas. `world.clearForces()` is called after every step to reset the physics model for the next step.

Example 5-20 provides the full code listing for *CH1EX20.html*. When you test this example, you will see 50 randomly created balls fall down and bounce off the bottom of the canvas. Some will bounce around for a long time, others will stop bouncing much sooner. Notice that balls appear to act the way you would expect balls to act. However, if you look back at the code we wrote, we did not create any functions for hit detection, angle of reflection, or linear movement. All of that was handled by Box2D.

Example 5-20. Box2dWeb balls demo

```
<!doctype html>
<html lang="en">
<head>
<meta charset="UTF-8">
<title>CH5EX20:  Box2dWeb Balls Demo</title>

<script src="modernizr.js"></script>
<script type="text/javascript" src="Box2dWeb-2.1.a.3.js"></script>
<script type="text/javascript">
window.addEventListener('load', eventWindowLoaded, false);

function eventWindowLoaded() {
    canvasApp();
}


function canvasSupport () {
    return Modernizr.canvas;
}

function canvasApp() {

  if (!canvasSupport()) {
    return;
  }
```

```
function  drawScreen () {

        world.Step(1 / 60, 10, 10);
        world.DrawDebugData();
        world.ClearForces();
}
    theCanvas = document.getElementById('canvasOne');
    context = theCanvas.getContext('2d');
    var     b2Vec2 = Box2D.Common.Math.b2Vec2
            ,   b2BodyDef = Box2D.Dynamics.b2BodyDef
            ,   b2Body = Box2D.Dynamics.b2Body
            ,   b2FixtureDef = Box2D.Dynamics.b2FixtureDef
            ,   b2World = Box2D.Dynamics.b2World
            ,   b2PolygonShape = Box2D.Collision.Shapes.b2PolygonShape
            ,   b2CircleShape = Box2D.Collision.Shapes.b2CircleShape
            ,   b2DebugDraw = Box2D.Dynamics.b2DebugDraw;
    var world = new b2World(new b2Vec2(0,10),  true);
    var numBalls = 50;
    var balls = new Array();
    for (var i=0; i < numBalls; i++) {
        var ballDef = new b2BodyDef;
        ballDef.type = b2Body.b2_dynamicBody;
        var ypos = (Math.random() * 8)+1;
        var xpos = (Math.random() * 14)+1;
        var size = (Math.random() * .4)+.2;
        ballDef.position.Set(xpos, ypos);
        var ballFixture = new b2FixtureDef;
        ballFixture.density = 10.0;
        ballFixture.friction = 0.5;
        ballFixture.restitution = 1;
        ballFixture.shape =  new b2CircleShape(size);
        var newBall = world.CreateBody(ballDef)
        newBall.CreateFixture(ballFixture);
        balls.push(newBall);
    }
    var wallDefs = new Array({x:8.3,y:.03,w:8.3 ,h:.03}, //top
            {x:8.3,y:13.33,w:8.3 ,h:.03},    //bottom
            {x:0,y:6.67,w:.03 ,h:6.67},      //left
            {x:16.7,y:6.67,w:.03 ,h:6.67} );     //right
    var walls = new Array();
    for (var i = 0; i <wallDefs.length; i++) {
       var wallDef = new b2BodyDef;
       wallDef.type = b2Body.b2_staticBody;
       wallDef.position.Set(wallDefs[i].x, wallDefs[i].y);
       var newWall = world.CreateBody(wallDef)
       var wallFixture = new b2FixtureDef;
       wallFixture.density = 10.0;
       wallFixture.friction = 0.5;
       wallFixture.restitution = 1;
       wallFixture.shape = new b2PolygonShape;
       wallFixture.shape.SetAsBox(wallDefs[i].w, wallDefs[i].h);
       newWall.CreateFixture(wallFixture);
```

```
        walls.push(newWall);
    }
    var debugDraw = new b2DebugDraw();
    debugDraw.SetSprite (context);
        debugDraw.SetDrawScale(30);        //define scale
        debugDraw.SetFillAlpha(0.3);       //define transparency
        debugDraw.SetLineThickness(1.0);
        debugDraw.SetFlags(b2DebugDraw.e_shapeBit | b2DebugDraw.e_jointBit);
    world.SetDebugDraw(debugDraw);
    function gameLoop() {
        window.setTimeout(gameLoop, 20);
        drawScreen()
    }
    gameLoop();
}
</script>

</head>
<body>
<div style="position: absolute; top: 0px; left: 0px;">
<canvas id="canvasOne" width="500" height="400">
 Your browser does not support the HTML 5 Canvas.
</canvas>
</div>
</body>
</html>
```

Bouncing Balls Revisited

Do you recall from *CH5EX7.html* how we created bouncing balls that bounce off one another? We are going to iterate the last example with just a few simple changes to create a world that acts a lot like that example.

First, we will change the gravity in the world definition so that there is no y-axis gravity at all. Instead of looking at balls from the side, we are looking at balls from the top (like it's a flat 2D world and we are looking down). We will also set our demo to have 50 balls instead of 30.

```
    var world = new b2World(new b2Vec2(0,0),  true);
    var numBalls = 50;
```

Because there is no gravity in this world, we need some way for the balls to move when the demo starts. To do this, we will add a random *x* and *y* velocity to each ball and then pass those as parameters of a new b2Vec2() object with a call to the ball's SetLinearVelocity() method.

```
    var xVelocity = Math.floor(Math.random() * 10) -5;
    var yVelocity = Math.floor(Math.random() * 10) -5;
    newBall.SetLinearVelocity(new b2Vec2(xVelocity,yVelocity))
```

That's all we need to do to change our falling balls demo into something similar to the bouncing balls demo from earlier in the chapter.

You can test this example by opening *CH5EX21.html* in the code distribution. The results will look something like what you see in Figure 5-26.

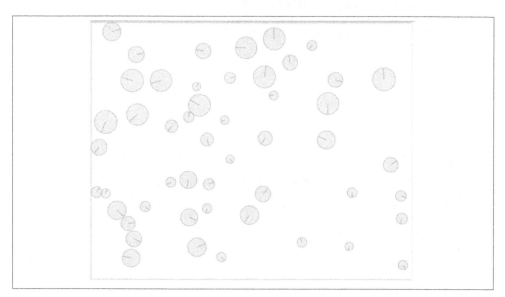

Figure 5-26. Bouncing balls in Box2D

As you can see, getting up to speed with Box2D might take a bit of time, but when you get the hang of it, you can make some dramatic changes with very little code.

Translating to the Canvas

So far, we have looked only at Box2D output with `b2DebigDraw`. While this looks neat, it's not really useful for Canvas applications. As we stated earlier, Box2D is just a "physics model." It is your job to apply that model to the HTML5 Canvas. In this next example, we will take the bouncing balls from the last example and show them running side-by-wide with the Canvas. (See Figure 5-27.)

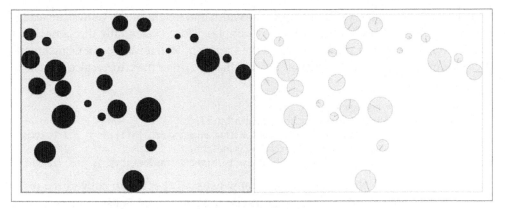

Figure 5-27. Bouncing balls in Box2D on the Canvas and in b2DebugDraw

The first thing we need to do is to define a second Canvas in our HTML to show the b2DebugDraw output:

```
<canvas id="canvasOne" width="450" height="350">
  Your browser does not support the HTML 5 Canvas.
</canvas>
<canvas id="canvasTwo" width="450" height="350">
  Your browser does not support the HTML 5 Canvas.
</canvas>
```

Notice that the Canvas is now smaller (450×350). We changed the size so that we could easily fit two Canvases side by side in the web browser. We also need to make sure to get a reference to both in our JavaScript code:

```
var theCanvas = document.getElementById('canvasOne');
var context = theCanvas.getContext('2d');

var theCanvasTwo = document.getElementById('canvasTwo');
var context2 = theCanvasTwo.getContext('2d');
```

Now that we have that out of the way, let's start by making our lives a lot easier. Instead of using a literal for our scale factor, we will create a variable named `scaleFactor` that we can use for scale conversions:

```
var scaleFactor = 30;
```

We can use `scaleFactor` when finding positions and sizes for our objects in Box2D. First, in the loop where we created the balls to display, we now use the entire canvas width and height, modified by the `scaleFactor` to randomly position the balls:

```
var ypos = (Math.random() * theCanvas.height)/scaleFactor;
var xpos = (Math.random() * theCanvas.width/scaleFactor);
var size = ((Math.random() * 20)+ 5)/scaleFactor;
```

We also now define the `wallDefs` using the width and height of the Canvas instead of the MTS values we used in the previous examples. This is essentially the same, but it makes it much easier to adjust the size of the Canvas now that we are not using literals. Because our Canvas is now smaller, it helps that we don't have to recalculate all the values:

```
var wallDefs = new Array (
  {x:theCanvas.width,y:0,w:theCanvas.width ,h:1},            //top
  {x:theCanvas.width,y:theCanvas.height,w:theCanvas.width ,h:1},    //bottom
  {x:0,y:theCanvas.height,w:1 ,h:theCanvas.height},          //left
  {x:theCanvas.width,y:theCanvas.height,w:1 ,h:theCanvas.height} );  //right
```

In the loop where we define the walls, we now use `scaleFactor` to convert the pixels values in our array to MTS values for positions and sizes of the walls:

```
wallDef.position.Set(wallDefs[i].x/scaleFactor, wallDefs[i].y/scaleFactor);
...
wallFixture.shape.SetAsBox(wallDefs[i].w/scaleFactor, wallDefs[i].h/scaleFactor);
```

When we define our instance of `b2DebugDraw`, we pass a reference to the second Canvas (`context2`) so that the debug output will display there, and we can draw on the first Canvas with the Canvas drawing API:

```
debugDraw.SetSprite (context2);
debugDraw.SetDrawScale(scaleFactor);     //define scale
```

The big changes for this example arrive in `drawScreen()`. The calls to the methods of the world object are the same as in the last example (even though `world.DrawDebugData()` is now using `context2`):

```
function  drawScreen () {

        world.Step(1 / 60, 10, 10);
        world.DrawDebugData();
        world.ClearForces();
```

Now we are going to translate the Box2D data in our model to the Canvas. Most of this `drawScreen()` function should look familiar, because it is not much different than some of the earlier bouncing ball demos. First we clear the Canvas, and then we look through the `balls` array to display each ball:

```
context.fillStyle = '#EEEEEE';
context.fillRect(0, 0, theCanvas.width, theCanvas.height);
//Box
context.strokeStyle = '#000000';
context.strokeRect(1,  1, theCanvas.width-2, theCanvas.height-2);
for (i =0;i <balls.length;i++) {
```

The first big difference is how we get the position and size of the ball we are going to draw. The items we have in our `balls` array are instances of the Box2D `b2Body` object. We use that object's `GetPosition()` method to find the current x and y coordinates of the ball. We then call the `GetFixtureList()` method of `b2Body`. This will give us the `b2Fixture` we created for the ball. Recall that for each fixture we set a `shape` property. We need to get that `shape` property by calling `fixtureList.GetShape()`:

```
var position = balls[i].GetPosition();
var fixtureList = balls[i].GetFixtureList();
var shape = fixtureList.GetShape();
```

With all the information we need, we can now draw the ball on the Canvas. Using the `context.arc()` method, we set the x and y position multiplied by the `scaleFactor` (because we are now converting from MTS units to pixels). We call `shape.GetRadius()` for the size of the circle and use the same conversion with `scaleFactor`:

```
context.fillStyle = "#000000";
context.beginPath();
context.arc(position.x * scaleFactor   , position.y *
scaleFactor ,shape.GetRadius() *scaleFactor ,0,Math.PI*2,true);
context.closePath();
context.fill();


}
```

When you run the example (*CH5EX22.html*), you will see something similar to what is in Figure 5-27 The Canvas on the left displays balls using the Canvas drawing objects and looks very similar to the demo we created in *CH5EX8.html*. The Canvas on the right shows the `b2DebugDraw` output from Box2D. We have now successfully applied a Box2D physics model to the HTML5 Canvas.

Again, notice that, besides getting familiar with the object model of Box2D, this example is very simple. We did not have to build any movement or collisions detection routines ourselves. Box2D takes care of all that stuff on its own. We just need to define a Box2D world and then put objects inside of it.

Interactivity with Box2D

So far, we have simply placed objects in a defined Box2D world and let them move on their own. While that type of application is great for teaching or instruction, creating an interactive world with Box2D is a path to creating exciting games and simulations on the Canvas.

For this example, we will create a game where you shoot balls at a pile of boxes and knock them over. However, before we get to that example, we will start with a simpler iteration where we display some boxes and model them falling and rotating. (See Figure 5-28.)

Figure 5-28. Boxes falling and rotating

Creating the Boxes

The world we are going to simulate is essentially the same as in the last example, with a positive y-axis gravitation force of 10 and a `scaleFactor` of 30.

```
var world = new b2World(new b2Vec2(0,10),  true);
var scaleFactor = 30;
```

In this world, we will create a set of eight 25×25 pixel boxes that are piled on top of each other, 100 pixels from the right side of the Canvas, and starting 100 pixels from the bottom so that they will fall to the ground when the demo starts:

```
var numBoxes = 8;
var boxes = new Array();
var boxHeight = 25;
var boxWidth  = 25;
var startX = (theCanvas.width-100);
var startY = (theCanvas.height-boxHeight)-100
```

When we loop through, creating the boxes, we perform essentially the same operations as when we create walls. We use the `scaleFactor` to convert to MTS units, but instead of defining a `b2_staticBody`, we define the box as a `b2_dynamicBody`, which means it can move and be affected by the physics-driven models in Box2D.

One other thing we do here is offset each box to the right by (`i*2`) pixels. We do this so that each successive box will fall a tiny bit to the right of the box under it. This will make the stack unstable so that the boxes fall over when they hit the ground. We want to do this so that we can illustrate rotating the boxes on the Canvas:

```
for (var i=0; i < numBoxes; i++) {
   var boxDef = new b2BodyDef;
```

```
boxDef.type = b2Body.b2_dynamicBody;
var ypos = (startY-(i*boxHeight))/scaleFactor;
var xpos = (startX+(i*2))/scaleFactor;
boxDef.position.Set(xpos, ypos);
  var newBox = world.CreateBody(boxDef)
var boxFixture = new b2FixtureDef;
boxFixture.density = 10.0;
boxFixture.friction = 0.5;
boxFixture.restitution = 1;
  boxFixture.shape = new b2PolygonShape;
boxFixture.shape.SetAsBox((boxWidth/scaleFactor)/2, (boxHeight/scaleFactor)/2);
newBox.CreateFixture(boxFixture);
```

The one addition we will add to the boxes that we did not have for the walls is using the `SetUserData()` method of the `b2Body` object. This allows us to create a dynamic object that holds any type of data we might need and attach it to the body. For our purposes, we will attach an object that holds the width and height of the boxes (in MTS units) so that we can easily model them on the Canvas in our `drawScreen()` function.

```
newBox.SetUserData({width:boxWidth/scaleFactor, height:boxHeight/scaleFactor})
boxes.push(newBox);
}
```

Rendering the Boxes

To render the boxes, we loop through the boxes array in `drawScreen()` in a similar manner to how we looped through the balls in *CH5EX22.html*. We retrieve the position and shape using `GetPosition()` and `GetShape()`, preparing to render the boxes:

```
for (i =0;i <boxes.length;i++) {
    var position = boxes[i].GetPosition();
    var fixtureList = boxes[i].GetFixtureList();
    var shape = fixtureList.GetShape();
```

However, because these are boxes that fall and rotate, we need to perform some significantly different operations to render the boxes correctly. First we retrieve the object we saved in the user data attached to the body by calling `GetUserData()`:

```
var userData = boxes[i].GetUserData();
```

Next we save the Canvas context, reset the transformation matrix, and translate to the center of the box. Because the origin of the objects in Box2D is set to the center, we don't have to offset to the center for our transformation. Next we rotate the Canvas to the angle of the box. We find the angle with a call to `GetAngle()`:

```
context.save();
context.setTransform(1,0,0,1,0,0);
context.translate(position.x * scaleFactor,position.y * scaleFactor);
context.rotate(boxes[i].GetAngle());
```

To draw the box, we need to offset the x and y from the position back to ½ width and height because we draw on the Canvas with an origin at the upper-left corner. Then we restore the context, and we are done with the box:

```
context.fillRect(0-(userData.width*scaleFactor/2), 0-
                    (userData.height*scaleFactor/2),
          userData.width * scaleFactor, userData.height * scaleFactor);
      context.restore();
  }
```

We have now modeled boxes falling and reacting to gravity and collisions with other boxes in Box2D. You can view this example by looking at *CH5EX23.html* in the code distribution.

Adding Interactivity

The final example in our foray into Box2D will add interactivity to the Canvas so that we can shoot balls that knock over the pile of boxes we created in the last example. Figure 5-29 shows what the example looks like when executed in a web browser.

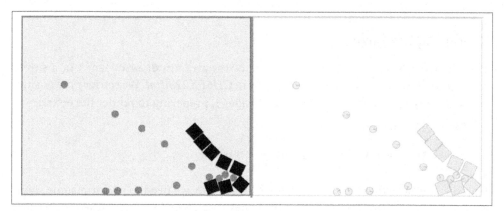

Figure 5-29. Shooting balls at boxes

Creating Boxes

There are a few changes we need to make for this example from *CH5EX23.html* when we create the boxes. In the loop, we set the x position for the boxes to be right on top of each other, instead of offset to the right. We no longer need the boxes to fall over on their own; the balls we shoot at the boxes will do that for us!

We also set the density of the boxes to 20 so that they are harder to knock over, and we reduce the restitution to .1 so that they don't bounce around as much as they did in the last example:

```
var xpos = (startX)/scaleFactor;
boxFixture.density = 20.0;
...
boxFixture.restitution = .1;
```

Also, when we create the walls, we set the wall restitution to .5, which means objects will be less apt to bounce around on top of them:

```
wallFixture.restitution = .5;
```

Handling the Balls

For this example, we want to listen for a mouse click on the Canvas. When the user clicks, we want to create a ball that flies across the Canvas towards the piles of boxes. The first thing we need to do is create an event listener for the mouseup event:

```
theCanvas.addEventListener("mouseup",createBall, false);
```

Next we need to create the createBall() function. First, we get the *x* and *y* position of the mouse from the event object passed to createBall(). Then we use some cross-browser code to figure out the mouse position relative to the Canvas. The following boilerplate code captured (at the time of this writing) the proper x and y mouse position on the Canvas:

```
function createBall(event) {
    var x;
    var y;
    if (event.pageX || event.pageY) {
        x = event.pageX;
        y = event.pageY;
    }
    else {
        x = e.clientX + document.body.scrollLeft +
                document.documentElement.scrollLeft;
        y = e.clientY + document.body.scrollTop +
                document.documentElement.scrollTop;
    }
    x -= theCanvas.offsetLeft;
    y -= theCanvas.offsetTop;

    mouseX=x;
    mouseY=y;
```

Because we are capturing the mouse x and y position relative to the Canvas, you need to make sure that the <canvas> element in the HTML page is styled with top and left values so that the offsetLeft and offsetTop values are correct. For example, if you position the Canvas inside a <div> at 50,50 and leave the left and top style values at 0, the mouse clicks will not be captured in the correct locations:

```
<canvas id="canvasOne" width="450" height="350"
        style="position: absolute; top: 0px; left: 0px;">
```

```
    Your browser does not support the HTML5 Canvas.
    </canvas>
    <canvas id="canvasTwo" width="450" height="350"
            style="position: absolute; top: 0px; left: 451px;">
    Your browser does not support the HTML5 Canvas.
    </canvas>
```

Next, we create a rigid body definition object, setting the *x* and *y* position in the b2Body
Def to the location of the mouse click, and we set the size of the ball radius to 7 pixels,
which we will use a few lines down:

```
    var ballDef = new b2BodyDef;
    ballDef.type = b2Body.b2_dynamicBody;
    var ypos = mouseY/scaleFactor;
    var xpos = mouseX/scaleFactor;
    var size = 7/scaleFactor;
    ballDef.position.Set(xpos, ypos);
```

Next we create the fixture, setting the density of the ball to 30 (harder than the boxes),
friction to .6 (only because it makes the simulation feel better when running), and set
the restitution to .2, which is more than both the boxes and the walls because we want
to balls to bounce a bit higher than the boxes when they hit another object:

```
    var ballFixture = new b2FixtureDef;
    ballFixture.density = 30.0;
    ballFixture.friction = 0.6;
    ballFixture.restitution = .2;
    ballFixture.shape =  new b2CircleShape(size);
    var newBall = world.CreateBody(ballDef)
    newBall.CreateFixture(ballFixture);
```

Then, we set the linear velocity of the balls to positive 15 on the x axis, which will have
them start moving across the Canvas to the right when they are created:

```
    var xVelocity = 15;
    var yVelocity = 0;
    newBall.SetLinearVelocity(new b2Vec2(xVelocity,yVelocity))
    balls.push(newBall);
}
```

Finally, we need to render the balls in drawScreen(). Except for the fact that we color
the balls red, the rendering we do here is essentially the same as we did in the bouncing
balls demo in *CH5EX22*:

```
for (i =0;i <balls.length;i++) {
    var position = balls[i].GetPosition();
    var fixtureList = balls[i].GetFixtureList();
    var shape = fixtureList.GetShape();
    context.fillStyle = "#FF0000";
    context.beginPath();
    context.arc(position.x * scaleFactor   , position.y * scaleFactor ,
            shape.GetRadius()
        *scaleFactor ,0,Math.PI*2,true);
```

```
        context.closePath();
        context.fill();
    }
```

Those are all the changes we need to make to convert the stacked boxes example (*CH5EX23.html*) into an interactive experience when the user shoots balls to knock down boxes. Load *CH5EX24.html* from the code distribution into your web browser, and check it out! The full code listing is provided in Example 5-21.

Example 5-21. Box2dWeb box battle

```
<!doctype html>
<html lang="en">
<head>
<meta charset="UTF-8">
<title>CH5EX24:  Box2dWeb Box Battle</title>

<script src="modernizr.js"></script>
<script type="text/javascript" src="Box2dWeb-2.1.a.3.js"></script>
<script type="text/javascript">
window.addEventListener('load', eventWindowLoaded, false);

function eventWindowLoaded() {
    canvasApp();
}


function canvasSupport () {
     return Modernizr.canvas;
}

function canvasApp() {

  if (!canvasSupport()) {
          return;
      }


  function  drawScreen () {

        world.Step(1 / 60, 10, 10);
        world.DrawDebugData();
        world.ClearForces();

        context.strokeStyle = '#000000';
        context.fillStyle = '#EEEEEE';
        context.fillRect(0, 0, theCanvas.width, theCanvas.height);
         //Box
        context.fillStyle = '#000000';
        context.strokeRect(1,  1, theCanvas.width-2, theCanvas.height-2);
        for (i =0;i <boxes.length;i++) {
            var position = boxes[i].GetPosition();
            var fixtureList = boxes[i].GetFixtureList();
```

```
            var shape = fixtureList.GetShape();
            var userData = boxes[i].GetUserData();
            context.save();
            context.setTransform(1,0,0,1,0,0);
            context.translate(position.x * scaleFactor,position.y *
                    scaleFactor);
            context.rotate(boxes[i].GetAngle());
            context.fillRect(0-(userData.width*scaleFactor/2)   ,
                0-(userData.height*scaleFactor/2), userData.width * scaleFactor,
                    userData.height
                * scaleFactor);
            context.restore();
    }

    for (i =0;i <balls.length;i++) {
        var position = balls[i].GetPosition();
        var fixtureList = balls[i].GetFixtureList();
        var shape = fixtureList.GetShape();
        context.fillStyle = "#FF0000";
        context.beginPath();
        context.arc(position.x * scaleFactor   , position.y * scaleFactor ,
                shape.GetRadius()
            *scaleFactor ,0,Math.PI*2,true);
        context.closePath();
        context.fill();
    }

}

function createBall(event) {
    var x;
    var y;
    if (event.pageX || event.pageY) {
        x = event.pageX;
        y = event.pageY;
    }
    else {
        x = e.clientX + document.body.scrollLeft +
        document.documentElement.scrollLeft;
        y = e.clientY + document.body.scrollTop +
        document.documentElement.scrollTop;
    }
    x -= theCanvas.offsetLeft;
    y -= theCanvas.offsetTop;

    mouseX=x;
    mouseY=y;
    var ballDef = new b2BodyDef;
    ballDef.type = b2Body.b2_dynamicBody;
    var ypos = mouseY/scaleFactor;
    var xpos = mouseX/scaleFactor;
    var size = 7/scaleFactor;
```

```
            ballDef.position.Set(xpos, ypos);
            var ballFixture = new b2FixtureDef;
            ballFixture.density = 30.0;
            ballFixture.friction = 0.6;
            ballFixture.restitution = .2;
            ballFixture.shape =  new b2CircleShape(size);
            var newBall = world.CreateBody(ballDef)
            newBall.CreateFixture(ballFixture);
            var xVelocity = 15;
            var yVelocity = 0;
            newBall.SetLinearVelocity(new b2Vec2(xVelocity,yVelocity))
            balls.push(newBall);

    }

    var theCanvas = document.getElementById('canvasOne');
    var context = theCanvas.getContext('2d');

    var theCanvasTwo = document.getElementById('canvasTwo');
    var context2 = theCanvasTwo.getContext('2d');

    theCanvas.addEventListener("mouseup",createBall, false);

    var scaleFactor = 30;
    var     b2Vec2 = Box2D.Common.Math.b2Vec2
            ,   b2BodyDef = Box2D.Dynamics.b2BodyDef
            ,   b2Body = Box2D.Dynamics.b2Body
            ,   b2FixtureDef = Box2D.Dynamics.b2FixtureDef
            ,   b2World = Box2D.Dynamics.b2World
            ,   b2PolygonShape = Box2D.Collision.Shapes.b2PolygonShape
            ,    b2CircleShape = Box2D.Collision.Shapes.b2CircleShape
            ,   b2DebugDraw = Box2D.Dynamics.b2DebugDraw;

    var world = new b2World(new b2Vec2(0,20),  true);
    var numBoxes = 8;
    var boxes = new Array();
    var balls = new Array();
    var boxHeight = 25;
    var boxWidth  = 25;
    var startX = (theCanvas.width-100);
    var startY = (theCanvas.height-boxHeight)-100
    for (var i=0; i < numBoxes; i++) {
        var boxDef = new b2BodyDef;
        boxDef.type = b2Body.b2_dynamicBody;
        var ypos = (startY-(i*boxHeight))/scaleFactor;
        var xpos = (startX)/scaleFactor;
        boxDef.position.Set(xpos, ypos);
        var newBox = world.CreateBody(boxDef)
        var boxFixture = new b2FixtureDef;
        boxFixture.density = 20.0;
        boxFixture.friction = .5;
        boxFixture.restitution = .1;
```

```
            boxFixture.shape = new b2PolygonShape;
            boxFixture.shape.SetAsBox((boxWidth/scaleFactor)/2,
                    (boxHeight/scaleFactor)/2);
            newBox.CreateFixture(boxFixture);
            newBox.SetUserData({width:boxWidth/scaleFactor,
                    height:boxHeight/scaleFactor})
            boxes.push(newBox);
        }

    var wallDefs = new Array(
            {x:theCanvas.width,y:0,w:theCanvas.width ,h:1},//top
            {x:theCanvas.width,y:theCanvas.height,w:theCanvas.width ,h:1},//bottom
            {x:0,y:theCanvas.height,w:1 ,h:theCanvas.height},          //left
            {x:theCanvas.width,y:theCanvas.height,w:1 ,h:theCanvas.height} );  //right
    var walls = new Array();
    for (var i = 0; i <wallDefs.length; i++) {
        var wallDef = new b2BodyDef;
        wallDef.type = b2Body.b2_staticBody;
        wallDef.position.Set(wallDefs[i].x/scaleFactor, wallDefs[i].y/scaleFactor);
        var newWall = world.CreateBody(wallDef)
        var wallFixture = new b2FixtureDef;
        wallFixture.density = 10.0;
        wallFixture.friction = 0.5;
        wallFixture.restitution = .5;
        wallFixture.shape = new b2PolygonShape;
        wallFixture.shape.SetAsBox(wallDefs[i].w/scaleFactor,
                wallDefs[i].h/scaleFactor);
        newWall.CreateFixture(wallFixture);
        walls.push(newWall);
    }

     var debugDraw = new b2DebugDraw();
    debugDraw.SetSprite (context2);
    debugDraw.SetDrawScale(scaleFactor);      //define scale
    debugDraw.SetFillAlpha(0.3);    //define transparency
    debugDraw.SetLineThickness(1.0);
    debugDraw.SetFlags(b2DebugDraw.e_shapeBit | b2DebugDraw.e_jointBit);
    world.SetDebugDraw(debugDraw);



    function gameLoop() {
            window.setTimeout(gameLoop, 20);
            drawScreen()
        }

    gameLoop();



}
```

```
</script>

</head>
<body>
<canvas id="canvasOne" width="450" height="350" style="position: absolute;
    top: 0px; left: 0px;">
 Your browser does not support the HTML 5 Canvas.
</canvas>
<canvas id="canvasTwo" width="450" height="350" style="position: absolute;
    top: 0px; left: 451px;">
 Your browser does not support the HTML 5 Canvas.
</canvas>
</body>
</html>
```

Box2D Further Reading

As you can see, Box2D has a steep learning curve, but after you get the hang of it, relatively minor changes to your code can create some very cool applications. We have covered only a very small percentage of what can be accomplished with Box2D. Here are some resources to continue your *Box2D* journey:

Box2dWeb basic usage
    http://code.google.com/p/box2dweb/wiki/BasicUsage

Box2D Manual
    http://box2d.org/manual.pdf

Box2D 2.1 Flash Reference
    http://www.box2dflash.org/docs/2.1a/reference/

What's Next?

We have shown you a plethora of examples for how you can use HTML5 Canvas to animate objects using some basic principles of math, physics, and Box2D. However, we have really only begun to scratch the surface of the multitude of ways that you can use math and physics in your applications. In the next couple chapters, we will switch gears, discussing audio and video, before we start applying many of the concepts we have learned in this book to a couple of in-depth game projects.

CHAPTER 6

Mixing HTML5 Video and Canvas

Using the new <video> tag, HTML5 lets sites show video directly in HTML without needing any plug-in technologies. However, the simple <video> tag opens up a whole slew of complexities and opportunities for developers. While we can't cover everything related to video in this chapter, we will introduce you to the HTML5 <video> tag and then show you ways in which video can be incorporated and manipulated by HTML5 Canvas.

HTML5 Video Support

HTML5 specifies a new tag, <video>, that allows developers to place video directly in an HTML page. With a few simple options, you can autoplay, loop, and add playback controls to the embedded video.

First, let's talk about video format support, which is a very complicated issue. Some video formats are free, and others are licensed. Some formats look better than others, some make smaller file sizes, and some are supported in one browser while others are supported in a different browser. In this chapter, we will concentrate on three formats that either have broad support now or promise to have broad support in the future: *.ogg*, *.mp4*, and *.webm*.

We will discuss these video formats in terms of *video codecs*. Each format uses one or more *codecs* to compress and decompress video. Codecs are usually the secret sauce of a video format because compression is the key to making video that, in the wild, can convert very large files into file sizes that can be easily transported on the Internet.

Theora + Vorbis = .ogg

Theora (*http://www.theora.org/*) is an open source, free video codec developed by Xiph.org. Vorbis (*http://www.vorbis.com*) is a free, open source audio codec that is used in conjunction with Theora. Both Theora and Vorbis are stored in an *.ogg* file. Ogg files have the broadest support among traditional web browsers but, unfortunately, not on handheld devices. These files can also be represented by *.ogv* (video) and *.oga* (audio). Many commercial companies (for example, Apple) have balked at using Theora/Vorbis because they are unsure about whether somewhere, someplace, someone might own a patent that covers part of the technology, and thus they might get sued for using it.

 Sometimes technology companies get hit with what is known as a *submarine patent*. This was a patent tactic—available up until 1995 in the United States—that allowed a filer to delay the publication of a patent. Because patents were only enforceable for 17 years, if someone filed one but delayed the publication, he could wait years (even decades) until someone else came up with the same idea and then hit that person with a lawsuit.

H.264 + $$$ = .mp4

H.264 is a high-quality video standard that has received the backing of some very big players, such as Apple, Adobe, and Microsoft. However, despite offering high-quality video, it defines only a standard—not a video codec. An organization named MPEG LA owns the intellectual property, and they license it out to software and hardware vendors. Many companies that have implemented H.264 have done so with their own proprietary codecs. As a result, the varying codecs are incompatible with one another, making this a tricky format to use across multiple platforms. H.264 videos have the *.mp4* extension. Most for-profit corporations have implemented support for this format on their platforms, but the developers of open source browsers like Firefox and Opera have not. In late 2010, Google dropped H.264 support in Chrome in favor of WebM.

VP8 + Vorbis = .webm

WebM is a new open source video standard supported by Google, Adobe, Mozilla, and Opera. It is based on the VP8 codec and includes Vorbis (just like Theora) as an audio codec. When YouTube (*http://youtube.com*) announced they had converted many of their videos to be HTML5-compatible, one of the formats they used was WebM. Currently, only Google Chrome and Opera support WebM, but broader support should be coming in the future.

To summarize, here is a chart of the video formats supported by various browsers.

Platform	.ogg	.mp4	.webm
Android	X	X	
Firefox	X		X
Chrome	X		X

Platform	.ogg	.mp4	.webm
iPhone		X	
Internet Explorer 9		X	
Opera	X		X
Safari		X	

As you can see, no one format is supported by all browsers or platforms. Because HTML5 Canvas supports video only in the format supported by the browser it is implemented within, we must apply a strategy that uses multiple formats to play video.

Combining All Three

The examples in this chapter will introduce a strategy that may seem crazy at first—using all three formats at once. While this might seem to be more work than necessary, right now it is the only way to ensure broad support across as many platforms as possible. The HTML5 <video> tag allows us to specify multiple formats for a single video, and this will help us achieve our goal of broad video support when working with HTML5 Canvas.

Converting Video Formats

Before we get into some video demonstrations, we should discuss video conversions. Because we are going to use *.ogg*, *.mp4*, and *.webm* videos in all our projects, we need to have a way to convert video to these formats. Converting video can be a daunting task for someone unfamiliar with all the existing and competing formats; luckily, there are some great free tools to help us do just that:

Miro Video Converter (http://www.mirovideoconverter.com/)
> This application will quickly convert most video types to *.ogg*, *.mp4*, and *.webm*. It is available for both Windows and Mac.

SUPER (http://www.erightsoft.com/SUPER.html)
> This is a free video-conversion tool for Windows only that creates *.mp4* and *.ogg* formats. If you can navigate through the maze of screens trying to sell you other products, it can be very useful for video conversions.

HandBrake (http://handbrake.fr/)
> This video-converter application for the Macintosh platform creates *.mp4* and *.ogg* file types.

FFmpeg (http://ffmpeg.org/)
> This is the ultimate cross-platform, command-line tool for doing video conversions. It works in Windows/Mac/Linux and can do nearly any conversion you desire. However, there is no GUI interface, so it can be daunting for beginners. Some

of the preceding tools listed here use FFmpeg as their engine to do video conversions.

Basic HTML5 Video Implementation

In the `<video>` tag's most minimal implementation, it requires only a valid `src` attribute. For example, if we took a nifty little video of the waves crashing at Muir Beach, California (just north of San Francisco), and we encoded it as an H.264 *.mp4* file, the code might look like this:

```
<video src="muirbeach.mp4" />
```

 To see an example of this basic code, look at the *CH6EX1.html* file in the code distribution.

There are many properties that can be set in an HTML5 video embed. These properties are actually part of the `HTMLMediaElement` interface, implemented by the `HTMLVideoEle ment` object. Some of the more important properties include:

`src`
> The URL to the video that you want to play.

`autoplay`
> `true` or `false`. Forces the video to play automatically when loaded.

`loop`
> `true` or `false`. Loops the video back to the beginning when it has finished playing.

`volume`
> A number between 0 and 1. Sets the volume level of the playing video.

`poster`
> A URL to an image that will be shown while the video is loading.

There are also some methods of `HTMLVideoElement` that are necessary when playing video in conjunction with JavaScript and Canvas:

`play()`
> A method used to start playing a video.

`pause()`
> A method used to pause a video that is playing.

Additionally, there are some properties you can use to check the status of a video, including:

duration
> The length of the video in seconds.

currentTime
> The current playing time of the video in seconds. This can be used in conjunction with `duration` for some interesting effects, which we will explore later.

ended
> `true` or `false`, depending on whether the video has finished playing.

muted
> `true` or `false`. Used to inquire whether the sound of the playing video has been muted.

paused
> `true` or `false`. Used to inquire whether the video is currently paused.

> There are even more properties that exist for `HTMLVideoElement`. Check them out at this site (*http://www.w3.org/2010/05/video/mediae vents.html*).

Plain-Vanilla Video Embed

To demonstrate a plain-vanilla embed, we are going to work under our previously established rules for video formats. We will use three formats because no one format will work in every browser. We have created a version of the Muir Beach video as a *.webm*, an *.ogg*, and an *.mp4*. For the rest of this chapter, we will use all three formats in all of our video embeds.

To support all three formats at once, we must use an alternative method for setting the `src` attribute of the `<video>` tag. Why? Because we need to specify three different video formats instead of one in our HTML page. To do this, we add `<source>` tags within the `<video>` tag:

```
<video id="thevideo"  width="320" height="240">
 <source src="muirbeach.webm" type='video/webm; codecs="vp8, vorbis" '>
 <source src="muirbeach.mp4" type='video/mp4; codecs="avc1.42E01E, mp4a.40.2" '>
 <source src="muirbeach.ogg" type='video/ogg; codecs="theora, vorbis" '>
</video>
```

> We put the *.mp4* file second in the `src` list because newer versions of Chrome will try to use the format, but performance is spotty. This might cause issues on iOS (iPhone, iPad) devices and with older versions of Safari. In those versions of Safari, the browser will not attempt to load any other `src` type than the first one listed.

When a web browser reads this HTML, it will attempt to load each video in succession. If it does not support one format, it will try the next one. Using this style of embed allows the code in Example 6-1 to execute on all HTML5-compliant browsers.

Also notice that we have set the width and height properties of the video. While these are not necessarily needed (as we saw earlier), it is proper HTML form to include them, and we will need them a bit later when we start to manipulate the video size in code.

Example 6-1. Basic HTML video

```
<!doctype html>
<html lang="en">
<head>
<meta charset="UTF-8">
<title>CH6EX1: Basic HTML5 Video</title>
</head>
<body>
<div>
<video id="thevideo"  width="320" height="240">
 <source src="muirbeach.webm" type='video/webm; codecs="vp8, vorbis"' >
 <source src="muirbeach.mp4" type='video/mp4; codecs="avc1.42E01E, mp4a.40.2"' >
 <source src="muirbeach.ogg" type='video/ogg; codecs="theora, vorbis"'>
</video>
</div>
<div>
(Right-click To Control)
</div>
</body>
</html>
```

Figure 6-1 shows an example of the plain-vanilla video embed in an HTML5 page. There are no controls displayed in the default settings, but if you right-click on the video, controls will appear that can be used in conjunction with the embedded video.

(Right click To Control)

Figure 6-1. HTML5 video embed

Video with Controls, Loop, and Autoplay

While a video displayed without controls might suit your needs, most users expect to see some way to control a video. Also, as the developer, you might want a video to play automatically or loop back to the beginning when it finishes. All of these things (if supported in the browser) are very easy to accomplish in HTML5.

Adding controls, looping, and autoplay to an HTML5 video embed is simple. All you need to do is specify the options controls, loop, and/or autoplay in the <video> tag, like this:

```
<video autoplay loop controls id="thevideo" width="320" height="240">
  <source src="muirbeach.webm" type='video/webm; codecs="vp8, vorbis"'>
  <source src="muirbeach.mp4" type='video/mp4; codecs="avc1.42E01E, mp4a.40.2"'>
  <source src="muirbeach.ogg" type='video/ogg; codecs="theora, vorbis"'>
</video>
```

 As of this writing, loop does not work in Firefox; however, support is expected in version 4.0.

The code to embed our Muir Beach video with controls, loop, and autoplay is in *CH6EX2.html* in the code distribution. Figure 6-2 shows what a video with controls looks like in Google Chrome.

(Autoplay, Loop, Controls)

Figure 6-2. HTML5 video embed with controls

You can see the full code in Example 6-2.

Example 6-2. HTML video with controls, loop, and autoplay

```
<!doctype html>
<html lang="en">
<head>
```

```
<meta charset="UTF-8">
<title>CH6EX2: Basic HTML5 Video With Controls</title>
</head>
<body>
<div>
<video autoplay loop controls id="thevideo" width="320" height="240">
 <source src="muirbeach.webm" type='video/webm; codecs="vp8, vorbis"' >
 <source src="muirbeach.mp4" type='video/mp4; codecs="avc1.42E01E, mp4a.40.2"' >
 <source src="muirbeach.ogg" type='video/ogg; codecs="theora, vorbis"'>
</video>
</div>
<div>
(Autoplay, Loop, Controls)
</div>
</body>
</html>
```

Altering the Width and Height of the Video

In our first example, we showed how you could embed a video without changing the default width or height. However, there are many good reasons why you might want to change the default width and height of a video in the HTML page, such as fitting it into a particular part of the page or enlarging it so that it is easier to see. Similar to embedding an image into HTML with the <img> tag, a video will scale to whatever width and height you provide in the <video> tag. Also, like with the <img> tag, this scale does not affect the size of the object downloaded. If the video is 5 megabytes at 640×480, it will still be 5 megabytes when displayed at 180×120—just scaled to fit that size.

In Example 6-3 (*CH6EX3.html*), we have scaled the same video to three different sizes and displayed them on the same page. Figure 6-3 shows what this looks like in HTML (again, rendered in the Google Chrome browser).

Figure 6-3. Controlling video width and height in the embed

Example 6-3. Basic HTML5 video in three sizes

```
<!doctype html>
<html lang="en">
<head>
<meta charset="UTF-8">
<title>CH6EX3: Basic HTML5 Video: 3 Sizes</title>
</head>
<body>
<div>
<video autoplay loop controls  width="640" height="480" id="thevideo">
 <source src="muirbeach.webm" type='video/webm; codecs="vp8, vorbis"' >
 <source src="muirbeach.mp4" type='video/mp4; codecs="avc1.42E01E, mp4a.40.2"' >
 <source src="muirbeach.ogg" type='video/ogg; codecs="theora, vorbis"'>
</video>
</div>
<div>
(640×480)
<div>
```

```
<video  autoplay loop controls  width="320" height="240"id="thevideo">
 <source src="muirbeach.webm" type='video/webm; codecs="vp8, vorbis"' >
 <source src="muirbeach.mp4" type='video/mp4; codecs="avc1.42E01E, mp4a.40.2"' >
 <source src="muirbeach.ogg" type='video/ogg; codecs="theora, vorbis"'>
</video>
</div>
<div>
(320×240)
</div>
<div>
<video autoplay loop controls  width="180" height="120"id="thevideo">
 <source src="muirbeach.webm" type='video/webm; codecs="vp8, vorbis"' >
 <source src="muirbeach.mp4" type='video/mp4; codecs="avc1.42E01E, mp4a.40.2"' >
 <source src="muirbeach.ogg" type='video/ogg; codecs="theora, vorbis"'>
</video>
</div>
 (180×120)
</body>
</html>
```

Now it is time for a more elaborate (and, we think, more effective) example of scaling a video. By changing the `width` and `height` attributes of the `<video>` tag, we can scale the video on the fly. While there might be a few practical reasons that you would do this in a real-world situation, it is also an effective way to demonstrate some of the power of the HTML5 `<video>` tag.

First, we need to add an HTML5 `range` control to the page:

```
<form>
 Video Size: <input type="range" id="videoSize"
        min="80"
        max="1280"
        step="1"
        value="320"/>
</form>
```

We discussed the details of the `range` control in Chapter 3, but just to refresh your memory, `range` is a new form control added to HTML5 that creates a slider of values. We are going to use this slider to set the video size.

 If the browser does not support the `range` element, a text box will appear that will allow the user to enter text directly.

To capture the change to the video size, we need to add some JavaScript. We create an event listener for the `load` event that calls the `eventWindowLoaded()` function when the page loads (this should look very familiar to you by now):

```
window.addEventListener('load', eventWindowLoaded, false);
```

We need to set up a couple things in the eventWindowLoaded() function. First, we need to add an event listener for a change to the videoSize form control we created in the HTML page. A "change" to the control (for example, someone slides it right or left) will create an event handled by the videoSizeChanged() event handler:

```
var sizeElement = document.getElementById("videoSize")
sizeElement.addEventListener('change', videoSizeChanged, false);
```

Next, we need to create a value that can be used to set both the width and the height of the video at once. This is because we want to keep the proper *aspect ratio* of the video (the ratio of width to height) when the video is resized. To do this, we create the variable widthtoHeightRatio, which is simply the width of the video divided by the height:

```
var widthtoHeightRatio = videoElement.width/videoElement.height;
```

Finally, when the user changes the videoSize range control, the videoSize Changed() event handler is called. This function sets the width property of the video to the value of the range control (target.value), sets the height of the video to the same value, and then divides by the widthtoHeightRatio value we just created. The effect is that the video resizes while playing. Figure 6-4 captures one moment of that:

```
function videoSizeChanged(e) {

    var target = e.target;
    var videoElement = document.getElementById("theVideo");
    videoElement.width = target.value;
    videoElement.height = target.value/widthtoHeightRatio;

}
```

 At the time of this writing, this example no longer works in Firefox.

Example 6-4 offers the full code listing for this application.

Figure 6-4. Controlling video width and height in JavaScript

Example 6-4. Basic HTML5 video with resize range control

```
<!doctype html>
<html lang="en">
<head>
<meta charset="UTF-8">
<title>CH6EX4: Basic HTML5 Video With Resize Range Control </title>

<script type="text/javascript">
window.addEventListener('load', eventWindowLoaded, false);
function eventWindowLoaded() {
   var sizeElement = document.getElementById("videoSize")
   sizeElement.addEventListener('change', videoSizeChanged, false);
   var videoElement = document.getElementById("theVideo");
   var widthtoHeightRatio = videoElement.width/videoElement.height;

function videoSizeChanged(e) {
     var target = e.target;
     var videoElement = document.getElementById("theVideo");
     videoElement.width = target.value;
     videoElement.height = target.value/widthtoHeightRatio;
```

```
        }

    }

</script>

</head>
<body>
<div>
<form>
 Video Size: <input type="range" id="videoSize"
        min="80"
        max="1280"
        step="1"
        value="320"/>
</form>
  <br>
</div>
<div>
<video autoplay loop controls id="theVideo" width="320" height="240">
 <source src="muirbeach.webm" type='video/webm; codecs="vp8, vorbis"' >
 <source src="muirbeach.mp4" type='video/mp4; codecs="avc1.42E01E, mp4a.40.2"' >
 <source src="muirbeach.ogg" type='video/ogg; codecs="theora, vorbis"'>
</video>
</div>
</body>
</html>
```

Preloading Video in JavaScript

It is often necessary to preload a video before you do anything with it. This is especially true when using video with HTML5 Canvas, because what you want to do often goes beyond the simple act of playing the video.

We are going to leverage the DOM and JavaScript to create a preload architecture that can be reused and expanded upon. We are still not using Canvas, but this process will lead directly to it.

To do this, we must first embed the video in the HTML page in the same way we have done previously in this chapter. However, this time, we are going to add <div> with the id of loadingStatus.

 In practice, you probably would not display the loading status on the HTML page.

This `<div>` will report the percentage of the video that has loaded when we retrieve it through JavaScript:

```
<div>
<video loop controls id="thevideo" width="320" height="240" preload="auto">
 <source src="muirbeach.webm" type='video/webm; codecs="vp8, vorbis"' >
 <source src="muirbeach.mp4" type='video/mp4; codecs="avc1.42E01E, mp4a.40.2"' >
 <source src="muirbeach.ogg" type='video/ogg; codecs="theora, vorbis"'>
</video>

</div>

<div id="loadingStatus">
0%
</div>
```

In JavaScript, we need to create the same type of `eventWindowLoaded()` function that we have created many times previously in this book. This function is called when the HTML page has finished loading. In `eventWindowLoaded()`, we need to create two listeners for two more events that are dispatched from the `HTMLVideoElement` object:

progress
Dispatched when the `video` object has updated information about the loading progress of a video. We will use this event to update the percentage text in the `loading Status <div>`.

canplaythrough
Dispatched when the video has loaded enough that it can play in its entirety. This event will let us know when to start playing the video.

Below is the code that creates the listeners for those events:

```
function eventWindowLoaded() {
    var videoElement = document.getElementById("thevideo");

    videoElement.addEventListener('progress',updateLoadingStatus,false);
    videoElement.addEventListener('canplaythrough',playVideo,false);
}
```

The `updateLoadingStatus()` function is called when the `progress` event is dispatched from the `video` element. This function calculates the percent loaded by calculating the ratio of the already-loaded bytes (`videoElement.buffered.end(0)`) by the total bytes (`videoElement.duration`) and then dividing that value by 100. That value is then displayed by setting the `innerHTML` property of the `loadingStatus <div>`, as shown in Figure 6-5. Remember, this is only for displaying the progress. We still need to do something after the video has loaded.

```
function updateLoadingStatus() {
    var loadingStatus = document.getElementById("loadingStatus");
    var videoElement = document.getElementById("thevideo");
    var percentLoaded = parseInt(((videoElement.buffered.end(0) /
```

```
            videoElement.duration) * 100));
        document.getElementById("loadingStatus").innerHTML =   percentLoaded + '%';
    }
```

Figure 6-5. Preloading a video in JavaScript

The playVideo() function is called when the video object dispatches a canplay through event. playVideo() calls the play() function of the video object, and the video starts to play:

```
function playVideo() {
    var videoElement = document.getElementById("thevideo");
    videoElement.play();

}
```

Example 6-5 gives the full code for preloading video.

Example 6-5. Basic HTML5 preloading video

```
<!doctype html>
<html lang="en">
<head>
<meta charset="UTF-8">
<title>CH6EX5: Basic HTML5 Preloading Video</title>

<script type="text/javascript">
window.addEventListener('load', eventWindowLoaded, false);
function eventWindowLoaded() {
    var videoElement = document.getElementById("thevideo");
    videoElement.addEventListener('progress',updateLoadingStatus,false);
    videoElement.addEventListener('canplaythrough',playVideo,false);

}

function updateLoadingStatus() {
```

```
    var loadingStatus = document.getElementById("loadingStatus");
    var videoElement = document.getElementById("thevideo");
    var percentLoaded = parseInt(((videoElement.buffered.end(0) /
        videoElement.duration) * 100));
    document.getElementById("loadingStatus").innerHTML =   percentLoaded + '%';

}

function playVideo() {
    var videoElement = document.getElementById("thevideo");
    videoElement.play();

}
</script>

</head>
<body>
<div>
<video loop controls id="thevideo" width="320" height="240" preload="auto">
 <source src="muirbeach.webm" type='video/webm; codecs="vp8, vorbis"' >
 <source src="muirbeach.mp4" type='video/mp4; codecs="avc1.42E01E, mp4a.40.2"' >
 <source src="muirbeach.ogg" type='video/ogg; codecs="theora, vorbis"'>
</video>

</div>

<div id="loadingStatus">
0%
</div>

</body>
</html>
```

Now that we have gone through this exercise, we have to give you some bad news. While the code we presented for *CH6EX5.html* works in most HTML5-compliant web browsers, the code stopped working in some cases. With a bit of investigation, we discovered that Chrome and Internet Explorer 10 were not firing progress events. At the same time, Firefox removed the load event. While these were anecdotal occurrences, they lead to one common truth: *the HTML5 specification is not finished*. This is an obvious but important fact to note. If you are developing for HTML5 or Canvas, you are developing with a moving target.

Video and the Canvas

The HTML video object already has a poster property for displaying an image before the video starts to play, as well as functions to autoplay and loop. So why is it necessary to preload the video? Well, as we alluded to in the previous section, simply playing a video is one thing—manipulating it with HTML5 Canvas is quite another. If you want to start manipulating video while it is displayed on the canvas, you first need to make sure it is loaded.

In this section, we will load video and then manipulate it in various ways so that you can see how powerful Canvas can be when it is mixed with other HTML5 elements.

Displaying a Video on HTML5 Canvas

First, we must learn the basics of displaying video on HTML5 Canvas. There are a few important things to note that are not immediately obvious when you start working with video and the canvas. We worked through them so that you don't have to do it yourself.

Video must still be embedded in HTML

Even though the video is displayed only on HTML5 Canvas, you still need a `<video>` tag in HTML. The key is to put the video in a `<div>` (or a similar construct) and to set the display CSS style property of that `<div>` to none in HTML. This will ensure that while the video is loaded in the page, it is not displayed. If we wrote the code in HTML, it might look like this:

```
<div style="position: absolute; top: 50px; left: 600px; display:none">
<video loop controls id="thevideo" width="320" height="240" preload="auto">
 <source src="muirbeach.webm" type='video/webm; codecs="vp8, vorbis"' >
 <source src="muirbeach.mp4" type='video/mp4; codecs="avc1.42E01E, mp4a.40.2"' >
 <source src="muirbeach.ogg" type='video/ogg; codecs="theora, vorbis"'>
</video>
```

However, we already know that we don't want to use an HTML embed. As we stated at the end of the last section, video events do not appear to fire reliably when video elements are embedded in the HTML page. For this reason, we need a new strategy to load video dynamically—we'll create the `<div>` and `<video>` elements in JavaScript.

The first thing we do in our JavaScript is add a couple variables to hold references to the dynamic HTML elements we will create. The videoElement variable will hold the dynamically created `<video>` tag, while videoDiv will hold the dynamically created `<div>`:

```
var videoElement;
var videoDiv;
```

We use this method to create global variables throughout this chapter. There are many reasons not to use global variables, but for these simple applications, it's the quickest way to get something on the canvas. If you want to learn a better way to handle loading assets, the last section of Chapter 7 employs a strategy to preload assets without the use of global variables.

Next, we create our dynamic form elements in the `eventWindowLoaded()` function. First, we use the `createElement()` method of the document DOM object to create a `<video>` element and a `<div>` element, placing references to them in the variables we just created:

```
function eventWindowLoaded() {

    videoElement = document.createElement("video");
    videoDiv = document.createElement('div');
    document.body.appendChild(videoDiv);
```

Next, we add `videoElement` as a child of `videoDiv`, essentially putting it inside of that `<div>` on the HTML page. We then set the style attribute of `<div>` to `display:none;`, which will make it invisible on the HTML page. We do this because, although we want the video to display on the canvas, we don't want to show it on the HTML page:

```
    videoDiv.appendChild(videoElement);
    videoDiv.setAttribute("style", "display:none;");
```

We then create another new variable named `videoType` that holds the results of a new function we will create, `supportedVideoFormat()`. This function returns the file extension of the supported video format for the browser; otherwise, it returns "" (an empty string), which means that we alert the user that there is no video support in the app for his browser:

```
    var videoType = supportedVideoFormat(videoElement);
    if (videoType == "") {
       alert("no video support");
       return;
    }
```

Finally, we set the `src` property of the `video` element using the file extension we just received from `supportedVideoFormat()` and create the event handler for the `canplaythrough` event:

```
    videoElement.addEventListener("canplaythrough",videoLoaded,false);
    videoElement.setAttribute("src", "muirbeach." + videoType);

}
```

When the video has finished loading, the `videoLoaded` event handler is called, which in turn calls the `canvasApp()` function:

```
function videoLoaded(event) {

    canvasApp();

}
```

Before the code in the last section will work, we need to define the supportedVideo
Format() function. The reason for this function is simple: because we are adding video
objects dynamically to the HTML page, we do not have a way to define multiple
<source> tags. Instead, we are going to use the canPlayType() method of the video
object to tell us which type of audio file to load.

The canPlayType() method takes a single parameter, a MIME type. It returns a text
string of maybe, probably, or nothing (an empty string).

"" *(nothing)*
 This is returned if the browser knows the type cannot be rendered.

maybe
 This is returned if the browser does not confidently know that the type can be
 displayed.

probably
 This is returned if the browser knows the type can be displayed using an audio or
 video element.

We are going to use these values to determine which media type to load and play. For
the sake of this exercise, we will assume that both maybe and probably equate to yes. If
we encounter either result with any of our three MIME types (*video/webm, video/mp4,
video/ogg*), we will return the extension associated with that MIME type so that the
sound file can be loaded.

In the following function, video represents the instance of HTMLVideoElement that we
are going to test. The returnExtension variable represents that valid extension for the
first MIME type found that has the value of maybe or probably returned from the call
to canPlayType():

```
function supportedVideoFormat(video) {
    var returnExtension = "";
    if (video.canPlayType("video/webm") =="probably" ||
        video.canPlayType("video/webm") == "maybe") {
            returnExtension = "webm";
    } else if(video.canPlayType("video/mp4") == "probably" ||
        video.canPlayType("video/mp4") == "maybe") {
            returnExtension = "mp4";
    } else if(video.canPlayType("video/ogg") =="probably" ||
        video.canPlayType("video/ogg") == "maybe") {
            returnExtension = "ogg";
    }
```

```
        return returnExtension;

    }
```

We do not check for a condition when no valid video format is found and the return value is "". If that is the case, the code that has called this function might need to be written in a way to catch that condition and alter the program execution. We did that with the test of the return value and alert(), which we described previously.

Video is displayed like an image

When you write code to display a video on the canvas, you use the context.draw Image() function, as though you were displaying a static image. Don't go looking for a drawVideo() function in the HTML5 Canvas spec because you won't find it. The following code will display a video stored in a variable named videoElement, displayed at the x,y position of 85,30:

```
    context.drawImage(videoElement , 85, 30);
```

However, when you draw a video for the first time, you will notice that it will not move —it stays on the first frame. At first you might think you have done something wrong, but you have not. You just need to add one more thing to make it work.

Set an interval to update the display

Just like when we discussed animation in the previous chapters, a video placed on HTML5 Canvas using drawImage() will not update itself. You need to call draw Image() in some sort of loop to continually update the image with new data from the playing video in the HTML page (hidden or not). To do this, we call the video's play() method and then use a setTimeout() loop to call the drawScreen() function every 20 milliseconds. We put this code in our canvasApp() function, which is called after we know the video has loaded:

```
    videoElement.play();
    function gameLoop() {
        window.setTimeout(gameLoop, 20);
        drawScreen();
    }

    gameLoop();
```

In drawScreen(), we will call drawImage() to display the video, but because it will be called every 20 milliseconds, the video will be updated and play on the canvas:

```
    function  drawScreen () {

        context.drawImage(videoElement , 85, 30);

    }
```

Example 6-6 gives the full code for displaying a video on the canvas and updating it using `setInterval()`. Figure 6-6 shows this code in the browser.

Example 6-6. Basic HTML5 loading video onto the canvas

```
<!doctype html>
<html lang="en">
<head>
<meta charset="UTF-8">
<title>CH6EX6: Basic HTML5 Load Video Onto The Canvas</title>

<script src="modernizr.js"></script>
<script type="text/javascript">
window.addEventListener('load', eventWindowLoaded, false);
var videoElement;
var videoDiv;
function eventWindowLoaded() {

    videoElement = document.createElement("video");
    videoDiv = document.createElement('div');
    document.body.appendChild(videoDiv);
    videoDiv.appendChild(videoElement);
    videoDiv.setAttribute("style", "display:none;");
    var videoType = supportedVideoFormat(videoElement);
    if (videoType == "") {
        alert("no video support");
        return;
    }
  videoElement.addEventListener("canplaythrough",videoLoaded,false);
  videoElement.setAttribute("src", "muirbeach." + videoType);

}

function supportedVideoFormat(video) {
    var returnExtension = "";
    if (video.canPlayType("video/webm") =="probably" ||
        video.canPlayType("video/webm") == "maybe") {
          returnExtension = "webm";
    } else if(video.canPlayType("video/mp4") == "probably" ||
        video.canPlayType("video/mp4") == "maybe") {
          returnExtension = "mp4";
    } else if(video.canPlayType("video/ogg") =="probably" ||
        video.canPlayType("video/ogg") == "maybe") {
          returnExtension = "ogg";
    }

    return returnExtension;

}

function canvasSupport () {
      return Modernizr.canvas;
}
```

```
function videoLoaded(event) {

    canvasApp();

}

function canvasApp() {

    if (!canvasSupport()) {
         return;
       }

function  drawScreen () {

        //Background
        context.fillStyle = '#ffffaa';
        context.fillRect(0, 0, theCanvas.width, theCanvas.height);
        //Box
        context.strokeStyle = '#000000';
        context.strokeRect(5,  5, theCanvas.width-10, theCanvas.height-10);
        //video
        context.drawImage(videoElement , 85, 30);

    }

    var theCanvas = document.getElementById("canvasOne");
    var context = theCanvas.getContext("2d");
    videoElement.play();

    function gameLoop() {
        window.setTimeout(gameLoop, 20);
        drawScreen();
    }

    gameLoop();
}

</script>

</head>
<body>
<div style="position: absolute; top: 50px; left: 50px;">

<canvas id="canvasOne" width="500" height="300">
 Your browser does not support HTML5 Canvas.
</canvas>
</div>
</body>
</html>
```

loaded 100%

Figure 6-6. Displaying a video on HTML5 Canvas

HTML5 Video Properties

We have already talked about some properties of HTMLVideoElement (inherited from HTMLMediaElement), but now that we have a video loaded onto the canvas, it would be interesting to see them in action.

In this example, we are going to display seven properties of a playing video, taken from the HTMLVideoElement object: duration, currentTime, loop, autoplay, muted, con trols, and volume. Of these, duration, loop, and autoplay will not update because they are set when the video is embedded. Also, because we call the play() function of the video after it is preloaded in JavaScript, autoplay can be set to false but the video will play anyway. The other properties will update as the video is played.

To display these values on the canvas, we will draw them as text in the drawScreen() function called by setInterval().The drawScreen() function that we have created to display these values is as follows:

```
function  drawScreen () {

    //Background
    context.fillStyle = '#ffffaa';
    context.fillRect(0, 0, theCanvas.width, theCanvas.height);
    //Box
    context.strokeStyle = '#000000';
    context.strokeRect(5,  5, theCanvas.width-10, theCanvas.height-10);
    //video
    context.drawImage(videoElement , 85, 30);
```

```
// Text
context.fillStyle = "#000000";
context.fillText ("Duration:" + videoElement.duration,  10 ,280);
context.fillText ("Current time:" + videoElement.currentTime,  260 ,280);
context.fillText ("Loop: " + videoElement.loop,  10 ,290);
context.fillText ("Autoplay: " + videoElement.autoplay,  100 ,290);
context.fillText ("Muted: " + videoElement.muted,  180 ,290);
context.fillText ("Controls: " + videoElement.controls,  260 ,290);
context.fillText ("Volume: " + videoElement.volume,  340 ,290);

}
```

Figure 6-7 shows what the attributes look like when displayed on the canvas. Notice that we have placed the <video> embed next to the canvas, and we have *not* set the CSS display style to none. We did this to demonstrate the relationship between the video embedded in the HTML page and the one playing on the canvas. If you roll over the video in the HTML page, you can see the control panel. If you set the volume, you will notice that the volume attribute displayed on the canvas will change. If you pause the embedded video, the video on the canvas will stop playing and the currentTime value will stop.

This demo should give you a very good idea of the relationship between the video on the canvas and the one embedded with the <video> tag. Even though they are displayed using completely different methods, they are in fact one and the same.

Figure 6-7. Video on the canvas with properties displayed and <video> embed

You can see Example 6-7 in action by executing *CH6EX7.html* from the code distribution.

Example 6-7. Video properties

```
<!doctype html>
<html lang="en">
<head>
```

```
<meta charset="UTF-8">
<title>CH6EX7: Video Properties</title>

<script src="modernizr.js"></script>
<script type="text/javascript">
window.addEventListener('load', eventWindowLoaded, false);
var videoElement;
var videoDiv;
function eventWindowLoaded() {

    videoElement = document.createElement("video");
    var videoDiv = document.createElement('div');
    document.body.appendChild(videoDiv);
    videoDiv.appendChild(videoElement);
    videoDiv.setAttribute("style", "position: absolute; top: 50px; left: 600px; ");
    var videoType = supportedVideoFormat(videoElement);
    if (videoType == "") {
        alert("no video support");
        return;
    }
    videoElement.addEventListener("canplaythrough",videoLoaded,false);
    videoElement.setAttribute("src", "muirbeach." + videoType);

}


function supportedVideoFormat(video) {
    var returnExtension = "";
    if (video.canPlayType("video/webm") =="probably" ||
        video.canPlayType("video/webm") == "maybe") {
            returnExtension = "webm";
    } else if(video.canPlayType("video/mp4") == "probably" ||
        video.canPlayType("video/mp4") == "maybe") {
            returnExtension = "mp4";
    } else if(video.canPlayType("video/ogg") =="probably" ||
        video.canPlayType("video/ogg") == "maybe") {
            returnExtension = "ogg";
    }

    return returnExtension;

}


function canvasSupport () {
    return Modernizr.canvas;
}

function videoLoaded() {
   canvasApp();

}
```

```
function canvasApp() {

  if (!canvasSupport()) {
     return;
  }

  function  drawScreen () {

      //Background
      context.fillStyle = '#ffffaa';
      context.fillRect(0, 0, theCanvas.width, theCanvas.height);
      //Box
      context.strokeStyle = '#000000';
      context.strokeRect(5,  5, theCanvas.width-10, theCanvas.height-10);
      //video
      context.drawImage(videoElement , 85, 30);
      // Text
      context.fillStyle = "#000000";
      context.fillText  ("Duration:" + videoElement.duration,  10 ,280);
      context.fillText  ("Current time:" + videoElement.currentTime,  260 ,280);
      context.fillText  ("Loop: " + videoElement.loop,  10 ,290);
      context.fillText  ("Autoplay: " + videoElement.autoplay,  100 ,290);
      context.fillText  ("Muted: " + videoElement.muted,  180 ,290);
      context.fillText  ("Controls: " + videoElement.controls,  260 ,290);
      context.fillText  ("Volume: " + videoElement.volume,  340 ,290);

  }

  var theCanvas = document.getElementById("canvasOne");
  var context = theCanvas.getContext("2d");
  videoElement.play();

  function gameLoop() {
     window.setTimeout(gameLoop, 20);
     drawScreen();
  }

  gameLoop();

}

</script>

</head>
<body>
<div style="position: absolute; top: 50px; left: 50px;">

<canvas id="canvasOne" width="500" height="300">
 Your browser does not support HTML5 Canvas.
</canvas>
</div>
</body>
</html>
```

You can see all the events and properties for the `HTMLVideoElement` at this site (*http://www.w3.org/2010/05/video/mediaevents.html*).

Video on the Canvas Examples

In the last section, we learned that the video playing on the canvas and the video embedded with the `<video>` tag are, in fact, the same video. It took a lot more code to play the video on the canvas than it did to embed and play the video in JavaScript. This begs the question: *why load video onto the canvas at all?*

Well, sometimes simply displaying a video and playing it is not enough. You might want events to occur as the video is playing, or perhaps you want to use transformations on it, use it in a game, create custom video controls, or animate it and move it on the canvas.

The following five examples will show you in very specific detail why the canvas can be an exciting way to display video.

Using the currentTime Property to Create Video Events

The first way we will use video in conjunction with Canvas is to use the `currentTime` property of a playing video to trigger events. Recall that the `currentTime` property is updated as the video plays, and it shows the video's elapsed running time.

For our example, we are going to create a dynamic object in JavaScript containing the following properties:

time
> The elapsed time to trigger the event

message
> A text message to display on the canvas

x
> The x position of the text message

y
> The y position of the text message

First, we will create an array of these objects and place them into a variable named `messages`. We will then create four events (messages that will appear) that will take place at the elapsed `currentTime` of 0, 1, 4, and 8 seconds:

```
var messages = new Array();
    messages[0] = {time:0,message:"", x:0 ,y:0};
    messages[1] = {time:1,message:"This Is Muir Beach!", x:90 ,y:200};
    messages[2] = {time:4,message:"Look At Those Waves!", x:240 ,y:240};
    messages[3] = {time:8,message:"Look At Those Rocks!", x:100 ,y:100};
```

To display the messages, we will call a `for:next` loop inside our `drawScreen()` function. Inside the loop, we test each message in the `messages` array to see whether the `current Time` property of the video is greater than the `time` property of the message. If so, we know that it is OK to display the message. We then display the message on the canvas using the `fillStyle` property and `fillText()` function of the Canvas context, producing the results shown in Figure 6-8:

```
for (var i = 0; i < messages.length ; i++) {
        var tempMessage = messages[i];
        if (videoElement.currentTime > tempMessage.time) {
            context.font = "bold 14px sans";
            context.fillStyle = "#FFFF00";
            context.fillText  (tempMessage.message,  tempMessage.x ,
                             tempMessage.y);
        }
    }
```

Figure 6-8. Canvas video displaying text overlay events

Of course, this is a very simple way to create events. The various text messages will not disappear after others are created, but that is just a small detail. The point of this exercise is that, with code like this, you could do almost anything with a running video. You could pause the video, show an animation, and then continue after the animation is done. Or you could pause to ask the user for input and then load a different video. Essentially, you can make the video completely interactive in any way you choose. The model for these events could be very similar to the one we just created.

Example 6-8 provides the full code listing for this application.

Example 6-8. Creating simple video events

```
<!doctype html>
<html lang="en">
<head>
<meta charset="UTF-8">
<title>CH6EX8: Creating Simple Video Events</title>

<script src="modernizr.js"></script>
<script type="text/javascript">
window.addEventListener('load', eventWindowLoaded, false);
var videoElement;
var videoDiv;
function eventWindowLoaded() {

    videoElement = document.createElement("video");
    videoDiv = document.createElement('div');
    document.body.appendChild(videoDiv);
    videoDiv.appendChild(videoElement);
    videoDiv.setAttribute("style", "display:none;");
    var videoType = supportedVideoFormat(videoElement);
    if (videoType == "") {
        alert("no video support");
        return;
    }
    videoElement.addEventListener("canplaythrough",videoLoaded,false);
    videoElement.setAttribute("src", "muirbeach." + videoType);

}
function supportedVideoFormat(video) {
    var returnExtension = "";
    if (video.canPlayType("video/webm") =="probably" ||
        video.canPlayType("video/webm") == "maybe") {
            returnExtension = "webm";
    } else if(video.canPlayType("video/mp4") == "probably" ||
        video.canPlayType("video/mp4") == "maybe") {
            returnExtension = "mp4";
    } else if(video.canPlayType("video/ogg") =="probably" ||
        video.canPlayType("video/ogg") == "maybe") {
            returnExtension = "ogg";
    }

    return returnExtension;

}

function canvasSupport () {
    return Modernizr.canvas;
}


function videoLoaded() {
```

```
        canvasApp();

}

function canvasApp() {

  if (!canvasSupport()) {
        return;
      }

  function  drawScreen () {

      //Background
      context.fillStyle = '#ffffaa';
      context.fillRect(0, 0, theCanvas.width, theCanvas.height);
      //Box
      context.strokeStyle = '#000000';
      context.strokeRect(5,  5, theCanvas.width-10, theCanvas.height-10);
      //video
      context.drawImage(videoElement , 85, 30);
      // Text
      context.fillStyle = "#000000";
      context.font = "10px sans";
      context.fillText ("Duration:" + videoElement.duration,  10 ,280);
      context.fillText ("Current time:" + videoElement.currentTime,  260 ,280);
      context.fillText ("Loop: " + videoElement.loop,  10 ,290);
      context.fillText ("Autoplay: " + videoElement.autoplay,  80 ,290);
      context.fillText ("Muted: " + videoElement.muted,  160 ,290);
      context.fillText ("Controls: " + videoElement.controls,  240 ,290);
      context.fillText ("Volume: " + videoElement.volume,  320 ,290);

      //Display Message
      for (var i =0; i < messages.length ; i++) {
         var tempMessage = messages[i];
         if (videoElement.currentTime > tempMessage.time) {
            context.font = "bold 14px sans";
            context.fillStyle = "#FFFF00";
            context.fillText (tempMessage.message,  tempMessage.x ,tempMessage.y);
         }
      }

  }

  var messages = new Array();
  messages[0] = {time:0,message:"", x:0 ,y:0};
  messages[1] = {time:1,message:"This Is Muir Beach!", x:90 ,y:200};
  messages[2] = {time:4,message:"Look At Those Waves!", x:240 ,y:240};
  messages[3] = {time:8,message:"Look At Those Rocks!", x:100 ,y:100};

  var theCanvas = document.getElementById("canvasOne");
  var context = theCanvas.getContext("2d");
  videoElement.play();
```

```
    function gameLoop() {
        window.setTimeout(gameLoop, 20);
        drawScreen();
    }

    gameLoop();
}

</script>

</head>
<body>
<div style="position: absolute; top: 50px; left: 50px;">

<canvas id="canvasOne" width="500" height="300">
 Your browser does not support HTML5 Canvas.
</canvas>
</div>
</body>
</html>
```

Canvas Video Transformations: Rotation

Showing a static video on the screen is one thing, but transforming it on the screen using alpha transparency and rotations is quite another. These types of transformations can be easily applied to video on the canvas in much the same way as you would apply them to an image or a drawing object.

In this example, we will create a video that rotates clockwise. To achieve this effect, we first create a variable, `rotation`, which we will use to hold the current values of the rotation property that we will apply to the video. We create this variable outside of the `drawScreen()` function, inside `canvasApp()`:

```
    var rotation = 0;
```

The `drawScreen()` function is where all the real action takes place for this example. First, we need to save the current canvas context so that we can restore it after we perform the transformation. We covered this in depth in Chapter 2, but here's a quick refresher. Transformations on the canvas are global in nature, which means they affect *everything*. Because the canvas works in immediate mode, there is no stack of objects to manipulate. Instead, we need to save the canvas context before the transformation, apply the transformation, and then restore the saved context afterward.

First, we save it:

```
    context.save();
```

Next we reset the context transformation to the identity, which clears anything that was set previously:

```
context.setTransform(1,0,0,1,0,0);
```

Then we need to set up some variables that will be used for the rotation calculation. The x and y variables set the upper-left location of the video on the canvas. The video Width and videoHeight variables will be used to help rotate the video from the center:

```
var x = 100;
var y = 100;
var videoWidth=320;
var videoHeight=240;
```

Now it is time to use the rotation variable, which represents the angle that we rotated the video on the canvas. It starts at 0, and we will increase it every time drawScreen() is called. However, the context.rotate() method requires an angle to be converted to radians when passed as its lone parameter. The following line of code converts the value in the rotation variable to radians and stores it in a variable named angleInRadians:

```
var angleInRadians = rotation * Math.PI / 180;
```

We need to find the video's center on the canvas so that we can start our rotation from that point. We find the x value by taking our videoX variable and adding half the width of the video. We find the y value by taking our videoY variable and adding half the height of the video. We supply both of those values as parameters to the context.trans late() function so that the rotation will begin at that point. We need to do this because we are not rotating the video object—we are rotating the entire canvas in relation to the displayed video:

```
context.translate(x+.5*videoWidth, y+.5*videoHeight);
```

The rest of the code is really straightforward. First, we call the rotate() function of the context, passing our angle (converted to radians) to perform the rotation:

```
context.rotate(angleInRadians);
```

Then we call drawImage(), passing the video object and the x,y positions of where we want the video to be displayed. This is a bit tricky but should make sense. Because we used the context.translate() function to move to the center of the video, we now need to place it in the upper-left corner. To find that corner, we need to subtract half the width to find the x position and half the height to find the y position:

```
context.drawImage(videoElement ,-.5*videoWidth, -.5*videoHeight);
```

Finally, we restore the canvas we saved before the transformation started, and we update the rotation variable so that we will have a new angle on the next call to drawScreen():

```
context.restore();
rotation++;
```

Now the video should rotate at 1 degree clockwise per call to drawScreen() while fading onto the canvas. You can easily increase the speed of the rotation by changing the value that you input for the rotation variable in the last line in the drawScreen() function.

Here is the code for the final `drawScreen()` function for this example:

```
function drawScreen () {

    //Background
    context.fillStyle = '#ffffaa';
    context.fillRect(0, 0, theCanvas.width, theCanvas.height);
    //Box
    context.strokeStyle = '#000000';
    context.strokeRect(5,  5, theCanvas.width-10, theCanvas.height-10);
    //video
    //*** Start rotation calculation
    context.save();
    context.setTransform(1,0,0,1,0,0);

    var angleInRadians = rotation * Math.PI / 180;
    var x = 100;
    var y = 100;
    var videoWidth=320;
    var videoHeight=240;
    context.translate(x+.5*videoWidth, y+.5*videoHeight);
    context.rotate(angleInRadians);
    //****
    context.drawImage(videoElement ,-.5*videoWidth, -.5*videoHeight);
    //*** restore screen
    context.restore();
    rotation++;
    //***
}
```

Figure 6-9 shows what the video will look like when rotating on the canvas. You can see the full code for this in Example 6-9.

loaded 100%

Figure 6-9. Canvas video rotation

Example 6-9. Rotating a video

```
<!doctype html>
<html lang="en">
<head>
<meta charset="UTF-8">
<title>CH6EX9: Video Rotation Transform</title>

<script src="modernizr.js"></script>
<script type="text/javascript">
window.addEventListener('load', eventWindowLoaded, false);
var videoElement;
var videoDiv;
function eventWindowLoaded() {

    videoElement = document.createElement("video");
    videoDiv = document.createElement('div');
    document.body.appendChild(videoDiv);
```

```
        videoDiv.appendChild(videoElement);
        videoDiv.setAttribute("style", "display:none;");
        var videoType = supportedVideoFormat(videoElement);
        if (videoType == "") {
            alert("no video support");
            return;
        }
        videoElement.addEventListener("canplaythrough",videoLoaded,false);
        videoElement.setAttribute("src", "muirbeach." + videoType);

}

function supportedVideoFormat(video) {
    var returnExtension = "";
    if (video.canPlayType("video/webm") =="probably" ||
        video.canPlayType("video/webm") == "maybe") {
            returnExtension = "webm";
    } else if(video.canPlayType("video/mp4") == "probably" ||
        video.canPlayType("video/mp4") == "maybe") {
            returnExtension = "mp4";
    } else if(video.canPlayType("video/ogg") =="probably" ||
        video.canPlayType("video/ogg") == "maybe") {
            returnExtension = "ogg";
    }

    return returnExtension;

}

function canvasSupport () {
        return Modernizr.canvas;
}


function videoLoaded() {
    canvasApp();

}

function canvasApp() {

  if (!canvasSupport()) {
        return;
      }

  //*** set rotation value
  var rotation = 0;
  //***

  function  drawScreen () {

      //Background
```

```
            context.fillStyle = '#ffffaa';
            context.fillRect(0, 0, theCanvas.width, theCanvas.height);
            //Box
            context.strokeStyle = '#000000';
            context.strokeRect(5,  5, theCanvas.width-10, theCanvas.height-10);
            //video
            //*** Start rotation calculation
            context.save();
            context.setTransform(1,0,0,1,0,0);

            var angleInRadians = rotation * Math.PI / 180;
            var x = 100;
            var y = 100;
            var videoWidth=320;
            var videoHeight=240;
            context.translate(x+.5*videoWidth, y+.5*videoHeight);
            context.rotate(angleInRadians);
            //****
            context.drawImage(videoElement ,-.5*videoWidth, -.5*videoHeight);
            //*** restore screen
            context.restore();
            rotation++;
            //***

        }


        var theCanvas = document.getElementById("canvasOne");
        var context = theCanvas.getContext("2d");
        videoElement.setAttribute("loop", "true");        videoElement.play();
        function gameLoop() {
            window.setTimeout(gameLoop, 20);
            drawScreen();
        }

        gameLoop();
}

</script>

</head>
<body>
<div style="position: absolute; top: 50px; left: 50px;">

<canvas id="canvasOne" width="500" height="500">
 Your browser does not support HTML5 Canvas.
</canvas>
</div>
</body>
</html>
```

Canvas Video Puzzle

Now we arrive at the most involved example of this section. We are going to create a puzzle game based on the video we have displayed on the canvas, illustrated in Figure 6-10. Here are the steps showing how the game will operate:

1. We will load the video onto the canvas but not display it.

2. We will decide how many parts we want to have in our puzzle.

3. We will create a `board` array that holds all the puzzle pieces.

4. The pieces will be displayed in a 4×4 grid.

5. We will randomize the pieces on the board to mix up the puzzle.

6. We will add an event listener for the mouse button.

7. We will set an interval to call `drawScreen()`.

8. We will wait for the user to click a puzzle piece.

9. While we are waiting, the various parts of the video will play just as though they were one video.

10. When a user clicks a puzzle piece, it will highlight in yellow.

11. If the user has selected two pieces, we will swap their positions.

12. The user will attempt to put the puzzle back together so that she can see the video as it was created.

Figure 6-10. Video puzzle

Setting up the game

To start, we are going to set up some variables that will define the game's playfield. Here is a rundown of the variables and how they will be used:

rows
> The numbers of rows in the grid of puzzle pieces.

cols
> The number of columns in the grid of puzzle pieces.

xPad
> The space, in pixels, between each column.

yPad
> The space, in pixels, between each row.

startXOffset
> The number of pixels from the left of the canvas to the location where we will start drawing the grid of puzzle pieces.

startYOffset
> The number of pieces from the top of the canvas to the location where we will start drawing the grid of puzzle pieces.

partWidth
> The width of each puzzle piece.

partHeight
> The height of each puzzle piece.

board
> A two-dimensional array that holds the puzzle pieces.

The following code includes values for each variable:

```
var rows = 4;
var cols = 4;
var xPad = 10;
var yPad = 10;
var startXOffset = 10;
var startYOffset = 10;
var partWidth = videoElement.width/cols;
var partHeight = videoElement.height/rows;
var board = new Array();
```

Next we need to initialize the board array and fill it with some dynamic objects that represent each piece of the puzzle. We loop through the number of cols in the board and create rows amount of dynamic objects in each one. The dynamic objects we are creating have these properties:

`finalCol`
> The final column-resting place of the piece when the puzzle is complete. We use this value to figure out what part of the video to cut out to make this piece.

`finalRow`
> The final row-resting place of the piece when the puzzle is complete. We use this value to figure out what part of the video to cut out to make this piece.

`selected`
> A Boolean that is initially set to `false`. We will use this to see whether we should highlight a piece or switch two pieces when the user clicks a piece.

Notice that we use two nested `for:next` loops to fill the `board` array with these objects. Familiarize yourself with this construct because we use it many times in this game. Two nested loops used like this are particularly useful for games and apps that require a 2D grid in order to be displayed and manipulated:

```
for (var i = 0; i < cols; i++) {
    board[i] = new Array();
    for (var j =0; j < rows; j++) {
        board[i][j] = { finalCol:i,finalRow:j,selected:false };
    }
}
```

Now that we have the `board` array initialized, we call `randomizeBoard()` (we will discuss this function shortly), which mixes up the puzzle by randomly placing the pieces on the screen. We finish the setup section of the game by adding an event listener for the `mouseup` event (when the user releases the mouse button) and by setting an interval to call `drawScreen()` every 20 milliseconds:

```
board = randomizeBoard(board);

theCanvas.addEventListener("mouseup",eventMouseUp, false);
function gameLoop() {
        window.setTimeout(gameLoop, 20);
        drawScreen()
    }

gameLoop();
```

Randomizing the puzzle pieces

The `randomizeBoard()` function requires you to pass in the `board` variable so that we can operate on it. We've set up the function this way so that it will be portable to other applications.

To randomize the puzzle pieces, we first need to set up an array named `newBoard` that will hold the randomized puzzle pieces. `newBoard` will be what we call a *parallel array*. Its purpose is to become the original array—but randomized. We then create a local cols variable and initialize it to the length of the board array that was passed in to the function, and we create a local rows variable, initialized to the length of the first column —board[0]—in the array. This works because all of our rows and columns are the same length, so the number of rows in the first column is the same as all the others. We now have the building blocks required to randomize the pieces:

```
function randomizeBoard(board) {
    var newBoard = new Array();
    var cols = board.length;
    var rows = board[0].length
```

Next we loop through every column and row, randomly choosing a piece from the board array and moving it into newBoard:

```
for (var i = 0; i < cols; i++) {
```

 We use two nested for:next loops here, once again.

Every time we come to an iteration of the outer nested loop, we create a new array that we will fill up in the second nested loop. Then we drop into that nested loop. The found variable will be set to true when we have found a random location to place the piece in the newBoard array. The rndRow and rndCol variables hold the random values that we will create to try and find a random location for the puzzle pieces:

```
newBoard[i] = new Array();
    for (var j =0; j < rows; j++) {
        var found = false;
        var rndCol = 0;
        var rndRow = 0;
```

Now we need to find a location in newBoard in which to put the puzzle piece from the board array. We use a while() loop that continues to iterate as long as the found variable is false. To find a piece to move, we randomly choose a row and column and then use them to see whether that space (board[rndCol][rndRow]) is set to false. If it is not false, we have found a piece to move to the newBoard array. We then set found equal to true so that we can get out of the while() loop and move to the next space in newBoard that we need to fill:

```
while (!found) {
    var rndCol = Math.floor(Math.random() * cols);
    var rndRow = Math.floor(Math.random() * rows);
    if (board[rndCol][rndRow] != false) {
        found = true;
    }
}
```

Finally, we move the piece we found in board to the current location we are filling in newBoard. Then we set the piece in the board array to false so that when we test for the next piece, we won't try to use the same piece we just found. When we are done filling up newBoard, we return it as the newly randomized array of puzzle pieces:

```
            newBoard[i][j] = board[rndCol][rndRow];
            board[rndCol][rndRow] = false;
        }

    }       return newBoard;

    }
```

Drawing the screen

The drawScreen() function is the heart of this application. It is called on an interval and then used to update the video frames and to draw the puzzle pieces on the screen. A good portion of drawScreen() looks like applications we have built many times already in this book. When it begins, we draw the background and a bounding box on the screen:

```
function drawScreen () {

        //Background
        context.fillStyle = '#303030';
        context.fillRect(0, 0, theCanvas.width, theCanvas.height);
        //Box
        context.strokeStyle = '#FFFFFF';
        context.strokeRect(5,  5, theCanvas.width-10, theCanvas.height-10);
```

However, the primary work of this function is—you guessed it—another set of two nested for:next loops that draw the puzzle pieces onto the canvas. This set needs to do three things:

1. Draw a grid of puzzle pieces on the canvas based on their placement in the board two-dimensional array.

2. Find the correct part of the video to render for each piece based on the finalCol and finalRow properties we set in the dynamic object for each piece.

3. Draw a yellow box around the piece that has its selected property set to true.

We start our loop by finding the x and y (imageX, imageY) locations to "cut" the puzzle piece from the video object. We do this by taking the finalRow and finalCol properties of the dynamic piece objects we created and multiplying them by the partWidth and partHeight, respectively. We then have the origin point (top-left x and y locations) for the piece of the video to display:

```
    for (var c = 0; c < cols; c++) {
        for (var r = 0; r < rows; r++) {
```

```
    var tempPiece = board[c][r];
    var imageX = tempPiece.finalCol*partWidth;
    var imageY = tempPiece.finalRow*partHeight;
```

Now that we know the origin point of the video we will display for a particular piece of the puzzle, we need to know where it will be placed on the canvas. While the code below might look confusing, it's really just simple arithmetic. To find the x location (`placeX`) of a piece, multiply the `partWidth` times the current iterated column (`c`), add the current iterated column multiplied by the `xPad` (the number of pixels between each piece), and then add the `startXOffset`, which is the x location of the upper-left corner of the entire board of pieces. Finding `placeY` is very similar, but you use the current row (`r`), `yPad`, and `partHeight` in the calculation:

```
    var placeX = c*partWidth+c*xPad+startXOffset;
    var placeY = r*partHeight+r*yPad+startYOffset;
```

Now it's time to draw the piece on the canvas. We need to "cut" out the part of the video that we will display for each piece of the puzzle. (We won't actually cut anything.) We will again use the `drawImage()` function, as we have many other times already. However, now we use the version of `drawImage()` that accepts nine parameters:

videoElement
: The image that we are going to display; in this case, it is the video.

imageX
: The x location of the upper-right order of the part of the image to display.

imageY
: The y location of the upper-right order of the part of the image to display.

partWidth
: The width from the x location of the rectangle to display.

partHeight
: The height from the y location of the rectangle to display.

placeX
: The x location to place the image on the canvas.

placeY
: The y location to place the image on the canvas.

partWidth
: The width of the image as displayed on the canvas.

partHeight
: The height of the image as displayed on the canvas.

We've already discussed how we calculated most of these values, so it is just a matter of knowing the drawImage() API function and plugging in the variables:

```
context.drawImage(videoElement, imageX, imageY, partWidth, partHeight,
    placeX, placeY, partWidth, partHeight);
```

There is one last thing we are going to do in this function. If a puzzle piece is marked as "selected" (the selected Boolean property is true), we will draw a yellow box around the piece:

```
            if (tempPiece.selected) {

                context.strokeStyle = '#FFFF00';
                context.strokeRect( placeX,  placeY, partWidth, partHeight);


            }
        }
    }

}
```

Detecting mouse interactions and the canvas

Recall that in the canvasApp() function we set an event listener for the mouseup action with the event handler function set to eventMouseUp. We now need to create that function:

```
theCanvas.addEventListener("mouseup",eventMouseUp, false);
```

The first thing we do in the eventMouseUp() function is test to find the x and y locations of the mouse pointer when the button was pressed. We will use those coordinates to figure out whether the user clicked on any of the puzzle pieces.

Because some browsers support the event.pageX/event.pageY properties of the event object and others support the e.clientX/e.clientX properties, we need to support both. No matter which one is set, we will use those properties to set our mouseX and mouseY variables to the x and y locations of the mouse pointer:

```
function eventMouseUp(event) {

    var mouseX;
    var mouseY;
    var pieceX;
    var pieceY;
    var x;
    var y;
    if (event.pageX || event.pageY) {
        x = event.pageX;
        y = event.pageY;
    } else {
        x = e.clientX + document.body.scrollLeft +
            document.documentElement.scrollLeft;
```

```
        y = e.clientY + document.body.scrollTop +
            document.documentElement.scrollTop;
    }
        x -= theCanvas.offsetLeft;
        y -= theCanvas.offsetTop;

    mouseX=x;
    mouseY=y;
```

Creating hit test point-style collision detection

Now that we know where the user clicked, we need to test whether that location "hits" any of the puzzle pieces. If so, we set the `selected` property of that piece to `true`. What we are going to perform is a simple *hit test point*–style hit detection. It will tell us whether the x,y position (*point*) of the mouse is inside (*hits*) any one of the puzzle pieces when the mouse button is clicked.

First, we create a local variable named `selectedList` that we will use when we need to swap the pieces in the `board` array. Next we will use a set of two nested `for:next` loops to traverse through all the pieces in the `board` array. Inside the `for:next` loops, the first thing we do is find the top-left corner x and y points of the current piece pointed to by `board[c][r]`. We calculate those values and put them into the `placeX` and `placeY` variables:

```
        var selectedList= new Array();
        for (var c = 0; c < cols; c++) {

            for (var r =0; r < rows; r++) {
                pieceX = c*partWidth+c*xPad+startXOffset;
                pieceY = r*partHeight+r*yPad+startYOffset;
```

Next, we use those calculated values to test for a hit test point collision. We do this with a semi-complicated `if:then` statement that tests the following four conditions simultaneously:

`mouseY >= pieceY`
:   The mouse pointer lies lower than or equal to the top of the piece.

`mouseY <= pieceY+partHeight`
:   The mouse pointer lies above or equal to the bottom of the piece.

`mouseX >= pieceX`
:   The mouse pointer lies to the right or equal to the left side of the piece.

`mouseX <= pieceX+partWidth`
:   The mouse pointer lies to the left or equal to the right side of the piece.

All of the above conditions must evaluate to `true` for a hit to be registered on any one piece on the board:

```
if ( (mouseY >= pieceY) && (mouseY <= pieceY+partHeight) && (mouseX >= pieceX) &&
     (mouseX <= pieceX+partWidth) ) {
```

If all these conditions are true, we set the selected property of the piece object to true
if it was already false, or we set it to false if it was already true. This allows the user
to "deselect" the selected piece if he has decided not to move it:

```
if ( board[c][r].selected) {
     board[c][r].selected = false;

} else {
     board[c][r].selected = true;

}
}
```

At the end of the nested for:next loop, we make sure to test each piece to see whether
its selected property is true. If so, we push it into the selectedList local array so that
we can perform the swap operation on the pieces:

```
if (board[c][r].selected) {
     selectedList.push({col:c,row:r})
}

}

}
```

Swapping two elements in a two-dimensional array

Now we need to test to see whether two pieces have been marked as selected. If so, we
swap the positions of those pieces. In this way, it appears that the player is clicking on
puzzle pieces and changing their locations to try to solve the puzzle.

To achieve the swap, we use a classic *three-way swap* programming construct utilizing
a temporary variable, tempPiece1, as a placeholder for the values we are going to swap.
First, we need to create a couple variables to hold the selected pieces. We will use
selected1 and selected2 for that purpose. Next, we move the reference to the piece
represented by selected1 into the tempPiece1 variable:

```
if (selectedList.length == 2) {
     var selected1 = selectedList[0];
     var selected2 = selectedList[1];
     var tempPiece1 = board[selected1.col][selected1.row];
```

Next, we move the piece referenced by selected2 to the location in the board array of
the piece represented by selected1 (the first swap). Then we apply the piece referenced
in selected1 to the position represented by selected2 (the second swap). Finally, now
that they are swapped, we make sure to set the selected properties of both pieces to
false:

```
            board[selected1.col][selected1.row] = board[selected2.col]
                                                  [selected2.row];
            board[selected2.col][selected2.row] = tempPiece1;
            board[selected1.col][selected1.row].selected = false;
            board[selected2.col][selected2.row].selected = false;
        }

    }
```

 This part of the function works because we have limited the number of pieces that can be selected to 2. For a game such as poker, which requires the player to select five cards, you would use a slightly different algorithm that tests for 5 cards instead of 2, and then calculate the value of the hand.

Testing the game

Believe it or not, that is all the code we need to talk about—the rest you have seen many times before. Try running the game (*CH6EX10.html*). When it loads, you should see the video organized in a 16-piece grid. Each part of the video will be playing, just like one of those magic tricks where a woman appears to be separated into multiple boxes but her legs, arms, and head are still moving. In fact, this game is sort of like one of those magic tricks because, in reality, the video was never "cut" in any way. We simply display the parts of the video to make it appear to be cut into 16 independent, moving pieces that can be swapped to re-form the original video.

Example 6-10 shows the full code listing for the Video Puzzle application.

Example 6-10. Video puzzle

```
<!doctype html>
<html lang="en">
<head>
<meta charset="UTF-8">
<title>CH6EX10: Video Puzzle</title>

<script src="modernizr.js"></script>
<script type="text/javascript">
window.addEventListener('load', eventWindowLoaded, false);
var videoElement;
var videoDiv;
function eventWindowLoaded() {

    videoElement = document.createElement("video");
    videoDiv = document.createElement('div');
    document.body.appendChild(videoDiv);
    videoDiv.appendChild(videoElement);
    videoDiv.setAttribute("style", "display:none;");
    var videoType = supportedVideoFormat(videoElement);
```

```
    if (videoType == "") {
        alert("no video support");
        return;
    }
    videoElement.addEventListener("canplaythrough",videoLoaded,false);
    videoElement.setAttribute("src", "muirbeach." + videoType);

}

function supportedVideoFormat(video) {
    var returnExtension = "";
    if (video.canPlayType("video/webm") =="probably" ||
        video.canPlayType("video/webm") == "maybe") {
            returnExtension = "webm";
    } else if(video.canPlayType("video/mp4") == "probably" ||
        video.canPlayType("video/mp4") == "maybe") {
            returnExtension = "mp4";
    } else if(video.canPlayType("video/ogg") =="probably" ||
        video.canPlayType("video/ogg") == "maybe") {
            returnExtension = "ogg";
    }

    return returnExtension;

}

function canvasSupport () {
        return Modernizr.canvas;
}


function videoLoaded() {
    canvasApp();

}

function canvasApp() {

    if (!canvasSupport()) {
            return;
        }

    function  drawScreen () {

        //Background
        context.fillStyle = '#303030';
        context.fillRect(0, 0, theCanvas.width, theCanvas.height);
        //Box
        context.strokeStyle = '#FFFFFF';
        context.strokeRect(5,   5, theCanvas.width-10, theCanvas.height-10);

        for (var c = 0; c < cols; c++) {
```

```
        for (var r = 0; r < rows; r++) {

            var tempPiece = board[c][r];
            var imageX = tempPiece.finalCol*partWidth;
            var imageY = tempPiece.finalRow*partHeight;
            var placeX = c*partWidth+c*xPad+startXOffset;
            var placeY = r*partHeight+r*yPad+startYOffset;
            //context.drawImage(videoElement , imageX, imageY, partWidth, partHeight);
            context.drawImage(videoElement, imageX, imageY, partWidth, partHeight,
                placeX, placeY, partWidth, partHeight);
            if (tempPiece.selected) {

                context.strokeStyle = '#FFFF00';
                context.strokeRect( placeX,  placeY, partWidth, partHeight);

            }
        }
    }

}

function randomizeBoard(board) {
    var newBoard = new Array();
    var cols = board.length;
    var rows = board[0].length
    for (var i = 0; i < cols; i++) {
        newBoard[i] = new Array();
        for (var j =0; j < rows; j++) {
            var found = false;
            var rndCol = 0;
            var rndRow = 0;
            while (!found) {
                var rndCol = Math.floor(Math.random() * cols);
                var rndRow = Math.floor(Math.random() * rows);
                if (board[rndCol][rndRow] != false) {
                    found = true;
                }
            }

            newBoard[i][j] = board[rndCol][rndRow];
            board[rndCol][rndRow] = false;
        }

    }

    return newBoard;

}

function eventMouseUp(event) {

    var mouseX;
```

```
var mouseY;
var pieceX;
var pieceY;
var x;
var y;
if (event.pageX || event.pageY) {
   x = event.pageX;
   y = event.pageY;
} else {
   x = e.clientX + document.body.scrollLeft +
       document.documentElement.scrollLeft;
   y = e.clientY + document.body.scrollTop +
       document.documentElement.scrollTop;
}
x -= theCanvas.offsetLeft;
y -= theCanvas.offsetTop;

mouseX=x;
mouseY=y;
var selectedList= new Array();
for (var c = 0; c < cols; c++) {

   for (var r =0; r < rows; r++) {
      pieceX = c*partWidth+c*xPad+startXOffset;
      pieceY = r*partHeight+r*yPad+startYOffset;
      if ( (mouseY >= pieceY) && (mouseY <= pieceY+partHeight) &&
          (mouseX >= pieceX) && (mouseX <= pieceX+partWidth) ) {

         if ( board[c][r].selected) {
              board[c][r].selected = false;

         } else {
              board[c][r].selected = true;

         }
      }
      if (board[c][r].selected) {
           selectedList.push({col:c,row:r})
      }

   }

}
if (selectedList.length == 2) {
   var selected1 = selectedList[0];
   var selected2 = selectedList[1];
   var tempPiece1 = board[selected1.col][selected1.row];
   board[selected1.col][selected1.row] =  board[selected2.col][selected2.row];
   board[selected2.col][selected2.row] = tempPiece1;
   board[selected1.col][selected1.row].selected = false;
   board[selected2.col][selected2.row].selected = false;
}
```

```
        }
        var theCanvas = document.getElementById("canvasOne");
        var context = theCanvas.getContext("2d");
        videoElement.play();

        //Puzzle Settings

        var rows = 4;
        var cols = 4;
        var xPad = 10;
        var yPad = 10;
        var startXOffset = 10;
        var startYOffset = 10;
        var partWidth = videoElement.width/cols;
        var partHeight = videoElement.height/rows;
        //320×240
        partWidth = 80;
        partHeight = 60;
        var board = new Array();

        //Initialize Board

        for (var i = 0; i < cols; i++) {
              board[i] = new Array();
              for (var j =0; j < rows; j++) {
                 board[i][j] = { finalCol:i,finalRow:j,selected:false };
              }
        }

        board = randomizeBoard(board);

        theCanvas.addEventListener("mouseup",eventMouseUp, false);

        function gameLoop() {
           window.setTimeout(gameLoop, 20);
           drawScreen();
        }

        gameLoop();
}

</script>

</head>
<body>
<canvas id="canvasOne" width="370" height="300" style="position: absolute;
    top: 50px; left: 50px;">
 Your browser does not support HTML5 Canvas.
</canvas>
</body>
</html>
```

Creating Video Controls on the Canvas

One obvious use of the HTML5 Canvas video display functionality is to create custom video controls to play, pause, stop, and so on. You might have already noticed that when a video is rendered on the canvas, it does not retain any of the HTML5 video controls. If you want to create controls on the canvas, you need to make them yourself. Thankfully, we have already learned almost everything we need to do this—now we just have to put it all together.

Creating video buttons

We are going to use some video control buttons that were created specifically for this example. Figure 6-11 shows a tile sheet that consists of *off* and *on* states for play, pause, and stop. The top row images are the on state; the bottom row images are the off state.

Figure 6-11. Video control button tile sheet

 We don't use the off state of the stop button in this application, but we included it in case you—the amazing reader and programmer that you are—want to use it later.

We will load this image dynamically onto the canvas and then place each 32×32 button onto the canvas individually. We use the width and height to calculate which part of the image to display as a control.

Preloading the buttons

The first thing we need to do is preload the button tile sheet. Because we are already testing for the video to preload before we display the canvas, we need a slightly new strategy to preload multiple objects. For this example, we will use a counter variable named loadCount that we will increment each time we detect that an item has loaded. In conjunction with that variable, we will create another named itemsToLoad, which will hold the number of things we are preloading. For this app, that number is two: the video and the tile sheet. These two variables are created outside of all functions at the top of our JavaScript:

```
var loadCount = 0;
var itemsToLoad = 2;
```

Along with `videoElement` and `videoDiv`, we also create another new variable, `button Sheet`. This is a reference to the image we load that holds the graphical buttons we will use for the video player interface:

```
var videoElement;
var videoDiv;
var buttonSheet;
```

In some web browsers, multiple `mouseup` events are fired for mouse clicks. To help fix this, we are going to create a counter to accept a click only every five frames. The `buttonWait` variable is the time to wait, while the `timeWaited` variable is the counter:

```
var buttonWait = 5;
var timeWaited = buttonWait;
```

We now must make some updates to our standard `eventWindowLoaded()` function that we have used for most of this chapter. First, we are going to change the `canplay` event handler for the video to a new function, `itemLoaded`:

```
videoElement.addEventListener("canplay",itemLoaded,false);
```

We used the `canplay` event instead of `canplaythrough` because, most of the time, a user wants to start watching a video as soon as enough data has been buffered to play, and not after the entire video has loaded.

Next we need to load our tile sheet. We create a new `Image` object and set the `src` property to *videobuttons.png*, which is the file shown in Figure 6-11. We also set its `onload` event handler to `itemLoaded`, just like the video:

```
    buttonSheet = new Image();
    buttonSheet.src = "videobuttons.png";
    buttonSheet.onload = itemLoaded;
}
```

Finally, we create the `itemLoaded()` event handler function. When this function is called, we increment the `loadCount` variable and test it against the `itemsToLoad` variable.

loadCount should never be greater than `itemsToLoad` if your application is running correctly. However, we find it safer to limit the use of the strict == test if possible. Why? Because if somehow, somewhere, something gets counted twice, the app will never load properly.

If `loadCount` is equal to or greater than `itemsToLoad`, we call `canvasApp()` to start the application:

```
function itemLoaded() {
    loadCount++;
    if (loadCount >= itemsToLoad) {
        canvasApp();
```

```
        }
    }
```

Placing the buttons

We need to set some variables in canvasApp() that will represent the locations of the three buttons we will display: play, pause, and stop. We start by specifying the standard button width and height as the variables bW and bH. All the images in the *videobut tons.png* tile sheet are 32×32 pixels, so we will set bW and bH accordingly. Then we proceed to create variables that represent the x and y locations of each button: playX, playY, pauseX, pauseY, stopX, and stopY. We could use literal values; however, these variables will make a couple of the more complicated calculations easier to swallow:

```
var bW = 32;
var bH = 32;
var playX = 190;
var playY = 300;
var pauseX = 230;
var pauseY = 300;
var stopX = 270
var stopY = 300;
```

In the drawImage() function, we need to test for the current state of the playing video and render the buttons accordingly. For this application, we will use the paused state of the video object's attribute to render the buttons properly in their "up" or "down" states.

When a video first loads on the page and is not yet playing, its paused attribute is set to true. When a video is playing, its paused attribute is set to false. Knowing this, we can create the actions for these simple buttons.

First, if we know that the video is not in a paused state, it must be playing, so we display the "down" version of the play button. The "down" position is in the second row on the tile sheet in Figure 6-11. The third parameter of the call to the drawImage() function is 32 because that is where the y position of the image we want to display starts on the tile sheet. If paused is true, it means that the video is not playing, so we display the "up" version of the play button. It starts at y position 0:

```
if (!videoElement.paused) {
    context.drawImage(buttonSheet, 0,32,bW,bH,playX,playY,bW,bH); //Play Down

} else {
    context.drawImage(buttonSheet, 0,0,bW,bH,playX,playY,bW,bH); //Play up
}
```

Displaying the pause button is simply the opposite of play. If the video paused property is true, we display the "down" version of the pause button. If the video is playing, it means the pause property is false, so we display the "up" version. Notice that the second parameter is 32 because to display the pause buttons in the tile sheet, we need to skip over the play button and start at the x position of the pause button:

```
if (videoElement.paused) {
    context.drawImage(buttonSheet,  32,32,bW,bH,pauseX,pauseY,bW,bH); //down
} else {
    context.drawImage(buttonSheet,  32,0,bW,bH,pauseX,pauseY,bW,bH); // up
}

context.drawImage(buttonSheet,  64,0,bW,bH,stopX,stopY,bW,bH); // Stop up
```

Finally, we update our timeCounter to limit the mouseUp events we listen to. We will show how this works in the next section:

```
timeWaited++;
```

Listening for the button presses

We also need to listen for the mouse button click. This process is very similar to how we accomplished much the same thing in the Video Puzzle application. First, in the canvasApp() function, we set an event handler, eventMouseUp(), for the mouseup event:

```
theCanvas.addEventListener("mouseup",eventMouseUp, false);
```

The way that the eventMouseUp() function works is very similar to the same function we created earlier for Video Puzzle. First, we test to see whether we have waited enough time (buttonWait) to accept another mouse click. If so, we drop in and set timeWai ted to 0 to reset the wait time. Next, we find the mouse pointer's x and y positions based on the way the browser tracks those values, and we put those values into local mouseX and mouseY variables:

```
function eventMouseUp(event) {
    if (timeWaited >= buttonWait) {
      timeWaited = 0;
      var mouseX;
      var mouseY;
      var x;
      var y;
      if (event.pageX || event.pageY) {
          x = event.pageX;
          y = event.pageY;
      } else {
        x = e.clientX + document.body.scrollLeft
            + document.documentElement.scrollLeft;
        y = e.clientY + document.body.scrollTop
            + document.documentElement.scrollTop;
      }
      x -= theCanvas.offsetLeft;
      y -= theCanvas.offsetTop;

      mouseX=x;
```

```
        mouseY=y;
        //Hit Play
```

Next, we test for a hit test point inside each button by checking the bounds (right, left, top, bottom) on the canvas to see whether the mouse pointer was over any of our buttons when it was clicked. If so, we detect a hit.

Then, we test the play button. Notice that those variables we created to represent the upper-left x and y locations of the button (playX and playY) help us make this calculation. They also help us because the names of the buttons self-document what we are trying to accomplish in each test of this function.

If the play button has been clicked and the video paused property is true, we call the play() function of the video to start playing:

```
    //Hit Play
        if ( (mouseY >= playY) && (mouseY <= playY+bH) && (mouseX >= playX) &&
            (mouseX <= playX+bW) ) {
          if (videoElement.paused) {
            videoElement.play();

        }
```

If the stop button was clicked, we set the paused property of the video to true and set the currentTime property to 0 so that the video will return to the first frame:

```
    //Hit Stop

        if ( (mouseY >= stopY) && (mouseY <= stopY+bH) && (mouseX >= stopX) &&
            (mouseX <= stopX+bW) ) {

          videoElement.pause();
          videoElement.currentTime = 0;
        }
```

If the pause button is clicked and the paused property of the video is false, we call the pause() function of the video to—you guessed it—pause the video on the current frame. If the paused property is true, we call the play() function of the video so that it will resume playing:

```
    //Hit Pause
        if ( (mouseY >= pauseY) && (mouseY <= pauseY+bH) && (mouseX >= pauseX) &&
            (mouseX <= pauseX+bW) ) {

          if (videoElement.paused == false) {
            videoElement.pause();
          } else {
            videoElement.play();
          }

        }
    }
```

Figure 6-12 shows what the canvas looks like when the video is displayed with controls.

 You will notice an odd relationship between the play and pause buttons. When one is "on," the other is "off." This is because we have only one property to look at: paused. There is a property named playing that exists in the HTML5 specification, but it did not work in all browsers, so we used only paused. In reality, you could have only one button and swap out the play or paused graphic, depending on the paused state. That would make these controls work more like the default HTML video controls.

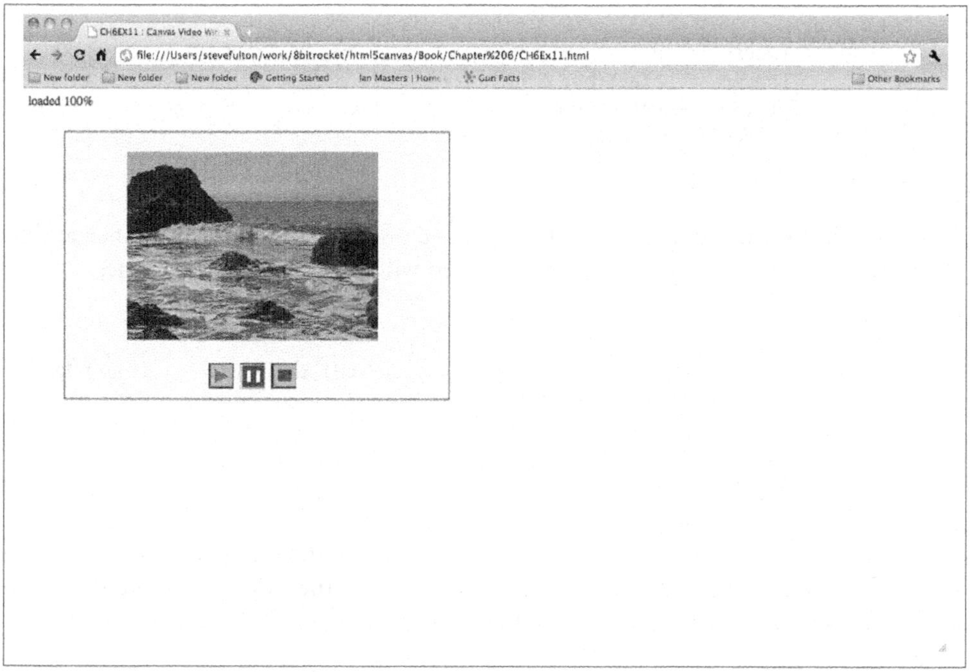

![Canvas video player buttons screenshot]

Figure 6-12. Canvas video player buttons

Example 6-11 shows the full source code for this application.

Example 6-11. Canvas video with controls

```
<!doctype html>
<html lang="en">
<head>
<meta charset="UTF-8">
<title>CH6EX11: Canvas Video With Controls</title>
```

```
<script src="modernizr.js"></script>
<script type="text/javascript">
window.addEventListener('load', eventWindowLoaded, false);
var loadCount= 0;
var itemsToLoad = 2;
var videoElement;
var videoDiv;
var buttonSheet;
var buttonWait = 5;
var timeWaited = buttonWait;

function eventWindowLoaded() {
   videoElement = document.createElement("video");
   videoDiv = document.createElement('div');
   document.body.appendChild(videoDiv);
   videoDiv.appendChild(videoElement);
   videoDiv.setAttribute("style", "display:none;");
   var videoType = supportedVideoFormat(videoElement);
   if (videoType == "") {
      alert("no video support");
      return;
   }
   videoElement.addEventListener("canplay",itemLoaded,false);
   videoElement.setAttribute("src", "muirbeach." + videoType);
   buttonSheet = new Image();
   buttonSheet.onload = itemLoaded;
   buttonSheet.src = "videobuttons.png";
}

function supportedVideoFormat(video) {
   var returnExtension = "";
   if (video.canPlayType("video/webm") =="probably" ||
      video.canPlayType("video/webm") == "maybe") {
         returnExtension = "webm";
   } else if(video.canPlayType("video/mp4") == "probably" ||
      video.canPlayType("video/mp4") == "maybe") {
         returnExtension = "mp4";
   } else if(video.canPlayType("video/ogg") =="probably" ||
      video.canPlayType("video/ogg") == "maybe") {
         returnExtension = "ogg";
   }

   return returnExtension;

}

function canvasSupport () {
    return Modernizr.canvas;
}
function itemLoaded() {
   loadCount++;
   if (loadCount >= itemsToLoad) {
```

```
                canvasApp();
        }

}
function canvasApp() {

    if (!canvasSupport()) {
            return;
          }

    function  drawScreen () {

        //Background
        context.fillStyle = '#ffffaa';
        context.fillRect(0, 0, theCanvas.width, theCanvas.height);
        //Box
        context.strokeStyle = '#000000';
        context.strokeRect(5,  5, theCanvas.width-10, theCanvas.height-10);
        //video
        context.drawImage(videoElement , 85, 30);
        //Draw Buttons
        //Play
        if (!videoElement.paused) {
            context.drawImage(buttonSheet, 0,32,bW,bH,playX,playY,bW,bH); //Play Down

        } else {
            context.drawImage(buttonSheet, 0,0,bW,bH,playX,playY,bW,bH); //Play up

        }

        if (videoElement.paused) {
            context.drawImage(buttonSheet,
                              32,32,bW,bH,pauseX,pauseY,bW,bH); // Pause down
        } else {
            context.drawImage(buttonSheet,  32,0,bW,bH,pauseX,pauseY,bW,bH); // Pause up
        }

        context.drawImage(buttonSheet,  64,0,bW,bH,stopX,stopY,bW,bH); // Stop up
        timeWaited++;
    }

        function eventMouseUp(event) {
        if (timeWaited >= buttonWait) {
            timeWaited = 0;
            var mouseX;
            var mouseY;

            var x;
            var y;
            if (event.pageX || event.pageY) {
                x = event.pageX;
                y = event.pageY;
```

```
        } else {
            x = e.clientX + document.body.scrollLeft
                + document.documentElement.scrollLeft;
            y = e.clientY + document.body.scrollTop
                + document.documentElement.scrollTop;
        }
        x -= theCanvas.offsetLeft;
        y -= theCanvas.offsetTop;

        mouseX=x;
        mouseY=y;
        //Hit Play
        if ( (mouseY >= playY) && (mouseY <= playY+bH) && (mouseX >= playX) &&
            (mouseX <= playX+bW) ) {
            if (videoElement.paused) {
                videoElement.play();

            }

        }

        //Hit Stop

        if ( (mouseY >= stopY) && (mouseY <= stopY+bH) && (mouseX >= stopX) &&
            (mouseX <= stopX+bW) ) {

            videoElement.pause();
            videoElement.currentTime = 0;
        }
        //Hit Pause
        if ( (mouseY >= pauseY) && (mouseY <= pauseY+bH) && (mouseX >= pauseX) &&
            (mouseX <= pauseX+bW) ) {

            if (videoElement.paused == false) {
                videoElement.pause();
            } else {
                videoElement.play();
            }

        }

    }
}

var theCanvas = document.getElementById("canvasOne");
var context = theCanvas.getContext("2d");

var bW = 32;
var bH = 32;
var playX = 190;
var playY = 300;
var pauseX = 230;
```

```
    var pauseY = 300;
    var stopX = 270
    var stopY = 300;


    theCanvas.addEventListener("mouseup",eventMouseUp, false);

    function gameLoop() {
        window.setTimeout(gameLoop, 20);
        drawScreen();
     }

    gameLoop();}

</script>

</head>
<body>
<canvas id="canvasOne" width="500" height="350" style="position: absolute;
    top: 50px; left: 50px;">
 Your browser does not support HTML5 Canvas.
</canvas>
</body>
</html>
```

Animation Revisited: Moving Videos

Now we are going to revisit the bouncing balls demo from Chapter 5 to show you how
you can achieve the same effect with images and videos. Because we covered this in
detail in Example 5-5 (*CH5EX5.html*), we don't need to examine all the code—just the
changes that make the videos move.

> Remember that videos are drawn in much the same way as images, so
> with very few changes, this application would work just as well with a
> static image.

While there are a few other changes, the most important is in the drawScreen() function
when we draw the videos onto the canvas. Recall that in Chapter 5 we created an array
named balls and a dynamic object to hold the properties of each ball that looked like
this:

```
tempBall = {x:tempX,y:tempY,radius:tempRadius, speed:tempSpeed, angle:tempAngle,
    xunits:tempXunits, yunits:tempYunits}
```

For videos, we will create a similar array, named videos, but we will alter the dynamic
object:

```
tempvideo = {x:tempX,y:tempY,width:180, height:120, speed:tempSpeed,
            angle:tempAngle,
   xunits:tempXunits, yunits:tempYunits}
```

The big difference here is that we no longer need a `radius` that represents the size of the ball; instead, we need the `width` and `height` so that we can render the video to our desired size in the `drawScreen()` function.

In Chapter 5, we used the canvas drawing command to draw balls on the screen like this:

```
context.beginPath();
context.arc(ball.x,ball.y,ball.radius,0,Math.PI*2,true);
context.closePath();
context.fill();
```

To draw videos, we need to change the code:

```
context.drawImage(videoElement, video.x, video.y, video.width, video.height);
```

That is pretty much all you need to do! There are some other changes here (for example, we start all the videos in the center of the screen before they start moving), but the items mentioned above are the main things you need to concentrate on to move video, not yellow balls, around the screen. Figure 6-13 shows what the example looks like with bouncing videos instead of balls. You can see the full code in Example 6-12.

Figure 6-13. Canvas video animation demo

Example 6-12. Multiple video bounce

```
<!doctype html>
<html lang="en">
<head>
<meta charset="UTF-8">
<title>CH6EX12: Multiple Video Bounce</title>

<script src="modernizr.js"></script>
<script type="text/javascript">
window.addEventListener('load', eventWindowLoaded, false);

var videoElement;
var videoDiv;
function eventWindowLoaded() {

    videoElement = document.createElement("video");
    var videoDiv = document.createElement('div');
```

```
        document.body.appendChild(videoDiv);
        videoDiv.appendChild(videoElement);
        videoDiv.setAttribute("style", "display:none;");
        var videoType = supportedVideoFormat(videoElement);
        if (videoType == "") {
            alert("no video support");
            return;
        }
        videoElement.addEventListener("canplaythrough",videoLoaded,false);
        videoElement.setAttribute("src", "muirbeach." + videoType);

}

function supportedVideoFormat(video) {
    var returnExtension = "";
    if (video.canPlayType("video/webm") =="probably" ||
        video.canPlayType("video/webm") == "maybe") {
            returnExtension = "webm";
    } else if(video.canPlayType("video/mp4") == "probably" ||
        video.canPlayType("video/mp4") == "maybe") {
            returnExtension = "mp4";
    } else if(video.canPlayType("video/ogg") =="probably" ||
        video.canPlayType("video/ogg") == "maybe") {
            returnExtension = "ogg";
    }

    return returnExtension;

}

function canvasSupport () {
        return Modernizr.canvas;
}

function videoLoaded() {
    canvasApp();

}

function canvasApp() {

    if (!canvasSupport()) {
            return;
        }

    function  drawScreen () {

        context.fillStyle = '#000000';
        context.fillRect(0, 0, theCanvas.width, theCanvas.height);
        //Box
        context.strokeStyle = '#ffffff';
        context.strokeRect(1,  1, theCanvas.width-2, theCanvas.height-2);
```

```
    //Place videos
    context.fillStyle = "#FFFF00";
    var video;

    for (var i =0; i <videos.length; i++) {
        video = videos[i];
        video.x += video.xunits;
        video.y += video.yunits;

        context.drawImage(videoElement ,video.x, video.y, video.width, video.height);

        if (video.x > theCanvas.width-video.width || video.x < 0 ) {
            video.angle = 180 - video.angle;
            updatevideo(video);
        } else if (video.y > theCanvas.height-video.height || video.y < 0) {
            video.angle = 360 - video.angle;
            updatevideo(video);
        }
    }

}

function updatevideo(video) {

    video.radians = video.angle * Math.PI/ 180;
    video.xunits = Math.cos(video.radians) * video.speed;
    video.yunits = Math.sin(video.radians) * video.speed;

}

var numVideos = 12 ;
var maxSpeed = 10;
var videos = new Array();
var tempvideo;
var tempX;
var tempY;
var tempSpeed;
var tempAngle;
var tempRadians;
var tempXunits;
var tempYunits;

var theCanvas = document.getElementById("canvasOne");
var context = theCanvas.getContext("2d");
videoElement.play();

for (var i = 0; i < numVideos; i++) {

    tempX = 160 ;
    tempY = 190 ;
    tempSpeed = 5;
```

```
        tempAngle = Math.floor(Math.random()*360);
        tempRadians = tempAngle * Math.PI/ 180;
        tempXunits = Math.cos(tempRadians) * tempSpeed;
        tempYunits = Math.sin(tempRadians) * tempSpeed;
        tempvideo = {x:tempX,y:tempY,width:180, height:120,
            speed:tempSpeed, angle:tempAngle,
            xunits:tempXunits, yunits:tempYunits}
        videos.push(tempvideo);
    }

    function gameLoop() {
        window.setTimeout(gameLoop, 20);
        drawScreen();
    }

    gameLoop();
}

</script>

</head>
<body>
<div style="position: absolute; top: 50px; left: 50px;">

<canvas id="canvasOne" width="500" height="500">
 Your browser does not support HTML5 Canvas.
</canvas>
</div>
</body>
</html>
```

 The HTML5 video element combined with the canvas is an exciting, emerging area that is being explored on the Web as you read this. One great example of this is the exploding 3D video at CraftyMind.com (*http://www.craftymind.com/2010/04/20/blowing-up-html5-video-and-mapping-it-into-3d-space/*).

Capturing Video with JavaScript

One of the big deficits in HTML for many years has been the lack of any pure HTML/ JavaScript interface to the microphone and camera on a user's machine. Up until now, most JavaScript APIs for media capture have leveraged Flash to capture audio and video. However, in the new (mostly) Flash-less mobile HTML5 world, relying on a nonexistent (on certain mobile devices) technology is no longer an answer. In recent months, the W3C's Device API Policy Working Group has stepped in to create a specification named *The HTML Media Capture API* to fill this hole.

Web RTC Media Capture and Streams API

Not too long ago, if you wanted to access a webcam or microphone in a web browser, you had to fall back to using Flash. There simply was no way to access media capture hardware in JavaScript. However, with HTML5 replacing Flash as the standard for web browser applications, applications that relied on Flash for "exotic" features (such as webcam and microphone access) need a new way to solve this problem. This is where the Media Capture and Streams API comes in. It is a new browser-based API access through JavaScript that gives access to microphones and webcams and (for our purposes) allows a developer to utilize this input on the HTML5 Canvas.

The main entry point to Media Capture and Streams is the `getUserMedia()` native function that bridges the gap between the web browser and media capture devices. At the time of this writing, `getUserMedia()` is still experimental. It is supported in the following browsers:

- Google Chrome Canary
- Opera (labs version)
- Firefox (very soon, but our tests proved not quite yet)

Because support is always changing, a great resource to find out about the compatibility of new browser features is *http://caniuse.com*. It will tell you which browsers can currently support which features.

It might seem obvious, but you will also need a webcam of some sort for the next three examples to work properly.

Example 1: Show Video

In our first example of Web RTC Media Capture, we will simply show a video from a webcam on an HTML5 page.

First we need a `<video>` tag in the HTML page to hold the video that we will capture from the webcam. We set it to `autoplay` so that we will see it moving as soon as it becomes available:

```
<div>
<video id="thevideo" autoplay></video>
</div>
```

Our next job is to try to figure out whether the browser supports video capture. We do this by creating a function named `userMediaSupported()` that returns a Boolean based on the availability of the `getUserMedia()` method in various browsers. We need to do this because `getUserMedia()` support is not the universal standard yet.

```
function userMediaSupported() {
    return !!(navigator.getUserMedia || navigator.webkitGetUserMedia ||
```

```
            navigator.mozGetUserMedia || navigator.msGetUserMedia);
    }
```

If we know that getUserMedia() is supported, we call startVideo(). If not, we display an alert box:

```
function eventWindowLoaded() {
    if (userMediaSupported()) {
        startVideo();
    } else {
        alert("getUserMedia() Not Supported")
    }
}
```

Next, we find the existing getUserMedia() method for the current browser and set the local navigator.getUserMedia() function to its value. Again, we do this because support is not universal, and this step will make it much easier to reference getUserMedia() in our code.

Next we call the getUserMedia() function, passing three arguments:

- An object with Boolean properties media that we want to capture (video:true and/ or audio:true) (At the time this was written, the audio property was not supported.)
- A success callback function.
- A fail callback function.

```
        function startVideo() {
            navigator.getUserMedia = navigator.getUserMedia ||
                                     navigator.webkitGetUserMedia ||
            navigator.mozGetUserMedia || navigator.msGetUserMedia;
            navigator.getUserMedia({video: true, audio:true}, mediaSuccess, mediaFail);
        }
```

The mediaFail() function simply creates an alert() box to show us an error. Most likely, when you try this example, you will get error code 1, which means "permission denied." This error will occur if you are trying to run the example locally from the file system. You need to try all the getUserMedia() examples from a web server, running either on your own machine or on the Internet.

```
function mediaFail(error) {
    //error code 1 = permission Denied
    alert("Failed To get user media:" + error.code)
}
```

The mediaSuccess() function is the heart of this application. It is passed a reference to the video object from the webcam (userMedia). To utilize this, we need to create a URL that points to the object representing the user media so that our <video> object has a source that it can use to start showing video.

First, we set `window.URL` to whatever version of `window.URL` the browser supports. We then retrieve a reference to the `<video>` in the HTML page. Next we use `window.URL.cre ateObjectURL()` to retrieve a usable URL that points to media that our video object can display. We set the `src` property of our video to that URL. Finally, we set a callback for the `onloadedmetadata` event so that we can proceed with our application after the video has started displaying:

```
function mediaSuccess(userMedia) {
    window.URL = window.URL || window.webkitURL || window.mozURL || window.msURL;
    var video = document.getElementById("thevideo");
    video.src = window.URL.createObjectURL(userMedia);
    video.onloadedmetadata = doCoolStuff;
}

function doCoolStuff() {
    alert("Do Cool Stuff");
}
```

And that's it! You can view the full code for this example in *CHX6EX13.HTML* in the code distribution.

If this does not work the first time you try it, check the following:

1. Make sure you are using one of the supported browsers:
   a. Google Chrome Canary
   b. Opera (labs version)
2. Verify that you have a webcam on your machine. You might have to find the webcam application on your computer and launch it. (We needed to do that on Microsoft Windows 7, but not on Microsoft Windows 8). It's clumsy, but it should work.
3. Verify that the app is served from a web server in an HTML page. Figure 6-14 shows what the app should look like when it works.

Figure 6-14. getUserMedia() displaying video capture of a stressed-out developer

Example 2: Put Video on the Canvas and Take a Screenshot

Next, we are going to modify the sixth example from this chapter (*CH6EX6.html*). As a refresher, in that example, we used the Canvas to display a video by dynamically adding an HTMLVideoElement object to the page and then using it as the source for video displayed on the Canvas. For this example, we will use getUserMedia() as the source for the video on the canvas and display it in the same way. However, we will add the ability to take a screenshot of the video by using the canvas context.toDataURL() method.

The first thing we do is create a dynamic video element (videoElement) and a dynamically created <div> to hold it on the page, and then we make both invisible by setting the style of videoDiv to display:none. This will get our video onto the page but hide it, because we want to display it on the canvas.

Next we check our userMediaSupported() function to see whether we can access the webcam. If so, we call startVideo() to start the media capture and then call canvasApp() to start our application:

```
function eventWindowLoaded() {

    videoElement = document.createElement("video");
```

```
videoDiv = document.createElement('div');
document.body.appendChild(videoDiv);
videoDiv.appendChild(videoElement);
videoDiv.setAttribute("style", "display:none;");
if (userMediaSupported()) {
    startVideo();
    canvasApp();
} else {
    alert("getUserMedia() Not Supported")
}
}
```

The startVideo() function is nearly identical to the one we created for the last example. We get a reference to the getUserMedia() function for this browser and then make a call to getUserMedia(), passing an object that represents features we want to capture, plus callback functions for success and fail:

```
function startVideo() {
    navigator.getUserMedia = navigator.getUserMedia ||
                             navigator.webkitGetUserMedia ||
    navigator.mozGetUserMedia || navigator.msGetUserMedia;
    navigator.getUserMedia({video: true, audio:true}, mediaSuccess, mediaFail);

}
```

After a successful call to getUserMedia(), we set the source of videoElement to the object represented by the userMedia argument passed automatically to mediaSuc cess() after a successful connection with getUserMedia():

```
function mediaSuccess(userMedia) {
    window.URL = window.URL || window.webkitURL || window.mozURL || window.msURL;
    videoElement.src = window.URL.createObjectURL(userMedia);
}
```

In the canvasApp() function, we need to make sure that we call the play() function of the video, or nothing will be displayed:

```
videoElement.play();
```

Just like in Example 6 (*CH6EX6.html*), we need to call drawScreen() in a loop to display new frames of the video. If we leave this out, the video will look like a static image:

```
function gameLoop() {
    window.setTimeout(gameLoop, 20);
    drawScreen();
}

gameLoop();
```

In the drawScreen() function, we call drawImage() to display the updated image data from videoElement:

```
function drawScreen () {

    context.drawImage(videoElement , 10, 10);
}
```

We also want to create a button for the user to press to take a screenshot of the image from the webcam. We will accomplish this essentially the same way that we did it in Chapter 3. First, we create a button on the HTML page with the id of createImageData:

```
<canvas id="canvasOne" width="660" height="500">
 Your browser does not support the HTML 5 Canvas.
</canvas>
<form>
<input type="button" id="createImageData" value="Take Photo!">
</form>
```

Then, in our JavaScript, we retrieve a reference to the button and add a click event handler:

```
formElement = document.getElementById("createImageData");
formElement.addEventListener("click", createImageDataPressed, false);
```

The click event handler calls toDataUrl() to open a new window, using the image taken from the video as the source:

```
function createImageDataPressed(e) {

window.open(theCanvas.toDataURL(),"canvasImage","left=0,top=0,width="
    + theCanvas.width + ",height=" + theCanvas.height +",toolbar=0,resizable=0");

}
```

Figure 6-15. getUserMedia() taking screenshot from Canvas

And that's it! Figure 6-15 shows what it might look like when you export the Canvas to an image. Now, not only are we showing the video from the web cam on the Canvas, we can manipulate it too! You can see the full code for this example in *CH6EX14.html* in the code distribution.

Example 3: Create a Video Puzzle out of User-Captured Video

For our final example of the `getUserMedia()` function, we will use video captured from a webcam to create the video puzzle from Example 10 (*CH6EX10.html*).

The first thing we need to note is that (currently) the video captured from `getUserMe dia()` is fixed to 640×480 and cannot be resized. For this reason, we need to update the code in *CH6EX10.html* to reflect a larger canvas with larger puzzle pieces.

In the HTML, we change the size of the Canvas to 690×530.

```
<canvas id="canvasOne" width="690" height="530"style="position: absolute; top:
    10px; left: 10px;" >
  Your browser does not support the HTML5 Canvas.
</canvas>
```

Then, in the JavaScript, we double the size of the pieces. In *CH6EX10.html*, we used 80×60 pieces, so in this example we make them 160×120:

```
partWidth=160;
partHeight=120;
```

The rest of the code changes are nearly identical to the last example. We create a <vid
eo> element in code as videoElement and use that as the object to capture video using
getUserMedia():

```
function eventWindowLoaded() {

    videoElement = document.createElement("video");
    videoDiv = document.createElement('div');
    document.body.appendChild(videoDiv);
    videoDiv.appendChild(videoElement);
    videoDiv.setAttribute("style", "display:none;");
    if (userMediaSupported()) {
        startVideo();
        canvasApp();
    } else {
        alert("getUserMedia() Not Supported")
    }

}

function userMediaSupported() {
    return !!(navigator.getUserMedia || navigator.webkitGetUserMedia ||
            navigator.mozGetUserMedia || navigator.msGetUserMedia);
}


function mediaFail(error) {
    //error code 1 = permission Denied
    alert("Failed To get user media:" + error.code)
}

function startVideo() {
    navigator.getUserMedia = navigator.getUserMedia ||
                            navigator.webkitGetUserMedia ||
    navigator.mozGetUserMedia || navigator.msGetUserMedia;
    navigator.getUserMedia({video: true, audio:true}, mediaSuccess, mediaFail);

}

function mediaSuccess(userMedia) {
    window.URL = window.URL || window.webkitURL || window.mozURL || window.msURL;
    videoElement.src = window.URL.createObjectURL(userMedia);
}
```

In our drawScreen() function, we use videoElement as the source for the puzzle pieces
we display with drawImage():

```
function  drawScreen () {
    ...
    context.drawImage(videoElement, imageX, imageY, partWidth, partHeight,
                    placeX, placeY, partWidth, partHeight);
```

```
    . . .
  }
```

There you go. Just a few simple changes, and we now can use a video stream from a webcam as the source for video on the canvas and then manipulate it into an interactive application. You can see what this might look like in Figure 6-16. You can see the full code for this example in *CH6EX15.html* in the code distribution.

Figure 6-16. Video puzzle on canvas using getUserMedia()

Video and Mobile

The dirty secret about video on the canvas and mobile web browsers is that, currently, it won't work at all. At the time of this writing, video could not be displayed on the canvas on any mobile browser that supports HTML5. While Apple claims it will work on Safari on the iPad, all of our tests were negative. We hope that Google, Apple, and Microsoft will fix this situation soon because, as you can see, there are some pretty cool things you can accomplish when you mix the HTML5 Canvas and HTML5 Video.

What's Next?

In this chapter, we introduced the HTML `<video>` tag and showed some basic ways that it could be used on an HTML page, including how to manipulate loaded video in numerous ways. While we showed you how to do some pretty cool stuff with the video and HTML5 Canvas, we went on to show you new ways to capture video and use it on the canvas. This is really just the tip of the iceberg. We believe that these two very powerful and flexible new features of HTML5 (video and the canvas) will prove to be a very potent combination for web applications of the future. In the next chapter, we will dive into HTML5 audio and how it can be used with applications created on the canvas.

CHAPTER 7

Working with Audio

You can't physically manipulate audio with HTML5 Canvas as directly as you can video, but many canvas applications can use that extra dimension of sound. Audio is represented by the `HTMLAudioElement` object manipulated through JavaScript and by the `<audio>` tag in HTML5. There is no Canvas API for audio nor, really, is one necessary. However, there are many ways that you might want to use audio with HTML5 Canvas. As you will see, the `HTMLAudioElement` has some limitations and can be frustrating. However, with developments like the Web Audio API on the horizon, the outlook for using audio with the HTML5 Canvas looks brighter every day.

The Basic <audio> Tag

The basic usage of the `<audio>` tag in HTML5 is very similar to that of the `<video>` tag. The only required property is `src`, which needs to point to an existing audio file to play in the browser. Of course, it's always nice to show some audio controls on the page, and this can be accomplished using the `controls` Boolean, just as we did with `<video>`.

The code in Example 7-1 will load and play *song1.ogg* in a web browser that supports *.ogg* file playback, as shown in Figure 7-1. (Reminder: not all browsers support all formats.)

Example 7-1. Basic HTML5 audio

```
<!doctype html>
<html lang="en">
<head>
<meta charset="UTF-8">
<title>CH7EX1: Basic HTML5 Audio</title>
</head>
<body>
<div>
<audio src="song1.ogg" controls>
```

```
Your browser does not support the audio element.
</audio>
</div>
</body>
</html>
```

Figure 7-1. The very basic HTML5 <audio> tag

Audio Formats

Similar to video formats, which we learned about in Chapter 6, not every web browser supports every audio format. In fact, audio support appears to be in worse shape than video. As you will soon discover in this chapter, audio is one place where HTML5 needs some serious work. However, we will show you some strategies and workarounds for making audio easier to use in your applications.

Supported Formats

Here is a quick chart to show you which audio formats are supported by which browsers. We are not going to use version numbers here, because we assume the latest version of each product:

Platform	.ogg	.mp3	.wav
Chrome	X	X	X
Firefox	X		X
Safari		X	X
Opera	X		X
Internet Explorer		X	

The situation is much like that of the <video> tag. To support <audio>, we will need to use multiple separate formats for each piece of audio we want to play. To be on the safe side, we will use three formats: *.mp3*, *.ogg*, and *.wav*. At this point, we will probably never see Opera and Firefox support for .mp3 files. The license fee associated with the format is prohibitive for those browsers.

Audacity

Fortunately, there is a great free audio tool available that will help you convert audio into any format. In our case, we need to convert to *.mp3*, *.ogg*, and *.wav*.

Audacity (*http://audacity.sourceforge.net/*) is an open source, cross-platform project designed to bring sophisticated audio editing to the desktop. The current version works on Mac, Windows, and Linux.

Figure 7-2 shows a sample screen from Audacity. When you load a sound into Audacity, it displays the waveform of the sound. You can manipulate the sound in many ways, including trimming, splitting, and duplicating, and then add effects such as fade, echo, reverse, and so on. After editing a sound, you export it to the sound format that you would like to create. In our case, that would be *.ogg*, *.wav*, and *.mp3*.

We don't have the space here to fully describe how to use an audio tool like Audacity, but we do need to give you one caveat: the distributed version of Audacity does not support the export of audio in the *.mp3* format. To export *.mp3* audio, you will need to download the LAME *.mp3* encoder (*http://lame.sourceforge.net/*). LAME is also an open source project.

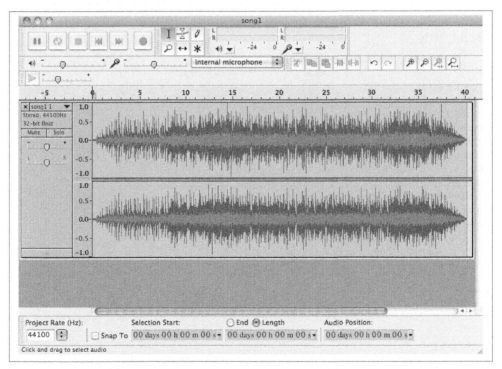

Figure 7-2. Editing an audio file in Audacity

Example: Using All Three Formats

In Example 7-2, we are going to embed a 40-second song, *song1*, in an HTML5 page and play it. To make sure *song1* can play in as many browsers as possible, we are going to embed it with three different sources. For this example, we are also going to set the `autoplay`, `loop`, and `controls` properties so that the song will start automatically, replay when it reaches the end, and display the default browser audio controls. Here is the code to embed *song1*:

```
<audio controls autoplay loop>
<source src="song1.mp3" type="audio/mp3">
<source src="song1.wav" type="audio/wav">
<source src="song1.ogg" type="audio/ogg">
</audio>
```

 Just as we did with video, we have placed the audio type with the broadest support for iOS devices first in the list. This is because handheld devices do not do well with multiple embedded sources.

We created *.ogg*, *.wav*, and *.mp3* versions of the song using Audacity. Example 7-2 gives the full code.

Example 7-2. Basic HTML5 audio revisited

```
<!doctype html>
<html lang="en">
<head>
<meta charset="UTF-8">
<title>CH7EX2: Basic HTML5 Audio Revisited</title>
</head>
<body>
<div>
<audio controls autoplay loop>
<source src="song1.mp3" type="audio/mp3">
<source src="song1.ogg" type="audio/ogg">
<source src="song1.wav" type="audio/wav">
Your browser does not support the audio element.
</audio>
</div>
</body>
</html>
```

song1 was created 10 years ago using Sonic Foundry's Acid music-looping software. Acid is an amazing tool for creating soundtracks because it can help even the musically inept (read: us) create songs that sound perfect for games and applications. Acid is now sold by Sony for Windows only. Songs can be created on the Mac in a similar way using GarageBand.

Audio Tag Properties, Functions, and Events

Similar to the `<video>` tag, the `<audio>` tag in HTML5 is based on the `HTMLAudioEle``ment` DOM object, which is derived from `HTMLMediaElement`.

Audio Functions

`load()`
> Starts loading the sound file specified by the `src` property of the `<audio>` tag.

`play()`
> Starts playing the sound file specified by the `src` property of the `<audio>` tag. If the file is not ready, it will be loaded.

`pause()`
> Pauses the playing audio file.

`canPlayType()`
> Accepts a MIME type as a parameter, and returns the value `maybe` or `probably` if the browser can play that type of audio file. It returns `""` (an empty string) if it cannot.

Important Audio Properties

There are many properties defined for the `audio` element in HTML5. We are going to focus on the following because they are the most useful for the applications we will build:

`duration`
> The total length, in seconds, of the sound represented by the `audio` object.

`currentTime`
> The current playing position, in seconds, of the playing audio file.

`loop`
> `true` or `false`: whether the audio clip should start playing at the beginning when `currentTime` reaches the `duration`.

autoplay
: true or false: whether the audio should start playing automatically when it has loaded.

muted
: true or false: Setting this to true silences the audio object regardless of volume settings.

controls
: true or false: Displays controls for an audio object in an HTML page. Controls will not display on the canvas unless they are created in HTML (for example, with a <div> overlay).

volume
: The volume level of the audio object; the value must be between 0 and 1.

paused
: true or false: whether the audio object is paused. Set with a call to the pause() function.

ended
: true or false. Set when an audio object has played through its entire duration.

currentSrc
: URL to the source file for the audio object.

preload
: Specifies whether the media file should be loaded before the page is displayed. At the time of this writing, this property has not been implemented across all browsers.

 To see which properties and events of the HTMLMediaObject are supported in which browsers, visit this site (*http://www.w3.org/2010/05/ video/mediaevents.html*).

Important Audio Events

Many events are defined for the HTML5 audio element. We are going to focus on the following events because they have proven to work when building audio applications:

progress
: Raised when the browser is retrieving data while loading the file. (This still has spotty support in browsers, so be careful with it.)

canplaythrough
: Raised when the browser calculates that the media element could be played from beginning to end if started immediately.

playing

Set to `true` when the audio is being played.

volumechange

Set when either the `volume` property or the `muted` property changes.

ended

Set when playback reaches the `duration` of the audio file and the file stops being played.

Loading and Playing the Audio

We are going to use the `canplaythrough` and `progress` events to load `<audio>` before we try to play it. Here is how we embed the audio for *song1*:

```
<audio id="theAudio" controls>
<source src="song1.mp3" type="audio/mp3">
<source src="song1.wav" type="audio/wav">
<source src="song1.ogg" type="audio/ogg">
Your browser does not support the audio element.
</audio>
```

Similar to most of the applications we have built thus far in this book, we will create event handlers for `progress` and `canplaythrough` after the `window` DOM object has finished loading, and then we will call the `load()` method of `audioElement` to force the audio file to start loading:

```
window.addEventListener('load', eventWindowLoaded, false);
function eventWindowLoaded() {
   var audioElement = document.getElementById("theAudio");
   audioElement.addEventListener('canplaythrough',audioLoaded,false);
   audioElement.addEventListener('progress',updateLoadingStatus,false);
   audioElement.load();

}
```

When the `canplaythrough` event is dispatched, `canvasApp()` is called. Then we start playing the audio by retrieving a reference to the `audio` element in the HTML page through the DOM, with a call to `getElementById()`. (We will create a variable named `audioElement` that we will use throughout the canvas application to reference the au dio element in the HTML page.) We then call the `play()` function of `audioElement`:

```
var audioElement = document.getElementById("theAudio");
audioElement.play();
```

You might be wondering why we didn't use the `preload` attribute of `HTMLAudioEle ment` instead of forcing it to load by listening for the `canplaythrough` event. There are two reasons for this, and both apply to the `video` element as well. First, you want to preload so that you are sure the assets you need are available to your program at runtime. Second, preloading ensures that the user will see something useful or interesting while

---

everything is loading. By using the standard `preload` attribute, you (in theory) force your audio assets to load before the page loads. Because Canvas apps are interactive and can require many more assets than those loaded when the page loads, we avoid the `preload` attribute and load the assets within the application.

Displaying Attributes on the Canvas

Now we are going to display the attribute values of an `audio` element playing on an HTML page. In this example (*CH7EX3.html*), we are also going to display the `audio` element in the HTML page so that you can see the relationship between what is shown on the canvas and the state of the `<audio>` tag in the page.

In the `drawScreen()` function, we will add the following code to display the attributes of the `audioElement` variable:

```
context.fillStyle = "#000000";
context.fillText ("Duration:" + audioElement.duration,  20 ,20);
context.fillText ("Current time:" + audioElement.currentTime,  20 ,40);
context.fillText ("Loop: " + audioElement.loop,  20 ,60);
context.fillText ("Autoplay: " +audioElement.autoplay,  20 ,80);
context.fillText ("Muted: " + audioElement.muted,  20 ,100);
context.fillText ("Controls: " + audioElement.controls,  20 ,120);
context.fillText ("Volume: " + audioElement.volume,  20 ,140);
context.fillText ("Paused: " + audioElement.paused,  20 ,160);
context.fillText ("Ended: " + audioElement.ended,  20 ,180);
context.fillText ("Source: " + audioElement.currentSrc,  20 ,200);
context.fillText ("Can Play OGG: " + audioElement.canPlayType("audio/ogg"),
                  20 ,220);
context.fillText ("Can Play WAV: " + audioElement.canPlayType("audio/wav"),
                  20 ,240);
context.fillText ("Can Play MP3: " + audioElement.canPlayType("audio/mp3"),
                  20 ,260);
```

You should already be familiar with most of these attributes. When you launch Example 7-3 (*CH7EX3.html*), play it with the audio controls in the browser. You will notice that the changes are reflected by the attribute values displayed on the canvas. This is just our first step toward integrating audio with the canvas, but it should give you a good idea of how we will start to use `audio` elements and manipulate them through JavaScript.

Figure 7-3 shows what this application looks like when it is executed in a web browser.

Figure 7-3. Showing audio properties on the canvas

There are also a few attributes displayed at the bottom of this list that we have not discussed. They all come from calls to the `canPlayType()` function of `HTMLAudioEle ment`. We are only displaying these right now, but in Example 7-3, we will make use of this function to help us decide which sound to dynamically load in JavaScript.

Example 7-3. Audio properties and the canvas

```
<!doctype html>
<html lang="en">
<head>
<meta charset="UTF-8">
<title>CH7EX3: Audio Properties And The Canvas</title>

<script src="modernizr.js"></script>
<script type="text/javascript">
window.addEventListener('load', eventWindowLoaded, false);
function eventWindowLoaded() {
    var audioElement = document.getElementById("theAudio");
    audioElement.addEventListener("canplaythrough",audioLoaded,false);
    audioElement.addEventListener("progress",updateLoadingStatus,false);
    audioElement.load();

}

function canvasSupport () {
    return Modernizr.canvas;
}

function updateLoadingStatus() {
    var loadingStatus = document.getElementById("loadingStatus");
    var audioElement = document.getElementById("theAudio");
    var percentLoaded = parseInt(((audioElement.buffered.end(0) /
      audioElement.duration) * 100));
    document.getElementById("loadingStatus").innerHTML =   'loaded '
      + percentLoaded + '%';
```

```
}

function audioLoaded() {

   canvasApp();

}

function canvasApp() {

  if (!canvasSupport()) {
        return;
      }

  function  drawScreen () {


      //Background
      context.fillStyle = "#ffffaa";
      context.fillRect(0, 0, theCanvas.width, theCanvas.height);

      //Box
      context.strokeStyle = "#000000";
      context.strokeRect(5,  5, theCanvas.width-10, theCanvas.height-10);

      // Text
      context.fillStyle  = "#000000";
      context.fillText  ("Duration:" + audioElement.duration,  20 ,20);
      context.fillText  ("Current time:" + audioElement.currentTime,  20 ,40);
      context.fillText  ("Loop: " + audioElement.loop,  20 ,60);
      context.fillText  ("Autoplay: " +audioElement.autoplay,  20 ,80);
      context.fillText  ("Muted: " + audioElement.muted,  20 ,100);
      context.fillText  ("Controls: " + audioElement.controls,  20 ,120);
      context.fillText  ("Volume: " + audioElement.volume,  20 ,140);
      context.fillText  ("Paused: " + audioElement.paused,  20 ,160);
      context.fillText  ("Ended: " + audioElement.ended,  20 ,180);
      context.fillText  ("Source: " + audioElement.currentSrc,  20 ,200);
      context.fillText  ("Can Play OGG: " + audioElement.canPlayType("audio/ogg"),
                        20 ,220);
      context.fillText  ("Can Play WAV: " + audioElement.canPlayType("audio/wav"),
                        20 ,240);
      context.fillText  ("Can Play MP3: " + audioElement.canPlayType("audio/mp3"),
                        20 ,260);

   }

  var theCanvas = document.getElementById("canvasOne");
  var context = theCanvas.getContext("2d");
  var audioElement = document.getElementById("theAudio");
  audioElement.play();
```

```
        function gameLoop() {
                window.setTimeout(gameLoop, 20);
                drawScreen()
        }

    gameLoop();

}

</script>

</head>
<body>
<div style="position: absolute; top: 50px; left: 50px;">

<canvas id="canvasOne" width="500" height="300">
 Your browser does not support HTML5 Canvas.
</canvas>
</div>

<div id="loadingStatus">
0%
</div>

<div style="position: absolute; top: 50px; left: 600px; ">
<audio id="theAudio" controls >
<source src="song1.mp3" type="audio/mp3">
<source src="song1.ogg" type="audio/ogg">
<source src="song1.wav" type="audio/wav">

Your browser does not support the audio element.
</audio>

</div>
</body>
</html>
```

 When tested, Internet Explorer 10 does not fire the Audio progress event.

Playing a Sound with No Audio Tag

Now that we have a sound playing in an HTML5 page and we are tracking the properties of the audio element on the canvas, it is time to step up their integration. The next step is to do away with the <audio> tag embedded in the HTML page.

If you recall from Chapter 6, we created a video element dynamically in the HTML page and then used the canPlayType() method of the HTMLVideoElement object to figure out what video file type to load for a particular browser. We will do something very similar for audio.

Dynamically Creating an Audio Element in JavaScript

The first step to dynamically creating `audio` elements is to create a global variable named `audioElement`. This variable will hold an instance of `HTMLAudioElement` that we will use in our canvas application. Recall that `audio` elements in an HTML page are instances of the `HTMLAudioElement` DOM object. We refer to them as `audio` objects when embedded in an HTML page and as instances of `HTMLAudioElement` when created dynamically in JavaScript. However, they are essentially the same.

 Don't fret if you don't like using global variables. By the end of this chapter, we will show you a way to make these variables local to your canvas application.

Next, we create our event handler for the window `load` event named `eventWindowLoaded()`. Inside that function, we call the `createElement()` function of the DOM document object, passing the value `audio` as the type of element to create. This will dynamically create an `audio` object and put it into the DOM. By placing that object in the `audioElement` variable, we can then dynamically place it onto the HTML page with a call to the `appendChild()` method of the `document.body` DOM object:

```
window.addEventListener('load', eventWindowLoaded, false);
var audioElement;
function eventWindowLoaded() {
    audioElement = document.createElement("audio");
    document.body.appendChild(audioElement);
```

However, just having a dynamically created `audio` element is not enough. We also need to set the `src` attribute of the `HTMLAudioElement` object represented by `audioElement` to a valid audio file to load and play. But the problem is that we don't yet know what type of audio file the current browser supports. We will get that information from a function we will create named `supportedAudioFormat()`. We will define this function so that it returns a string value representing the extension of the file type we want to load. When we have that extension, we concatenate it with the name of the sound we want to load, and we set the `src` with a call to the `setAttribute()` method of the `HTMLAudioElement` object:

```
var audioType = supportedAudioFormat(audioElement);
```

If a valid extension from `supportedAudioFormat()` is not returned, something has gone wrong and we need to halt execution. To handle this condition in a simple way, we create an `alert()` message and then `return` from the function, effectively halting execution.

While this is not a very robust form of error handling, it will work for the sake of this example:

```
if (audioType == "") {
    alert("no audio support");
    return;
}
audioElement.setAttribute("src", "song1." + audioType);
```

Finally, like we did with video, we will listen for the `canplaythrough` event of `audio Element` so that we know when the sound is ready to play:

```
audioElement.addEventListener("canplaythrough",audioLoaded,false);
```

Finding the Supported Audio Format

Before the code in the previous section will work, we need to define the `supportedAu dioFormat()` function. Because we are adding `audio` objects dynamically to the HTML page, we do not have a way to define multiple `<source>` tags like we can in HTML. Instead, we are going to use the `canPlayType()` method of the `audio` object to tell us which type of audio file to load. We already introduced you to the `canPlayType()` method in Chapter 6, but to refresh your memory, `canPlayType()` takes a single parameter—a MIME type. It returns a text string of `maybe`, `probably`, or `""` (nothing). We are going to use these values to figure out which media type to load and play. Just like in Chapter 6, and for the sake of this exercise, we are going to assume that both `maybe` and `probably` equate to yes. If we encounter either result with any of our three MIME types (*audio/ogg*, *audio/wav*, *audio/mp3*), we will return the extension associated with that MIME type so that the sound file can be loaded.

 The next function is essentially the same as the one we created in Chapter 6 to handle video formats. The obvious changes here are with the MIME types for audio.

In the following function, `audio` represents the instance of `HTMLAudioElement` that we will test. The `returnExtension` variable represents that valid extension for the first MIME type found that has the value of `maybe` or `probably` returned:

```
function supportedAudioFormat(audio) {
    var returnExtension = "";
    if (audio.canPlayType("audio/ogg") =="probably" ||
        audio.canPlayType("audio/ogg") == "maybe") {
            returnExtension = "ogg";    }
      else if(audio.canPlayType("audio/wav") =="probably" ||
        audio.canPlayType("audio/wav") == "maybe") {
            returnExtension = "wav";
    } else if(audio.canPlayType("audio/mp3") == "probably" ||
        audio.canPlayType("audio/mp3") == "maybe") {
```

```
            returnExtension = "mp3";
    }

    return returnExtension;

}
```

Notice that we do not check for a condition when no valid audio format is found and the return value is "". If that is the case, the code that has called this function might need to be written in a way to catch that condition and alter the program execution. We did that with the test of the `return` value and the `alert()` message, which we described in the previous section.

 If you want to test the error condition with no valid `return` value from this function, simply add an extra character to the MIME type (for example, *audio/oggx*) to make sure an empty string is always returned.

Alternatively, you can use Modernizr to test for audio support. If you have included the Modernizr JavaScript library in your HTML page (as we have done in every application we have written thus far), you can access the static values of *Modernizr.audio.ogg*, *Modernizr.audio.wav*, and *Modernizr.audio.mp3* to test to see whether those types are valid. These are not Booleans—they evaluate to the same `probably`, `maybe`, and `""` values that we get from a call to `canPlayType()`. If you are comfortable using Modernizr for all your tests, you can replace the test in the code with tests of these Modernizr static values.

Playing the Sound

Finally, we get to the point where we can play a sound inside our `canvasApp()` function. Because we preloaded the sound originally outside the context of this function into a variable with a global scope, we just need to call the `play()` function `audioElement` to start playing the sound:

```
audioElement.play();
```

Figure 7-4 shows what this Canvas application will look like when executed in an HTML5-compliant web browser. (Notice that we have left the display of the audio properties in this application.)

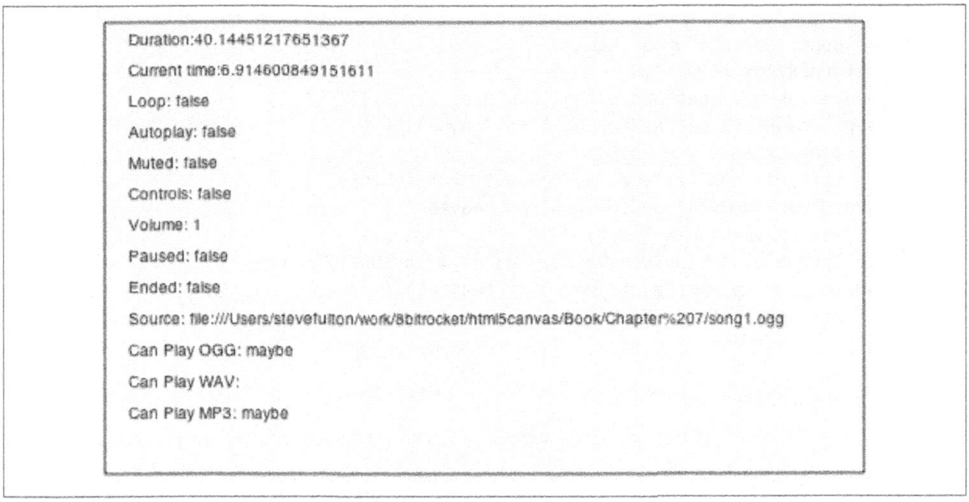

```
Duration:40.14451217651367

Current time:6.914600849151611

Loop: false

Autoplay: false

Muted: false

Controls: false

Volume: 1

Paused: false

Ended: false

Source: file:///Users/stevefulton/work/8bitrocket/html5canvas/Book/Chapter%207/song1.ogg

Can Play OGG: maybe

Can Play WAV:

Can Play MP3: maybe
```

Figure 7-4. Sound loaded and played "on" the canvas

No Tag!

out the full application in Example 7-4. Notice that there is no <audio> tag
he HTML, but the sound still plays. This is our first step toward integrating
Element objects with HTML5 Canvas.

-4. Playing a sound with no tag

```html
                html>
<html lang="en">
<head>
<meta charset="UTF-8">
<title>CH7EX4: Playing A Sound With No Tag</title>

<script src="modernizr.js"></script>
<script type="text/javascript">
window.addEventListener('load', eventWindowLoaded, false);
var audioElement;
function eventWindowLoaded() {

    audioElement = document.createElement("audio");
    document.body.appendChild(audioElement);
    var audioType = supportedAudioFormat(audioElement);
    if (audioType == "") {
        alert("no audio support");
        return;
    }
    audioElement.addEventListener("canplaythrough",audioLoaded,false);
    audioElement.setAttribute("src", "song1." + audioType);

}
```

```
function supportedAudioFormat(audio) {
    var returnExtension = "";
    if (audio.canPlayType("audio/ogg") =="probably" ||
        audio.canPlayType("audio/ogg") == "maybe") {
            returnExtension = "ogg";
    } else if(audio.canPlayType("audio/wav") =="probably" ||
        audio.canPlayType("audio/wav") == "maybe") {
            returnExtension = "wav";
    } else if(audio.canPlayType("audio/mp3") == "probably" ||
        audio.canPlayType("audio/mp3") == "maybe") {
            returnExtension = "mp3";
    }

    return returnExtension;

}

function canvasSupport () {
        return Modernizr.canvas;
}


function audioLoaded(event) {

    canvasApp();

}

function canvasApp() {

    if (!canvasSupport()) {
            return;
        }

    function  drawScreen () {

        //Background
        context.fillStyle = '#ffffaa';
        context.fillRect(0, 0, theCanvas.width, theCanvas.height);

        //Box
        context.strokeStyle = '#000000';
        context.strokeRect(5,  5, theCanvas.width-10, theCanvas.height-10);

        // Text
        context.fillStyle = "#000000";
        context.fillText ("Duration:" + audioElement.duration,  20 ,20);
        context.fillText ("Current time:" + audioElement.currentTime,  20 ,40);
        context.fillText ("Loop: " + audioElement.loop,  20 ,60);
        context.fillText ("Autoplay: " +audioElement.autoplay,  20 ,80);
        context.fillText ("Muted: " + audioElement.muted,  20 ,100);
```

```
            context.fillText  ("Controls: " + audioElement.controls,  20 ,120);
            context.fillText  ("Volume: " + audioElement.volume,  20 ,140);
            context.fillText  ("Paused: " + audioElement.paused,  20 ,160);
            context.fillText  ("Ended: " + audioElement.ended,  20 ,180);
            context.fillText  ("Source: " + audioElement.currentSrc,  20 ,200);
            context.fillText  ("Can Play OGG: " + audioElement.canPlayType("audio/ogg"),
                               20 ,220);
            context.fillText  ("Can Play WAV: " + audioElement.canPlayType("audio/wav"),
                               20 ,240);
            context.fillText  ("Can Play MP3: " + audioElement.canPlayType("audio/mp3"),
                               20 ,260);

    }

    var theCanvas = document.getElementById("canvasOne");
    var context = theCanvas.getContext("2d");
    audioElement.play()

    function gameLoop() {
            window.setTimeout(gameLoop, 20);
            drawScreen()
        }

    gameLoop();
}

</script>

</head>
<body>
<div style="position: absolute; top: 50px; left: 50px;">

<canvas id="canvasOne" width="500" height="300">
 Your browser does not support HTML5 Canvas.
</canvas>
</div>
</body>
</html>
```

Creating a Canvas Audio Player

Now that we can play an audio file directly in an HTML page using the <audio> tag or
through JavaScript by creating a dynamic HTMLAudioElement object, it's time to step up
our game. We are going to create an audio player on the canvas that we can use to control
dynamically loaded audio files. Why do we want to do this? Well, while the audio controls baked into HTML5-compliant browsers might look decent, it is often necessary
for developers to implement a design that more closely matches a particular website.
HTML5 Canvas provides a way to create a dynamic set of audio controls with nearly
any look-and-feel you desire.

However, this flexibility comes at a cost. HTML5 Canvas does not natively support common GUI controls such as push buttons, toggle buttons, and sliders. So to create a decent audio player, we need to make these types of GUI user controls from scratch. We could create these controls in HTML and JavaScript, but we have already covered communication between HTML and Canvas via form controls several times in this book. You wanted to know how to make HTML5 Canvas apps when you started reading, so we won't pull any punches in this chapter.

Creating Custom User Controls on the Canvas

For this application we are going to create four elements:

Play/pause push button
> The audio file is either playing or is paused. Whichever state it is currently in, we show the other button (for example, show pause when playing).

A sliding progress bar
> This is a non-interactive slider. It displays how much of the audio track has played and how much is left to play. The movement of this bar needs to be dynamic and based on the `duration` and `currentTime` properties of the `HTMLAudioElement` object.

An interactive volume slider
> We want to create a sliding volume control that the user can manipulate with a click-and-drag operation. This is the trickiest control we will build because Canvas has no native support for click-and-drag.

A loop toggle button
> This is a bonus. Most of the default embedded HTML5 audio players do not have a loop/no-loop toggle button, but we are going to add one. Already, we are outstripping the functionality of standard HTML5!

Figure 7-5 shows the *audiocontrols.png* image that we created. It holds all the images we will use for the audio player. The top row consists of:

- The play state of the play/pause button
- The background of the play slider
- The moving slider we will use for the play and volume sliders

The second row consists of:

- The pause state of the play/pause button
- The background of the volume slider
- The "off" state of the loop button

- The "on" state of the loop button

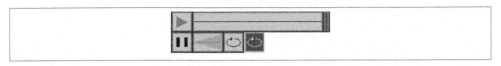

Figure 7-5. audiocontrols.png

Loading the Button Assets

Because we are going to load in both an audio file and an image file for this application, we need to employ a strategy that will allow us to preload two assets instead of just one. This process is much like the one we employed in Chapter 6 when we created controls for a video. Previously in this chapter, we used a function named `audioLoaded()` to make sure the audio was loaded before we started use it. However, that strategy will not work when we have two assets to load. We could create two separate event listeners, but what if we need to load 3, 4, or 10 assets? What we need is a simple way to ensure that we can preload any number of assets before our application executes.

We will start this process by creating some variables that are global in scope to all the functions in the applications. First, outside of all the JavaScript functions, we will create three new variables—`loadCount`, `itemsToLoad`, and `buttonSheet`:

`loadCount`
> This variable will be used as a counter. When an asset has preloaded we will increment this value.

`itemsToLoad`
> This is a numeric value that represents the number of assets we need to load before we can execute the application in the HTML page.

`buttonSheet`
> This variable will hold a reference to the *audiocontrols.png* image shown in Figure 7-5. We will use it to create our audio controls.

Here is the code with values included:

```
var loadCount = 0;
var itemsToLoad = 2;
var buttonSheet;
var audioElement;
```

To make these variables scope only to the Canvas app and not globally to all of JavaScript, you can encapsulate this code in a `function()`. The final version of the code in Example A-1 shows that process.

Also, like in the video player application from the last chapter (*CH6EX11.html*), we need to create some variables to set a wait time between button presses:

```
var buttonWait = 5;
var timeWaited = buttonWait;
```

Inside the `eventWindowLoaded()` function, we now need to set the event handlers for the assets to load. For the `audioElement`, we will change the handler from `audioLoaded` to `itemLoaded`:

```
audioElement.addEventListener("canplaythrough",itemLoaded,false);
```

To load and use the *audiocontrols.png* image, we first create a new `Image()` object and place a reference to it into the `buttonSheet` variable. Next, we set the `src` attribute of the new `Image` object to the image file we want to load—in this case, *audiocontrols.png*. We then set the `onload` event handler of the `Image` object to `itemLoaded`, which is the same event handler we used for the audio file:

```
buttonSheet = new Image();
buttonSheet.onload = itemLoaded;
buttonSheet.src = "audiocontrols.png";
```

Now we need to create the `itemLoaded()` event handler. This function is quite simple. Every time it is called, we increment the `loadCount` variable. We then test `loadCount` to see whether it is equal to or has surpassed the number of items we want to preload, which is represented by the `itemsToLoad` variable. If so, we call the `canvasApp()` function to start our application:

```
function itemLoaded(event) {

    loadCount++;
    if (loadCount >= itemsToLoad) {
        canvasApp();

    }

}
```

Setting Up the Audio Player Values

Inside the `canvasApp()` function, we need to create some values to help us place all the various buttons and sliders on the canvas.

First, `bH` represents the height of all the controls; `bW` represents the width of a standard button (play/pause, loop/not loop):

```
var bW = 32;
var bH = 32;
```

Next we set the width of the playback area, `playBackW`, and the width of the volume background, `volBackW`. We also set the slider's width (`sliderW`) and height (`sliderH`):

```
var playBackW = 206;
var volBackW = 50;
var sliderW = 10;
var sliderH = 32;
```

We also need a couple variables to represent the x and y locations on the canvas where we will start to build our audio controls. We will define those as `controlStartX` and `controlStartY`:

```
var controlStartX = 25;
var controlStartY = 200;
```

Finally, we need to specify the x and y locations for the play/pause button (`playX`, `playY`), the playing slider background (`playBackX`, `playBackY`), the volume slider background (`volBackX`, `volBackY`), and the location of the loop/no loop toggle button (`loopX`, `loopY`):

```
var playX = controlStartX;
var playY = controlStartY;
var playBackX = controlStartX+bW
var playBackY = controlStartY;
var volBackX = controlStartX+bW+playBackW;
var volBackY = controlStartY;
var loopX = controlStartX+bW+playBackW+volBackW
var loopY = controlStartY;
```

We are going to use all of these values to help design and add functionality to our audio controls. It might seem like overkill to create so many variables, but when trying to "roll your own" collision detection and drag-and-drop functionality into the canvas, having variable names to manipulate instead of literals makes the job much easier.

Mouse Events

Because we are going to create our own functions for interactivity between the mouse and our custom canvas audio controls, we need to add some event handlers for certain common mouse events.

First, we need to create a couple variables—`mouseX` and `mouseY`—that will hold the current x and y locations of the mouse pointer:

```
var mouseX;
var mouseY;
```

Next we need to create the event handlers. First, we listen for the `mouseup` event. This event fires when a user stops pressing the mouse button. We will listen for this event when we are trying to determine whether we should stop dragging the volume slider:

```
theCanvas.addEventListener("mouseup",eventMouseUp, false);
```

We also need to listen for the mousedown event to determine whether the play/pause button was pressed, the loop on/off toggle button was pressed, and/or the volume slider was clicked, so that we can start dragging it:

```
theCanvas.addEventListener("mousedown",eventMouseDown, false);
```

Finally, we listen for the mousemove event so that we can figure out the current x and y locations of the mouse pointer. We use this value to determine whether buttons have been pressed, as well as whether the volume slider has been clicked and/or dragged:

```
theCanvas.addEventListener("mousemove",eventMouseMove, false);
```

Sliding Play Indicator

The sliding play indicator is the simplest control we are going to draw onto the canvas. It is not interactive—it just gives the user a visual indication of how much of the audio clip is left to play.

First of all, in canvasApp() we need to make sure that we call the drawScreen() function on an interval so that our updated controls will be displayed:

```
function gameLoop() {
        window.setTimeout(gameLoop, 20);
        drawScreen()
    }

gameLoop();
```

 Unlike when displaying video on the canvas, we do not have to call drawScreen() to update the playing audio. In JavaScript, audio plays completely separate from the canvas. Our need to call drawScreen() on an interval is necessary because the audio controls we are creating need to be updated as the audio plays.

In the drawScreen() function, we need to draw the slider and background on the canvas. We are going to "cut" all the images we display from the single buttonSheet image we loaded from *audiocontrols.png*. To draw the background, we use the values we set up earlier. We use literals (32,0) to locate the starting point of the image because those values do not change on the buttonSheet image. However, we use the variables we created to find the width and height, and to locate the final position of the background on the canvas:

```
context.drawImage(buttonSheet, 32,0,playBackW,bH,playBackX,playBackY,
                  playBackW,bH);
```

Drawing the play slider is only a bit more complicated. Before we draw it, we need to create a variable that represents the relationship between the length of playing audio and the width of slider area. This is so we will know how far on the x-axis to move the slider based on how much of the song has played. This might sound complicated, but it's just a simple fraction. Divide the width of the play background (`playBackW`) by the duration of the playing audio (`audioElement.duration`). We will store that ratio in `sliderIncrement` and use it to place the play slider on the canvas:

```
var slideIncrement = playBackW/audioElement.duration;
```

Now we need to calculate the x position of the slider. The x position is the sum of the slider's starting position (the place on the canvas where the controls start) plus the width of the play/pause button (`controlStartX+bW`), plus the audio's current play position. We calculate the play position by taking the ratio we just created, `sliderIncrement`, and multiplying it by the current play time of the audio clip (`audioElement.currentTime`). That's it!

```
var sliderX = (controlStartX+bW) + (slideIncrement*audioElement.currentTime);
```

Now all we need to do is draw the image onto the canvas and then test to see whether the audio clip has ended. If it has ended, we put the play position back to the beginning of the playback area and call `audioElement.pause()` to pause the audio clip. That is, unless the `loop` property is sent, in which case we start playing the audio clip from the beginning by setting the `currentTime` property to `0`:

```
context.drawImage(buttonSheet, 238,0,sliderW,bH,sliderX,controlStartY,sliderW,bH);

if (audioElement.ended && !audioElement.loop) {
    audioElement.currentTime = 0;
    audioElement.pause();
}
```

We also need to make sure to update `timeWaited` so that we don't accept too many events:

```
timeWaited++;
```

This leads us right into our next topic, handling the play/pause button.

Play/Pause Push Button: Hit Test Point Revisited

The first thing we need to do when implementing the play/pause button is create the event handler for the `mousemove` event. The function really is just the standard cross-browser code we introduced earlier in the book for tracking the mouse position, depending on which properties the DOM in browsers supports: `pageX`/`pageY` or `e.clienX`/`e.clientY`. This function is called every time the mouse is moved on the canvas to update the `mouseX` and `mouseY` variables. Those variables are scoped to `canvasApp()` so that all functions defined inside of it can access them:

```
function eventMouseMove(event) {
    var x;
    var y;
```

```
        if (event.pageX || event.pageY) {
             x = event.pageX;
             y = event.pageY;
        }
        else {
             x = e.clientX + document.body.scrollLeft +
             document.documentElement.scrollLeft;
             y = e.clientY + document.body.scrollTop +
                 document.documentElement.scrollTop;
        }
        x -= theCanvas.offsetLeft;
        y -= theCanvas.offsetTop;

        mouseX=x;
        mouseY=y;
    }
```

Now we need to create the eventMouseUp() handler function. This function is called when the user releases the mouse button after clicking. Why *after*, and not when the mouse is clicked? Well, one reason is because we generally use the mousedown event for the start of a "dragging" operation, which we will show you shortly.

The first thing we do here, just like in *CH6EX11.html* in the last chapter, is test to see whether timeWaited is greater than buttonWait. If so, we will accept a new mouseUp event. If not, we skip it.

The heart of this function is a hit test point-style collision detection check for the buttons. We discussed this in depth in Chapter 6 when we created the buttons for the video puzzle game (*CH6EX10.html*). Notice that here we are using the variables we create to represent the x and y locations of the button (playX, playY) and the width and height of a button (bW, bH) to form the bounds of the area we will test. If the mouse pointer is within those bounds, we know the button has been clicked:

```
function eventMouseUp(event) {
    if (timeWaited >= buttonWait) {
        timeWaited = 0;
        if ( (mouseY >= playY) && (mouseY <= playY+bH) && (mouseX >= playX) &&
            (mouseX <= playX+bW) ) {
```

 If you had images stacked on top of one another, you would need to store some kind of stacking value or z-index to know which item was on top and was clicked at any one time. Because the canvas works in immediate mode, you would have to "roll your own," just like the other functionality we have discussed.

After a hit is detected, we need to determine whether we are going to call the play() or pause() method of the HTMLAudioElement object represented by the audioElement variable. To figure out which method to call, we simply test to see whether the audio is paused by checking the `audioElement.paused` property. If so, we call the `play()` method; if not, we call `pause()`. Recall that the `HTMLAudioElement.paused` property is set to `true` if the audio is not playing, regardless of whether the `paused()` function was called. This means that when the application starts but we have not set `autoplay`, we can easily display the proper button (play or pause) just by testing this property:

```
        if (audioElement.paused) {
            audioElement.play();

        } else {
            audioElement.pause();

        }

      }
    }
  }
```

Now, in `drawScreen()`, we need to choose which button to display: the one representing play (green triangle) or pause (two horizontal boxes). The play button is displayed when the audio is paused, and the pause button is displayed when the audio is playing. This button is a "call to action," so it displays what will happen when you click on it, not the status of the audio element that is playing. This *inverse relationship* exists because it is the standard way audio players work.

If the `audioElement` is paused, we display the graphic from the top row of the *audio controls.png* image represented by `buttonSheet`. (See Figure 7-5.) If it is not paused, we display the button on the second row right below it. Because that button starts at the y position of 32, we use that literal value in the call to `drawImage()`:

```
if (audioElement.paused) {
    context.drawImage(buttonSheet, 0,0,bW,bH,playX,playY,bW,bH);//show play

} else {
    context.drawImage(buttonSheet, 0,32,bW,bH,playX,playY,bW,bH); //show pause

}
```

 Again, we could have represented the literal values of locations in the `buttonSheet` with variables, but we decided to use literals to show you the difference between how we specify `buttonSheet` pixel locations and how we calculate widths and distances for placing those elements.

Loop/No Loop Toggle Button

Implementing the loop/no loop toggle button is nearly identical to implementing the play/pause button. In Figure 7-5, you can see that the last two buttons on the bottom row represent the "on" and "off" states of the loop/no loop button. Unlike the play/pause button, this button shows the "state" of looping: the lighter, 3D-looking "out" button is displayed when the audio is not set to loop. The inverse, darker button is displayed when the audio is set to loop (because it looks like the button has been pressed).

In the `eventMouseUp()` function, we need to add support for loop/no loop. First, we test for a hit test point on the button with the current location of the mouse pointer. This is identical to the test we did for the play/pause button, except that we use `loopX` and `loopY` to find the current location of the loop/no loop button.

Next we check the value of `audioElement.loop`. We need to update the value to the opposite of the current setting. If `loop` is `true`, we set it to `false`; if it is `false`, we set it to `true`:

```
if ( (mouseY >=loopY) && (mouseY <= loopY+bH) && (mouseX >= loopX) &&
    (mouseX <= loopX+bW) ) {
  if (audioElement.loop) {
        audioElement.loop = false;

      } else {
        audioElement.loop = true;

      }
```

Finally, in `drawScreen()`, we will display the proper part of the `buttonSheet` image for whichever state of loop/no loop is currently set. Unlike play/pause, we display the "off" state when `loop` is `false` and the "on" state when it is set to `true`, because, again, there is not an inverse relationship to the states of the button:

```
if (audioElement.loop) {
        context.drawImage(buttonSheet, 114,32,bW,bH,loopX,loopY,bW,bH); // loop

      } else {
        context.drawImage(buttonSheet, 82,32,bW,bH,loopX,loopY,bW,bH);
        // no loop
      }
```

Click-and-Drag Volume Slider

So now we make it to the last, but certainly not least, piece of functionality for the audio player: the volume slider. The volume slider is an interactive control allowing the user to manipulate it by sliding it right or left to control the volume of the playing audio element. Before we create the volume slider, we need to define some boundaries for its usage:

- The slider never moves on the y-axis; it will always keep a y value.
- The farther the volume slider is to the right (the greater the x value), the higher the volume.
- The slider moves on the x-axis but is bounded by the starting x value of the volume slider image—`volumeSliderStart` on the left and `volumeSliderEnd` on the right.
- When the user clicks on the volume slider, we will assume that the user wants to set the volume, so we will start "dragging" the slider. This means that if the user moves the mouse on the x-axis, we will move the slider accordingly.
- When the user takes his finger off the mouse button, we will assume that he no longer wishes to set the volume, and we still stop "dragging" the slider.
- The volume will be set based on the slider's position on the x-axis in relation to the `volumeSliderStart` plus a ratio (`volumeIncrement`) that we create describing how much volume to increase or decrease based on where the slider rests.

Volume slider variables

Now that we have thoroughly confused you, let's talk about the process in depth. First, we start with the `canvasApp()` function. In `canvasApp()`, we need to set up some variables to set the rules we defined in the list above.

The starting x position for the volume slider is `volumeSliderStart`. When the application starts, it is equal to the x position of the volume background, or `volBackX`. This means that it will start at the leftmost edge of the volume slider where the `volume` will be set to 0. We will update this to the correct position based on the `volume` as soon as we calculate that value:

```
var volumeSliderStart = volBackX;
```

The final x position for the volume slider is `volumeSliderEnd`, which is the rightmost position. It is the position where the volume will be set to 100% (or 1). This position lies at the x position of `volumeSliderStart` plus the width of the volume slider background (`volBackW`), less the width of the volume slider itself (`sliderW`):

```
var volumeSliderEnd = volumeSliderStart + volBackW - sliderW;
```

`volumeSliderX` and `volumeSliderY` are the slider's x and y positions on the canvas. The y position is the same as the other elements in the audio player, `controlStartY`. However, the x position is calculated in quite a different way. First, we take the value of `volumeSliderStart` and add the difference between slider volume background width and the slider width (`volBackW - sliderW`), multiplied by the `volume` property of the `audioElement`, which is a number between 0 and 1. This will give us the position relative to the starting point from which we want to draw the volume slider for any given volume setting:

```
var volumeSliderX  = volumeSliderStart + (audioElement.volume*
    (volBackW - sliderW));
var volumeSliderY  = controlStartY;
```

Next we create the `volumeSliderDrag` variable, which we will use as a switch to tell us whether the volume slider is being dragged by the user at any given moment:

```
var volumeSliderDrag = false;
```

Finally, we create the `volumeIncrement` variable. This variable tells us how much volume to increase or decrease on the `audioElement.volume` property based on where the slider is positioned on the volume background. Because the maximum value of the volume is 1, we simply find the total width that the volume slider can move on the x-axis (`volBackW - sliderW`) and divide 1 by that value. This will give us a product that we can multiply by the x position of the slider, relative to `volumeSliderStart`, to give us the volume we should set for the `audioElement`:

```
var volumeIncrement = 1/(volBackW - sliderW);
```

Volume slider functionality

Now that we have discussed the variables we need for the volume slider, we will talk about how we use them in the various functions of the audio player. The good news is that the implementation is simple now that you know how the variables work.

In the `eventMouseDown()` handler, we perform a hit test point-style test, just like we did with the play/pause and loop/no loop buttons to see whether the volume slider was clicked. If so, we set the `volumeSliderDrag` variable to `true`. This means that the volume slider will now to move to the x position of the mouse when we call `drawScreen()`:

```
function eventMouseDown(event) {

if ( (mouseY >= volumeSliderY) && (mouseY <=volumeSliderY+sliderH) &&
     (mouseX >= volumeSliderX) && (mouseX <= volumeSliderX+sliderW) ) {
        volumeSliderDrag = true;

    }

}
```

In the `eventMouseUp()` handler, we test to see whether `volumeSliderDrag` is set to `true`. If so, it means that the user has released the mouse button and no longer wants to drag the volume slider. We set `volumeSliderDrag` to `false` so that the slider will not move with the mouse:

```
if (volumeSliderDrag) {
        volumeSliderDrag = false;
    }
```

Also, make sure this test is *outside* the test of (`timeWaited >= buttonWait`), or the slider will stick to the mouse (in some browsers).

In drawScreen(), we actually put the pixels to the canvas, so to speak, with the volume slider. First, we draw the background image from buttonSheet:

```
//vol Background
      context.drawImage(buttonSheet, 32,32,volBackW,bH,volBackX,volBackY,
                        volBackW,bH);
```

Next, we check to see whether volumeSliderDrag is true. If so, we make the volume SliderX variable equal to the mouse's x position. Then we drop in a couple more tests to determine whether the x position of the volume slider falls outside the bounds of the volume background. These two tests make sure that the volume slider does not move past the rightmost or leftmost sides of the volume slider background, and in turn, the volume property of audioElement is not calculated to be more than 1 or less than 0:

```
if (volumeSliderDrag) {
   volumeSliderX = mouseX;
   if (volumeSliderX > volumeSliderEnd) {
      volumeSliderX = volumeSliderEnd;
   }
   if (volumeSliderX < volumeSliderStart) {
      volumeSliderX = volumeSliderStart;
   }
```

If the volumeSliderDrag is false, we still need an x position at which to draw the slider graphic. We get this the same way we calculated the volumeSliderX value when we initialized the variable in the canvasApp() function:

```
} else {
   volumeSliderX = volumeSliderStart + (audioElement.volume*
   (volBackW -sliderW));
}
```

Finally, we draw the slider onto the canvas:

```
context.drawImage(buttonSheet, 238,0,sliderW,bH,volumeSliderX,
volumeSliderY, sliderW,bH);
audioElement.volume = (volumeSliderX-volumeSliderStart) * volumeIncrement;
```

Figure 7-6 displays the custom controls in the browser.

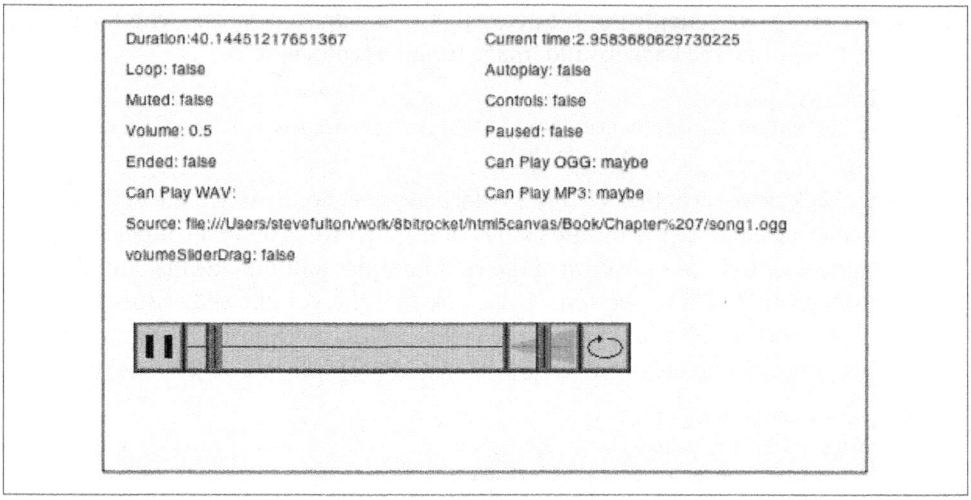

Figure 7-6. Canvas sound player with custom controls

So there you have it. You can test the audio player as *CH7EX5.html* in the source code. The full code listing for the HTML5 Canvas audio player is shown in Example 7-5.

Example 7-5. A custom audio player on the canvas

```
<!doctype html>
<html lang="en">
<head>
<meta charset="UTF-8">
<title>CH7EX5: A Custom Sound Player On The Canvas</title>

<script src="modernizr.js"></script>
<script type="text/javascript">
window.addEventListener('load', eventWindowLoaded, false);
var loadCount = 0;
var itemsToLoad = 2;
var buttonSheet;
var audioElement;
var buttonWait = 5;
var timeWaited = buttonWait;

function eventWindowLoaded() {

    audioElement = document.createElement("audio");
    document.body.appendChild(audioElement);
    var audioType = supportedAudioFormat(audioElement);
    if (audioType == "") {
        alert("no audio support");
        return;
    }
    audioElement.addEventListener("canplaythrough",itemLoaded,false);
    audioElement.setAttribute("src", "song1." + audioType);
```

```
        buttonSheet = new Image();
        buttonSheet.onload = itemLoaded;
        buttonSheet.src = "audiocontrols.png";

}

function supportedAudioFormat(audio) {
    var returnExtension = "";
    if (audio.canPlayType("audio/ogg") =="probably" ||
        audio.canPlayType("audio/ogg") == "maybe") {
            returnExtension = "ogg";
    } else if(audio.canPlayType("audio/wav") =="probably" ||
        audio.canPlayType("audio/wav") == "maybe") {
            returnExtension = "wav";
    } else if(audio.canPlayType("audio/mp3") == "probably" ||
        audio.canPlayType("audio/mp3") == "maybe") {
            returnExtension = "mp3";
    }

    return returnExtension;

}

function canvasSupport () {
     return Modernizr.canvas;
}

function itemLoaded(event) {

    loadCount++;
    if (loadCount >= itemsToLoad) {
        canvasApp();

    }

}

function canvasApp() {

  if (!canvasSupport()) {
          return;
        }

  function  drawScreen () {

      //Background

      context.fillStyle = "#ffffaa";
      context.fillRect(0, 0, theCanvas.width, theCanvas.height);

      //Box
```

```
context.strokeStyle = "#000000";
context.strokeRect(5,  5, theCanvas.width-10, theCanvas.height-10);

// Text
context.fillStyle = "#000000";
context.fillText ("Duration:" + audioElement.duration,  20 ,20);
context.fillText ("Current time:" + audioElement.currentTime,  250 ,20);
context.fillText ("Loop: " + audioElement.loop,  20 ,40);
context.fillText ("Autoplay: " +audioElement.autoplay,  250 ,40);
context.fillText ("Muted: " + audioElement.muted,  20 ,60);
context.fillText ("Controls: " + audioElement.controls,  250 ,60);
context.fillText ("Volume: " + audioElement.volume,  20 ,80);
context.fillText ("Paused: " + audioElement.paused,  250 ,80);
context.fillText ("Ended: " + audioElement.ended,  20 ,100);
context.fillText ("Can Play OGG: " + audioElement.canPlayType("audio/ogg"),
                  250 ,100);
context.fillText ("Can Play WAV: " + audioElement.canPlayType("audio/wav"),
                  20 ,120);
context.fillText ("Can Play MP3: " + audioElement.canPlayType("audio/mp3"),
                  250 ,120);
context.fillText ("Source: " + audioElement.currentSrc, 20 ,140);
context.fillText ("volumeSliderDrag: " + volumeSliderDrag, 20 ,160);

//Draw Controls

//play or pause

if (audioElement.paused) {
   context.drawImage(buttonSheet, 0,0,bW,bH,playX,playY,bW,bH);//show play

} else {
   context.drawImage(buttonSheet, 0,32,bW,bH,playX,playY,bW,bH); //show pause

}

//loop

if (audioElement.loop) {
   context.drawImage(buttonSheet, 114,32,bW,bH,loopX,loopY,bW,bH);//show loop
} else {
   context.drawImage(buttonSheet, 82,32,bW,bH,loopX,loopY,bW,bH); //show no loop
}

//play background
context.drawImage(buttonSheet, 32,0,playBackW,bH,playBackX,playBackY,
   playBackW,bH);

//vol Background
context.drawImage(buttonSheet, 32,32,volBackW,bH,volBackX,volBackY,volBackW,bH);

//play slider
var slideIncrement = playBackW/audioElement.duration;
```

```
    var sliderX = (controlStartX+bW) +
        (slideIncrement*audioElement.currentTime);
    context.drawImage(buttonSheet, 238,0,sliderW,bH,sliderX,
        controlStartY,sliderW,bH);

    //Go back to start
    if (audioElement.ended && !audioElement.loop) {
        audioElement.currentTime = 0;
        audioElement.pause();
    }

    //Volume slider
    //Test Volume Drag

    if (volumeSliderDrag) {
        volumeSliderX = mouseX;
        if (volumeSliderX > volumeSliderEnd) {
            volumeSliderX = volumeSliderEnd;
        }
        if (volumeSliderX < volumeSliderStart) {
            volumeSliderX = volumeSliderStart;
        }
    } else {
        volumeSliderX = volumeSliderStart +
            (audioElement.volume*(volBackW -sliderW));
    }

    context.drawImage(buttonSheet, 238,0,sliderW,bH,volumeSliderX,volumeSliderY,
        sliderW,bH);
    audioElement.volume = (volumeSliderX-volumeSliderStart) * volumeIncrement;
    timeWaited++;

}

function eventMouseDown(event) {

    //Hit Volume Slider
    if ( (mouseY >= volumeSliderY) && (mouseY <=volumeSliderY+sliderH) &&
        (mouseX >= volumeSliderX) && (mouseX <= volumeSliderX+sliderW) ) {
        volumeSliderDrag = true;

    }

}

function eventMouseMove(event) {
    var x;
    var y;
    if (event.pageX || event.pageY) {
        x = event.pageX;
        y = event.pageY;
    } else {
```

```
                x = e.clientX + document.body.scrollLeft +
                   document.documentElement.scrollLeft;
                y = e.clientY + document.body.scrollTop +
                   document.documentElement.scrollTop;
        }
        x -= theCanvas.offsetLeft;
        y -= theCanvas.offsetTop;

        mouseX=x;
        mouseY=y;
    }

    function eventMouseUp(event) {
        if (timeWaited >= buttonWait) {
            timeWaited = 0;
            //Hit Play
            if ( (mouseY >= playY) && (mouseY <= playY+bH) && (mouseX >= playX) &&
                (mouseX <= playX+bW) ) {
                if (audioElement.paused) {
                    audioElement.play();

                } else {
                    audioElement.pause();

                }

            }

            //Hit loop
            if ( (mouseY >=loopY) && (mouseY <= loopY+bH) && (mouseX >= loopX) &&
                (mouseX <= loopX+bW) ) {
                if (audioElement.loop) {
                    audioElement.loop=false;

                } else {
                    audioElement.loop = true;

                }

            }
        }

        if (volumeSliderDrag) {
            volumeSliderDrag = false;
        }

    }

    var theCanvas = document.getElementById("canvasOne");
    var context = theCanvas.getContext("2d");

    var bW = 32;
```

```
    var bH = 32;
    var playBackW = 206;
    var volBackW = 50;
    var sliderW = 10;
    var sliderH = 32;
    var controlStartX = 25;
    var controlStartY =200;
    var playX = controlStartX;
    var playY = controlStartY;
    var playBackX = controlStartX+bW;
    var playBackY = controlStartY;
    var volBackX = controlStartX+bW+playBackW;
    var volBackY = controlStartY;
    var loopX = controlStartX+bW+playBackW+volBackW;
    var loopY = controlStartY;
    var mouseX;
    var mouseY;

    theCanvas.addEventListener("mouseup",eventMouseUp, false);
    theCanvas.addEventListener("mousedown",eventMouseDown, false);
    theCanvas.addEventListener("mousemove",eventMouseMove, false);

    audioElement.play();
    audioElement.loop = false;
    audioElement.volume = .5;
    var volumeSliderStart = volBackX;
    var volumeSliderEnd = volumeSliderStart + volBackW -sliderW;
    var volumeSliderX = volumeSliderStart + (audioElement.volume*(volBackW -sliderW));
    var volumeSliderY = controlStartY;
    var volumeSliderDrag = false;
    var volumeIncrement = 1/(volBackW -sliderW);

    function gameLoop() {
            window.setTimeout(gameLoop, 20);
            drawScreen()
        }

    gameLoop();

}

</script>

</head>
<body>
<canvas id="canvasOne" width="500" height="300"
    style="position: absolute; top: 50px; left: 50px;"  >
 Your browser does not support HTML5 Canvas.
</canvas>
</body>
</html>
```

Case Study in Audio: Space Raiders Game

If we were writing a book about standard HTML5, we might be able to stop here and continue on with another topic. However, there is a lot more to playing audio in an application than simply getting a song to play and tracking its progress. In the last part of this chapter, we will look at a case study: *Space Raiders*. We will iterate through several ideas and attempts to get audio working in an efficient way in conjunction with action on HTML5 Canvas.

Why Sounds in Apps Are Different: Event Sounds

Why make a game as an example for playing sounds in HTML5? Well, a game is a perfect example because it is difficult to predict how many sounds might be playing at any one time.

Games are some of the most demanding applications when it comes to sound. In most games, sounds are played based on user interactions, and those interactions are usually both asynchronous and unpredictable. Because of those factors, we need to create a strategy for playing sounds that is flexible and resource-efficient.

To demonstrate how tricky sounds can be when using JavaScript and HTML5 with a Canvas game, we will iterate this game several times until we have a working model.

Here are some assumptions we will make regarding sound in *Space Raiders*, based on what we know about the HTML5 `audio` object:

1. After loading a sound, you can make another object with the same source and "load" it without having to wait for it to load. (Flash sort of works this way.)

2. Playing sounds locally is the same as playing them on a remotely hosted web page.

It turns out that both of these assumptions are *wrong*. As we continue through this case study, we will show you why, as well as how to accommodate them.

Because this is not a chapter about making games, *Space Raiders* is going to be only a façade. In Hollywood, a façade is a structure built for filming, containing only the parts the camera will see. For example, a building façade might have only the front wall and windows—with nothing behind them. *Space Raiders* is like this because we are going to create only the parts necessary to include the dynamic sounds we will be using. It will be most of a game, leading you into Chapters 8 and 9, which take a deep dive into making complete games with HTML5 Canvas.

Iterations

In this case study, we will create four iterations of *Space Raiders*. Each one will attempt to solve a dynamic audio problem in a different way. First, we will show you the basics

---

of the *Space Raiders* game structure, and then we will discuss how to solve the audio problem.

Space Raiders Game Structure

Space Raiders is an iconic action game where a swarm of alien invaders attack from the top of the screen, and the player's job is to defend the world. The raiders move in horizontal lines near the top of the screen. When each raider reaches the side of the playfield, it moves down the screen and then switches direction.

The player controls a spaceship by moving the mouse and fires missiles using the left mouse button. We need to play a "shoot" sound every time the player fires a missile. When the missiles hit the enemy space raiders, we need to remove them from the screen and then play an "explosion" sound. We are not limiting the number of shots the player can fire, which means that there could be any number of shoot and explode sounds playing simultaneously. Our goal is to manage all these dynamic sounds.

State machine

This game runs using a very simple state machine. A *state machine* is a construct that allows an application to exist in only one state at a time, which means it is only doing one thing. This kind of construct is great for single-player games because it removes the need to hold a bunch of Booleans describing what is going on at any one moment.

Space Raiders has four states plus a variable named `appState` that holds the value of the current state. Those states include:

STATE_INIT
> A state to set up the loading of assets:

```
var STATE_INIT = 10;
```

STATE_LOADING
> A wait state that has the application sleep until all assets have been loaded:

```
var STATE_LOADING = 20;
```

STATE_RESET
> A state to set up the initial game values:

```
var STATE_RESET = 30;
```

STATE_PLAYING
> A state that handles all game-play logic:

```
var STATE_PLAYING = 40;
```

A final game of this type might have a few more states, such as STATE_END_GAME and STATE_NEXT_LEVEL, but our case study does not require them.

Also note that these are designated as var but they should really be const. However, because Internet Explorer does not support the use of const, we left them as var.

The heart of our state machine is the run() function, which is called on an interval of every 20 milliseconds. The appState variable determines what function to call at any given time using a switch() statement. appState is updated to a different state any time the program is ready to move on and do something else. The process of calling a function such as run() on an interval and switching states is commonly known as a *game loop*:

```
function run() {
    switch(appState) {
        ccase STATE_INIT:
            initApp();
            break;
        case STATE_LOADING:
            //wait for call backs
            break;
        case STATE_RESET:
            resetApp();
            break;
        case STATE_PLAYING:
            drawScreen();
            break;

    }
}
```

Initializing the game: no global variables

Now that we know a bit about the state machine varruct we will use for this game, it's time to set up the preload for our assets. As we mentioned previously, this game has two sounds, shoot and explode, but it also has three images: a player, an alien, and a missile.

Remember how we kept saying we'd do away with global variables in these applications? Well, here's where it happens. With the state machine, we now have a mechanism to allow our application to wait for loading assets instead of leveraging only the DOM's window load event.

In the canvasApp() function, we set up the following variables to use in the game.

The appState variable holds the current state variable:

```
var appState = STATE_INIT;
```

We use the `loadCount` and `itemsToLoad` variables in exactly the same way we used them in the audio player application—except here we will be loading more items:

```
var loadCount= 0;
var itemsToLoad = 0;
```

The variables `alienImage`, `missileImage`, and `playerImage` will hold the loaded images we use in the game:

```
var alienImage = new Image();
var missileImage = new Image();
var playerImage = new Image();
```

`explodeSound` and `shootSound` will hold the references to the `HTMLAudioElement` objects we will load:

```
var explodeSound ;
var shootSound;
```

The `audioType` variable will hold the extension of the valid audio file type for the browser displaying the application:

```
var audioType;
```

The `mouseX` and `mouseY` variables will hold the current x and y location of the mouse:

```
var mouseX;
var mouseY;
```

The `player` variable will hold a dynamic object with the x and y location of the player ship (controlled with the mouse):

```
var player = {x:250,y:475};
```

Both the `aliens` and `missiles` arrays will hold lists of dynamic objects for displaying aliens and missiles on the canvas:

```
var aliens = new Array();
var missiles = new Array();
```

The next five variables set the number of aliens (ALIEN_ROWS, ALIEN_COLS), their starting location (ALIEN_START_X, ALIEN_START_Y), and their spacing on screen (ALIEN_SPACING):

```
var ALIEN_START_X = 25;
var ALIEN_START_Y = 25;
var ALIEN_ROWS = 5;
var ALIEN_COLS = 8;
var ALIEN_SPACING = 40;
```

Also, in the `canvasApp()` function, we need to set up event handlers for `mouseup` and `mousemove`. To create the game loop, we need to set up our interval to call the `run()` function:

```
theCanvas.addEventListener("mouseup",eventMouseUp, false);
theCanvas.addEventListener("mousemove",eventMouseMove, false);

function gameLoop() {
        window.setTimeout(gameLoop, 20);
        run()
    }

gameLoop();
```

At this point, run() will be called and our game loop will start by calling the function associated with the value of appState.

Preloading all assets without global variables

We just showed that the appState variable was initialized to STATE_INIT, which means that when the run() function is called for the first time, the initApp() function will be called. The good news (at least for this discussion) is that initApp() does very little that we have not already seen—it just does it in the context of the Canvas application. The result? Now we don't need any global variables.

In the following code, notice that we are using the same strategy. We have a single event handler for all loaded assets (itemLoaded()), we set itemsToLoad to 5 (three graphics and two sounds), and we set the appState to STATE_LOADING at the end of the function. The rest of the code is all simple review:

```
function initApp() {
    loadCount=0;
    itemsToLoad = 5;
    explodeSound = document.createElement("audio");
    document.body.appendChild(explodeSound);
    audioType = supportedAudioFormat(explodeSound);
    explodeSound.addEventListener("canplaythrough",itemLoaded,false);
    explodeSound.setAttribute("src", "explode1." + audioType);

    shootSound = document.createElement("audio");
    document.body.appendChild(shootSound);
    shootSound.addEventListener("canplaythrough",itemLoaded,false);
    shootSound.setAttribute("src", "shoot1." + audioType);

    alienImage = new Image();
    alienImage.onload = itemLoaded;
    alienImage.src = "alien.png";
    playerImage = new Image();
    playerImage.onload = itemLoaded;
    playerImage.src = "player.png";
    missileImage = new Image();
    missileImage.onload = itemLoaded;
    missileImage.src = "missile.png"; appState = STATE_LOADING;
    }
```

If you recall, STATE_LOADING does nothing in our run() function; it just waits for all events to occur. The action here is handled by the itemLoaded() event handler, which works exactly like the itemLoaded() function we wrote for the audio player, except that it has two additional functions:

1. It must remove the event listeners from the two sound objects we created. This is because, in some browsers, calling the play() method of an HTMLAudioElement object—or changing the src attribute of an HTMLAudioElement object—initiates a load operation, which will then call the itemLoaded event handler a second time. This will cause unexpected results in your application. Furthermore, it is always a good idea to remove unneeded event handlers from your objects.

2. We set the appState to STATE_RESET, which will initialize the game the next time the run() function is called on the interval.

Here is the code with the two additional functions:

```
function itemLoaded(event) {

    loadCount++;
    if (loadCount >= itemsToLoad) {

        shootSound.removeEventListener("canplaythrough",itemLoaded, false);
        explodeSound.removeEventListener("canplaythrough",itemLoaded,false);

        appState = STATE_RESET;

    }

}
```

Resetting the game

In the run() function, the STATE_RESET state calls the resetApp() function, which in turn calls startLevel(). It also sets the volume of our two sounds to 50% (.5) before setting the appState to STATE_PLAYING:

```
function resetApp() {

    startLevel();
    shootSound.volume = .5;
    explodeSound.volume = .5;
    appState = STATE_PLAYING;

}
```

The startLevel() function traverses through two nested for:next loops, creating the rows of aliens by column. Each time we create an alien, we push a dynamic object into the aliens array with the following properties:

speed
: The number of pixels the aliens will move left or right on each call to drawScreen().

x
: The starting x position of the alien on the screen. This value is set by the column (c) multiplied by ALIEN_SPACING, added to ALIEN_START_X.

y
: The starting y position of the alien on the screen. This is set by the row (r) multiplied by ALIEN_SPACING, added to ALIEN_START_Y.

width
: The width of the alien image.

height
: The height of the alien image.

Here is the code for the startLevel() function:

```
function startLevel() {

    for (var r = 0; r < ALIEN_ROWS; r++) {
      for( var c= 0; c < ALIEN_COLS; c++) {
        aliens.push({speed:2,x:ALIEN_START_X+c*ALIEN_SPACING,
            y:ALIEN_START_Y+r*
            ALIEN_SPACING,width:alienImage.width, height:alienImage.height});
      }
    }
  }
```

Mouse control

Before we talk about the game play itself, let's quickly discuss mouse event handlers, which will collect all user input for the game. When the player moves the mouse, the eventMouseMove() handler is called. This function operates just like the same function we created for the audio player, except for the last two lines. Those two lines set the x and y properties of the player object we created back in the variable definition section of canvasApp(). We will use these two properties to position the playerImage on the canvas in the drawScreen() function:

```
function eventMouseMove(event) {
    var x;
    var y;
    if (event.pageX || event.pageY) {
        x = event.pageX;
        y = event.pageY;
    } else {
        x = e.clientX + document.body.scrollLeft +
            document.documentElement.scrollLeft;
        y = e.clientY + document.body.scrollTop +
            document.documentElement.scrollTop;
```

```
    }
    x -= theCanvas.offsetLeft;
    y -= theCanvas.offsetTop;

    mouseX=x;
    mouseY=y;        player.x = mouseX;
      player.y = mouseY;

    }
```

The eventMouseUp() handler is called when the player presses and releases the left mouse button. When this event occurs, a missile will fire. The missile object is almost identical to the alien object, because it includes speed, x, y, width, and height properties. Because the player is firing the missile, we set the missile's x and y positions to the center of the player's ship on the x-axis (player.x+.5*playerImage.width) and to the y position of the player's ship, minus the height of the missile (player.y - missileImage.height):

```
    function eventMouseUp(event) {

    missiles.push({speed:5, x: player.x+.5*playerImage.width,
        y:player.y-missileImage.height,width:missileImage.width,
        height:missileImage.height});
```

Next is the first really critical line of code for the subject at hand: audio. For this first iteration of *Space Raiders*, we simply call the play() function of shootSound. This will play the shoot sound as often as the player presses the left mouse button (in theory):

```
    shootSound.play();
    }
```

Bounding box collision detection

Before we get to the main part of the game logic, we should discuss bounding box collision detection. We need to detect collisions between the missiles the player fires and the aliens the player is firing upon. To do this, we will create a function that tests to see whether two objects are overlapping. For lack of a better name, we call this function hitTest().

The type of hit test we are going to perform is called a bounding box collision test. This means that we are going to ignore the intricate details of the bitmapped graphics and simply test to see whether an invisible "box" drawn around the bounds of each object overlaps with a similar box drawn around the other objects.

Recall that both the alien and missile dynamic objects were created with similar properties: x, y, width, height. This was so that the hitTest() function could test them as generic objects, unspecific to the type of on-screen object that they represent. This means that we can add any other type of object to this game (boss alien, power-ups, enemy missiles, and so on), and if it is created with similar properties, we can use the same function to test collisions against it.

The function works by finding the top, left, bottom, and right values for each object and then testing to see whether any of those values overlap. Bounding box collision detection will be discussed in detail in Chapter 8, but we just wanted to give you a preview of what it looks like for *Space Raiders*:

```
function hitTest(image1,image2)  {
      r1left = image1.x;
      r1top = image1.y;
      r1right = image1.x + image1.width;
      r1bottom = image1.y + image1.height;
      r2left = image2.x;
      r2top = image2.y;
      r2right = image2.x + image2.width;
      r2bottom = image2.y + image2.height;
      retval = false;

      if ( (r1left > r2right) || (r1right < r2left) || (r1bottom < r2top) ||
         (r1top > r2bottom) ) {
        retval = false;
      } else {
        retval = true;
      }


      return retval;
   }
```

Playing the game

Now the game is ready to play. STATE_PLAYING calls the drawScreen() function, which is the heart of *Space Raiders*. The first part of this function simply moves the missiles and aliens on the screen. Moving the missiles is quite easy. We loop through the array (backward), updating the y property of each with the speed property. If they move off the top of the screen, we remove them from the array. We move through the array backward so that we can splice() array elements out of the array and not affect loop length. If we did not do this, elements would be skipped after we splice() the array:

```
for (var i=missiles.length-1; i>= 0;i--) {
   missiles[i].y -= missiles[i].speed;
   if (missiles[i].y < (0-missiles[i].height)) {
      missiles.splice(i,1);
   }

}
```

Drawing the aliens is similar to drawing missiles—with a few exceptions. Aliens move left and right, and when they reach the side of the canvas, they move down 20 pixels and then reverse direction. To achieve the reversal in direction, multiply the speed property by –1. If the aliens are moving to the right (speed = 2), this will make the speed property equal to –2, which will subtract from the x position and move the aliens to the left. If the aliens hit the left side of the canvas, the speed property will again be multiplied by –1 (–2 * –1), which will equal 2. The alien will then move to the right because 2 will be added to the x value for the alien each time drawScreen() is called:

```
//Move Aliens
    for (var i=aliens.length-1; i>= 0;i--) {
        aliens[i].x += aliens[i].speed;
        if (aliens[i].x > (theCanvas.width-aliens[i].width) ||
        aliens[i].x < 0) {
            aliens[i].speed *= -1;
            aliens[i].y += 20;
        }
        if (aliens[i].y > theCanvas.height) {
            aliens.splice(i,1);
        }

    }
```

The next step in drawScreen() is to detect collisions between the aliens and the missiles. This part of the code loops through the missiles array backward while nesting a loop through the aliens array. It will test every missile against every alien to determine whether there is a collision. Because we have already covered the hitTest() function, we need to discuss only what happens if a collision is detected. First, we call the play() function of the explodeSound. This is the second critical line of code in this iteration of *Space Raiders*, because it plays (or attempts to play) the explosion sound every time a collision is detected. After that, it splices the alien and missile objects out of their respective arrays and then breaks out of the nested for:next loop. If there are no aliens left to shoot, we set the appState to STATE_RESET, which will add more aliens to the canvas so that the player can continue shooting:

```
missile: for (var i=missiles.length-1; i>= 0;i--) {
        var tempMissile = missiles[i]
        for (var j=aliens.length-1; j>= 0;j--) {
            var tempAlien =aliens[j];
            if (hitTest(tempMissile,tempAlien)) {
                explodeSound.play();
                missiles.splice(i,1);
                aliens.splice(j,1);
                break missile;
            }
        }

        if (aliens.length <=0) {
            appState = STATE_RESET;
        }
    }
```

The last few lines of code in drawScreen() loop through the missiles and aliens arrays and draw them onto the canvas. This is done using the drawImage() method of the context object and using the x and y properties we calculated earlier. Finally, it draws the playerImage on the canvas, and the function is finished:

```
//Draw Missiles
      for (var i=missiles.length-1; i>= 0;i--) {
          context.drawImage(missileImage,missiles[i].x,missiles[i].y);

      }
//draw aliens
      for (var i=aliens.length-1; i>= 0;i--) {
          context.drawImage(alienImage,aliens[i].x,aliens[i].y);

      }

//Draw Player
          context.drawImage(playerImage,player.x,player.y);
```

As we stated previously, *Space Raiders* is not a full game. We have implemented only enough to get the player to shoot missiles so that we can play the shoot sound and to detect collisions so that we can play the explode sound.

Iteration #1: Playing Sounds Using a Single Object

We just described the first iteration of the dynamic audio code. It works by attempting to call the play() function of both shootSound and explodeSound as often as necessary. This appears to work at first, but if you listen carefully (and this is apparent on some browsers more than others), the sounds start to play "off," or not play at all. This is because we are using a single object and attempting to play and replay the same sound over and over. A single HTMLAudioElement was not designed to operate this way. You can test this example in the code distribution by running *CH7EX6.html* in your HTML5-compliant web browser. Press the fire button as quickly as possible, and listen to when and how the sounds play. After a bit, they start to play at the wrong time, don't finish, or don't play at all. Figure 7-7 shows what the first iteration of *Space Raiders* looks like in a web browser.

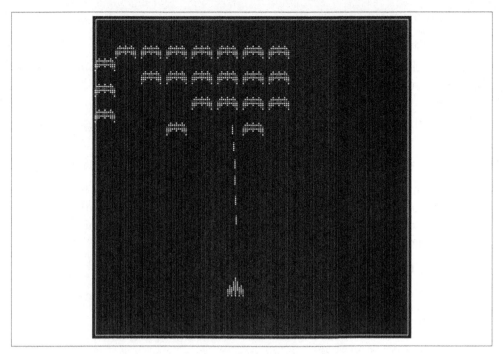

Figure 7-7. Space Raiders playing sounds from two objects

Iteration #2: Creating Unlimited Dynamic Sound Objects

So, we almost got what we wanted with the first iteration, but we ran into some oddities when calling the `play()` function on a single `HTMLAudioElement` multiple times before the sound had finished playing.

For our second iteration, we are going to try something different. Let's see what happens when we simply create a new `HTMLAudioElement` object every time we want to play a sound. If this doesn't sound like an efficient use of memory or resources in the web browser, you are a keen observer. It's actually a horrible idea. However, let's proceed just to see what happens.

In `canvasApp()`, we will create a couple variables that represent the filenames of the sounds we want to play, but without the associated extension. We will still retrieve the extension with a call to `supportedAudioFormat()`, just as we did in the first iteration, and store that value in the `audioType` variable.

We will also create an array named `sounds` that we will use to hold all the `HTMLAudioEle ment` objects we create. This array will tell us how many objects we have created so that we can visually see when all heck breaks loose:

```
var SOUND_EXPLODE = "explode1";
var SOUND_SHOOT  = "shoot1";
var sounds = new Array();
```

Instead of calling the play() function of each sound directly, we are going to create a function named playSound(). This function accepts two parameters:

sound

> One of the variables we created above that contains the name of the sound file

volume

> A number between 0 and 1 that represents the volume of the sound to play

The function here creates a new sound object every time it is called by calling the createElement() function of the document DOM object. It then sets the properties (src, loop, volume) and attempts to play the sound. Just for fun, let's push the object into the sounds array:

```
function playSound(sound,volume) {
    var tempSound = document.createElement("audio");
    tempSound.setAttribute("src", sound + "." + audioType);
    tempSound.loop = false;
    tempSound.volume = volume;
    tempSound.play();
    sounds.push(tempSound);
}
```

To play the sounds, we call playSound(), passing the proper parameters.

The call in eventMouseUp() looks like this:

```
playSound(SOUND_SHOOT,.5);
```

And in drawScreen(), it looks like this:

```
playSound(SOUND_EXPLODE,.5);
```

To display on the canvas how many sounds we have created, we add this code to the drawScreen() function:

```
context.fillStyle  = "#FFFFFF";
context.fillText  ("Active Sounds: " + sounds.length,  200 ,480);
```

Now, go ahead and try this example (*CH7EX7.html* in the code distribution). Figure 7-8 shows what *Space Raiders* iteration #2 looks like. Notice that we have added some display text at the bottom of the screen to show how many sounds are in the sounds array. You will discover two issues with this iteration:

1. The sounds play with almost no pauses when loaded from a local drive. But when the page is loaded from a remote website, there is a defined pause before each sound is loaded and played.

2. The number of sound objects created is a huge problem. For some browsers, such as Chrome, the number of active sounds caps out at about 50. After that, no sounds play at all.

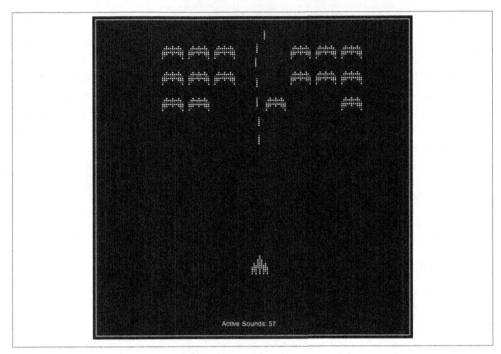

Figure 7-8. Space Raiders creating sounds on the fly

Iteration #3: Creating a Sound Pool

So, now we know we don't want to play an HTMLAudioElement object repeatedly or create unlimited sound objects on the fly. However, what if we cap the number of audio objects we create and put those objects in a pool so that we can use them over and over? This will save us memory, and after the sounds are loaded, we shouldn't see any loading pause before they are played, right?

We will implement a solution that uses HTMLAudioElement objects as general-purpose sound objects. We will keep a pool of them and change the src attribute to whatever sound we want to play. This appears to be an elegant solution that reuses as much as possible, in addition to giving us a lot of flexibility as to which sounds we want to play.

In canvasApp(), we will create a new variable named MAX_SOUNDS. This will represent the maximum number of sound objects we can create at any one time. We will also rename our sounds array to soundPool to better describe its purpose:

```
var MAX_SOUNDS = 8;
var soundPool = new Array();
```

The big change here is the playSound() function. It uses the same parameters as the one from iteration #2, but the functionality is very different:

```
function playSound(sound,volume) {
```

The first half of the function loops through the soundPool array to see whether any of the HTMLAudioElement objects in the pool are available to play a sound. We determine this by checking the ended property. Because only HTMLAudioElement objects that have previously been used to play a sound are put into the pool, the ended property will be set to true when the sound has finished playing. By replaying sounds that have finished, we remove the issue of trying to reuse an HTMLAudioElement object to play a sound while it is already in use:

```
var soundFound = false;
var soundIndex = 0;
var tempSound;

if (soundPool.length> 0) {
    while (!soundFound && soundIndex < soundPool.length) {

        var tSound = soundPool[soundIndex];

        if (tSound.ended) {
            soundFound = true;
        } else {
            soundIndex++;
        }
    }
}
if (soundFound) {
    tempSound = soundPool[soundIndex];
    tempSound.setAttribute("src", sound + "." + audioType);
    tempSound.loop = false;
    tempSound.volume = volume;
    tempSound.play();
```

If we don't find a sound, and if the size of the pool is less than MAX_SOUNDS, we go ahead and create a new HTMLAudioElement object, call its play() function, and push it into the sound pool. This keeps the pool from getting too large while making sure there are not too many HTMLAudioElement objects in the browser at any one time:

```
} else if (soundPool.length < MAX_SOUNDS){
    tempSound = document.createElement("audio");
    tempSound.setAttribute("src", sound + "." + audioType);
    tempSound.volume = volume;
    tempSound.play();
    soundPool.push(tempSound);
}
}
```

You can go ahead and try this iteration by loading *CH7EX8.html* in your HTML5-compliant web browser. In this case, it works! You hear every sound, and the browser doesn't die like it would with iteration #2.

Unfortunately, there are some issues. On some browsers, there is still a pause before a sound plays, just like with iteration #2. Again, this happens more often when the page is loaded from an external website than when it is loaded locally in a web browser.

The worst manifestation of this comes in Google Chrome, where the sounds pause every time they are played. Also, in Firefox, the `src` doesn't change for all the objects, making the shoot sound play when the explode sound should play, and vice versa.

Uh-oh, it looks like we need another iteration. Figure 7-9 shows *Space Raiders* playing with a pool size governed by MAX_SOUNDS.

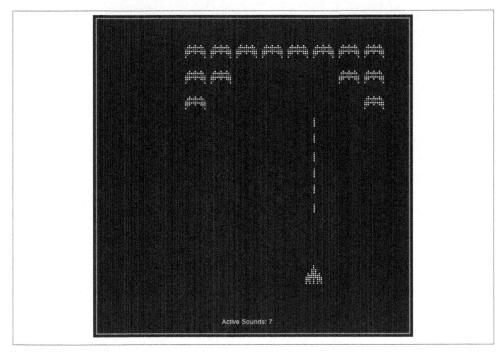

Figure 7-9. Space Raiders with a sound pool

Iteration #4: Reusing Preloaded Sounds

Even though the code in iteration #3 was pretty clean, it simply did not work for us. Instead, we need to compromise and implement a solution that is less elegant but that works to play sounds nearly every time they are needed. This solution must also work both locally and when loaded from a website.

For this final iteration, we are going to use a sound pool just like in iteration #3, but it will operate in a different way. We will not reuse sound objects for different sound files. Instead, we will load all our sounds up front and simply play a sound object that is currently not being used. In effect, we will "prime the pump," creating three sound objects for each of our two sounds, for a total of six sound objects when we start the application. While this might not seem like the perfect solution, it appears to work fairly well in all browsers and plays sounds in the most effective way.

In canvasApp(), we set our MAX_SOUNDS variables to 6. We could make it higher, but for this example, we will limit it to the number of sounds we will create and preload:

```
var MAX_SOUNDS = 6;
```

We then create six variables to hold our HTMLAudioElement objects—three for the explode sound:

```
var explodeSound ;
var explodeSound2 ;
var explodeSound3 ;
```

And three for the shoot sound:

```
var shootSound;
var shootSound2;
var shootSound3;
```

In the initApp() function, we preload all of these sound objects. Yes, we load the same object multiple times:

```
explodeSound = document.createElement("audio");
document.body.appendChild(explodeSound);
audioType = supportedAudioFormat(explodeSound);
explodeSound.addEventListener("canplaythrough",itemLoaded,false);
explodeSound.setAttribute("src", "explode1." + audioType);

explodeSound2 = document.createElement("audio");
document.body.appendChild(explodeSound2);
explodeSound2.addEventListener("canplaythrough",itemLoaded,false);
explodeSound2.setAttribute("src", "explode1." + audioType);

explodeSound3 = document.createElement("audio");
document.body.appendChild(explodeSound3);
explodeSound3.addEventListener("canplaythrough",itemLoaded,false);
explodeSound3.setAttribute("src", "explode1." + audioType);

shootSound = document.createElement("audio");
document.body.appendChild(shootSound);
shootSound.addEventListener("canplaythrough",itemLoaded,false);
shootSound.setAttribute("src", "shoot1." + audioType);

shootSound2 = document.createElement("audio");
document.body.appendChild(shootSound2);
```

```
shootSound2.addEventListener("canplaythrough",itemLoaded,false);
shootSound2.setAttribute("src", "shoot1." + audioType);

shootSound3 = document.createElement("audio");
document.body.appendChild(shootSound3);
shootSound3.addEventListener("canplaythrough",itemLoaded,false);
shootSound3.setAttribute("src", "shoot1." + audioType);
```

In the `itemLoaded()` function, we remove the event listeners for all six loaded sounds:

```
shootSound.removeEventListener("canplaythrough",itemLoaded, false);
shootSound2.removeEventListener("canplaythrough",itemLoaded, false);
shootSound3.removeEventListener("canplaythrough",itemLoaded, false);
explodeSound.removeEventListener("canplaythrough",itemLoaded,false);
explodeSound2.removeEventListener("canplaythrough",itemLoaded,false);
explodeSound3.removeEventListener("canplaythrough",itemLoaded,false);
```

Then we push each sound into our `soundPool` array. However, this time, we push them as dynamic objects so that we can set the following properties, which don't exist in the `HTMLAudioElement` object:

name

> The name of the sound file to play (again, without the extension).

element

> The reference to the `HTMLAudioElement` object.

played

> A Boolean that tells us whether this sound has played once or not. We need this property because we are putting all of these sound objects into our array, but they have not been played yet. That means their ended property has not yet been set to true. The `played` property tells us whether the sound is ready to play—that is, it has not been played yet. We will set this to true after we play the sound once:

```
soundPool.push({name:"explode1", element:explodeSound, played:false});
soundPool.push({name:"explode1", element:explodeSound2, played:false});
soundPool.push({name:"explode1", element:explodeSound3, played:false});
soundPool.push({name:"shoot1", element:shootSound, played:false});
soundPool.push({name:"shoot1", element:shootSound2, played:false});
soundPool.push({name:"shoot1", element:shootSound3, played:false});
```

Now we need to make a change in our `resetApp()` function. This change is to support sounds playing in Chrome, which appears to be the only browser that has a slight issue with loading sounds in this manner. The first time you play a sound in Chrome, there is a pause before it starts. To alleviate this, we play each sound type once but set the volume to 0. This will make sure a sound is loaded and ready to play the first time we call `playSound()` in Chrome:

```
function resetApp() {

    playSound(SOUND_EXPLODE,0);
```

```
        playSound(SOUND_SHOOT,0);
        startLevel();
        appState = STATE_PLAYING;


    }
```

The playSound() function operates in a similar way to iteration #3. It loops through the soundPool array looking for a sound that it can play. However, in this version, we check to see whether the HTMLAudioElement object has ended (tSound.ele ment.ended) or whether it has not been played (!tSound.played) yet. We also check whether the value in the sound parameter matches the name property of the sound object in soundPool (tSound.name == sound):

```
    function playSound(sound,volume) {

            var soundFound = false;
            var soundIndex = 0;
            var tempSound;

            if (soundPool.length > 0) {
                while (!soundFound && soundIndex < soundPool.length) {

                    var tSound = soundPool[soundIndex];
                    if ((tSound.element.ended || !tSound.played) &&
                    tSound.name == sound) {
                        soundFound = true;
                        tSound.played = true;
                    } else {
                        soundIndex++;
                    }

                }
            }
```

Using this method, we play a sound only if it has not been played, it has ended, and it already has the sound file loaded that we need to play. There is no pause to load (most of the time), and sounds play at pretty much the time that we need them to play. If we need more sounds, we can load more up front, or we can set MAX_SOUNDS to a number greater than the number of preloaded sounds. If we do that, we will create new sound objects on the fly (although this might still give you a pause when loading from a web server):

```
    if (soundFound) {
            tempSound = soundPool[soundIndex].element;
            tempSound.volume = volume;
            tempSound.play();

        } else if (soundPool.length < MAX_SOUNDS){
            tempSound = document.createElement("audio");
            tempSound.setAttribute("src", sound + "." + audioType);
```

```
            tempSound.volume = volume;
            tempSound.play();
            soundPool.push({name:sound, element:tempSound, type:audioType,
                            played:true});
    }
```

Go ahead and try this code. It is *CH7EX9.html* in the code distribution, or you can type in the program listing.

Other stuff you could do to improve the game

The next couple chapters introduce game concepts, so we really shouldn't go much further with *Space Raiders*. Still, if you were going to finish this game, you might consider doing the following:

1. Add a score.
2. Increase the aliens' speed on each new level.
3. Collision-detect the aliens and the player.
4. Make an object pool for missiles and aliens.
5. Slow down firing with a `wait()` state or frame counter.
6. Add explosions.
7. Include a title sequence, level sequence, and end game sequence.
8. Add a looping soundtrack.

The final code for Space Raiders

Example A-1 shows the final code for the *Space Raiders* game (*CH7EX9.html*).

Web Audio API

The Web Audio API is a relatively new specification that allows for more direct access to the audio playing in the web browser than is possible with the `<audio>` tag. One day, this promises to completely alter the way audio is handled in the web browser. However, at the time of this writing, the Web Audio API is only partially supported in webkit browsers (Chrome, Chrome for Android, Safari (Mountain Lion), and Safari mobile (iOS)), and support was only being planned for Firefox. Firefox has its own proprietary audio API named *The Audio Data API*. Furthermore, Chrome was the only browser we could find that worked reliably. Still, it looks like the Web Audio API will become a future standard, and that is why we are taking a quick look at this emerging technology in this book.

What Is the Web Audio API?

The Web Audio API uses the `XMLHttpRequest()` functionality of the web browser to load a sound as an array of binary bytes that is decoded into an audio buffer and then used to play your sound. An audio buffer is a memory-resident copy of your sound. It remains in memory, and you can access it as many times and as often as you like without the need to make multiple copies, using up precious memory. There is no need to create multiple copies of an `audio` object, as we did in earlier examples. Using the Web Audio API promises to one day be the most efficient way to play audio clips in games and applications.

 The Web Audio API specifies that it should be used for short sounds and audio clips, but music and longer audio should be streamed with the Audio element.

Space Raiders with the Web Audio API Applied

We are now going to create another version of *Space Raiders*, this time using the Web Audio API. The first thing we need to do is to get a reference to the `AudioContext` object. However, because the only implementation (at the time of this writing) is in Google Chrome, we need to use its object for `AudioContext`, which is `webkitAudioContext`. (In theory, this should also work in Safari, but our tests were not successful.)

```
var audioContext = new webkitAudioContext();
```

Next we will set up a couple variables to hold the sound buffers for our two sounds (shoot and explode):

```
var shootSoundBuffer;
var explodeSoundBuffer;
```

Now we need to load each sound. To make things straightforward, we will create a function to load each sound that accepts one parameter, named `url`, that represents the location and name of the sound file. In the `initApp()` function, we will get the `audioType` value as before, but now it will also call our two new functions to load the sounds:

```
audioType = supportedAudioFormat(tempSound);
loadExplodeSound("explode1." + audioType);
loadShootSound("shoot1."+ audioType);
```

Next, we need to create the functions that will load the sounds. The first thing the function needs to do is create an instance of `XMLHttpRequest()`and configure it for binary data. We do this by setting the `responseType` of `XMLHttpRequest` to `arraybuffer`. This is a new way to load data with `XMLHttpRequest` that allows us to open binary files, such as audio files.

We then set the `onload` callback to an inline anonymous function. We will use this to create a buffer for the sound it has loaded. In that function, we call `audioContext.de codeAudioData()` to retrieve the binary loaded data as an audio buffer that we can reference. That method requires three parameters:

1. The audio data (`request.response` from the call to `XMLHttpRequest`)
2. A `Success` callback (another inline anonymous function that we will describe next)
3. A `Failure` callback function named `onSoundError()`

The success callback function receives an argument containing the `buffer` of the loaded audio data. We set our variable named `shootSoundBuffer` to this argument, and we are ready to play the sound in the game. We then call `itemLoaded()` so that we can increment the `loadCount` variable in the *Space Raiders* game.

```
function loadShootSound(url) {

        var request = new XMLHttpRequest();
        request.open('GET', url, true);
        request.responseType = 'arraybuffer';

        request.onload = function() {
            audioContext.decodeAudioData(request.response, function(buffer) {
            shootSoundBuffer = buffer;
            itemLoaded();
            }, onSoundError);
    };
    request.send();
    }
function onSoundError(e) {
    alert("error loading sound")
}
```

We then create a similar function like the above for the "explode" sound. The only difference is that we set `explodeSoundBuffer` to the value of the buffer in the success callback function:

```
explodeSoundBuffer = buffer;
```

Now, inside the game when we want to play a sound, we call the `playSound()` function, passing the name of the sound buffer we want to play:

```
playSound(shootSoundBuffer);
```

The `playSound()` function is now totally different than the one we created in the previous iteration of *Space Raiders* because we don't have to manage multiple copies of each sound. First, we create an instance of `AudioBufferSourceNode` by calling `audioCon text.createBufferSource()` and save it in a variable named `source`. This object will hold the sound that we will be playing. We set the `buffer` property of `source` to the buffer that we passed into the function. Again, this buffer represents one of our sounds in memory (shoot or explode). We then call the connect function of `audioContext` to set the destination for the sound. For our purposes, we are using the default destination value, which should be the speakers on your computer. Finally, we call the `noteOn()` function of the source, passing 0, which means "start playing immediately."

You can call the `noteOn()` function on an instance of `AudioBufferSourceNode` only once. After that, it will never play a second time. You need to create another instance if you want hear the sound again. This is why we don't save the source after we start playing it. When the sound is done playing, the browser will garbage collect the reference for us. There is nothing else we need to do.

```
function playSound(soundBuffer) {
    var source = audioContext.createBufferSource();
    source.buffer = soundBuffer;
    source.connect(audioContext.destination);
    source.noteOn(0);
}
```

One last thing: we have updated the game to fire automatically. To accomplish this, we added two variables: `shootWaitFrames` (the amount to wait before we shoot) and `shoot Wait`, a counter that keeps track of how long we have waited before we shoot.

```
var shootWaitedFrames = 8;
var shootWait = 8;
```

We also added the following code to `drawScreen()` to accomplish this. This code makes the game wait for eight calls to `drawScreen()` before the player fires a shot. You can alter `shootWaitFrames` to make the player fire more or less often. By making this value less, you can really put the Web Audio API through its paces, with more sounds playing more often.

```
shootWaitedFrames++;
if (shootWaitedFrames > shootWait) {
        shoot();
        shootWaitedFrames = 0;;
}
```

 Google Chrome was the only web browser that supported this example at the time of publication. Also, the `noteOn()` function will soon be deprecated for `start()`.

You can try this new version of *Space Raiders* by loading *CH7EX10.html* from the code distribution. Here are some things to note when you try the example:

1. You need to run this example from a web server; otherwise, `XMLHttpRequest()` might not work.

2. You might need to add MIME types for audio files to your web server configuration if they will not load.

As you can see, the Web Audio API provides an efficient architecture for playing sounds in apps created on the Canvas. There is a lot more you can do with the Web Audio API, including adding filters and getting access to the audio data for further audio processing and visualization. We have only scratched the surface in relation to the problem we were trying to solve with *Space Raiders*. While the Web Audio API is still in flux, the best way to learn about new changes regarding this new technology is to look at the W3C specification (*https://dvcs.w3.org/hg/audio/raw-file/tip/webaudio/specification.html*).

What's Next?

This is not a book about the HTML5 `<audio>` tag, so we did not cover every aspect of that new feature. Instead, we focused on the elements of `audio` that could be used with HTML5 Canvas. We created two in-depth applications that make use of sound with HTML5 Canvas in very different ways: an audio player that plays one song, and a game that plays many sounds dynamically. During that process, we learned that audio in HTML5, while being a wonderful new feature, is not without its pitfalls and gotchas.

In the next two chapters, we will expand upon the last section we presented here and discuss how to implement games on HTML5 Canvas.

Canvas Games: Part I

Games are the reason why many of us initially became interested in computers, and they continue to be a major driving force that pushes computer technology to new heights. In this chapter, we will examine how to build a mini game framework that can be used to create games on the canvas. We will explore many of the core building blocks associated with game development and apply them to HTML5 Canvas with the Java-Script API.

We don't have the space to cover every type of game you might want to create, but we will discuss many elementary and intermediate topics necessary for most games. At the end of this chapter, we will have a basic clone of Atari's classic *Asteroids* game. We will step through the creation of this game by first applying some of the techniques for drawing and transformations specific to our game's visual objects. This will help get our feet wet by taking some of the techniques we covered in previous chapters and applying them to an arcade game application. Next, we will create a basic game framework that can be applied to any game we want to make on the canvas. Following this, we will dive into some game techniques and algorithms, and finally, we will apply everything we have covered to create the finished product.

Two-dimensional flying space shooter games are just the beginning of what can be accomplished on the Canvas. In the rest of the chapter, we will dig further into the 2D tile map structure we create in Chapter 4 and apply it to an application In doing so, we will take a look at using the A* path-finding algorithm to navigate the 2D tile map.

Why Games in HTML5?

Playing games in a browser has become one of the most popular activities for Internet users. HTML5 Canvas gives web developers an API to directly manage drawing to a specific area of the browser. This functionality makes game development in JavaScript much more powerful than ever before.

Canvas Compared to Flash

We've covered this topic in earlier chapters, but we expect that a large portion of readers might have previously developed games in Flash. If so, you will find that Canvas offers similar functionality in certain areas, but lacks some of the more refined features of Flash.

No Flash timeline
> There is no frame-based timeline for animation intrinsic to Canvas. This means that we will need to code all of our animations using images and/or paths, and apply our own frame-based updates.

No display list
> Flash AS3 offers the very powerful idea of an object display list; a developer can add hundreds of individual physical display objects to the game screen. HTML5 Canvas has only a single display object (the canvas itself).

What Does Canvas Offer?

Even though Canvas lacks some of the features that make the Flash platform very nice for game development, it also has some strengths.

A powerful single stage
> HTML5 Canvas is closely akin to the Flash Stage. It is a rectangular piece of screen real estate that can be manipulated programmatically. Advanced Flash developers might recognize Canvas as a close cousin to both the `BitmapData` and `Shape` objects in ActionScript. We can draw directly to the canvas with paths and images and transform them on the fly.

Logical display objects
> Canvas gives us a single physical display object, but we can create any number of logical display objects. We will use JavaScript objects to hold all of the logical data and methods we need to draw and transform our logical game objects to the physical canvas.

Our Basic Game HTML5 File

Before we start to develop our arcade game, let's look at Example 8-1, the most basic HTML file we will use in this chapter (*CH8EX1.html*). We'll start by using the basic HTML5 template we defined in Chapter 1. Our canvas will be a 200×200 square.

Example 8-1. The Basic HTML file for Chapter 8

```
<!doctype html>
<html lang="en">
<head>
```

```
<meta charset="UTF-8">
<title>CH8EX1: Filled Screen With Some Text</title>

<script type="text/javascript">
    window.addEventListener('load', eventWindowLoaded, false);
    function eventWindowLoaded() {
        canvasApp();
    }
    function canvasApp(){
        var theCanvas = document.getElementById("canvas");
        if (!theCanvas || !theCanvas.getContext) {
            return;
        }
        var context = theCanvas.getContext("2d");
        if (!context) {
            return;
        }
        drawScreen();
        function drawScreen() {
            context.fillStyle = '#aaaaaa';
            context.fillRect(0, 0, 200, 200);
            context.fillStyle = '#000000';
            context.font = '20px sans-serif';
            context.textBaseline = 'top';
            context.fillText  ("Canvas!", 0, 0);
        }
    }
</script>

</head>
    <body>
        <div style="position: absolute; top: 50px; left: 50px;">
            <canvas id="canvas" width="200" height="200">
            Your browser does not support HTML5 Canvas.
            </canvas>
        </div>
    </body>
</html>
```

This example will do nothing more than place a 200×200 gray box on the canvas and write "Canvas!" starting at 0,0. We will be replacing the drawScreen() function for most of the next few examples. Figure 8-1 illustrates Example 8-1.

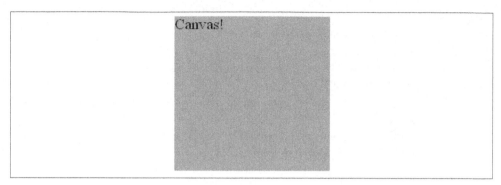

Figure 8-1. The basic HTML file for Chapter 8

Next, we will begin to make our *Asteroids*-like game, which we've named *Geo Blaster Basic*. See Figure 8-7 for an example of the final game in action.

Our Game's Design

We are not going to assume that everyone who reads this chapter knows of or understands Atari's classic arcade game *Asteroids*. So let's start by taking a peek at the *Asteroids* game-play elements.

Asteroids, designed by Ed Logg and Lyle Rains, was released by Atari in 1979. The game pitted a lone triangular two-dimensional vector spaceship (the player ship) against screen after screen of asteroid rocks that needed to be dodged and destroyed. Every so often a space saucer would enter the screen attempting to destroy the player ship.

All asteroids started the game as large rocks; when they were hit, they would split into two medium-sized rocks. When hit by a player missile, these medium-sized rocks would then split into two small rocks. The small rocks would simply be destroyed when hit. (Small was the final size for all asteroids.)

When the player destroyed all the asteroids, a new screen of more and slightly faster asteroids would appear. This went on until the player exhausted his three ships. At each 10,000-point score mark, the player was awarded an extra ship.

All of the game objects moved (thrusting, rotating, and/or floating) freely across the entire screen, which represented a slice of space as a flat plane. When an object went off the side of the screen, it would reappear on the opposite side, in warp-like fashion.

Game Graphics: Drawing with Paths

Let's jump into game development on Canvas by first taking a look at some of the graphics we will use in our game. This will help give us a visual feel for what type of code we will need to implement.

Needed Assets

For our *Asteroids*-like game, *Geo Blaster Basic*, we will need some very simple game graphics, including:

- A solid black background.
- A player ship that will rotate and thrust (move on a vector) across the game screen. There will be two frames of animation for this ship: a "static" frame and a "thrust" frame.
- A saucer that flies across the screen and shoots at the player.
- Some "rocks" for the player to shoot. We will use a simple square as our rock.

There are two different methods we can employ to draw the graphics for our game: bitmap images or paths. For the game in this chapter, we will focus on using paths. In Chapter 9, we will explore how to manipulate bitmap images for our game graphics.

Using Paths to Draw the Game's Main Character

Paths offer us a very simple but powerful way to mimic the vector look of the classic *Asteroids* game. We could use bitmap images for this purpose, but in this chapter we are going to focus on creating our game in code with no external assets. Let's take a look at the two frames of animation we will create for our player ship.

The static player ship (frame 1)

The main frame of the player ship will be drawn with paths on a 20×20 grid, as shown in Figure 8-2.

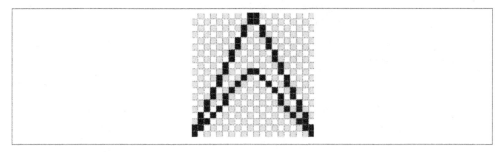

Figure 8-2. The player ship

Using the basic HTML file presented in Example 8-1, we can simply swap the drawScreen() function with the code in Example 8-2 to draw the ship.

Example 8-2. Drawing the player ship

```
function drawScreen() {
    // draw background and text
    context.fillStyle = '#000000';
    context.fillRect(0, 0, 200, 200);
    context.fillStyle = '#ffffff';
    context.font = '20px sans-serif';
    context.textBaseline = 'top';
    context.fillText  ("Player Ship - Static", 0, 180);

    //drawShip
    context.strokeStyle = '#ffffff';
    context.beginPath();
    context.moveTo(10,0);
    context.lineTo(19,19);
    context.lineTo(10,9);
    context.moveTo(9,9);
    context.lineTo(0,19);
    context.lineTo(9,0);

    context.stroke();
    context.closePath();
}
```

Drawing with Paths

As a refresher on drawing with paths, review the following steps:

1. Always start a new path with the `context.beginPath()` function call.

2. Set `context.strokeStyle()` before starting to draw the path.

3. Use a combination of the `context.moveTo()` and `context.drawTo()` stroke commands to paint the path lines.

4. End the drawing with the `context.stroke()` call, and close off the path with `context.closePath()`.

We are drawing to the upper-left corner of the screen, starting at 0,0. Figure 8-3 shows what this will look like.

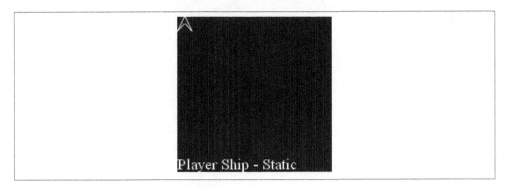

Figure 8-3. The player ship on the canvas

The ship with thrust engaged (frame 2)

Now let's take a look at the second frame of animation for the player ship, which is shown in Figure 8-4.

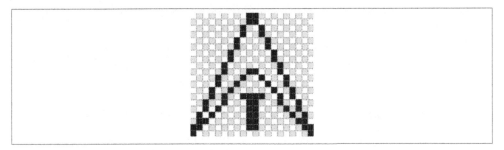

Figure 8-4. The player ship with thrust engaged

The drawScreen() function code to add this extra "thrust" graphic is very simple; see Example 8-3.

Example 8-3. Drawing the player ship with thrust

```
function drawScreen() {
   // draw background and text
   context.fillStyle = '#000000';
   context.fillRect(0, 0, 200, 200);
   context.fillStyle = '#ffffff';
   context.font = '20px sans-serif';
   context.textBaseline = 'top';
   context.fillText ("Player Ship - Thrust", 0, 180);

   //drawShip
   context.strokeStyle = '#ffffff';
   context.beginPath();
   context.moveTo(10,0);
```

```
    context.lineTo(19,19);
    context.lineTo(10,9);
    context.moveTo(9,9);
    context.lineTo(0,19);
    context.lineTo(9,0);

    //draw thrust
    context.moveTo(8,13);
    context.lineTo(11,13);
    context.moveTo(9,14);
    context.lineTo(9,18);
    context.moveTo(10,14);
    context.lineTo(10,18);

    context.stroke();
    context.closePath();
}
```

Animating on the Canvas

The player ship we just created has two frames (static and thrust), but we can display only a single frame at a time. Our game will need to switch out the frame of animation based on the state of the player ship, and it will need to run on a timer so that this animation can occur. Let's take a quick look at the code necessary to create our game timer.

Game Timer Loop

Games on HTML5 Canvas require the use of the repeated update/render loop to simulate animation. We do this by using the setTimeout() JavaScript function, which will repeatedly call a function of our choosing at millisecond intervals. Each second of game/animation time is made up of 1,000 milliseconds. If we want our game to run at 30 update/render cycles per second, we call this a 30 frames per second (FPS) rate. To run our interval at 30 FPS, we first need to divide 1,000 by 30. The result is the number of milliseconds in each interval:

```
const FRAME_RATE = 30;
var intervalTime = 1000/FRAME_RATE;

gameLoop()

function gameLoop() {
        drawScreen();
        window.setTimeout(gameLoop, intervalTime);
    }
```

By calling the drawScreen() function repeatedly on each interval time-out, we can simulate animation.

Sometimes we will refer to each of the frame intervals as a *frame tick*.

The Player Ship State Changes

We simply need to switch between the static and thrust states to simulate the animation. Let's take a look at the full HTML file to do this. In Example 8-4, we will start to place canvasApp class-level variables in a new section just above the drawScreen() function. This will be the location going forward for all variables needing a global scope inside the canvasApp() object.

Example 8-4. The player ship state changes for thrust animation

```
<!doctype html>
<html lang="en">
<head>
<meta charset="UTF-8">
<title>CH8EX4: Ship Animation Loop</title>

<script type="text/javascript">
window.addEventListener('load', eventWindowLoaded, false);
function eventWindowLoaded() {

    canvasApp();
}

function canvasApp(){

    var theCanvas = document.getElementById("canvas");
    if (!theCanvas || !theCanvas.getContext) {
            return;
    }

    var context = theCanvas.getContext("2d");

    if (!context) {
            return;
    }

    //canvasApp level variables
    var shipState = 0; //0 = static, 1 = thrust

    function drawScreen() {
        //update the shipState
        shipState++;
        if (shipState >1) {
            shipState=0;
      }
```

```
        // draw background and text
        context.fillStyle = '#000000';
        context.fillRect(0, 0, 200, 200);
        context.fillStyle = '#ffffff';
        context.font = '20px sans-serif';
        context.textBaseline = 'top';
        context.fillText ("Player Ship - animate", 0, 180);

        //drawShip
        context.strokeStyle = '#ffffff';
        context.beginPath();
        context.moveTo(10,0);
        context.lineTo(19,19);
        context.lineTo(10,9);
        context.moveTo(9,9);
        context.lineTo(0,19);
        context.lineTo(9,0);

        if (shipState==1) {
            //draw thrust
            context.moveTo(8,13);
            context.lineTo(11,13);
            context.moveTo(9,14);
            context.lineTo(9,18);
            context.moveTo(10,14);
            context.lineTo(10,18);
        }

        context.stroke();
        context.closePath();
    }

    var FRAME_RATE = 40;
    var intervalTime = 1000/FRAME_RATE;

    gameLoop();

    function gameLoop() {
            drawScreen();
            window.setTimeout(gameLoop, intervalTime);
    }

}

</script>

</head>
<body>
<div style="position: absolute; top: 50px; left: 50px;">

<canvas id="canvas" width="200" height="200">
 Your browser does not support HTML5 Canvas.
</canvas>
```

```
</div>
</body>
</html>
```

When we run Example 8-4, we will see the player ship in the upper-left corner of the canvas. The static and thrust states will alternate on each frame.

Applying Transformations to Game Graphics

Our game will probably have many individual logical display objects that need to be updated on a single frame tick. We can make use of the Canvas stack (`save()` and `restore()` functions) and use the transformation matrix to ensure that the final output affects only the current object we are working on—not the entire canvas.

The Canvas Stack

The Canvas state can be saved to a stack and retrieved. This is important when we are transforming and animating game objects because we want our transformations to affect only the current game object and not the entire canvas. The basic workflow for using the Canvas stack in a game looks like this:

1. Save the current canvas to the stack.
2. Transform and draw the game object.
3. Retrieve the saved canvas from the stack.

As an example, let's set up a basic rotation for our player ship. We will rotate it by 1 degree on each frame. Because we are currently drawing the player ship in the top-left corner of the canvas, we are going to move it to a new location. We do this because the basic rotation will use the top-left corner of the ship as the *registration point*: the axis location used for rotation and scale operations. Therefore, if we kept the ship at the 0,0 location and rotated it by its top-left corner, you would not see it half the time because its location would be off the top and left edges of the canvas. Instead, we will place the ship at 50,50.

We will be using the same HTML code as in Example 8-4, changing out only the draw Canvas() function. To simplify this example, we will remove the shipState variable and concentrate on the static state only. We will be adding in three new variables above the drawCanvas() function:

```
var rotation = 0; - holds the current rotation of the player ship
var x = 50; - holds the x location to start drawing the player ship
var y = 50; - holds the y location to start drawing the player ship
```

Example 8-5 gives the full code.

Example 8-5. Rotating an image

```
//canvasApp level variables
   var rotation = 0;
   var x = 50;
   var y = 50;

   function drawScreen() {

       // draw background and text
       context.fillStyle = '#000000';
       context.fillRect(0, 0, 200, 200);
       context.fillStyle = '#ffffff';
       context.font = '20px sans-serif';
       context.textBaseline = 'top';
       context.fillText  ("Player Ship - rotate", 0, 180);

       //transformation
       var angleInRadians = rotation * Math.PI / 180;
       context.save(); //save current state in stack
       context.setTransform(1,0,0,1,0,0); // reset to identity

       //translate the canvas origin to the center of the player
       context.translate(x,y);
       context.rotate(angleInRadians);

       //drawShip
       context.strokeStyle = '#ffffff';
       context.beginPath();
       context.moveTo(10,0);
       context.lineTo(19,19);
       context.lineTo(10,9);
       context.moveTo(9,9);
       context.lineTo(0,19);
       context.lineTo(9,0);

       context.stroke();
       context.closePath();

       //restore context
       context.restore(); //pop old state on to screen

       //add to rotation
       rotation++;
   }
```

As you can see, the player ship rotates clockwise one degree at a time. As we've mentioned many times already, we must convert from degrees to radians because the con
text.rotate() transformations use radians for calculations. In the next section, we'll take a deeper look at some of the transformations we will use in our *Geo Blaster Basic* game.

Game Graphic Transformations

As we saw in the previous section, we can easily rotate a game graphic at the top-left corner by using the `context.rotate()` transformation. However, our game will need to rotate objects at the center rather than the top-left corner. To do this, we must change the transformation point to the center of our game graphic object.

Rotating the Player Ship from the Center

The code to rotate the player ship from its center point is almost exactly like the code used to rotate it at the top-left corner. What we need to modify is the point of the translation. In Example 8-5, we placed the immediate-mode drawing context at the x and y coordinates of our game object (50,50). This had the effect of rotating the object from the top-left corner. Now we must move the translation to the center of our object:

```
context.translate(x+.5*width,y+.5*height);
```

 The `width` and `height` variables represent attributes of our drawn player ship. We will create these attributes in Example 8-6.

This is not the only change we need to make; we also need to draw our ship as though it is the center point. To do this, we will subtract half the `width` from each x attribute in our path draw sequence, and we will subtract half the `height` from each y attribute:

```
context.moveTo(10-.5*width,0-.5*height);
context.lineTo(19-.5*width,19-.5*height);
```

As you can see, it might get a little confusing trying to draw coordinates in this manner. It is also slightly more processor-intensive than using constants. In that case, we would simply hardcode in the needed values. Remember, the `width` and `height` attributes of our ship are both `20`. The hardcoded version would look something like this:

```
context.moveTo(0,-10);  //10-10, 0-10
context.lineTo(9,9); //19-10, 19-10
```

The method where we use the calculated values (using the `width` and `height` variables) is much more flexible, while the hardcoded method is much less processor-intensive. Example 8-6 contains all the code to use either method. We have commented out the calculated version of the code.

Example 8-6. Rotating an image from its center point

```
//canvasApp level variables
   var rotation = 0;
   var x = 50;
   var y = 50;    var width = 20;
```

```
var height = 20;

function drawScreen() {
    // draw background and text
    context.fillStyle = '#000000';
    context.fillRect(0, 0, 200, 200);
    context.fillStyle = '#ffffff';
    context.font = '20px sans-serif';
    context.textBaseline = 'top';
    context.fillText  ("Player Ship - rotate", 0, 180);

    //transformation
    var angleInRadians = rotation * Math.PI / 180;
    context.save(); //save current state in stack
    context.setTransform(1,0,0,1,0,0); // reset to identity

    //translate the canvas origin to the center of the player
    context.translate(x+.5*width,y+.5*height);
    context.rotate(angleInRadians);

    //drawShip

    context.strokeStyle = '#ffffff';
    context.beginPath();

    //hardcoding in locations
    context.moveTo(0,-10);
    context.lineTo(9,9);
    context.lineTo(0,-1);
    context.moveTo(-1,-1);
    context.lineTo(-10,9);
    context.lineTo(-1,-10);

    /*
    //using the width and height to calculate
    context.moveTo(10-.5*width,0-.5*height);
    context.lineTo(19-.5*width,19-.5*height);
    context.lineTo(10-.5*width,9-.5*height);
    context.moveTo(9-.5*width,9-.5*height);
    context.lineTo(0-.5*width,19-.5*height);
    context.lineTo(9-.5*width,0-.5*height);
    */

    context.stroke();
    context.closePath();

    //restore context
    context.restore(); //pop old state on to screen

    //add to rotation
    rotation++;
}
```

Alpha Fading the Player Ship

When a new player ship in *Geo Blaster Basic* enters the game screen, we will have it fade from transparent to opaque. Example 8-7 shows how we will create this transformation in our game.

To use the `context.globalAlpha` attribute of the canvas, we simply set it to a number between 0 and 1 before we draw the game graphics. We will create a new variable in our code called `alpha`, which will hold the current alpha value for our player ship. We will increase it by `.01` until it reaches 1. When we actually create our game, we will stop it at 1 and then start the game level. However, for this demo, we will just repeat it over and over.

Example 8-7. Alpha fading to the player ship

```
//canvasApp level variables
   var x = 50;
   var y = 50;
   var width = 20;
   var height = 20;
   var alpha = 0;
   context.globalAlpha  = 1;

   function drawScreen() {

       context.globalAlpha = 1;
       context.fillStyle = '#000000';
       context.fillRect(0, 0, 200, 200);
       context.fillStyle = '#ffffff';
       context.font = '20px sans-serif';
       context.textBaseline = 'top';
       context.fillText  ("Player Ship - alpha", 0, 180);
       context.globalAlpha = alpha;
       context.save(); //save current state in stack
       context.setTransform(1,0,0,1,0,0); // reset to identity

       //translate the canvas origin to the center of the player
       context.translate(x+.5*width,y+.5*height);

       //drawShip
       context.strokeStyle = '#ffffff';
       context.beginPath();

       //hardcoding in locations
       context.moveTo(0,-10);
       context.lineTo(9,9);
       context.lineTo(0,-1);
       context.moveTo(-1,-1);
       context.lineTo(-10,9);
       context.lineTo(-1,-10);
```

```
        context.stroke();
        context.closePath();

        //restore context
        context.restore(); //pop old state on to screen

        //add to rotation
        alpha+=.01;
        if (alpha > 1) {
        alpha=0;
        }
    }
```

Game Object Physics and Animation

All of our game objects will move on a two-dimensional plane. We will use basic directional movement vectors to calculate the change in the x and y coordinates for each game object. At its very basic level, we will be updating the delta x (dx) and delta y (dy) of each of our game objects on each frame to simulate movement. These dx and dy values will be based on the angle and direction in which we want the object to move. All of our logical display objects will add their respective dx and dy values to their x and y values on each frame of animation. The player ship will not use strict dx and dy because it needs to be able to float and turn independently. Let's take a closer look at the player movement now.

How Our Player Ship Will Move

Our player ship will change its angle of center axis rotation when the game player presses the left and right arrow keys. When the game player presses the up arrow key, the player ship will accelerate (thrust) in the angle it is facing. Because there is no friction applied to the ship, it will continue to float in the current accelerated angle until a different angle of acceleration is applied. This happens when the game player rotates to a new angle and presses the up (thrust) key once again.

The difference between facing and moving

Our player ship can rotate the direction it is facing while it is moving in a different direction. For this reason, we cannot simply use classic dx and dy values to represent the movement vector on the x and y axes. We must keep both sets of values for the ship at all times. When the player rotates the ship but does not thrust it, we need to draw the ship in the new rotated angle. All missile projectiles that the ship fires must also move in the direction the ship is facing. On the x-axis, we will name this value facingX; on the y-axis, it's facingY. movingX and movingY values will handle moving the ship in the direction it was pointed in when the thrust was applied. All four values are needed to thrust the ship in a new direction. Let's take a look at this next.

Thrusting in the rotated direction

After the ship is rotated to the desired direction, the player can thrust it forward by pressing the up arrow key. This thrust will accelerate the player ship only while the key is pressed. Because we know the rotation of the ship, we can easily calculate the angle of the rotation. We will then add new `movingX` and `movingY` values to the ship's x and y attributes to move it forward.

First, we must change the rotation value from degrees to radians:

```
var angleInRadians = rotation * Math.PI / 180;
```

You have seen this before—it's identical to how we calculated the rotation transformation before it was applied to the player ship.

When we have the angle of the ship's rotation, we must calculate the `facingX` and `facingY` values for this current direction. We do this only when we are going to thrust because it is an expensive calculation, processor-wise. We could calculate these each time the player changes the ship's rotation, but doing so would add unnecessary processor overhead:

```
facingX = Math.cos(angleInRadians);
facingY = Math.sin(angleInRadians);
```

When we have values on the x and y axes that represent the direction the player ship is currently facing, we can calculate the new `movingX` and `movingY` values for the player:

```
movingX = movingX+thrustAcceleration*facingX;
movingY = movingY+thrustAcceleration*facingY;
```

To apply these new values to the player ship's current position, we need to add them to its current x and y positions. *This does not occur only when the player presses the up key.* If it did, the player ship would not float; it would move only when the key was pressed. We must modify the x and y values on each frame with the `movingX` and `movingY` values:

```
x = x+movingX;
y = y+movingY;
```

Redrawing the player ship to start at angle 0

As you might recall, when we first drew the image for our player ship, we had the pointed end (the top) of the ship pointing up. We did this for ease of drawing, but it's not really the best direction in which to draw our ship when we intend to apply calculations for rotational thrust. The pointing-up direction is actually the −90 (or 270) degree angle. If we want to leave everything the way it currently is, we will need to modify the `angleIn Radians` calculation to look like this:

```
var angleInRadians = (Math.PI * (player.rotation -90 ))/ 180;
```

This is some ugly code, but it works fine if we want our player ship to be pointing up before we apply rotation transformations. A better method is to keep the current an gleInRadians calculation but draw the ship pointing in the actual angle 0 direction (to the right). Figure 8-5 shows how we would draw this.

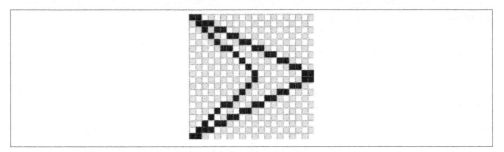

Figure 8-5. The player ship drawn at the 0 degree rotation

The drawing code for this direction would be modified to look like this:

```
//facing right
context.moveTo(-10,-10);
context.lineTo(10,0);
context.moveTo(10,1);
context.lineTo(-10,10);
context.lineTo(1,1);
context.moveTo(1,-1);
context.lineTo(-10,-10);
```

Controlling the Player Ship with the Keyboard

We will add in two keyboard events and an array object to hold the state of each key press. This will allow the player to hold down a key and have it repeat without a pause. Arcade games require this type of key-press response.

The array to hold our key presses

An array will hold the true or false value for each keyCode associated with key events. The keyCode will be the index of the array that will receive the true or false value:

```
var keyPressList = [];
```

The key events

We will use separate events for both key down and key up. The key down event will put a true value in the keyPressList array at the index associated with the event's key Code. Conversely, the key up event will place a false value in that array index:

```
document.onkeydown = function(e){
```

```
        e=e?e:window.event;
        //ConsoleLog.log(e.keyCode + "down");
        keyPressList[e.keyCode] = true;
    }

    document.onkeyup = function(e){

        e = e?e:window.event;
        //ConsoleLog.log(e.keyCode + "up");
        keyPressList[e.keyCode] = false;
    };
```

Evaluating key presses

Our game will need to include code to look for `true` (or `false`) values in the `keyPress
List` array and use those values to apply game logic:

```
if (keyPressList[38]==true){
    //thrust
    var angleInRadians = player.rotation * Math.PI / 180;
    facingX = Math.cos(angleInRadians);
    facingY = Math.sin(angleInRadians);

    movingX = movingX+thrustAcceleration*facingX;
    movingY = movingY+thrustAcceleration*facingY;
}

if (keyPressList[37]==true) {
    //rotate counterclockwise
    rotation-=rotationalVelocity;
}

if (keyPressList[39]==true) {
    //rotate clockwise
    rotation+=rotationalVelocity;;
}
```

Let's add this code to our current set of rotation examples and test it out. We have made
some major changes, so Example 8-8 presents the entire HTML file once again.

Example 8-8. Controlling the player ship

```
<!doctype html>
<html lang="en">
<head>
<meta charset="UTF-8">
<title>CH8EX8: Ship Turn With Keys</title>

<script type="text/javascript">
window.addEventListener('load', eventWindowLoaded, false);
function eventWindowLoaded() {

    canvasApp();
```

```
}

function canvasApp(){

    var theCanvas = document.getElementById("canvas");
    if (!theCanvas || !theCanvas.getContext) {
        return;
    }

    var context = theCanvas.getContext("2d");

    if (!context) {
        return;
    }

    //canvasApp level variables

    var rotation = 0;
    var x = 50;
    var y = 50;
    var facingX = 0;
    var facingY = 0;
    var movingX = 0;
    var movingY = 0;
    var width = 20;
    var height = 20;
    var rotationalVelocity = 5; //how many degrees to turn the ship
    var thrustAcceleration = .03;
    var keyPressList = [];
    function drawScreen() {

    //check keys

    if (keyPressList[38]==true){
        //thrust
        var angleInRadians = rotation * Math.PI / 180;
        facingX = Math.cos(angleInRadians);
        facingY = Math.sin(angleInRadians);

        movingX = movingX+thrustAcceleration*facingX;
        movingY = movingY+thrustAcceleration*facingY;

    }

    if (keyPressList[37]==true) {
        //rotate counterclockwise
        rotation -= rotationalVelocity;
    }

    if (keyPressList[39]==true) {
        //rotate clockwise
```

```
        rotation += rotationalVelocity;;
    }    x = x+movingX;
y = y+movingY;

// draw background and text
context.fillStyle = '#000000';
context.fillRect(0, 0, 200, 200);
context.fillStyle = '#ffffff';
context.font = '20px sans-serif';
context.textBaseline = 'top';
context.fillText  ("Player Ship - key turn", 0, 180);

//transformation
var angleInRadians = rotation * Math.PI / 180;
context.save(); //save current state in stack
context.setTransform(1,0,0,1,0,0); // reset to identity

//translate the canvas origin to the center of the player
context.translate(x+.5*width,y+.5*height);
context.rotate(angleInRadians);

//drawShip

context.strokeStyle = '#ffffff';
context.beginPath();

//hardcoding in locations
//facing right
context.moveTo(-10,-10);
context.lineTo(10,0);
context.moveTo(10,1);
context.lineTo(-10,10);
context.lineTo(1,1);
context.moveTo(1,-1);
context.lineTo(-10,-10);

context.stroke();
context.closePath();

//restore context
context.restore(); //pop old state on to screen
}

var FRAME_RATE = 40;
var intervalTime = 1000/FRAME_RATE;
gameLoop();

  function gameLoop() {
      drawScreen();
      window.setTimeout(gameLoop, intervalTime);
  }
```

```
        document.onkeydown = function(e){
            e = e?e:window.event;
            //ConsoleLog.log(e.keyCode + "down");
            keyPressList[e.keyCode] = true;
        }

        document.onkeyup = function(e){
            //document.body.onkeyup = function(e){
            e = e?e:window.event;
            //ConsoleLog.log(e.keyCode + "up");
            keyPressList[e.keyCode] = false;
        };

    }

</script>

</head>
<body>
<div style="position: absolute; top: 50px; left: 50px;">
<canvas id="canvas" width="200" height="200">
 Your browser does not support HTML5 Canvas.
</canvas>
</div>
</body>
</html>
```

When this file is run in a browser, you should be able to press the left and right keys to rotate the ship on its center axis. If you press the up key, the ship will move in the direction it is facing.

Giving the Player Ship a Maximum Velocity

If you play with the code in Example 8-8, you will notice two problems:

1. The ship can go off the sides of the screen and get lost.
2. The ship has no maximum speed.

We'll resolve the first issue when we start to code the complete game, but for now, let's look at how to apply a maximum velocity to our current movement code. Suppose we give our player ship a maximum acceleration of two pixels per frame. It's easy to calculate the current velocity if we are moving in only the four primary directions: up, down, right, left. When we are moving left or right, the movingY value will always be 0. If we are moving up or down, the movingX value will always be 0. The current velocity we are moving on one axis would be easy to compare to the maximum velocity.

But in our game, we are almost always moving in the *x* and *y* directions at the same time. To calculate the current velocity and compare it to a maximum velocity, we must use a bit more math.

First, let's assume that we will add a maximum velocity variable to our game:

```
var maxVelocity = 2;
```

Next, we must make sure to calculate and compare the `maxVelocity` to the current velocity *before* we calculate the new `movingX` and `movingY` values. We will do this with local variables used to store the new values for `movingX` and `movingY` before they are applied:

```
var movingXNew = movingX+thrustAcceleration*facingX;
var movingYNew = movingY+thrustAcceleration*facingY;
```

The current velocity of our ship is the square root of `movingXNew^2 + movingYNew^2`:

```
var currentVelocity = Math.sqrt ((movingXNew*movingXNew) +
                      (movingYNew*movingYNew));
```

If the `currentVelocity` is less than the `maxVelocity`, we set the `movingX` and `movingY` values:

```
if (currentVelocity < maxVelocity) {
    movingX = movingXNew;
    movingY = movingYNew;
}
```

A Basic Game Framework

Now that we have gotten our feet wet (so to speak) by taking a peek at some of the graphics, transformations, and basic physics we will use in our game, let's look at how we will structure a simple framework for all games that we might want to create on HTML5 Canvas. We will begin by creating a simple state machine using constant variables. Next, we will introduce our game timer interval function to this structure, and finally, we will create a simple reusable object that will display the current frame rate our game is running in. Let's get started.

The Game State Machine

A state machine is a programming construct that allows for our game to be in only a single application state at any one time. We will create a state machine for our game, called *application state*, which will include seven basic states (we will use constants to refer to these states):

- GAME_STATE_TITLE
- GAME_STATE_NEW_GAME
- GAME_STATE_NEW_LEVEL
- GAME_STATE_PLAYER_START
- GAME_STATE_PLAY_LEVEL

- GAME_STATE_PLAYER_DIE
- GAME_STATE_GAME_OVER

We will create a `function` object for each state that will contain game logic necessary for the state to function and to change to a new state when appropriate. By doing this, we can use the same structure for each game we create by simply changing out the content of each *state function* (as we will refer to them).

Let's take a look at a very basic version of this in action. We will use a function reference variable called `currentGameStateFunction`, as well as an integer variable called `cur rentGameState` that will hold the current application state constant value:

```
var currentGameState = 0;
var currentGameStateFunction = null;
```

We will create a function called `switchAppState()` that will be called only when we want to switch to a new state:

```
function switchGameState(newState) {
    currentGameState = newState;
    switch (currentGameState) {

        case GAME_STATE_TITLE:
            currentGameStateFunction = gameStateTitle;
            break;

        case GAME_STATE_PLAY_LEVEL:
            currentGameStateFunctionappStatePlayeLevel;
            break;

        case GAME_STATE_GAME_OVER:
            currentGameStateFunction = gameStateGameOver;
            break;

    }

}
```

The `gameLoop()` function call will start the application by triggering the iteration of the `runGame()` function by use of the `setTimeout()` method. We will call the `runGame()` function repeatedly in this `setTimeout()` method. `runGame()` will call the `currentGa meStateFunction` reference variable on each frame tick. This allows us to easily change the function called by `runGame()` based on changes in the application state:

```
gameLoop();

function gameLoop() {
    runGame();
    window.setTimeout(gameLoop, intervalTime);
}
```

```
function runGame(){
    currentGameStateFunction();
}
```

Let's look at the complete code. We will create some shell functions for the various application state functions. Before the application starts, we will call the `switchGameS` `tate()` function and pass in the constant value for the new function we want as the `currentGameStateFunction`:

```
//*** application start
    switchGameState(GAME_STATE_TITLE);
```

In Example 8-9, we will use the `GAME_STATE_TITLE` state to draw a simple title screen that will be redrawn on each frame tick.

Example 8-9. The tile screen state

```
<script type="text/javascript">
window.addEventListener('load', eventWindowLoaded, false);
function eventWindowLoaded() {

    canvasApp();

}

    function canvasApp(){

    var theCanvas = document.getElementById("canvas");
    if (!theCanvas || !theCanvas.getContext) {
        return;
    }

    var context = theCanvas.getContext("2d");

    if (!context) {
        return;
    }

    //application states

    const GAME_STATE_TITLE = 0;
    const GAME_STATE_NEW_LEVEL = 1;
    const GAME_STATE_GAME_OVER = 2;

    var currentGameState = 0;
    var currentGameStateFunction = null;

    function switchGameState(newState) {
        currentGameState = newState;
        switch (currentGameState) {

            case GAME_STATE_TITLE:
                currentGameStateFunction = gameStateTitle;
```

```
                break;

            case GAME_STATE_PLAY_LEVEL:
                currentGameStateFunctionappStatePlayeLevel;
                break;

            case GAME_STATE_GAME_OVER:
                currentGameStateFunction = gameStateGameOver;
                break;

        }

    }

    function gameStateTitle() {
        ConsoleLog.log("appStateTitle");
        // draw background and text
        context.fillStyle = '#000000';
        context.fillRect(0, 0, 200, 200);
        context.fillStyle = '#ffffff';
        context.font = '20px sans-serif';
        context.textBaseline = 'top';
        context.fillText  ("Title Screen", 50, 90);

    }

    function gameStatePlayLevel() {
        ConsoleLog.log("appStateGamePlay");
    }

    function gameStateGameOver() {
        ConsoleLog.log("appStateGameOver");
    }

    function runGame(){
        currentGameStateFunction();
    }

    //*** application start
    switchGameState(GAME_STATE_TITLE);

    //**** application loop
    var FRAME_RATE = 40;
    var intervalTime = 1000/FRAME_RATE;
    gameLoop();

     function gameLoop() {
         runGame();
         window.setTimeout(gameLoop, intervalTime);
     }
}
```

```
//***** object prototypes *****

//*** consoleLog util object
//create constructor
function ConsoleLog(){

}

//create function that will be added to the class
console_log = function(message) {
   if(typeof(console) !== 'undefined' && console != null) {
      console.log(message);
   }
}
//add class/static function to class by assignment
ConsoleLog.log = console_log;

//*** end console log object

</script>
```

 Example 8-9 added in the `ConsoleLog` object from the previous chapters. We will continue to use this utility to create helpful debug messages in the JavaScript log window of the browser. This was added for browsers that crashed when no console was turned on. However, this is a rare occurrence in most browsers that support Canvas.

We will continue to explore the application state machine and then create one for our game logic states in the upcoming section, "Putting It All Together" on page 471.

The Update/Render (Repeat) Cycle

In any of our application states, we might need to employ animation and screen updates. We will handle these updates by separating our code into distinct `update()` and `render()` operations. For example, as you might recall, the player ship can move around the game screen, and when the player presses the up arrow key, the ship's thrust frame of animation will be displayed rather than its static frame. In the previous examples, we contained all the code that updates the properties of the ship, as well as the code that actually draws the ship, in a single function called `drawScreen()`. Starting with Example 8-10, we will rid ourselves of this simple `drawScreen()` function and instead employ `update()` and `render()` functions separately. We will also separate out the code that checks for the game-specific key presses into a `checkKeys()` function.

Let's reexamine the contents of the `drawScreen()` function from Example 8-8, but this time, we'll break the function up into separate functions for each set of tasks, as shown in Example 8-10.

Example 8-10. Splitting the update and render cycles

```
function gameStatePlayLevel() {
    checkKeys();
    update();
    render();
}

function checkKeys() {

    //check keys

    if (keyPressList[38]==true){
        //thrust
        var angleInRadians = rotation * Math.PI / 180;
        facingX = Math.cos(angleInRadians);
        facingY = Math.sin(angleInRadians);

        movingX = movingX+thrustAcceleration*facingX;
        movingY = movingY+thrustAcceleration*facingY;

    }

    if (keyPressList[37]==true) {
        //rotate counterclockwise
        rotation-=rotationalVelocity;
    }

    if (keyPressList[39]==true) {
        //rotate clockwise
        rotation+=rotationalVelocity;;
    }
}

function update() {
    x = x+movingX;
    y = y+movingY;
}

function render() {
    //draw background and text
    context.fillStyle = '#000000';
    context.fillRect(0, 0, 200, 200);
    context.fillStyle = '#ffffff';
    context.font = '20px sans-serif';
    context.textBaseline = 'top';
    context.fillText ("render/update", 0, 180);

    //transformation
    var angleInRadians = rotation * Math.PI / 180;
    context.save(); //save current state in stack
    context.setTransform(1,0,0,1,0,0); // reset to identity
```

```
    //translate the canvas origin to the center of the player
    context.translate(x+.5*width,y+.5*height);
    context.rotate(angleInRadians);

    //drawShip

    context.strokeStyle = '#ffffff';
    context.beginPath();

    //hardcoding in locations
    //facing right
    context.moveTo(-10,-10);
    context.lineTo(10,0);
    context.moveTo(10,1);
    context.lineTo(-10,10);
    context.lineTo(1,1);
    context.moveTo(1,-1);
    context.lineTo(-10,-10);

    context.stroke();
    context.closePath();

    //restore context
    context.restore(); //pop old state on to screen
}
const FRAME_RATE = 40;
var intervalTime = 1000/FRAME_RATE;
gameLoop();

    function gameLoop() {
        runGame();
        window.setTimeout(gameLoop, intervalTime);
    }
```

We left out the entire application state machine from Example 8-9 to save space. In Example 8-10, we are simply showing what the `gameStatePlayLevel()` function might look like.

In the section "Putting It All Together" on page 471, we will go into this in greater detail as we start to build out the entire application.

The FrameRateCounter Object Prototype

Arcade games such as *Asteroids* and *Geo Blaster Basic* rely on fast processing and screen updates to ensure that all game-object rendering and game-play logic are delivered to the player at a reliable rate. One way to tell whether your game is performing up to par is to employ the use of a frame rate per second (FPS) counter. Below is a simple one that can be reused in any game you create on the canvas:

```
//*** FrameRateCounter  object prototype
function FrameRateCounter() {

    this.lastFrameCount = 0;
    var dateTemp = new Date();
    this.frameLast = dateTemp.getTime();
    delete dateTemp;
    this.frameCtr = 0;
}

FrameRateCounter.prototype.countFrames=function() {
    var dateTemp = new Date();
    this.frameCtr++;

    if (dateTemp.getTime() >=this.frameLast+1000) {
        ConsoleLog.log("frame event");
        this.lastFrameCount = this.frameCtr;
        this.frameLast = dateTemp.getTime();
        this.frameCtr = 0;
    }

    delete dateTemp;
}
```

Our game will create an instance of this object and call the countFrames() function on each frame tick in our update() function. We will write out the current frame rate in our render() function.

Example 8-11 shows these functions by adding code to Example 8-10. Make sure you add the definition of the FrameRateCounter prototype object to the code in Example 8-10 under the canvasApp() function but before the final <script> tag. Alternatively, you can place it in its own <script\> tags or in a separate *.js* file and set the URL as the src= value of a <script> tag. For simplicity's sake, we will keep all our code in a single file.

Example 8-11 contains the definition for our FrameRateCounter object prototype, as well as the code changes to Example 8-10 that are necessary to implement it.

Example 8-11. The FrameRateCounter is added

```
function update() {
    x = x+movingX;
    y = y+movingY;
    frameRateCounter.countFrames();
}

function render() {
    // draw background and text
    context.fillStyle = '#000000';
    context.fillRect(0, 0, 200, 200);
    context.fillStyle = '#ffffff';
```

```
        context.font = '20px sans-serif';
        context.textBaseline = 'top';
        context.fillText  ("FPS:" + frameRateCounter.lastFrameCount, 0, 180);

        //...Leave everything else from Example 8-10 intact here
}

frameRateCounter = new FrameRateCounter();
const FRAME_RATE = 40;
var intervalTime = 1000/FRAME_RATE;
gameLoop();

    function gameLoop() {
        runGame();
        window.setTimeout(gameLoop, intervalTime);
    }
```

Putting It All Together

We are now ready to start coding our game. First, we will look at the structure of the game and some of the ideas behind the various algorithms we will employ to create it. After that, we will present the full source code for *Geo Blaster Basic*.

Geo Blaster Game Structure

The structure of the game application is very similar to the structure we started to build earlier in this chapter. Let's take a closer look at the state functions and how they will work together.

Game application states

Our game will have seven distinct game application states. We will store these in constants:

```
const GAME_STATE_TITLE = 0;
const GAME_STATE_NEW_GAME = 1;
const GAME_STATE_NEW_LEVEL = 2;
const GAME_STATE_PLAYER_START = 3;
const GAME_STATE_PLAY_LEVEL = 4;
const GAME_STATE_PLAYER_DIE = 5;
const GAME_STATE_GAME_OVER = 6;
```

Game application state functions

Each individual state will have an associated function that will be called on each frame tick. Let's look at the functionality for each:

`gameStateTitle()`
> Displays the title screen text and waits for the space bar to be pressed before the game starts.

`gameStateNewGame()`
> Sets up all the defaults for a new game. All of the arrays for holding display objects are reinitialized—the game `level` is reset to 0, and the game `score` is set to 0.

`gameStateNewLevel()`
> Increases the `level` value by one and then sets the "game knob" values to control the level difficulty. See the upcoming section "Level Knobs" on page 479 for details.

`gameStatePlayerStart()`
> Fades the player graphic onto the screen from 0 alpha to 1. When this is complete, level play will start.

`gameStatePlayLevel()`
> Controls the play of the game level. It calls the `update()` and `render()` functions, as well as the functions for evaluating keyboard input for player ship control.

`gameStatePlayerDie()`
> Starts up an explosion at the location where the player ship was when it was hit by a rock, saucer, or saucer missile. When the explosion is complete (all particles in the explosion have exhausted their individual life values), it sets the move to the `GAME_STATE_PLAYER_START` state.

`gameStateGameOver()`
> Displays the "Game Over" screen and starts a new game when the space bar is pressed.

Game application functions

Aside from the game application state functions, there are a number of functions we need for the game to run. Each state function will call these functions as needed:

`resetPlayer()`
> Resets the player to the center of the game screen and readies it for game play.

`checkForExtraShip()`
> Checks to see whether the player should be awarded an extra ship. See the section "Awarding the Player Extra Ships" on page 481 for details about this algorithm.

`checkForEndOfLevel()`
> Checks to see whether all the rocks have been destroyed on a given level and, if so, starts up a new level. See the section "Level and Game End" on page 480 for details about this algorithm.

`fillBackground()`
Fills the canvas with the background color on each frame tick.

`setTextStyle()`
Sets the base text style before text is written to the game screen.

`renderScoreBoard()`
Is called on each frame tick. It displays the updated score, number of ships remaining, and the current FPS for the game.

`checkKeys()`
Checks the `keyPressList` array and then modifies the player ship attributes based on the values found to be `true`.

`update()`
Is called from `GAME_STATE_PLAY_LEVEL`. It in turn calls the `update()` function for each individual display object array.

Individual display object `update()` *functions*
The unique functions listed below update each different type of display object. These functions (with the exception of `updatePlayer()`) will loop through the respective array of objects associated with its type of display object and update the x and y values with dx and dy values. The `updateSaucer()` function contains the logic necessary to check whether to create a new saucer and whether any current saucers on the screen should fire a missile at the player.

- `updatePlayer()`
- `updatePlayerMissiles()`
- `updateRocks()`
- `updateSaucers()`
- `updateSaucerMissiles()`
- `updateParticles()`

`render()`
Is called from `GAME_STATE_PLAY_LEVEL`. It in turn calls the `render()` function for each individual display object array.

Individual display object `render()` *functions*
Like the `update()` functions, the unique functions listed below render each different type of display object. Again, with the exception of the `renderPlayer()` object (because there is only a single player ship), each of these functions will loop through the array of objects associated with its type and draw them to the game screen. As we saw when drawing the player ship earlier in this chapter, we will draw each object by moving and translating the canvas to the

point at which we want to draw our logical object. We will then transform our object (if necessary) and paint the paths to the game screen.

- renderPlayer()
- renderPlayerMissiles()
- renderRocks()
- renderSaucers()
- renderSaucerMissiles()
- renderParticles()

checkCollisions()
Loops through the individual game display objects and checks them for collisions. See the section "Applying Collision Detection" on page 481 for a detailed discussion of this topic.

firePlayerMissile()
Creates a playerMissile object at the center of the player ship and fires it in the direction the player ship is facing.

fireSaucerMissile()
Creates a saucerMissile object at the center of the saucer and fires it in the direction of the player ship.

playerDie()
Creates an explosion for the player by calling createExplode(), as well as changing the game application state to GAME_STATE_PLAYER_DIE.

createExplode()
Accepts in the location for the explosion to start and the number of particles for the explosion.

boundingBoxCollide()
Determines whether the rectangular box that encompasses an object's width and height is overlapping the bounding box of another object. It takes in two logical display objects as parameters and returns true if they are overlapping and false if they are not. See the section "Applying Collision Detection" on page 481 for details about this function.

splitRock()
Accepts in the scale and x and y starting points for two new rocks that will be created if a large or medium rock is destroyed.

addToScore()
Accepts in a value to add to the player's score.

Geo Blaster Global Game Variables

Now let's look at the entire set of game application scope variables needed for our game.

Variables that control screen flow

These variables will be used when the title and "Game Over" screens first appear. They will be set to true after the screen is drawn. When these variables are true, the screens will look for the space bar to be pressed before moving on to the next application state:

```
var titleStarted = false;
var gameOverStarted = false;
```

Game environment variables

These variables set up the necessary defaults for a new game. We will discuss the extraShipAtEach and extraShipsEarned in the section "Awarding the Player Extra Ships" on page 481:

```
var score = 0;
var level = 0;
var extraShipAtEach = 10000;
var extraShipsEarned = 0;
var playerShips = 3;
```

Playfield variables

These variables set up the maximum and minimum x and y coordinates for the game stage:

```
var xMin = 0;
var xMax = 400;
var yMin = 0;
var yMax = 400;
```

Score value variables

These variables set the score value for each of the objects the player can destroy:

```
var bigRockScore = 50;
var medRockScore = 75;
var smlRockScore = 100;
var saucerScore = 300;
```

Rock size constants

These variables set up some human-readable values for the three rock sizes, allowing us to simply use the constant instead of a literal value. We can then change the literal value if needed:

```
const ROCK_SCALE_LARGE = 1;
const ROCK_SCALE_MEDIUM = 2;
const ROCK_SCALE_SMALL = 3;
```

Logical display objects

These variables set up the single player object and arrays to hold the various other logical display objects for our game. See the upcoming sections "The Player Object" on page 476 and "Arrays of Logical Display Objects" on page 477 for further details about each:

```
var player = {};
var rocks = [];
var saucers = [];
var playerMissiles = [];
var particles = []
var saucerMissiles = [];
```

Level-specific variables

The level-specific variables handle the difficulty settings when the game level increases. See the section "Level Knobs" on page 479 for more details about how these are used:

```
var levelRockMaxSpeedAdjust = 1;
var levelSaucerMax = 1;
var levelSaucerOccurrenceRate = 25
var levelSaucerSpeed = 1;
var levelSaucerFireDelay = 300;
var levelSaucerFireRate = 30;
var levelSaucerMissileSpeed = 1;
```

The Player Object

The player object contains many of the variables we encountered earlier in this chapter when we discussed animating, rotating, and moving the player ship about the game screen. We have also added in three new variables that you have not seen before:

```
player.maxVelocity = 5;
player.width = 20;
player.height = 20;
player.halfWidth = 10;
player.halfHeight = 10;
player.rotationalVelocity = 5
player.thrustAcceleration = .05;
player.missileFrameDelay = 5;
player.thrust = false;
```

The new variables are halfWidth, halfHeight, and missileFrameDelay. halfWidth and halfHeight simply store half the width and half the height values, so these need not be calculated on each frame tick in multiple locations inside the code. The missile FrameDelay variable contains the number of frame ticks the game will count between firing player missiles. This way, the player cannot simply fire a steady stream of ordnance and destroy everything with little difficulty.

The `player.thrust` variable will be set to `true` when the player presses the up key.

Geo Blaster Game Algorithms

The game source code covers a lot of ground that we did not touch on earlier in this chapter. Let's discuss some of those topics now; the rest will be covered in detail in Chapter 9.

Arrays of Logical Display Objects

We have used arrays to hold all our logical display objects, and we have an array for each type of object (`rocks`, `saucers`, `playerMissiles`, `saucerMissiles`, and `particles`). Each logical display object is a simple object instance. We have created a separate function to draw and update each of our objects.

The use of an object class prototype similar to `FrameRateCounter` can be implemented easily for the various display object types. To conserve space, we have not implemented them in this game. However, these objects would allow us to separate the update and draw code from the current common functions and then place that code into the individual object prototypes. We have included a Rock prototype at the end of this chapter as an example. (See Example 8-13.)

You will notice that saucers and rocks are drawn with points in the same manner as the player ship.

Rocks

The rocks will be simple squares that rotate clockwise or counterclockwise. The rock instances will be in the `rocks` array. When a new level starts, these will all be created in the upper-right corner of the game screen.

Here are the variable attributes of a `rock` object:

```
newRock.scale = 1;
newRock.width = 50;
newRock.height = 50;
newRock.halfWidth = 25;
newRock.halfHeight = 25;
newRock.x
newRock.y
newRock.dx
newRock.dy
newRock.scoreValue = bigRockScore;
newRock.rotation = 0;
```

The rock scale will be set to one of the three rock-scale constants discussed earlier. halfWidth and halfHeight will be set based on the scale, and they will be used in calculations in the same manner as the player object versions. The dx and dy values represent the values to apply to the x and y axes when updating the rock on each frame tick.

Saucers

Unlike Atari's *Asteroids* game, which has both small and large saucers, we are going to have only one size in *Geo Blaster Basic*. It will be stored in the saucers array. On a 28×13 grid (using paths), it looks like Figure 8-6.

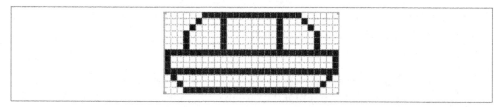

Figure 8-6. The saucer design

The variable attributes of the saucer object are very similar to the attributes of a rock object, although without the rock scale attribute. Also, saucers don't have a rotation; it is always set at 0. The saucer also contains variables that are updated on each new level to make the game more challenging for the player. Here are those variables, which will be discussed in more detail in the upcoming section "Level Knobs" on page 479:

```
newSaucer.fireRate = levelSaucerFireRate;
newSaucer.fireDelay = levelSaucerFireDelay;
newSaucer.fireDelayCount = 0;
newSaucer.missileSpeed = levelSaucerMissileSpeed;
```

Missiles

Both the player missiles and saucer missiles will be 2×2-pixel blocks. They will be stored in the playerMissiles and saucerMissiles arrays, respectively.

The objects are very simple. They contain enough attributes to move them across the game screen and to calculate life values:

```
newPlayerMissile.dx = 5*Math.cos(Math.PI*(player.rotation)/180);
newPlayerMissile.dy = 5*Math.sin(Math.PI*(player.rotation)/180);
newPlayerMissile.x = player.x+player.halfWidth;
newPlayerMissile.y = player.y+player.halfHeight;
newPlayerMissile.life = 60;
newPlayerMissile.lifeCtr = 0;
newPlayerMissile.width = 2;
newPlayerMissile.height = 2;
```

Explosions and particles

When a rock, saucer, or the player ship is destroyed, that object explodes into a series of particles. The createExplode() function creates this so-called particle explosion. Particles are simply individual logical display objects with their own life, dx, and dy values. Randomly generating these values makes each explosion appear to be unique. Particles will be stored in the particles array.

Like missiles, particle objects are rather simple. They also contain enough information to move them across the screen and to calculate their life span in frame ticks:

```
newParticle.dx = Math.random()*3;
newParticle.dy = Math.random()*3;
newParticle.life = Math.floor(Math.random()*30+30);
newParticle.lifeCtr = 0;
newParticle.x = x;
newParticle.y = y;
```

Level Knobs

Even though we never show the level number to the game player, we are adjusting the difficulty every time a screen of rocks is cleared. We do this by increasing the level variable by 1 and then recalculating these values before the level begins. We refer to the variance in level difficulty as *knobs*, which refers to dials or switches. Here are the variables we will use for these knobs:

level+3
: Number of rocks

levelRockMaxSpeedAdjust = level*.25;
: Rock max speed

levelSaucerMax = 1+Math.floor(level/10);
: Number of simultaneous saucers

levelSaucerOccurrenceRate = 10+3*level;
: Percent chance a saucer will appear

levelSaucerSpeed = 1+.5*level;
: Saucer speed

levelSaucerFireDelay = 120-10*level;
: Delay between saucer missiles

levelSaucerFireRate = 20+3*level;
: Percent chance a saucer will fire at the player

levelSaucerMissileSpeed = 1+.2*level;
: Speed of saucer missiles

Level and Game End

We need to check for game and level end so we can transition to either a new game or to the next level.

Level end

We will check for level end on each frame tick. The function to do so will look like this:

```
function checkForEndOfLevel(){
    if (rocks.length==0) {
        switchGameState(GAME_STATE_NEW_LEVEL);
    }
}
```

When the `rocks` array length is 0, we switch the state to GAME_STATE_NEW_LEVEL.

Game end

We do not need to check for the end of the game on each frame tick. We need to check only when the player loses a ship. We do this inside the `gameStatePlayerDie()` function:

```
function gameStatePlayerDie(){
    if (particles.length >0 || playerMissiles.length>0) {
        fillBackground();
        renderScoreBoard();
        updateRocks();
        updateSaucers();
        updateParticles();
        updateSaucerMissiles();
        updatePlayerMissiles();
        renderRocks();
        renderSaucers();
        renderParticles();
        renderSaucerMissiles();
        renderPlayerMissiles();
        frameRateCounter.countFrames();

    }else{
        playerShips--;
        if (playerShips<1) {
            switchGameState(GAME_STATE_GAME_OVER);
        }else{
            resetPlayer();
            switchGameState(GAME_STATE_PLAYER_START);
        }
    }
}
```

This is the state function that is called on each frame tick during the GAME_STATE_PLAYER_DIE state. First, it checks to see that there are no longer any particles on the screen. This ensures that the game will not end until the player ship has finished exploding. We also check to make sure that all the player's missiles have finished their lives. We do this so that we can check for collisions between the `playerMissiles` and for collisions of rocks against `saucers`. This way the player might earn an extra ship before `playerShips--` is called.

When the `particles` and `missiles` have all left the game screen, we subtract 1 from the `playerShips` variable and then switch to `GAME_STATE_GAME_OVER` if the `playerShips` number is less than 1.

Awarding the Player Extra Ships

We want to award the player extra ships at regular intervals based on her score. We do this by setting an amount of points that the game player must achieve to earn a new ship —this also helps us keep a count of the number of ships earned:

```
function checkForExtraShip() {
    if (Math.floor(score/extraShipAtEach) > extraShipsEarned) {
        playerShips++
        extraShipsEarned++;
    }
}
```

We call this function on each frame tick. The player earns an extra ship if the `score/extraShipAtEach` variable (with the decimals stripped off) is greater than the number of ships earned. In our game, we have set the `extraShipAtEach` value to `10000`. When the game starts, `extraShipsEarned` is `0`. When the player's score is `10000` or more, `score/extraShipAtEach` will equal 1, which is greater than the `extraShipsEarned` value of `0`. An extra ship is given to the player, and the `extraShipsEarned` value is increased by 1.

Applying Collision Detection

We will be checking the bounding box around each object when we do our collision detection. A bounding box is the smallest rectangle that will encompass all four corners of a game logic object. We have created a function for this purpose:

```
function boundingBoxCollide(object1, object2) {

    var left1 = object1.x;
    var left2 = object2.x;
    var right1 = object1.x + object1.width;
    var right2 = object2.x + object2.width;
    var top1 = object1.y;
    var top2 = object2.y;
    var bottom1 = object1.y + object1.height;
    var bottom2 = object2.y + object2.height;

    if (bottom1 < top2) return(false);
    if (top1 > bottom2) return(false);
```

```
if (right1 < left2) return(false);
if (left1 > right2) return(false);

return(true);

};
```

We can pass any two of our game objects into this function as long as each contains x, y, width, and height attributes. If the two objects are overlapping, the function will return true. If not, it will return false.

The checkCollision() function for *Geo Blaster Basic* is quite involved. The full code listing is given in Example 8-12. Rather than reprint it here, let's examine some of the basic concepts.

One thing you will notice is the use of "labels" next to the for loop constructs. Using labels, such as in the following line, can help streamline collision detection:

```
rocks: for (var rockCtr=rocksLength;rockCtr>=0;rockCtr--){
```

We will need to loop through each of the various object types that must be checked against one another. But we do not want to check an object that was previously destroyed against other objects. To ensure that we do the fewest amount of collision checks necessary, we have implemented a routine that employs label and break statements.

Here is the logic behind the routine:

1. Create a rocks: label, and then start to loop through the rocks array.

2. Create a missiles: label inside the rocks iteration, and loop through the player Missiles array.

3. Do a bounding box collision detection between the last rock and the last missile. Notice that we loop starting at the end of each array so that we can remove elements (when collisions occur) in the array without affecting array members that have not been checked yet.

4. If a rock and a missile collide, remove them from their respective arrays, and then call break rocks and then break missiles. We must break back to the next element in an array for any object type that is removed.

5. Continue looping through the missiles until they have all been checked against the current rock (unless break rocks was fired off for a rock/missile collision).

6. Check each saucer, each saucer missile, and the player against each of the rocks. The player does not need a label because there is only a single instance of the player. The saucers and saucerMissiles will follow the same logic as missiles. If there is a collision between one and a rock, break back to their respective labels after removing the objects from their respective arrays.

7. After we have checked the rocks against all the other game objects, check the `playerMissiles` against the saucers, using the same basic logic of loop labels, looping backward through the arrays and breaking back to the labels when objects are removed.

8. Check the `saucerMissiles` against the player in the same manner.

Over the years, we have found this to be a powerful way to check multiple objects' arrays against one another. It certainly is not the only way to do so. If you are not comfortable using loop labels, you can employ a method such as the following:

1. Add a Boolean `hit` attribute to each object, and set it to `false` when an object is created.

2. Loop through the `rocks`, and check them against the other game objects. This time the direction (forward or backward) through the loops does not matter.

3. Before calling the `boundingBoxCollide()` function, be sure that each object's `hit` attribute is `false`. If not, skip the collision check.

4. If the two objects collide, set each object's `hit` attribute to `true`. There is no need to remove objects from the arrays at this time.

5. Loop though `playerMissiles` and check against the `saucers`, and then loop through the `saucers` to check against the `player`.

6. When all the collision-detection routines are complete, reloop through each object array (backward this time) and remove all the objects with `true` as a `hit` attribute.

We have used both methods—and variations—on each. While the second method is a little cleaner, this final loop through all of the objects might add more processor overhead when dealing with a large number of objects. We will leave the implementation of this second method to you as an exercise, in case you want to test it.

The Geo Blaster Basic Full Source

The full source code and assets for *Geo Blaster Basic* are located at this site (*http://examples.oreilly.com/0636920013327/*).

Figure 8-7 shows a screenshot of the game in action.

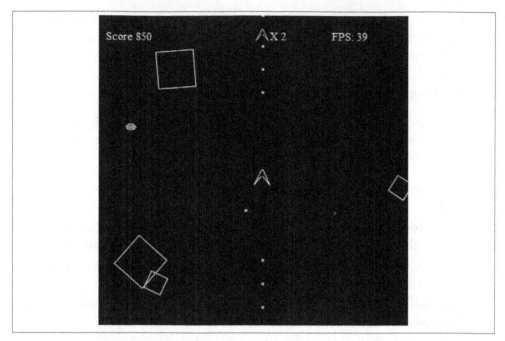

Figure 8-7. Geo Blaster Basic in action

Rock Object Prototype

To conserve space, we did not create separate object prototypes for the various display objects in this game. However, Example 8-12 is a Rock prototype object that can be used in a game such as *Geo Blaster Basic*.

Example 8-12. The Rock.js prototype

```
//*** Rock Object Prototype

function Rock(scale, type) {

    //scale
    //1 = large
    //2 = medium
    //3 = small
    //these will be used as the divisor for the new size
    //50/1 = 50
    //50/2 = 25
    //50/3 = 16

    this.scale = scale;
    if (this.scale <1 || this.scale >3){
        this.scale=1;
    }
```

```
        this.type = type;
        this.dx = 0;
        this.dy = 0;
        this.x = 0;
        this.y = 0;
        this.rotation = 0;
        this.rotationInc = 0;
        this.scoreValue = 0;

        //ConsoleLog.log("create rock. Scale=" + this.scale);
        switch(this.scale){

            case 1:
                this.width = 50;
                this.height = 50;
                break;
            case 2:
                this.width = 25;
                this.height = 25;
                break;
            case 3:
                this.width = 16;
                this.height = 16;
                break;
        }

}

Rock.prototype.update = function(xmin,xmax,ymin,ymax) {
    this.x += this.dx;
    this.y += this.dy;
    this.rotation += this.rotationInc;
    if (this.x > xmax) {
        this.x = xmin-this.width;
    }else if (this.x<xmin-this.width){
        this.x = xmax;
    }

    if (this.y > ymax) {
        this.y = ymin-this.width;
    }else if (this.y<ymin-this.width){
        this.y = ymax;
    }
}

Rock.prototype.draw = function(context) {

    var angleInRadians = this.rotation * Math.PI / 180;
    var halfWidth = Math.floor(this.width*.5); //used to find center of object
    var halfHeight = Math.floor(this.height*.5)// used to find center of object
    context.save(); //save current state in stack
    context.setTransform(1,0,0,1,0,0); // reset to identity
```

```
                                                // translate the canvas origin to
                                                // the center of the player
        context.translate(this.x+halfWidth,this.y+halfHeight);
        context.rotate(angleInRadians);
        context.strokeStyle = '#ffffff';

        context.beginPath();

        // draw everything offset by 1/2. Zero Relative 1/2 is if .5*width -1.
        // Same for height

        context.moveTo(-(halfWidth-1),-(halfHeight-1));
        context.lineTo((halfWidth-1),-(halfHeight-1));
        context.lineTo((halfWidth-1),(halfHeight-1));
        context.lineTo(-(halfWidth-1),(halfHeight-1));
        context.lineTo(-(halfWidth-1),-(halfHeight-1));

        context.stroke();
        context.closePath();
        context.restore(); //pop old state on to screen

}

//*** end Rock Class
```

Simple A* Path Finding on a Tile Grid

Next we are going to take a look at a subject that applies to many games, *Path Finding*.
We are going to revisit the tile-based grid drawing from Chapter 4 and apply JavaScript
path finding algorithms to the game screen. This type of logic can be used in many types
of games, from the simplest Pac-Man style contests to the most complicated 3D shooters.
We are not going to develop our own path finding algorithms in this chapter; instead,
we will make use of a pre-existing A-Star (or A* as we will continue to call it over the
next few sections) and use the canvas to display the results.

What Is A*?

A* is a grid-based path finding algorithm used to find the shortest "node" path from
point A to point B. A* is best implemented on a grid-based game screen where we
consider each tile of the grid to be a "node." For example, Figure 8-8 shows a simple grid
made up of tiles from a tile sheet.

Figure 8-8. Simple 5×5 tile map

In this simple five-column and five-row tile map, we have only two types of tiles. The gray tiles are "movable" tiles, meaning that game characters can occupy those tiles, while the blue tiles are "walls." Wall tiles are tiles that no game character can occupy. As you can see, there are only three movable tiles on the Figure 8-8 tile map.

A* can be used to find the shortest path between two points on a map, as illustrated in Figure 8-8. As you can see, there is only one straight line that an object can move in on this simple map. Using 0,0 as the index of the first tile, the column that extends from row 0, column 1 to row 2, column 1 is this straight vertical line. This is of no use to us in practice, because you would not need any type of path finding algorithm to figure out that a game character can move on only those three tiles, but we are going to start simple and get more complicated as we proceed. A* is a very useful tool, and although we are not going to code our own library here, we will go over the basic pseudocode for the algorithm.

David M. Bourg and Glenn Seeman, in *AI for Game Developers* (O'Reilly), describe A* this way:

> A* uses nodes to create a simplified search area to find the shortest path between any two points.

They also provide the following simplified A* pseudocode:

```
//*** A* Pseudo code from AI For Game Developers
//*** David M. Bourg
//*** Glenn Seeman
//*** O'Reilly (R)

add the starting node to the open node list
while the open list is not empty
   current node=node from open list with lowest cost
   if current node == goal then
      path complete
   else
      move current node to the closed list
      examine each node adjacent to the current node
      for each adjacent node
```

```
        if node is not on the open list
        and node is not on the closed list
        and node is not an obstacle
        then
            move node to open list and calculate cost of entire path
}
```

Nodes can contain obstacles (like our blue walls) or other terrain, such as water or grass. For our purposes, the blue tiles can *never* be passed, but we will add in a grass tile in later examples that, while not easily passable, is not impassable like the blue tiles. We are not going to use the available chapter space to create our own version of A* in JavaScript. Rather, we are going to use a version created by Brian Grinstead (*http://www.briangrinstead.com/blog/*).

 Brian's A* algorithm in JavaScript can be found at this site (*http://www.briangrinstead.com/blog/astar-search-algorithm-in-javascript-updated*).

We will be using both the *graph.js* and the *astar.js* files that Brian created and has supplied for download at his site. The one caveat to using an algorithm that we did not create is that we will need to make some minor modifications to our display code. Brian's code expects a tile map made up of columns of rows, while our tile map is made up of rows of columns. For example purposes, you can treat one of our tile maps from Chapter 4 as being turned on its side if it's to be used with Brian's code. (That is, we simply swap the x and y components.) However, it is easy to compensate for this. Let's get into the first example, and then we can describe what we mean and how the JavaScript and Canvas code is affected.

You will need to have downloaded the example files for this chapter from the book's website to use the use the first example. We have provided a new, very simple tile sheet called *tiles.png*, as well as the *astar.js* and *graph.js* files from Brian Grinstead's algorithm library.

Figure 8-9 shows the *tiles.png* tile sheet that we will use as the source graphic material for the A* examples throughout the rest of this section.

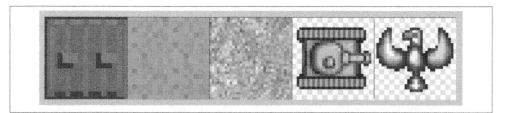

Figure 8-9. The tiles sheet for the A* examples

Here is the full code listing for Example 8-13. We will be modifying this code in the following sections to add to the size of the map and to demonstrate further A* functionality. This simple example shows the basics of using the algorithm with our tile sheet and tile map and shows how to display the results on the Canvas.

Example 8-13. A* Example 1

```
<!doctype html>
<html lang="en">
<head>
<meta charset="UTF-8">
<title>Chapter 8 Example 14: A* Example 1</title>

<script src="modernizr.js"></script>
<script type='text/javascript' src='graph.js'></script>
<script type='text/javascript' src='astar.js'></script>
<script type="text/javascript">
window.addEventListener('load', eventWindowLoaded, false);
function eventWindowLoaded() {
    canvasApp();
}
function canvasSupport () {
    return Modernizr.canvas;
}
function canvasApp(){
    if (!canvasSupport()) {
        return;
    }else{
        var theCanvas = document.getElementById('canvas');
        var context = theCanvas.getContext('2d');
    }
    //set up tile map
    var mapRows=5;
    var mapCols=5;
    var tileMap=[
    [0,1,0,0,0]
    ,[0,1,0,0,0]
    ,[0,1,0,0,0]
    ,[0,0,0,0,0]
    ,[0,0,0,0,0]
    ];
    //set up a* graph
    var graph = new Graph(tileMap);
    var startNode={x:0,y:1}; // use values of map turned on side
    var endNode={x:2,y:1};

    //create node list
    var start = graph.nodes[startNode.x][startNode.y];
    var end = graph.nodes[endNode.x][endNode.y];
    var result = astar.search(graph.nodes, start, end, false);

    //load in tile sheet image
```

```
    var tileSheet=new Image();
    tileSheet.addEventListener('load', eventSheetLoaded , false);
    tileSheet.src="tiles.png";

    function eventSheetLoaded() {
        drawScreen();
    }
    function drawScreen() {
        for (var rowCtr=0;rowCtr<mapRows;rowCtr++) {
            for (var colCtr=0;colCtr<mapCols;colCtr++){
                var tileId=tileMap[rowCtr][colCtr];
                var sourceX=Math.floor(tileId % 5) *32;
                var sourceY=Math.floor(tileId / 5) *32;
              context.drawImage(tileSheet,sourceX,sourceY,32,32,colCtr*32,
                            rowCtr*32,32,32);
            }
        }
        //draw green circle at start node
        context.beginPath();
        context.strokeStyle="green";
        context.lineWidth=5;
        context.arc((startNode.y*32)+16,(startNode.x*32)+16,10,0,
                (Math.PI/180)*360,false);
        context.stroke();
        context.closePath();

        //draw red circle at end node
        context.beginPath();
        context.strokeStyle="red";
        context.lineWidth=5;
        context.arc((endNode.y*32)+16, (endNode.x*32)+16, 10, 0,
                (Math.PI/180)*360,false);
        context.stroke();
        context.closePath();

        //draw black circles on path
        for (var ctr=0;ctr<result.length-1;ctr++) {
            var node=result[ctr];
            context.beginPath();
            context.strokeStyle="black";
            context.lineWidth=5;
            context.arc((node.y*32)+16, (node.x*32)+16, 10, 0,
                    (Math.PI/180)*360,false);
            context.stroke();
            context.closePath();
        }
    }
}
</script>

</head>
<body>
<div style="position: absolute; top: 50px; left: 50px;">
```

```
<canvas id="canvas" width="500" height="500">
Your browser does not support the HTML5 Canvas.
</canvas>
</div>
</body>
</html>
```

Example 8-13 presents some new concepts and some review from Chapter 4. Let's take a look at the most important parts of the code before we take a look at what it does in action.

In the example code, we first set up our tile map. This describes the look of the game screen and which tiles to display:

```
var mapRows=5;
var mapCols=5;
var tileMap=[
[0,1,0,0,0]
,[0,1,0,0,0]
,[0,1,0,0,0]
,[0,0,0,0,0]
,[0,0,0,0,0]
];
```

Our tile map will be made up of five rows and five columns. The tile map is laid out in a two-dimensional array of rows and columns that mimic how it will look on the screen. Notice that the second column is made up of the number 1 in the first three rows. When displayed on the canvas (without including the path finding code from Example 8-13), it will look like Figure 8-10. This amounts to simply swapping the x and y values we use for displaying the map when we use and evaluate the data that comes back from the *astar.js* functions.

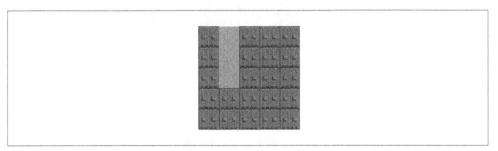

Figure 8-10. The Example 8-13 tile map with no path finding code applied

The goal of Example 8-13 is to use this very simple tile map with only three movable tiles to show an example of how the *astar.as* and *graph.as* functions work to find a path of nodes.

The first task is to create a new `Graph` object from the prototype code in the *graph.as* file. We do this by passing a two-dimensional array into to new `Graph()` constructor function. As mentioned earlier, the problem is that the `Graph` prototype is looking for columns of rows rather than rows of columns. Therefore, when we create the `start Node` and `endNode` objects that are used by *astar.js*, we need to flip our idea of the tile map on its side and pass in the values as if the tile map was set up in this manner. (Again, simply swapping the x and y values will do the trick.)

```
//set up a* graph
var graph = new Graph(tileMap);
var startNode={x:0,y:1}; // use values of map turned on side
var endNode={x:2,y:1};
```

Figure 8-11 shows this flipping concept in an easy-to-understand fashion. The x and y values for our tile map are simply swapped for use with *astar.js*.

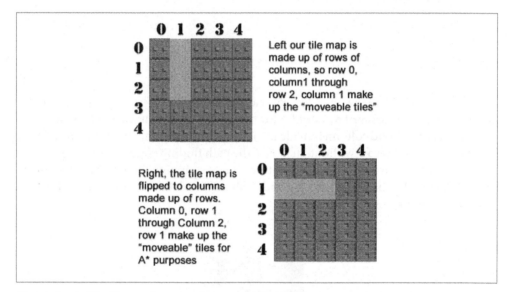

Figure 8-11. The Example 8-13 tile map vs. the A* tile map

Figure 8-11 shows the difference between the two-dimensional array structure for the tile map we have created and the two-dimensional structure that the *graphs.js* expects its graph map to be in. When we create the `startNode` object, we use 0 for the x value and 1 for the y value because these map to the *graph.js* expected values. The actual values on our tile map are 0 for the row (y) and 1 for the column (x). We needed to use the same logic to transpose the end node from row 2, column 1 (or, y=2 and x=1) into x=2, y=1.

To find an actual path, the start and end nodes are passed into the `astar.search` function:

```
var result = astar.search(graph.nodes, start, end, false);
```

The `false` value passed into the function as the final parameter tells the function to *not* consider diagonal nodes in the search. We will use this option in an example further along in this section. The result that is returned is an array of nodes that is the shortest path through the movable tiles.

When we do the actual Canvas drawing, we use the exact same code as we used in Chapter 4 for drawing the tile map from the tile sheet. This uses the rows of columns. The tile map is first drawn in its entirety by looping through the rows and then each element in each row (or the column) and drawing that tile to the screen.

To show the path, we draw a green circle at the starting node and a red circle at the end node. In between, we draw a black circle on each path node. The interesting thing to note here is that when we loop through the result array of objects for the nodes, we use the y value returned as the x coordinate (or row) and the x returned as the y coordinate (or column):

```
context.arc((node.y*32)+16, (node.x*32)+16, 10, 0,(Math.PI/180)*360,false);
```

The final output from the example will return the simplest path that can be drawn between two points. Figure 8-12 shows this final output.

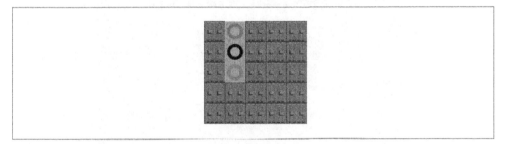

Figure 8-12. The final output from Example 8-13

A* Applied to a Larger Tile Map

To demonstrate A* path finding in a more real-world way, we must first create a new tile map. For our next example, we are going to create a more maze-like structure that still uses just the first two tile types.

The following code example shows the changes to the Example 8-13 tile map for Example 8-14. We will also be changing the `startNode` and `endNode` for Example 8-14. We have not provided the full code listing for this example, just the changes needed to turn Example 8-13 into Example 8-14:

```
//Example 8-14 changes to Example 8-13 to make a larger tile map
var mapRows=15;
var mapCols=15;
```

```
var tileMap=[
 [0,0,0,0,0,0,0,0,0,0,0,0,0,0,0]
,[0,1,1,1,1,1,1,1,1,1,1,1,1,1,0]
,[0,1,0,1,0,0,1,0,1,0,0,1,0,1,0]
,[0,1,0,1,0,0,1,0,1,0,0,1,0,1,0]
,[0,1,0,1,0,0,1,1,1,0,0,1,0,1,0]
,[0,1,1,1,1,1,0,0,0,1,1,1,1,1,0]
,[0,1,0,0,0,1,0,0,0,1,0,0,0,1,0]
,[0,1,1,1,1,1,0,0,0,1,1,1,1,1,0]
,[0,0,0,0,0,1,1,1,1,1,0,0,0,0,0]
,[0,1,1,1,1,1,0,0,0,1,1,1,1,1,0]
,[0,1,0,1,0,0,1,1,1,0,0,1,0,1,0]
,[0,1,0,1,0,0,1,0,1,0,0,1,0,1,0]
,[0,1,0,1,0,0,1,0,1,0,0,1,0,1,0]
,[0,1,1,1,1,1,1,1,1,1,1,1,1,1,0]
,[0,0,0,0,0,0,0,0,0,0,0,0,0,0,0]
];
```

If we create a tile map like the above, it will result in a map that looks like Figure 8-13, which shows the output from the new, larger tile map that will be generated from this data.

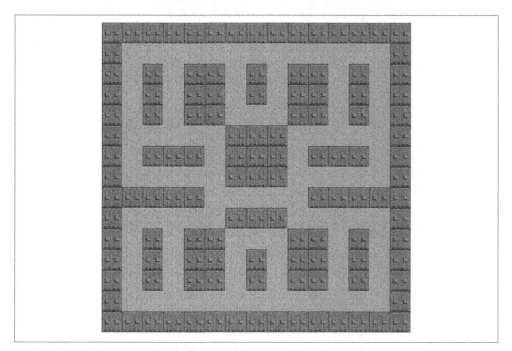

Figure 8-13. The Example 8-14 15×15 tile map with no path finding applied

Along with changing the map data for Example 8-14, we will also be adding new start and end nodes to reflect the larger map size. Let's choose a start node of row 4, column

1, and end node of row 13, column 10. This would require us to make changes to the new `startNode` and `endNode` variables. The changes for Example 8-14 are simple, but they will create this larger map and provide a better demonstration of the capabilities of the *graph.as* and *astar.js* functions:

In Example 8-14 we will demonstrate what happens when we increase the size of the Example 8-13 tile map and run the A* functions. The following code shows the changes to the `startNode` and `endNode` for this larger tile map.

```
//Example 8-14 startNode and endNode
var graph = new Graph(tileMap);
var startNode={x:4,y:1}; // use values of map turned on side
var endNode={x:13,y:10};
```

If you make all of the changes to Example 8-13 listed previously, the result will be Example 8-14. The result of Example 8-14 is shown in Figure 8-14.

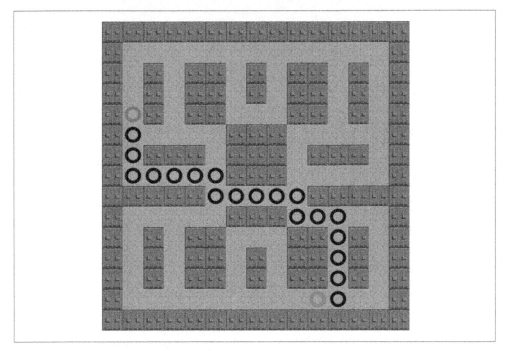

Figure 8-14. Example 8-14 A* applied to the 15x15 tile map

Example 8-14. Larger A* example

```
<!doctype html>
<html lang="en">
<head>
<meta charset="UTF-8">
<title>Chapter 8 Example 14 - Larger A* Example</title>
```

```
<script src="modernizr.js"></script>
<script type='text/javascript' src='graph.js'></script>
<script type='text/javascript' src='astar.js'></script>
<script type="text/javascript">
window.addEventListener('load', eventWindowLoaded, false);
function eventWindowLoaded() {

    canvasApp();

}

function canvasSupport () {
    return Modernizr.canvas;
}

function canvasApp(){

    if (!canvasSupport()) {
                return;
    }else{
        var theCanvas = document.getElementById('canvas');
        var context = theCanvas.getContext('2d');
    }

    //set up tile map
    var mapRows=15;
    var mapCols=15;
    var tileMap=[
    [0,0,0,0,0,0,0,0,0,0,0,0,0,0,0]
    ,[0,1,1,1,1,1,1,1,1,1,1,1,1,1,0]
    ,[0,1,0,1,0,0,1,0,1,0,0,1,0,1,0]
    ,[0,1,0,1,0,0,1,0,1,0,0,1,0,1,0]
    ,[0,1,0,1,0,0,1,1,1,0,0,1,0,1,0]
    ,[0,1,1,1,1,1,0,0,0,1,1,1,1,1,0]
    ,[0,1,0,0,0,1,0,0,0,1,0,0,0,1,0]
    ,[0,1,1,1,1,1,0,0,0,1,1,1,1,1,0]
    ,[0,0,0,0,0,1,1,1,1,1,0,0,0,0,0]
    ,[0,1,1,1,1,1,0,0,0,1,1,1,1,1,0]
    ,[0,1,0,1,0,0,1,1,1,0,0,1,0,1,0]
    ,[0,1,0,1,0,0,1,0,1,0,0,1,0,1,0]
    ,[0,1,0,1,0,0,1,0,1,0,0,1,0,1,0]
    ,[0,1,1,1,1,1,1,1,1,1,1,1,1,1,0]
    ,[0,0,0,0,0,0,0,0,0,0,0,0,0,0,0]
    ];


    console.log("tileMap.length=" , tileMap.length);

    //set up a* graph
    var graph = new Graph(tileMap);
    var startNode={x:4,y:1}; // use values of map turned on side
    var endNode={x:13,y:10};
```

```
//create node list
var start = graph.nodes[startNode.x][startNode.y];
var end = graph.nodes[endNode.x][endNode.y];
var result = astar.search(graph.nodes, start, end, false);

//load in tile sheet image
var tileSheet=new Image();
tileSheet.addEventListener('load', eventSheetLoaded , false);
tileSheet.src="tiles.png";

function eventSheetLoaded() {
     drawScreen()
}

function drawScreen() {
     for (var rowCtr=0;rowCtr<mapRows;rowCtr++) {
         for (var colCtr=0;colCtr<mapCols;colCtr++){

             var tileId=tileMap[rowCtr][colCtr];
             var sourceX=Math.floor(tileId % 5) *32;
             var sourceY=Math.floor(tileId / 5) *32;

             context.drawImage(tileSheet, sourceX, sourceY,32,32,
                         colCtr*32,rowCtr*32,32,32);


         }
     }


     //draw green circle at start node
     context.beginPath();
     context.strokeStyle="green";
     context.lineWidth=5;
     context.arc((startNode.y*32)+16, (startNode.x*32)+16, 10, 0,
             (Math.PI/180)*360,false);
     context.stroke();
     context.closePath();

     //draw red circle at end node
     context.beginPath();
     context.strokeStyle="red";
     context.lineWidth=5;
     context.arc((endNode.y*32)+16, (endNode.x*32)+16, 10, 0,
             (Math.PI/180)*360,false);
     context.stroke();
     context.closePath();

     //draw black circles on path
     for (var ctr=0;ctr<result.length-1;ctr++) {
         var node=result[ctr];
```

```
                    context.beginPath();
                    context.strokeStyle="black";
                    context.lineWidth=5;
                    context.arc((node.y*32)+16, (node.x*32)+16, 10, 0,
                            (Math.PI/180)*360,false);
                    context.stroke();
                    context.closePath();
                }


        }

}

</script>

</head>
<body>
<div style="position: absolute; top: 50px; left: 50px;">
<canvas id="canvas" width="500" height="500">
 Your browser does not support the HTML 5 Canvas.
</canvas>
</div>
</body>
</html>
```

A* Taking Diagonal Moves into Account

For Example 8-15, we will be making changes to Example 8-14 to add in diagonal movement to the A* path.

So far, each of our examples has used the *astar.js* functions, which ignore diagonal movements between nodes. We can easily add this capability. Example 8-15 does this with one simple change. We will be changing the `false` in the A* search function to `true`:

```
//For example 8-15 we will add true to the end of the search function

var result = astar.search(graph.nodes, start, end, true);
```

By simply changing `false` to `true` at the end of the call to the `astar.search()`, we can change the result node path dramatically. Figure 8-15 shows the path difference.

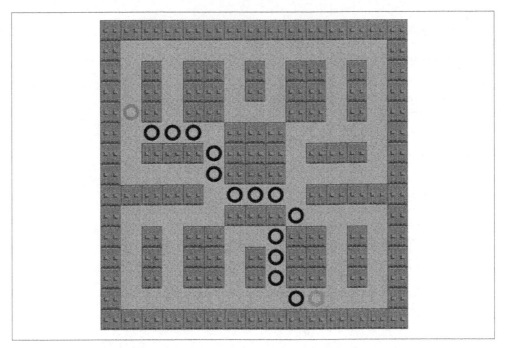

Figure 8-15. A* applied to the 15x15 tile map with diagonals

Each node on the movable tiles has the same weight (1). When A* calculates the shortest node path, it does so by taking these weights into account. Next we will add in some nodes with a higher weight value.

Example 8-15. Larger A* example with diagonals

```
<!doctype html>
<html lang="en">
<head>
<meta charset="UTF-8">
<title>Chapter 8 Example 15 - Larger A* Example with Diagonals</title>

<script src="modernizr.js"></script>
<script type='text/javascript' src='graph.js'></script>
<script type='text/javascript' src='astar.js'></script>
<script type="text/javascript">
window.addEventListener('load', eventWindowLoaded, false);
function eventWindowLoaded() {

    canvasApp();

}

function canvasSupport () {
    return Modernizr.canvas;
}
```

```
function canvasApp(){

    if (!canvasSupport()) {
            return;
    }else{
        var theCanvas = document.getElementById('canvas');
        var context = theCanvas.getContext('2d');
    }

    //set up tile map
    var mapRows=15;
    var mapCols=15;
    var tileMap=[
    [0,0,0,0,0,0,0,0,0,0,0,0,0,0,0]
    ,[0,1,1,1,1,1,1,1,1,1,1,1,1,1,0]
    ,[0,1,0,1,0,0,1,0,1,0,0,1,0,1,0]
    ,[0,1,0,1,0,0,1,0,1,0,0,1,0,1,0]
    ,[0,1,0,1,0,0,1,1,1,0,0,1,0,1,0]
    ,[0,1,1,1,1,1,0,0,0,1,1,1,1,1,0]
    ,[0,1,0,0,0,1,0,0,0,1,0,0,0,1,0]
    ,[0,1,1,1,1,1,0,0,0,1,1,1,1,1,0]
    ,[0,0,0,0,0,1,1,1,1,1,0,0,0,0,0]
    ,[0,1,1,1,1,1,0,0,0,1,1,1,1,1,0]
    ,[0,1,0,1,0,0,1,1,1,0,0,1,0,1,0]
    ,[0,1,0,1,0,0,1,0,1,0,0,1,0,1,0]
    ,[0,1,0,1,0,0,1,0,1,0,0,1,0,1,0]
    ,[0,1,1,1,1,1,1,1,1,1,1,1,1,1,0]
    ,[0,0,0,0,0,0,0,0,0,0,0,0,0,0,0]
    ];


    console.log("tileMap.length=" , tileMap.length);

    //set up a* graph
    var graph = new Graph(tileMap);
    var startNode={x:4,y:1}; // use values of map turned on side
    var endNode={x:13,y:10};

    //create node list
    var start = graph.nodes[startNode.x][startNode.y];
    var end = graph.nodes[endNode.x][endNode.y];
    var result = astar.search(graph.nodes, start, end, true);

    //load in tile sheet image
    var tileSheet=new Image();
    tileSheet.addEventListener('load', eventSheetLoaded , false);
    tileSheet.src="tiles.png";

    function eventSheetLoaded() {
        drawScreen()
    }
```

```javascript
function drawScreen() {
    for (var rowCtr=0;rowCtr<mapRows;rowCtr++) {
        for (var colCtr=0;colCtr<mapCols;colCtr++){

            var tileId=tileMap[rowCtr][colCtr];
            var sourceX=Math.floor(tileId % 5) *32;
            var sourceY=Math.floor(tileId / 5) *32;

            context.drawImage(tileSheet, sourceX, sourceY,32,32,colCtr*32,
                            rowCtr*32,32,32);

        }
    }



    //draw green circle at start node
    context.beginPath();
    context.strokeStyle="green";
    context.lineWidth=5;
    context.arc((startNode.y*32)+16, (startNode.x*32)+16, 10, 0,
            (Math.PI/180)*360,false);
    context.stroke();
    context.closePath();

    //draw red circle at end node
    context.beginPath();
    context.strokeStyle="red";
    context.lineWidth=5;
    context.arc((endNode.y*32)+16, (endNode.x*32)+16, 10, 0,
            (Math.PI/180)*360,false);
    context.stroke();
    context.closePath();

    //draw black circles on path
    for (var ctr=0;ctr<result.length-1;ctr++) {
        var node=result[ctr];
        context.beginPath();
        context.strokeStyle="black";
        context.lineWidth=5;
        context.arc((node.y*32)+16, (node.x*32)+16, 10, 0,
                (Math.PI/180)*360,false);
        context.stroke();
        context.closePath();
    }


}

}
```

```
</script>

</head>
<body>
<div style="position: absolute; top: 50px; left: 50px;">
<canvas id="canvas" width="500" height="500">
 Your browser does not support the HTML 5 Canvas.
</canvas>
</div>
</body>
</html>
```

A* with Node Weights

For Example 8-16, we will be adding weighs to our nodes. We'll do this by simply adding in some grass tiles to the tile map we have been using in the previous examples. By doing this, we can change the A* search result in a path avoiding the grass tiles has a lower total node value sum than one that travels over the grass tiles.

We can add to the weight of each open node by simply giving it a number higher than 1. We have created our tile sheet to make this very simple. The third tile (or tile index 2) is a grass tile. With *astar.as*, as long as a tile has a node value greater than 0, it is considered a movable tile. If a path can be made through the maze and the total value of the path, taking the node values into account, is the lowest, the path will cross these nodes with higher values. To demonstrate this, we will now add some grass tiles to the tile map. The changes for Example 8-16 are below. Notice that we are also removing the diagonal movement from Example 8-15, but it is not mandatory that you do so. We will look at that in Example 8-17:

```
//Example 8-16 changes to example 8-15 tile map
 var mapRows=15;
 var mapCols=15;
 var tileMap=[
[0,0,0,0,0,0,0,0,0,0,0,0,0,0,0]
,[0,1,2,1,1,1,1,1,1,1,1,1,1,1,0]
,[0,1,0,1,0,0,1,0,1,0,0,1,0,1,0]
,[0,1,0,1,0,0,1,0,1,0,0,1,0,1,0]
,[0,1,0,1,0,0,1,1,1,0,0,1,0,1,0]
,[0,2,1,1,1,1,0,0,0,1,1,1,1,1,0]
,[0,1,0,0,0,1,0,0,0,1,0,0,0,1,0]
,[0,1,1,1,2,1,0,0,0,1,1,1,1,1,0]
,[0,0,0,0,0,1,1,1,1,1,0,0,0,0,0]
,[0,1,1,1,1,1,0,0,0,1,1,1,1,1,0]
,[0,1,0,1,0,0,1,1,1,0,0,1,0,1,0]
,[0,1,0,1,0,0,2,0,1,0,0,1,0,1,0]
,[0,1,0,1,0,0,1,0,1,0,0,1,0,1,0]
,[0,1,1,1,1,1,1,2,1,1,1,1,1,1,0]
,[0,0,0,0,0,0,0,0,0,0,0,0,0,0,0]
];
```

```
//set up a* graph
var graph = new Graph(tileMap);
var startNode={x:4,y:1}; // use values of map turned on side
var endNode={x:13,y:10};

//create node list
var start = graph.nodes[startNode.x][startNode.y];
var end = graph.nodes[endNode.x][endNode.y];
var result = astar.search(graph.nodes, start, end, false);
```

This will result in Figure 8-16, showing the path running through a grass tile because it does not add enough to the total path cost to force a new direction change.

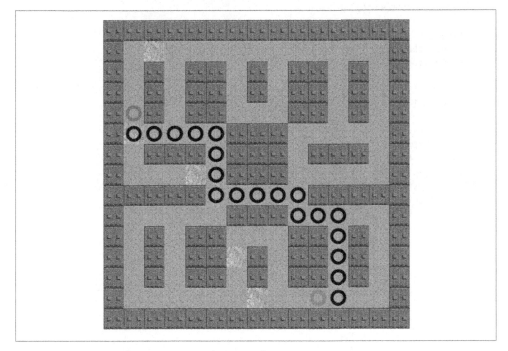

Figure 8-16. Example 8-16—A* with grass tiles

Example 8-16. Larger A* example with grass tiles

```
<!doctype html>
<html lang="en">
<head>
<meta charset="UTF-8">
<title>Chapter 8 Example 16 - Larger A* Example with Grass Tiles</title>

<script src="modernizr.js"></script>
<script type='text/javascript' src='graph.js'></script>
<script type='text/javascript' src='astar.js'></script>
```

```
<script type="text/javascript">
window.addEventListener('load', eventWindowLoaded, false);
function eventWindowLoaded() {

    canvasApp();

}

function canvasSupport () {
    return Modernizr.canvas;
}

function canvasApp(){

    if (!canvasSupport()) {
                return;
    }else{
        var theCanvas = document.getElementById('canvas');
        var context = theCanvas.getContext('2d');
    }

  //set up tile map
   var mapRows=15;
   var mapCols=15;
   var tileMap=[
   [0,0,0,0,0,0,0,0,0,0,0,0,0,0,0]
  ,[0,1,2,1,1,1,1,1,1,1,1,1,1,1,0]
  ,[0,1,0,1,0,0,1,0,1,0,0,1,0,1,0]
  ,[0,1,0,1,0,0,1,0,1,0,0,1,0,1,0]
  ,[0,1,0,1,0,0,1,1,1,0,0,1,0,1,0]
  ,[0,2,1,1,1,1,0,0,0,1,1,1,1,1,0]
  ,[0,1,0,0,0,1,0,0,0,1,0,0,0,1,0]
  ,[0,1,1,1,2,1,0,0,0,1,1,1,1,1,0]
  ,[0,0,0,0,0,1,1,1,1,1,0,0,0,0,0]
  ,[0,1,1,1,1,1,0,0,0,1,1,1,1,1,0]
  ,[0,1,0,1,0,0,1,1,1,0,0,1,0,1,0]
  ,[0,1,0,1,0,0,2,0,1,0,0,1,0,1,0]
  ,[0,1,0,1,0,0,1,0,1,0,0,1,0,1,0]
  ,[0,1,1,1,1,1,1,2,1,1,1,1,1,1,0]
  ,[0,0,0,0,0,0,0,0,0,0,0,0,0,0,0]
  ];

    //set up a* graph
    var graph = new Graph(tileMap);
    var startNode={x:4,y:1}; // use values of map turned on side
    var endNode={x:13,y:10};

    //create node list
    var start = graph.nodes[startNode.x][startNode.y];
    var end = graph.nodes[endNode.x][endNode.y];
    var result = astar.search(graph.nodes, start, end, false);
```

```
//load in tile sheet image
var tileSheet=new Image();
tileSheet.addEventListener('load', eventSheetLoaded , false);
tileSheet.src="tiles.png";

function eventSheetLoaded() {
      drawScreen()
}

function drawScreen() {
      for (var rowCtr=0;rowCtr<mapRows;rowCtr++) {
          for (var colCtr=0;colCtr<mapCols;colCtr++){

                var tileId=tileMap[rowCtr][colCtr];
                var sourceX=Math.floor(tileId % 5) *32;
                var sourceY=Math.floor(tileId / 5) *32;

                context.drawImage(tileSheet, sourceX, sourceY,32,32,
                                  colCtr*32,rowCtr*32,32,32);


          }
      }



      //draw green circle at start node
      context.beginPath();
      context.strokeStyle="green";
      context.lineWidth=5;
      context.arc((startNode.y*32)+16, (startNode.x*32)+16, 10, 0,
              (Math.PI/180)*360,false);
      context.stroke();
      context.closePath();

      //draw red circle at end node
      context.beginPath();
      context.strokeStyle="red";
      context.lineWidth=5;
      context.arc((endNode.y*32)+16, (endNode.x*32)+16, 10, 0,
              (Math.PI/180)*360,false);
      context.stroke();
      context.closePath();

      //draw black circles on path
      for (var ctr=0;ctr<result.length-1;ctr++) {
          var node=result[ctr];
          context.beginPath();
          context.strokeStyle="black";
          context.lineWidth=5;
          context.arc((node.y*32)+16, (node.x*32)+16, 10, 0,
                  (Math.PI/180)*360,false);
          context.stroke();
```

```
                context.closePath();
            }


        }

}

</script>

</head>
<body>
<div style="position: absolute; top: 50px; left: 50px;">
<canvas id="canvas" width="500" height="500">
 Your browser does not support the HTML5 Canvas.
</canvas>
</div>
</body>
</html>
```

In Example 8-16 (shown in Figure 8-16), you can see that even though the grass tile increased the total node path value by 1, it was still the shortest path through the maze to the end goal node. This resulted in a path that ran through the grass node. In the next example, Example 8-17, we will add back in the diagonal movement to the node path. By doing so, the tank will avoid the grass node because the A* function will be able to find a path that has a lower total combined node weight than one that travels over the grass tiles.

A* with Node Weights and Diagonals

In Example 8-17 we will add back in the diagonal node capability to see whether this will allow for a path that will bypass the grass tiles. A diagonal will add 1.41 (the square root of 2) to the total node path weight, while a grass tile will add 2. For that reason, adding in the use of diagonals will cost less than moving over grass.

```
//Example 8-17 changes to Example 8-16 to add node weights
var result = astar.search(graph.nodes, start, end, true);
```

After simply adding true back into astar.search(), Figure 8-17 shows that the grass tiles can be avoided because even though a diagonal adds 1.41 to the path cost, that amount is still less than grass tile movement.

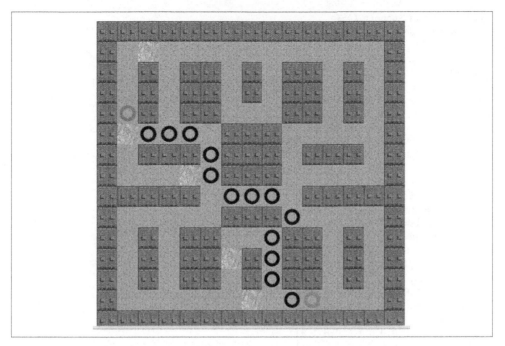

Figure 8-17. A* with grass tiles and diagonals

Wow...just adding in diagonal path node capability changed the node structure of the result path dramatically and allowed us to avoid a path that moves over grass tiles. As a final example, and because this book really is about making cool things happen on the canvas, we are going add the green tank from the tile sheet to the demo and have it follow the A* created path.

Example 8-17. Larger A* Example with grass tiles and diagonal movement

```
<!doctype html>
<html lang="en">
<head>
<meta charset="UTF-8">
<title>Chapter 8 Example 17 - A* with Grass Tiles and Diagonal Moves</title>

<script src="modernizr.js"></script>
<script type='text/javascript' src='graph.js'></script>
<script type='text/javascript' src='astar.js'></script>
<script type="text/javascript">
window.addEventListener('load', eventWindowLoaded, false);
function eventWindowLoaded() {

    canvasApp();

}
```

```
function canvasSupport () {
    return Modernizr.canvas;
}

function canvasApp(){

    if (!canvasSupport()) {
                return;
    }else{
        var theCanvas = document.getElementById('canvas');
        var context = theCanvas.getContext('2d');
    }

  //set up tile map
   var mapRows=15;
   var mapCols=15;
   var tileMap=[
   [0,0,0,0,0,0,0,0,0,0,0,0,0,0,0]
   ,[0,1,2,1,1,1,1,1,1,1,1,1,1,1,0]
   ,[0,1,0,1,0,0,1,0,1,0,0,1,0,1,0]
   ,[0,1,0,1,0,0,1,0,1,0,0,1,0,1,0]
   ,[0,1,0,1,0,0,1,1,1,0,0,1,0,1,0]
   ,[0,2,2,1,1,1,0,0,0,1,1,1,1,1,0]
   ,[0,1,0,0,0,1,0,0,0,1,0,0,0,1,0]
   ,[0,1,1,1,2,1,0,0,0,1,1,1,1,1,0]
   ,[0,0,0,0,0,1,1,1,1,1,0,0,0,0,0]
   ,[0,1,1,1,1,1,0,0,0,1,1,1,1,1,0]
   ,[0,1,0,1,0,0,1,1,1,0,0,1,0,1,0]
   ,[0,1,0,1,0,0,2,0,1,0,0,1,0,1,0]
   ,[0,1,0,1,0,0,1,0,1,0,0,1,0,1,0]
   ,[0,1,1,1,1,1,1,2,1,1,1,1,1,1,0]
   ,[0,0,0,0,0,0,0,0,0,0,0,0,0,0,0]
];

    //set up a* graph
    var graph = new Graph(tileMap);
    var startNode={x:4,y:1}; // use values of map turned on side
    var endNode={x:13,y:10};

    //create node list
    var start = graph.nodes[startNode.x][startNode.y];
    var end = graph.nodes[endNode.x][endNode.y];
    var result = astar.search(graph.nodes, start, end, true);

    //load in tile sheet image
    var tileSheet=new Image();
    tileSheet.addEventListener('load', eventSheetLoaded , false);
    tileSheet.src="tiles.png";

    function eventSheetLoaded() {
            drawScreen()
    }
```

```
function drawScreen() {
    for (var rowCtr=0;rowCtr<mapRows;rowCtr++) {
        for (var colCtr=0;colCtr<mapCols;colCtr++){

            var tileId=tileMap[rowCtr][colCtr];
            var sourceX=Math.floor(tileId % 5) *32;
            var sourceY=Math.floor(tileId / 5) *32;

            context.drawImage(tileSheet, sourceX, sourceY,32,32,
                        colCtr*32,rowCtr*32,32,32);

        }
    }


    //draw green circle at start node
    context.beginPath();
    context.strokeStyle="green";
    context.lineWidth=5;
    context.arc((startNode.y*32)+16, (startNode.x*32)+16, 10, 0,
            (Math.PI/180)*360,false);
    context.stroke();
    context.closePath();

    //draw red circle at end node
    context.beginPath();
    context.strokeStyle="red";
    context.lineWidth=5;
    context.arc((endNode.y*32)+16, (endNode.x*32)+16, 10, 0,
            (Math.PI/180)*360,false);
    context.stroke();
    context.closePath();

    //draw black circles on path
    for (var ctr=0;ctr<result.length-1;ctr++) {
        var node=result[ctr];
        context.beginPath();
        context.strokeStyle="black";
        context.lineWidth=5;
        context.arc((node.y*32)+16, (node.x*32)+16, 10, 0,
                (Math.PI/180)*360,false);
        context.stroke();
        context.closePath();
    }


}

}
```

```
    </script>

</head>
<body>
<div style="position: absolute; top: 50px; left: 50px;">
<canvas id="canvas" width="500" height="500">
 Your browser does not support the HTML5 Canvas.
</canvas>
</div>
</body>
</html>
```

In the final next A* example, Example 8-18, we'll get to the fun part of Canvas and A*. We are going to actually animate and move the tank through the node path.

The full code listing for Example 8-18 follows. We'll explain the more interesting parts after you have taken a look and have had a chance to see the example in action. The movement code combines the animation and transformation code from Chapter 4 with the A* node path result to create a really cool animated implementation of A* path finding.

Example 8-18. Full code listing of A* with tank animation

```
<!doctype html>
<html lang="en">
<head>
<meta charset="UTF-8">
<title>Chapter 8 Example 18 - Larger A* With Tank Animation</title>

<script src="modernizr.js"></script>
<script type='text/javascript' src='graph.js'></script>
<script type='text/javascript' src='astar.js'></script>
<script type="text/javascript">
window.addEventListener('load', eventWindowLoaded, false);
function eventWindowLoaded() {
 canvasApp();
}

function canvasSupport () {
    return Modernizr.canvas;
}

function canvasApp(){

 if (!canvasSupport()) {
   return;
 }else{
   var theCanvas = document.getElementById('canvas');
   var context = theCanvas.getContext('2d');
 }

 var currentNodeIndex=0;
```

```
var nextNode;
var currentNode;
var rowDelta=0;
var colDelta=0;
var tankX=0;
var tankY=0;
var angleInRadians=0;
var tankStarted=false;
var tankMoving=false;
var finishedPath=false;
//set up tile map
var mapRows=15;
var mapCols=15;
var tileMap=[
[0,0,0,0,0,0,0,0,0,0,0,0,0,0,0]
,[0,1,2,1,1,1,1,1,1,1,1,1,1,1,0]
,[0,1,0,1,0,0,1,0,1,0,0,1,0,1,0]
,[0,1,0,1,0,0,1,0,1,0,0,1,0,1,0]
,[0,1,0,1,0,0,1,1,1,0,0,1,0,1,0]
,[0,2,1,1,1,0,0,0,1,1,1,1,1,0]
,[0,1,0,0,0,1,0,0,0,1,0,0,0,1,0]
,[0,1,1,1,2,1,0,0,0,1,1,1,1,1,0]
,[0,0,0,0,0,1,1,1,1,0,0,0,0,0,0]
,[0,1,1,1,1,1,0,0,1,1,1,1,1,1,0]
,[0,1,0,1,0,0,1,1,1,0,0,1,0,1,0]
,[0,1,0,1,0,0,2,0,1,0,0,1,0,1,0]
,[0,1,0,1,0,0,1,0,1,0,0,1,0,1,0]
,[0,1,1,1,1,1,1,2,1,1,1,1,1,1,0]
,[0,0,0,0,0,0,0,0,0,0,0,0,0,0,0]
 ];

//set up a* graph
var graph = new Graph(tileMap);
var startNode={x:4,y:1}; // use values of map turned on side
var endNode={x:13,y:10};

//create node list
var start = graph.nodes[startNode.x][startNode.y];
var end = graph.nodes[endNode.x][endNode.y];
var result = astar.search(graph.nodes, start, end, false);
console.log("result", result);

//load in tile sheet image
var tileSheet=new Image();
tileSheet.addEventListener('load', eventSheetLoaded , false);
tileSheet.src="tiles.png";

const FRAME_RATE=40;
var intervalTime=1000/FRAME_RATE;
function eventSheetLoaded() {
  gameLoop();
}
```

```
function gameLoop() {
  drawScreen();
  window.setTimeout(gameLoop, intervalTime);
}

function drawScreen() {
  for (var rowCtr=0;rowCtr<mapRows;rowCtr++) {
   for (var colCtr=0;colCtr<mapCols;colCtr++){
     var tileId=tileMap[rowCtr][colCtr];
     var sourceX=Math.floor(tileId % 5) *32;
     var sourceY=Math.floor(tileId / 5) *32;
     context.drawImage(tileSheet,sourceX,
         sourceY,32,32,colCtr*32,rowCtr*32,32,32);
   }
   }

//draw green circle at start node
context.beginPath();
context.strokeStyle="green";
context.lineWidth=5;
context.arc((startNode.y*32)+16, (startNode.x*32)+16, 10, 0,(Math.PI/180)*360,false);
context.stroke();
context.closePath();

//draw red circle at end node
context.beginPath();
context.strokeStyle="red";
context.lineWidth=5;
context.arc((endNode.y*32)+16, (endNode.x*32)+16, 10, 0,(Math.PI/180)*360,false);
context.stroke();
context.closePath();

//draw black circles on path
for (var ctr=0;ctr<result.length-1;ctr++) {
  var node=result[ctr];
  context.beginPath();
  context.strokeStyle="black";
  context.lineWidth=5;
  context.arc((node.y*32)+16, (node.x*32)+16, 10, 0,(Math.PI/180)*360,false);
  context.stroke();
  context.closePath();
}

if (!finishedPath) {
  if (!tankStarted) {
   currentNode=startNode;
   tankStarted=true;
   nextNode=result[0];
   tankX=currentNode.x*32;
   tankY=currentNode.y*32
  }
```

```
  if (tankX==nextNode.x*32 && tankY==nextNode.y*32) {
   //node change
   currentNodeIndex++;
   if (currentNodeIndex == result.length) {
     finishedPath=true;
   }
   currentNode=nextNode;
   nextNode=result[currentNodeIndex]
   tankMoving=false;
  }

  if (!finishedPath) {
   if (nextNode.x > currentNode.x) {
     colDelta=1;
   }else if (nextNode.x < currentNode.x) {
     colDelta=-1
   }else{
     colDelta=0
   }

   if (nextNode.y > currentNode.y) {
    rowDelta=1;
   }else if (nextNode.y < currentNode.y) {
     rowDelta=-1
   }else{
     rowDelta=0
   }
   angleInRadians=Math.atan2(colDelta,rowDelta);
   tankMoving=true;

  }
  tankX+=colDelta;
  tankY+=rowDelta;
 }

 var tankSourceX=Math.floor(3 % 5) *32;
 var tankSourceY=Math.floor(3 / 5) *32;
 context.save(); //save current state in stack
 context.setTransform(1,0,0,1,0,0); // reset to identity
 context.translate((tankY)+16,(tankX)+16);
 context.rotate(angleInRadians);
 context.drawImage(tileSheet, tankSourceX, tankSourceY,32,32,-16,-16,32,32);
 context.restore();
 }
}

</script>

</head>
<body>
<div style="position: absolute; top: 50px; left: 50px;">
<canvas id="canvas" width="500" height="500">
```

```
  Your browser does not support the HTML 5 Canvas.
</canvas>
</div>
</body>
</html>
```

Moving a Game Character Along the A* Path

Let's dig deeper into the logic behind Example 8-18. To add a game character to the path, we will need to use the *x* and *y* coordinates returned in the result array from the as tar.search() function. This function does not return the starting point of our path, so we must use the startNode object values for the first node. After that, we can use the nodes from the path to have our tank follow. There is a lot of new code for this example, so let's take it in small pieces, starting with the variable we will need.

Game variables for tank movement and node changes

Here are the variables we'll use for tank movement and node changes:

```
var currentNodeIndex=0;
var nextNode;
var currentNode;
var rowDelta=0;
var colDelta=0;
var tankX=0;
var tankY=0;
var angleInRadians=0;
var tankStarted=false;
var tankMoving=false;
var finishedPath=false;
```

Following are brief descriptions of what these variables do:

currentNodeIndex
:   This will hold the integer of the current node on the path. Because the result array does not contain the entire path, we will need to calculate the location to draw the tank on the starting node in a slightly different manner than when the tank is moving along the A* node path.

nextNode
:   Contains the object values for the next node that the tank is moving *to*.

currentNode
:   Contains the object values for the node the tank is moving *from*.

rowDelta
:   Calculated each time the tank changes nodes. This represents the pixel change on the y-axis for the moving tank.

colDelta

> Calculated each time the tank changes nodes. This represents the pixel change on the x-axis for the moving tank.

tankX

> The current Canvas screen x-axis coordinates used to draw the tank on the screen.

tankY

> The current Canvas screen y-axis coordinate used to draw the tank on the screen.

angleInRadians

> Calculated each time the tank changes nodes. This is the angle that we must rotate the tank so that it is pointing in the right direction as it moves along the node path.

tankStarted

> This remains false until the tank has moved the first time from the starting node. After the tank has moved from the starting node, we can use the result array node values.

tankMoving

> When this is false, the tank has made it to the center of the next node (or the tank has not yet moved from the starting node. The code will calculate new rowDelta, colDelta, and angleInRadians values at this time.

finishedPath

> This is set to true after the tank has moved completely into the final node on the path.

In the drawScreen() function, we are going to add code to test whether or not the tank has started down the path. First we are going to enclose everything but the actual tank drawing code inside the following if conditional:

```
if (!finishedPath) {
//Logic for updating he tank node and position
}
```

Logic for updating the tank node and position

Next we will update the node the tank is positioned on. First we must check to see whether the tank has started moving at all, If not, we will use the result[0] value returned by the A* function.

```
if (!tankStarted) {
 currentNode=startNode;
 tankStarted=true;
 nextNode=result[0];
 tankX=currentNode.x*32;
 tankY=currentNode.y*32
}
```

If the tank is in the first `startNode`, `tankStarted` will be `false`. In this case, we must set `currentNode` to the `startNode` value. `nextNode` will be the first node in the result array node path. The `tankX` and `tankY` coordinates are the path *x* and *y* values (respectively) multiplied by the tile size (32).

Now that the tank is actually moving, we check to determine when it has made it to the center of the next node. We did this the simplest manner possible because each step that the tank takes in any direction will be the value 1.

 If the tank were to move at a speed other than 1, it would be better to calculate the vector between the center of each of the nodes and count the steps in between the nodes. We would then move the tank that number of steps before it stopped to change nodes. Examples of this type of movement are provided in Chapter 5.

```
if (tankX==nextNode.x*32 && tankY==nextNode.y*32) {
 //node change
 currentNodeIndex++;
 if (currentNodeIndex == result.length) {
   finishedPath=true;
 }
 currentNode=nextNode;
 nextNode=result[currentNodeIndex]
 tankMoving=false;
}
```

Next we check to see whether the tank has moved to the center of the next node. We do this by comparing the tank x and y values with the node x and y values. First we add 1 to `currentNodeIndex`. Using that new value, we either stop the tank from moving by setting `finishedPath` to `true`, or we set `currentNode` to be `nextNode`, set `nextNode` to the new node in the result path using `currentNodeIndex`, and we set `tankMoving` to `false`.

When the tank is not moving, we know that we must be at the center of the current node. This requires us to calculate how and where to move the tank to the next node and what angle it should be rotated in.

```
if (!finishedPath) {
 if (nextNode.x > currentNode.x) {
   colDelta=1;
 }else if (nextNode.x < currentNode.x) {
   colDelta=-1
 }else{

   colDelta=0
 }
 if (nextNode.y > currentNode.y) {
```

```
      rowDelta=1;
    }else if (nextNode.y < currentNode.y) {
      rowDelta=-1
    }else{
      rowDelta=0
    }
    angleInRadians=Math.atan2(colDelta,rowDelta);
    tankMoving=true;
  }
```

If the x value of `nextNode` is greater than the x value of `currentNode`, the tank will need to move to the right. If the opposite is true, the tank will move to the left. If the x values are equal, there will be no movement on the x-axis.

If the y value of `nextNode` is greater than the y value of `currentNode`, the tank will need to move down. If the opposite is true, the tank will move up. If the y values are equal, there will be no movement on the y-axis.

After we have calculated the `rowDelta` and `colDelta` values, we can use those to find the angle to rotate the tank. This is accomplished by passing them into the `Mathy.atan2` function. Notice that we swap the normal y,x (row, col) in the `atan2` function with x,y (col,row) to match the screen coordinates for our tile map rather than the `astar.search()` returned coordinates. This goes back to the tile map being laid out in rows of columns rather than columns of rows (the way the *graph.as* uses them).

Finally, if the tank has not finished its path, we need to add the `colDelta` value to *the* `tankX` position and the `rowDelta` value to the `tankY` position:

```
tankX+=colDelta;
tankY+=rowDelta;
```

Drawing the tank on the screen

This is a review of the discussion in Chapter 4 about using the Canvas transformations to rotate the tank to the correct angle based on the `angleInRadians` value we have stored on each node change:

```
var tankSourceX=Math.floor(3 % 5) *32;
var tankSourceY=Math.floor(3 / 5) *32;
context.save(); //save current state in stack
context.setTransform(1,0,0,1,0,0); // reset to identity
context.translate((tankY)+16,(tankX)+16);
context.rotate(angleInRadians);
context.drawImage(tileSheet, tankSourceX, tankSourceY,32,32,-16,-16,32,32);
context.restore();
```

First, we find the tile location of the tile sheet (top-left corner) of the tank tile and place those values into the `tankSourceX` and `tankSourceY` variables. Next we save the current canvas to the stack and reset the transformation matrix to the reset identity. We then translate the entire canvas to the center of the current node (tile) and rotate it using the angleInRadians value. The image is then drawn to the Canvas as if the drawing pen is sitting at 0,0. To draw the tank in the center, we must offset –16 on each.

Figure 8-18 shows the tank following the path created in Example 8-18. If we change var result = astar.search(graph.nodes, start, end, false) to var result = astar.search(graph.nodes, start, end, true), we will get the result shown in Figure 8-19. The path will actually take the tank diagonally through walls, so if you plan to use the true (use diagonal path node) parameter, you will want to take this into consideration when you are creating your tile maps. An extra block at that intersection would prevent the tank from moving through that path, as can be seen in Figure 8-20.

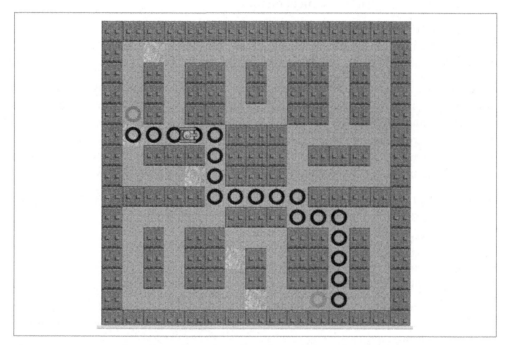

Figure 8-18. A* tank moving through path with no diagonal nodes

Tanks That Pass Through Walls?

In Example 8-19, we are going to demonstrate how a poorly designed tile map can allow for a node path to seemingly go through solid walls when diagonal movement is allow. Figure 8-19 shows this occurring. Here is the full code listing for Example 8-19.

Example 8-19. Maze design with tank going through walls

```
<!doctype html>
<html lang="en">
<head>
```

```
<meta charset="UTF-8">
<title>Chapter 8 Example 19 - A* With Tank Animation with diagoinal moves</title>

<script src="modernizr.js"></script>
<script type='text/javascript' src='graph.js'></script>
<script type='text/javascript' src='astar.js'></script>
<script type="text/javascript">
window.addEventListener('load', eventWindowLoaded, false);
function eventWindowLoaded() {

    canvasApp();

}

function canvasSupport () {
    return Modernizr.canvas;
}

function canvasApp(){

    if (!canvasSupport()) {
                return;
    }else{
        var theCanvas = document.getElementById('canvas');
        var context = theCanvas.getContext('2d');
    }

    var currentNodeIndex=0;
    var nextNode;
    var currentNode;
    var rowDelta=0;
    var colDelta=0;
    var tankX=0;
    var tankY=0;
    var angleInRadians=0;
    var tankStarted=false;
    var tankMoving=false;
    var finishedPath=false;
  //set up tile map
  var mapRows=15;
  var mapCols=15;
  var tileMap=[
  [0,0,0,0,0,0,0,0,0,0,0,0,0,0,0]
  ,[0,1,2,1,1,1,1,1,1,1,1,1,1,1,0]
  ,[0,1,0,1,0,0,1,0,1,0,0,1,0,1,0]
  ,[0,1,0,1,0,0,1,0,1,0,0,1,0,1,0]
  ,[0,1,0,1,0,0,1,1,1,0,0,1,0,1,0]
  ,[0,2,1,1,1,1,0,0,0,1,1,1,1,1,0]
  ,[0,1,0,0,0,1,0,0,0,1,0,0,0,1,0]
  ,[0,1,1,1,1,2,1,0,0,0,1,1,1,1,0]
  ,[0,0,0,0,0,0,1,1,1,1,1,0,0,0,0]
  ,[0,1,1,1,1,1,0,0,0,1,1,1,1,1,0]
  ,[0,1,0,1,0,0,1,1,1,0,0,1,0,1,0]
```

```
        ,[0,1,0,1,0,0,2,0,1,0,0,1,0,1,0]
        ,[0,1,0,1,0,0,1,0,1,0,0,1,0,1,0]
        ,[0,1,1,1,1,1,1,2,1,1,1,1,1,1,0]
        ,[0,0,0,0,0,0,0,0,0,0,0,0,0,0,0]
];

    //set up a* graph
    var graph = new Graph(tileMap);
    var startNode={x:4,y:1}; // use values of map turned on side
    var endNode={x:13,y:10};

    //create node list
    var start = graph.nodes[startNode.x][startNode.y];
    var end = graph.nodes[endNode.x][endNode.y];
    var result = astar.search(graph.nodes, start, end, true);
    console.log("result", result);
    //load in tile sheet image
    var tileSheet=new Image();
    tileSheet.addEventListener('load', eventSheetLoaded , false);
    tileSheet.src="tiles.png";

    const FRAME_RATE=40;
    var intervalTime=1000/FRAME_RATE;

        function eventSheetLoaded() {
        gameLoop();
    }

function gameLoop() {
        drawScreen()
        window.setTimeout(gameLoop, intervalTime);
}

function drawScreen() {
        for (var rowCtr=0;rowCtr<mapRows;rowCtr++) {
            for (var colCtr=0;colCtr<mapCols;colCtr++){

                    var tileId=tileMap[rowCtr][colCtr];
                    var sourceX=Math.floor(tileId % 5) *32;
                    var sourceY=Math.floor(tileId / 5) *32;
                    context.drawImage(tileSheet, sourceX, sourceY,32,32,
                                    colCtr*32,rowCtr*32,32,32);
            }
        }

        //draw green circle at start node
        context.beginPath();
        context.strokeStyle="green";
        context.lineWidth=5;
        context.arc((startNode.y*32)+16, (startNode.x*32)+16, 10, 0,
                (Math.PI/180)*360,false);
        context.stroke();
```

```
context.closePath();

//draw red circle at end node
context.beginPath();
context.strokeStyle="red";
context.lineWidth=5;
context.arc((endNode.y*32)+16, (endNode.x*32)+16, 10, 0,
            (Math.PI/180)*360,false);
context.stroke();
context.closePath();

//draw black circles on path
for (var ctr=0;ctr<result.length-1;ctr++) {
    var node=result[ctr];
    context.beginPath();
    context.strokeStyle="black";
    context.lineWidth=5;
    context.arc((node.y*32)+16, (node.x*32)+16, 10, 0,
                (Math.PI/180)*360,false);
    context.stroke();
    context.closePath();
}

if (!finishedPath) {
    if (!tankStarted) {
            currentNode=startNode;
            tankStarted=true;
            nextNode=result[0];
            tankX=currentNode.x*32;
            tankY=currentNode.y*32
    }

    if (tankX==nextNode.x*32 &&  tankY==nextNode.y*32) {
            //node change
            currentNodeIndex++;
            if (currentNodeIndex == result.length) {
                    finishedPath=true;
            }
            currentNode=nextNode;
            nextNode=result[currentNodeIndex]
            tankMoving=false;
    }

    if (!finishedPath) {

            if (nextNode.x > currentNode.x) {
                colDelta=1;
            }else if (nextNode.x < currentNode.x) {
                colDelta=-1
            }else{
                colDelta=0
            }
```

```
                    if (nextNode.y > currentNode.y) {
                        rowDelta=1;
                    }else if (nextNode.y < currentNode.y) {
                        rowDelta=-1
                    }else{
                        rowDelta=0
                    }

                    angleInRadians=Math.atan2(colDelta,rowDelta);
                    tankMoving=true;
                }


            tankX+=colDelta;
            tankY+=rowDelta;
        }

        var tankSourceX=Math.floor(3 % 5) *32;
        var tankSourceY=Math.floor(3 / 5) *32;
        context.save(); //save current state in stack
        context.setTransform(1,0,0,1,0,0); // reset to identity
        context.translate((tankY)+16,(tankX)+16);
        context.rotate(angleInRadians);
        context.drawImage(tileSheet, tankSourceX, tankSourceY,
                        32,32,-16,-16,32,32);
        context.restore();

    }

}

</script>

</head>
<body>
<div style="position: absolute; top: 50px; left: 50px;">
<canvas id="canvas" width="500" height="500">
 Your browser does not support the HTML 5 Canvas.
</canvas>
</div>
</body>
</html>
```

Figure 8-19 demonstrates Example 8-19. The poorly designed tile map with diagonal node paths turned on results in a path where the tank can move through the walls. In the next example, we will fix this problem with a new tile map.

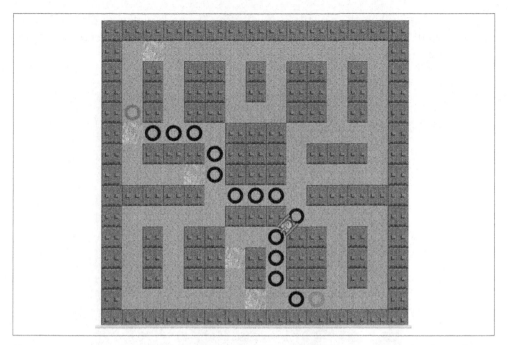

Figure 8-19. A* tank moving through path with diagonal and possible pass through

In Example 8-20, we will modify the maze to add an extra block at the intersection where the tank passed through the walls with a diagonal path. Here is the new tile map for Example 8-20:

```
var mapCols=15;
var tileMap=[
[0,0,0,0,0,0,0,0,0,0,0,0,0,0,0]
,[0,1,2,1,1,1,1,1,1,1,1,1,1,1,0]
,[0,1,0,1,0,0,1,0,1,0,0,1,0,1,0]
,[0,1,0,1,0,0,1,0,1,0,0,1,0,1,0]
,[0,1,0,1,0,0,1,1,1,0,0,1,0,1,0]
,[0,2,1,1,1,1,0,0,0,1,1,1,1,1,0]
,[0,1,0,0,0,1,0,0,0,1,0,0,0,1,0]
,[0,1,1,1,2,1,0,0,0,1,1,1,1,1,0]
,[0,0,0,0,0,1,1,1,1,1,0,0,0,0,0]
,[0,1,1,1,1,1,0,0,0,1,1,1,1,1,0]
,[0,1,0,1,0,0,1,1,1,0,0,1,0,1,0]
,[0,1,0,1,0,0,2,0,0,0,0,1,0,1,0]
,[0,1,0,1,0,0,1,0,1,0,0,1,0,1,0]
,[0,1,1,1,1,1,1,2,1,1,1,1,1,1,0]
,[0,0,0,0,0,0,0,0,0,0,0,0,0,0,0]
];
```

Figure 8-20 shows how the new tile map will affect the node path with diagonal movement applied. The new tiles will block the diagonal path through the *seemingly* impassable walls and create *real* impassable diagonal walls.

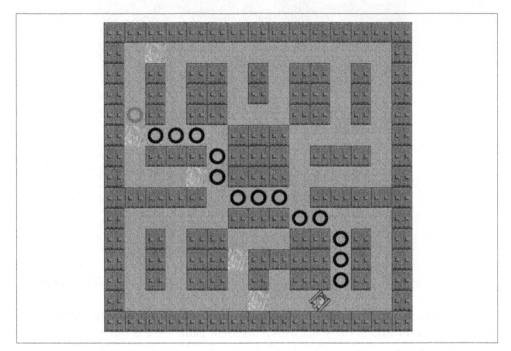

Figure 8-20. A* tank moving through the maze, with added walls to create impassible diagonal barriers

Example 8-20. New maze design with impassable walls

```
<!doctype html>
<html lang="en">
<head>
<meta charset="UTF-8">
<title>Chapter 8 Example 20 - A* With Tank Animation with new maze to prevent
        passable walls </title>

<script src="modernizr.js"></script>
<script type='text/javascript' src='graph.js'></script>
<script type='text/javascript' src='astar.js'></script>
<script type="text/javascript">
window.addEventListener('load', eventWindowLoaded, false);
function eventWindowLoaded() {

    canvasApp();
}
```

```
function canvasSupport () {
    return Modernizr.canvas;
}

function canvasApp(){

    if (!canvasSupport()) {
            return;
    }else{
        var theCanvas = document.getElementById('canvas');
        var context = theCanvas.getContext('2d');
    }

    var currentNodeIndex=0;
    var nextNode;
    var currentNode;
    var rowDelta=0;
    var colDelta=0;
    var tankX=0;
    var tankY=0;
    var angleInRadians=0;
    var tankStarted=false;
    var tankMoving=false;
    var finishedPath=false;
//set up tile map
 var mapRows=15;
 var mapCols=15;
 var tileMap=[
 [0,0,0,0,0,0,0,0,0,0,0,0,0,0,0]
,[0,1,2,1,1,1,1,1,1,1,1,1,1,1,0]
,[0,1,0,1,0,0,1,0,1,0,0,1,0,1,0]
,[0,1,0,1,0,0,1,0,1,0,0,1,0,1,0]
,[0,1,0,1,0,0,1,1,1,0,0,1,0,1,0]
,[0,2,1,1,1,0,0,0,1,1,1,1,1,1,0]
,[0,1,0,0,0,1,0,0,0,1,0,0,0,1,0]
,[0,1,1,1,2,1,0,0,0,1,1,1,1,1,0]
,[0,0,0,0,0,1,1,1,1,1,0,0,0,0,0]
,[0,1,1,1,1,1,0,0,0,1,1,1,1,1,0]
,[0,1,0,1,0,0,1,1,1,0,0,1,0,1,0]
,[0,1,0,1,0,0,2,0,0,0,0,1,0,1,0]
,[0,1,0,1,0,0,1,0,1,0,0,1,0,1,0]
,[0,1,1,1,1,1,1,2,1,1,1,1,1,1,0]
,[0,0,0,0,0,0,0,0,0,0,0,0,0,0,0]
];

    //set up a* graph
    var graph = new Graph(tileMap);
    var startNode={x:4,y:1}; // use values of map turned on side
    var endNode={x:13,y:10};

    //create node list
    var start = graph.nodes[startNode.x][startNode.y];
```

```
var end = graph.nodes[endNode.x][endNode.y];
var result = astar.search(graph.nodes, start, end, true);
console.log("result", result);
//load in tile sheet image
var tileSheet=new Image();
tileSheet.addEventListener('load', eventSheetLoaded , false);
tileSheet.src="tiles.png";

const FRAME_RATE=40;
var intervalTime=1000/FRAME_RATE;

    function eventSheetLoaded() {
    gameLoop();
}

function gameLoop() {
    drawScreen()
    window.setTimeout(gameLoop, intervalTime);
}

function drawScreen() {
    for (var rowCtr=0;rowCtr<mapRows;rowCtr++) {
        for (var colCtr=0;colCtr<mapCols;colCtr++){

            var tileId=tileMap[rowCtr][colCtr];
            var sourceX=Math.floor(tileId % 5) *32;
            var sourceY=Math.floor(tileId / 5) *32;
            context.drawImage(tileSheet, sourceX, sourceY,32,32,
                        colCtr*32,rowCtr*32,32,32);
        }
    }

    //draw green circle at start node
    context.beginPath();
    context.strokeStyle="green";
    context.lineWidth=5;
    context.arc((startNode.y*32)+16, (startNode.x*32)+16, 10, 0,
            (Math.PI/180)*360,false);
    context.stroke();
    context.closePath();

    //draw red circle at end node
    context.beginPath();
    context.strokeStyle="red";
    context.lineWidth=5;
    context.arc((endNode.y*32)+16, (endNode.x*32)+16, 10, 0,
            (Math.PI/180)*360,false);
    context.stroke();
    context.closePath();

    //draw black circles on path
    for (var ctr=0;ctr<result.length-1;ctr++) {
```

```
        var node=result[ctr];
        context.beginPath();
        context.strokeStyle="black";
        context.lineWidth=5;
        context.arc((node.y*32)+16, (node.x*32)+16, 10, 0,
                    (Math.PI/180)*360,false);
        context.stroke();
        context.closePath();
}

if (!finishedPath) {
    if (!tankStarted) {
            currentNode=startNode;
            tankStarted=true;
            nextNode=result[0];
            tankX=currentNode.x*32;
            tankY=currentNode.y*32
    }

    if (tankX==nextNode.x*32 &&  tankY==nextNode.y*32) {
            //node change
            currentNodeIndex++;
            if (currentNodeIndex == result.length) {
                  finishedPath=true;
            }
            currentNode=nextNode;
            nextNode=result[currentNodeIndex]
            tankMoving=false;
    }

    if (!finishedPath) {

            if (nextNode.x > currentNode.x) {
                colDelta=1;
            }else if (nextNode.x < currentNode.x) {
                colDelta=-1
            }else{
                colDelta=0
            }

            if (nextNode.y > currentNode.y) {
                rowDelta=1;
            }else if (nextNode.y < currentNode.y) {
                rowDelta=-1
            }else{
                rowDelta=0
            }

            angleInRadians=Math.atan2(colDelta,rowDelta);
            tankMoving=true;
    }
```

```
                tankX+=colDelta;
                tankY+=rowDelta;
            }

        var tankSourceX=Math.floor(3 % 5) *32;
        var tankSourceY=Math.floor(3 / 5) *32;
        context.save(); //save current state in stack
        context.setTransform(1,0,0,1,0,0); // reset to identity
        context.translate((tankY)+16,(tankX)+16);
        context.rotate(angleInRadians);
        context.drawImage(tileSheet, tankSourceX, tankSourceY,
                          32,32,-16,-16,32,32);
        context.restore();


    }
}

</script>

</head>
<body>
<div style="position: absolute; top: 50px; left: 50px;">
<canvas id="canvas" width="500" height="500">
 Your browser does not support the HTML5 Canvas.
</canvas>
</div>
</body>
</html>
```

We have now covered some basic, intermediate, and more advanced topics on A* path finding. These are easy to apply to any tile-based application where you need to find the shortest path between two points.

What's Next?

We covered quite a bit in this chapter. HTML5 Canvas might lack some of the more refined features common to web game development platforms such as Flash, but it contains powerful tools for manipulating the screen in immediate mode. These features allow us to create a game application with many individual logical display objects—even though each canvas can support only a single physical display object (the canvas itself). We also covered a more advanced topic of tile-based path finding on a 2D map using the A* algorithm.

In Chapter 9, we will explore some more advanced game topics, such as replacing paths with bitmap images, creating object pools, and adding a sound manager. We'll extend the game we built in this chapter and create a new turn-based strategy game, and we'll cover scrolling a tile-based game screen.

Canvas Games: Part II

Geo Blaster Basic was constructed using pure paths for drawing. In its creation, we began to cover some game-application-related topics, such as basic collision detection and state machines. In this chapter, we focus on using bitmaps and tile sheets for our game graphics, and we add sound, using techniques introduced in Chapter 7.

Along the way, we update the `FrameRateCounter` from Chapter 8 by adding in a step timer. We also examine how we can eliminate the use of a tile sheet for rotations by precreating an array of `imageData` instances using the `getImageData()` and `putImage Data()` Canvas functions.

In the second half of this chapter, we create another small turn-based strategy game using bitmaps. This game is roughly based on the classic computer game, *Daleks*.

Geo Blaster Extended

We create a new game, *Geo Blaster Extended*, by adding bitmaps and sound to the *Geo Blaster Basic* game from Chapter 8. Much of the game logic is the same, but adding bitmaps to replace paths enables us to optimize the game for rendering. Optimized rendering is very important when you are targeting limited-processor devices, such as mobile phones. We also add sound to *Geo Blaster Extended* and apply an object pool to the particles used for game explosions. Figure 9-1 shows an example screen of the finished game.

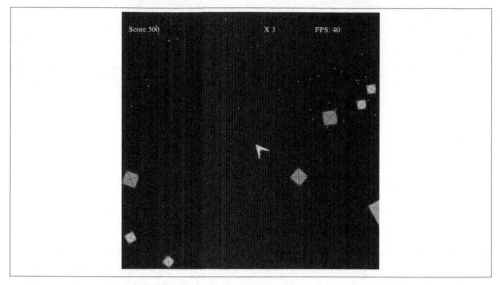

Figure 9-1. Geo Blaster Extended

First, let's look at the tile sheets we will use for our new game.

Geo Blaster Tile Sheet

In Chapter 4, we examined applying bitmap graphics to the canvas, and we explored using tile sheet methods to render images. In Chapter 8, we drew all our game graphics as paths and transformed them on the fly. In this chapter, we apply the concepts from Chapter 4 to optimizing the rendering of the *Geo Blaster Basic* game. We do this by prerendering all our game graphics and transformations as bitmaps. We then use these bitmaps instead of paths and the immediate-mode transformations that were necessary in Chapter 8 to create *Geo Blaster Extended*.

Figure 9-2 shows one of the tile sheets we use for this game (*ship_tiles.png*).

These tiles are the 36 rotations for our player ship. We are canning the rotations in a tile sheet to avoid spending processor cycles transforming them on each frame tick as we draw them to the canvas.

Figure 9-2. The ship_tiles.png tile sheet

Figure 9-3 shows a second set of tiles for the ship with the thruster firing (*ship_tiles2.png*). We use this set to depict the ship when the user is pressing the up arrow key.

Figure 9-3. The ship_tiles2.png tile sheet

The next three sets of tiles are for the rocks the player will destroy. We have three sheets for these: *largerocks.png* (Figure 9-4), *mediumrocks.png* (Figure 9-5), and *small rocks.png* (Figure 9-6).

Figure 9-4. The largerocks.png tile sheet

Figure 9-5. The mediumrocks.png tile sheet

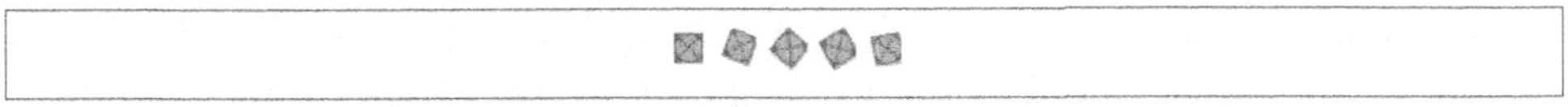

Figure 9-6. The smallrocks.png tile sheet

These three tile sheets need to be only five tiles each. Because the rock is a square, we can simply repeat the five frames to simulate rotation in either the clockwise or counterclockwise direction.

The saucer that attempts to shoot the player is a single tile, *saucer.png*, shown in Figure 9-7.

Figure 9-7. The saucer.png tile

Finally, *parts.png* (Figure 9-8) is a tiny 8×2 tile sheet that contains four 2×2 particle tiles. These are used for the explosions and missiles the player and the saucer fire.

Figure 9-8. The parts.png tile sheet

You cannot see the colors in a black-and-white printed book, but you can view them by downloading the files from this book's website. The first tile is green, and it is used for the small rock and saucer explosions. The second tile is light blue, and it depicts the player's missiles and the player explosion. The third tile is reddish pink (salmon, if you will), and it illustrates the large rock explosions. The final, purple tile is used for the medium rock explosions.

Now that we have our tiles in place, let's look at the methods we'll use to transform *Geo Blaster Basic*'s immediate-mode path, rendering it to *Geo Blaster Extended*'s tile-based bitmap.

Refresher: Calculating the tile source location

In Chapter 4, we examined the method to calculate a tile's location on a tile sheet if we know the single-dimension ID of that tile. Let's briefly look back at this, because it is reused to render all the tiles for the games in this chapter.

Given that we have a tile sheet such as *ship_tiles.png*, we can locate the tile we want to display with a simple math trick.

ship_tiles.png is a 36-tile animation with the player ship starting in the 0-degree angle, or pointing-right direction. Each of the remaining 35 tiles displays the ship rotating in 10-degree increments.

If we would like to display tile 19 (the ship pointing to the left, or in the 190-degree angle), we first need to find the x and y coordinates for the top-left corner of the tile by calculating sourceX and sourceY.

Here is pseudocode for the sourceX calculation:

```
sourceX = integer(current_frame_index modulo
the_number_columns_in_the_tilesheet) * tile_width
```

The modulo (%) operator returns the remainder of the division calculation. Following is the actual code (with variables replaced with literals) we use for this calculation:

```
var sourceX = Math.floor(19 % 10) *32;
```

The result is x = 9*32 = 288;.

The calculation for the `sourceY` value is similar, except we divide rather than use the modulo operator:

```
sourceY = integer(current_frame_index divided by
the_number_columns_in_the_tilesheet) *tile_height
```

Here's the actual code we use for this calculation:

```
var sourceY = Math.floor(19 / 10) *32;
```

This works out to y = 1*32 = 32;. Therefore, the top-left location on the *ship_tiles.png* from which to start copying pixels is 288,32.

To copy this to the canvas, we use this statement:

```
context.drawImage(shipTiles, sourceX, sourceY,32,32,player.x,player.y,32,32);
```

In Chapter 8, we needed quite a lot of code to draw and translate the player ship at the current rotation. When we use a tile sheet, this code is reduced considerably.

Here is the code we use to render the player ship. It replaces the `renderPlayer()` function in Example 8-12 in Chapter 8:

```
function renderPlayerShip(x,y,rotation, scale) {
    //transformation
    context.save(); //save current state in stack
    context.globalAlpha = parseFloat(player.alpha);
    var angleInRadians = rotation * Math.PI / 180;
    var sourceX = Math.floor((player.rotation/10) % 10) * 32;
    var sourceY = Math.floor((player.rotation/10) /10) *32;
    if (player.thrust){
        context.drawImage(shipTiles2, sourceX, sourceY, 32, 32,
            player.x,player.y,32,32);
    }else{
        context.drawImage(shipTiles, sourceX, sourceY, 32, 32,
            player.x,player.y,32,32);
    }

    //restore context
    context.restore(); //pop old state on to screen

    context.globalAlpha = 1;

}
```

 You can find the entire source code for *Geo Blaster Extended* (Example A-2) in Appendix A.

The renderPlayer() function divides the player.rotation by 10 to determine which of the 36 tiles in the shipTiles image instance to display on the canvas. If the player is in thrust mode, the shipTiles2 image is used instead of shipTiles.

This works because we have set the ship to rotate by 10 degrees with each press of the left or right arrow key. In the Chapter 8 version of the game, we set this to 5 degrees. If we had created a 72-frame tile sheet, with the player ship rotated in 5-degree increments, we could have kept the player.rotationalVelocity at 5. For *Geo Blaster Extended*, we drew only 36 tiles for the player ship, so we are using the value 10 for the rotational velocity. We certainly could use 72 or even 360 frames for the player ship rotation tiles. This is limited only by creative imagination (and patience with a drawing tool).

Let's look at the rotationalVelocity value assigned earlier in the gameStateNew Game() function:

```
function gameStateNewGame(){
    ConsoleLog.log("gameStateNewGame")
    //setup new game
    level = 0;
    score = 0;
    playerShips = 3;
    player.maxVelocity = 5;
    player.width = 32;
    player.height = 32;
    player.halfWidth = 16;
    player.halfHeight = 16;
    player.hitWidth = 24;
    player.hitHeight = 24;
    player.rotationalVelocity = 10; //how many degrees to turn the ship
    player.thrustAcceleration = .05;
    player.missileFrameDelay = 5;
    player.thrust = false;
    player.alpha = 1;
    player.rotation = 0;
    player.x = 0;
    player.y = 0;

    fillBackground();
    renderScoreBoard();
    switchGameState(GAME_STATE_NEW_LEVEL)

}
```

Other new player attributes

Along with the change in the rotational velocity, we have also modified the player's width and height attributes. These are both now 32, which is the same as the tile width and height. If you look at the first frame of the *ship_tiles.png* tile sheet, you see that the player ship does not fill the entire 32×32 tile. It is centered in the middle, taking up roughly 24×24 of the tile, which leaves enough space around the edges of the tile to eliminate clipping when the ship is rotated. We also used this concept when we created the rock rotations.

The extra pixels of padding added to eliminate clipping during frame rotation pose a small problem for collision detection. In the Chapter 8 version of the game, we used the width and height values for bounding box collision detection. We will not use those values in this new version because we have created two new variables to use for collision detection: hitWidth and hitHeight. Instead of setting these values to 32, they are 24. This new, smaller value makes our collision detection more accurate than if we used the entire tile width and height.

The new boundingBoxCollide() algorithm

All the other game objects also have new hitWidth and hitHeight attributes. We modify the boundingBoxCollide() function from *Geo Blaster Basic* to use these new values for all collision testing:

```
function boundingBoxCollide(object1, object2) {

    var left1 = object1.x;
    var left2 = object2.x;
    var right1 = object1.x + object1.hitWidth;
    var right2 = object2.x + object2.hitWidth;
    var top1 = object1.y;
    var top2 = object2.y;
    var bottom1 = object1.y + object1.hitHeight;
    var bottom2 = object2.y + object2.hitHeight;

    if (bottom1 < top2) return(false);
    if (top1 > bottom2) return(false);

    if (right1 < left2) return(false);
    if (left1 > right2) return(false);

    return(true);

}
```

Next, we take a quick look at how we use these same ideas to render the rest of the game objects with the new tile sheets.

Rendering the Other Game Objects

The rocks, saucers, missiles, and particles are all rendered in a manner similar to the method implemented for the player ship. Let's first look at the code for the saucer's render function.

Rendering the saucers

The saucers do not have a multiple-cell tile sheet, but to be consistent, we render them as though they do. This allows us to add more animation tiles for the saucers later:

```
function renderSaucers() {
    var tempSaucer = {};
    var saucerLength = saucers.length-1;
    for (var saucerCtr=saucerLength;saucerCtr>=0;saucerCtr--){
        //ConsoleLog.log("saucer: " + saucerCtr);
        tempSaucer = saucers[saucerCtr];

        context.save(); //save current state in stack
        var sourceX = 0;
        var sourceY = 0;
        context.drawImage(saucerTiles, sourceX, sourceY, 30, 15,
        tempSaucer.x,tempSaucer.y,30,15);
        context.restore(); //pop old state on to screen
    }
}
```

There is no need to calculate the `sourceX` and `sourceY` values for the saucer because the saucer is only a single tile. In this instance, we can just set them to 0. We have hardcoded the `saucer.width` (30) and `saucer.height` (15) as an example, but with all the rest of the game objects, we use the object `width` and `height` attributes rather than literals.

Next, let's look at the rock rendering, which varies slightly from both the player ship and the saucers.

Rendering the rocks

The rock tiles are contained inside three tile sheets based on their size (large, medium, and small), and we have used only five tiles for each rock. The rocks are square with a symmetrical pattern, so we only need to precreate a single quarter-turn rotation for each of the three sizes.

Here is the `renderRocks()` function. Notice that we must switch based on the scale of the rock (1=large, 2=medium, 3=small) to choose the right tile sheet to render:

```
function renderRocks() {
    var tempRock = {};
    var rocksLength = rocks.length-1;
    for (var rockCtr=rocksLength;rockCtr>=0;rockCtr--){
    context.save(); //save current state in stack
    tempRock = rocks[rockCtr];
    var sourceX = Math.floor((tempRock.rotation) % 5) * tempRock.width;
    var sourceY = Math.floor((tempRock.rotation) /5) *tempRock.height;

    switch(tempRock.scale){
        case 1:
        context.drawImage(largeRockTiles, sourceX, sourceY,
          tempRock.width,tempRock.height,tempRock.x,tempRock.y,
```

```
        tempRock.width,tempRock.height);
        break;
        case 2:
        context.drawImage(mediumRockTiles, sourceX,
          sourceY,tempRock.width,tempRock.height,tempRock.x,tempRock.y,
          tempRock.width,tempRock.height);
        break;
        case 3:
        context.drawImage(smallRockTiles, sourceX,
          sourceY,tempRock.width,tempRock.height,tempRock.x,tempRock.y,
          tempRock.width,tempRock.height);
        break;

    }

    context.restore(); //pop old state on to screen

    }
  }
```

In the `renderRocks()` function, we are no longer using the `rock.rotation` attribute as the angle of rotation as we did in *Geo Blaster Basic*. Instead, we have repurposed the `rotation` attribute to represent the tile ID (0–4) of the current tile on the tile sheet to render.

In the Chapter 8 version, we could simulate faster or slower speeds for the rock rotations by simply giving each rock a random `rotationInc` value. This value, either negative for counterclockwise or positive for clockwise, was added to the `rotation` attribute on each frame. In this new tilesheet-based version, we only have five frames of animation, so we don't want to skip frames because it will look choppy. Instead, we are going to add two new attributes to each rock: `animationCount` and `animationDelay`.

The `animationDelay` represents the number of frames between each tile change for a given rock. The `animationCount` variable restarts at 0 after each tile frame change and increases by 1 on each subsequent frame tick. When `animationCount` is greater than `animationDelay`, the `rock.rotation` value is increased (clockwise) or decreased (counterclockwise). Here is the new code in our `updateRocks()` function:

```
    tempRock.animationCount++;
      if (tempRock.animationCount > tempRock.animationDelay){
        tempRock.animationCount = 0;
        tempRock.rotation += tempRock.rotationInc;        if (tempRock.rotation > 4){
          tempRock.rotation = 0;
        }else if (tempRock.rotation <0){
          tempRock.rotation = 4;
        }
      }
```

Notice that we have hardcoded the values 4 and 0 into the tile ID maximum and minimum checks. We could have just as easily used a constant or two variables for this purpose.

Rendering the missiles

Both the player missiles and saucer missiles are rendered in the same manner. For each, we simply need to know the tile ID on the four-tile `particleTiles` image representing the tile we want to display. For the player missiles, this tile ID is 1; for the saucer missile, the tile ID is 0.

Let's take a quick look at both of these functions:

```
function renderPlayerMissiles() {
    var tempPlayerMissile = {};
    var playerMissileLength = playerMissiles.length-1;
    //ConsoleLog.log("render playerMissileLength=" + playerMissileLength);
    for (var playerMissileCtr=playerMissileLength; playerMissileCtr>=0;
     playerMissileCtr--){

    //ConsoleLog.log("draw player missile " + playerMissileCtr)
    tempPlayerMissile = playerMissiles[playerMissileCtr];
    context.save(); //save current state in stack
    var sourceX = Math.floor(1 % 4) * tempPlayerMissile.width;
    var sourceY = Math.floor(1 / 4) * tempPlayerMissile.height;

    context.drawImage(particleTiles, sourceX, sourceY,
     tempPlayerMissile.width,tempPlayerMissile.height,
     tempPlayerMissile.x,tempPlayerMissile.y,tempPlayerMissile.width,
     tempPlayerMissile.height);

    context.restore(); //pop old state on to screen
    }
    }

function renderSaucerMissiles() {
    var tempSaucerMissile = {};
    var saucerMissileLength = saucerMissiles.length-1;
    //ConsoleLog.log("saucerMissiles= " + saucerMissiles.length)
    for (var saucerMissileCtr=saucerMissileLength;
    saucerMissileCtr >= 0;saucerMissileCtr--){
    //ConsoleLog.log("draw player missile " + playerMissileCtr)
    tempSaucerMissile = saucerMissiles[saucerMissileCtr];
    context.save(); //save current state in stack
    var sourceX = Math.floor(0 % 4) * tempSaucerMissile.width;
    var sourceY = Math.floor(0 / 4) * tempSaucerMissile.height;

    context.drawImage(particleTiles, sourceX, sourceY,
     tempSaucerMissile.width,tempSaucerMissile.height,
     tempSaucerMissile.x,tempSaucerMissile.y,tempSaucerMissile.width,
     tempSaucerMissile.height);
```

```
        context.restore(); //pop old state on to screen

    }
  }
```

The particle explosion is also rendered using a bitmap tile sheet, and its code is very similar to the code for the projectiles. Let's examine the particles next.

Rendering the particles

The particles will use the same four-tile *parts.png* file (as shown in Figure 9-8) that rendered the projectiles. The *Geo Blaster Basic* game from Chapter 8 used only a single white particle for all explosions. We replace the `createExplode()` function from this previous game with a new one that can use a different-colored particle for each type of explosion. This way, the rocks, saucers, and player ship can all have uniquely colored explosions.

The new `createExplode()` function handles this by adding a final `type` parameter to its parameter list. Let's look at the code:

```
function createExplode(x,y,num,type) {

    playSound(SOUND_EXPLODE,.5);
    for (var partCtr=0;partCtr<num;partCtr++){
       if (particlePool.length > 0){
          newParticle = particlePool.pop();
       newParticle.dx = Math.random()*3;
       if (Math.random()<.5){
          newParticle.dx *= -1;
       }
       newParticle.dy = Math.random()*3;
       if (Math.random()<.5){
       newParticle.dy *= -1;
       }

       newParticle.life = Math.floor(Math.random()*30+30);
       newParticle.lifeCtr = 0;
       newParticle.x = x;
       newParticle.width = 2;
       newParticle.height = 2;
       newParticle.y = y;
       newParticle.type = type;
       //ConsoleLog.log("newParticle.life=" + newParticle.life);
       particles.push(newParticle);
       }

    }

}
```

As the `particle` objects are created in `createExplode()`, we add a new `type` attribute to them. When an explosion is triggered in the `checkCollisions()` function, the call to `createExplode()` now includes this type value based on the object that was destroyed. Each rock already has a `scale` parameter that varies from 1 to 3 based on its size. We use those as our base `type` value to pass in for the rocks. Now we only need `type` values for the player and the saucer. For the saucer, we use 0, and for the player, we use 4. We pulled these id values out of the air. We very well could have used 99 for the saucer and 200 for the player. We just could not use 1, 2, or 3 because those values are used for the rocks. The `type` breakdown looks like this:

- Saucer: type=0
- Large rock: type=1
- Medium rock: type=2
- Small rock: type=3
- Player: type=4

This `type` value will need to be used in a switch statement inside the `renderParti cles()` function to determine which of the four tiles to render for a given particle. Let's examine this function now:

```
function renderParticles() {

    var tempParticle = {};
    var particleLength = particles.length-1;
    for (var particleCtr=particleLength;particleCtr>=0;particleCtr--){
        tempParticle = particles[particleCtr];
        context.save(); //save current state in stack

        var tile;

        console.log("part type=" + tempParticle.type)
        switch(tempParticle.type){
            case 0: // saucer
              tile = 0;
              break;
            case 1: //large rock
              tile = 2
              break;
            case 2: //medium rock
              tile = 3;
              break;
            case 3: //small rock
              tile = 0;
              break;
            case 4: //player
              tile = 1;
              break;
```

```
}       var sourceX = Math.floor(tile % 4) * tempParticle.width;
var sourceY = Math.floor(tile / 4) * tempParticle.height;

context.drawImage(particleTiles, sourceX, sourceY,
tempParticle.width, tempParticle.height, tempParticle.x,
tempParticle.y,tempParticle.width,tempParticle.height);

context.restore(); //pop old state on to screen


    }
```

In `checkCollisions()`, we need to pass the `type` parameter to the `createExplode()` function so the `type` can be assigned to the particles in the explosion. Here is an example of a `createExplode()` function call used for a rock instance:

```
createExplode(tempRock.x+tempRock.halfWidth,tempRock.y+tempRock.halfHeight,
    10,tempRock.scale);
```

We pass the `tempRock.scale` as the final parameter because we are using the rock's scale as the `type`.

For a saucer:

```
createExplode(tempSaucer.x+tempSaucer.halfWidth,
  tempSaucer.y+tempSaucer.halfHeight,10,0);
```

For the saucers and the player, we pass a number literal into the `createExplode()` function. In the saucer's case, we pass in a `0`. For the player ship, we pass in a `4`:

```
createExplode(player.x+player.halfWidth, player.y+player.halfWidth,50,4);
```

Note that the `createExplode()` function call for the player is in the `playerDie()` function, which is called from `checkCollisions()`.

 After we discuss adding sound and a particle pool to this game, we present the entire set of code (Example A-2), replacing the *Geo Blaster Basic* code. There is no need to make the changes to the individual functions.

Adding Sound

In Chapter 7, we covered everything we need to know to add robust sound management to our canvas applications. If you are unfamiliar with the concepts presented in Chapter 7, please review that chapter first. In this chapter, we cover only the code necessary to include sound in our game.

Arcade games need to play many sounds simultaneously, and sometimes those sounds play very rapidly in succession. In Chapter 7, we used the HTML5 `<audio>` tag to create a pool of sounds, solving the problems associated with playing the same sound instance multiple times.

 As of this writing, the Opera browser in Windows offers the best support for playing sounds. If you are having trouble with the sound in this game, any other sound example in the book, or in your own games, please test them in the Opera browser.

The sounds for our game

We add three sounds to our game:

- A sound for when the player shoots a projectile (*shoot1.mp3, .ogg, .wav*)

- A sound for explosions (*explode1.mp3, .ogg, .wav*)

- A sound for when the saucer shoots a projectile (*saucershoot.mp3, .ogg, .wav*)

In the file download for this chapter, we have provided each of the three sounds in three formats: *.wav*, *.ogg*, and *.mp3*.

Adding sound instances and management variables to the game

In the variable definition section of our game code, we create variables to work with the sound manager code from Chapter 7. We create three instances of each sound that goes into our pool:

```
var explodeSound;
var explodeSound2;
var explodeSound3;
var shootSound;
var shootSound2;
var shootSound3;
var saucershootSound;
var saucershootSound2;
var saucershootSound3;
```

We also need to create an array to hold our pool of sounds:

```
var soundPool = new Array();
```

To control which sound we want to play, we assign a constant string to each, and to play the sound, we just need to use the constant. This way, we can change the sound names easily, which will help in refactoring code if we want to modify the sounds later:

```
var SOUND_EXPLODE = "explode1";
var SOUND_SHOOT = "shoot1";
var SOUND_SAUCER_SHOOT = "saucershoot"
```

Finally, we need an `audioType` variable, which we use to reference the current file type (*.ogg*, *.mp3*, or *.wav*) by the sound manager code.

Loading in sounds and tile sheet assets

In Chapter 7, we used a function to load all the game assets while our state machine waited in an idle state. We add this code to our game in a `gameStateInit()`function.

 Sound does not work the same in all browsers. In this example game, we are preloading all the images and sounds. For Internet Explorer 9 and 10, this preloading sometimes does not work. You can change the number of items to preload from 16 to 7 to test the game without sound in Internet Explorer browsers that have trouble with the preloading.

```
function gameStateInit() {
    loadCount = 0;
    itemsToLoad  = 16; // change to 7 for IE

    explodeSound = document.createElement("audio");
    document.body.appendChild(explodeSound);
    audioType = supportedAudioFormat(explodeSound);
    explodeSound.setAttribute("src", "explode1." + audioType);
    explodeSound.addEventListener("canplaythrough",itemLoaded,false);

    explodeSound2 = document.createElement("audio");
    document.body.appendChild(explodeSound2);
    explodeSound2.setAttribute("src", "explode1." + audioType);
    explodeSound2.addEventListener("canplaythrough",itemLoaded,false);

    explodeSound3 = document.createElement("audio");
    document.body.appendChild(explodeSound3);
    explodeSound3.setAttribute("src", "explode1." + audioType);
    explodeSound3.addEventListener("canplaythrough",itemLoaded,false);

    shootSound = document.createElement("audio");
    audioType = supportedAudioFormat(shootSound);
    document.body.appendChild(shootSound);
    shootSound.setAttribute("src", "shoot1." + audioType);
    shootSound.addEventListener("canplaythrough",itemLoaded,false);

    shootSound2 = document.createElement("audio");
    document.body.appendChild(shootSound2);
    shootSound2.setAttribute("src", "shoot1." + audioType);
    shootSound2.addEventListener("canplaythrough",itemLoaded,false);

    shootSound3 = document.createElement("audio");
    document.body.appendChild(shootSound3);
    shootSound3.setAttribute("src", "shoot1." + audioType);
    shootSound3.addEventListener("canplaythrough",itemLoaded,false);
```

```
saucershootSound = document.createElement("audio");
audioType = supportedAudioFormat(saucershootSound);
document.body.appendChild(saucershootSound);
saucershootSound.setAttribute("src", "saucershoot." + audioType);
saucershootSound.addEventListener("canplaythrough",itemLoaded,false);

saucershootSound2 = document.createElement("audio");
document.body.appendChild(saucershootSound2);
saucershootSound2.setAttribute("src", "saucershoot." + audioType);
saucershootSound2.addEventListener("canplaythrough",itemLoaded,false);

saucershootSound3 = document.createElement("audio");
document.body.appendChild(saucershootSound3);
saucershootSound3.setAttribute("src", "saucershoot." + audioType);
saucershootSound3.addEventListener("canplaythrough",itemLoaded,false);

shipTiles = new Image();
shipTiles.src = "ship_tiles.png";
shipTiles.onload = itemLoaded;

shipTiles2 = new Image();
shipTiles2.src = "ship_tiles2.png";
shipTiles2.onload = itemLoaded;

saucerTiles= new Image();
saucerTiles.src = "saucer.png";
saucerTiles.onload = itemLoaded;

largeRockTiles = new Image();
largeRockTiles.src = "largerocks.png";
largeRockTiles.onload = itemLoaded;

mediumRockTiles = new Image();
mediumRockTiles.src = "mediumrocks.png";
mediumRockTiles.onload = itemLoaded;

smallRockTiles = new Image();
smallRockTiles.src = "smallrocks.png";
smallRockTiles.onload = itemLoaded;

particleTiles = new Image();
particleTiles.src = "parts.png";
particleTiles.onload = itemLoaded;

switchGameState(GAME_STATE_WAIT_FOR_LOAD);

}
```

Notice that we must create and preload three instances of each sound, even though they share the same sound file (or files). In this function, we also load our tile sheets. The application scope itemsToLoad variable checks against the application scope load

Count variable in the load event callback itemLoaded() function, which is shared by all assets to be loaded. This makes it easy for the application to change state so that it can start playing the game when all assets have loaded. Let's briefly look at the itemLoaded() function now:

```
function itemLoaded(event) {

    loadCount++;
    //console.log("loading:" + loadCount)
    if (loadCount >= itemsToLoad) {

        shootSound.removeEventListener("canplaythrough",itemLoaded, false);
        shootSound2.removeEventListener("canplaythrough",itemLoaded, false);
        shootSound3.removeEventListener("canplaythrough",itemLoaded, false);
        explodeSound.removeEventListener("canplaythrough",itemLoaded,false);
        explodeSound2.removeEventListener("canplaythrough",itemLoaded,false);
        explodeSound3.removeEventListener("canplaythrough",itemLoaded,false);
        saucershootSound.removeEventListener("canplaythrough",itemLoaded,false);
        saucershootSound2.removeEventListener("canplaythrough",itemLoaded,false);
        saucershootSound3.removeEventListener("canplaythrough",itemLoaded,false);

        soundPool.push({name:"explode1", element:explodeSound, played:false});
        soundPool.push({name:"explode1", element:explodeSound2, played:false});
        soundPool.push({name:"explode1", element:explodeSound3, played:false});
        soundPool.push({name:"shoot1", element:shootSound, played:false});
        soundPool.push({name:"shoot1", element:shootSound2, played:false});
        soundPool.push({name:"shoot1", element:shootSound3, played:false});
        soundPool.push({name:"saucershoot", element:saucershootSound,
         played:false});
        soundPool.push({name:"saucershoot", element:saucershootSound2,
         played:false});
        soundPool.push({name:"saucershoot", element:saucershootSound3,
         played:false});

        switchGameState(GAME_STATE_TITLE)
    }

}
```

In this function, we first remove the event listener from each loaded item and then add the sounds to our sound pool. Finally, we call the switchGameState() to send the game to the title screen.

Playing sounds

Sounds play using the playSound() function from Chapter 7. We will not reprint that function here, but it is in Example A-2, where we give the entire set of code for the game. We call the playSound() function at various instances in our code to play the needed sounds. For example, the createExplode() function presented earlier in this chapter included this line:

```
playSound(SOUND_EXPLODE,.5);
```

When we want to play a sound instance from the pool, we call the playSound() function and pass in the constants representing the sound and the volume for the sound. If an instance of the sound is available in the pool, it is used, and the sound will play.

Now, let's move on to another type of application pool—the object pool.

Pooling Object Instances

We have looked at object pools as they relate to sounds, but we have not applied this concept to our game objects. Object pooling is a technique designed to save processing time, so it is very applicable to an arcade game application such as the one we are building. By pooling object instances, we avoid the sometimes processor-intensive task of creating object instances on the fly during game execution. This is especially applicable to our particle explosions because we create multiple objects on the same frame tick. On a lower-powered platform, such as a handheld device, object pooling can help increase frame rate.

Object pooling in Geo Blaster Extended

In our game, we apply the pooling concept to the explosion particles. Of course, we can extend this concept to rocks, projectiles, saucers, and any other type of object that requires multiple instances. For this example, though, let's focus on the particles. As we will see, adding pooling in JavaScript is a relatively simple but powerful technique.

Adding pooling variables to our game

We need to add four application scope variables to our game to use pooling for our game particle:

```
var particlePool = [];
var maxParticles = 200;
var newParticle;
var tempParticle;
```

The particlePool array holds the list of particle object instances that are waiting to be used. When createExplode() needs to use a particle, it first sees whether any are available in this array. If one is available, it is popped off the top of the particlePool stack and placed in the application scope newParticle variable—which is a reference to the pooled particle. The createExplode() function sets the properties of the new Particle and then pushes it to the end of the existing particles array.

When a particle's life has been exhausted, the updateParticles() function splices the particle from the particles array and pushes it back into the particlePool array. We have created the tempParticle reference to alleviate the updateParticles() function's need to create this instance on each frame tick.

The maxParticles value is used in a new function called createObjectPools(). We call this function in the gameStateInit() state function before we create the sound and tile sheet loading events.

Let's take a look at the createObjectPools() function now:

```
function createObjectPools(){
    for (var ctr=0;ctr<maxParticles;ctr++){
        var newParticle = {};
        particlePool.push(newParticle)
    }
    console.log("particlePool=" + particlePool.length)
}
```

As you can see, we simply iterate from 0 to 1 less than the maxParticles value and place a generic object instance at each element in the pool. When a particle is needed, the createExplode() function sees whether particlePool.length is greater than 0. If a particle is available, it is added to the particles array after its attributes are set. If no particle is available, none is used.

 This functionality can be extended to add a particle as needed to the pool when none is available. We have not added that functionality to our example, but it is common in some pooling algorithms.

Here is the newly modified createExplode() function in its entirety:

```
function createExplode(x,y,num,type) {

    playSound(SOUND_EXPLODE,.5);
    for (var partCtr=0;partCtr<num;partCtr++){
        if (particlePool.length > 0){

        newParticle = particlePool.pop();
        newParticle.dx = Math.random()*3;
        if (Math.random()<.5){
            newParticle.dx* = -1;
        }
        newParticle.dy = Math.random()*3;
        if (Math.random()<.5){
        newParticle.dy* = -1;
        }

        newParticle.life = Math.floor(Math.random()*30+30);
        newParticle.lifeCtr = 0;
        newParticle.x = x;
        newParticle.width = 2;
        newParticle.height = 2;
        newParticle.y = y;
        newParticle.type = type;
```

```
        //ConsoleLog.log("newParticle.life=" + newParticle.life);
        particles.push(newParticle);
        }

    }

}
```

The `updateParticles()` function will loop through the `particles` instances, update the attributes of each, and then check whether the particle's life has been exhausted. If it has, the function places the particle back in the pool. Here is the code we add to `updateParticles()` to replenish the pool:

```
if (remove) {
    particlePool.push(tempParticle)
    particles.splice(particleCtr,1)

}
```

Adding a Step Timer

In Chapter 8, we created a simple `FrameRateCounter` object prototype that displayed the current frame rate as the game was running. We now extend the functionality of this counter to add a step timer. The step timer uses the time difference calculated between frames to create a step factor. This step factor is used when updating the positions of the objects on the canvas. The result will be smoother rendering of the game objects when there are drops in frame rate and relatively consistent game play on browsers and systems that cannot maintain the frame rate needed to play the game effectively.

We update the constructor function for `FrameRateCounter` to accept in a new single parameter called `fps`. This value represents the frames per second we want our game to run:

```
function FrameRateCounter(fps) {
    if (fps == undefined){
        this.fps = 40
    }else{
        this.fps = fps
    }
```

If no `fps` value is passed in, the value `40` is used.

We also add two new object-level scope variables to calculate the `step` in our step timer:

```
this.lastTime = dateTemp.getTime();
this.step = 1;
```

The `lastTime` variable contains the time in which the previous frame completed its work.

We calculate the step by comparing the current time value with the lastTime value on each frame tick. This calculation occurs in the FrameRateCounter countFrames() function:

```
FrameRateCounter.prototype.countFrames=function() {

    var dateTemp = new Date();

    var timeDifference = dateTemp.getTime()-this.lastTime;
    this.step = (timeDifference/1000)*this.fps;
    this.lastTime = dateTemp.getTime();
```

The local timeDifference value is calculated by subtracting the lastTime value from the current time (represented by the dateTemp.getTime() return value).

To calculate the step value, divide the timeDifference by 1000 (the number of milliseconds in a single second) and multiply the result by the desired frame rate. If the game is running with no surplus or deficit in time between frame ticks, the step value is 1. If the current frame tick took longer than a single frame to finish, the value is greater than 1 (a deficit). If the current frame took less time than a single frame, the step value is less than 1 (a surplus).

For example, if the last frame took too long to process, the current frame will compensate by moving each object a little bit more than the step value of 1. Let's illustrate this with a simple example.

Let's say we want the saucer to move five pixels to the right on each frame tick. This would be a dx value of 5.

For this example, we also say that our desired frame rate is 40 FPS. This means that we want each frame tick to use up 25 milliseconds (1000/40 = 25).

Let's also suppose that the timeDifference between the current frame and the last frame is 26 milliseconds. Our game is running at a deficit of 1 millisecond per frame—this means that the game processing is taking more time than we want it to.

To calculate the step value, divide the timeDifference by 1000: 26/1000 = .026.

We multiply this value by the desired fps for our game: .026 * 40 = 1.04

Our step value is 1.04 for the current frame. Because of the deficit in processing time, we want to move each game object slightly more than a frame so there is no surplus or deficit. In the case of no surplus or deficit, the step value would be 1. If there is a surplus, the step value would be less than 1.

This step value is multiplied by the changes in movement vectors for each object in the update functions. This allows the game to keep a relatively smooth look even when there are fluctuations in the frame rate. In addition, the game updates the screen in a relatively consistent manner across the various browsers and systems, resulting in game play that is relatively consistent for each user.

Here are the new movement vector calculations for each object:

player

```
player.x += player.movingX*frameRateCounter.step;
player.y += player.movingY*frameRateCounter.step;
```

playerMissiles

```
tempPlayerMissile.x += tempPlayerMissile.dx*frameRateCounter.step;
tempPlayerMissile.y += tempPlayerMissile.dy*frameRateCounter.step;
```

rocks

```
tempRock.x += tempRock.dx*frameRateCounter.step;
tempRock.y += tempRock.dy*frameRateCounter.step;
```

saucers

```
tempSaucer.x += tempSaucer.dx*frameRateCounter.step;
tempSaucer.y += tempSaucer.dy*frameRateCounter.step;
```

saucerMissiles

```
tempSaucerMissile.x += tempSaucerMissile.dx*frameRateCounter.step;
tempSaucerMissile.y += tempSaucerMissile.dy*frameRateCounter.step;
```

particles

```
tempParticle.x += tempParticle.dx*frameRateCounter.step;
tempParticle.y += tempParticle.dy*frameRateCounter.step;
```

We have now covered all the major changes to turn *Geo Blaster Basic* into *Geo Blaster Extended*. Take a look at Example A-2, which has the entire code for the final game.

Creating a Dynamic Tile Sheet at Runtime

In Chapter 4, we briefly examined two principles we can use to help eliminate the need to precreate rotations of objects in tile sheets. Creating these types of tile sheets can be cumbersome and use up valuable time that's better spent elsewhere in the project.

The idea is to take a single image of a game object (e.g., the first tile in the medium rock tile sheet), create a dynamic tile sheet at runtime, and store it in an array rather than using the prerendered image rotation tiles.

To accomplish this, we need to use a second canvas as well as the `getImageData()` and `putImageData()` Canvas functions. Recall from Chapter 4 that `getImageData()` throws a security error if the HTML page using it is not on a web server.

Currently, only the Safari browser doesn't throw this error if the file is used on a local filesystem, so we have separated this functionality from the *Geo Blaster Extended* game and simply demonstrate how it could be used instead of replacing all the tile sheets in the game with this type of prerendering.

We start by creating two <canvas> elements on our HTML page:

```
<body>
<div>
<canvas id="canvas" width="256" height="256" style="position: absolute; top:
50px; left: 50px;">
 Your browser does not support HTML5 Canvas.
</canvas>

<canvas id="canvas2" width="32" height="32"  style="position: absolute; top:
 256px; left: 50px;">
 Your browser does not support HTML5 Canvas.
</canvas>
</div>
</body>
```

The first <canvas>, named canvas, represents our hypothetical game screen, which displays the precached dynamic tile sheet animation.

The second <canvas>, named canvas2, is used as a drawing surface to create the dynamic tile frames for our tile sheet.

We need to separate context instances in the JavaScript, one for each <canvas>:

```
var theCanvas = document.getElementById("canvas");
var context = theCanvas.getContext("2d");
var theCanvas2 = document.getElementById("canvas2");
var context2= theCanvas2.getContext("2d");
```

We use the *mediumrocks.png* file (Figure 9-9) from the *Geo Blaster Extended* game as our source for the dynamic tile sheet. Don't let this confuse you. We will not use all five tiles on this tile sheet—only the first tile.

Figure 9-9. The mediumrocks.png tile sheet

In *Geo Blaster Extended*, we used all five tiles to create a simulated rotation animation. Here, we use only the first tile. We draw this first tile, rotate it on theCanvas2 by 10 degrees, and then copy the current imageData pixels from this canvas to an array of imageData instances called rotationImageArray.

We then repeat this process by rotating theCanvas2 by 10 more degrees and in a loop until we have 36 individual frames of imageData representing the rotation animation for our medium rock in an array:

```
var rotationImageArray = [];
var animationFrame = 0;
var tileSheet = new Image();
```

```
tileSheet.addEventListener('load', eventSheetLoaded , false);
tileSheet.src = "mediumrocks.png";
```

The `rotationImageArray` variable holds the generated `imageData` instances, which we create by using a rotation transformation on `theCanvas2`.

The `animationFrame` is used when redisplaying the rotation animation frames in `rotationImageArray` back to the first `theCanvas` to demo the animation.

When the `tileSheet` is loaded, the `eventSheetLoaded()` function is called, which in turn calls the `startup()` function. The `startup()` function uses a loop to create the 36 frames of animation:

```
function startUp(){

    for (var ctr=0;ctr<360;ctr+=10){
        context2.fillStyle = "#ffffff";
        context2.fillRect(0,0,32,32);
        context2.save();
        context2.setTransform(1,0,0,1,0,0)
        var angleInRadians = ctr * Math.PI / 180;
        context2.translate(16, 16);
        context2.rotate(angleInRadians);
        context2.drawImage(tileSheet, 0, 0,32,32,-16,-16,32,32);
        context2.restore();
        var imagedata = context2.getImageData(0, 0, 32, 32)
        rotationImageArray.push(imagedata);
    }
    setInterval(drawScreen, 100 );
}
```

This loop first clears `theCanvas2` with a white color and then saves it to the stack. We then translate to the center of our object and rotate the canvas by the current `ctr` value (an increment of `10`). Next, we draw the first tile from *mediumrocks.png* and save the result in a new local `imageData` instance, using the `getImageData()` function.

 This is where the security error will be thrown if the domain of the image and the domain of the HTML file are not the same. On a local machine (not running on a local web server, but from the filesystem), this error will be thrown on all browsers but Safari (currently).

Finally, the new `imageData` is pushed into the `rotationImageArray`. When the loop is complete, we set up an interval to run and call the `drawScreen()` function every 100 milliseconds.

To display the animation on the first canvas, we use this timer loop interval and call `putImageData()` to draw each frame in succession, creating the simulation of animation. As with the tile sheet, we didn't have to use 36 frames of animation; we could use just five. Naturally, the animation is much smoother with more frames, but this process shows how easy it is to create simple transformation animations on the fly rather than precreating them in image files:

```
function drawScreen() {

        //context.fillStyle = "#ffffff";
        //context.fillRect(50,50,32,32);
        context.putImageData(rotationImageArray[animationFrame],50,50);
        animationFrame++;
        if (animationFrame ==rotationImageArray.length){
            animationFrame=0;
        }
    }
```

Example 9-1 shows the entire code.

Example 9-1. A dynamic tile sheet example

```
<!doctype html>
<html lang="en">
<head>
<meta charset="UTF-8">
<title>CH9EX2: Canvas Copy</title>

<script src="modernizr-1.6.min.js"></script>
<script type="text/javascript">
window.addEventListener('load', eventWindowLoaded, false);
function eventWindowLoaded() {
    canvasApp();
}

function canvasSupport () {
    return Modernizr.canvas;
}

function canvasApp(){

    if (!canvasSupport()) {
            return;      }else{
        var theCanvas = document.getElementById("canvas");
        var context = theCanvas.getContext("2d");

        var theCanvas2 = document.getElementById("canvas2");
        var context2= theCanvas2.getContext("2d");
    }
    var rotationImageArray = [];
    var tileSheet = new Image();
    var animationFrame = 0;
    tileSheet.addEventListener('load', eventSheetLoaded , false);
    tileSheet.src = "mediumrocks.png";
    function eventSheetLoaded() {
        startUp();
```

```
        }

    function startUp(){
        //context.drawImage(tileSheet, 0, 0);
        //context2.drawImage(theCanvas, 0, 0,32,32,0,0,32,32);

        for (var ctr=0;ctr<360;ctr+=10){
            context2.fillStyle="#ffffff";
            context2.fillRect(0,0,32,32);

            context2.save();
            context2.setTransform(1,0,0,1,0,0)
            var angleInRadians = ctr * Math.PI / 180;
            context2.translate(16, 16);
            context2.rotate(angleInRadians);
            context2.drawImage(tileSheet, 0, 0,32,32,-16,-16,32,32);
            context2.restore();

            var imagedata = context2.getImageData(0, 0, 32, 32);

            rotationImageArray.push(imagedata);
        }
        setInterval(drawScreen, 100 );
    }

    function drawScreen() {
        //context.fillStyle="#ffffff";
        //context.fillRect(50,50,32,32);
        context.putImageData(rotationImageArray[animationFrame],50,50);
        animationFrame++;
        if (animationFrame ==rotationImageArray.length){
            animationFrame = 0;
        }
    }

}

</script>

</head>
<body>
<div>
<canvas id="canvas" width="256" height="256" style="position: absolute; top:
 50px; left: 50px;">
 Your browser does not support the HTML 5 Canvas.
</canvas>

<canvas id="canvas2" width="32" height="32" style="position: absolute; top:
 256px; left: 50px;">
 Your browser does not support HTML5 Canvas.
</canvas>

</div>
```

```
</body>
</html>
```

In the rest of the chapter, we look at creating a simple tile-based game using some of the techniques first discussed in Chapter 4.

A Simple Tile-Based Game

Let's move from *Asteroids* to another classic game genre, the tile-based maze-chase game. When you're discussing early tile-based games, undoubtedly *Pac-Man* enters the conversation. *Pac-Man* was one of the first commercially successful tile-based games, although it certainly was not the first of its kind. The maze-chase genre was actually well covered by budding game developers before microcomputers were even thought possible. Many minicomputer and mainframe tile-based games, such as *Daleks*, were crafted in the '60s and '70s. In this section, we create a simple turn-based maze-chase game. Our game, *Micro Tank Maze*, is based loosely on *Daleks*, but we use the tank sprites from Chapter 4. Figure 9-10 is a screenshot from the finished game.

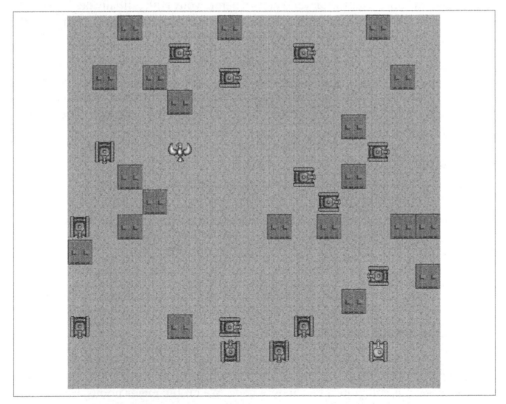

Figure 9-10. Micro Tank Maze in action

Micro Tank Maze Description

Micro Tank Maze is a simple turn-based strategy game played on a 15×15 tile-based grid. At the beginning of each game, the player (the green tank), 20 enemy tanks (the blue tanks), 25 wall tiles, and a single goal tile (the phoenix) are randomly placed on the grid. The rest of the grid is simply road tiles on which the tanks move. The player must get to the goal object without running into any walls or any of the enemy tanks. On each turn, the player and all enemy tanks move a single space (tile) on the grid. Neither the player nor the enemy tanks can move off the grid edges. If the player runs into a wall tile or an enemy tank, his game is over. If an enemy tank runs into a wall or another tank, it is destroyed and removed from the game board. If an enemy tank runs into the player tank, it and the player are destroyed. If the player hits the goal tile without an enemy tank also hitting the tile on the same turn, the player wins.

Game progression

Each time the player collects the goal object and wins the game, the next game starts with one more enemy tank (up to 50 enemy tanks). The ultimate goal of the game is to see how many times you (the player) can win before your tank is finally destroyed. The game keeps a session-based high score, and even if you lose, you always start from the last completed level.

This is a simple game, and much more can be added to it to enhance the gaming experience. In this chapter, though, we want to cover the basics of creating a tile-based game on HTML5 Canvas. By combining what you have learned throughout this book, you should have enough skill and knowledge to extend this simple contest into a much more robust game-play experience.

Game strategy

The player must try to reach the goal while avoiding the enemy tanks. The enemy follows or chases the player to a fault. Most of the time (75%), each enemy tank stupidly follows the player, even if that means moving into a wall and destroying itself. The player then has the advantage of intelligence to compensate for the large number of tanks the enemy employs. The other 25% of the time, an enemy tank randomly chooses a direction to move in.

Now, let's get into the game by looking at the tile sheet we will be using.

The Tile Sheet for Our Game

Make sure you've read Chapter 4 and the Chapter 8 section, "A Basic Game Framework" on page 463, before moving on. Even though *Micro Tank Maze* is a relatively simple game, it is still quite a few lines of code. We hit the major points, but we don't have space to discuss every detail.

The tile sheet (*tanks_sheet.png*) we use looks very familiar if you've read Chapter 4. Figure 9-11 shows *tanks_sheet.png*.

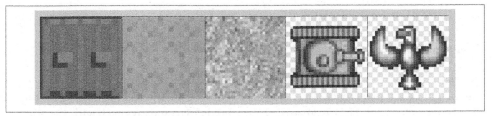

Figure 9-11. The Micro Tank Maze tile sheet

We are using only a very small portion of these tiles for *Micro Tank Maze*.

Road tile
> This is the tile on which the player and the enemy tanks can move. Tile 0, the road tile, is in the top-left corner.

Wall tile
> The wall tile causes any tank moving on it to be destroyed. Tile 30, the second-to-last tile on the sheet, is the wall tile.

Goal tile
> This is the tile the player must reach to win the game. It is the last tile in the second-to-last row (the phoenix).

Player tiles
> The player is made up of the eight green tank tiles. Each tile simulates the tank treads moving from tile to tile.

Enemy tiles
> The enemy is made up of the eight blue tank tiles. These tiles animate the tank treads as the tank moves from tile to tile.

Our game code stores the tile IDs needed for each of these game objects in application scope variables:

```
var playerTiles = [1,2,3,4,5,6,7,8];
var enemyTiles = [9,10,11,12,13,14,15,16];
var roadTile = 0;
var wallTile = 30;
var goalTile = 23;
var explodeTiles = [17,18,19,18,17];
```

The tile sheet is loaded into an application scope Image instance and given the name tileSheet:

```
var tileSheet;
```

In the application's initialization state, we load and assign the `Image` instance:

```
tileSheet = new Image();
tileSheet.src = "tanks_sheet.png";
```

Next, we examine the setup of the game playfield.

The Playfield

The game playfield is a 15×15 grid of 32×32 tiles. This is a total of 225 tiles with a width and height of 480 pixels each. Every time we start a new game, all the objects are placed randomly on the grid. The `playField[]` array holds 15 row arrays each with 15 columns. This gives us 225 tiles that can be easily accessed with the simple `playField[row][col]` syntax.

We first place a road tile on each of the 225 `playField` array locations. We then randomly place all the wall tiles. (These actually replace some of the road tiles at locations in the `playField` array.)

Next, we randomly place all the enemy tank tiles. Unlike the wall tiles, the tank tiles do *not* replace road tiles in the `playField` array. Instead, they are placed in an array of their own called `enemy`. To ensure that neither the player nor the goal object occupies the same tile space as the enemy tanks, we create another array, `items`.

The `items` array is also a 15×15 two-dimensional array of rows and columns, which can be considered the second layer of playfield data. Unlike the `playField` array, it is used only to make sure no two objects (player, enemy, or goal) occupy the same space while building the playfield. We must do this because the player and enemy objects are not added to the `playField` array.

After we have placed the enemy, we randomly place the player at a spot that is not currently occupied by an enemy or a wall. Finally, we place the goal tile in a spot not taken by the player, a wall, or an enemy tank.

The code for this is in the `createPlayField()` function. If you would like to review it now, go to the "Micro Tank Maze Complete Game Code" on page 570 section (Example 9-2).

All the data about the `playField` is stored in application scope variables:

```
//playfield
var playField = [];
var items = [];
var xMin = 0;
var xMax = 480;
var yMin = 0;
var yMax = 480;
```

To create the `playField`, the game code needs to know the maximum number of each type of tile. These are also application scope variables:

```
var wallMax = 25;
var playerMax = 1;
var enemyMax = 20;
var goalMax = 1;
```

The Player

The player and all its current attributes are contained in the `player` object. Even a game as simple as *Micro Tank Maze* requires quite a few attributes. Here is a list and description of each:

`player.row`

    The current row on the 15×15 `playField` grid where the player resides.

`player.col`

    The current column on the 15×15 `playField` grid where the player resides.

`player.nextRow`

    The row the player moves to next, after a successful key press in that direction.

`player.nextCol`

    The column the player moves to next, after a successful key press in that direction.

`player.currentTile`

    The id of the current tile that displays the player from the `playerTiles` array.

`player.rotation`

    The player starts pointed up, so this is the 0 rotation. When the player moves in one of the four basic directions, this rotation changes and moves the player in the direction it is facing.

`player.speed`

    The number of pixels the `player` object moves on each frame tick.

`player.destinationX`

    The final x location for the 32×32 `player` object while it is moving to a new tile. It represents the top-left corner x location for this new location. During the player movement and animation phase of the game, this value determines when the player has arrived at its new x-axis location.

`player.destinationY`

    The final y location for the 32×32 `player` object while it is moving to a new tile. It represents the top-left corner y location for this new location. During the player movement and animation phase of the game, this value determines when the player has arrived at its new y-axis location.

`player.x`
> The current x location of the top-left corner of the 32×32 player object.

`player.y`
> The current y location of the top-left corner of the 32×32 player object.

`player.dx`
> The player's change in x direction on each frame tick while it is animating. This will be –1, 0, or 1, depending on the direction in which the player is moving.

`player.dy`
> The player's change in y direction on each frame tick while it is animating. This will be –1, 0, or 1, depending on the direction in which the player is moving.

`player.hit`
> Set to `true` when the player moves to a new square that is occupied by an enemy tank or a wall.

`player.dead`
> When `player.hit` is `true`, it is replaced on the `playField` by an explosion sprite. With `dead` set to `true`, it is not rendered to the game screen.

`player.win`
> Set to `true` if the player collects the goal object.

The enemy and the player share many of the same attributes because they both use the same type of calculations to move about the grid. Now let's examine how the enemy object is constructed.

The Enemy

Each enemy object has its own set of attributes that are very similar to those of the player. Like the player, each enemy is an object instance.

Here is the code from the `createPlayField()` function that sets up the attributes for a new enemy object:

```
EnemyLocationFound = true;
var tempEnemy = {};
tempEnemy.row = randRow;
tempEnemy.col = randCol;
tempEnemy.nextRow = 0;
tempEnemy.nextCol = 0;
tempEnemy.currentTile = 0;
tempEnemy.rotation = 0;
tempEnemy.x = tempEnemy.col*32;
tempEnemy.y = tempEnemy.row*32;
tempEnemy.speed = 2;
tempEnemy.destinationX = 0;
tempEnemy.destinationY = 0;
```

```
tempEnemy.dx = 0;
tempEnemy.dy = 0;
tempEnemy.hit = false;
tempEnemy.dead = false;
tempEnemy.moveComplete = false;
enemy.push(tempEnemy);
items[randRow][randCol] = 1;
```

A few extra things are worth pointing out in this code. The first is that each enemy object needs a moveComplete attribute. This is used in the animateEnemy() game state function. When the entire enemy battalion has moved to its new location, the game transitions to the next game state. This is discussed in detail in the next section, "Turn-Based Game Flow and the State Machine" on page 562.

Notice, too, that the new enemy objects are added to the enemy array and to the items multidimensional array. This ensures that the player and the goal cannot be placed on an enemy location. After the enemy moves from its initial location, the playField array still has a road tile to show in its place. We call the player and the enemy moving-object tiles because they can move about the game board. When they move, they must uncover the road tile in the spot they were in before moving.

Now let's take a quick look at the goal tile to solidify your understanding of the difference between the playField and the moving object tiles.

The Goal

The tile ID of the goal tile is stored in the playField array along with the road and wall tiles. It is not considered a separate item because, unlike the player and enemy objects, it does not need to move. As we have described previously, because the enemy and player tiles move on top of the playfield, they are considered moving items and not part of the playfield.

The Explosions

The explosion tiles are unique. They are rendered on top of the playfield when an enemy tank or the player's hit attribute has been set to true. The explosion tiles animate through a list of five tiles and then are removed from the game screen. Again, tiles for the explosion are set in the explodeTiles array:

```
var explodeTiles = [17,18,19,18,17];
```

Next, we examine the entire game flow and state machine to give you an overall look at how the game logic is designed.

Turn-Based Game Flow and the State Machine

Our game logic and flow is separated into 16 discrete states. The entire application runs on a 40-frames-per-second interval timer:

```
switchGameState(GAME_STATE_INIT);
var FRAME_RATE = 40;
var intervalTime = 1000/FRAME_RATE;
setInterval(runGame, intervalTime )
```

As with the other games, in Chapter 8 and earlier in this chapter, we use a function reference state machine to run our current game state. The switchGameState() function transitions to a new game state. Let's discuss this function briefly and then move through the rest of the game functions.

 We do not reprint each line of code or dissect it in detail here. Use this section as a guide for perusing the entire set of game code included at the end of this chapter (in Example 9-2). By now, you have seen most of the code and ideas that create this game logic. We break out the new ideas and code in the sections that follow.

GAME_STATE_INIT

This state loads the assets we need for our game. We are loading only a single tile sheet and no sounds for *Micro Tank Maze*.

After the initial load, it sends the state machine to the GAME_STATE_WAIT_FOR_LOAD state until the load event has occurred.

GAME_STATE_WAIT_FOR_LOAD

This state simply makes sure that all the items in GAME_STATE_INIT have loaded properly. It then sends the state machine to the GAME_STATE_TITLE state.

GAME_STATE_TITLE

This state shows the title screen and then waits for the space bar to be pressed. When this happens, it sends the state machine to GAME_STATE_NEW_GAME.

GAME_STATE_NEW_GAME

This state resets all the game arrays and objects and then calls the createPlay Field() function. The createPlayField() function creates the playField and ene my arrays for the new game and sets the player object's starting location. When it has finished, it calls the renderPlayField() function a single time to display the initial board on the game screen.

When this completes, the state machine is now ready to start the real game loop by moving the game state machine to the GAME_STATE_WAIT_FOR_PLAYER_MOVE state.

GAME_STATE_WAIT_FOR_PLAYER_MOVE

This state waits for the player to press one of the four arrow buttons. When the player has done so, the switch statement checks which arrow was pressed. Based on the direction pressed, the checkBounds() function is called.

 This state contains a bit of the new code for tile movement logic that we have not seen previously in this book. See the upcoming section, "Simple Tile Movement Logic Overview" on page 566, for more details on these concepts.

The checkBounds() function accepts three parameters:

- The number to increment the row the player is currently in
- The number to increment the column the player is currently in
- The object being tested (either the player or one of the enemy tanks)

The sole purpose of this function is to determine whether the object being tested can move in the desired direction. In this game, the only illegal moves are off the side of the screen. In games such as *Pac-Man*, this would check to make sure that the tile was not a wall tile. Our game does not do this because we want the player and the enemy objects to be able to move mistakenly onto the wall tiles (and be destroyed).

If a valid move is found for the player in the direction pressed, the setPlayerDestina tion() function is called. This function simply sets the player.destinationX and player.destinationY attributes based on the new tile location.

checkBounds() sets the player.nextRow and player.nextCol attributes. The set PlayerDestination() function multiplies the player.nextRow and the player.next Col by the tile size (32) to determine the player.destinationX and player.destina tionY attributes. These move the player to its new location.

GAME_STATE_ANIMATE_PLAYER is then set as the current game state.

GAME_STATE_ANIMATE_PLAYER

This function moves the player to its destinationX and destinationY locations. Because this is a turn-based game, we don't have to do any other processing while this movement is occurring.

On each iteration, the `player.currentTile` is incremented by 1. This changes the tile that is rendered to be the next tile in the `playerTiles` array. When `destinationX` and `destinationY` are equal to the x and y values for the player, the movement and animation stop, and the game state is changed to the `GAME_STATE_EVALUATE_PLAYER_MOVE` state.

GAME_STATE_EVALUATE_PLAYER_MOVE

Now that the player has moved to the next tile, the `player.row` and `player.col` attributes are set to `player.nextRow` and `player.nextCol`, respectively.

Next, if the player is on a goal tile, the `player.win` attribute is set to `true`. If the player is on a wall tile, the `player.hit` is set to `true`.

We then loop though all the enemy objects and see whether any occupy the same tile as the player. If they do, both the player and the enemy `hit` attributes are set to `true`.

Next, we move the game to the `GAME_STATE_ENEMY_MOVE` state.

GAME_STATE_ENEMY_MOVE

This state uses the homegrown chase AI—discussed in "Simple Homegrown AI Overview"—to choose a direction in which to move each enemy tank. It does this by looping through all the tanks and applying the logic to them individually.

This function first uses a little tile-based math to determine where the player is in relation to an enemy tank. It then creates an array of directions to test based on these calculations. It stores these as string values in a `directionsToTest` variable.

Next, it uses the `chanceRandomMovement` value (25%) to determine whether it will use the list of directions it just compiled or throw them out and simply choose a random direction to move in.

In either case, it must check all the available directions (either in the list of `direction sToMove` or in all four directions for random movement) to see which is the first that will not move the tank off the side of the screen.

When it has the direction to move in, it sets the `destinationX` and `destinationY` values of the enemy tank, using the same `tile size * x` and `tile size * y` trick used for the player.

Finally, it sets the game state to `GAME_STATE_ANIMATE_ENEMY`.

GAME_STATE_ANIMATE_ENEMY

Like `GAME_STATE_ANIMATE_PLAYER`, this state moves and animates the tank to its new location represented by its `destinationX` and `destinationY` values. It must do this for each of the enemy tanks, so it uses the enemyMoveCompleteCount variable to keep count of how many of the enemy tanks have finished their moves.

When all the enemy tanks have completed their moves, the game state is changed to the GAME_STATE_EVALUATE_ENEMY_MOVE state.

GAME_STATE_EVALUATE_ENEMY_MOVE

Like GAME_STATE_EVALUATE_PLAYER_MOVE, this state looks at the location of each tank to determine which ones need to be destroyed.

If a tank occupies the same tile as the player, a wall, or another tank, the tank is "to be destroyed." If the player and enemy tank occupy the same tile, the player is also "to be destroyed." This "to be destroyed" state is set by placing true in the hit attribute of the enemy tank or the player.

The game is then moved to the GAME_STATE_EVALUATE_OUTCOME state.

GAME_STATE_EVALUATE_OUTCOME

This function looks at each of the enemy tanks and the player tank to determine which have a hit attribute set to true. If any do, that tank's dead attribute is set to true, and an explosion is created by calling createExplode() and passing in the object instance (player or enemy tank). In the case of the enemy, a dead enemy is also removed from the enemy array.

The GAME_STATE_ANIMATE_EXPLODE state is called next.

GAME_STATE_ANIMATE_EXPLODE

If the explosions array length is greater than 0, this function loops through each instance and animates it, using the explodeTiles array. Each explosion instance is removed from the explosions array after it finishes its animation. When the explosions array length is 0, the game moves to the GAME_STATE_CHECK_FOR_GAME_OVER state.

GAME_STATE_CHECK_FOR_GAME_OVER

This state first checks whether the player is dead and then checks to see whether she has won. The player cannot win if an enemy tank makes it to the goal on the same try as the player.

If the player has lost, the state changes to GAME_STATE_PLAYER_LOSE; if the player has won, it moves to the GAME_STATE_PLAYER_WIN state. If neither of those has occurred, the game is set to GAME_STATE_WAIT_FOR_PLAYER_MOVE. This starts the game loop iteration over, and the player begins her next turn.

GAME_STATE_PLAYER_WIN

If the player wins, the maxEnemy is increased for the next game. The player's score is also checked against the current session high score to determine whether a new high score has been achieved. This state waits for a space bar press and then moves to the GAME_STATE_NEW_GAME state.

GAME_STATE_PLAYER_LOSE

The player's score is checked against the current session high score to determine whether a new high score has been achieved. This state waits for a space bar press and then moves to the GAME_STATE_NEW_GAME state.

Simple Tile Movement Logic Overview

Micro Tank Maze employs simple tile-to-tile movement by using the "center of a tile" logic. This logic relies on making calculations when the game character has reached the center of a tile. The origin point of our game character tiles is the top-left corner. Because of this, we can easily calculate that a game character is in the center of a tile when its x and y coordinates are equal to the destination tile's x and y coordinates.

When the user presses a movement key (up, down, right, or left arrow), we first must check whether the player is trying to move to a legal tile on the playField. In *Micro Tank Maze*, all tiles are legal. The only illegal moves are off the edges of the board. So, if the player wants to move up, down, left, or right, we must first check the tile in that direction based on the key pressed in the gameStateWaitForPlayerMove() function. Here is the switch statement that determines whether the player pressed an arrow key:

```
if (keyPressList[38]==true){
     //up
     if (checkBounds(-1,0, player)){
     setPlayerDestination();
     }
}else if (keyPressList[37]==true) {
     //left
     if (checkBounds(0,-1, player)){
     setPlayerDestination();
     }
}else if (keyPressList[39]==true) {
     //right
     if (checkBounds(0,1, player)){
     setPlayerDestination();
     }
}else if  (keyPressList[40]==true){
     //down
     if (checkBounds(1,0, player)){
     setPlayerDestination();
     }
}
```

Notice that the checkBounds() function takes a row increment and then a column increment to test. It is important to note that we don't access tiles in the same manner we would access pixels on the screen. Tiles in the playField array are accessed by addressing the vertical (row) and then the horizontal (column) (using [row][column], not [column][row]). This is because a simple array is organized into a set of rows. Each row has a set of 15 columns. Therefore, we do not access a tile in playField by using the [horizontal][vertical] coordinates. Instead, we use the [row][column] syntax that simple arrays use to powerful and elegant effect.

In the checkBounds() function, enter the row increment, then the column increment, and then the object to be tested. If this is a legal move, the checkBounds() function sets nextRow and nextCol to be row+rowInc and col+colInc, respectively:

```
function checkBounds(rowInc, colInc, object){
    object.nextRow = object.row+rowInc;
    object.nextCol = object.col+colInc;

    if (object.nextCol >=0 && object.nextCol<15 &&
     object.nextRow>=0 && object.nextRow<15){
        object.dx = colInc;
        object.dy = rowInc;

        if (colInc==1){
        object.rotation = 90;
        }else if (colInc==-1){
        object.rotation = 270;
        }else if (rowInc==-1){
        object.rotation = 0;
        }else if (rowInc==1){
        object.rotation = 180;
        }

        return(true);

    }else{
        object.nextRow = object.row;
        object.nextCol = object.col;
        return(false);

    }

}
```

If the move is legal, the dx (delta, or change in x) and dy (delta, or change in y) are set to colInc and rowInc, respectively.

The animatePlayer() function is called next. Its job is to move the player object to its new location while running through its animation frames. Here is the code from the animatePlayer() function:

```
player.x += player.dx*player.speed;
player.currentTile++;if (player.currentTile==playerTiles.length){
    player.currentTile = 0;
}
renderPlayField();
if (player.x==player.destinationX && player.y==player.destinationY){
    switchGameState(GAME_STATE_EVALUATE_PLAYER_MOVE);
}
```

First, the `player` object's x and y locations are increased by the `player.speed * play` `er.dx` (or dy). The tile size is 32, so we must use a speed value that is evenly divided into 32. The values 1, 2, 4, 8, 16, and 32 are all valid.

This function also runs though the `playerTiles` array on each game loop iteration. This renders the tank tracks moving, simulating a smooth ride from one tile to the next.

Next, let's take a closer look at how we render `playField`.

Rendering Logic Overview

Each time the game renders objects to the screen, it runs through the entire `render()` function. It does this to ensure that even the nonmoving objects are rendered back to the game screen. The `render()` function looks like this:

```
function renderPlayField() {
    fillBackground();
    drawPlayField();
    drawPlayer();
    drawEnemy();
    drawExplosions();
}
```

First, we draw the plain black background, and then we draw `playField`. After that, we draw the game objects. `drawPlayField()` draws the map of tiles to the game screen. This function is similar to the functions in Chapter 4 but with some additions for our game. Let's review how it is organized:

```
function drawPlayField(){
    for (rowCtr=0;rowCtr<15;rowCtr++){

        for (colCtr=0;colCtr<15;colCtr++) {
        var sourceX = Math.floor((playField[rowCtr][colCtr]) % 8) * 32;
        var sourceY = Math.floor((playField[rowCtr][colCtr]) /8) *32;

        if (playField[rowCtr][colCtr] != roadTile){
            context.drawImage(tileSheet, 0, 0,32,32,colCtr*32,rowCtr*32,32,32);
        }
        context.drawImage(tileSheet, sourceX, sourceY, 32,32,
         colCtr*32,rowCtr*32,32,32);
         }
```

```
        }
    }
```

The drawPlayField() function loops through the rows in the playField array and then through each column inside each row. If the tile ID number at playField[rowCtr] [colCtr] is a road tile, it simply paints that tile at the correct location on playField. If the tile ID is a game object (not a road tile), it first paints a road tile in that spot and then paints the object tile in that spot.

Simple Homegrown AI Overview

The enemy tanks chase the player object based on a set of simple rules. We have coded those rules into the gameStateEnemyMove() function, which is one of the longest and most complicated functions in this book. Let's first step through the logic used to create the function, and then you can examine it in Example 9-2.

This function starts by looping through the enemy array. It must determine a new tile location on which to move each enemy. To do so, it follows some simple rules that determine the order in which the testBounds() function will test the movement directions:

1. First, it tests to see whether the player is closer to the enemy vertically or horizontally.

2. If vertically, and the player is above the enemy, it places up and then down in the directionsToTest array.

3. If vertically, and the player is below the enemy, it places down and then up in the directionsToTest array.

The up and then down, or down and then up, directions are pushed into the directionsTest array to simplify the AI. The logic here is if the player is up from the enemy, but the enemy is blocked by an object, the enemy will try the opposite direction first. In our game, there will be no instance when an object blocks the direction the enemy tank wants to move in, because the only illegal direction is trying to move off the bounds of the screen. If we add tiles to our playfield that block the enemy, this entire set of AI code suddenly becomes very useful and necessary. We have included this entire homegrown chase AI in our game in case more of these tile types are added.

4. It then looks where to add the left and right directions. It does this based on which way will put it closer to the player.

5. If the horizontal direction and not the vertical direction is the shortest, it runs through the same type of logic, but this time using `left` and then `right`, then `up` and then `down`.

6. When this is complete, all four directions will be in the `directionsToTest` array.

Next, the logic finds a number between 0 and 99 and checks whether it is less than the `chanceRandomEnemyMovement` value. If it is, it ignores the `directionsToTest` array and simply tries to find a random direction to move in. In either case, all the directions (either in the `directionsToTest` array or in order up, down, left, and right) are tested until the `testBounds()` function returns `true`.

That's all there is to this code. In Example 9-2, you find the entire set of code for this game.

Micro Tank Maze Complete Game Code

The full source code and assets for *Micro Tank Maze* are located at this site (*http://examples.oreilly.com/0636920013327/*).

Scrolling a Tile-Based World

One of the advantages of using a tile-based world is that it can be virtually any size we want it to be. Although some memory and processor limitations (especially on mobile devices) might cause problems when trying to scroll or pan over an image that is much larger than the canvas size, as we did in Chapter 4, there is virtually no limit to the size of a game world that can be created with tiles.

The power comes from the use of the simple two-dimensional arrays we use to hold the game world. As we examined in Chapter 8, the concept of painting the game screen with tiles is pretty simple. Here's a short review of the process of painting the screen from a tile-based grid.

First, a Tile Sheet That Contains the Tiles We Want to Paint to the Screen

We will be using the same tile sheet as in Chapter 8 (see Figure 9-12).

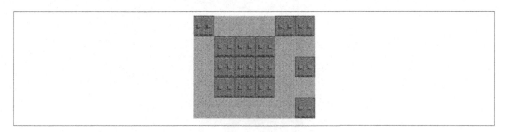

Figure 9-12. The tiles sheet for the scrolling examples

Next, we use the data from a two-dimensional array to paint these tiles to the game screen to create our game world.

Second, a Two-Dimensional Array to Describe Our Game World

We put this game world into an array. Each number in the array rows and columns represents a tile number in our game world. So, a 0 would paint the first tile in the tile sheet (the blue wall), a 1 would be gray road tile, and so on.

```
world.map=[
  [0,0,0,0,0,0,0,0,0,0,0,0,0,0,0]
  ,[0,1,2,1,1,1,1,1,1,1,1,1,1,1,0]
  ,[0,1,0,1,0,0,1,0,1,0,0,1,0,1,0]
  ,[0,1,0,1,0,0,1,0,1,0,0,1,0,1,0]
  ,[0,1,0,1,0,0,1,1,1,0,0,1,0,1,0]
  ,[0,2,1,1,1,0,0,0,1,1,1,1,1,0]
  ,[0,1,0,0,0,1,0,0,0,1,0,0,0,1,0]
  ,[0,1,1,1,2,1,0,0,0,1,1,1,1,1,0]
  ,[0,0,0,0,0,1,1,1,1,1,0,0,0,0,0]
  ,[0,1,1,1,1,1,0,0,0,1,1,1,1,1,0]
  ,[0,1,0,1,0,0,1,1,1,0,0,1,0,1,0]
  ,[0,1,0,1,0,0,2,0,0,0,0,1,0,1,0]
  ,[0,1,0,1,0,0,1,0,1,0,0,1,0,1,0]
  ,[0,1,1,1,1,1,1,2,1,1,1,1,1,1,0]
  ,[0,0,0,0,0,0,0,0,0,0,0,0,0,0,0]
];
```

Third, Paint the Tile-Based World to the Canvas

Our world is built using a 15x15 grid. Figure 9-13 shows the entire world we will use in our scrolling examples.

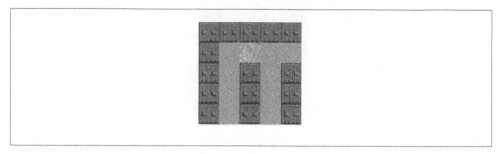

Figure 9-13. A 15×15 tile map

For the scrolling examples, we use a canvas that is smaller than the world. We are using a small canvas (160×160) and a small world (480×480) simply to make sure that the code is easily understood in book form. In a real-world example, the tile-based world might be 100+ tiles in each dimension, drawn onto a canvas that is 640×480. Here is the HTML5 Canvas object we will be using:

```
<canvas id="canvas" width="160" height="160">
```

Coarse Scrolling vs. Fine Scrolling

There are two methods by which we can scroll the game screen: coarse scrolling and fine scrolling. Coarse scrolling is a method by which we scroll the screen a single tile at a time. Therefore, because our tiles are 32×32 pixels, we would scroll 32 pixels in the direction the user presses with the keys. We allow the user to use the up, down, left, and right arrow keys in our examples to move a viewable window over the tile world map.

Fine scrolling is a method by which the user scrolls just a few pixels at a time. This is a much more powerful and user-friendly method for scrolling the game screen and would be useful for most games.

Each method has its uses, though. Coarse scrolling can be applied to strategy-based games, board games, or any game in which scrolling a single tile at a time does not distract from the user experience. Fine scrolling, however, is useful for most scrolling applications because it allows simple physics, such as delta x and y changes, to be applied to the scrolling at a rate that is smaller than an entire tile size. A platform game such as *Super Mario Brothers* or a scrolling shooter such as *Raiden* would be good uses for fine scrolling.

Next, let's define some of the concepts we will apply in our code.

The Camera Object

The viewable window the user will see is called the Camera. It displays just a portion of the tile-based world at a single time. We allow the user to move the camera with the arrow keys to scroll through our tile-map.

The camera will have these attributes:

```
camera.height=theCanvas.height;
camera.width=theCanvas.width;
camera.rows=camera.height / world.tileHeight;
camera.cols=camera.width / world.tileWidth;
camera.dx=0;
camera.dy=0;
camera.x=0;
camera.y=0;
```

The camera object is not complicated. It contains just the necessary attributes to move and paint it to the screen during a `setTimeOut` interval based on user key presses. Its `height` and `width` come directly from the Canvas size (160×160). The *x* and *y* values represent the upper left corner of the camera of the game world. In coarse scrolling, this is either 0 or a multiple of 32 (our tile height and width). The maximum value for the upper left corner of the camera on the x-axis is the world width (480 in our example) minus the camera width (160 in our example). This way, the camera never tries to paint tiles that do not exist in our world map array.

Fine scrolling is similar, but the values for x and y top left corner, or the camera, can each be 0 or any number up to a maximum we calculate to ensure that we are not trying to paint tiles that do not exist off the right side or bottom of the tile-map. In essence, we don't need to scroll 32 pixels at a time but, rather, any number from 1 to 32 (or more, but that would result in extra coarse scrolling and is not examined here as a practical application).

The dx and dy values will be the number of pixels to move the x and y on an interval based on the user key press.

As you can see, the camera dynamically calculates the number of rows and columns it needs to be, based on the `tileHeight` and `tileWidth` from the world. On that note, let's examine the world now.

The World Object

The `world` object contains just the necessary information to create the world the camera will scroll around on and display to the user. The actual world is never shown to the user as a visible object:

```
world.cols=15;
world.rows=15;
world.tileWidth=32;
world.tileHeight=32;
world.height=world.rows*world.tileHeight;
world.width=world.cols*world.tileWidth;
world.map=[];
```

The cols and rows depict the entire size of the world, and the tileHeight and tile Width values are used in calculations when determining the camera position and painting the world tiles to the Camera. The height and width are calculated from the first four values, and the map array is filled in with the map data we examined previously.

Fine Scrolling the Row and Column Buffers

The secret in fine scrolling the canvas is in the row and column buffers. These contain an extra tile (outside the viewable Camera area) that is not needed in coarse scrolling. The buffer is very important because when we fine scroll, we are usually painting only part of the tiles that are on the left, right, top, and bottom edges of the viewable camera.

If camera.x and camera.y are both at 0 (the top left edge of the tile map), we don't need a scroll buffer. If camera.x or camera.y is at ANY other position on the game map screen, we need a scroll buffer for whichever (or both) dimensions are greater than 0, but not at the far right or bottom edge of the viewable world (as described earlier). As you can probably imagine, when playing a game, these x and y values will seldom be 0. Let's take a close look at some examples of this now, because it is the crux of how we calculate and paint the game screen when fine scrolling.

Here is the code we will use to decide whether to use a row or column buffer when we draw our tile map when fine scrolling:

```
if (camera.x<=0) {
    camera.x=0;
    colBuffer=0;
}else if (camera.x > (world.width - camera.width)-scrollRate) {
    camera.x=world.width - camera.width;
    colBuffer=0;
}else{
    colBuffer=1;
}

if (camera.y<=0) {
    camera.y=0;
    rowBuffer=0;
}else if (camera.y > (world.height - camera.height)-scrollRate) {
    camera.y=world.height - camera.height;
    rowBuffer=0;
}else{
    rowBuffer=1;
}
```

The algorithm finds the necessary colBuffer and rowBuffer values, depending on the x and y values of the camera object.

1. If the camera x or y value is 0 or less than 0, we first set it to 0 (so that we are not trying to draw from the negative space of the game map that does not exist), and we set the corresponding `colBuffer` or `rowBuffer` to 0.

2. If the x or y value is not 0 or greater than 0, we next check to see whether the camera will draw from outside the far right or far bottom of the tile map (those tiles do not exist). If that is true, we also set the corresponding `rowBuffer` or `colBuffer` to 0.

3. If on either the x or y axis the camera is in the middle of the tile map, the corresponding `colBuffer` or `rowBuffer` is set to 1. This adds an extra tile row or column to the drawn screen and allows the partial tile to be displayed.

Rather than simply going through this line by line, let's look at four examples and how they would be displayed and calculated in our code.

The camera top-left position

At the upper-left position in our game world, the values to be plugged in would be those in the list that follows. This is the simplest version of scrolling because, in effect, there is no scrolling.

- `scrollRate = 4`
- `camera.x = 0`
- `camera.y = 0`

Subtracting `camera.width` (160) from `world.width` (480) = 320. Next, we subtract `scrollRate` from this result to use in calculating the value of `colBuffer`.

We use the same algorithm for the y axis to get `rowBuffer`: *camera.y > (world.height – camera.height) – scrollRate*:

```
(world.width - camera.width) - scrollRate = 316
(world.height - camera.height) - scrollRate = 316
```

In this example, because the window is at the top-left corner, these values (316, 316) are not needed, but we wanted to demonstrate them because they will be used in the examples. Because we are in the upper left corner of the map, we simply need to check for `camera.x` and `camera.y` being less than or equal to 0.

```
if (camera.x<=0) {
    camera.x=0;
    colBuffer=0;
colBuffer= 0
if (camera.y<=0) {
    camera.y=0;
    rowBuffer=0;
rowBuffer= 0
```

Figure 9-14 shows how the upper left corner would be drawn.

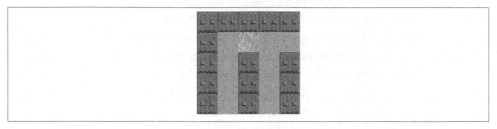

Figure 9-14. The fine scrolling camera at position 0,0

Now let's take a look at the most common type of calculation. This occurs when the viable camera is not right at the edge or bottom of the game screen and not at the top left corner of either of the row or column tiles.

The camera scrolled position

The camera in a scrolled position means that it is *not* in the upper corner of the screen. In this example, we place the camera in about the middle of the screen.

```
scrollRate = 4
camera.x = 180
camera.y = 120
```

Subtracting `camera.width` (160) from `world.width` = 320. Next, we subtract `scrollRate` from this result to use in calculating the value of `colBuffer`.

We use the same algorithm for the y axis to get `rowBuffer`: `camera.y > (world.height - camera.height) -scrollRate`:

```
(world.width - camera.width) - scrollRate = 316
(world.height - camera.height) - scrollRate = 316
colBuffer= 1
rowBuffer= 1
```

In this case, we need to add a scroll buffer on each axis. Figure 9-15 shows what would be painted to the canvas at this camera position.

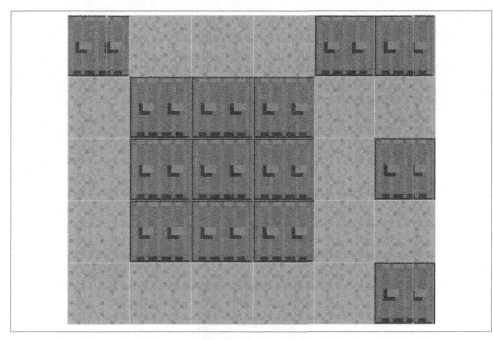

Figure 9-15. The fine scrolling camera at position 180,120 with scroll buffers

What you don't see are the scroll buffers on each axis that actually allow for the fine scrolling to take place. Figure 9-15 shows what is painted to the canvas and the extra map image data that is *not* painted to the canvas. This figure has been zoomed in to show that we actually need to draw an extra row and extra column to the canvas when the camera is in a fine-scrolled state. To display the actual position of the scrolled tiles, we first use a matrix transformation to translate the canvas to the actual point we want to paint to the screen:

```
context.setTransform(1,0,0,1,0,0);
context.translate(-camera.x%world.tileWidth, -camera.y%world.tileHeight);
```

The mod (%) operation returns us just the number of pixels on each axis we need to move *back* in the negative direction to show the portion of all the tiles in Figure 9-15.

We then loop though all the tiles and paint them starting at that position. Therefore, the first tile in each row painted starts in the negative position, off the canvas, and only a portion of it is actually painted to the canvas. The last tile in each row is painted onto only a portion of the canvas. The corresponding paint operations on the columns work the same way. By doing this, we are fine scrolling by simply translating the canvas over the entire subset of tiles (including the extra buffer tiles, see Figure 9-16).

Here is the code that loops through the rows and tiles and paints them to the screen, starting at the newly translated point:

```
for (rowCtr=0;rowCtr<camera.rows+rowBuffer;rowCtr++) {
    for (colCtr=0;colCtr<camera.cols+colBuffer;colCtr++) {

        tileNum=(world.map[rowCtr+tiley][colCtr+tilex]);

        var tilePoint={};
        tilePoint.x=colCtr*world.tileWidth;
        tilePoint.y=rowCtr*world.tileHeight;
        var source={};
        source.x=Math.floor(tileNum % 5) * world.tileWidth;
        source.y=Math.floor(tileNum /5) *world.tileHeight;
        context.drawImage(tileSheet, source.x,
          source.y,world.tileWidth,world.tileHeight, tilePoint.x, tilePoint.y,
                world.tileWidth, world.tileHeight);
        }

    }
```

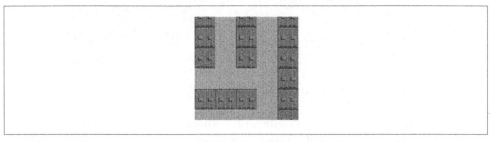

Figure 9-16. The fine scrolling camera at position 180,120

Notice in the code that we add the `rowBuffer` value (in this case, 1) to the `rowCtr` loop, and we add the `colBuffer` value to the `colCtr` loop. Next, we look at edge cases (literally). These occur when the camera has been scrolled to the far right or far bottom of the tile map.

The camera far-right scrolled position

When the camera scrolls past the point where an extra tile would need to be on the far right of the game screen map, we need to set it back to the position it was and *not* try to paint an extra column in `colBuffer`, because the tile map world does not have any more tiles to display. If we didn't do this, an error would be thrown in JavaScript, telling us that we had hit a null in the `world.map` array. In essence, we are subtracting the `dx` or `scrollRate` value from the current camera position.

We have seen this code previously, but here it is one more time. This edge case is the first else: (bold and larger type):

```
if (camera.x<=0) {
    camera.x=0;
```

```
        colBuffer=0;
    }else if (camera.x > (world.width - camera.width)-scrollRate) {
        camera.x=world.width - camera.width;
        colBuffer=0;
    }else{
        colBuffer=1;
    }
```

Figure 9-16 shows an example of the right-side edge case.

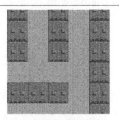

Figure 9-17. The fine scrolling camera at position right-side edge

The data for the algorithm would look like this:

```
scrollRate= 4
camera.x= 320
camera.y= 80
```

This returns buffer values as follows data:

```
colBuffer= 0
rowBuffer= 1
```

Because we are scrolled all the way to the right, the camera.x value is 320. When we add
the camera.width of 160 to this value 320, we get 480. This just so happens to be the
width of the world (world.width). Notice that we have to subtract the scrollRate to
ensure that we are always comparing a value that is less than where the player wants to
go; if we didn't do this, we could actually throw a null pointer error in the column array
lookup.

The camera far down scrolled position

When the camera scrolls past the point at which an extra tile would need to be on the
far bottom of the game screen map, we need to set it back to the position it was and *not*
try to paint an extra row in rowBuffer, because the tile map world does not have any
more tiles to display. If we didn't do this, an error would be thrown in JavaScript, telling
us we had hit a null in the world.map array. In essence, we are subtracting the dy or
scrollRate value from the current camera position.

We have seen this code previously, but here it is one more time. This edge case is the
first else: (bold and larger type):

```
if (camera.y<=0) {
    camera.y=0;
    rowBuffer=0;
}else if (camera.y > (world.height - camera.height)-scrollRate) {
    camera.y=world.height - camera.height;
    rowBuffer=0;
}else{
    rowBuffer=1;
}
```

Figure 9-18 shows an example of the bottom edge case.

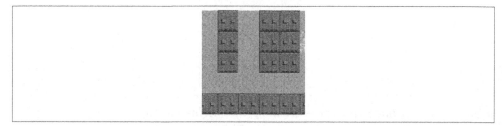

Figure 9-18. The fine scrolling camera at position bottom edge

The data for the algorithm would look like this:

```
scrollRate= 4
camera.x= 40
camera.y= 320
```

This will return buffer values as follows data:

```
colBuffer= 1
rowBuffer= 0
```

Because we are scrolled all the way down, the camera.y value is 320. When we add camera.height of 160 to this value 320, we get 480. This just so happens to be the height of the world (world.height). Notice that we have to subtract scrollRate to ensure that we are always comparing a value that is less than where the player wants to go; if we didn't do this, we could actually throw a null pointer error in the row array lookup.

Coarse Scrolling Full Code Example

Example 9-2, shows the full code listing for the Coarse Scrolling example. The code for this is a little bit simpler than the Fine Scrolling version because we do not need the rowBuffer and colBuffer variables. We also do not need to the matrix transformation to translate the Canvas. We simply need to paint the current set of tiles and will never need to paint any partial tiles as we would with Fine scrolling.

Example 9-2. Coarse scrolling

```
<!doctype html>
<html lang="en">
<head>
<meta charset="UTF-8">
<title>CH9 EX3 - Scrolling Test 1 coarse scrolling</title>

<script src="modernizr.min.js"></script>
<script type="text/javascript">
window.addEventListener('load', eventWindowLoaded, false);
function eventWindowLoaded() {

    canvasApp();

}


</script>


<script language="Javascript">

function canvasSupport () {
      return Modernizr.canvas;
}


function canvasApp(){

    if (!canvasSupport()) {
            return;
      }else{
        var theCanvas = document.getElementById('canvas');
        var context = theCanvas.getContext('2d');
      }


    document.onkeydown=function(e){
        e=e?e:window.event;
        keyPressList[e.keyCode]=true;
    }

    document.onkeyup=function(e){
    //document.body.onkeyup=function(e){
        e=e?e:window.event;
        keyPressList[e.keyCode]=false;
    };

    //key presses
    var keyPressList=[];

    //images
```

```
var tileSheet = new Image();
tileSheet.src = "scrolling_tiles.png";

//mapdata
var world={};

//camera
var camera={}

//key presses
var keyPressList={};


function init() {

    world.cols=15;
    world.rows=15;
    world.tileWidth=32;
    world.tileHeight=32;
    world.height=world.rows*world.tileHeight;
    world.width=world.cols*world.tileWidth;

    camera.height=theCanvas.height;
    camera.width=theCanvas.width;
    camera.rows=camera.height / world.tileHeight;
    camera.cols=camera.width / world.tileWidth;

    camera.dx=0;
    camera.dy=0;
    camera.x=0;
    camera.y=0;

    keyPressList=[];
    gameLoop()
}

function runGame() {
    camera.dx=0;
    camera.dy=0;
    //check input
    if (keyPressList[38]){
        console.log("up");
        camera.dy=-world.tileHeight;
    }
    if (keyPressList[40]){
        console.log("down");
        camera.dy=world.tileHeight;
    }

    if (keyPressList[37]){
        console.log("left");
        camera.dx=-world.tileWidth;
```

```
        }
        if (keyPressList[39]){
            console.log("right");
            camera.dx=world.tileWidth;
        }

        camera.x+=camera.dx;
        camera.y+=camera.dy;

        if (camera.x<0) {
            camera.x=0;

        }else if (camera.x > (world.width - camera.width)-world.tileWidth) {
            camera.x=world.width - camera.width;
        }

        if (camera.y<0) {
            camera.y=0;

        }else if (camera.y > (world.height - camera.height)-world.tileHeight) {
            camera.y=world.height - camera.height;
        }

        context.fillStyle = '#000000';
        context.fillRect(0, 0, theCanvas.width, theCanvas.height);

        //draw camera
        //calculate starting tile position

        var tilex=Math.floor(camera.x/world.tileWidth);
        var tiley=Math.floor(camera.y/world.tileHeight);
        var rowCtr;
        var colCtr;
        var tileNum;

        for (rowCtr=0;rowCtr<camera.rows;rowCtr++) {
            for (colCtr=0;colCtr<camera.cols;colCtr++) {

                tileNum=(world.map[rowCtr+tiley][colCtr+tilex]);
                var tilePoint={};
                tilePoint.x=colCtr*world.tileWidth;
                tilePoint.y=rowCtr*world.tileHeight;
                var source={};
                source.x=Math.floor(tileNum % 5) * world.tileWidth;
                source.y=Math.floor(tileNum /5) *world.tileHeight;
                context.drawImage(tileSheet, source.x, source.y,world.tileWidth,
                            world.tileHeight,tilePoint.x,tilePoint.y,
                            world.tileWidth,world.tileHeight);
            }

        }
```

```
        }

    world.map=[
     [0,0,0,0,0,0,0,0,0,0,0,0,0,0,0,0]
    ,[0,1,2,1,1,1,1,1,1,1,1,1,1,1,1,0]
    ,[0,1,0,1,0,0,1,0,1,0,0,1,0,1,0]
    ,[0,1,0,1,0,0,1,0,1,0,0,1,0,1,0]
    ,[0,1,0,1,0,0,1,1,1,0,0,1,0,1,0]
    ,[0,2,1,1,1,0,0,0,1,1,1,1,1,0]
    ,[0,1,0,0,0,1,0,0,0,1,0,0,0,1,0]
    ,[0,1,1,1,2,1,0,0,0,1,1,1,1,1,0]
    ,[0,0,0,0,0,1,1,1,1,1,0,0,0,0,0]
    ,[0,1,1,1,1,1,0,0,0,1,1,1,1,1,0]
    ,[0,1,0,1,0,0,1,1,1,0,0,1,0,1,0]
    ,[0,1,0,1,0,0,2,0,0,0,0,1,0,1,0]
    ,[0,1,0,1,0,0,1,0,1,0,0,1,0,1,0]
    ,[0,1,1,1,1,1,1,2,1,1,1,1,1,1,0]
    ,[0,0,0,0,0,0,0,0,0,0,0,0,0,0,0,0]
    ];


    init();

    var FRAME_RATE=10;
    var intervalTime=1000/FRAME_RATE;

    function gameLoop() {
        runGame();
        window.setTimeout(gameLoop, intervalTime);
    }

}



</script>

</head>
<body>
<div style="position: absolute; top: 50px; left: 50px;">
<canvas id="canvas" width="160" height="160">
 Your browser does not support the HTML5 Canvas.
</canvas>
</div>
</body>
</html>
```

When you try this in a browser, you can use the arrow keys to scroll the 160×160 camera around the game world. Each key press moves the window 32 pixels at a time in the direction pressed. Now let's take a look at the full code listing for the fine scrolling version.

Fine Scrolling Full Code Example

Example 9-3 shows the full code listing for the Fine Scrolling example. Notice that this code adds in the colBuffer and rowBuffer variables as well as the matrix transformation secret that performs the actual smooth fine scrolling.

Example 9-3. Fine scrolling

```html
<!doctype html>
<html lang="en">
<head>
<meta charset="UTF-8">
<title>CH9 EX4 Scrolling Test 2 fine scrolling</title>

<script src="modernizr.js"></script>
<script type="text/javascript">
window.addEventListener('load', eventWindowLoaded, false);
function eventWindowLoaded() {

    canvasApp();

}

</script>


<script language="Javascript">

function canvasSupport () {
      return Modernizr.canvas;
}


function canvasApp(){

    if (!canvasSupport()) {
            return;
     }else{
        var theCanvas = document.getElementById('canvas');
        var context = theCanvas.getContext('2d');
    }


    document.onkeydown=function(e){
        e=e?e:window.event;
        keyPressList[e.keyCode]=true;
    }

    document.onkeyup=function(e){
    //document.body.onkeyup=function(e){
        e=e?e:window.event;
        keyPressList[e.keyCode]=false;
    };
```

```
//key presses
var keyPressList=[];

//images
var tileSheet = new Image();
tileSheet.src = "scrolling_tiles.png";

//mapdata
var world={};

//camera
var camera={};

//key presses
var keyPressList={};

var rowBuffer=1;
var colBuffer=1;

var scrollRate=4;

function init() {

    world.cols=15;
    world.rows=15;
    world.tileWidth=32;
    world.tileHeight=32;
    world.height=world.rows*world.tileHeight;
    world.width=world.cols*world.tileWidth;

    camera.height=theCanvas.height;
    camera.width=theCanvas.width;
    camera.rows=camera.height / world.tileHeight;
    camera.cols=camera.width / world.tileWidth;

    camera.dx=0;
    camera.dy=0;
    camera.x=0;
    camera.y=0;

    keyPressList=[];
    //console.log("camera.rows=", camera.rows, "camera.cols=", camera.cols);
    gameLoop()
}

function runGame() {
    camera.dx=0;
    camera.dy=0;
    //check input
    if (keyPressList[38]){
        console.log("up");
```

```
            camera.dy=-scrollRate;
    }
    if (keyPressList[40]){
        console.log("down");
        camera.dy=scrollRate;
    }

    if (keyPressList[37]){
        console.log("left");
        camera.dx=-scrollRate;
    }
    if (keyPressList[39]){
        console.log("right");
        camera.dx=scrollRate;
    }

    camera.x+=camera.dx;
    camera.y+=camera.dy;



    if (camera.x<=0) {
        camera.x=0;
        colBuffer=0;
    }else if (camera.x > (world.width - camera.width)-scrollRate) {
        camera.x=world.width - camera.width;
        colBuffer=0;
    }else{
        colBuffer=1;
    }

    if (camera.y<=0) {
        camera.y=0;
        rowBuffer=0;
    }else if (camera.y > (world.height - camera.height)-scrollRate) {
        camera.y=world.height - camera.height;
        rowBuffer=0;
    }else{
        rowBuffer=1;
    }

    console.log("scrollRate=", scrollRate);

    var xDistance=(world.width - camera.width)-scrollRate;
    console.log("camera.x=", camera.x);
    console.log("(world.width - camera.width)-scrollRate =", xDistance);

    var yDistance=(world.height - camera.height)-scrollRate;
    console.log("camera.y=", camera.y);
    console.log("(world.height - camera.height)-scrollRate =", yDistance);
```

```
        console.log("colBuffer=", colBuffer);
        console.log("rowBuffer", rowBuffer);

        context.fillStyle = '#000000';
        context.fillRect(0, 0, theCanvas.width, theCanvas.height);

        //draw camera
        //calculate starting tile position

        var tilex=Math.floor(camera.x/world.tileWidth);
        var tiley=Math.floor(camera.y/world.tileHeight);
        var rowCtr;
        var colCtr;
        var tileNum;

        context.setTransform(1,0,0,1,0,0);
        context.translate(-camera.x%world.tileWidth, -camera.y%world.tileHeight);

        for (rowCtr=0;rowCtr<camera.rows+rowBuffer;rowCtr++) {
            for (colCtr=0;colCtr<camera.cols+colBuffer;colCtr++) {

                tileNum=(world.map[rowCtr+tiley][colCtr+tilex]);

                var tilePoint={};
                tilePoint.x=colCtr*world.tileWidth;
                tilePoint.y=rowCtr*world.tileHeight;
                var source={};
                source.x=Math.floor(tileNum % 5) * world.tileWidth;
                source.y=Math.floor(tileNum /5) *world.tileHeight;
                context.drawImage(tileSheet, source.x, source.y, world.tileWidth,
                                world.tileHeight,tilePoint.x,tilePoint.y,
                                world.tileWidth,world.tileHeight);
            }

        }

    }


  world.map=[
  [0,0,0,0,0,0,0,0,0,0,0,0,0,0,0]
  ,[0,1,2,1,1,1,1,1,1,1,1,1,1,1,0]
  ,[0,1,0,1,0,0,1,0,1,0,0,1,0,1,0]
  ,[0,1,0,1,0,0,1,0,1,0,0,1,0,1,0]
  ,[0,1,0,1,0,0,1,1,1,0,0,1,0,1,0]
  ,[0,2,1,1,1,1,0,0,0,1,1,1,1,1,0]
  ,[0,1,0,0,0,1,0,0,0,1,0,0,0,1,0]
  ,[0,1,1,1,2,1,0,0,0,1,1,1,1,1,0]
  ,[0,0,0,0,0,1,1,1,1,1,0,0,0,0,0]
  ,[0,1,1,1,1,1,0,0,0,1,1,1,1,1,0]
  ,[0,1,0,1,0,0,1,1,1,0,0,1,0,1,0]
  ,[0,1,0,1,0,0,2,0,0,0,0,1,0,1,0]
```

```
    ,[0,1,0,1,0,0,1,0,1,0,0,1,0,1,0]
    ,[0,1,1,1,1,1,1,2,1,1,1,1,1,1,0]
    ,[0,0,0,0,0,0,0,0,0,0,0,0,0,0,0]
   ];

      init();

      var FRAME_RATE=10;
      var intervalTime=1000/FRAME_RATE;

      function gameLoop() {
          runGame();
          window.setTimeout(gameLoop, intervalTime);
      }

   }



</script>

</head>
<body>
<div style="position: absolute; top: 50px; left: 50px;">
<canvas id="canvas" width="160" height="160">
 Your browser does not support the HTML5 Canvas.
</canvas>
</div>
</body>
</html>
```

We have left in the console.log statements that show how the algorithm is detecting the `rowBuffer` and `colBuffer` values. These are the same values we saw previously in Example 9-3.

When you run this page in a browser, the arrow keys allow you to move the camera 4 pixels in each of the up, down, left, and right directions. You can change this value by setting `scrollRate` to a new value.

That's all there is to both fine and coarse scrolling a tile-based screen. By using some of the examples in previous chapters, you can extend this to add path finding, physics, and even pixel-based collision detection to create any type of game you want that uses a scrolling screen.

What's Next?

Throughout this book, we have used game and entertainment-related subjects to demonstrate canvas application building concepts. Over these last two chapters, we've sped up the game discussion and covered many game concepts directly by creating two unique games and optimizing a third with bitmaps and object pooling. We also introduced the powerful concept of tile-based coarse and fine scrolling and A* path finding to the mix. In doing so, we have applied many of the concepts from the earlier chapters in full-blown game applications and have added a new secret technique that can be applied to make some very powerful games and game engines. The techniques used to create a game on Canvas can be applied to almost any Canvas application, from image viewers to stock charting. The sky is really the limit because the canvas allows the developer a full suite of powerful, low-level capabilities that can be molded into any application.

In Chapter 10, we look at porting a simple game from Canvas into a native iPhone application and optimizing *Geo Blaster Extended* for a touch-based interface.

Going Mobile!

Nowadays, it seems that everyone is making, planning to make, or thinking of making applications for mobile devices. Mobile is the next great (or maybe actually the current) place to make money by selling applications. While HTML5 applications can be packaged up with tools such as Cordova Phone Gap and other systems, we are going to focus this chapter on targeting the mobile browser from a website to play games. We will first build our applications to work in a desktop web browser, and then we will modify them to scale full screen on iOS devices.

The First Application

The application we are going to create is a simple *BS Bingo* game. BS Bingo was designed on paper well before mobile devices were available. This cynical game concept is based on the feeling (by some) that the typical business workplace has been overtaken with *Dilbert-* or *Office Space*-esque annoying corporate jargon and doublespeak. This doublespeak seems to have deeply rooted itself in the workplace over the last 20 years, mostly to the annoyance of software developers (such as ourselves).

In the pen-and-paper version of the game, each player brings a "bingo card" to a meeting where he expects to hear a lot of this corporate doublespeak. The bingo card is a 5×5 grid, and each of the 25 squares is filled with one of the annoying words or jargon phrases. During the meeting, each player marks off squares as the words or phrases are said aloud by the unsuspecting (and not playing) members of the meeting. When a player has a full column or row of his card marked off, he is supposed to jump up from the meeting table and yell "BS!"

Whether this game was ever widely played (or even played at all) is a debatable urban legend, but the simple concept of clicking squares to highlight them makes for a useful piece of code that we can build easily and then port to the iPhone. We are not even going to build the entire game here; we will leave extending it into a full application (possibly adding multiplayer, which is discussed in Chapter 11) for you, the reader.

The Code

Example 10-1 gives the code for our game. We'll discuss the various functions in the next section before we move on to testing it in a desktop browser and then modifying it to run full screen on an iOS device. This version of the game will work fine on a Safari desktop browser. We will highlight the modifications necessary to port it to the iPhone/ iPad in the next section.

Example 10-1. BSBingo.html full source listing

```
<!doctype html>
 <html lang="en">
 <head>
    <meta charset="UTF-8">

 <title>BS Bingo</title>

 <script src="modernizr-min.js"></script>
 <script src="TextButton.js"></script>
 <script src="ConsoleLog.js"></script>
 <script type="text/javascript">

window.addEventListener('load', eventWindowLoaded, false);
function eventWindowLoaded() {

    canvasApp();

}

function canvasSupport () {
    return Modernizr.canvas;
}

function canvasApp(){

    if (!canvasSupport()) {
          return;
      }else{
        theCanvas = document.getElementById("canvas");
        context = theCanvas.getContext("2d");
    }

    var bingoCard = [];
    var buttons = [];

    var standardJargonList = [];
    var tempButton = {};
    var clickSound;
```

```
function initLists(){

    standardJargonList=[
     "Actionable", "Assessment" ,"Bandwidth", "Benchmark",
     "Best\nPractices", "Bottle neck" , "Change\nManagement",  "Coach",
     "Competitive\nAdvantage", "Constraints", "Core\nCompetencies",
     "Core values", "Critical\nthinking", "Cutting\nedge",
     "Dashboard", "Deliverables", "Enterprise","Gatekeeper",
     "Individual\nContributor", "Leadership", "Matrix\norganisation",
     "Metrics", "Milestones", "Momentum", "Moving target",
     "Initiative","Partnership", "Process", "Process\nmanagement",
     "Re-engineer", "Requirements", "Rightsize", "Seat at\nthe table",
     "Tentpole", " Silo", "Standards", "State of the art",
     "Supply chain", "Synergy","Teamwork", "Thought\nleader",
     "Touchpoints", "Value\nadded", "Drink the\nKool Aid",
     "Baked In", "Champion", "Circle Back", "Dialogue", "Emerge",
     "Enhance", "Evolve", "Execute", "Facilitate" ,"Incentivise",
     "Leverage", "Partner", "Spearhead", "Strategize","Synergise",
     "Throw\na\nCurve", "Touch Base", "Outside\nthe\nBox",
     "Opportunity", "Open Door\nPolicy","Win-Win\n(Anything)",
     "Risk\n(Anything)","Proactive","Reactive","Buy-In",
     "Paradigm\nShift","Task-Oriented","Empower","Team\nPlayer",
     "Enterprise\nWide","Globalization","Localization",
     "Mission-critical", "Magic\nQuadrant","Agile\n(Anything)",
     "Waterfall","Outsourcing","Off-Shoring","Blue Sky",
     "20/20\nhindsight","Low\nHanging\nFruit","10,000\nFoot View",
     "Take\nOwnership","Ramp up", "Out of\nthe Box", "24x7",
     "Fast Track", "Out of\nthe Loop", "In the\nLoop","Touch Base",
     "Mindset", "Game Plan", "Bring to \nthe Table", "Drill Down",
     "Elevator\nSpeech", "Level the\nPlaying field",
     "Ping\n(Someone)","Pushback","Retool", "Take Away",
     "Life-Time\nValue", "Thought\nLeadership", "Up Sell"
      ];

}

function initButtons(){
    buttons = [
       [

       new TextButton(0,0,"Button
           0,0",85,50,gr,"#000000","#ffff00","#000000"),

       new TextButton(92,0,"Button
           0,1",85,50,gr,"#000000","#ffff00","#000000"),

       new TextButton(184,0,"Button
           0,2",85,50,gr,"#000000","#ffff00","#000000"),

       new TextButton(276,0,"Button
           0,3",85,50,gr,"#000000","#ffff00","#000000"),
```

```
  new TextButton(368,0,"Button
     0,4",85,50,gr,"#000000","#ffff00","#000000")

],

[

 new TextButton(0,57,"Button
     1,0",85,50,gr,"#000000","#ffff00","#000000"),

 new TextButton(92,57,"Button
     1,1",85,50,gr,"#000000","#ffff00","#000000"),

 new TextButton(184,57,"Button
     1,2",85,50,gr,"#000000","#ffff00","#000000"),

 new TextButton(276,57,"Button
     1,3",85,50,gr,"#000000","#ffff00","#000000"),

 new TextButton(368,57,"Button
     1,4",85,50,gr,"#000000","#ffff00","#000000")

],

[

 new TextButton(0,114,"Button
     2,0",85,50,gr,"#000000","#ffff00","#000000"),

 new TextButton(92,114,"Button
     2,1",85,50,gr,"#000000","#ffff00","#000000"),

 new TextButton(184,114,"Button
     2,2",85,50,gr,"#000000","#ffff00","#000000"),

 new TextButton(276,114,"Button
     2,3",85,50,gr,"#000000","#ffff00","#000000"),

 new TextButton(368,114,"Button
     2,4",85,50,gr,"#000000","#ffff00","#000000")

],

[

 new TextButton(0,171,"Button
     3,0",85,50,gr,"#000000","#ffff00","#000000"),

 new TextButton(92,171,"Button
     3,1",85,50,gr,"#000000","#ffff00","#000000"),
```

```
      new TextButton(184,171,"Button
          3,2",85,50,gr,"#000000","#ffff00","#000000"),

      new TextButton(276,171,"Button
          3,3",85,50,gr,"#000000","#ffff00","#000000"),

      new TextButton(368,171,"Button
          3,4",85,50,gr,"#000000","#ffff00","#000000")

    ],

    [

      new TextButton(0,228,"Button
          4,0",85,50,gr,"#000000","#ffff00","#000000"),

      new TextButton(92,228,"Button
          4,1",85,50,gr,"#000000","#ffff00","#000000"),

      new TextButton(184,228,"Button
          4,2",85,50,gr,"#000000","#ffff00","#000000"),

      new TextButton(276,228,"Button
          4,3",85,50,gr,"#000000","#ffff00","#000000"),

      new TextButton(368,228,"Button
          4,4",85,50,gr,"#000000","#ffff00","#000000")

    ]
  ];
}

function initSounds(){
    clickSound = document.getElementById('clicksound');
}

function chooseButtonsForCard(){
    //copy jargon into temp array
    var tempArray = [];
    for (var arrayctr=0;arrayctr<standardJargonList.length;arrayctr++){
        tempArray.push(standardJargonList[arrayctr]);
    }

    for (var ctr1=0;ctr1<buttons.length;ctr1++){

        for (var ctr2=0; ctr2<buttons[ctr1].length;ctr2++){
            var randInt = Math.floor(Math.random()*tempArray.length);
            buttons[ctr1][ctr2].text = tempArray[randInt];
            tempArray.splice(randInt,1);
        }
    }
}
```

```
    }


    function drawScreen() {
       //ConsoleLog.log("standardAcronymList="+standardAcronymList.length);
       //ConsoleLog.log("standardJargonList="+standardJargonList.length);
       for (var ctr1=0;ctr1<buttons.length;ctr1++){
          ConsoleLog.log("ctr1="+ctr1)
          for (var ctr2=0; ctr2<buttons[ctr1].length;ctr2++){
             buttons[ctr1][ctr2].draw(context);
          }
       }

    }

    function onMouseClick(e) {

       //select case through states and then the locations of
       //buttons in those states
       mouseX = e.clientX-theCanvas.offsetLeft;
       mouseY = e.clientY-theCanvas.offsetTop;
       ConsoleLog.log("click " + mouseX + "," + mouseY);
       //find the button clicked

       var col = Math.floor(mouseX/92);
       var row = Math.floor(mouseY/57);

       console.log("row",row,"col", col);
       tempButton = buttons[row][col];
       clickSound.play();
       tempButton.pressDown();
       tempButton.draw(context);

    }

    function onMouseMove(e) {
       mouseX = e.clientX-theCanvas.offsetLeft;
       mouseY = e.clientY-theCanvas.offsetTop;
    }

       //**** start application
    var gr = context.createLinearGradient(0, 0, 85, 50);

    // Add the color stops.
    gr.addColorStop(0,'#ffffff');
         gr.addColorStop(.5,'#bbbbbb');
    gr.addColorStop(1,'#777777');

    theCanvas.addEventListener("mousemove", onMouseMove, false);
    theCanvas.addEventListener("click", onMouseClick, false);
```

```
    initSounds();
    initButtons();
    initLists();
    chooseButtonsForCard();
    drawScreen();

}

</script>

</head>
<body>
<div style="position: absolute; top: 0px; left: 0px;">
<canvas id="canvas" width="570" height="418">
 Your browser does not support HTML5 Canvas.
</canvas>
<audio id ="clicksound"  preload="auto">
   <source src="click.mp3" type="audio/mpeg" />

Your browser does not support the audio element.
</audio>
</div>
</body>
</html>
```

Name this file *bsbingo.html*, and save it in a folder. If you are going to follow along and create the example project, you will also want to create a folder to hold the project files.

Examining the Code for BSBingo.html

 When designing an application for the iOS platform, we are actually targeting the Safari Mobile browser. This means that we can make concessions rather than having to target all available HTML5-compatible devices. You will notice this especially when we discuss <audio> tag usage.

The TextButton.js file

Our BS Bingo game will be played on a grid of 25 squares. We have created a class (an object prototype, actually) called `TextButton.js` to help us create buttons with the text, as well as a "press" state that we can use to show that the button has been clicked. You will want to save this file in the project folder along with the *BSBingo.html* file. Here is the code for this file:

```
function TextButton(x,y,text, width, height, backColor, strokeColor,
  overColor, textColor){
    this.x = x;
    this.y = y;
```

```
        this.text = text;
        this.width = width;
        this.height = height;
        this.backColor = backColor;
        this.strokeColor = strokeColor;
        this.overColor = overColor;
        this.textColor = textColor;
        this.press = false;
}

TextButton.prototype.pressDown=function() {
    if (this.press==true){
        this.press = false;
    }else{
        this.press = true;
    }
}

TextButton.prototype.draw = function(context){

    context.save();
    context.setTransform(1,0,0,1,0,0); // reset to identity
    context.translate(this.x, this.y);

    context.shadowOffsetX = 3;
    context.shadowOffsetY = 3;
    context.shadowBlur = 3;
    context.shadowColor = "#222222";

    context.lineWidth = 4;
    context.lineJoin = 'round';
    context.strokeStyle = this.strokeColor;

    if (this.press==true){
        context.fillStyle = this.overColor;
    }else{
        context.fillStyle = this.backColor;
    }

    context.strokeRect(0, 0, this.width,this.height);
    context.fillRect(0, 0, this.width,this.height);

    //text
    context.shadowOffsetX = 1;
    context.shadowOffsetY = 1;
    context.shadowBlur = 1;
    context.shadowColor = "#ffffff";
    context.font = "14px serif"
    context.fillStyle = this.textColor;
    context.textAlign = "center";
    context.textBaseline = "middle";
    var metrics = context.measureText(this.text);
```

```
var textWidth = metrics.width;
var xPosition = this.width/2;
var yPosition = (this.height/2);

var splitText = this.text.split('\n');
var verticalSpacing = 14;

for (var ctr1=0; ctr1<splitText.length;ctr1++) {
    context.fillText ( splitText[ctr1], xPosition,
    yPosition+ (ctr1*verticalSpacing));
}

    context.restore();
}
```

This object prototype contains functions for creating, drawing, and clicking a gray square button with black text on it. When clicked, the button will be drawn with a yellow background. We have covered all these drawing functions earlier in this book, so they will look familiar to you if you have read those chapters. If you have not, it's especially a good idea to read Chapter 2, which covers drawing and shading objects drawn with paths.

Let's now take a quick look at the functions we have created in *bsbingo.html*.

The initLists() function

The first game-related function you will encounter is initLists(). For our simple game implementation, we have created a single list of words based on some common business jargon. The standardJargonList application scope variable will contain a single-dimension array of words that will be placed randomly on the player's bingo card. We can add more types of lists if we would like to target other types of jargon-speak, such as pure IT process-speak, marketing-speak, or even sports- or geek-speak.

The initButtons() function

This function creates a grid of 25 TextButton instances, 85 pixels in width and 25 in height. These are stored in the application scope buttons two-dimensional array so that they can be accessed via the [row][column] syntax.

The initSounds() function

The initSounds() function needs to initialize only a single sound referenced in an HTML5 <audio> tag. Because we are targeting the iOS platform, we need to provide only a single *.mp3*-formatted sound. We do not need *.ogg* or *.wav* because we are not targeting any other browsers. Here is the HTML5 <audio> tag:

```
<audio id="clicksound" preload="auto">
    <source src="click.mp3" type="audio/mpeg" />
```

```
Your browser does not support the audio element.
</audio>
```

The chooseButtonsForCard() function

This function creates a local array called tempArray and fills it with the contents of the standardJargonList. Next, it randomly chooses an element from the tempArray for each of the 25 row/column combinations on the bingo card. As it selects a word, it splices it from the tempArray so that it cannot be selected again, leaving the card with no duplicates.

The drawScreen() function

This function loops through the buttons two-dimensional array and draws the initial 25 buttons with text onto the canvas.

The onMouseClick() function

When the user clicks the mouse on the game screen, this event listener function determines which of the 25 squares was clicked. It calls the appropriate TextButton instance's pressDown() function and then its draw() function, passing in the context.

The onMouseMove() function

When the mouse is moved, this event listener function will set the mouseX and mouseY values to the current mouse position on the canvas.

The Application Code

After all the functions and the TextButton object prototype are created, the actual application code is very simple. Because this is a completely event-based application, we don't need a main loop. We also have not put in any other states or buttons, such as a title screen or a reset button. This makes the app less user-friendly, but it is fine for this simple example. It also makes the application code very simple:

```
//**** start application
   var gr = context.createLinearGradient(0, 0, 100, 100);

   // Add the color stops.
   gr.addColorStop(0,'#ffffff');
   gr.addColorStop(.5,'#bbbbbb');
   gr.addColorStop(1,'#777777');

   theCanvas.addEventListener("mousemove", onMouseMove, false);
   theCanvas.addEventListener("click", onMouseClick, false);
   initSounds();
   initButtons();
   initLists();
```

```
        chooseButtonsForCard();
        drawScreen();
```
First, we create a shared linear gradient that can be used by all the TextButton instances. Next we add the mouse event listeners for click and move. Finally, we run through our functions to set up the card, and then we simply wait for the user to click a button. That's all there is to it. We haven't even added a way to announce that the player has won. Extending this into a full-fledged application would be very simple, so we leave this task up to the reader if you have the desire to do so.

Figure 10-1 shows the screen for the finished application.

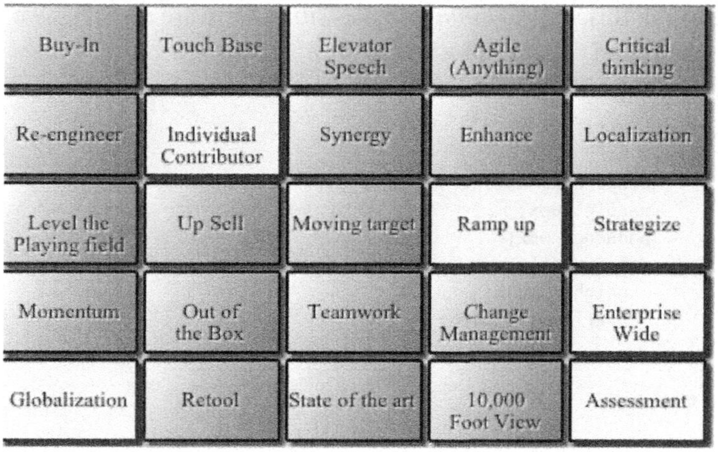

Figure 10-1. BS Bingo in Safari Desktop Edition

Next we will look at how to scale the game as a web-based, full-screen iOS application.

Scaling the Game for the Browser

The cool thing about HTML5 Canvas, especially when it comes to Mobile Safari, is that we can easily create applications that scale to the full screen of an iOS device and allow the user to add an icon to their Home screen interface. This icon will play the application in full screen (without the top browser bar) and will function just like an app downloaded from iTunes. The only caveat us that the app is actually on a web page, hosted on a web server, and the user will need Internet access to use it.

Starting to create a full screen mobile version of BS Bingo

We now have a game that is shoved up into the top-left corner of the browser window, and while it plays fine, it will be too small on a phone browser and will be shoved up into the corner on a tablet browser. Scaling the game to work on the desktop and mobile devices is not difficult, but it will require some changes and additions to the current code in the *bsbingo.html* file.

The game's aspect ratio is not ideal for a mobile Safari full screen application, so we will see soon enough that the buttons and text will look a little pixilated and not fit perfectly on the iOS screens. However, this is only the first of two examples, and it will be good to see it in action to educate ourselves about what changes we should make for the second application in the chapter so that it will fit better on an iOS screen.

Changing the Canvas style properties

We will need to add some new styles to the file to help position and scale the *.html* file. I am going to call this version *bsbingo_scaled.html*. Here are the styles we will need to add to take the scaled Canvas full screen:

```
<style>
<style type="text/css">
        html, body {
            background-color: #2f9acc;
            margin: 0px;
            padding: 0px;
            color: #fff;
              height: 100%;
              overflow: hidden;
        }

        #canvas {

            overflow: hidden;
            image-rendering: optimizeSpeed;
            -ms-interpolation-mode: nearest-neighbor;
            -webkit-optimize-contrast;
              width:100%;
              height:100%;

        }

         :webkit-full-screen {
            width: 100%;
            height: 100%;
        }


    </style>
```

What these styles do is force both the HTML <BODY> tag and the canvas to scale to fit the entire screen and limit the size of the scroll bars.

See Figure 10-2 for an example of *bsbingo_scaled.html* in a desktop browser.

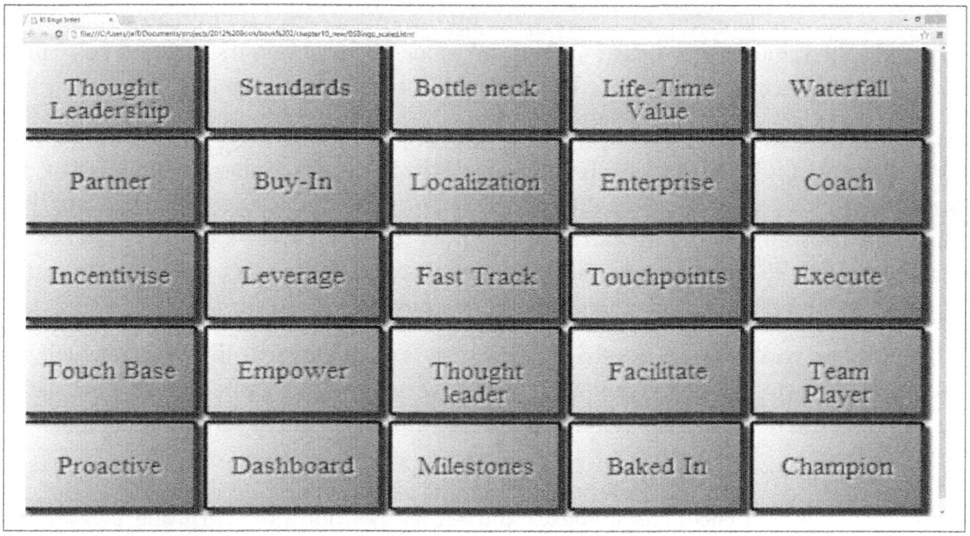

Figure 10-2. BS Bingo scaled to fit the Chrome browser

Updating the mouse listening code

Now that the game has been scaled, the current mouse listener code that determines clicks will not work. We need to add in the following code to determine the new scale of the Canvas and translate that into mouse clicks:

```
function onMouseClick(e) {

    var mouseX;
    var mouseY;

    var xFactor = theCanvas.width / window.innerWidth;
    var yFactor = theCanvas.height / window.innerHeight;

    var mouseX1 = event.clientX - theCanvas.offsetLeft;
    var mouseY1 = event.clientY - theCanvas.offsetTop;
    mouseX = mouseX1 * xFactor;
    mouseY = mouseY1 * yFactor;
    //find the button clicked

    var col = Math.floor(mouseX/(92));
    var row = Math.floor(mouseY/(57));

    console.log("row",row,"col", col);
    tempButton=buttons[row][col];
    clickSound.play();
    tempButton.pressDown();
    tempButton.draw(context);

}
```

The xFactor and yFactor variables make up the secret sauce that creates values that are multiplied against the mouseX and mouseY values. This allows the col and row values to be easily determined now that that the scale factor has been applied.

These are determined by dividing the current canvas width and height by the current actual size of the web browser (window.innerWidth and window.innerHeight), respectively. This will provide us with a scale factor in each dimension that we apply to the mouse position to find the canvas pixel rather than the browser pixel. This takes the scaling out of the equation and allows the application to use its original math rather than worry about the actual scaled size of the Canvas.

One problem you will notice is that if the screen is scrolled vertically, this code will not work. This is why we will create a full screen version of the game that can be played from the Home screen of the iOS device and eliminate as much scrolling as possible.

 If you encounter a mouseX and mouseY position problem using the event.clientX and event.clientY values on a scrolling browser window, you can substitute them with event.pageX and event.page. In most browsers, this substitution will help if the screen is scrolled.

Adding meta-tags for iOS devices

Meta-tags are added to help the iOS devices determine the correct size of the viewport in a scaled mode and also to define an icon. With the icon, the user can add a link from the web-published game to their iOS device that can be clicked just like any other application.

```
<meta name="viewport" content="initial-scale=1 maximum-scale=1
    user-scalable=0" />
<meta name="apple-mobile-web-app-capable" content="yes" />
<meta name="apple-touch-fullscreen" content="yes">
<link rel="apple-touch-icon" href="bsicon.png" >
```

Figures 10-3 and 10-4 show the icon and banner that we will use for the app.

Figure 10-3. 57x57 icon (scaled up for viewing)

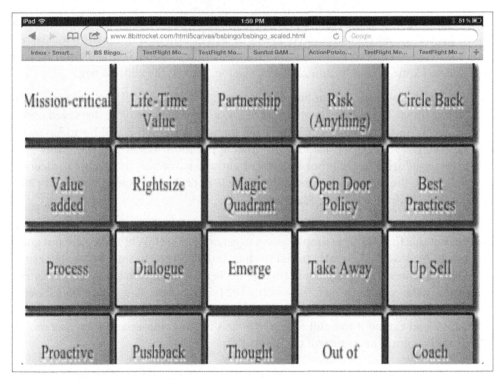

Figure 10-4. Add to Home Screen button at top

Testing the Game on an Actual Device

We have placed a folder with the live files at this site (*http://www.8bitrocket.com/html5canvas/bsbingo/bsbingo_scaled.html*).

You can find also these files in the *bsbingo_scaled* folder, inside the Chapter 10 directory in the book's download files at O'Reilly's website (*http://oreil.ly/html5-canvas-2edition*).

The folder contains the following files:

1. *bsbingo_scaled.html*
2. *bsicon.png*
3. *click.mp3*
4. *ConsoleLog.js*
5. *modernizr-min.js*
6. *TextButton.js*

To add this page (or your own live page) to the iPad or iPhone desktop, simply navigate to the page and then click the Add to Home Screen button next to the browser address bar. Figure 10-4 shows *bsbingo_scaled.html* running in mobile Safari on an iPad with the Add to Home Screen button circled at the top, next to the address bar.

When the Add to Home Screen button is pressed, it will ask you if you want to use the *bsicon.png* image that we designated. It will also ask for a name to be displayed on the home screen under the icon. Click the icon, name it, and then it will be added to the home screen of your device just like any other application. When you run it this time, the browser address bar will not be present and the game will fit nicely (as nicely as possible given the aspect ratio we chose) on the iPad or iPhone Screen. See Figure 10-5 for the game running in this mode.

You will notice that we did not choose an aspect ratio that looks really pretty on the scale screen, but this first example simply serves to get our feet wet. While were are not going to do it here, it would be pretty trivial to change the code to fit into a 640×480 aspect ratio with borders around the application to make it look nicer on the screen. If you do choose to make your game on a 640×480 or 1024×768 canvas, you will get much better results. Next, we will create a new version of the GeoBlaster Extended game from Chapter 9 and extend it to a full screen app, first in the browser and then as a mobile Safari application. The game will use a better aspect ratio.

iPad		2:09 PM		⅜ 50%
Tentpole	Drill Down	Competitive Advantage	Level the Playing field	Ping (Someone)
Mission-critical	Supply chain	Partnership	Enhance	Change Management
Waterfall	Deliverables	Win-Win (Anything)	Open Door Policy	Benchmark
Re-engineer	Value added	Process	Touchpoints	Matrix organisation
Throw	Critical thinking	Fast Track	Dashboard	Standards

Figure 10-5. Game launched from the Home screen

Retro Blaster Touch

We are going to use the guts of the GeoBlaster Extended game from Chapter 9, change it up a bit graphically, and then modify it for touch controls. Mouse movement and touch movement are handled in different manners between the desktop and mobile Safari browsers, so most of our code changes will be in this area. We will also be adding in auto-fire to the game, because we don't want the user to have to press any complicated on-screen buttons to fire missiles.

The original Retro Blaster was one of the first indie Flash games that we ever completed. If you search for "8bitrocket Retro Blaster" on the Internet, you will find it in a number of places. It is a much more complicated and intricate game than we are going to create here. What we have done is replace the tile sheets from GeoBlaster Extended with game graphics from Retro Blaster, and we have added a background graphic and title screen.

Figures 10-6 and 10-7 show the new player ship tile sheets that we will be using.

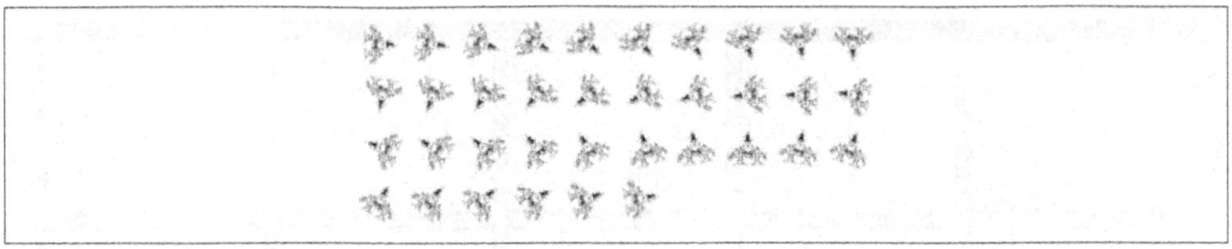

Figure 10-6. Retro Blaster ship tiles 1

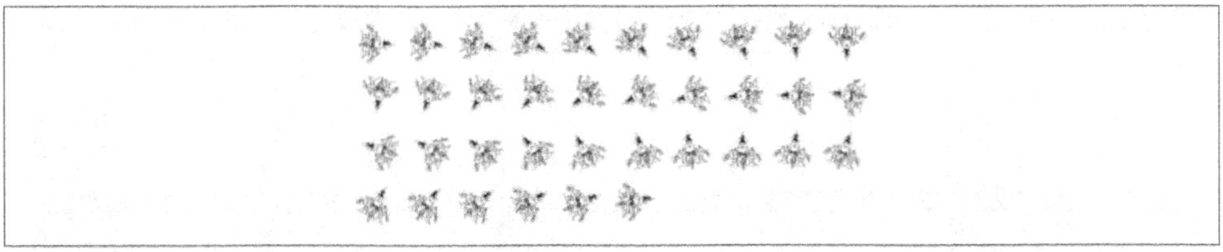

Figure 10-7. Retro Blaster ship tiles 2 (with thrust)

Figures 10-8, 10-9, and 10-10 show examples of the large, medium, and small rock tile sheets that we will use in this version of the Retro Blaster Touch game.

Figure 10-8. Retro Blaster large rock tiles

Figure 10-9. Retro Blaster medium rock tiles

Figure 10-10. Retro Blaster small rock tiles

We also have a set of tiles for the particle explosions and a single image that will be that saucer that attacks the player. Figures 10-11 and 10-12 show these two files, respectively.

Figure 10-11. 10x enlarged version of the Retro Blaster particle explosion tiles

Figure 10-12. Enlarged version of the Retro Blaster enemy saucer

Aside from these game-play elements, we have created a title screen, background screen, and home screen icon for the game. These are shown in Figures 10-13, 10-14, and 10-15.

Figure 10-13. Retro Blaster title screen

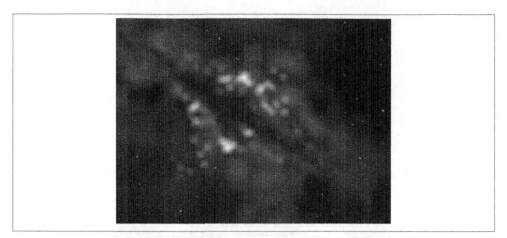

Figure 10-14. Retro Blaster game background screen

Figure 10-15. 64x64 Home screen icon (enlarged for print)

Now that we have taken a good look at the new assets, let's go through the code necessary to scale the game to the browser window and then add both the mouse and the touch events.

Mobilizing Retro Blaster Touch

The full code for the Retro Blaster Touch game is in a folder called *retroblaster_touch* in the Chapter 10 files downloaded from the O'Reilly (*http://shop.oreilly.com/product/ 0636920026266.do*) website. We are not going to go through the full set of changes or provide the entire code listing here (one giant code listing in Chapter 9 was quite enough). Retro Blaster Touch is a modification of that full code listing for GeoBlaster Extended game from Chapter 9. We will go though the most important changes in the next few sections.

Jumping to Full Screen

The changes to HTML and CSS necessary to jump to full screen are almost identical to those for the BSBingo game. The one change we have made is to create this game at a

480×320 aspect ratio that will scale more evenly to various device sizes in landscape mode.

Canvas element

We will be using the following HTML Canvas element code:

```
<div style="top: 0px; left: 0px; height: 100%; width: 100%;">
<canvas id="canvas" width="480" height="320" >
 Your browser does not support the HTML 5 Canvas.
</canvas>
```

Notice that we have moved the DIV element that holds the game from the GeoBlaster Extended 50x, 50y starting point to 0,0, using the top and left style attributes.

Meta-tags

We also need to add in a set of meta-tags for Mobile Safari that will aid in informing the device to run the application at full screen when the Home Screen icon is clicked.

```
<meta name="viewport" content="initial-scale=1 maximum-scale=1
     user-scalable=0" />
<meta name="apple-mobile-web-app-capable" content="yes" />
<meta name="apple-touch-fullscreen" content="yes">
<link rel="apple-touch-icon" href="icon.png" >
```

Also note that we have added the *icon.png* image as the referenced Home Screen icon when the user adds the game to their Home screen from the website.

Style sheets

Next we need to add in the same style attributes for the canvas that we did with the BSBingo game:

```
<style type="text/css">
      html, body {
          background-color: #2f9acc;
          margin: 0px;
          padding: 0px;
          color: #fff;
            height: 100%;
            overflow: hidden;
      }

      #canvas {

          overflow: hidden;
          image-rendering: optimizeSpeed;
          -ms-interpolation-mode: nearest-neighbor;
          -webkit-optimize-contrast;
            width:100%;
            height:100%;
```

```
        }

    :webkit-full-screen {
        width: 100%;
        height: 100%;
    }
</style>
```

These changes will cosmetically put the game into full screen, but we still have not added in the mouse movement and touch controls to allow the game to be played full screen in either a desktop or a mobile Safari browser. Let's look at those now.

Touch Move Events

The one difference between a desktop mouse and a mobile device is the finger touch. The finger-touch movement when "tapped" is identical to the mouse-click, so we were able to use the same basic code for each in the *bsbingo_scaled* game. For Retro Blaster Touch, we will need to have two separate events set up. One will be for the finger-touch events, and one will be for the mouse events. The same scale factor algorithm as in *bsbingo_scaled* can be applied to each set of events to determine the correct *x* and *y* coordinate for the mouse for whichever device (Safari Desktop or Safari Mobile) the game is played on.

New global variables

We will be defining a new set of global variables that will be used to move the player ship on the game screen:

```
//touch
var mouseX;
var mouseY;
var touchX;
var touchY;
```

The touch and mouse listener functions will translate the position of the finger or mouse on the game screen to the mouseX and mouseY variables. touchX and touchY will be caught and used to set mouseX and mouseY when using a mobile device, while mouseX and mouseY will be used directly when using a desktop browser. We will demonstrate this code in the following section.

New listener functions

When the player ship starts, we will add these new functions to the gameStatePlayer Start() function from GeoBlaster Extended.

```
theCanvas.addEventListener("mousemove", onMouseMove, false);
theCanvas.addEventListener("touchmove", onTouchMove, false);
```

We are going to add a listener function for each of these and also a separate function that will translate the touchX and touchY values into mouseX and mouseY. This way, the game doesn't need to know what type of device it is running on; it will work with both mouse and touch events in the same manner.

```
function onMouseMove(e) {
    var xFactor = theCanvas.width / window.innerWidth;
    var yFactor = theCanvas.height / window.innerHeight;

    var mouseX1 = event.clientX - theCanvas.offsetLeft;
    var mouseY1 = event.clientY - theCanvas.offsetTop;
    mouseX = mouseX1 * xFactor;
    mouseY = mouseY1 * yFactor;

    allMoveHandler(mouseX,mouseY);

}


function onTouchMove(e) {
    if (e.touches.item(0)) {
        targetEvent =  e.touches.item(0);
    }else{
        targetEvent =  e;
    }

    touchX1=targetEvent.clientX-theCanvas.offsetLeft;
    touchY1=targetEvent.clientY-theCanvas.offsetTop;
    xFactor =  theCanvas.width/window.innerWidth;
    yFactor = theCanvas.height/window.innerHeight;
    touchX=touchX1*xFactor;
    touchY=touchY1*yFactor;

    allMoveHandler(touchX,touchY);

    e.preventDefault();

}


function allMoveHandler(x, y) {
    mouseX=x;
    mouseY=y;
}
```

The onMouseMove() function creates the xFactor and yFactor values by using the current size of the canvas and browser window. It does this on each event just in case the window has changed sizes since the last event. These are translated into mouseX and mouseY coordinates that are passed into the allMoveHandler() function.

The `allMoveHandler` function takes whatever is passed in and sets the `mouseX` and `mouseY` values. This is not 100% necessary here, because they are global values, but the next function, `onTouchMove`, will set the `touchX` and `touchY` values and pass those in. Just in case we wanted to do more in the `allMoveHander()` function, we made it accept in the parameters and be called from both functions. This might be a little redundant in this example, but it could prove useful in a larger game as a reusable function.

The `onTouchMove` function looks a little strange. This is because not all browsers give off the same touch events. Some give a touch event off as an array, and some give it off as the actual event. To make sure we cover as many devices as possible, we first look to see whether the first element in the `e.touches` array exists. If it does, we use its attributes in the algorithm to find the current touch location. If not, we use the attributes of the event passed in directly (`e`).

Beyond that, the `touchX` and `touchY` values are calculated in the same manner as the `mouseX` and `mouseY` values for `onMouseMove`. We also need to make sure that the finger move event is *not* passed to the mobile Safari web browser. This would result in the browser window moving rather than the ship moving. We do this with the `e.prevent Default()` function call.

 If you encounter `mouseX` and `mouseY` position problems when using the `event.clientX` and `event.clientY` values on a scrolling browser window, you can substitute them with `event.pageX` and `event.page`. In most browsers, these will help if the screen is scrolled.

Auto-fire

One other change we've made is to remove the need for the player to press any keys or tap the screen to fire bullets. We have added this code to the `updatePlayer()` function.

```
player.missileFrameCount++;
    if (player.missileFrameCount>player.missileFrameDelay){
        playSound(SOUND_SHOOT,.5);
        firePlayerMissile();
        player.missileFrameCount=0;

    }
```

The `player.missileFrameCount` and `player.missileFrameDelay` attributes were added to the player object in the `gameStateNewgame()` function from GeoBlaster Extended:

```
player.missileFrameDelay=5;
player,missileFrameCount=0;
```

Player movement

The player ship must now follow the mouse rather than respond to the arrow keys pressed by the user. We have removed checkKeys() function from the GeoBlaster Extended code base as well as all references to it. In its place, we have added the following code to the updatePlayer() function:

```
var radians=Math.atan2((mouseY)-player.y, (mouseX)-player.x);
var degrees=(radians * (180/ Math.PI));
var yChange=(mouseY-player.y);
var xChange=(mouseX-player.x);
var delay=16;
var yMove=(yChange/delay)*frameRateCounter.step;
var xMove=(xChange/delay)*frameRateCounter.step;

player.x=player.x+xMove;
player.y=player.y+yMove;


if (degrees <0) {
    player.rotation=359+degrees;
}else{
    player.rotation = degrees;
}
```

First, we find the radians value for the direction the player needs to point to follow the mouse. Next, we use the yChange and xChange values to find the difference in screen pixel location between the player position and the mouse position. Finally, we create the actual delta for the player movement (xMove and yMove). We have put in a delay value of 16. This value acts like a smooth easing function so that the player doesn't zoom straight to the mouse (or finger) on each click. This value can be changed to easily modify the easing look and feel.

Finally we check to make sure the degrees value is not less than 0. If it is, we add 359 to the value. If it is not, we simply use the degree value as calculated. This keeps the player rotation between 0 and 359 and doesn't allow any negative values.

Checking out the game

Now it's time to check out how this all comes together. I have placed the live files at this site (*http://bit.ly/14Hve2L*).

You can place them at any location you like. The game will be fully playable from a local folder, but to play it from a mobile device, you will need to go to the link above or place the files on the web server of your choice.

Let's take a look at the three different versions of the game. First, Figure 10-16 shows the game being played in the desktop Safari Browser. (It will also work fine in Chrome as of this writing.)

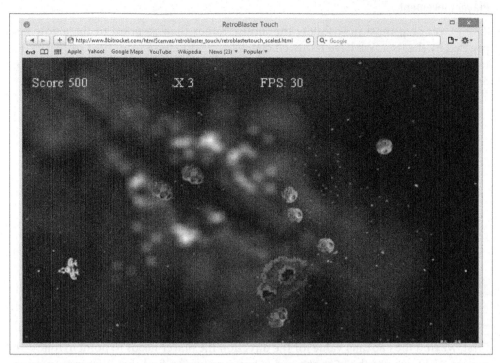

Figure 10-16. Retro Blaster Touch scaled in the Safari desktop browser

Next, Figure 10-17 shows the mobile Safari version before it has been added the Home screen.

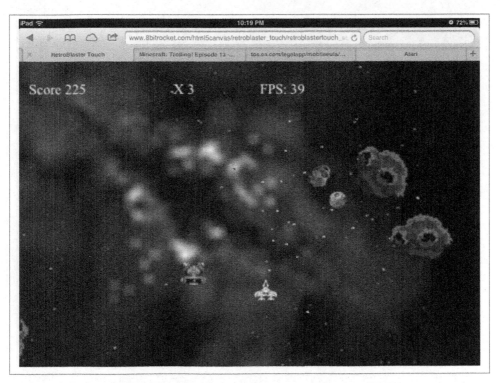

Figure 10-17. Retro Blaster Touch scaled in the Safari Mobile browser

Finally, Figure 10-18 shows the game being played from the Home Screen icon. Notice that the browser bar and other navigation elements are eliminated from this version.

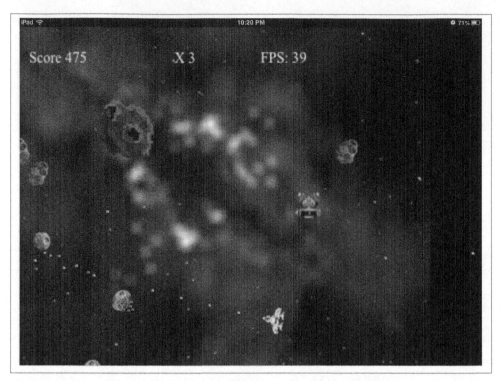

Figure 10-18. Retro Blaster Touch played from the iOS Home screen icon

That's as far as we are going to go with creating scaled, mobile versions of your applications. Both of these games and the ideas presented can be fully fleshed out to create much more elaborate applications. The goal was to demonstrate that HTML5 Canvas applications can easily be turned into apps that work on both the desktop and mobile Safari browsers in a similar manner and that it is very easy to turn them into apps that can be played right from the Home screen of an iOS device, just like an application downloaded from the iTunes store.

 Sound does not work the same in all current browsers and platforms. For example, sounds in the Mobile Safari browser need to be triggered on an event, such as a button click. We could have added an HTML "fire" button to the screen, and this would have allowed us to play a shooting sound when the player's missiles are fired.

Retro Blaster Touch Complete Game Code

The full source code and assets for *Retro Blaster Touch* are located at this site (*http://examples.oreilly.com/0636920013327/*).

Beyond the Canvas

A nice set of tools and frameworks are available (with more emerging every day) that can help transform the look and feel of an HTML or an HTML5 application (not necessarily just on Canvas) into an iPhone-like application. These can be used in conjunction with a canvas app to provide a seamless iPhone look and feel for the user.

If you would like to explore mobile functionality further, we recommend the following technologies, which can be combined with other technologies, such as Cordova PhoneGap, to create very powerful mobile applications:

jQT

> jQT (*http://jqtjs.com*) is a framework that makes use of jQuery to target mobile-device-specific features across platforms that use WebKit (iOS, Palm, Nexus, and so on).

jQuery Mobile Framework

> The jQuery Mobile Framework (*http://jquerymobile.com/*) is another jQuery-based mobile framework for building cross-platform applications. It can be used to create a unified user interface across mobile platforms.

What's Next?

As you can see, HTML5 Canvas is a powerful and easy way to target the iOS Safari browser. In this chapter, we built a small game to run in the Safari browser and then modified the application to run on the iPhone in full screen. After the simulation was successful, we modified the GeoBlaster Extended game from Chapter 9 to create a new game called Retro Blaster Touch. Finally, we were able to see this completed application running on an actual iOS device.

In Chapter 11, we will look at applying multiplayer capabilities to a canvas application using ElectroServer. We'll also take a small tour of 3D in Canvas. We will continue to explore the Canvas by creating a framework for a drag-and-drop application, and finally, we will take a look at HTML5 in Microsoft Windows 8.

Further Explorations

There are many emerging technologies and frameworks that can help take HTML5 Canvas into rarely explored areas. In this chapter, we will cover a couple of those areas: using Canvas for 3D with WebGL, and using Canvas for multiplayer applications. Both of these areas are still experimental, requiring you either to download beta/developer versions of browsers or to launch browsers using command-line switches so that you can turn various technologies off and on.

We will also cover a couple more topics that, while still involving the Canvas, veer into software design and emerging platforms. We will create a sample structure for our Canvas code and then apply it to a drag-and-drop application. After that, we will take that application and deploy it on the Microsoft Windows 8 desktop.

This chapter is structured a bit differently. The discussions are focused on giving you some tools and information about these new and emerging areas for Canvas. While we will offer code, examples, and some explanation, it's geared more toward getting you started on the path to learning than on teaching you how every detail works.

3D with WebGL

The 2D capabilities of HTML5 Canvas are impressive, but what about 3D? There is no "production" 3D context available in the standard version of any web browser at this time. However, the best support for a 3D context will probably come in the form of WebGL.

What Is WebGL?

WebGL is a JavaScript API that gives programmers access to the 3D hardware on the user's machine. Currently, it is supported only by the debug/development versions of Opera, Firefox, and Chrome. The API is managed by Kronos, the same organization that manages OpenGL. In fact, much of WebGL is similar to programming in OpenGL. This is both good and bad. It's good because it's a standard programming interface that is recognizable to many developers, but it is bad because it is not as easy to learn as the 2D Canvas context.

How Does One Test WebGL?

First, you need to find a web browser that supports WebGL. When trying to run a WebGL application, a browser that does not support WebGL might give a message like the one shown in Figure 11-1.

Figure 11-1. Trying to run WebGL in a standard web browser

Currently, the release versions of both Google Chrome and Firefox support WebGL. When you have a browser that can display WebGL, you need to write the code to make it happen. You start that process by accessing the WebGL context instead of the Canvas 2d context. So, instead of the following code, which we have used throughout this book:

```
context = theCanvas.getContext("2d");
```

We reference the experimental-webgl context, like this:

```
gl = theCanvas.getContext("experimental-webgl");
```

How Do I Learn More About WebGL?

The best place to learn about WebGL is at *http://learningwebgl.com/*. This site has an FAQ, a blog, and some helpful low-level lessons on how to create apps using WebGL. You can also find a ton of great content about WebGL at *http://developer.mozilla.org*.

One warning, however: programming WebGL is not for the uninitiated. Although WebGL is based on OpenGL, it is still a very low-level API, meaning that you will need to create everything by hand. At the end of this section, we will guide you toward some higher-level libraries that should make this process a bit easier.

What Does a WebGL Application Look Like?

Now we are going to show you a WebGL application demo that rotates a 3D cube on Canvas (see Figure 11-2). Because we are not experts in 3D graphics, we will forgo our practice of describing every line of code in the example; instead, we will highlight interesting sections of code to help you understand what is happening.

This demo is based on Lesson 4 from Giles Thomas's Learning WebGL website (*http://learningwebgl.com/blog/?p=370*). While this is only one short demo, it should give you a very good idea of how to structure and build code for a WebGL application.

 Much of this code has been adapted from the work of Giles Thomas with his express written permission.

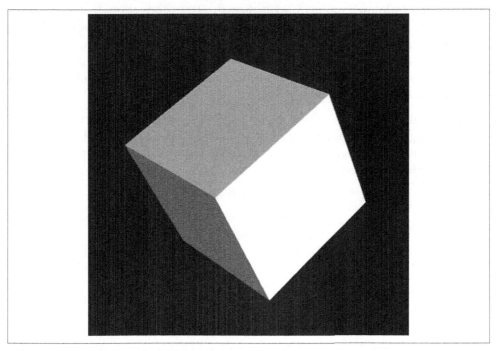

Figure 11-2. 3D rotating cube (CH11EX1.html)

JavaScript libraries

First, we add some JavaScript libraries. Modernizr includes a test for WebGL support in a web browser. This version was freshly released, but it could be updated with new features at any time (in fact, at the time of this writing, this had been updated to version 2.6). It is necessary to make sure that you have the most recent versions of your libraries:

```
<script src="modernizr.js"></script>
```

We now need to include some JavaScript libraries to assist with our application. *sylvest er.js* and *glUtils.js* are two libraries that you will find included for most apps that use WebGL. *sylvester.js* (*http://sylvester.jcoglan.com/*) is a library that helps when performing vector and matrix math calculations in JavaScript. *glUtils.js* is an extension for *sylvester.js*, specifically for helping with math related to WebGL:

```
<script type="text/javascript" src="sylvester.js"></script>
<script type="text/javascript" src="glUtils.js"></script>
```

Shaders

Shaders are pieces of code that run directly on a graphics card. They describe how a *scene*—how you refer to a 3D canvas when working with WebGL—should be rendered. Many of these little programs perform mathematical transformations that would otherwise run very slowly in JavaScript. In fact, we are pointing these out because they are *not* JavaScript; they are written in a way that WebGL can understand. These sections of code will be read in like text files and passed to the graphics hardware. Full discussions of topics like shaders are far out of scope for this little section of the book, but we will tell you a bit about each one of them to help set the tone for what comes next.

The first shader below is a *fragment shader*, which tells the graphics card that we will be using floating-point numbers and blended colors. The second shader is the *vertex shader*. It works with the vertices (defined points in 3D space used to create 3D objects) and will be used for every vertex we draw onto the Canvas 3D context:

```
<script id="shader-fs" type="x-shader/x-fragment">
  #ifdef GL_ES
  precision highp float;
  #endif

  varying vec4 vColor;

  void main(void) {
    gl_FragColor = vColor;
  }
</script>

<script id="shader-vs" type="x-shader/x-vertex">
  attribute vec3 aVertexPosition;
  attribute vec4 aVertexColor;

  uniform mat4 uMVMatrix;
  uniform mat4 uPMatrix;

  varying vec4 vColor;
```

```
    void main(void) {
      gl_Position = uPMatrix * uMVMatrix * vec4(aVertexPosition, 1.0);
      vColor = aVertexColor;
    }
</script>
```

Testing for WebGL support with Modernizr

The structure of the code in this example is much like the other applications we have
written in this book. However, it has been modified to work with the specific needs of
the 3D context. In the canvasApp() function, we need to test to see whether the browser
has WebGL support. This is easily accomplished by using the Modernizr.webgl static
constant in Modernizr:

```
if ( !webglSupport()) {
    alert("Unable to initialize WebGL");
    return;
}
function webglSupport() {
    return Modernizr.webgl;
}
```

Initialization in canvasApp()

In canvasApp(), we still get a context, but this time it is the experimental-webgl
context. Also, just like in our other apps, we still call drawScreen() on an interval to
render the canvas:

```
var theCanvas = document.getElementById("canvasOne");
webGLContext = theCanvas.getContext("experimental-webgl");

setInterval(drawScreen, 33);
```

However, there is additional code in canvasApp() required to set up the application to
rotate the cube. A couple of the most important initialization steps are the calls to
initShaders() and initBuffers():

```
initShaders();
initBuffers();
```

The initShaders() function itself calls a function named getShader() to load in the
text of the shader programs we have already defined. You can see the code for these
functions in the code listing in Example A-3.

 You can learn about the shaders used in this program in "Lesson 2—
Adding colour" on the LearningWebGL website (*http://learning
webgl.com/blog/?p=134*).

After we have loaded the shader programs, we need to create the buffers. *Buffers* refer to space in the video card's memory that we set aside to hold the geometry describing our 3D objects. In our case, we need to create buffers to describe the cube we will rotate on the canvas. We do this in initBuffers().

The initBuffers() function contains a lot of code, but we'll discuss only a couple very interesting sections. The first is the Vertex Position buffer, which describes the vertices that make up the sides of the cube:

```
webGLContext.bindBuffer(webGLContext.ARRAY_BUFFER, cubeVertexPositionBuffer);
    vertices = [
      // Front face
      -1.0, -1.0,  1.0,
       1.0, -1.0,  1.0,
       1.0,  1.0,  1.0,
      -1.0,  1.0,  1.0,

      // Back face
      -1.0, -1.0, -1.0,
      -1.0,  1.0, -1.0,
       1.0,  1.0, -1.0,
       1.0, -1.0, -1.0,

      // Top face
      -1.0,  1.0, -1.0,
      -1.0,  1.0,  1.0,
       1.0,  1.0,  1.0,
       1.0,  1.0, -1.0,

      // Bottom face
      -1.0, -1.0, -1.0,
       1.0, -1.0, -1.0,
       1.0, -1.0,  1.0,
      -1.0, -1.0,  1.0,          // Right face
       1.0, -1.0, -1.0,
       1.0,  1.0, -1.0,
       1.0,  1.0,  1.0,
       1.0, -1.0,  1.0,

      // Left face
      -1.0, -1.0, -1.0,
      -1.0, -1.0,  1.0,
      -1.0,  1.0,  1.0,
      -1.0,  1.0, -1.0,
    ];
```

The Vertex Color buffer holds information about the color that will appear on each side of the cube. These values are set as percentages of RGBA values (red, green, blue, alpha):

```
webGLContext.bindBuffer(webGLContext.ARRAY_BUFFER, cubeVertexColorBuffer);
    var colors = [
      [1.0, 1.0, 1.0, 1.0],      // Front face
```

```
    [0.9, 0.0, 0.0, 1.0],    // Back face
    [0.6, 0.6, 0.6, 1.0],    // Top face
    [0.6, 0.0, 0.0, 1.0],    // Bottom face
    [0.3 ,0.0, 0.0, 1.0],    // Right face
    [0.3, 0.3, 0.3, 1.0],    // Left face
];
```

The Vertex Index buffer is kind of like a map that builds the object (our cube) based on the colors specified in Vertex Color (the order of these elements) and the vertices specified in the Vertex Position buffer. Each of these sets of three values represents a triangle that will be drawn onto the 3D context:

```
webGLContext.bindBuffer(webGLContext.ELEMENT_ARRAY_BUFFER, cubeVertexIndexBuffer);
    var cubeVertexIndices = [
    0, 1, 2,      0, 2, 3,    // Front face
    4, 5, 6,      4, 6, 7,    // Back face
    8, 9, 10,     8, 10, 11,  // Top face
    12, 13, 14,   12, 14, 15, // Bottom face
    16, 17, 18,   16, 18, 19, // Right face
    20, 21, 22,   20, 22, 23  // Left face
    ]
```

Again, there is more code in `initBuffers()` than we described here, but start with these three sections when you want to play with the code and make your own objects.

Animating the cube

Now that you know a bit about creating an object in WebGL, let's learn about animating the cube on the canvas. Similar to what we did in the 2D context, we use the `drawScreen()` function to position, draw, and animate objects in the 3D context. The first thing we do here is set up the viewport, which defines the canvas's view of the 3D scene. Next, we clear the canvas and then set up the perspective:

```
function drawScreen() {

    webGLContext.viewport(0, 0, webGLContext.viewportWidth,
        webGLContext.viewportHeight);
    webGLContext.clear(webGLContext.COLOR_BUFFER_BIT |
        webGLContext.DEPTH_BUFFER_BIT);

    perspective(25, (webGLContext.viewportWidth / webGLContext.viewportHeight),
        0.1, 100.0);
```

The perspective has four parameters:

Field of view
> The angle at which we will view the 3D scene (25 degrees).

Width-to-height ratio
> The radio of width to height of the current size of the canvas (500×500).

Minimum units

The smallest unit size away from our viewport that we want to display (0.1).

Maximum units

The furthest unit size away from our viewport that we want to see (100.0).

Next, we move to the center of the 3D scene, calling loadIdentity() so that we can start drawing. We then call mvTranslate(), passing the locations on the x-, y-, and z-axes to draw the cube. To rotate the cube, we call a function named mvPushMatrix(), and later mvPopMatrix(), which is similar to how we called context.save() and con text.restore() when rotating objects on the 2D canvas. The call to mvRotate() then makes the cube rotate from the center, tilted up and to the right:

```
loadIdentity();

mvTranslate([0, 0.0, -10.0]);

mvPushMatrix();
mvRotate(rotateCube, [0, .5, .5]);
```

Next, we draw the cube by binding the buffers that hold the vertices and color information that we set up earlier for the cube's sides. We then draw each side, made up of two triangles each:

```
webGLContext.bindBuffer(webGLContext.ARRAY_BUFFER, cubeVertexPositionBuffer);
webGLContext.vertexAttribPointer(shaderProgram.vertexPositionAttribute,
    cubeVertexPositionBuffer.itemSize, webGLContext.FLOAT, false, 0, 0);

webGLContext.bindBuffer(webGLContext.ARRAY_BUFFER, cubeVertexColorBuffer);
webGLContext.vertexAttribPointer(shaderProgram.vertexColorAttribute,
    cubeVertexColorBuffer.itemSize, webGLContext.FLOAT, false, 0, 0);

webGLContext.bindBuffer(webGLContext.ELEMENT_ARRAY_BUFFER, cubeVertexIndexBuffer);
setMatrixUniforms();webGLContext.drawElements(webGLContext.TRIANGLES,
    cubeVertexIndexBuffer.numItems, webGLContext.UNSIGNED_SHORT, 0);

mvPopMatrix();
```

Finally, we increase the rotateCube variable so that the next time drawScreen() is called, the cube will be updated with a new angle. The following code adds 2 degrees to the rotation angle each time drawScreen() is called:

```
rotateCube += 2;

}
```

Further Explorations with WebGL

Obviously, we cannot teach you all about WebGL in this chapter. We opted to include this demo and short discussion to introduce you to WebGL and show you what it looks like. In reality, a full discussion of WebGL, even the basic concepts, could take up an entire volume.

If you are interested in WebGL, we strongly recommend that you consult *http://lear ningwebgl.com* for more examples and the latest information about this exciting yet still experimental context for HTML5 Canvas.

WebGL JavaScript Libraries

At the start of this section, we promised to show you some libraries that can be used with WebGL to make it easier to develop applications. Here are some of the more interesting libraries and projects.

Google O3D

Google's O3D library (*http://code.google.com/p/o3d/*) was once a browser plug-in, but has now been released as a standalone JavaScript library for WebGL. The examples of using O3D with JavaScript—including a fairly spectacular 3D pool game—are very impressive. O3D allows you to load COLLADA 3D models created with Google Sketch-Up (as well as other 3D packages).

The required code looks about as complex as straight WebGL code, so while this is very powerful, you might want to look at some of the other libraries here first if you are just starting out.

C3DL

The tagline for C3DL (*http://www.c3dl.org/*) is "WebGL made easy!" C3DL, or "Canvas 3D JS Library," is similar to GLGE, but it seems to have a head start thanks to a larger API and more support. This library also appears to be slanted toward games; a real-time strategy (RTS) and an arcade game are featured as its more prominent demos. The library supports COLLADA models, and the code also appears very straightforward to implement.

SpiderGL

"3D Graphics for Next-Generation WWW" is how SpiderGL (*http://spidergl.org/*) bills itself to the world. This library appears to be very similar to GLGE and C3DL, except that the demos focus more on lighting, color, and textures than on games and applications. It also supports COLLADA models.

SceneJS

SceneJS (*http://scenejs.org/*) is geared toward rendering 3D scenes built as COLLADA JSON models in WebGL. You can also define and manipulate 3D scenes. Loading and rendering the models is a straightforward process, and the results are quite impressive.

CopperLicht

This commercial library (*http://www.ambiera.com/copperlicht/*) advertises itself as the "fast WebGL JavaScript 3D Engine." All the demos are game-oriented, and the library supports many commercial 3D formats. It has both collision detection and physics built in. The demos are fast and are fun to play. This library appears to be centered on loading and using external 3D assets, so if that is what you are looking for, this might be your best choice.

GLGE

"WebGL for the lazy" is the tagline for this JavaScript library (*http://www.glge.org/*). The author of the library, Paul Brunt, says this about GLGE:

> The aim of GLGE is to mask the involved nature of WebGL from the web developer, who can then spend his/her time creating richer content for the Web.

This is a high-level API that is still in development. Just like O3D, it has the ability to load COLLADA models. Applications written with GLGE are created with a combination of XML and JavaScript. It looks very promising.

Of all of these libraries, GLGE appears to be a favorite among indie developers. It takes a lot of the pain out of WebGL by using XML to define 3D objects, meshes, materials, and so on.

Three.js

The most promising WebGL library might be *three.js (https://github.com/mrdoob/three.js/)*. It's a free, lightweight API that is gaining popularity because it is easy to use and implement.

 One final note about WebGL: Microsoft has vowed to not support WebGL in the IE browser. They believe that it poses a security threat, and they balk at it because it is not a W3C standard. However, there is a plug-in named iewebgl (*http://www.iewebgl.com/*) that will run most WebGL content in Internet Explorer.

Multiplayer Applications with ElectroServer 5

Because Flash has built-in support for communication via sockets, its applications have had the ability to open socket communications with server-side applications for many years. HTML (until Web Sockets), on the other hand, has never had the ability to reliably communicate to a socket server without performing some sleight of hand, usually involving constant polling by the web browser for new information from the web server.

ElectroServer from Electrotank was one of the first reliable socket-server applications built to communicate with Flash clients. Over the past couple years, ElectroServer has been updated with APIs for iOS, C#, C++, and now JavaScript. This first iteration of the ElectroServer JavaScript API does not use WebSockets but instead implements JavaScript polling. However, with the availability of ElectroServer's simplified JavaScript API, you can still start to write multiplayer applications using HTML5 Canvas.

 While this portion of the chapter is specific to ElectroServer, many of the multiplayer/multiuser concepts are applicable to other technologies as well.

Installing ElectroServer

To get started with multiplayer development using HTML5 Canvas and the ElectroServer socket server, you first need to download the free, 25-user version of the software from Electrotank. You can download the appropriate version for your operating system (Windows, Mac, Linux) at this site (*http://www.electrotank.com/resources/down loads.html*).

 There are some installation prerequisites, such as having Java version 1.6. For detailed installation instructions for every OS, visit this site (*http://www.electrotank.com/docs/es5/manual/index.html?operat ing_system.htm*).

The install package includes the server software, client APIs, documentation, and sample applications. After you have installed the server software, you should have a folder named something like *Electroserver_5_x_* on your computer. We used Mac OS X for this test, so this folder was created inside the Mac Applications folder. On Windows, it will be created in the location you specify upon installation.

Starting the server

After you have the files installed, you need to start the ElectroServer socket server by finding the installation directory and executing the file *Start_ElectroServer_5_0_1*. (Note: the three numbers at the end of this file will change as the version is upgraded, but the concept will remain the same.)

When ElectroServer starts, you should see a screen similar to Figure 11-3.

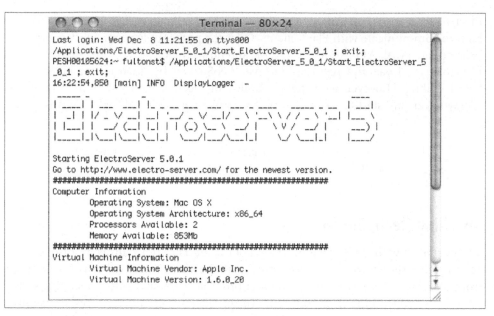

Figure 11-3. ElectroServer started

The server will run on your local machine for testing purposes. However, for any real-world application, you will need to install a production version of the software on a web server.

The ElectroServer admin tool

Because ElectroServer is a socket server, it listens on a specified port for communication from the JavaScript client using one of the supported protocols. ElectroServer supports multiple protocols, but we need to make sure we are using the *BinaryHTTP* protocol for the JavaScript API. The default port for BinaryHTTP in ElectroServer is 8989.

 When the ElectroServer JavaScript API is updated to support Web-Sockets, the port and protocol will likely be different.

There is a nifty admin tool for ElectroServer that allows you to view and modify all the supported protocols and ports, as well as many other cool features of the socket server. In the */admin* directory of the install folder, you should find both an installer for an Adobe AIR admin tool (named something like *es5-airadmin-5.0.0.air*), and a */webadmin* directory with an HTML file named *webadmin.html*. Either one will work for this exercise.

For the admin console to display properly, the server needs to be started.

When you launch the admin tool, you will be asked to supply a username and password. The default is administrator and password, unless you changed them upon installation.

After you log in, click the Server Management button on the top menu, and then choose the Gateways option from the side menu. You should see a screen that looks similar to Figure 11-4.

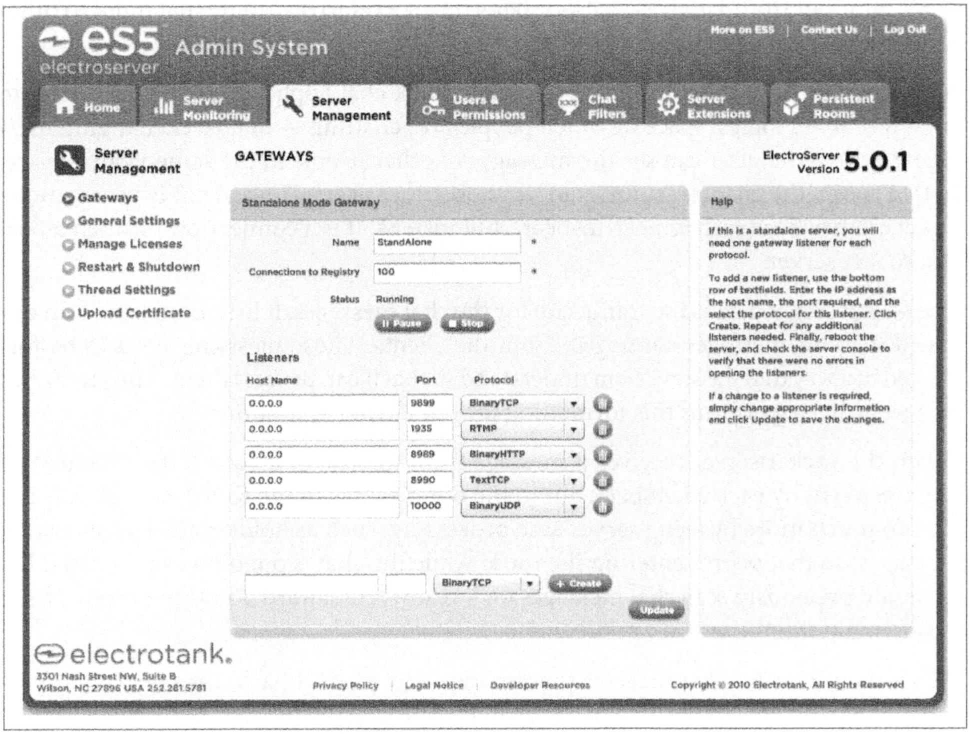

Figure 11-4. ElectroServer ports and protocols

This screen shows you the port settings for each protocol that ElectroServer supports. For the JavaScript API, we are most interested in the BinaryHTTP setting, which you can see is set to port 8989.

The JavaScript API

Besides starting ElectroServer, you will also need the JavaScript API so that you can begin building Canvas apps that connect to the server. You should be able to find the JavaScript API in the */apis/client/javascript* directory of the folder in which you installed ElectroServer. (This name might change in the final version.) The API should be named *ElectroServer-5-Client-JavaScript.js*.

The Basic Architecture of a Socket-Server Application

Now that you have ElectroServer ready to go and you have the JavaScript API, it is time to learn a bit about how socket-server-based multiplayer/multiuser applications are designed. Using a socket server means you are creating an application that relies on a client for input from a user, as well as relying on a server to distribute that input to other users who are connected to the first user.

A good example of this is a chat application. Most chat applications require a user to enter a *room* (a logical space in which people are "chatting"—that is, exchanging messages), where that user can see the messages of other people in the same virtual space. In that room, the client is "connected" to those other users. However, it is usually not a direct connection (such as peer-to-peer), but instead, it is a connection through a port to a socket server.

The socket server acts as the traffic cop for the chat messages. It listens on a port (in our case, 8989) for messages coming in from the clients. Those messages need to be formatted in a way that the server can understand so that it can process them. The JavaScript API we will use performs this formatting for our client applications.

When the socket server receives a message from the client, it routes the various text messages sent by each client back out to the other clients in the room. However, it can also do much more by using server-side processing, such as holding the list of current messages, so that people entering the room while the chat is ongoing can see what has been said previously, scan chat messages for swear words, award points to users for their input, or anything else you can dream up.

When the server finally processes the message and sends it back, the client then processes that message. In the case of the chat, that processing usually involves displaying the message on the canvas.

The Basic Architecture of an ElectroServer Application

ElectroServer acts very much like the socket-server application we described in the previous section. It listens on specified ports for different protocols; when messages arrive, they are routed back to the connected clients.

However, ElectroServer has some specific features that we should discuss. Some of these exist on other socket-server platforms, while some don't. However, much of this discussion will still be applicable to other socket servers when they make JavaScript APIs available.

Client

The client for an ElectroServer application is a program written in one of the API-supported language platforms, including Flash ActionScript 2, Flash ActionScript 3, Java, Objective-C, C#/.NET, and now JavaScript. The client is the application, which the user will manipulate to send messages through the API to ElectroServer. This is usually a game, a chat room, a virtual world, or some other kind of multiuser social or communication application.

All the communication with ElectroServer is *event*-based. The client application uses the JavaScript API to send events, and the client defines event handlers that listen for messages from ElectroServer. All of these messages and events are communicated through the API, which in turn is communicating through port 8989 using the BinaryHTTP protocol (at least for our examples).

Zones, rooms, and games

When a user first connects to ElectroServer, she needs to join or create a *zone*, which is simply a collection of rooms. If the user tries to create a zone that already exists, she will be added to that zone without creating a new one.

After entering a zone, the user needs to join a room in that zone. If a user attempts to create a new room that already exists, she will be added to that room instead.

 Beyond zones and rooms, ElectroServer also offers a GameManager API that allows you to further segment users into specific instances of a game that is being played. We do not get this granular for the examples in this chapter.

Extensions

Extensions are server-side code modules that can process data sent by clients before that data is sent back to other clients. Extensions can also process and create their own events. For many games, the extension contains much of the game logic, relying on the clients for displaying and gathering user input.

At the very minimum, an extension contains what is known as a *plug-in*. A plug-in is a code module written in ActionScript 1 (basically JavaScript) or Java that can be instantiated and scoped to a room. For example, if you were making a card game, you would want a card game plug-in on the server to handle things like shuffling the deck and making sure the correct player wins a hand. In this way, the server holds the true state of the game. Using an extension helps keep a game flowing and lessens the users' ability to cheat. For the simple examples in this chapter, we will not be using any server-side extensions. However, if you delve further into ElectroServer or other socket-server applications, you should make sure to learn as much as possible about them.

Creating a Chat Application with ElectroServer

As an example, we are going to create a single chat application using the ElectroServer JavaScript API. Users will submit a chat message through an HTML form, and the displayed chat will be in HTML5 Canvas. We are also going to create and display some messages from ElectroServer so that you can see the status of the connection to the server.

Establishing a connection to ElectroServer

First, a client application is written so that it includes the ElectroServer JavaScript API:

```
<script src="ElectroServer-5-Client-JavaScript.js"></script>
```

The client application makes a connection to ElectroServer running on a server at a specific URL, listening on a specific port, using a specific protocol. For our examples, this will be `localhost`, `8989`, and `BinaryHTTP`, respectively.

We need to use these values to make a connection from the client to the server. We do this by first creating an instance of the `ElectroServer` object and then calling its methods. We start by creating an instance of an ElectroServer server connection named `server`. We then configure a new variable named `availableConnection` with the previous properties we described, and then we add it to the server variable with a call to the method `addAvailableConnection()`. We will create all of this code inside our `canvasApp()` function:

```
var server = new ElectroServer.Server("server1");
var availableConnection = new ElectroServer.AvailableConnection
    ("localhost", 8989, ElectroServer.TransportType.BinaryHTTP);
server.addAvailableConnection(availableConnection);
```

Now we need to use the `server` variable we just configured to establish a connection to ElectroServer. We do this by setting a new variable, `es`, as an instance of the class `ElectroServer`. We then call its `initialize()` method and add the server we just configured to the es object by calling the `addServer()` method of the `ElectroServer` server engine property:

```
var es = new ElectroServer();
es.initialize();
es.engine.addServer(server);
```

We are almost ready to try to connect to ElectroServer. However, first we need to create some event handlers for `ElectroServer` events. Remember when we told you that all the communication with ElectroServer is done through creating and listening for events? This is where that process begins. We need to listen for the following events: `ConnectionResponse`, `LoginResponse`, `JoinRoomEvent`, `JoinZoneEvent`, `ConnectionAttemptResponse`, and `PublicMessageEvent`:

```
es.engine.addEventListener(MessageType.ConnectionResponse, onConnectionResponse);
es.engine.addEventListener(MessageType.LoginResponse, onLoginResponse);
es.engine.addEventListener(MessageType.JoinRoomEvent, onJoinRoomEvent);
es.engine.addEventListener(MessageType.JoinZoneEvent, onJoinZoneEvent);
es.engine.addEventListener(MessageType.ConnectionAttemptResponse,
    onConnectionAttemptResponse);
es.engine.addEventListener(MessageType.PublicMessageEvent, onPublicMessageEvent);
```

Finally, when we have everything ready, we call the `connect` method of the `ElectroServer` object and wait for events to be handled by the event listener functions we have just established:

```
es.engine.connect();
```

When the `ElectroServer` API object tries to connect to an ElectroServer server, a `ConnectionAttemptResponse` event will be fired back to the client from the server. We handle that event with the `onConnectionAttemptResponse()` event handler. For our application, we don't do anything with this event except create a status message for it that we will display. The `statusMessages` variable is an array of messages that we keep around to display back as debug information for our chat application. We will discuss this briefly in the next section:

```
function onConnectionAttemptResponse(event) {
  statusMessages.push("connection attempt response!!");
}
```

At this point, the client waits for a `ConnectionResponse` event to be sent back from the ElectroServer server. When the client application receives a `ConnectionResponse` event, it handles it with the `onConnectionResponse()` event handler. When the connection is established, the client then attempts to log on to the server. To make a logon attempt, we need a username. We will create a random username, but it could come from an account on a web server, a `form` field or cookie, Facebook Connect, or any other location or service you might have available.

After we have a username, we create a `LoginRequest()` object, set the `userName` property, and then call the `send()` method of the `es.engine` object. This is how we will send all messages to ElectroServer from this point forward:

```
function onConnectionResponse(event) {
    statusMessages.push("Connect Successful?: "+event.successful);
    var r = new LoginRequest();
    r.userName = "CanvasUser_" + Math.floor(Math.random() * 1000);
```

```
        es.engine.send(r);
    }
```

When ElectroServer responds from the LoginRequest, it is time to join a zone and a room. Recall that any user connected to ElectroServer needs to belong to a room, and every room belongs to a zone. Therefore, we need to make a user belong to one of each, which we accomplish with a CreateRoomRequest(). We set the zoneName property to TestZoneChat and the roomName property to TestRoomChat. If either of these does not already exist, it will be created by the server. If they do exist, the user will be added to them. We then send the message to ElectroServer:

```
function onLoginResponse(event) {
    statusMessages.push("Login Successful?: "+event.successful);

    username = event.userName;

    var crr = new CreateRoomRequest();
    crr.zoneName = "TestZoneChat";
    crr.roomName = "TestRoomChat";

    es.engine.send(crr);
}
```

We still need to wait for a couple responses from ElectroServer events that come back through the API via port 8989. We know we have to join a zone, and we handle the event with the function onJoinZoneEvent(), but we don't need to do anything with it:

```
function onJoinZoneEvent(event) {
    statusMessages.push("joined a zone");
}
```

The most important event we are waiting to handle is JoinRoomEvent. When we receive this event, we know that we have joined both a zone and a room, and the application is ready to run. For the chat application, this means the user can start typing and sending messages. First, we set the _room variable equal to the Room object, which was returned by the event from ElectroServer. We will use this variable for our further communications with ElectroServer. The other thing we do in this function is set an HTML <div> with the id of inputForm, which is made visible by changing its style. The input Form <div> is invisible when the page loads. We do this so that the user won't send chat messages before the connection to ElectroServer is established. Now that everything is ready to go, we display the inputForm <div> so that chatting can start:

```
function onJoinRoomEvent(event) {
        statusMessages.push("joined a room");
        _room = es.managerHelper.zoneManager.zoneById
            (event.zoneId).roomById(event.roomId);
        var formElement = document.getElementById("inputForm");
        formElement.setAttribute("style", "display:true");
    }
```

Creating the chat functionality

Now that we have established a connection to ElectroServer and joined a zone and a room, the chat application can start.

First, let's talk a bit about a few more variables we have created in our canvasApp() function, which we must scope to the rest of the chat application. The statusMessages array will hold a set of messages that we want to keep about the connection to ElectroServer. We will display these in a box on the right side of the canvas. The chatMessages array holds all the messages users have sent into the chat room. The username variable holds the name of the user who is running the Canvas application, and _room is a reference to the room object that user has joined:

```
var statusMessages = new Array();
var chatMessages = new Array();
var username;
var _room;
```

The HTML page holds a <form> that we will use to collect the chat messages from the user. It contains a text box for the user to type into (the id of textBox), and a button with the id of sendChat. This is the same form that was invisible until we received the JoinRoomEvent event:

```
<form>
<input id="textBox" placeholder="your text" />
<input type="button" id ="sendChat" value="Send"/>
</form>
```

In canvasApp(), we set up an event listener for when the user clicks the sendChat button. When a click event occurs, the function sendMessage handles the event:

```
var formElement = document.getElementById("sendChat");
formElement.addEventListener('click', sendMessage, false);
```

The sendMessage() function is one of the most important functions in this application. This is where we create a couple very critical objects for communicating with Electro-Server. The first is a PublicMessageRequest, which is one of several types we can make to the ElectroServer socket server. Others include a PrivateMessageRequest and a PluginMessageRequest. A PublicMessageRequest is a message that will be sent to everyone in the room. We send that data using an EsObject, which is native to the ElectroServer API. It allows you to create and access ad hoc data elements for any type of information you want to send to other users in the same room.

For a full discussion of EsObject and ElectroServer events, see the ElectroServer documentation. It is installed with the server on your local machine in *[your install folder]//documentation/html/index.html* *.

For this simple chat example, we want to send the chat message the user typed and submitted. To do this, we will use the setString() method of EsObject. This method takes two parameters: the text you want to send, and an identifier you can use to access the text. We also set another element named type, which will tell us what kind of message we are sending. We do this because, in a more complicated application, you might send all sorts of messages and need a way to identify what they are so that you can process them.

After we have configured our PublicMessageEvent with the roomId, the zoneId, and the EsObject, we call es.engine.send(pmr) to send it to the rest of the room:

```
function sendMessage(event) {
    var formElement = document.getElementById("textBox");
    var pmr = new PublicMessageRequest();
    pmr.message = "";
    pmr.roomId = _room.id;
    pmr.zoneId = _room.zoneId;
    var esob = new ElectroServer.EsObject();
    esob.setString("message", formElement.value);
    esob.setString("type","chatmessage");
    pmr.esObject = esob;
    es.engine.send(pmr);
    statusMessages.push("message sent");
}
```

Notice that we did not print the user's chat message to the canvas when it was submitted. Instead, we will wait for the PublicMessageEvent to return from ElectroServer and then handle it like all the other chats. This keeps the interface clean, while preserving a create event/handle event processing model across the entire application.

After the socket server processes the chat message, it is broadcast out to all the users in the room. All the users must create an event handler for a PublicMessageEvent so that they can receive and process the message; we have created the onPublicMessageE vent handler for this purpose. This function is very simple. It checks the type EsOb ject variable we set to see whether it is a chatmessage. If so, it pushes a string that includes the user who submitted the message (event.userName) and the message itself (esob.getString("message")) into the chatMessages array. This is what will be displayed on the canvas:

```
function onPublicMessageEvent(event) {

    var esob = event.esObject;
    statusMessages.push("message received");
    if (esob.getString("type") == "chatmessage") {

        chatMessages.push(event.userName + ":" + esob.getString("message"));
        }
}
```

Now all that remains is to display the messages that we have collected. We do this (where else?) in `drawScreen()`. For both the `statusMessages` and `chatMessages` arrays, we need to display the "current" 22 messages (if we have 22) and start them at the y position of 15 pixels. We display only the last 22 messages so that both the chat and the status messages will appear to scroll up the screen as more chatting and status messages are generated:

```
var starty = 15;
var maxMessages = 22;
```

If the array is larger than `maxMessages`, we display only the latest 22. To find those messages, we set a new variable named `starti` to the length of the `statusMessages` array, subtracted by the value in `maxMessages`. This gives us the index into the array of the first message we want to display. We do the exact same thing for the `chatMessag es` array:

```
//status box
   context.strokeStyle = '#000000';
    context.strokeRect(345,  10, 145, 285);
        var starti = 0;

        if (statusMessages.length > maxMessages) {
            starti = (statusMessages.length) - maxMessages;

        }
        for (var i = starti;i< statusMessages.length;i++) {
            context.fillText  (statusMessages[i], 350, starty );
            starty+=12;
//chat box
        context.strokeStyle = '#000000';
        context.strokeRect(10,   10, 335, 285);

        starti = 0;
        lastMessage = chatMessages.length-1;
        if (chatMessages.length > maxMessages) {
            starti = (chatMessages.length) - maxMessages;
        }
        starty = 15;
        for (var i = starti;i< chatMessages.length;i++) {
            context.fillText  (chatMessages[i], 10, starty );
            starty+=12;
        }
    }
```

That's it! We've finished developing our multiuser chat application.

Testing the Application in Google Chrome

To test the current ElectroServer JavaScript API, you need to start Google Chrome with web security disabled. The method of doing this varies by operating system, but on Mac

OS X, you can open a Terminal session and execute the following command (which will open Chrome if you have it in your Applications folder):

```
/Applications/Google\ Chrome.app/Contents/MacOS/Google\
    Chrome --disable-web-security
```

On a Windows-based PC, input a command similar to this from a command prompt or from a *.bat* file:

```
"C:\Program Files (x86)\Google\Chrome\Application\chrome.exe"
    --disable-web-security
```

 Obviously this is not a workable solution for a production application. As Electrotank (and other companies who make similar products) continue to improve the functionality of their APIs and add support for HTML5 WebSockets, this limitation should disappear.

The best way to test a multiplayer application on your own development machine is to open two web browsers or two web browser windows at the same time. When you look at *CH11EX2.html* in Google Chrome using this method, you should see something that looks like Figure 11-5.

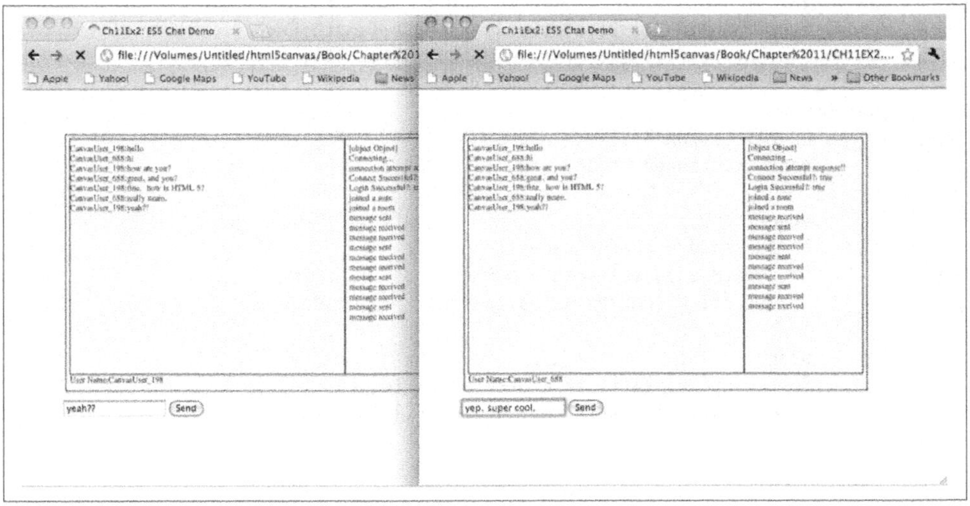

Figure 11-5. ElectroServer chat demo on the canvas with JavaScript API

Further Explorations with ElectroServer

Displaying text on HTML5 Canvas is interesting, but as we have shown you in this book, you can do much more. Let's add some graphics to the previous demo. We have added a second application for you to peruse, named *CH11EX3.html*. This application adds the bouncing ball demo app from Chapter 5 to the chat application we just created. It allows chatters to "send" bouncing balls to each other by clicking on the Canvas.

The heart of the app is simply another use of the EsObject instance from the chat application, which is created when the user clicks on the canvas. This EsObject instance adds information about a ball that one user created for the others in the room:

```
function eventMouseUp(event) {
    var mouseX;
    var mouseY;
    if (event.layerX ||  event.layerX == 0) { // Firefox
        mouseX = event.layerX ;
        mouseY = event.layerY;
    } else if (event.offsetX || event.offsetX == 0) { // Opera
        mouseX = event.offsetX;
        mouseY = event.offsetY;
    }
    ballcounter++;
    var maxSize = 8;
    var minSize = 5;
    var maxSpeed = maxSize+5;
    var tempRadius = Math.floor(Math.random()*maxSize)+minSize;
    var tempX = mouseX;
    var tempY = mouseY;
    var tempSpeed = maxSpeed-tempRadius;
    var tempAngle = Math.floor(Math.random()*360);
    var tempRadians = tempAngle * Math.PI/ 180;
    var tempvelocityx = Math.cos(tempRadians) * tempSpeed;
    var tempvelocityy = Math.sin(tempRadians) * tempSpeed;
    var pmr = new PublicMessageRequest();
    pmr.message = "";
    pmr.roomId = _room.id;
    pmr.zoneId = _room.zoneId;
    var esob = new ElectroServer.EsObject();
    esob.setFloat("tempX",tempX );
    esob.setFloat("tempY",tempY );
    esob.setFloat("tempRadius",tempRadius );
    esob.setFloat("tempSpeed",tempSpeed );
    esob.setFloat("tempAngle",tempAngle );
    esob.setFloat("velocityx",tempvelocityx );
    esob.setFloat("velocityy",tempvelocityy );
    esob.setString("usercolor",usercolor );
    esob.setString("ballname",username+ballcounter);
    esob.setString("type", "newball");
    pmr.esObject = esob;
    es.engine.send(pmr);
    statusMessages.push("send ball");

}
```

When a user connected in the same room receives this public message, we handle the newball event in a similar manner to how we handled the chat text, by using the onPublicMessageEvent() function. When the function sees an event with the type newball, it calls createNetBall(). The createNetBall() function creates ball objects to bounce around the canvas, much like the ones we created in Chapter 5:

```
function onPublicMessageEvent(event) {
    statusMessages.push("message received");
    var esob = event.esObject;
    if (esob.getString("type") == "chatmessage") {
     chatMessages.push(event.userName + ":" + esob.getString("message"));
    } else if (esob.getString("type") == "newball") {
        statusMessages.push("create ball")
        createNetBall(esob.getFloat("tempX"),esob.getFloat("tempY"),
            esob.getFloat("tempSpeed"),esob.getFloat("tempAngle"),
            esob.getFloat("tempRadius"),esob.getFloat("velocityx"),
            esob.getFloat("velocityy"),event.userName,esob.getString("usercolor"),
            esob.getString("ballname") );
    }

}

function createNetBall(tempX,tempY,tempSpeed,tempAngle,tempRadius,tempvelocityx,
                    tempvelocityy, user, usercolor, ballname) {

    tempBall = {x:tempX,y:tempY,radius:tempRadius, speed:tempSpeed,
        angle:tempAngle,
        velocityx:tempvelocityx, velocityy:tempvelocityy,nextx:tempX,
        nexty:tempY,
        mass:tempRadius, usercolor:usercolor, ballname:ballname}
    balls.push(tempBall);
    }
```

Figure 11-6 shows what this demo looks like when users click the mouse button to send balls to other users. The colors of the balls are assigned randomly. You can see the full set of code for this example in *CH11EX3.html*.

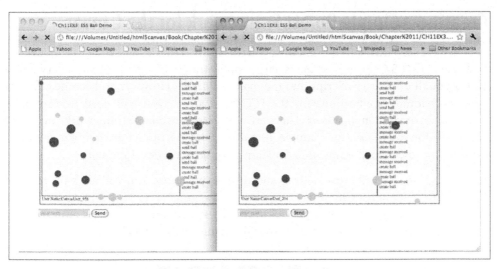

Figure 11-6. ElectroServer chat ball demo

This Is Just the Tip of the Iceberg

There is much more you can do with ElectroServer than what we showed you in this chapter. Sending and receiving `PublicMessage` events can get you only so far when designing multiuser/multiplayer applications.

To start designing multiplayer applications seriously, you will need to delve into the extension and plug-in architecture of ElectroServer, as well as explore plug-in events, which are used to communicate to the server portion of an application. We suggest you check out *http://www.electrotank.com/es5.html* for more information about the socket server. You can also read *ActionScript for Multiplayer Games and Virtual Worlds* by Jobe Makar (New Riders). Even though it centers on Flash and an earlier version of ElectroServer, the architectural information about designing apps for a socket server is well worth your time. You can check out the current ElectroServer JavaScript Client API (*http://www.electrotank.com/docs/es5/client/javascript/*).

At the same time, ElectroServer can be used with technologies other than Canvas (such as Flash, iOS, and so on), so Canvas will be able to communicate with other socket servers via JavaScript and WebSockets. We chose to base this example on ElectroServer because it allowed us to create a full application for you to test and work through. Other libraries and tools are bound to appear very soon that can work with Canvas—for example, the SmartFox server (*http://docs2x.smartfoxserver.com/GettingStarted/web-sockets*), which now supports WebSockets and JavaScript without add-ons.

Creating a Simple Object Framework for the Canvas

As you have seen throughout this book, you can easily create a lot of code when working with the HTML5 Canvas. The fact is, large applications can get out of hand very easily if you put all of your JavaScript into the main *.html* file. However, to become efficient when developing applications for the HTML5 Canvas, you will need to develop a framework for your applications. There are many freely available frameworks that exist right now for you to use (for example, *Impact.js*, *Easel.js*), but we are going to focus on creating our own small framework for Canvas application development.

In this section, we will create a drag-and drop-application. You will click on colored "bulbs" and decorate a Christmas tree, shown in Figure 11-7. This might seem like a simple application, but it will require us to create a system that recognizes mouse clicks, dragging items, and keeping track of an infinite number of objects.

Figure 11-7. Drag-and-drop application example

Creating the Drag-and-Drop Application

When creating our drag-and-drop application, we need to accomplish the following:

- We will create objects that can be clicked on to decorate a Christmas tree and can be dragged, dropped, and dragged again.
- We need to make the Canvas think it works in "retained mode" so that we can keep track of multiple objects. To do this, we need to create a "display list" of objects.
- We need to add the ability for these Canvas objects to listen to "events," and we need to have a way for mouse events to be "broadcast" events to objects that need to "hear" them.
- We want to change the mouse pointer to a hand cursor when it is over objects that can be clicked to make the application act like it might in Flash or Silverlight.

- The application will actually be a "click and stick" version of drag and drop. This means that when you click on an item, it sticks to the mouse until you click the mouse again.

Application Design

To create our framework, we will be creating objects and resource files that will help us design our application. Here is a brief run-down of what we will be creating:

EventDispatcher.js
> The base class for objects that need to broadcast events to other objects

Ornament.js
> A class that represents the draggable objects in the application

DisplayList.js
> A class that represents the "retained mode" that we will simulate for our application

GameUtilities.js
> A recourse file filled with nifty functions that we can reuse

DragAndDrop.js
> The main application class

DragAndDrop.html
> The HTML file that pulls all of our code together

You can find these files in the Chapter 11 */draganddrop* folder in the code distribution.

EventDispatcher.js

The first thing we need to do is to create a way for our JavaScript object to subscribe to and dispatch events. Standard DOM objects can have event listeners to listen for events —for example:

```
theCanvas.addEventListener("mouseup",onMouseUp, false);
```

However, Canvas images and drawing paths cannot create events because they are not kept in a retained mode. Our task is to create an event dispatcher object in JavaScript that we can use as the base class for other objects. We will use the `EventDispatcher` object as the base class for our `Ornament` class, so when an ornament is clicked, we can dispatch an event and the subscriber to that event can take some action.

`EventDispatcher.js` needs the following three methods:

`addEventListener()`
> Allows us to add a listener (subscriber) for a particular event

`dispatch()`
> Allows us to send events to listeners

`removeEventListener()`
> Allows us to remove a listener when it is no longer needed

By defining all the preceding methods as properties of the `EventDispatcher` prototype (`EventDispatcher.prototype.addEventListener()`), another class will be able to use this class as a base class and inherit all of them.

```
//Adapted from code Copyright (c) 2010 Nicholas C. Zakas. All rights reserved.
//MIT License


function EventDispatcher(){
    this._listeners = {};
}
EventDispatcher.prototype.addEventListener = function(type, listener){
        if (typeof this._listeners[type] == "undefined"){
            this._listeners[type] = [];
        }
        this._listeners[type].push(listener);
 }
EventDispatcher.prototype.dispatch = function(event){
        if (typeof event == "string"){
            event = { type: event };
        }
        if (!event.target){
            event.target = this;
        }
        if (!event.type){   //false
            throw new Error("Event object missing 'type' property.");
        }
        if (this._listeners[event.type] instanceof Array){
            var listeners = this._listeners[event.type];
            for (var i=0, len=listeners.length; i < len; i++){
                listeners[i].call(this, event);
            }
        }
    }
EventDispatcher.prototype.removeEve ntListener = function(type, listener){
        if (this._listeners[type] instanceof Array){
            var listeners = this._listeners[type];
            for (var i=0, len=listeners.length;
                i < len; i++){
                if (listeners[i] === listener){
                    listeners.splice(i, 1);
                    break;
                }
            }
        }
    }
```

```
}
```

Ornament.js

The `Ornament` class defined in *Ornamant.js* will use `EventDispatcher` as its' base class. Instances of `Ornament` will represent the bulbs we create and then drag and drop onto our Christmas tree.

To inherit all the methods and properties from `EventListener`, we need to create an object and then set the prototype of the object to `EventDispatcher`. We also need to set the constructor to be the `Ornament` function that holds all of the other functions in the `Ornament` class. It will look something like this:

```
function Ornament(color,height,width,context) {
...(all code goes here)
}
Ornament.prototype = new EventDispatcher();
Ornament.prototype.constructor = Ornament;
```

Because the `Ornament` class is the heart of this application, it contains many essential properties that form the basis of how this application will function:

bulbColor
: Color of bulb (red, green, blue, yellow, orange, purple).

file
: Filename of bulb image to load. We generate this name when we know the color of the bulb.

height
: Height of bulb image.

width
: Width of bulb image.

x
: x position of bulb.

y
: y position of bulb.

context
: Canvas context.

loaded
: Boolean value; set when bulb image has loaded.

image
: Image to load.

EVENT_CLICKED

Event to dispatch when clicked.

type

"Factory" or "copy." (Factory bulbs are the ones you click on to make a copy.)

dragging

Boolean value: Is the bulb being dragged? This is essential information for a drag-and-drop application.

Here is the code to create the previous variables:

```
this.bulbColor = color;
this.file = "bulb_"+ this.bulbColor + ".gif";
this.height = height;
this.width = width;
this.x = 0;
this.y = 0;
this.context = context;
this.loaded = false;
this.image = null;
this.EVENT_CLICKED = "clicked";
this.type = "factory";
this.dragging = false;
```

When a user clicks on an instance of Ornament, the mouseUp() method is called (by way of DisplayList, but we will get to that in the next section) and we dispatch an event to subscribers to say the bulb has been clicked. In this app, the only subscribers will be an instance of the DragAndDrop class, but in theory, there could be many more.

```
this.onMouseUp = function (mouseX,mouseY) {
    this.dispatch(this.EVENT_CLICKED);
}
```

Instead of drawing everything in a main drawScreen() function of DragAndDrop.js, as we have done throughout the rest of this book, our display objects (like Ornament) will have their own draw() functions. This function draws the bulb image at the specified x and y location at the size of width and height.

This helps keep the draw() function in the main app class as simple as possible:

```
this.draw = function() {
this.context.drawImage(this.image,this.x,this.y, this.width,this.height);
    }
```

The last thing we do in our class is call the loadImage() function, which loads the image file associated with the file property:

```
this.loadImage = function (file) {
        this.image = new Image();
        this.image.onload = this.imageLoaded;
        this.image.src = file;
```

```
    }

    this.imageLoaded = function() {
        this.loaded = true;
    }



    this.loadImage(this.file);
```

You can see the final code listing in *Ornament.js* in the code distribution.

DisplayList.js

DisplayList is a JavaScript object that will hold a list of items we are displaying on the canvas. It will send mouse click events to the items in the list when a user clicks on them on the canvas. It will function as our "retained mode" for this application.

DisplayList has two properties:

objectList *(array)*
>   A list of the items to display.

theCanvas
>   Reference to the Canvas context. We need this so that we can find the proper mouse *x* and *y* coordinates when a user clicks on an item in the display list.

The addChild() function of DisplayList adds an object to the objectList array by pushing it into the array. All the items in objectList will have their draw() functions called when the displayList draw() function is called:

```
    this.addChild = function(child) {
        this.objectList.push(child);
    }
```

The removeChild() function finds the first instance of the object in the display list passed as a parameter and then removes it from objectList. We do this using the array.indexOf() method, which finds the first instance of an object in an array and removes it:

```
    this.removeChild = function(child) {
    var removeIndex = null;
        removeIndex = this.objectList.indexOf(child,0);
        if (removeIndex != null) {
            this.objectList.splice(removeIndex,1);
        }
    }
```

The draw() function of DisplayList loops through all the objects in objectList and calls their draw() functions:

```
this.draw = function() {
    for (var i = 0; i < this.objectList.length; i++) {
        tempObject = this.objectList[i];
        tempObject.draw();
    }
}
```

The mouseUp function finds the current x and y position of the mouse pointer in a similar fashion to how we have done it previously in this book. (See Chapter 6.) Then, using a "hit test Point" collision detection (again, as we saw in Chapter 6), we check to see whether the mouse was clicked on any of the items in objectList. If so, it calls that object's mouseUp() function:

```
this.onMouseUp = function(event) {
    var x;
    var y;
    if (event.pageX || event.pageY) {
        x = event.pageX;
        y = event.pageY;
    } else {
     x = e.clientX + document.body.scrollLeft +
            document.documentElement.scrollLeft;
     y = e.clientY + document.body.scrollTop +
            document.documentElement.scrollTop;
    }
    x -= this.theCanvas.offsetLeft;
    y -= this.theCanvas.offsetTop;

    var mouseX=x;
    var mouseY=y;

    for (i=0; i< this.objectList.length; i++) {
        var to = this.objectList[i];
        if ( (mouseY >= to.y) && (mouseY <= to.y+to.height)
                && (mouseX >= to.x) && (mouseX <=
            to.x+to.width) ) {
            to.onMouseUp(mouseX,mouseY);
            }
        }

    }
```

You can see the final code listing in *DisplayList.js* in the code distribution.

GameUtilities.js

GameUtilities.js is where we will put our debugger function and our check for can vasSupport(). In the future, you could plan to put any utility functions in here that do not need to exist in a class.

```
var Debugger = function () { };
Debugger.log = function (message) {
```

```
    try {
        console.log(message);
    } catch (exception) {
        return;
    }
}


function canvasSupport () {
    return Modernizr.canvas;
}
```

DragAndDrop.js

`DragAndDrop.js` is the main class for the drag-and-drop application. It acts as the controller for all the other code and classes we have already created.

The first things we do in `DragAndDrop.js` are as follows:

1. Check for Canvas support using the new function in `GameUtilities.js`.

2. Get a reference to the Canvas context (`theCanvas`).

We would begin to define this class as follows:

```
function DragAndDrop() {

    if (!canvasSupport()) {
        return;
        }

    var theCanvas =  document.getElementById("canvasOne");
    var context = theCanvas.getContext("2d");

    ...(code goes here)...
}
```

Next, we begin to create properties that we will use to create the application:

```
var backGround;
var bulbColors = new Array ("red","blue","green","yellow","orange","pink",
                            "purple");
var bulbs;
```

backGround

Holds the background image (a black field with snow and a Christmas tree)

bulbColors

An array of color values we will use when placing bulbs on the canvas

bulbs

An array to hold the bulbs that we are manipulating on the canvas

Now we define some variable that we will use to place objects on the canvas. These variables will be used to place the factory bulbs. Factory bulbs are the ones the user clicks on to create new bulbs to drag and drop. Now they could be defined as const, but we elected to use var. This is because Internet Explorer does not support the JavaScript const keyword.

```
var BULB_START_X = 40;
var BULB_START_Y = 50;
var BULB_Y_SPACING = 10;
var BULB_WIDTH = 25;
var BULB_HEIGHT = 25;
```

Next we create an array to hold to hold the factory bulbs:

```
var clickBulbs;
```

The following two variables are used to limit the number of clicks the application responds to. clickWait is the number of calls to gameLoop() to wait until we allow the user to click again. The value of clickWaitedFrames is set to 0 when the user clicks a bulb, so the process can restart. If you don't have some kind of limit to the number of mouse clicks you listen for, you can get into a situation where objects never get dragged and dropped, because as soon as you click, the event fires multiple times.

```
var clickWait = 5;
var clickWaitedFrames = 5;
```

Next we create an instance of DisplayList passing a reference to the Canvas context. This will hold all the Ornament objects we display on the canvas.

```
var displayList = new DisplayList(theCanvas);
```

We also need to create listeners for mousemove and mouseup, so we use the events to click and/or drag bulbs on the screen:

```
theCanvas.addEventListener("mouseup",onMouseUp, false);
theCanvas.addEventListener("mousemove",onMouseMove, false);
```

Next we initialize the arrays for bulbs and clickBulbs and load the background image:

```
bulbs = new Array();
clickBulbs = new Array();
backGround = new Image();
backGround.src = "background.gif";
```

The factory bulbs are the ones we click on the canvas to create the bulbs that are dragged and dropped. To create them, we loop through all the colors in the bulbColors array, creating a new Ornament instance for each color. We then set the type property to factory, place it on the canvas using our placement variables (x,y), and then add it to the clickBulbs array and add it to the instance of displayList:

```
for (var i=0;i < bulbColors.length; i++) {
    var tempBulb = new     Ornament(bulbColors[i],BULB_WIDTH,
```

```
        BULB_HEIGHT,context);
    tempBulb.addEventListener(
        tempBulb.EVENT_CLICKED ,
        onBulbClicked);
    tempBulb.x = BULB_START_X;
    tempBulb.y = BULB_START_Y +
        i*BULB_Y_SPACING +i*BULB_HEIGHT;
    tempBulb.type = "factory";
    clickBulbs.push(tempBulb);
    displayList.addChild(tempBulb);
}
```

Next we create our game loop. We create a `setTimeout` loop that calls `draw()` every 20 milliseconds. This is also where we update `clickWaitedFrames` to test whether we will accept another mouse click:

```
function gameLoop() {
    window.setTimeout(gameLoop, 20);
    clickWaitedFrames++;
    draw();
}
```

Our `draw()` function is slimmed down considerably from others we have created previously in this book. First, it draws a background image, and then it calls `display List.draw()` to draw all objects in `displayList`. For this simple display list to work, you need to add objects to the list in the opposite order that you want them layered because the later ones will be drawn on top of the earlier ones:

```
function  draw () {
    context.drawImage(backGround,0,0);
    displayList.draw();
}
```

The `onBulbClicked()` function is the heart of the `DragAndDrop` class. This function does several things:

1. It tests to see whether a click is valid by checking `clickWaitedFrames` against `clickWait`.

2. If a click is valid, it tests to see whether we have clicked on a factory bulb (so that we can make a new one) or whether it is a draggable bulb instance and sets `click WaitedFrames` to 0 so that the app will wait a few frames until another click is valid.

3. We find the instance of `Ornament` that was clicked on by using the `event.target` property. It will be a reference to the object that dispatched the event.

4. If it is a factory bulb and if we are not currently dragging any bulbs, we create a new instance of `Ornament` and start dragging it. We set its type to `copy`, which means it is draggable.

5. If it is a draggable instance of `Ornament`, we check to see whether we are currently dragging it. If so, we drop it by setting the `dragging` property to `false`. If not and

if we are not dragging another bulb, we start dragging the new one by setting its dragging property to true.

The following code matches the previous description:

```
function onBulbClicked(event) {
    if (clickWaitedFrames >= clickWait) {
        clickWaitedFrames = 0;
        var clickedBulb = event.target;
        if ( clickedBulb.type  == "factory" && !currentlyDragging()) {
            var tempBulb = new Ornament(clickedBulb.bulbColor,BULB_WIDTH,
                                    BULB_HEIGHT,context);
            tempBulb.addEventListener(tempBulb.EVENT_CLICKED , onBulbClicked);
            tempBulb.y =  clickedBulb.y+10;
            tempBulb.x =  clickedBulb.x+10;
            tempBulb.type = "copy";
            tempBulb.dragging = true;
            bulbs.push(tempBulb);
            displayList.addChild(tempBulb);

        } else {
            if (clickedBulb.dragging) {
                clickedBulb.dragging = false;
            } else {
                if (!currentlyDragging()) {
                    clickedBulb.dragging = true;
                }
            }

        }
    }

}
```

Now we need to create the function to test whether the bulb being dragged is the same one we are testing in onCBulbClicked(). To do this, we simply loop through the bulbs array and see whether any bulb has its dragging property set to true:

```
function currentlyDragging() {
    isDragging = false
    for (var i =0; i < bulbs.length; i++) {
        if (bulbs[i].dragging) {
            isDragging = true;
        }
    }
    return isDragging;
}
```

When the user clicks (a mouseup event is fired on the Canvas DOM object), we want to send a message to the display list so that we can check to see whether any of the objects in the list have been clicked:

```
function onMouseUp(event) {
    displayList.onMouseUp(event);
}
```

When a mousemove event is fired on the Canvas DOM object, we want to do two things:

1. Move the bulb that is currently being dragged to be under the mouse pointer by setting its x and y properties to the *x* and *y* location of the mouse.

2. Check to see whether the mouse is over any clickable objects, and if so, change the look of the pointer to "hand" (to signify a button), using CSS. We do this by looping through all of the Ornament objects (both factory and copy ones) and checking a hit test point collision detection routine to see whether the mouse is over any of them. If it is over one, we set the style of the mouse to "pointer" (by setting the cursor variable). If not, we set it to "default". Then we update the style like this:

```
theCanvas.style.cursor = cursor;
function onMouseMove(event) {

    var x;
        var y;
    if (event.pageX || event.pageY) {
            x = event.pageX;
            y = event.pageY;
    } else {
            x = e.clientX + document.body.scrollLeft +
                document.documentElement.scrollLeft;
            y = e.clientY + document.body.scrollTop +
                document.documentElement.scrollTop;
    }
    x -= theCanvas.offsetLeft;
    y -= theCanvas.offsetTop;

    var mouseX=x;
    var mouseY=y;
    for (var i =0; i < bulbs.length; i++) {

        if (bulbs[i].dragging) {
            bulbs[i].x = mouseX - BULB_WIDTH/2;
            bulbs[i].y = mouseY - BULB_HEIGHT/2;
        }
    }

    var cursor ="default";
    for (i=0; i< bulbs.length; i++) {
        var tp = bulbs[i];
        if ( (mouseY >= tp.y) && (mouseY <= tp.y+tp.height) &&
            (mouseX >= tp.x)
            && (mouseX <= tp.x+tp.width) ) {
                cursor = "pointer";
        }
    }
```

```
        for (i=0; i< clickBulbs.length; i++) {
            var tp = clickBulbs[i];
            if ( (mouseY >= tp.y) && (mouseY <= tp.y+tp.height) &&
                (mouseX >= tp.x)
                    && (mouseX <= tp.x+tp.width) ) {
                cursor = "pointer";
            }
        }
        theCanvas.style.cursor = cursor;
    }
```

DragAndDrop.html

Because we have moved almost all the code out of the HTML file, here is our "almost" bare-bones HTML file that starts the drag-and-drop application.

We need to include all the files we just created:

```
<script type="text/javascript" src="EventDispatcher.js"></script>
<script type="text/javascript" src="DisplayList.js"></script>
<script type="text/javascript" src="GameUtilities.js"></script>
<script type="text/javascript" src="DragAndDrop.js"></script>
<script type="text/javascript" src="Ornament.js"></script>
<script type="text/javascript" src="modernizr.js"></script>
```

We need to create the canvas in HTML. For this application, we will center it on the screen:

```
<div align="center">
<canvas id="canvasOne" width="640" height="480" style="cursor: default;">
 Your browser does not support the HTML 5 Canvas.
</canvas>
</div>
```

Finally, we need to start the app when the window has loaded:

```
<script type="text/javascript">
window.addEventListener("load", eventWindowLoaded, false);
function eventWindowLoaded () {
    DragAndDrop();
}
</script>
```

We have now created a very simple object-oriented structure for a Canvas application. With this application, we have attempted to solve some glaring application development issues that occur when creating Canvas applications. We have created a way to subscribe to and broadcast events from logical objects on the canvas, a way to find and click on individual objects on the canvas, and we keep track of those objects using a display list that simulates "retained mode." While there are many ways this object model could be improved, we feel that this is a good starting point for your future endeavors with the HTML5 Canvas.

You can test this example by finding *dragandrop.html* in the code distribution (in the Chapter 11 */draganddrop* folder) and opening it in your web browser.

Windows 8 Apps and the HTML5 Canvas

One very interesting development that occurred as this book was going to press was the release of Windows 8. Windows 8 offers some very interesting ways for developers to create applications for the operating system and for the Windows Store. One of those methods is to package HTML5 using Visual Studio 2012.

To demonstrate how easy it is to create an HTML5 Canvas application for Windows 8, we will take the previous drag-and-drop example and show you the changes that are required to get it running under Windows 8 as a bare-bones application.

The first thing you need to do is download Visual Studio Express for Windows 8 (if you don't already have Visual Studio 2012 installed).

Next, you want to create a new *Blank App* project using the JavaScript template. (See Figure 11-8.)

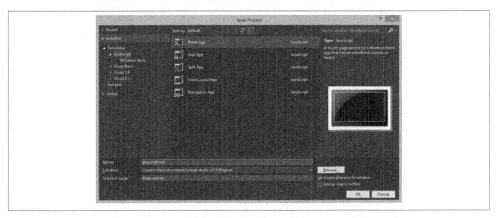

Figure 11-8. Creating a new JavaScript project in Visual Studio 2012

Next, you need to add all the files we created for the drag-and-drop example to the new project. Copy the files to the solution directory Visual Studio created for you. (This is usually in documents\visual studio 2012\projects\[project name]\[project name].)

After you do this, right-click in the Solution Explorer and select Add->Existing Item. Choose all the files you just copied to the directory. (See Figure 11-9.)

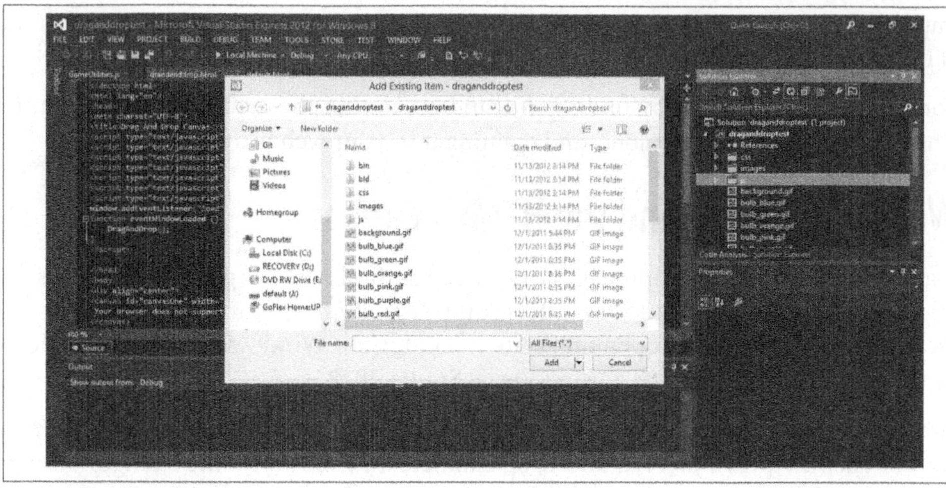

Figure 11-9. Add drag-and-drop files to the project

Now you are ready to edit the files and get the app running. We are going to describe the quickest route to having a running application.

Start with opening *default.html*. You need to copy all the JavaScript included (except for *modernizr.js*) from *draganddrop.html* to *default.html*. You also need to copy the HTML tags from *draganddrop.html* (<div> and <canvas>) and put them into the body of *default.html*. Leave everything else intact. The final file should look like this:

```html
<!DOCTYPE html>
<html>
<head>
    <meta charset="utf-8" />
    <title>draganddroptest</title>

    <!-- WinJS references -->
    <link href="//Microsoft.WinJS.1.0/css/ui-dark.css" rel="stylesheet" />
    <script src="//Microsoft.WinJS.1.0/js/base.js"></script>
    <script src="//Microsoft.WinJS.1.0/js/ui.js"></script>

    <!-- draganddroptest references -->
    <link href="/css/default.css" rel="stylesheet" />
    <script src="/js/default.js"></script>

    <script type="text/javascript" src="EventDispatcher.js"></script>
    <script type="text/javascript" src="DisplayList.js"></script>
    <script type="text/javascript" src="GameUtilities.js"></script>
    <script type="text/javascript" src="DragAndDrop.js"></script>
    <script type="text/javascript" src="Ornament.js"></script>

</head>
<body>
<div align="center">
```

```
<canvas id="canvasOne" width="640" height="480" style="cursor: default;">
  Your browser does not support the HTML 5 Canvas.
</canvas>
</div>
</body>
</html>
```

Next, we need to update default.js. This time, we will add the call to DragAnd
Drop() that is in *draganddrop.js* so that the application will start when Windows 8 is
ready. Add the call in the section with the following comment:

```
// TODO: This application has been newly launched. Initialize
// your application here.
```

Leave everything else untouched. This will make sure our app starts as soon as Windows
8 is ready for our program to run.

```
// For an introduction to the Blank template, see the following documentation:
// http://go.microsoft.com/fwlink/?LinkId=232509
(function () {
    "use strict";

    WinJS.Binding.optimizeBindingReferences = true;

    var app = WinJS.Application;
    var activation = Windows.ApplicationModel.Activation;

    app.onactivated = function (args) {
        if (args.detail.kind === activation.ActivationKind.launch) {
            if (args.detail.previousExecutionState !==
                activation.ApplicationExecutionState.terminated) {
                // TODO: This application has been newly launched. Initialize
                // your application here.
                DragAndDrop();
            } else {
                // TODO: This application has been reactivated from suspension.
                // Restore application state here.
            }
            args.setPromise(WinJS.UI.processAll());
        }
    };

    app.oncheckpoint = function (args) {
        // TODO: This application is about to be suspended. Save any state
        // that needs to persist across suspensions here. You might use the
        // WinJS.Application.sessionState object, which is automatically
        // saved and restored across suspension. If you need to complete an
        // asynchronous operation before your application is suspended, call
        // args.setPromise().
    };

    app.start();
})();
```

Finally, edit `GameUtilities.js` and change `canvasSupport()` to always return `true`. We do this because the Canvas will always be available, and we removed the reference to `moderizr.js` in *default.html*.

```
function canvasSupport () {
    return true;
}
```

Believe it or not, we are now ready to test the app. Click on the green arrow on the menu bar to test. (See Figure 11-10.) Be sure to have Local Machine selected from the drop-down menu.

Figure 11-10. Test application in Visual Studio

When you test the app, you should see what is shown in Figure 11-11.

Figure 11-11. Drag and drop running as a Windows 8 application

To get back to Visual Studio, roll the mouse pointer to the upper-left corner of the screen, and click on the thumbnail of the Visual Studio interface. You can close the app by doing the same thing while in Visual Studio, right-clicking on the drag-and-drop app, and choosing close.

You can find all the code for this application in the Chapter 11 *windows8* folder in the code distribution.

From there you should be able to take your HTML5 Canvas apps and Visual Studio 12 and start making all kinds of stuff for Windows 8.

If you are wondering why we did not cover Windows Phone, it's because at this moment there is no support for HTML5 to create apps for the Windows Phone using Visual Studio (although it is supported in the Internet Explorer 10 web browser). However, as we went to press, there was an effort underway in the Phonegap/Cordova community to create templates for the Windows Phone. When that happens, you can test your HTML5 Canvas apps on that platform too.

What's Next in HTML5.1 and Canvas Level 2?

At the end of 2012, the W3C specs for HTML5.1 and Canvas Level 2 were unleashed into the world. While many of these features are a long way away from being supported in the browser, we thought we would highlight some of the most interesting new functions that will arrive for Canvas developers in the next few years.

HTML5.1 Canvas Context

In HTML5.1, the Canvas context will include some methods beyond `toDataURL()` and `getContext()`.

supportsContext()

This method will allow a developer to test for support for different Canvas contexts in a web browser. In this book, we used the 2D context most of the time, but we added "experimental-wbgl" in this chapter, or "moz-3d." In the future, the new Canvas context will be registered at this site (*http://wiki.whatwg.org/wiki/CanvasContexts.*).

toDataURLHD(), toBlob(), toBlobHD()

If you recall from earlier in the book, `toDataURL()` allows a developer to export a base64 encoded string that represents the Canvas display, which can then be converted to an image. This image is restricted to 96 dpi. In HTML5.1, this ability will be expanded to include several new variations:

`toDataURLHD()`
　Returns canvas data at native resolution instead of 96 dpi

`toBlob()`
　Returns data as a blob at 96 dpi instead of a base64 encoded string

`toBlobHD()`
　Returns data as a blob at native resolution

Canvas Level-2

The next version of the Canvas, dubbed "Level 2," is slated to have changes and updates to the API. The new features and functionality are in a constant state of flux. It appears that most of these new features are being added so that the Canvas can be more DOM accessible. At press time, it appeared that some of the following would make it into the final specification:

- A way to define "hit regions" for mouse events instead of listening across the entire Canvas.
- The TextMetrics object returned from context.measureText will include many more properties, including bounding box and height information.
- New ways to create and use patterns from images and image data.
- New Path objects that can have text applied.

For more information about the Canvas updates in HTML5.1, check out this site (*http:// bit.ly/10w3Pwq*).

For more information about Canvas Level 2, check out this site (*http://www.w3.org/ html/wg/drafts/2dcontext/html5_canvas/*).

Conclusion

Over the past 11 chapters, you have been immersed in the world of HTML5 Canvas. We have given you dozens of examples and applications to work from and through so that you can start building your own creations. From simple text displays to high-performance games, we have shown you many ways to bring some of the magic of previous RIA (Rich Internet Application) technologies into the plug-in-*less* browser experience.

We offered many strategies for integrating Canvas with other HTML5 technologies, as well as techniques for handling text, displaying graphics, scrolling bitmaps, creating animation, detecting multiple types of collisions, embedding and manipulating video, playing music, handling sound effects, creating user interfaces, optimizing code, and preparing apps for the mobile web and Windows 8. We even introduced you to the future of 3D and multiuser applications directly in the web browser and showed you how to get started creating an object model for the HTML5 Canvas.

However, the true future is up to you. HTML5 and Canvas are dynamic topics that are still in a rapid state of change and adoption. While this book is a good starting point, you will need to keep abreast of new changes to the technology. Visit our website (*http:// www.8bitrocket.com*) for news and updates on HTML5 Canvas.

O'Reilly also has several books that you might find useful, including:

- *HTML5: Up and Running* by Mark Pilgrim
- *Supercharged JavaScript Graphics* by Raffaele Cecco

If you are interested in learning how some of the game-development techniques described in this book (as well as many others) can be applied to Flash, check out our other most recent book, *The Essential Guide to Flash Games* (friendsofED).

There is a real paradigm shift occurring right now on the Web. For most of the first decade of the 21st century, Java, Flash, Silverlight, and other plug-in RIA technologies dominated application development and design. At the time, there appeared to be no better solution for the development of rich applications in a web browser than to bolt on technology that was not native to the browser.

The emergence of the "connected apps" culture is changing this. Every platform—from tablets and phones to TVs, e-readers to tablets, wireless printers to desktop PCs—is targeted for web-enabled applications sold or distributed through an app store. In many ways, these apps are replacing RIA applications or, at the very least, offering a compelling new platform for their development and distribution.

Where RIA technologies of the past—like Java, Flash, and Silverlight—could target nearly all web browsers and PCs, they are having trouble finding a true foothold in the area of connected apps (especially on platforms where they are restricted from running, like iOS). This is where HTML5 Canvas can really make a difference. With true cross-platform execution, applications run in the web browser can be made available to the widest audience possible. Soon these applications will be enhanced with 3D graphics and have the ability to communicate with one another via technologies like the ElectroServer socket server. One can envision a day in the near future where technology platforms fade away, and the web-connected app world simply works, regardless of screen or location. This is the promise of HTML5—especially HTML5 Canvas. So, now that you have the tools to begin, what do you plan to build?

Full Code Listings

Code from Chapter 7

Example A-1. Space Raiders with optimized dynamic network sound and state loader

```html
<!doctype html>
<html lang="en">
<head>
<meta charset="UTF-8">
<title>CH7EX9: Space Raiders With Optimized Dynamic Network
        Sound And State Loader</title>

<script src="modernizr.js"></script>
<script type="text/javascript">
window.addEventListener('load', eventWindowLoaded, false);

function eventWindowLoaded() {

    canvasApp();

}

function supportedAudioFormat(audio) {
    var returnExtension = "";
    if (audio.canPlayType("audio/ogg") =="probably" ||
        audio.canPlayType("audio/ogg") == "maybe") {
          returnExtension = "ogg";   } else if(audio.canPlayType("audio/wav")
             =="probably" ||
        audio.canPlayType("audio/wav") == "maybe") {
          returnExtension = "wav";
    } else if(audio.canPlayType("audio/mp3") == "probably" ||
        audio.canPlayType("audio/mp3") == "maybe") {
          returnExtension = "mp3";
    }

    return returnExtension;
```

```
}

function canvasSupport () {
    return Modernizr.canvas;
}

function canvasApp() {

  var STATE_INIT  = 10;
  var STATE_LOADING = 20;
  var STATE_RESET  = 30;
  var STATE_PLAYING = 40;
  var appState = STATE_INIT;
  var loadCount= 0;
  var itemsToLoad = 0;
  var alienImage = new Image();
  var missileImage = new Image();
  var playerImage = new Image();

  var SOUND_EXPLODE = "explode1";
  var SOUND_SHOOT  = "shoot1";
  var MAX_SOUNDS = 6;
  var soundPool = new Array();
  var explodeSound ;
  var explodeSound2 ;
  var explodeSound3 ;
  var shootSound;
  var shootSound2;
  var shootSound3;
  var audioType;

  var mouseX;
  var mouseY;
  var player = {x:250,y:475};
  var aliens = new Array();
  var missiles = new Array();

  var ALIEN_START_X = 25;
  var ALIEN_START_Y = 25;
  var ALIEN_ROWS = 5;
  var ALIEN_COLS = 8;
  var ALIEN_SPACING = 40;
  if (!canvasSupport()) {
        return;
      }

  var theCanvas = document.getElementById("canvasOne");
  var context = theCanvas.getContext("2d");

  function itemLoaded(event) {
```

```
    loadCount++;
    if (loadCount >= itemsToLoad) {

        shootSound.removeEventListener("canplaythrough",itemLoaded, false);
        shootSound2.removeEventListener("canplaythrough",itemLoaded, false);
        shootSound3.removeEventListener("canplaythrough",itemLoaded, false);
        explodeSound.removeEventListener("canplaythrough",itemLoaded,false);
        explodeSound2.removeEventListener("canplaythrough",itemLoaded,false);
        explodeSound3.removeEventListener("canplaythrough",itemLoaded,false);
        soundPool.push({name:"explode1", element:explodeSound, played:false});
        soundPool.push({name:"explode1", element:explodeSound2, played:false});
        soundPool.push({name:"explode1", element:explodeSound3, played:false});
        soundPool.push({name:"shoot1", element:shootSound, played:false});
        soundPool.push({name:"shoot1", element:shootSound2, played:false});
        soundPool.push({name:"shoot1", element:shootSound3, played:false});

        appState = STATE_RESET;

    }

}

function initApp() {
    loadCount=0;
    itemsToLoad = 9;
    explodeSound = document.createElement("audio");
    document.body.appendChild(explodeSound);
    audioType = supportedAudioFormat(explodeSound);
    explodeSound.addEventListener("canplaythrough",itemLoaded,false);
    explodeSound.setAttribute("src", "explode1." + audioType);

    explodeSound2 = document.createElement("audio");
    document.body.appendChild(explodeSound2);
    explodeSound2.addEventListener("canplaythrough",itemLoaded,false);
    explodeSound2.setAttribute("src", "explode1." + audioType);

    explodeSound3 = document.createElement("audio");
    document.body.appendChild(explodeSound3);
    explodeSound3.addEventListener("canplaythrough",itemLoaded,false);
    explodeSound3.setAttribute("src", "explode1." + audioType);

    shootSound = document.createElement("audio");
    document.body.appendChild(shootSound);
    shootSound.addEventListener("canplaythrough",itemLoaded,false);
    shootSound.setAttribute("src", "shoot1." + audioType);

    shootSound2 = document.createElement("audio");
    document.body.appendChild(shootSound2);
    shootSound2.addEventListener("canplaythrough",itemLoaded,false);
    shootSound2.setAttribute("src", "shoot1." + audioType);

    shootSound3 = document.createElement("audio");
```

```
document.body.appendChild(shootSound3);
shootSound3.addEventListener("canplaythrough",itemLoaded,false);
shootSound3.setAttribute("src", "shoot1." + audioType);

alienImage = new Image();
alienImage.onload = itemLoaded;
alienImage.src = "alien.png";
playerImage = new Image();
playerImage.onload = itemLoaded;
playerImage.src = "player.png";
missileImage = new Image();
missileImage.onload = itemLoaded;
missileImage.src = "missile.png";
appState = STATE_LOADING;
}

function startLevel() {

    for (var r = 0; r < ALIEN_ROWS; r++) {
       for( var c= 0; c < ALIEN_COLS; c++) {
          aliens.push({speed:2,x:ALIEN_START_X+c*ALIEN_SPACING, y:ALIEN_START_Y+r*
             ALIEN_SPACING,width:alienImage.width, height:alienImage.height});
       }
    }
 }

function resetApp() {

 playSound(SOUND_EXPLODE,0);
 playSound(SOUND_SHOOT,0);
 startLevel();
 appState = STATE_PLAYING;

}

function  drawScreen () {

    //Move missiles
    for (var i=missiles.length-1; i>= 0;i--) {
      missiles[i].y -= missiles[i].speed;
      if (missiles[i].y < (0-missiles[i].height)) {
         missiles.splice(i,1);
       }

    }

    //Move Aliens
    for (var i=aliens.length-1; i>= 0;i--) {
      aliens[i].x += aliens[i].speed;
      if (aliens[i].x > (theCanvas.width-aliens[i].width) || aliens[i].x < 0) {
         aliens[i].speed *= -1;
         aliens[i].y += 20;
```

```
        }
        if (aliens[i].y > theCanvas.height) {
            aliens.splice(i,1);
        }

    }

    //Detect Collisions
    missile: for (var i=missiles.length-1; i>= 0;i--) {
        var tempMissile = missiles[i]
        for (var j=aliens.length-1; j>= 0;j--) {
            var tempAlien =aliens[j];
            if (hitTest(tempMissile,tempAlien)) {
                playSound(SOUND_EXPLODE,.5);
                missiles.splice(i,1);
                aliens.splice(j,1);
                break missile;
            }
        }

        if (aliens.length <=0) {
            appState = STATE_RESET;
        }
    }

    //Background
    context.fillStyle = "#000000";
    context.fillRect(0, 0, theCanvas.width, theCanvas.height);
    //Box
    context.strokeStyle = "#EEEEEE";
    context.strokeRect(5,  5, theCanvas.width-10, theCanvas.height-10);

    //Draw Player
    context.drawImage(playerImage,player.x,player.y);

    //Draw Missiles
    for (var i=missiles.length-1; i>= 0;i--) {
        context.drawImage(missileImage,missiles[i].x,missiles[i].y);

    }

    //draw aliens
    for (var i=aliens.length-1; i>= 0;i--) {
        context.drawImage(alienImage,aliens[i].x,aliens[i].y);

    }

    //Draw Text
    context.fillStyle = "#FFFFFF";
    context.fillText ("Active Sounds: " + soundPool.length,  200 ,480);

}
```

```
function hitTest(image1,image2)  {
   r1left = image1.x;
   r1top = image1.y;
   r1right = image1.x + image1.width;
   r1bottom = image1.y + image1.height;
   r2left = image2.x;
   r2top = image2.y;
   r2right = image2.x + image2.width;
   r2bottom = image2.y + image2.height;
   retval = false;

   if ( (r1left > r2right) || (r1right < r2left) || (r1bottom < r2top) ||
       (r1top > r2bottom) ) {
      retval = false;
   } else {
      retval = true;
   }

   return retval;
}

function eventMouseMove(event) {
   var x;
   var y;
   if (event.pageX || event.pageY) {
      x = event.pageX;
      y = event.pageY;
   } else {
      x = e.clientX + document.body.scrollLeft
         + document.documentElement.scrollLeft;
      y = e.clientY + document.body.scrollTop
         + document.documentElement.scrollTop;
   }
   x -= theCanvas.offsetLeft;
   y -= theCanvas.offsetTop;

   mouseX=x;
   mouseY=y;
   player.x = mouseX;
   player.y = mouseY;

}

function eventMouseUp(event) {

   missiles.push({speed:5, x: player.x+.5*playerImage.width,
      y:player.y-missileImage.height,width:missileImage.width,
      height:missileImage.height});

   playSound(SOUND_SHOOT,.5);
}
```

```
function playSound(sound,volume) {

    var soundFound = false;
    var soundIndex = 0;
    var tempSound;

    if (soundPool.length> 0) {
        while (!soundFound && soundIndex < soundPool.length) {
            var tSound = soundPool[soundIndex];
            if ((tSound.element.ended || !tSound.played) && tSound.name == sound) {
                soundFound = true;
                tSound.played = true;
            } else {
                soundIndex++;
            }

        }
    }
    if (soundFound) {
        tempSound = soundPool[soundIndex].element;
        tempSound.volume = volume;
        tempSound.play();

    } else if (soundPool.length < MAX_SOUNDS){
        tempSound = document.createElement("audio");
        tempSound.setAttribute("src", sound + "." + audioType);
        tempSound.volume = volume;
        tempSound.play();
        soundPool.push({name:sound, element:tempSound, type:audioType, played:true});
    }

}

function run() {
    switch(appState) {
    case STATE_INIT:
        initApp();
        break;
    case STATE_LOADING:
        //wait for call backs
        break;
    case STATE_RESET:
        resetApp();
        break;
    case STATE_PLAYING:
        drawScreen();
        break;

    }

}
```

```
        theCanvas.addEventListener("mouseup",eventMouseUp, false);
        theCanvas.addEventListener("mousemove",eventMouseMove, false);

        function gameLoop() {
                window.setTimeout(gameLoop, 20);
                run()
         }

        gameLoop();
}


</script>

</head>

<body>
<canvas id="canvasOne" width="500" height="500"
        style="position: absolute; top: 50px; left: 50px;">>
 Your browser does not support HTML5 Canvas.
</canvas>
</body>
</html>
```

Code from Chapter 9

Geo Blaster Extended Full Source

Example A-2. Geo Blaster Extended full source code listing

```
<!doctype html>
<html lang="en">
<head>
<meta charset="UTF-8">
<title>CH9EX1: Geo Blaster Extended</title>

<script src="modernizr-1.6.min.js"></script>
<script type="text/javascript">
window.addEventListener('load', eventWindowLoaded, false);
function eventWindowLoaded() {

    canvasApp();

}

function canvasSupport () {
    return Modernizr.canvas;
}

function supportedAudioFormat(audio) {
    var returnExtension = "";
```

```
    if (audio.canPlayType("audio/ogg") =="probably" ||
        audio.canPlayType("audio/ogg") == "maybe") {
            returnExtension = "ogg";
    } else if(audio.canPlayType("audio/wav") =="probably" ||
        audio.canPlayType("audio/wav") == "maybe") {
            returnExtension = "wav";
    } else if(audio.canPlayType("audio/wav") == "probably" ||
        audio.canPlayType("audio/wav") == "maybe") {
            returnExtension = "mp3";
    }

    return returnExtension;

}

function canvasApp(){

    if (!canvasSupport()) {
            return;
      }else{
        theCanvas = document.getElementById("canvas");
        context = theCanvas.getContext("2d");
    }

    //sounds
    var SOUND_EXPLODE = "explode1";
    var SOUND_SHOOT = "shoot1";
    var SOUND_SAUCER_SHOOT = "saucershoot"
    var MAX_SOUNDS = 9;
    var soundPool = new Array();
    var explodeSound;
    var explodeSound2;
    var explodeSound3;
    var shootSound;
    var shootSound2;
    var shootSound3;
    var saucershootSound;
    var saucershootSound2;
    var saucershootSound3;
    var audioType;

    //application states
    var GAME_STATE_INIT = 0;
    var GAME_STATE_WAIT_FOR_LOAD = 5;
    var GAME_STATE_TITLE = 10;
    var GAME_STATE_NEW_GAME = 20;
    var GAME_STATE_NEW_LEVEL = 30;
    var GAME_STATE_PLAYER_START = 40;
    var GAME_STATE_PLAY_LEVEL = 50;
    var GAME_STATE_PLAYER_DIE = 60;
    var GAME_STATE_GAME_OVER = 70;
    var currentGameState = 0;
```

```
var currentGameStateFunction = null;

//title screen
var titleStarted = false;

//game over screen
var gameOverStarted = false;

//objects for game play

//game environment
var score = 0;
var level = 0;    var extraShipAtEach = 10000;
var extraShipsEarned = 0;
var playerShips = 3;

//playfield
var xMin = 0;
var xMax = 400;
var yMin = 0;
var yMax = 400;

//score values
var bigRockScore = 50;
var medRockScore = 75;
var smlRockScore = 100;
var saucerScore = 300;

//rock scale constants
var ROCK_SCALE_LARGE = 1;
var ROCK_SCALE_MEDIUM = 2;
var ROCK_SCALE_SMALL = 3;

//create game objects and arrays
var player = {};
var rocks = [];
var saucers = [];
var playerMissiles = [];
var particles = [];
var saucerMissiles = [];
var particlePool = [];
var maxParticles = 200;
var newParticle;
var tempParticle;

//level specific
var levelRockMaxSpeedAdjust = 1;
var levelSaucerMax = 1;
var levelSaucerOccurrenceRate = 25;
var levelSaucerSpeed = 1;
var levelSaucerFireDelay = 300;
var levelSaucerFireRate = 30;
```

```
var levelSaucerMissileSpeed = 1;

//keyPresses
var keyPressList=[];

//tile sheets
var shipTiles;
var shipTiles2;
var saucerTiles;
var largeRockTiles;
var mediumRockTiles;
var smallRockTiles;
var particleTiles;

//loading
var loadcCount=0;
var itemsToLoad=0;

function itemLoaded(event) {

  loadCount++;
  //console.log("loading:" + loadCount)
  if (loadCount >= itemsToLoad) {

    shootSound.removeEventListener("canplaythrough",itemLoaded, false);
    shootSound2.removeEventListener("canplaythrough",itemLoaded, false);
    shootSound3.removeEventListener("canplaythrough",itemLoaded, false);
    explodeSound.removeEventListener("canplaythrough",itemLoaded,false);
    explodeSound2.removeEventListener("canplaythrough",itemLoaded,false);
    explodeSound3.removeEventListener("canplaythrough",itemLoaded,false);
    saucershootSound.removeEventListener("canplaythrough",itemLoaded,false);
    saucershootSound2.removeEventListener("canplaythrough",itemLoaded,
     false);
    saucershootSound3.removeEventListener("canplaythrough",itemLoaded,
     false);

    soundPool.push({name:"explode1", element:explodeSound, played:false});
    soundPool.push({name:"explode1", element:explodeSound2, played:false});
    soundPool.push({name:"explode1", element:explodeSound3, played:false});
    soundPool.push({name:"shoot1", element:shootSound, played:false});
    soundPool.push({name:"shoot1", element:shootSound2, played:false});
    soundPool.push({name:"shoot1", element:shootSound3, played:false});
    soundPool.push({name:"saucershoot", element:saucershootSound,
     played:false});
    soundPool.push({name:"saucershoot", element:saucershootSound2,
     played:false});
    soundPool.push({name:"saucershoot", element:saucershootSound3,
     played:false});

    switchGameState(GAME_STATE_TITLE)

  }
```

```
        }
function playSound(sound,volume) {
    ConsoleLog.log("play sound" + sound);
    var soundFound = false;
    var soundIndex = 0;
    var tempSound;

    if (soundPool.length> 0) {
        while (!soundFound && soundIndex < soundPool.length) {

            var tSound = soundPool[soundIndex];
            if ((tSound.element.ended || !tSound.played) && tSound.name == sound) {
                soundFound = true;
                tSound.played = true;
            } else {
                soundIndex++;
            }

        }
    }

  if (soundFound) {
        ConsoleLog.log("sound found");
        tempSound = soundPool[soundIndex].element;
        //tempSound.setAttribute("src", sound + "." + audioType);
        //tempSound.loop = false;
        //tempSound.volume = volume;
        tempSound.play();

    } else if (soundPool.length < MAX_SOUNDS){
        ConsoleLog.log("sound not found");
        tempSound = document.createElement("audio");
        tempSound.setAttribute("src", sound + "." + audioType);
        tempSound.volume = volume;
        tempSound.play();
        soundPool.push({name:sound, element:tempSound, type:audioType,
         played:true});
    }

}
function runGame(){
    currentGameStateFunction();
}

function switchGameState(newState) {
    currentGameState = newState;
    switch (currentGameState) {

        case GAME_STATE_INIT:
            currentGameStateFunction = gameStateInit;
            break;
```

```
            case GAME_STATE_WAIT_FOR_LOAD:
                currentGameStateFunction = gameStateWaitForLoad;
                break;
            case GAME_STATE_TITLE:
                 currentGameStateFunction = gameStateTitle;
                 break;
            case GAME_STATE_NEW_GAME:
                currentGameStateFunction = gameStateNewGame;
                break;
            case GAME_STATE_NEW_LEVEL:
                currentGameStateFunction = gameStateNewLevel;
                break;
            case GAME_STATE_PLAYER_START:
                currentGameStateFunction = gameStatePlayerStart;
                break;
            case GAME_STATE_PLAY_LEVEL:
                currentGameStateFunction = gameStatePlayLevel;
                break;
            case GAME_STATE_PLAYER_DIE:
                currentGameStateFunction = gameStatePlayerDie;
                break;
            case GAME_STATE_GAME_OVER:
                currentGameStateFunction = gameStateGameOver;
                break;

    }

}

function gameStateWaitForLoad(){
    //do nothing while loading events occur
    console.log("doing nothing...")
}

function createObjectPools(){
    for (var ctr=0;ctr<maxParticles;ctr++){
        var newParticle = {};
        particlePool.push(newParticle)
    }
    console.log("particlePool=" + particlePool.length)
}

function gameStateInit() {
    createObjectPools();

    loadCount = 0;
    itemsToLoad = 16; //change to 7 if experiencing problems in IE

    explodeSound = document.createElement("audio");
    document.body.appendChild(explodeSound);
    audioType = supportedAudioFormat(explodeSound);
    explodeSound.setAttribute("src", "explode1." + audioType);
```

```
explodeSound.addEventListener("canplaythrough",itemLoaded,false);

explodeSound2 = document.createElement("audio");
document.body.appendChild(explodeSound2);
explodeSound2.setAttribute("src", "explode1." + audioType);
explodeSound2.addEventListener("canplaythrough",itemLoaded,false);

explodeSound3 = document.createElement("audio");
document.body.appendChild(explodeSound3);
explodeSound3.setAttribute("src", "explode1." + audioType);
explodeSound3.addEventListener("canplaythrough",itemLoaded,false);

shootSound = document.createElement("audio");
audioType = supportedAudioFormat(shootSound);
document.body.appendChild(shootSound);
shootSound.setAttribute("src", "shoot1." + audioType);
shootSound.addEventListener("canplaythrough",itemLoaded,false);

shootSound2 = document.createElement("audio");
document.body.appendChild(shootSound2);
shootSound2.setAttribute("src", "shoot1." + audioType);
shootSound2.addEventListener("canplaythrough",itemLoaded,false);

shootSound3 = document.createElement("audio");
document.body.appendChild(shootSound3);
shootSound3.setAttribute("src", "shoot1." + audioType);
shootSound3.addEventListener("canplaythrough",itemLoaded,false);

saucershootSound = document.createElement("audio");
audioType = supportedAudioFormat(saucershootSound);
document.body.appendChild(saucershootSound);
saucershootSound.setAttribute("src", "saucershoot." + audioType);
saucershootSound.addEventListener("canplaythrough",itemLoaded,false);

saucershootSound2 = document.createElement("audio");
document.body.appendChild(saucershootSound2);
saucershootSound2.setAttribute("src", "saucershoot." + audioType);
saucershootSound2.addEventListener("canplaythrough",itemLoaded,false);

saucershootSound3 = document.createElement("audio");
document.body.appendChild(saucershootSound3);
saucershootSound3.setAttribute("src", "saucershoot." + audioType);
saucershootSound3.addEventListener("canplaythrough",itemLoaded,false);

shipTiles = new Image();
shipTiles.src = "ship_tiles.png";
shipTiles.onload = itemLoaded;

shipTiles2 = new Image();
shipTiles2.src = "ship_tiles2.png";
shipTiles2.onload = itemLoaded;
```

```
        saucerTiles= new Image();
        saucerTiles.src = "saucer.png";
        saucerTiles.onload = itemLoaded;

        largeRockTiles = new Image();
        largeRockTiles.src = "largerocks.png";
        largeRockTiles.onload = itemLoaded;

        mediumRockTiles = new Image();
        mediumRockTiles.src = "mediumrocks.png";
        mediumRockTiles.onload = itemLoaded;

        smallRockTiles = new Image();
        smallRockTiles.src = "smallrocks.png";
        smallRockTiles.onload = itemLoaded;

        particleTiles = new Image();
        particleTiles.src = "parts.png";
        particleTiles.onload = itemLoaded;

        switchGameState(GAME_STATE_WAIT_FOR_LOAD);
}

function gameStateTitle() {
    if (titleStarted !=true){
        fillBackground();
        setTextStyleTitle();
        context.fillText  ("Geo Blaster X-ten-d", 120, 70);
        setTextStyle();
        context.fillText  ("Press Space To Play", 130, 140);

        setTextStyleCredits();
        context.fillText  ("An HTML5 Example Game", 125, 200);
        context.fillText  ("From our upcoming HTML5 Canvas", 100, 215);
        context.fillText  ("book on O'Reilly Press", 130, 230);

        context.fillText  ("Game Code - Jeff Fulton", 130, 260);
        context.fillText  ("Sound Manager - Steve Fulton", 120, 275);


        titleStarted = true;
    }else{
        //wait for space key click
        if (keyPressList[32]==true){
            ConsoleLog.log("space pressed");
            switchGameState(GAME_STATE_NEW_GAME);
            titleStarted = false;

        }

    }
```

```
    }

function gameStateNewGame(){
    ConsoleLog.log("gameStateNewGame")
    //set up new game
    level = 0;
    score = 0;
    playerShips = 3;
    player.maxVelocity = 5;
    player.width = 32;
    player.height = 32;
    player.halfWidth = 16;
    player.halfHeight = 16;
    player.hitWidth = 24;
    player.hitHeight = 24;
    player.rotationalVelocity = 10; //how many degrees to turn the ship
    player.thrustAcceleration = .05;
    player.missileFrameDelay = 5;
    player.thrust = false;
    player.alpha = 1;
    player.rotation = 0;
    player.x = 0;
    player.y = 0;

    fillBackground();
    renderScoreBoard();
    switchGameState(GAME_STATE_NEW_LEVEL)

}
function gameStateNewLevel(){
    rocks = [];
    saucers = [];
    playerMissiles = [];
    particles = [];
    saucerMissiles = [];
    level++;
    levelRockMaxSpeedAdjust = level*.25;
    if (levelRockMaxSpeedAdjust > 3){
        levelRockMaxSpeed = 3;
    }

    levelSaucerMax = 1+Math.floor(level/10);
    if (levelSaucerMax > 5){
        levelSaucerMax = 5;
    }
    levelSaucerOccurrenceRate = 10+3*level;
    if (levelSaucerOccurrenceRate > 35){
        levelSaucerOccurrenceRate = 35;
    }
    levelSaucerSpeed = 1+.5*level;
    if (levelSaucerSpeed>5){
        levelSaucerSpeed = 5;
```

```
    }
    levelSaucerFireDelay = 120-10*level;
    if (levelSaucerFireDelay<20) {
        levelSaucerFireDelay = 20;
    }

    levelSaucerFireRate = 20 + 3*level;
    if (levelSaucerFireRate<50) {
        levelSaucerFireRate = 50;
    }

    levelSaucerMissileSpeed = 1+.2*level;
    if (levelSaucerMissileSpeed > 4){
        levelSaucerMissileSpeed = 4;
    }
    //create level rocks
    for (var newRockctr=0;newRockctr<level+3;newRockctr++){
        var newRock = {};

        newRock.scale = 1;
        //scale
        //1 = large
        //2 = medium
        //3 = small
        //these will be used as the divisor for the new size
        //50/1 = 50
        //50/2 = 25
        //50/3 = 16
        newRock.width = 64;
        newRock.height = 64;
        newRock.halfWidth = 32;
        newRock.halfHeight = 32;

        newRock.hitWidth = 48;
        newRock.hitHeight = 48;

        //start all new rocks in upper left for ship safety
        newRock.x = Math.floor(Math.random()*50);
        //ConsoleLog.log("newRock.x=" + newRock.x);
        newRock.y = Math.floor(Math.random()*50);
        //ConsoleLog.log("newRock.y=" + newRock.y);
        newRock.dx = (Math.random()*2)+levelRockMaxSpeedAdjust;
        if (Math.random()<.5){
            newRock.dx *= -1;
        }
        newRock.dy=(Math.random()*2)+levelRockMaxSpeedAdjust;
        if (Math.random()<.5){
            newRock.dy *= -1;
        }
        //rotation speed and direction

        if (Math.random()<.5){
```

```
                newRock.rotationInc = -1;
            }else{
                newRock.rotationInc = 1;
            }

            newRock.animationDelay = Math.floor(Math.random()*3+1);
            newRock.animationCount = 0;

            newRock.scoreValue = bigRockScore;
            newRock.rotation = 0;

            rocks.push(newRock);
            //ConsoleLog.log("rock created rotationInc=" + newRock.rotationInc);
        }
    resetPlayer();
    switchGameState(GAME_STATE_PLAYER_START);

}

function gameStatePlayerStart(){

    fillBackground();
    renderScoreBoard();
    if (player.alpha < 1){
        player.alpha += .01;

        ConsoleLog.log("player.alpha=" + context.globalAlpha)
    }else{
        switchGameState(GAME_STATE_PLAY_LEVEL);
        player.safe = false; // added chapter 9

    }

    //renderPlayerShip(player.x, player.y,270,1);
    context.globalAlpha = 1;
    //new in chapter 9
    checkKeys();
    update();
    render(); //added chapter 9
    checkCollisions();
    checkForExtraShip();
    checkForEndOfLevel();
    frameRateCounter.countFrames();

}

function gameStatePlayLevel(){
    checkKeys();
    update();
    render();
    checkCollisions();
    checkForExtraShip();
```

```
        checkForEndOfLevel();
        frameRateCounter.countFrames();

}

function resetPlayer() {
    player.rotation = 270;
    player.x = .5*xMax;
    player.y = .5*yMax;
    player.facingX = 0;
    player.facingY = 0;
    player.movingX = 0;
    player.movingY = 0;
    player.alpha = 0;
    player.missileFrameCount = 0;
    //added chapter 9
    player.safe = true;
}

function checkForExtraShip() {
    if (Math.floor(score/extraShipAtEach) > extraShipsEarned) {
        playerShips++
        extraShipsEarned++;
    }
}

function checkForEndOfLevel(){
    if (rocks.length==0) {
        switchGameState(GAME_STATE_NEW_LEVEL);
    }
}

function gameStatePlayerDie(){
    if (particles.length >0 || playerMissiles.length>0) {
        fillBackground();
        renderScoreBoard();
        updateRocks();
        updateSaucers();
        updateParticles();
        updateSaucerMissiles();
        updatePlayerMissiles();
        renderRocks();
        renderSaucers();
        renderParticles();
        renderSaucerMissiles();
        renderPlayerMissiles();
        frameRateCounter.countFrames();

    }else{
        playerShips--;
        if (playerShips<1) {
            switchGameState(GAME_STATE_GAME_OVER);
```

```
        }else{
            //resetPlayer();
            switchGameState(GAME_STATE_PLAYER_START);
        }
    }
}

function gameStateGameOver() {
    //ConsoleLog.log("Game Over State");
    if (gameOverStarted !=true){
        fillBackground();
        renderScoreBoard();
        setTextStyle();
        context.fillText  ("Game Over!", 160, 70);
        context.fillText  ("Press Space To Play", 130, 140);

        gameOverStarted = true;
    }else{
        //wait for space key click
        if (keyPressList[32]==true){
            ConsoleLog.log("space pressed");
            switchGameState(GAME_STATE_TITLE);
            gameOverStarted = false;

        }

    }
}

function fillBackground() {
    // draw background and text
    context.fillStyle = '#000000';
    context.fillRect(xMin, yMin, xMax, yMax);

}

function setTextStyle() {
    context.fillStyle = '#ffffff';
    context.font = '15px _sans';
    context.textBaseline = 'top';
}

function setTextStyleTitle() {
    context.fillStyle  = '#54ebeb';
    context.font = '20px _sans';
    context.textBaseline = 'top';
}

function setTextStyleCredits() {
    context.fillStyle = '#ffffff';
    context.font = '12px _sans';
    context.textBaseline = 'top';
```

```
}

function renderScoreBoard() {

    context.fillStyle = "#ffffff";
    context.fillText('Score ' + score, 10, 20);
    renderPlayerShip(200,16,270,.75)
    context.fillText('X ' + playerShips, 220, 20);

    context.fillText('FPS: ' + frameRateCounter.lastFrameCount, 300,20)

}

function checkKeys() {
    //check keys

    if (keyPressList[38]==true){
    //thrust
        var angleInRadians = player.rotation * Math.PI / 180;
        player.facingX = Math.cos(angleInRadians);
        player.facingY = Math.sin(angleInRadians);

        var movingXNew = player.movingX+player.thrustAcceleration*player.facingX;
        var movingYNew = player.movingY+player.thrustAcceleration*player.facingY;

        var currentVelocity = Math.sqrt ((movingXNew*movingXNew) +
        (movingXNew*movingXNew));

        if (currentVelocity < player.maxVelocity) {
            player.movingX = movingXNew;
            player.movingY = movingYNew;
        }
        player.thrust = true;

    }else{
        player.thrust = false;
    }

    if (keyPressList[37]==true) {
        //rotate counterclockwise
        player.rotation -= player.rotationalVelocity;
        if (player.rotation <0) {
            player.rotation = 350
        }

    }

    if (keyPressList[39]==true) {
        //rotate clockwise
        player.rotation += player.rotationalVelocity;
        if (player.rotation >350) {
            player.rotation = 10
```

```
        }
    }

    if (keyPressList[32]==true) {
        if (player.missileFrameCount>player.missileFrameDelay){
        playSound(SOUND_SHOOT,.5);
        firePlayerMissile();
        player.missileFrameCount = 0;

        }
    }
}

function update() {
    updatePlayer();
    updatePlayerMissiles();
    updateRocks();
    updateSaucers();
    updateSaucerMissiles();
    updateParticles();
}

function render() {
    fillBackground();
    renderScoreBoard();
    renderPlayerShip(player.x,player.y,player.rotation,1);
    renderPlayerMissiles();
    renderRocks();
    renderSaucers();
    renderSaucerMissiles();
    renderParticles();
}

function updatePlayer() {
    player.missileFrameCount++;

    player.x += player.movingX*frameRateCounter.step;
    player.y += player.movingY*frameRateCounter.step;

    if (player.x > xMax) {
        player.x =- player.width;
    }else if (player.x<-player.width){
        player.x = xMax;
    }

    if (player.y > yMax) {
        player.y =- player.height;
    }else if (player.y<-player.height){
        player.y = yMax;
    }
}
```

```
function updatePlayerMissiles() {
    var tempPlayerMissile = {};
    var playerMissileLength=playerMissiles.length-1;
    //ConsoleLog.log("update playerMissileLength=" + playerMissileLength);
    for (var playerMissileCtr=playerMissileLength;playerMissileCtr>=0;
     playerMissileCtr--){
        //ConsoleLog.log("update player missile" + playerMissileCtr)
        tempPlayerMissile = playerMissiles[playerMissileCtr];
        tempPlayerMissile.x += tempPlayerMissile.dx*frameRateCounter.step;
        tempPlayerMissile.y += tempPlayerMissile.dy*frameRateCounter.step;
        if (tempPlayerMissile.x > xMax) {
            tempPlayerMissile.x =- tempPlayerMissile.width;
        }else if (tempPlayerMissile.x<-tempPlayerMissile.width){
            tempPlayerMissile.x = xMax;
        }

        if (tempPlayerMissile.y > yMax) {
            tempPlayerMissile.y =- tempPlayerMissile.height;
        }else if (tempPlayerMissile.y<-tempPlayerMissile.height){
            tempPlayerMissile.y = yMax;
        }

        tempPlayerMissile.lifeCtr++;
        if (tempPlayerMissile.lifeCtr > tempPlayerMissile.life){
            //ConsoleLog.log("removing player missile");
            playerMissiles.splice(playerMissileCtr,1)
            tempPlayerMissile = null;
        }
    }
}

function updateRocks(){

    var tempRock = {};
    var rocksLength = rocks.length-1;
    //ConsoleLog.log("update rocks length=" + rocksLength);
    for (var rockCtr=rocksLength;rockCtr>=0;rockCtr--){
        tempRock = rocks[rockCtr];
        tempRock.x += tempRock.dx*frameRateCounter.step;
        tempRock.y += tempRock.dy*frameRateCounter.step;

        tempRock.animationCount++;
        if (tempRock.animationCount > tempRock.animationDelay){
            tempRock.animationCount = 0;
            tempRock.rotation += tempRock.rotationInc;

            if (tempRock.rotation > 4){
                tempRock.rotation = 0;
            }else if (tempRock.rotation <0){
                tempRock.rotation = 4;
            }
        }
```

```
        if (tempRock.x > xMax) {
            tempRock.x = xMin-tempRock.width;
        }else if (tempRock.x<xMin-tempRock.width){
            tempRock.x = xMax;
        }

        if (tempRock.y > yMax) {
            tempRock.y = yMin-tempRock.width;
        }else if (tempRock.y<yMin-tempRock.width){
            tempRock.y = yMax;
        }
    }
}

function updateSaucers() {
    //first check to see if we want to add a saucer

    if (saucers.length< levelSaucerMax){
        if (Math.floor(Math.random()*100)<=levelSaucerOccurrenceRate){
            //ConsoleLog.log("create saucer")
            var newSaucer = {};

            newSaucer.width = 30;
            newSaucer.height = 13;
            newSaucer.halfHeight = 6.5;
            newSaucer.halfWidth = 15;
            newSaucer.hitWidth = 30;
            newSaucer.hitHeight = 13;
            newSaucer.scoreValue = saucerScore;
            newSaucer.fireRate = levelSaucerFireRate;
            newSaucer.fireDelay = levelSaucerFireDelay;
            newSaucer.fireDelayCount = 0;
            newSaucer.missileSpeed = levelSaucerMissileSpeed;
            newSaucer.dy = (Math.random()*2);
            if (Math.floor(Math.random)*2==1){
                newSaucer.dy *= -1;
            }

            //choose betweeen left or right edge to start
            if (Math.floor(Math.random()*2)==1){
                //start on right and go left
                newSaucer.x = 450;
                newSaucer.dx = -1*levelSaucerSpeed;

            }else{
                //left to right
                newSaucer.x = -50;
                newSaucer.dx = levelSaucerSpeed;
            }

            newSaucer.missileSpeed = levelSaucerMissileSpeed;
```

```
        newSaucer.fireDelay = levelSaucerFireDelay;
        newSaucer.fireRate = levelSaucerFireRate;
        newSaucer.y = Math.floor(Math.random()*400);

        saucers.push(newSaucer);
    }

}

var tempSaucer = {};
var saucerLength = saucers.length-1;
//ConsoleLog.log("update rocks length=" + rocksLength);
for (var saucerCtr=saucerLength;saucerCtr>=0;saucerCtr--){
    tempSaucer = saucers[saucerCtr];

    //should saucer fire
    tempSaucer.fireDelayCount++;
    if (Math.floor(Math.random()*100) <=tempSaucer.fireRate &&
     tempSaucer.fireDelayCount>tempSaucer.fireDelay ){
        playSound(SOUND_SAUCER_SHOOT,.5);
        fireSaucerMissile(tempSaucer);
        tempSaucer.fireDelayCount=0;
    }

    var remove = false;
    tempSaucer.x += tempSaucer.dx*frameRateCounter.step;
    tempSaucer.y += tempSaucer.dy*frameRateCounter.step;

    //remove saucers on left and right edges
    if (tempSaucer.dx > 0 && tempSaucer.x >xMax){
        remove = true;
    }else if (tempSaucer.dx <0 &&tempSaucer.x<xMin-tempSaucer.width){
        remove = true;
    }

    //bounce saucers off over vertical edges
    if (tempSaucer.y > yMax || tempSaucer.y<yMin-tempSaucer.width) {
        tempSaucer.dy *= -1;
    }


    if (remove==true) {
        //remove the saucer
        saucers.splice(saucerCtr,1);
        tempSaucer = null;
    }

}

}
function updateSaucerMissiles() {
    var tempSaucerMissile = {};
```

```
    var saucerMissileLength = saucerMissiles.length-1;
    for (var saucerMissileCtr = saucerMissileLength;saucerMissileCtr>=0;
     saucerMissileCtr--){
        //ConsoleLog.log("update player missile" + playerMissileCtr)
        tempSaucerMissile = saucerMissiles[saucerMissileCtr];
        tempSaucerMissile.x += tempSaucerMissile.dx*frameRateCounter.step;
        tempSaucerMissile.y += tempSaucerMissile.dy*frameRateCounter.step;
        if (tempSaucerMissile.x > xMax) {
            tempSaucerMissile.x =- tempSaucerMissile.width;
        }else if (tempSaucerMissile.x<-tempSaucerMissile.width){
            tempSaucerMissile.x = xMax;
        }

        if (tempSaucerMissile.y > yMax) {
            tempSaucerMissile.y =- tempSaucerMissile.height;
        }else if (tempSaucerMissile.y<-tempSaucerMissile.height){
            tempSaucerMissile.y = yMax;
        }

        tempSaucerMissile.lifeCtr++;
        if (tempSaucerMissile.lifeCtr > tempSaucerMissile.life){
            //remove
            saucerMissiles.splice(saucerMissileCtr,1);
            tempSaucerMissile = null;
        }
    }
}

function updateParticles() {

    var particleLength=particles.length-1;
    for (var particleCtr=particleLength;particleCtr>=0;particleCtr--){
        var remove = false;
        tempParticle = particles[particleCtr];
        tempParticle.x += tempParticle.dx*frameRateCounter.step;
        tempParticle.y += tempParticle.dy*frameRateCounter.step;

        tempParticle.lifeCtr++;

        if (tempParticle.lifeCtr > tempParticle.life){
            remove = true;

        } else if ((tempParticle.x > xMax) || (tempParticle.x<xMin)
          || (tempParticle.y > yMax) || (tempParticle.y<yMin)){
            remove=true;

        }
        if (remove) {
            particlePool.push(tempParticle)
            particles.splice(particleCtr,1)

        }
```

```
        }
    }

    function renderPlayerShip(x,y,rotation, scale) {
        //transformation
        context.save(); //save current state in stack
        context.globalAlpha = parseFloat(player.alpha);
        var angleInRadians = rotation * Math.PI / 180;
        var sourceX = Math.floor((player.rotation/10) % 10) * 32;
        var sourceY = Math.floor((player.rotation/10) /10) *32;
        if (player.thrust){
            context.drawImage(shipTiles2, sourceX, sourceY, 32,32,
              player.x,player.y,32,32);
        }else{
            context.drawImage(shipTiles, sourceX, sourceY, 32,32,
              player.x,player.y,32,32);
        }

        //restore context
        context.restore(); //pop old state on to screen

        context.globalAlpha = 1;

    }

    function renderPlayerMissiles() {
        var tempPlayerMissile = {};
        var playerMissileLength=playerMissiles.length-1;
        //ConsoleLog.log("render playerMissileLength=" + playerMissileLength);
        for (var playerMissileCtr=playerMissileLength;playerMissileCtr>=0;
         playerMissileCtr--){
            //ConsoleLog.log("draw player missile " + playerMissileCtr)
            tempPlayerMissile = playerMissiles[playerMissileCtr];
            context.save(); //save current state in stack
            var sourceX=Math.floor(1 % 4) * tempPlayerMissile.width;
            var sourceY=Math.floor(1 / 4) * tempPlayerMissile.height;

            context.drawImage(particleTiles, sourceX, sourceY,
             tempPlayerMissile.width,tempPlayerMissile.height,
             tempPlayerMissile.x,tempPlayerMissile.y,
             tempPlayerMissile.width,tempPlayerMissile.height);

            context.restore(); //pop old state on to screen
        }
    }
    function renderRocks() {
        var tempRock = {};
        var rocksLength = rocks.length-1;
        for (var rockCtr = rocksLength;rockCtr>=0;rockCtr--){
            context.save(); //save current state in stack
```

```
        tempRock = rocks[rockCtr];
        var sourceX = Math.floor((tempRock.rotation) % 5) * tempRock.width;
        var sourceY = Math.floor((tempRock.rotation) /5) *tempRock.height;

        switch(tempRock.scale){
            case 1:
                context.drawImage(largeRockTiles, sourceX, sourceY,
                 tempRock.width,tempRock.height,tempRock.x,tempRock.y,
                 tempRock.width,tempRock.height);
                break;
            case 2:
                context.drawImage(mediumRockTiles, sourceX,
                 sourceY,tempRock.width,tempRock.height,tempRock.x,tempRock.y,
                 tempRock.width,tempRock.height);
                break;
            case 3:
                context.drawImage(smallRockTiles, sourceX,
                 sourceY,tempRock.width,tempRock.height,tempRock.x,tempRock.y,
                 tempRock.width,tempRock.height);
                break;

        }
        context.restore(); //pop old state on to screen

    }
}

function renderSaucers() {
    var tempSaucer = {};
    var saucerLength = saucers.length-1;
    for (var saucerCtr = saucerLength;saucerCtr>=0;saucerCtr--){
        //ConsoleLog.log("saucer: " + saucerCtr);
        tempSaucer = saucers[saucerCtr];

        context.save(); //save current state in stack
        var sourceX = 0;
        var sourceY = 0;
        context.drawImage(saucerTiles, sourceX, sourceY, 30,15,
         tempSaucer.x,tempSaucer.y,30,15);
        context.restore(); //pop old state on to screen
    }
}
function renderSaucerMissiles() {
    var tempSaucerMissile = {};
    var saucerMissileLength = saucerMissiles.length-1;
    //ConsoleLog.log("saucerMissiles= " + saucerMissiles.length)
    for (var saucerMissileCtr=saucerMissileLength;saucerMissileCtr>=0;
     saucerMissileCtr--){
        //ConsoleLog.log("draw player missile " + playerMissileCtr)
        tempSaucerMissile = saucerMissiles[saucerMissileCtr];
        context.save(); //save current state in stack
        var sourceX = Math.floor(0 % 4) * tempSaucerMissile.width;
```

```
            var sourceY = Math.floor(0 / 4) * tempSaucerMissile.height;

            context.drawImage(particleTiles, sourceX, sourceY,
              tempSaucerMissile.width,tempSaucerMissile.height,
              tempSaucerMissile.x,tempSaucerMissile.y,tempSaucerMissile.width,
              tempSaucerMissile.height);

            context.restore(); //pop old state on to screen

    }
}

function renderParticles() {

    var tempParticle = {};
    var particleLength = particles.length-1;
    for (var particleCtr=particleLength;particleCtr>=0;particleCtr--){
        tempParticle = particles[particleCtr];
        context.save(); //save current state in stack

        var tile;

        //console.log("part type=" + tempParticle.type)
        switch(tempParticle.type){
            case 0: // saucer
                tile = 0;
                break;
            case 1: //large rock
                tile = 2
                break;
            case 2: //medium rock
                tile = 3;
                break;
            case 3: //small rock
                tile = 0;
                break;
            case 4: //player
                tile = 1;
                break;

        }

        var sourceX = Math.floor(tile % 4) * tempParticle.width;
        var sourceY = Math.floor(tile / 4) * tempParticle.height;

        context.drawImage(particleTiles, sourceX, sourceY,
          tempParticle.width,tempParticle.height,tempParticle.x,
          tempParticle.y,tempParticle.width,tempParticle.height);

        context.restore(); //pop old state on to screen

    }
```

```
    }

function checkCollisions() {

    //loop through rocks then missiles.
    //There will always be rocks and a ship,
    //but there will not always be missiles.
    var tempRock = {};
    var rocksLength = rocks.length-1;
    var tempPlayerMissile = {};
    var playerMissileLength = playerMissiles.length-1;
    var saucerLength = saucers.length-1;
    var tempSaucer = {};
    var saucerMissileLength = saucerMissiles.length-1;

    rocks: for (var rockCtr=rocksLength;rockCtr>=0;rockCtr--){
        tempRock = rocks[rockCtr];

        missiles:for (var playerMissileCtr=playerMissileLength;
         playerMissileCtr>=0;playerMissileCtr--){
            tempPlayerMissile = playerMissiles[playerMissileCtr];

            if (boundingBoxCollide(tempRock,tempPlayerMissile)){
                //ConsoleLog.log("hit rock");
                createExplode(tempRock.x+tempRock.halfWidth,
                 tempRock.y+tempRock.halfHeight,10,tempRock.scale);
                if (tempRock.scale<3) {
                    splitRock(tempRock.scale+1, tempRock.x, tempRock.y);
                }
                addToScore(tempRock.scoreValue);
                playerMissiles.splice(playerMissileCtr,1);
                tempPlayerMissile = null;


                rocks.splice(rockCtr,1);
                tempRock = null;

                break rocks;
                break missiles;
            }
        }

        saucers:for (var saucerCtr=saucerLength;saucerCtr>=0;saucerCtr--){
            tempSaucer = saucers[saucerCtr];

            if (boundingBoxCollide(tempRock,tempSaucer)){
                //ConsoleLog.log("hit rock");
                createExplode(tempSaucer.x+tempSaucer.halfWidth,
                 tempSaucer.y+tempSaucer.halfHeight,10,0);
                createExplode(tempRock.x+tempRock.halfWidth,
                 tempRock.y+tempRock.halfHeight,10,tempRock.scale);
```

```
                    if (tempRock.scale<3) {
                        splitRock(tempRock.scale+1, tempRock.x, tempRock.y);
                    }

                    saucers.splice(saucerCtr,1);
                    tempSaucer = null;

                    rocks.splice(rockCtr,1);
                    tempRock = null;

                    break rocks;
                    break saucers;
                }
            }
        //saucer missiles against rocks
        //this is done here so we don't have to loop through
        //rocks again as it would probably
        //be the biggest array
        saucerMissiles:for (var saucerMissileCtr=saucerMissileLength;
                        saucerMissileCtr>=0;saucerMissileCtr--){

            tempSaucerMissile = saucerMissiles[saucerMissileCtr];
            if (boundingBoxCollide(tempRock,tempSaucerMissile)){
                    //ConsoleLog.log("hit rock");

                    createExplode(tempRock.x+tempRock.halfWidth,
                     tempRock.y+tempRock.halfHeight,10,tempRock.scale);
                    if (tempRock.scale<3) {
                        splitRock(tempRock.scale+1, tempRock.x, tempRock.y);
                    }

                    saucerMissiles.splice(saucerCtr,1);
                    tempSaucerMissile = null;

                    rocks.splice(rockCtr,1);
                    tempRock = null;

                    break rocks;
                    break saucerMissiles;
                }
            }

        //check player against rocks

        if (boundingBoxCollide(tempRock,player) && player.safe==false){
            //ConsoleLog.log("hit player");
            createExplode(tempRock.x+tempRock.halfWidth,
             tempRock.halfHeight,10,tempRock.scale);
            addToScore(tempRock.scoreValue);
            if (tempRock.scale<3) {
                splitRock(tempRock.scale+1, tempRock.x, tempRock.y);
            }
```

```
            rocks.splice(rockCtr,1);
            tempRock=null;

            playerDie();
        }

    }

    //now check player against saucers and then saucers against player missiles
    //and finally player against saucer missiles
    playerMissileLength = playerMissiles.length-1;
    saucerLength = saucers.length-1;
    saucers:for (var saucerCtr=saucerLength;saucerCtr>=0;saucerCtr--){
        tempSaucer = saucers[saucerCtr];

        missiles:for (var playerMissileCtr=playerMissileLength;
         playerMissileCtr>=0;playerMissileCtr--){

        tempPlayerMissile = playerMissiles[playerMissileCtr];

            if (boundingBoxCollide(tempSaucer,tempPlayerMissile)){
                //ConsoleLog.log("hit rock");
                createExplode(tempSaucer.x+tempSaucer.halfWidth,
                 tempSaucer.y+tempSaucer.halfHeight,10,0);
                addToScore(tempSaucer.scoreValue);

                playerMissiles.splice(playerMissileCtr,1);
                tempPlayerMissile = null;

                saucers.splice(saucerCtr,1);
                tempSaucer = null;

                break saucers;
                break missiles;
            }
        }

        //player against saucers
        if (boundingBoxCollide(tempSaucer,player) & player.safe==false){
            ConsoleLog.log("hit player");
            createExplode(tempSaucer.x+16,tempSaucer.y+16,10,tempRock.scale);
            addToScore(tempSaucer.scoreValue);

            saucers.splice(rockCtr,1);
            tempSaucer = null;

            playerDie();
        }
    }

    //saucerMissiles against player
    saucerMissileLength = saucerMissiles.length-1;
```

```
    saucerMissiles:for (var saucerMissileCtr=saucerMissileLength;
                        saucerMissileCtr>=0;saucerMissileCtr--){

        tempSaucerMissile = saucerMissiles[saucerMissileCtr];

        if (boundingBoxCollide(player,tempSaucerMissile) & player.safe==false){
            ConsoleLog.log("saucer missile hit player");

            playerDie();
            saucerMissiles.splice(saucerCtr,1);
            tempSaucerMissile = null;

            break saucerMissiles;
        }
    }

}

function firePlayerMissile(){

    //ConsoleLog.log("fire playerMissile");
    var newPlayerMissile = {};
    newPlayerMissile.dx = 5*Math.cos(Math.PI*(player.rotation)/180);
    newPlayerMissile.dy = 5*Math.sin(Math.PI*(player.rotation)/180);
    newPlayerMissile.x = player.x+player.halfWidth;
    newPlayerMissile.y = player.y+player.halfHeight;
    newPlayerMissile.life = 60;
    newPlayerMissile.lifeCtr = 0;
    newPlayerMissile.width = 2;
    newPlayerMissile.height = 2;
    newPlayerMissile.hitHeight = 2;
    newPlayerMissile.hitWidth = 2;
    playerMissiles.push(newPlayerMissile);
}

function fireSaucerMissile(saucer) {
    var newSaucerMissile = {};
    newSaucerMissile.x = saucer.x+.5*saucer.width;
    newSaucerMissile.y = saucer.y+.5*saucer.height;
    newSaucerMissile.width = 2;
    newSaucerMissile.height = 2;
    newSaucerMissile.hitHeight = 2;
    newSaucerMissile.hitWidth = 2;
    newSaucerMissile.speed = saucer.missileSpeed;

    //ConsoleLog.log("saucer fire");
    //fire at player from small saucer
    var diffx = player.x-saucer.x;
    var diffy = player.y-saucer.y;
    var radians = Math.atan2(diffy, diffx);
    var degrees = 360 * radians / (2 * Math.PI);
```

```
        newSaucerMissile.dx = saucer.missileSpeed*Math.cos(Math.PI*(degrees)/180);
        newSaucerMissile.dy = saucer.missileSpeed*Math.sin(Math.PI*(degrees)/180);
        newSaucerMissile.life = 160;
        newSaucerMissile.lifeCtr = 0;
        saucerMissiles.push(newSaucerMissile);
}

function playerDie() {

    ConsoleLog.log("player die");
    createExplode(player.x+player.halfWidth, player.y+player.halfWidth,50,4);
    resetPlayer();
    switchGameState(GAME_STATE_PLAYER_DIE);

}

function createExplode(x,y,num,type) {

    playSound(SOUND_EXPLODE,.5);
    for (var partCtr=0;partCtr<num;partCtr++){
        if (particlePool.length > 0){

            newParticle = particlePool.pop();
        newParticle.dx = Math.random()*3;
            if (Math.random()<.5){
                newParticle.dx *= -1;
            }
        newParticle.dy = Math.random()*3;
        if (Math.random()<.5){
            newParticle.dy *= -1;
        }

        newParticle.life = Math.floor(Math.random()*30+30);
        newParticle.lifeCtr = 0;
        newParticle.x = x;
        newParticle.width = 2;
        newParticle.height = 2;
        newParticle.y = y;
        newParticle.type = type;
        //ConsoleLog.log("newParticle.life=" + newParticle.life);
        particles.push(newParticle);
        }

    }

}

function boundingBoxCollide(object1, object2) {

    var left1 = object1.x;
    var left2 = object2.x;
    var right1 = object1.x + object1.hitWidth;
```

```
        var right2 = object2.x + object2.hitWidth;
        var top1 = object1.y;
        var top2 = object2.y;
        var bottom1 = object1.y + object1.hitHeight;
        var bottom2 = object2.y + object2.hitHeight;

        if (bottom1 < top2) return(false);
        if (top1 > bottom2) return(false);

        if (right1 < left2) return(false);
        if (left1 > right2) return(false);

        return(true);

};

function splitRock(scale,x,y){
    for (var newRockctr=0;newRockctr<2;newRockctr++){
        var newRock = {};
        //ConsoleLog.log("split rock");

        if (scale==2){
            newRock.scoreValue = medRockScore;
            newRock.width = 32;
            newRock.height = 32;
            newRock.halfWidth = 16;
            newRock.halfHeight = 16;
            newRock.hitWidth = 24;
            newRock.hitHeight = 24;

        }else {
            newRock.scoreValue = smlRockScore;
            newRock.width = 24;
            newRock.height = 24;
            newRock.halfWidth = 12;
            newRock.halfHeight = 12;
            newRock.hitWidth = 16;
            newRock.hitHeight = 16;
        }

        newRock.scale = scale;
        newRock.x = x;
        newRock.y = y;
        newRock.dx = Math.random()*3;
        if (Math.random()<.5){
            newRock.dx *= -1;
        }
        newRock.dy = Math.random()*3;
        if (Math.random()<.5){
            newRock.dy *= -1;
        }
        if (Math.random()<.5){
```

```
                newRock.rotationInc = -1;
        }else{
            newRock.rotationInc = 1;
        }

        newRock.animationDelay = Math.floor(Math.random()*3+1);
        newRock.animationCount = 0;

        newRock.rotation = 0;
        ConsoleLog.log("new rock scale"+(newRock.scale));
        rocks.push(newRock);

    }

  }
  function addToScore(value){
     score += value;
  }

  document.onkeydown = function(e){

     e = e?e:window.event;
     //ConsoleLog.log(e.keyCode + "down");
     keyPressList[e.keyCode] = true;
  }

  document.onkeyup = function(e){
  //document.body.onkeyup = function(e){
     e = e?e:window.event;
     //ConsoleLog.log(e.keyCode + "up");
     keyPressList[e.keyCode] =  false;
  };


  //*** application start

     switchGameState(GAME_STATE_INIT);
     var FRAME_RATE = 40;
     frameRateCounter = new FrameRateCounter(FRAME_RATE);
     //**** application loop
     var intervalTime = 1000/FRAME_RATE;
     setInterval(runGame, intervalTime );

}

//***** object prototypes *****

//*** consoleLog util object
//create constructor
function ConsoleLog(){
```

```
}

//create function that will be added to the class
console_log = function(message) {
   if(typeof(console) !== 'undefined' && console != null) {
      console.log(message);
   }
}
//add class/static function to class by assignment
ConsoleLog.log = console_log;

//*** end console log object

//***  new FrameRateCounter object prototype
function FrameRateCounter(fps) {
   if (fps == undefined){

      this.fps = 40
   }else{
      this.fps = fps
   }

   this.lastFrameCount = 0;
   var dateTemp = new Date();
   this.frameLast = dateTemp.getTime();
   delete dateTemp;
   this.frameCtr = 0;
   this.lastTime = dateTemp.getTime();

   this.step = 1;

}

FrameRateCounter.prototype.countFrames = function() {

   var dateTemp = new Date();
   var timeDifference = dateTemp.getTime()-this.lastTime;
   this.step = (timeDifference/1000)*this.fps;
   this.lastTime = dateTemp.getTime();
   this.frameCtr++;

    if (dateTemp.getTime() >=this.frameLast+1000) {
      ConsoleLog.log("frame event");
      this.lastFrameCount = this.frameCtr;
      this.frameCtr = 0;
      this.frameLast = dateTemp.getTime();
   }
   delete dateTemp;

}
</script>
```

```
</head>
<body>
<div style="position: absolute; top: 50px; left: 50px;">

<canvas id="canvas" width="400" height="400">
 Your browser does not support HTML5 Canvas.
</canvas>

</div>
</body>
</html>
```

Code from Chapter 11

Example A-3 gives the full code listing for *CH11EX1.html*. Notice that many of the code styles and constructs we have used through the course of this book are still in place in this application. Besides the obvious inclusion of code related directly to WebGL, this application operates essentially the same way as the other apps we discussed in this book.

Example A-3. WebGL test

```
<!doctype html>
<html lang="en">
<head>
<meta charset="UTF-8">
<title>CH11EX1: WebGL Test </title>

<script src="modernizr.js"></script>
<script type="text/javascript" src="sylvester.js"></script>
<script type="text/javascript" src="glUtils.js"></script>

<script id="shader-fs" type="x-shader/x-fragment">
   #ifdef GL_ES
   precision highp float;
   #endif

   varying vec4 vColor;

   void main(void) {
     gl_FragColor = vColor;
   }
</script>

<script id="shader-vs" type="x-shader/x-vertex">
   attribute vec3 aVertexPosition;
   attribute vec4 aVertexColor;

   uniform mat4 uMVMatrix;
   uniform mat4 uPMatrix;

   varying vec4 vColor;    void main(void) {
     gl_Position = uPMatrix * uMVMatrix * vec4(aVertexPosition, 1.0);
```

```
      vColor = aVertexColor;
   }
</script>

<script type="text/javascript">
window.addEventListener("load", eventWindowLoaded, false);

function eventWindowLoaded () {
   canvasApp();
}

function canvasSupport () {
   return Modernizr.canvas;
}

function webglSupport() {
   return Modernizr.webgl;
}
function canvasApp () {

function drawScreen() {

    webGLContext.viewport(0, 0, webGLContext.viewportWidth,
        webGLContext.viewportHeight);
    webGLContext.clear(webGLContext.COLOR_BUFFER_BIT | webGLContext.DEPTH_BUFFER_BIT);

    perspective(25, (webGLContext.viewportWidth / webGLContext.viewportHeight),
        0.1, 100.0);
    loadIdentity();

    mvTranslate([0, 0.0, -10.0]);

    mvPushMatrix();
    mvRotate(rotateCube, [0, .5, .5]);

    webGLContext.bindBuffer(webGLContext.ARRAY_BUFFER, cubeVertexPositionBuffer);
    webGLContext.vertexAttribPointer(shaderProgram.vertexPositionAttribute,
        cubeVertexPositionBuffer.itemSize, webGLContext.FLOAT, false, 0, 0);

    webGLContext.bindBuffer(webGLContext.ARRAY_BUFFER, cubeVertexColorBuffer);
    webGLContext.vertexAttribPointer(shaderProgram.vertexColorAttribute,
        cubeVertexColorBuffer.itemSize, webGLContext.FLOAT, false, 0, 0);

    webGLContext.bindBuffer(webGLContext.ELEMENT_ARRAY_BUFFER,
        cubeVertexIndexBuffer);
    setMatrixUniforms();
    webGLContext.drawElements(webGLContext.TRIANGLES,
        cubeVertexIndexBuffer.numItems, webGLContext.UNSIGNED_SHORT, 0);

    mvPopMatrix();
    rotateCube += 2;
```

```
    }

    if (!canvasSupport() ) {
        alert("Unable to initialize Canvas");
        return;
    }

    if ( !webglSupport()) {
        alert("Unable to initialize WebGL");
        return;
    }

    var webGLContext;
    var rotateCube = 0;

    var theCanvas = document.getElementById("canvasOne");
    webGLContext =theCanvas.getContext("experimental-webgl");
    webGLContext.viewportWidth =theCanvas.width;
    webGLContext.viewportHeight = theCanvas.height;

    initShaders();
    initBuffers();

    webGLContext.clearColor(0.0, 0.0, 0.0, 1.0);
    webGLContext.clearDepth(1.0);
    webGLContext.enable(webGLContext.DEPTH_TEST);
    webGLContext.depthFunc(webGLContext.LEQUAL);

    setInterval(drawScreen, 33);

function getShader(webglcontext, id) {
    var shaderScript = document.getElementById(id);
    if (!shaderScript) {
      return null;
    }

    var str = "";
    var scriptChild = shaderScript.firstChild;
    while (scriptChild) {
      if (scriptChild.nodeType == 3) {
       str += scriptChild.textContent;
      }
      scriptChild = scriptChild.nextSibling;
    }

    var shader;
    if (shaderScript.type == "x-shader/x-fragment") {
      shader = webGLContext.createShader(webGLContext.FRAGMENT_SHADER);
    } else if (shaderScript.type == "x-shader/x-vertex") {
      shader = webGLContext.createShader(webGLContext.VERTEX_SHADER);
    } else {
      return null;
```

```
  }

  webGLContext.shaderSource(shader, str);
  webGLContext.compileShader(shader);

  if (!webGLContext.getShaderParameter(shader, webGLContext.COMPILE_STATUS)) {
    alert(webGLContext.getShaderInfoLog(shader));
    return null;
  }

  return shader;
}

var shaderProgram;
function initShaders() {
  var fragmentShader = getShader(webGLContext, "shader-fs");
  var vertexShader = getShader(webGLContext, "shader-vs");

  shaderProgram = webGLContext.createProgram();
  webGLContext.attachShader(shaderProgram, vertexShader);
  webGLContext.attachShader(shaderProgram, fragmentShader);
  webGLContext.linkProgram(shaderProgram);

  if (!webGLContext.getProgramParameter(shaderProgram, webGLContext.LINK_STATUS)) {
    alert("Could not initialize shaders");
  }

  webGLContext.useProgram(shaderProgram);

  shaderProgram.vertexPositionAttribute = webGLContext.getAttribLocation
      (shaderProgram, "aVertexPosition");
  webGLContext.enableVertexAttribArray(shaderProgram.vertexPositionAttribute);

  shaderProgram.vertexColorAttribute = webGLContext.getAttribLocation
      (shaderProgram, "aVertexColor");
  webGLContext.enableVertexAttribArray(shaderProgram.vertexColorAttribute);

  shaderProgram.pMatrixUniform = webGLContext.getUniformLocation
      (shaderProgram, "uPMatrix");
  shaderProgram.mvMatrixUniform = webGLContext.getUniformLocation
      (shaderProgram, "uMVMatrix");
}

var mvMatrix;
var mvMatrixStack = [];

function mvPushMatrix(matrix) {
  if (matrix) {
    mvMatrixStack.push(matrix.dup());
    mvMatrix = matrix.dup();
  } else {
    mvMatrixStack.push(mvMatrix.dup());
```

```
    }
  }

function mvPopMatrix() {
  if (mvMatrixStack.length == 0) {
    throw "Invalid popMatrix!";
  }        mvMatrix = mvMatrixStack.pop();
  return mvMatrix;
}

function loadIdentity() {
  mvMatrix = Matrix.I(4);
}

function multMatrix(matrix) {
  mvMatrix = mvMatrix.x(matrix);
}

function mvTranslate(vector) {
  var matrix = Matrix.Translation($V([vector[0], vector[1],
      vector[2]])).ensure4x4();
  multMatrix(matrix);
}

function mvRotate(angle, vector) {
  var radians = angle * Math.PI / 180.0;
  var matrix = Matrix.Rotation(radians, $V([vector[0],
      vector[1], vector[2]])).ensure4x4();
  multMatrix(matrix);
}

  var pMatrix;
  function perspective(fovy, aspect, znear, zfar) {
  pMatrix = makePerspective(fovy, aspect, znear, zfar);
  }

function setMatrixUniforms() {
  webGLContext.uniformMatrix4fv(shaderProgram.pMatrixUniform, false,
      new Float32Array(pMatrix.flatten()));
  webGLContext.uniformMatrix4fv(shaderProgram.mvMatrixUniform, false,
      new Float32Array(mvMatrix.flatten()));
}

  var cubeVertexPositionBuffer;
  var cubeVertexColorBuffer;
  var cubeVertexIndexBuffer;
function initBuffers() {

  cubeVertexPositionBuffer = webGLContext.createBuffer();
  webGLContext.bindBuffer(webGLContext.ARRAY_BUFFER, cubeVertexPositionBuffer);
  vertices = [
    // Front face
```

```
    -1.0, -1.0,  1.0,
     1.0, -1.0,  1.0,
     1.0,  1.0,  1.0,
    -1.0,  1.0,  1.0,

    // Back face
    -1.0, -1.0, -1.0,
    -1.0,  1.0, -1.0,
     1.0,  1.0, -1.0,
     1.0, -1.0, -1.0,

    // Top face
    -1.0,  1.0, -1.0,
    -1.0,  1.0,  1.0,
     1.0,  1.0,  1.0,
     1.0,  1.0, -1.0,

    // Bottom face
    -1.0, -1.0, -1.0,
     1.0, -1.0, -1.0,
     1.0, -1.0,  1.0,
    -1.0, -1.0,  1.0,

    // Right face
     1.0, -1.0, -1.0,
     1.0,  1.0, -1.0,
     1.0,  1.0,  1.0,
     1.0, -1.0,  1.0,

    // Left face
    -1.0, -1.0, -1.0,
    -1.0, -1.0,  1.0,
    -1.0,  1.0,  1.0,
    -1.0,  1.0, -1.0,
];
webGLContext.bufferData(webGLContext.ARRAY_BUFFER, new Float32Array(vertices),
    webGLContext.STATIC_DRAW);
cubeVertexPositionBuffer.itemSize = 3;
cubeVertexPositionBuffer.numItems = 24;

cubeVertexColorBuffer = webGLContext.createBuffer();
webGLContext.bindBuffer(webGLContext.ARRAY_BUFFER, cubeVertexColorBuffer);
var colors = [
  [1.0, 1.0, 1.0, 1.0],     // Front face
  [0.9, 0.0, 0.0, 1.0],     // Back face
  [0.6, 0.6, 0.6, 1.0],     // Top face
  [0.6, 0.0, 0.0, 1.0],     // Bottom face
  [0.3 ,0.0, 0.0, 1.0],     // Right face
  [0.3, 0.3, 0.3, 1.0],     // Left face
];

var unpackedColors = []
```

```
          for (var i in colors) {
            var color = colors[i];
            for (var j=0; j < 4; j++) {
              unpackedColors = unpackedColors.concat(color);
            }
          }
          webGLContext.bufferData(webGLContext.ARRAY_BUFFER,
            new Float32Array(unpackedColors),
              webGLContext.STATIC_DRAW);
          cubeVertexColorBuffer.itemSize = 4;
          cubeVertexColorBuffer.numItems = 24;

          cubeVertexIndexBuffer = webGLContext.createBuffer();
          webGLContext.bindBuffer(webGLContext.ELEMENT_ARRAY_BUFFER,
            cubeVertexIndexBuffer);
          var cubeVertexIndices = [
            0, 1, 2,      0, 2, 3,     // Front face
            4, 5, 6,      4, 6, 7,     // Back face
            8, 9, 10,     8, 10, 11,   // Top face
            12, 13, 14,   12, 14, 15,  // Bottom face
            16, 17, 18,   16, 18, 19,  // Right face
            20, 21, 22,   20, 22, 23   // Left face
          ]
          webGLContext.bufferData(webGLContext.ELEMENT_ARRAY_BUFFER,
              new Uint16Array(cubeVertexIndices), webGLContext.STATIC_DRAW);
          cubeVertexIndexBuffer.itemSize = 1;
          cubeVertexIndexBuffer.numItems = 36;

      }

}

</script>

</head>
<body>
<div style="position: absolute; top: 50px; left: 50px;">
<canvas id="canvasOne" width="500" height="500">
 Your browser does not support HTML5 Canvas or WebGLContext.
</canvas>
</div>
</body>
</html>
```

Index

Symbols

% (modulo) operator, 146, 532

A

A* path finding
  about, 486–493
  adding node weights, 502–514
  applied to larger tile map, 493–498
  moving game characters along paths, 514–518
  poorly designed tile maps and, 518–528
  taking diagonal moves into account, 498–502, 506–514
Acid music-looping software, 384
alignment (text)
  about, 96, 98
  horizontal, 98
  vertical, 97
angle of incidence, 204
angle of reflection, 204
angles, 200
  (see also bouncing effects)
  converting to radians, 200
  finding in radians, 151, 457
animation
  bouncing objects off walls, 204–238
  Box2D library and, 281–303
  cell-based, 142–149

curve and circular movement, 239–259
easing technique, 273–281
in Geo Blaster Basic game, 445–451, 456–463
in Geo Blaster Extended game, 536, 550–555
gradients and, 128–132
Hello World application, 25–29
moving in a straight line, 191–204
moving video, 364–369
rotating cube application, 627
ship movement, 456–458
simple forces of nature in, 259–273
for transformed images, 153–155
animation loops, 27, 153
application states, 463–467, 471
arcs, drawing, 42
Array object
  indexOf() method, 22, 651
  push() method, 22
  toString() method, 23
arrays
  in Geo Blaster Basic game, 458, 477–479
  holding tiles for animation, 145
  numbering in, 145, 158
  scrolling tile-based worlds, 570, 571
  Space Raiders game, 419
  storing map data, 158
  tracing movement with, 196–199
  Video Puzzle example, 349

We'd like to hear your suggestions for improving our indexes. Send email to index@oreilly.com.

<article> tag, 3
astar.js
    about, 488
    search function, 492, 498, 506, 514, 518
Asteroids game (see Geo Blaster games)
Atari Asteroids game (see Geo Blaster games)
Audacity tool, 382
audio
    creating audio player, 397–416
    displaying attributes on Canvas, 388–391
    events supported, 386–388, 400
    in Geo Blaster Extended game, 541–546
    HTML5 formats supported, 382–385, 393
    loading and playing, 387
    mobile devices and, 384
    playing sounds without <audio> tag, 391–397
    properties, functions, and events, 385–387
    Space Raiders game, 416–435
audio codecs, 305
audio controls
    click-and-drag volume slider, 406–416
    creating custom, 398
    inverse relationship, 405
    loading button assets, 399–400
    loop/noloop toggle button, 406
    mouse events, 401
    play/pause button, 403–405
    setting up values, 400
    sliding play indicator, 402
Audio Data API, 435
audio element (see HTMLAudioElement object)
audio formats, 382–385, 393
audio player example
    about, 397
    click-and-drag volume slider, 406–416
    creating custom controls for, 398
    inverse relationship in, 405
    loading button assets, 399–400
    loop/noloop toggle button, 406
    mouse events, 401
    play/pause button, 403–405
    setting up player values, 400
    sliding play indicator, 402
<audio> tag
    about, 381
    autoplay attribute, 384
    controls attribute, 381, 384
    creating audio player, 397–416

displaying attributes on Canvas, 388–391
formats supported, 382–385
HTMLAudioElement object and, 385
loading and playing audio, 387
loop attribute, 384
playing sound without, 391–397
src attribute, 381, 385

B
b2Body class
    GetAngle() method, 295
    GetFixtureList() method, 293
    GetPosition() method, 292, 295
    GetUserData() method, 295
    SetLinearVelocity() method, 289
    SetUserData() method, 295
b2debugDraw class
    about, 286
    e_jointBit property, 286
    e_shapeBit property, 286
    SetFillAlpha() method, 286
    SetFlag() method, 286
    SetLineThickness() method, 286
    SetScaleFactor() method, 286
    SetSprite() method, 286
b2Fixture class, 295
b2World class
    ClearForces() method, 287
    DrawDebugData() method, 287, 292
    Step() method, 287
background, clearing and displaying, 28
balls
    bouncing multiple, 208–238
    bouncing single, 205–208
    bouncing with friction, 233–238
    Box2D example, 289–293
    collisions with, 219–232
    creating with Box2D, 285
    curve and circular movement, 239–259
    drawing, 195
    interactions in physics, 220
    shooting balls at boxes game, 293–303
    simulating forces of nature, 259–273
    updating positions of, 224
baseline (font), 97, 98
Bezier curves
    about, 44
    creating loops, 255–259
    moving images along, 251–255

moving objects along, 245–251
Bezier, Pierre, 245
BinaryHTTP protocol, 632
BitMapData object, 442
bitmaps
    current, 38
    Geo Blaster Basic game and, 445
    Geo Blaster Extended game and, 529
<body> tag
    about, 3
    BS Bingo game and, 602
    <canvas> tag and, 18
bouncing effects
    about, 204
    bouncing videos, 364–369
    Box2D example, 289–293
    elasticity and, 266–273
    gravity and, 263–273
    multiple balls off walls, 208–238
    single ball off wall, 205–208
bounding box theory
    about, 59
    Geo Blaster Extended game, 535
    Space Raiders game, 423
Bourg, David M., 487
Box2D library
    about, 281
    additional information, 303
    b2debugDraw class, 286–289
    bouncing balls example, 289–293
    creating balls, 285
    defining walls in, 284
    downloading Box2DWeb engine, 281
    Hello World application, 282
    including, 282
    interactivity with, 293–303
Box2DWeb engine
    about, 281
    downloading, 281
    initializing world, 282
    units in, 283–284
browsers (see web browsers)
BS Bingo game
    about, 591
    application code for, 600
    examining code for, 597–600
    full source code, 592–597
    scaling, 601–606
    testing, 606–606

buffers, 626
bull's eyes, as moving targets, 251–255

C

C3DL library, 629
Canvas (see HTML5 Canvas)
Canvas 2D Drawing API (see drawing on Canvas)
Canvas games (see game development)
Canvas Image API (see images on Canvas)
Canvas object
    clearElementPath() method, 33
    createImageData() method, 170
    creating, 18
    dir property, 98
    dynamically resizing, 114–116, 214–219
    getContext() method, 11, 12, 17, 18
    height property, 18, 77, 114–116, 206, 215–219
    mouse events and, 174
    scaling dynamically, 116
    setAttribute() method, 116
    setElementPath() method, 33
    supportsContext() method, 663
    Time Stamper application and, 174
    toBlob() method, 19, 663
    toBlobHD() method, 663
    toDataURL() method, 19, 24, 117, 373, 375, 663
    toDataURLHD() method, 663
    width property, 18, 77, 114–116, 206, 215–219
Canvas Pixel Manipulation API, 170–172
<canvas tag>
    bitmap drawing operations and, 179
<canvas> tag
    about, 3, 7
    <body> tag and, 18
    <div> tag and, 5, 7
    DOM support, 7
    in Geo Blaster Extended game, 551
    height attribute, 11
    id attribute, 10
    width attribute, 11
Canvas Text API (see Text API)
CanvasGradient object
    about, 82
    addColorStop() method, 107, 129
CanvasPattern object, 82

CanvasPixelArray object, 170
CanvasRenderingContext2D object
    about, 17
    arc() method, 42, 293
    arcTo() method, 44
    beginPath() method, 39, 446
    bezierCurveTo() method, 44
    clearRect() method, 37, 77–79
    clip() method, 17, 38, 45
    closePath() method, 39, 446
    createLinearGradient() method, 62, 66, 67,
        107, 129
    createPattern() method, 71, 109, 110
    createRadialGradient() method, 68, 109
    current state and, 17
    drawImage() method, 14, 136, 137–142,
        162–164, 166, 324, 357, 377, 405, 426
    fill() method, 65
    fillRect() method, 13, 37
    fillStyle property, 13, 17, 23, 38, 60, 62, 82,
        94, 332
    fillText() method, 13, 82, 82, 85–89, 332
    font property, 13, 17, 23, 38, 82, 85, 89–93
    getImageData() method, 171, 172, 182, 550,
        552
    globalAlpha property, 17, 26, 28–29, 38, 47–
        50, 101–103, 455
    globalCompositeOperation property, 17, 38,
        47–50
    isPointInPath() method, 79
    lineCap property, 17, 38, 39, 42
    lineJoin property, 17, 38, 40, 42
    lineTo() method, 39, 446
    lineWidth property, 17, 38, 40
    measureText() method, 84, 100, 112
    miterLimit property, 17, 38
    moveTo() method, 39, 446
    putImageData() method, 171, 550, 552
    quadraticCurveTo() method, 44
    rect() method, 45
    restore() method, 38, 46, 150, 451
    rotate() method, 38, 52, 57, 336, 452
    save() method, 38, 46, 150, 451
    scale() method, 56–58, 57
    setTransform() method, 38, 51
    shadowBlur property, 17, 38, 75–77, 104
    shadowColor property, 17, 38, 75–77, 104
    shadowOffsetX property, 17, 38, 75–77, 104
    shadowOffsetY property, 17, 38, 75–77, 104

stroke() method, 40, 446
strokeRect() method, 14, 37, 64
strokeStyle property, 17, 38, 39, 40, 60, 94,
    446
strokeText() method, 86–89
textAlign property, 17, 38, 98, 100
textBaseline property, 13, 17, 23, 38, 97
translate() method, 53, 336, 453
Cartesian coordinate system, 17
Cascading Style Sheets (CSS)
    about, 5
    future of text on Canvas, 133
    Text API and, 81
Catto, Erin, 281
Cecco, Raffaele, 664
cell-based animation
    advanced, 145–149
    simple, 142–144
chat applications
    about, 634
    creating with ElectroServer, 636–641
    testing, 641
Christmas tree application
    about, 646
    application design, 647–659
    creating, 646
    Windows 8 support, 659–663
circles
    collision detection for, 222
    update-collide-render cycle, 223
circular movement (see curve and circular
    movement)
clearing the Canvas, 77–79
click-and-drag volume slider, 406–416
coarse scrolling method
    about, 572
    full code example, 580–584
codecs
    audio, 305
    video, 305–307
COLLADA 3D models, 629
collision detection
    about, 182–184
    audio player example, 401
    checking intersection between two objects,
        184–190
    Geo Blaster Basic game, 481–483
    Geo Blaster Extended game, 535, 539–541
    for multiple balls, 219–232

Space Raiders game, 423
testing for, 184
using pixel data, 182–190
Video Puzzle example, 348
color stops, 129–132
colors
gradient color stop and, 130
linear gradients with, 107
setting basic fill, 60
setting for fonts, 94–96
setting for text, 82
compositing operations, 47–50
conservation of momentum law, 220
console.log, debugging with, 16
context object (see CanvasRenderingContext2D
    object)
controls
audio, 397–416
touch, 607–618
video, 355–364
CopperLicht library, 630
copying
images to another Canvas, 179–181
parts of images to Canvas, 140
Cordova PhoneGap, 619
cosine, 200, 239
CraftyMind.com site, 369
Crockford, Douglas, 7
CSS (Cascading Style Sheets)
about, 5
future of text on Canvas, 133
Text API and, 81
cubic Bezier curves
creating loops, 255–259
moving images along, 251–255
moving objects along, 245
current bitmap, 38
current path
about, 38
checking if points in, 79
saved states and, 38
current transformation matrix, 39
curve and circular movement
about, 239
cubic Bezier curve loops, 255–259
cubic Bezier curve movement, 245–251
moving images, 251–255
moving in simple spiral, 243–245
uniform circular motion, 239–243

D

Daleks game (see Micro Tank Maze game)
Date.getTime() method, 549
debugging with console.log, 16
delta x (dx), 456
delta y (dy), 456
descenders (font), 97
diagonal gradients, 67
display CSS attribute, 321
distance equation, 194
<div> tag
about, 5
<canvas> tag and, 5, 7
display attribute, 321
id attribute, 317
left attribute, 611
in Retro Blaster Touch game, 611
style attribute, 6
top attribute, 611
<video> tag and, 321
<!doctype html> tag, 3
document object
about, 7
addEventListener() method, 83
appendChild() method, 392
body property, 392
createElement() method, 322, 392, 428
dir property, 98
getElementById() method, 11, 25, 83, 116,
    387
Document Object Model (DOM)
about, 7
Fallback DOM Concept, 31–33
DOM (Document Object Model)
about, 7
Fallback DOM Concept, 31–33
DOM Exception 17, 110
DOM Exception 18, 119
drag-and drop-application
about, 646
application design, 647–659
creating, 646
Windows 8 support, 659–663
Drawing API (see drawing on Canvas)
drawing on Canvas
advanced path methods, 42–47
basic file setup, 35
basic rectangle shape, 36
checking if points in current path, 79

clearing the Canvas, 77–79
compositing operations, 47–50
creating lines with paths, 38–42
creating shadows on shapes, 75–77
drawing arcs, 42
drawing balls, 195
drawing focus ring, 80
drawing states, 37
filling shapes with colors and gradients, 60–71
filling shapes with patterns, 71–75
manipulating large images, 161–170
simple transformations, 50–58
drawing states, 37
dx (delta x), 456
dy (delta y), 456

E

easing technique
about, 273
easing in, 277–281
easing out, 273–277
elastic collisions, 220
elasticity
about, 266
bouncing effects and, 266–273
ElectroServer 5
about, 630
additional applications, 642
additional information, 645
admin tool for, 632
basic application architecture, 634
creating chat applications, 636–641
establishing connection to, 636–638
event support, 635, 637–641
installing, 631–634
JavaScript API, 634
socket-server application, 634
testing chat applications, 641
em square (fonts), 97
embedding video
altering width and height, 312–317
with controls, loop, and autoplay, 311–312
plain-vanilla example, 309
ESObject object
about, 639, 643
setString() method, 640
eval() function, 88

event handlers
for button presses, 358
creating for keyup event, 83
defining, 92
setting for range controls, 116
setting in functions, 92
event listeners
adding, 9
BS Bingo game, 603
listening for button presses, 358–364
Retro Blaster Touch game, 612–614
Space Raiders game, 421
event object
pageX property, 347, 403
pageY property, 347, 403
preventDefault() method, 614
target property, 83, 655
events
about, 8
audio, 386–388, 400
drag-and drop-application, 647
ElectroServer 5 support, 635
ElectroServer support, 637–641
HTML5 continuing development, 321
keyboard, 458–463
mouse, 174, 347, 401, 408, 422, 656
multiple events firing for mouse clicks, 356
occurring while video is playing, 331
playing sounds, 416
Space Raiders game, 422
touch controls and, 612–618
video, 318, 322, 331–335
explosions
in Geo Blaster Basic game, 479
in Geo Blaster Extended game, 529, 539–541
in Micro Tank Maze game, 561
exporting Canvas to an image, 24
extensions, 635

F

façades, 416
Fallback DOM Concept, 31–33
Fangs screen reader emulator, 32
Feldman, Ari, 138
FFmpeg tool, 307
Fibonacci sequence, 243
fill colors, 60, 112
fill patterns, 71–75, 107

filling shapes
    with colors and gradients, 60–71
    with patterns, 71–75
fine scrolling method
    about, 572
    full code example, 585–589
    row and column buffers, 574–580
Flash comparison to Canvas, 442
flip-book animation (see cell-based animation)
focus ring, drawing, 80
font color, 94–96
font faces
    creating necessary variables, 92
    custom, 91
    fallback, 91
    generic, 90
    handling in Text Arranger, 89–93
    setting, 89
    setting in functions, 93
font size
    creating necessary variables, 92
    handling in Text Arranger, 89–93
    HTML5 range control and, 91
    setting, 13, 89
    setting in functions, 93
font styles
    creating necessary variables, 92
    setting, 89
    supported, 90
font weights
    available, 90
    creating necessary variables, 92
    setting, 13, 89
font-face CSS attribute, 82
@font-face CSS rule, 81, 91
font-size CSS attribute, 82
font-style CSS attribute, 82
font-weight CSS attribute, 82
<footer> tag, 3
for:next loops
    Space Raiders game, 421, 425
    Video Puzzle example, 343, 348
<form> tag, 24, 83, 83
formats
    audio, 382–385, 393
    video, 305
FPS (frames per second)
    in Geo Blaster Basic game, 448, 469
    in Geo Blaster Extended game, 548

    in Micro Tank Maze game, 562
fragment shaders, 624
frame counters, 143
frame ticks, 143, 153
FrameRateCounter object prototype
    in Geo Blaster Basic game, 469, 477
    in Geo Blaster Extended game, 548
frames per second (FPS)
    in Geo Blaster Basic game, 448, 469
    in Geo Blaster Extended game, 548
    in Micro Tank Maze game, 562
friction
    about, 270
    ball bouncing with gravity, elasticity, and,
        270–273
    multiple balls bouncing with, 233–238

G

game development, 441
    (see also specific games)
    about, 441–442
    adding sound, 541–546
    adding step timers, 548–550
    animation and, 445–451, 456–463
    applying transformations to game graphics,
        451–456
    basic game framework, 463–470
    basic HTML5 file for, 442–444
    calculating tile source location, 532–534
    creating dynamic tile sheets at runtime, 550–
        555
    drawing with paths, 444–448
    FrameRateCounter object prototype, 469,
        477, 548
    game object physics and, 456–463
    for game state machines, 463–467
    game timer loop, 448
    graphic transformations, 453–456
    handling state changes, 449–451, 451–452
    path finding, 486–528
    pooling object instances, 546–548
    rendering game objects, 535–541, 568
    scaling games, 601–606
    scrolling tile-based worlds, 570–589
    testing games on actual devices, 606–606
    tile movement logic overview, 566–568
    turn-based game flow, 562–566
    update/render (repeat) cycle, 467–469
GarageBand software, 384

Geo Blaster Basic game
    animation in, 445–451, 456–463
    applying collision detection, 481–483
    applying transformations to game graphics,
      451–456
    awarding player extra ships, 481
    basic design, 444
    basic structure, 471–476
    controlling ship with keyboard, 458–463
    full source code, 483
    game algorithms, 477–483
    game objects physics, 456–463
    game timer loop, 448
    giving ship maximum velocity, 462
    graphic transformations, 453–456
    level and game end, 480
    level knobs in, 479
    player object, 476
    Rock prototype object, 484–486
    ship movement in, 456–458
    state changes in, 449–451, 451–452, 471
Geo Blaster Extended game
    about, 529
    adding sound, 541–546
    adding step timers, 548–550
    animation in, 536, 550–555
    full source code, 550–550
    pooling object instances, 546–548
    rendering other game objects, 535–541
    tile sheets in, 530–535, 550–555
GLGE library, 630
Google O3D library, 629
gradients
    animated, 128–132
    filling shapes with, 61–71
    linear, 61–67, 107, 107, 112
    radial, 68–71, 107, 109, 112
    Text Arranger handling, 110–114
gravity
    about, 260–263
    bouncing effects and, 263–273
grid-based path finding (see A* path finding)
Grinstead, Brian, 488
Guess The Letter example
    about, 19, 20
    drawScreen() function, 23
    eventKeyPressed() function, 21–23
    exporting Canvas to an image, 24
    final game code, 25

    initGame() function, 21
    variables used in, 20

H

H.264 video standard, 306
HandBrake tool, 307
<head> tag, 3, 8
<header> tag, 3
Hello World application
    about, 8
    adding <canvas> tag to HTML page, 10
    animated edition, 25–29
    animation loop, 27–29
    Box2D and, 282
    canvasSupport() function, 12
    determining browser support, 11
    with <div> tag, 6
    drawScreen() function, 12–14
    encapsulating code for Canvas, 9
    referencing <canvas> tag with document ob-
      ject, 11
    retrieving 2D context, 12
Hit Testing proposal, 32
horizontal alignment of text, 98
horizontal gradients, 61–65
HTML (HyperText Markup Language), 1, 5–7
HTML forms, 83, 639
<html lang="en"> tag, 4
HTML5
    about, 2
    basic page, 3–5
    upcoming enhancements, 663
HTML5 Canvas
    about, 1
    accessibility for, 31–33
    creating object framework, 646–659
    debugging with console.log, 16
    DOM support, 7
    Guess The Letter example, 19–25
    Hello World application, 8–14, 25–29
    JavaScript support, 7
    upcoming enhancements, 663
    Windows 8 apps and, 659–663
HTML5 Canvas Drawing API (see drawing on
    Canvas)
HTML5 Canvas Image API (see images on Can-
    vas)
HTML5 Canvas Text API (see Text API)

HTMLAudioElement object
    about, 381, 385
    additional information, 386
    audio formats supported, 393
    autoplay property, 386
    canplaythrough event, 386, 387, 393
    canPlayType() method, 385, 389, 393
    controls property, 386
    creating audio player, 397–416
    currentSrc property, 386
    currentTime property, 385, 398, 403
    displaying attributes on Canvas, 388–391
    duration property, 385, 398, 403
    ended event, 387
    ended property, 386, 430, 434
    load() method, 385
    loop property, 385, 406, 428
    muted property, 386
    pause() method, 385, 403, 405
    paused property, 386, 405
    play() method, 385, 394, 405, 421, 423, 426,
        427, 430
    playing event, 387
    playing sound without <audio> tag, 391–397
    preload property, 386, 387
    progress event, 386, 387
    setAttribute() method, 392
    Space Raiders game, 419
    src property, 392, 421, 428
    volume property, 386, 407, 428
    volumechange event, 387
HTMLMediaElement interface
    HTMLAudioElement object and, 385
    HTMLVideoElement object and, 308
HTMLVideoElement interface
    autoplay property, 308
    loop property, 308
    poster property, 308
    src property, 308
    volume property, 308
HTMLVideoElement object
    about, 308
    additional information, 331
    autoplay property, 327
    buffered property, 318
    canplaythrough event, 318, 319, 322
    canPlayType() method, 323
    controls property, 327
    currentTime property, 309, 327, 331–335

    duration property, 309, 318, 327
    ended property, 309
    loop property, 327
    muted property, 309, 327
    pause() method, 308
    paused property, 309, 357
    play() method, 308, 319, 327, 374
    progress event, 318
    screenshot of video example, 373
    src property, 322
    volume property, 327
HyperText Markup Language (HTML), 1, 5

I

if:then statement, 348
Image object
    as fill pattern, 109
    as fill pattern, 107
    filling shapes with patterns, 71–73
    height property, 423
    onload event, 14, 400
    src property, 13, 136, 400
    width property, 423
image windows
    changing source scale settings, 166
    changing viewport settings, 164
    creating, 162
    drawing, 162–163
    panning in, 167–170
    scaling operations in, 168–170
ImageData object
    about, 171–172
    checking for intersections between objects,
        184
    Time Stamper application and, 172
images on Canvas
    about, 135
    advanced cell-based animation, 145–149
    applying rotation transformations to, 149–
        155
    basic file setup, 135
    copying to another Canvas, 179–181
    detecting object collisions, 182–190
    displaying Guess The Letter, 20, 23
    displaying Hello World, 10, 12–14, 27–29
    drawing properties, 161–170
    exporting Canvas to images, 24
    image basics, 136–142
    moving, 148–149, 251–255

No Tanks! game, 155–161
pixel manipulation, 170–179
simple cell-based animation, 142–144
source scale settings, 166
Tile Stamper application, 172–179
viewport settings, 164
immediate mode, 1, 17, 129
incidence, angle of, 204
<input> tag
placeholder attribute, 83
range control type, 91
value attribute, 83
intersection between objects, 184–190
iOS devices
adding meta-tags for, 604
audio and, 384, 435
designing applications for, 597
Retro Blaster Touch game on, 607–618
scaling BS Bingo game for, 601–606
testing BS Bingo game on, 606–606
video and, 310

J

JavaScript language
Canvas support, 7
capturing video with, 369–378
DOM support, 7
dynamically creating audio elements, 392
ElectroServer API, 634
placement of functions, 3
preloading video in, 317–321
rotating cube application, 623
WebGL libraries, 629–630
jQTouch framework, 619
jQuery Mobile Framework, 619
JSColor color picker, 94, 104, 111

K

keyboard events, 458–463

L

LAME .mp3 encoder, 383
law of conservation of momentum, 220
linear gradients
about, 61
with colors, 107
diagonal style, 67
horizontal style, 61–65
text and, 107
Text Arranger example, 112
vertical style, 65
lines
advanced drawing examples, 40–42
creating with paths, 38–40
distance of, 194–199
moving in straight, 191–204
Logg, Ed, 444
loop/noloop toggle button, 406

M

Makar, Jobe, 220, 227, 645
mass (physics), 220
Math object
atan2 function, 517
cos function, 201
floor function, 175
max function, 185
min function, 185
PI function, 200
random function, 291
sin function, 201
maze-chase games (see Micro Tank Maze game)
<meta charset="UTF-8"> tag, 4
meta-tags
for iOS devices, 604
for Retro Blaster Touch game, 611
Micro Tank Maze game
about, 555–556
enemy object in, 560
explosions in, 561
full source code, 570
game playfield, 558
goal tile in, 561
player object in, 559
rendering logic overview, 568
simple rules overview, 569
state machine in, 562–566
tile movement logic overview, 566–568
tile sheets in, 556–558
turn-based game flow in, 562–566
MIME types, 393
Miro Video Converter, 307
mobile devices
audio and, 384, 435
designing applications for, 597
Retro Blaster Touch game on, 607–618

scaling BS Bingo game for, 601–606
testing BS Bingo game on, 606–606
video and, 310, 378
Modernizr library
about, 623
testing with, 12, 394, 625
webgl static constant, 625
modulo (%) operator, 146, 532
mouse events
adding to Canvas, 174
audio player example, 401, 408
detecting interactions, 347
drag-and drop-application, 656
Space Raiders game, 422
movement (see animation)
.mp3 file extension, 382
mp3 file extension, 394
.mp4 file extension, 306
MTS units, 283, 293
multiplayer applications (see ElectroServer 5)

N

<nav> tag, 3
No Tanks! game
A* path finding for, 486–528
about, 155
choosing tile to display, 146
creating animation array, 145
creating tile maps, 156–158
defining tile map, 155
displaying tile maps, 158–161
drawing tiles, 147
examining tile sheets, 145
example sprite sheet, 145
looping through tiles, 146
moving images in, 148–149

O

O3D library (Google), 629
.oga file extension, 306
.ogg file extension, 306, 382, 394
.ogv file extension, 306
Open Web Platform, 2

P

Pac-Man game, 555
panning in image windows, 167–170

particles
in Geo Blaster Basic game, 479
in Geo Blaster Extended game, 529, 539–541
path finding (see A* path finding)
paths
about, 35, 38
advanced methods for, 42–47
checking if points in, 79
creating lines with, 38–42
current, 38, 38
drawing during game development, 444–448
finding a point on the current, 79
moving characters along, 514–518
of points, 196–199
subpaths and, 39
patterns
filling shapes with, 71–75
Image objects as, 107, 109
Text Arranger handling, 110–114
with video element, 110
Penner, Robert, 281
percentage of gradient color stop, 130
PhoneGap (Cordova), 619
physics
in animation, 456–463
ball interactions in, 220
in Geo Blaster Basic game, 456–463
simple forces of nature, 259–273
Pilgrim, Mark, 664
pixel manipulation
about, 170–179
detecting object collisions, 182–190
play/pause button
audio example, 403–405
video example, 355–364
plug-ins, 635
points
calculating distance between, 194–199, 273
checking if in current path, 79
preloading
images, 137
Space Raiders game assets, 420–421
video buttons, 355
video in JavaScript, 317–321
puzzle example (see Video Puzzle example)
Pythagorean theorem, 194

Q

quadratic Bezier curves, 255

R

radial gradients
    about, 68–71
    with colors, 107
    text and, 109
    Text Arranger example, 112
radians, 200
    (see also bouncing effects)
    converting angles to, 200
    finding angles in, 151, 457
Rains, Lyle, 444
range controls
    adding, 115
    dynamically resizing Canvas, 215–219
    setting event handlers for, 116
    setting font size, 91
    setting video size, 314
    updating shadow settings, 104
rectangles
    drawing basic, 36
    rotation and scale of, 59
reflection, angle of, 204
repeat pattern, 71–75
resetting
    Canvas width and height, 77
    Space Raiders game, 421
    transformation matrix, 150
resizing
    Canvas dynamically, 114–116, 214–219
    images painted to Canvas, 139
retained mode, 1, 18
Retro Blaster Touch game
    about, 607–610
    full source code, 610
    jumping to full screen, 610–612
    meta-tags for, 611
    tile sheets in, 607
    touch move events, 612–618
rgb() method, 61
rgba() method, 61
Rock prototype object, 484–486
rotating cube application
    building, 623–628
    full code listing, 704–628
rotation transformations
    about, 50–58
    applying to images, 149–155
    Geo Blaster Basic game, 452–455
    Geo Blaster Extended game, 552

    video example, 335–341

S

scale transformations, 56–58
scaling BS Bingo game, 601–606
scaling Canvas
    drawing large images, 161–170
    dynamically, 116
    panning combined with, 168–170
SceneJS library, 629
scenes, 624
screenshots for videos, 373–376
<script> tag
    FrameRateCounter object prototype and,
        470
    src attribute, 470
scrolling tile-based worlds
    about, 570
    arrays for, 570, 571
    building, 571
    camera object for, 572, 574–580
    coarse scrolling in, 572, 580–584
    fine scrolling in, 572, 574–580, 585–589
    tile sheets for, 570
    world object for, 573
SECURITY_ERR error, 119
Seeman, Glenn, 487
shaders
    defined, 624
    fragment, 624
    vertex, 624
shadows, creating on shapes, 75–77
Shape object, 442
shapes
    applying transformations to, 51
    creating shadows on, 75–77
    filling with colors and gradients, 60–71
    filling with patterns, 71–75
    finding center of, 59
    translating point of origin, 52–56
shooting balls at boxes game
    adding interactivity, 296
    creating boxes, 294–295, 296
    handling balls, 297–303
    rendering boxes, 295
sine, 200, 239
sliding play indicator, 402
SmartFox server, 645
socket-server application, 634

Sonic Foundry Acid software, 384
sound management (see audio)
sounds (see audio)
<source> tag, 309
Space Raiders game
    about, 416
    bounding box collision detection, 423
    creating sound pool, 429–431
    creating unlimited dynamic sound objects,
        427–429
    event listeners, 421
    event sounds, 416
    improving, 435
    initializing, 418–420
    mouse control, 422
    playing, 424–426
    playing sounds using single object, 426
    preloading assets, 420–421
    resetting, 421
    reusing preloaded sounds, 431–435
    state machine, 417, 420
    structure of, 417–426
    Web Audio API and, 436–439
spaceship example
    copying parts of images, 140–142
    displaying images, 137–139
    resizing images, 139
SpiderGL library, 629
spiral, moving in, 243–245
sprite sheets (see tile sheets)
SpriteLib library, 138, 145
states and state machines
    about, 417
    basic game framework for, 463–467
    current state, 17
    drawing states, 37
    Geo Blaster Basic game, 449–451, 451–452,
        471
    Micro Tank Maze game, 562–566
    saving and restoring, 38
    Space Raiders game, 417, 420
step timers, 548–550
straight lines (see lines)
<style> tag, 611
sub dom concept, 31–33
submarine patents, 306
subpaths, 39
Super Mario Brothers game, 572
SUPER tool, 307

switch statements, 418

T
tank games (see Micro Tank Maze game; No
    Tanks! game)
testing
    BS Bingo game, 606–606
    chat applications, 641
    for collisions, 184
    with Modernizr library, 12, 394, 625
    Video Puzzle example, 350–355
    WebGL, 622, 625
text, 109
    (see also Text Arranger application)
    accessibility of, 133
    aligning, 96–101
    Canvas context and, 101–106
    CSS future considerations, 133
    displaying, 82
    font settings for, 89–101
    handling in Text Arranger, 82
    image patterns and, 109
    linear gradients and, 107
    radial gradients and, 109
    setting colors for, 82
Text API
    about, 81
    animated gradients, 128–132
    context properties and, 101–105
    CSS and, 81
    displaying basic text, 82–89
    dynamically resizing the Canvas, 114–115
    dynamically scaling the Canvas, 116
    future considerations, 132
    gradients and patterns, 106–113
    outputting image data, 117
    setting text font, 89–101
    Text Arranger example, 82, 119–128
Text Arranger application
    about, 81
    final version, 119–128
    handling basic text in, 82
    handling font faces in, 89–93
    handling font size in, 89–93
    handling gradients in, 110–114
    handling patterns in, 110–114
    version 2, 101
TextButton object prototype, 600

TextMetrics object
    about, 84
    height property, 84
    upcoming enhancements, 664
    width property, 84
texture sheets (see tile sheets)
Theora video codec, 305
Thomas, Giles, 623
three.js library, 630
3D with WebGL (see WebGL)
thrust force, 457
tile maps, 156
    (see also A* path finding)
    creating, 156–158
    defining, 155
    displaying on Canvas, 158–161
    poorly designed, 518–528
tile sheets
    about, 140
    advanced cell-based animation, 145–149
    applying rotation transformations to images, 149–155
    examining, 145
    in Geo Blaster Extended game, 530–535, 543–545, 550–555
    in Micro Tank Maze game, 556–558
    No Tanks! game, 155–161
    in Retro Blaster Touch game, 607
    scrolling tile-based worlds, 570
    simple cell-based animation, 142–144
    video buttons, 355
Tile Stamper application, 172–179
tile-based games (see scrolling tile-based worlds; specific games)
Tiled tile map editor, 156–158
timer loops
    drag-and drop-application, 655
    Geo Blaster Basic game, 448
    simple cell-based animation, 143
timer ticks, 143
<title> tag, 4
toggle button (audio player), 406
touch controls
    about, 607
    jumping to full screen, 610–612
    touch move events, 612–618
tracing movement of objects, 196–199
transformations
    about, 50

applying to game graphics, 451–456
    rotation, 50–58, 149–155, 335–341, 452–455, 552
    scale, 56–58
    translation, 50–56
translation transformations, 50–56
transparency settings, 28–29, 101
TYPE_MISMATCH_ERR error, 110

U

update-collide-render cycle, 223
update/render (repeat) cycle, 467–469

V

vectors
    Geo Blaster Basic game and, 445
    Geo Blaster Extended game and, 550
    moving on, 199–204
velocity
    ball collision example, 225–232
    in Geo Blaster Basic game, 462
vertex shaders, 624
vertical alignment of text, 97
vertical gradients, 65
video
    altering width and height of, 312–317
    animations in, 364–369
    capturing with JavaScript, 369–378
    with controls, loop, and autoplay, 311–312
    creating video controls, 355–364
    displaying on HTML5 Canvas, 321–331
    embedding, 308
    events supported, 318, 322, 331–335
    HTML5 formats supported, 305–307
    HTML5 properties, 327–331
    mobile devices and, 310, 378
    plain-vanilla video embed, 309
    preloading in JavaScript, 317–321
    rotation transformations, 335–341
    taking screenshots for, 373–376
    Video Puzzle example, 341–355, 376–378
<video> tag
    Video Puzzle example, 377
video codecs, 305–307
video controls
    about, 355
    creating video buttons, 355
    listening for button presses, 358–364

placing buttons, 357
preloading buttons, 355
video element (see HTMLVideoElement object)
video formats, 305–308
Video Puzzle example
    about, 341
    creating collision detection, 348
    creating out of user-captured video, 376–378
    detecting mouse interactions, 347
    drawing screen for, 345–347
    randomizing puzzle pieces, 343
    setting up game, 342–343
    swapping array elements, 349
    testing game, 350–355
<video> tag
    about, 305
    autoplay attribute, 311, 370
    controls attribute, 311
    <div> tag and, 321
    formats supported, 305–307
    height attribute, 310, 312–317
    implementing, 308–317
    loop attribute, 311
    patterns with, 110
    preloading video in JavaScript, 317–321
    <source> tag and, 309
    src attribute, 308, 309
    width attribute, 310, 312–317
viewport settings for images, 164
Visual Studio Express for Windows 8, 659
volume slider (audio player), 406–416
Vorbis audio codec, 305

W

W3C
    on future of text accessibility, 133
    Hit Testing proposal, 32
    HTML Media Capture API, 369
    on HTML5, 2
.wav file extension, 382, 394
Web Audio API
    about, 435
    Space Raiders game and, 436–439
web browsers
    audio events and, 391
    audio formats and, 382, 393
    Canvas support, 2
    event listeners and, 421
    HTML5 page example, 4

iOS platform and, 597
multiple events firing for mouse clicks, 356
patterns with videos, 110
range controls and, 91
Retro Blaster Touch game on, 607–618
scaling BS Bingo game for, 601–606
screen reader emulators, 32
Space Raiders game, 431
testing chat applications, 641
video formats and, 306, 310
Web Audio API and, 435
Web RTC Media Capture and Streams API
    and, 370
Web RTC Media Capture and Streams API
    about, 370
    getUserMedia() method, 370, 370
    show video example, 370–373
WebGL
    about, 621
    additional information, 622, 628
    application demo, 623–628
    JavaScript libraries, 629–630
    testing, 622, 625
.webm file extension, 306
WebM video standard, 306
while loop, 344
window object
    about, 7
    addEventListener() method, 9
    innerHeight property, 604
    innerWidth property, 604
    load event, 8, 418
    open() method, 25
    requestAnimationFrame() method, 27
    setInterval() method, 27, 325, 327
    setTimeout() method, 27, 77, 129, 324, 448,
        464, 655
    URL property, 372
Windows 8 platform, 659–663
Winiarczyk, Ben, 220, 227

X

Xiph.org, 305
XMLHttpRequest object
    about, 436
    responseType property, 436

Y

YouTube site, 306

Z

zones, 635

About the Authors

Steve Fulton is an author, speaker, and game development professional. He works at Mattel Toys as Sr. Manager of Software Development for the Digital Play division.

Jeff Fulton is an R.I.A. web and mobile game/application developer who has been cultivating an audience for news, stories, blogs, and tutorials about Flash, Corona, and now the HTML5 Canvas at his own website (*http://www.8bitrocket.com*) for the past five and a half years. Jeff is currently the Chief Technology Officer at Producto Studios (*Producto studios.com*) and can easily be found on Twitter daily using the handle @8bitrocket.

Jeff previously worked as a web development manager at Mattel Toys for 14 years, helping to create Mattel's extensive online presence.

Colophon

The animal on the cover of *HTML5 Canvas, Second Edition* is the New Zealand kaka (*Nestor meridionalis*), a parrot endemic to that country. The kaka's name comes from the Maori word for parrot (a duplication of the word *kā*, Maori for "to screech"). It is part of the Strigopidae family, which diverged from other parrots 80–100 million years ago when the landmass that is now New Zealand broke apart from the supercontinent Gondwana. A defining characteristic of this family of parrots is the bristles on their tongues, which are used to collect nectar.

A medium-sized parrot about 18 inches in length, the kaka is stocky and has a short, square tail. Its feathers are primarily olive-brown, with brighter splashes of crimson on the underwings and rump. It also has yellow-brown spots on its cheeks and a gray crown. It possesses the sharp curved beak common to many parrot species, which it uses to pry seeds loose from cones and dig up insects. The kaka also eats fruit, berries, nectar, and flowers.

These birds are primarily arboreal, living in the canopies of New Zealand forests. Very social creatures, kakas live in large flocks that sometimes include other local parrot species as well. In winter, breeding pairs build nests in hollow trees, and lay a clutch of two to four eggs. Both parents help feed their young.

The kaka is currently endangered due to deforestation, predators, and competition for food with non-native species. The closely related kea and kakapo parrots are facing similar challenges—and in fact, two species within the *Nestor* genus have already gone extinct (most recently in 1851).

The cover image is from Cassell's *Natural History*. The cover font is Adobe ITC Garamond. The text font is Adobe Minion Pro; the heading font is Adobe Myriad Condensed; and the code font is Dalton Maag's Ubuntu Mono.

Have it your way.

Get even more for your money.

Join the O'Reilly Community, and register the O'Reilly books you own. It's free, and you'll get:

- $4.99 ebook upgrade offer
- 40% upgrade offer on O'Reilly print books
- Membership discounts on books and events
- Free lifetime updates to ebooks and videos
- Multiple ebook formats, DRM FREE
- Participation in the O'Reilly community
- Newsletters
- Account management
- 100% Satisfaction Guarantee

Signing up is easy:

1. **Go to: oreilly.com/go/register**
2. **Create an O'Reilly login.**
3. **Provide your address.**
4. **Register your books.**

Note: English-language books only

To order books online:
oreilly.com/store

For questions about products or an order:
orders@oreilly.com

To sign up to get topic-specific email announcements and/or news about upcoming books, conferences, special offers, and new technologies:
elists@oreilly.com

For technical questions about book content:
booktech@oreilly.com

To submit new book proposals to our editors:
proposals@oreilly.com

O'Reilly books are available in multiple DRM-free ebook formats. For more information:
oreilly.com/ebooks

Spreading the knowledge of innovators   oreilly.com

CPSIA information can be obtained at www.ICGtesting.com
Printed in the USA
BVOW08s1457021114

373356BV00008B/74/P